THE ROLE OF LAW IN
INTERNATIONAL POLITICS

THE ROLE OF LAW IN INTERNATIONAL POLITICS

*Essays in International Relations
and International Law*

MICHAEL BYERS

OXFORD

UNIVERSITY PRESS

OXFORD
UNIVERSITY PRESS

Great Clarendon Street, Oxford OX2 6DP

Oxford University Press is a department of the University of Oxford.
It furthers the University's objective of excellence in research, scholarship,
and education by publishing worldwide in

Oxford New York

Auckland Bangkok Buenos Aires Cape Town Chennai
Dar es Salaam Delhi Hong Kong Istanbul Karachi Kolkata
Kuala Lumpur Madrid Melbourne Mexico City Mumbai Nairobi
São Paulo Shanghai Taipei Tokyo Toronto

Oxford is a registered trade mark of Oxford University Press
in the UK and in certain other countries

Published in the United States
by Oxford University Press Inc., New York

First published 2000
First published new in paperback 2001

British Library Cataloguing in Publication Data

Data available

Library of Congress Cataloging in Publication Data
The role of law in international politics: essays in international relations and
international law/[edited by] Michael Byers.
Includes bibliographical references.
1. International law.   2. International relations.   3. World politics—1989–
I. Byers, Michael, 1966–
KZ3092.R65 1999   341.21—dc21   99-045592
ISBN 0-19-826887-4
ISBN 0-19-924402-2 (pbk)

7 9 10 8

Typeset in Times by
Cambrian Typesetters, Frimley, Surrey
Printed in Great Britain
on acid-free paper by
Biddles Ltd., King's Lynn, Norfolk

Foreword

It is a very great honour for me to have been asked to write a foreword to this distinguished collection of essays. My own experience of international law has, I fear, been at best sporadic. Unlike almost any other foreign service that I know of, and certainly unlike most other European foreign services, the British Diplomatic Service requires no prior training in the law before appointment to the senior branch. Indeed, until recently, very little *subsequent* legal training of any sort has been provided for our mainstream diplomats—at least during my thirty-six years in the Service. One of the contributors to this volume, Sir Arthur Watts, deserves congratulations for having instituted, during his time as Legal Adviser, annual week-long courses for British diplomats, arranged by the Research Centre for International Law at Cambridge. However, I fear that I myself never found the opportunity to benefit from any of those courses.

True, I was given some training in the law of the Persian Gulf, during my training in Arabic at the Middle East Centre for Arabic Studies in Lebanon in the 1950s. In those days, young Arabists in the Diplomatic Service could expect an early posting to one of our Political Agencies in the Persian Gulf, where they would be expected to sit in expatriate courts to judge non-Sharia cases. As it happened, and perhaps just as well for both myself and the defendants, I never had the opportunity to test this training. My first posting to the Gulf came only some fifteen years later when, as the last Deputy Political Resident in Bahrain, I found myself responsible for helping to wind up the non-Sharia courts as we repatriated our special military, legal, and political responsibilities to the Gulf rulers and their governments.

As I have said, this lack of any requirement of legal training for diplomats seems to be peculiar to the British Diplomatic Service. It may perhaps be worth considering for a moment whether we are wise to let our diplomats loose on international diplomacy without the sort of legal training that our French and German colleagues, for instance, enjoy. Personally, I believe that we *are* right to separate policy-making from legal advice in this way—though as an ex-Head of the Diplomatic Service, I suppose that—like the reply of Miss Mandy Rice-Davies to Lord Denning—'I would say that, wouldn't I?'

In this context I would like to quote something that Sir Franklin Berman, the current Legal Adviser, has written about the structural model in other foreign ministries, where the legal function is carried out by a 'legal department' or 'legal division' which actually runs the files on those matters classified as wholly or predominantly 'legal'. 'On those matters', Sir Franklin has written, 'the lawyer has to make, propose or execute the policy on the basis of the legal advice which he himself has given—in all probability in answer to questions which he himself has formulated.'

Speaking personally, I would feel more comfortable—even if I had had much more extensive training in the law at an early age—to rely on the professional and experienced advice of lawyers like Sir Arthur and Sir Franklin. They have not only devoted a lifetime to the study and practice of international law within a foreign ministry and its missions abroad, but have also exemplified at all times the quality of legal advice which a former senior British diplomat and late Master of Pembroke College, Oxford, Sir Geoffrey Arthur, once described as 'trying to solve problems, rather than invent them'. Significantly, they have also continued to be regarded officially, and to regard themselves, as practising members of the legal profession.

I believe that this reliance by the British Diplomatic Service on a separate but integrated cadre of international lawyers, who remain practising barristers or solicitors while putting their legal knowledge at the service of the State, adds a very real strength to the legal input of the diplomatic and political advice which permanent officials are required to submit to Ministers.

Perhaps I am guilty of the alleged British devotion to amateurism, in arguing against the requirement of professional or extended legal training for members of the Diplomatic Service, or indeed for their mainstream colleagues in the Home Civil Service. I was reminded very recently of Harold Nicholson's claim that sheer common sense was perhaps the most important qualification for a diplomat. In March 1998, when I joined a parliamentary delegation on a visit to a United Nations demarcation post in southern Syria, near the cease-fire line with Israeli-occupied Golan, a United Nations officer commented to us that members of the United Nations Observer Force were required to operate 'not as lawyers, but as ordinary, well-meaning individuals'. I hope that international lawyers will not misinterpret that as an offensive contrast, or as implying in any sense that they are not thoroughly well-meaning. However, the remark contained, I think, an important distinction between the application of common sense and the benchmark of law.

Of course, the system only works if the diplomat remembers at all times the need to check his advice against what I have called the 'legal benchmark'. Woe betide the official who puts a submission to Ministers without having copied it first to the Legal Advisers, or without having first discussed the issue with them. In my experience, this essential rubric applies as much to such obviously legal questions as the Law of the Sea as it did to votes on issues in the United Nations Security Council. Sometimes, the advice might not be particularly welcome to Ministers. Indeed, Sir Franklin has pointed out to me that such few references as there are to lawyers in the memoirs of statesmen are usually on the lines of 'had to keep the lawyers out of it, and a good thing too'. I can only say that, on those very rare occasions when the lawyers were 'kept out of it'—either deliberately, or more usually by oversight—the issue nearly always went wrong, sometimes leading to a formal challenge, as for instance in the International or European Courts of Justice.

However, it would be wrong of me to suggest that, for the practising diplomat, the law is merely a benchmark against which to measure policy. International law—whether in the field of human rights, humanitarian law, environmental protection, or Security Council resolutions—increasingly forms the *substance* of international relations. To take two examples of international crises with which I was closely involved—the Argentine invasion of the Falkland Islands and the Gulf War—international law played a crucial and central role in resolving these two crises. In the first case, our diplomatic effort was radically altered by our ability to obtain a binding Chapter VII resolution from the Security Council. In the second case, the whole of our policy centred on the Security Council, and the constant efforts, through diplomatic and legal channels, to hold the coalition together, and to obtain the sanctions and collective military operation leading to an elaborate and unprecedented cease-fire regime.

I well remember how, through this latter crisis, the lawyers and diplomats, both in London and in New York, worked in close harmony to achieve our political objective. The law here was much more than a mere benchmark; it was an integral tool in the conduct of foreign policy.

Throughout my thirty-six years in the Diplomatic Service, and more recently at Chatham House, I have also become increasingly aware of the extent to which governments are now recognized as interdependent on each other, and on the international community at large. Of course, this was always true, but it was by no means universally acknowledged. Part of the trauma engendered in this country by the Suez Crisis of 1956 was the realization that, even at the height of British imperial self-confidence, the concept of total national sovereignty had been largely a myth. Similarly, part of the basis for what is crudely called 'Euroscepticism' in Britain today is the gradual but reluctant public realization that our own law courts and governments can be overruled by the European Court of Justice in Luxembourg.

Looking back on my five years as Permanent Under-Secretary from 1986 to 1991, I am struck by how many of the main political and international issues with which the Foreign and Commonwealth Office had to deal were intimately involved in international law. I have already referred to the Falklands Crisis and to the Gulf War. However, to take some other examples: the Iran/Iraq war involved frequent breaches by both sides of their obligations under international humanitarian law, and also, on occasion, raised issues concerning the Vienna Convention on Diplomatic Relations. The same war also required our lawyers to advise on attacks against British merchant shipping in the Gulf, and our right to take counter-action. The United States bombing raid on Libya raised questions—not all of them comfortable for British Ministers—about the legality of the use of force. The Stockholm Accord on Confidence Building and Disarmament in Europe raised new issues of observing and verifying military activities on the territory of other States. Many legal issues also arose from the international effort to suppress terrorism, whether by hijacking, or by attacks against aircraft and shipping.

I could go on. However, the two points I want to make are: (i) nearly all the diplomatic and political issues with which I was involved in those five years had a crucial legal dimension to them; (ii) the international legal agenda during my time as Permanent Under-Secretary impressed on me the significant change which has taken place over recent years in the attitude of sovereign governments to what used to be rejected as interference in their domestic affairs.

In April 1998, on the eve of a visit to Beijing by President Clinton, the release of a prominent civil rights activist represented an acknowledgement by the Chinese government that their treatment of dissidents is not purely a matter of domestic policy. Yet, when I accompanied Harold Wilson in the mid-1970s to Moscow and to Helsinki for the Conference of the Council on Security and Co-operation in Europe (CSCE), he twice tried to hand over to Mr Brezhnev a list of human rights cases in which the British government had a legitimate interest. On both occasions, the list was abruptly rejected as improper interference, and was left lying on the table.

Fifteen years later, when I visited Prague as Permanent Under-Secretary at the time of the Wenceslas Marches, I was able to make representations, to an admittedly rather frosty Secretary-General of the Czechoslovak communist government, about a young Czech who had been held without trial for over a year. His release the next day was something of a personal triumph for me; unlike lawyers, who lose or win cases, diplomats are seldom able to pin-point triumphs or failures in the stream of international relations. However, the point I want to make is not that my representations in that case were successful; it is remarkable that they were accepted at all.

Discussion of human rights cases under what is now called the Organisation for Security and Co-operation in Europe (OSCE) may seem to be straying somewhat from my theme. However, the change in the attitude of even communist governments towards the handling of what would previously have been regarded as matters of exclusively domestic policy illustrates a significant shift—and one not always acceptable to public opinion—in the concept of sovereignty.

In a remarkable address to Chatham House three years ago, Professor Sir Elihu Lauterpacht posed the question whether sovereignty was now myth or reality. His conclusion, I recall, was a finely balanced one. However, I would argue, from my own diplomatic experience, that much of the so-called Euroscepticism in the United Kingdom springs from the fallacy that we have always enjoyed unfettered sovereignty, which beastly foreigners in Brussels, Luxembourg, or Strasbourg are only now trying to take away from us.

Within our own country, the old adage that an Englishman's home is his castle reflects a fairly widespread fallacy that what we do behind the walls of our own homes is our own business, and no one else's. One has only to mention the issues of environmental protection, planning regulations, noise abatement, animal rights, and child abuse, to realize the extent to which we are now acknowledged, both by law and by custom, to be interdependent on each other.

So it is with governments, though I have to say that public opinion is sometimes readier to accept, and even to expect, our interference in other countries' affairs than to welcome their interference in ours. However, the more we all become, and acknowledge that we have become, interdependent nations, the more vital the contributions of international lawyers will become to the diplomats and politicians who conduct international affairs.

Lord Wright of Richmond
Chairman of the Royal Institute of International Affairs

Acknowledgements

Perhaps more than any other exercise engaged in by academics, the organization of a conference and the publication of the resulting essays require an enormous amount of co-operation and support. As the editor of this volume—indeed, during my entire time at Oxford—I was fortunate to have had the assistance of many remarkable people, only a few of whom I am able to acknowledge here.

Alan Boyle, the Honorary Secretary of the British Branch of the International Law Association, not only asked me to host the Branch's 1998 conference, he also gave me complete liberty to choose a topic and design a programme. I am grateful to him for his inspiration and trust. My Oxford colleagues Adam Roberts and Andrew Hurrell then commented on a series of draft programmes, thus adding an essential international relations perspective to the enterprise.

Another colleague, Carolyn Evans, helped with innumerable organizational tasks in the months leading up to the conference. Without her, it simply would not have happened. Four graduate students—Nicky Artemi, Simon Chesterman, Michelle Gavin, and Carol McQueen—provided essential assistance during the busiest three days.

Sir Franklin Berman, the Foreign Office Legal Adviser, threw his support behind the project at an early stage, making it possible to invite numerous speakers from overseas. He, along with Alan Boyle, Jeremy Carver, James Crawford, Denis Galligan, and Bruno Simma, served as genial yet provocative chairmen during the conference itself, while Anne Denise, my research assistant, helped bring the essays together afterwards.

I also wish to express my heartfelt thanks to the speakers and contributors. They have made my task much easier, not only by submitting essays of the highest calibre, but also by demonstrating great tolerance towards my largely unrefined editing skills.

Lastly, Jesus College Oxford, the Foreign and Commonwealth Office, the Oxford Centre for Socio-Legal Studies, the Oxford Centre for International Studies, Oxford University Press, the Rhodes Trust, and the British Academy were generous beyond expectation. I am grateful to them all.

M. B.

Duke University Law School
Durham, North Carolina

Contents

List of Contributors   xiii

Introduction
MICHAEL BYERS   1

1. The Importance of International Law
   SIR ARTHUR WATTS KCMG QC   5

2. Carl Schmitt, Hans Morgenthau, and the Image of Law
   in International Relations
   MARTTI KOSKENNIEMI   17

3. How Do Norms Matter?
   FRIEDRICH V. KRATOCHWIL   35

4. The Concept of International Law
   PHILIP ALLOTT   69

5. Emerging Patterns of Governance and International Law
   STEPHEN J. TOOPE   91

6. Domestic Politics and International Resources: What Role for
   International Law?
   EYAL BENVENISTI   109

7. Human Rights and the Politics of Representation: Is There a Role
   for International Law?
   CHRISTINE CHINKIN   131

8. Politics and Human Rights: An Essential Symbiosis
   MAKAU WA MUTUA   149

9. Governing the Global Economy through Government Networks
   ANNE-MARIE SLAUGHTER   177

10. The Politics of Law-Making: Are the Method and Character of Norm
    Creation Changing?
    VAUGHAN LOWE   207

11. Regulating the International Economy: What Role for the State?
    EDWARD KWAKWA   227

12. How to Regulate Globalization?
    BRIGITTE STERN   247

13. The Role of the United Nations Security Council in the
    International Legal System
    MARC PERRIN DE BRICHAMBAUT   269

14. The Functions of the United Nations Security Council in the
    International Legal System
    VERA GOWLLAND-DEBBAS   277

15. The Limits of the Security Council's Powers and its Functions in the
    International Legal System: Some Reflections
    GEORG NOLTE   315

Conclusion: International Law and the Changing Constitution
of International Society
ANDREW HURRELL   327

Index   349

Contributors

PHILIP ALLOTT is a Fellow of Trinity College and Reader in International Public Law, Cambridge University. He was formerly a Legal Counsellor in the Foreign and Commonwealth Office. He was Legal Counsellor in the British Permanent Representation to the European Communities at the time of the United Kingdom's accession in 1972–3, and an Alternate Representative in the United Kingdom delegation to the United Nations Law of the Sea Conference. He is the author of *Eunomia: New Order for a New World* (Oxford University Press, 1990), a general theory of international society and international law, as well as *Eutopia: The Return of the Ideal* (forthcoming).

EYAL BENVENISTI is Professor of Law at the Faculty of Law, Hebrew University of Jerusalem and Visiting Professor of Law at Columbia Law School. In 1998–99 he was Visiting Professor of Law at Harvard Law School. He received his LL B from the Hebrew University, and his LL M and JSD from Yale Law School. His main research interests are in the areas of human rights, freshwater law, and judicial review of administrative action. He is the author of *The International Law of Occupation* (Princeton University Press, 1993) and is currently working on his forthcoming book, *Sharing Freshwater: International Law and Optimal Water Use* (Cambridge University Press).

MICHAEL BYERS is Associate Professor of Law at Duke University. From 1996 to 1999 he was a Fellow of Jesus College, Oxford, and a Visiting Fellow of the Max Planck Institute for Comparative Public Law and International Law in Heidelberg. He is the author of *Custom, Power and the Power of Rules* (Cambridge University Press, 1999) and the translator of Wilhelm Grewe, *The Epochs of International Law* (Walter de Gruyter, 2000).

CHRISTINE CHINKIN is Professor of International Law at the London School of Economics and Political Science. She has previously taught in university law schools in Southampton, Sydney, Singapore, New York, London, and Oxford. Her teaching and research interests are in international law, including international dispute resolution processes, human rights, and the application of feminist theories to the international legal process. She is the author of *Third Parties in International Law* (Oxford University Press, 1993) and *Halsbury's Laws of Australia: Title on Foreign Relations* (1993) and *Dispute Resolution in Australia* (with H. Astor, Butterworth, 1993).

VERA GOWLLAND-DEBBAS is Associate Professor of Public International Law at the Graduate Institute of International Studies in Geneva. In 1995 she was Visiting Professor of United Nations Law at the University of California, Berkeley. She is the author of *Collective Responses to Illegal Acts in International Law: United Nations Action in the Question of Southern Rhodesia* (Martinus Nijhoff, 1990) and the editor of *The Problem of Refugees in the Light of International Law Issues* (Martinus Nijhoff,

1990). Her articles have focused in particular on Security Council sanctions, UN constitutional issues, such as the relationship between the Security Council and the International Court of Justice and International Criminal Court, and on the links between human rights and refugee law.

ANDREW HURRELL is a University Lecturer in International Relations and Fellow of Nuffield College, Oxford. His research interests include international relations theory, with particular reference to the study of institutions, and the international relations of Latin America. His publications include *The International Politics of the Environment* (co-edited with Benedict Kingsbury, Oxford University Press, 1992), *Regionalism in World Politics* (co-edited with Louise Fawcett, Oxford University Press, 1995), and *Inequality, Globalization and World Politics* (co-edited with Ngaire Woods, Oxford University Press, 1999).

MARTTI KOSKENNIEMI has been Professor of International Law at the University of Helsinki since 1996. From 1978 to 1996 he was a member of the Finnish foreign service, lastly as Counsellor (legal affairs) and acting director of the international law division. He served as Legal Adviser to Finnish delegations in the United Nations General Assembly from 1981, and in the Security Council in 1989–1990. He received his LL D from Turku University in 1989, and a Diploma in International Law from Oxford University in 1983. He is the author of *From Apology to Utopia: The Structure of International Legal Argument* (Lakimieeliiton Kustannus, 1989), and some fifty articles on international law and legal theory.

FRIEDRICH KRATOCHWIL is Professor of International Politics at the Geschwister-Scholl-Institute for Political Science at Ludwig Maximilians University in Munich. Prior to taking up the chair in Munich, he taught at Columbia University and the University of Pennsylvania. He is the co-editor of *The Return of Culture and Identity* (with Yosef Lapid, Lynne Rienner Publishers, 1996) and the author of *Rules, Norms, and Decisions: On the Conditions of Practical Legal Reasoning in International Relations and Domestic Affairs* (Cambridge University Press, 1989), as well as numerous articles on international relations, and the connections between international relations and international law.

EDWARD KWAKWA, a national of Ghana, is Assistant Legal Counsel at the World Intellectual Property Organization (WIPO) in Geneva. He holds law degrees from the University of Ghana, Queen's University, and Yale University. Before joining WIPO, he practised corporate and international trade law and investment with the law firm of O'Melveny and Myers in Washington, DC, worked as International Legal Adviser at the Commission on Global Governance in Geneva, as Senior Legal Adviser at the Office of the UN High Commissioner for Refugees, and briefly as Legal Affairs Officer at the World Trade Organisation. His publications include *The Legal Profession and the Protection of Human Rights in Africa* (co-edited with Evelyn Ankumah, Africa Legal Aid, 1999), *The International Law of Armed Conflict* (Martinus Nijhoff/Kluwer, 1992) and numerous articles on international law.

VAUGHAN LOWE is Chichele Professor of International Law at Oxford University and a Fellow of All Souls College. He has taught at the universities of Cardiff, Manchester and Cambridge and, as a visiting professor, at Duke University. He practises as a barrister from Essex Court Chambers, London, and is a consultant on international law to the Foreign and Commonwealth Office. He has published widely on international dispute settlement, economic law, and the law of the sea.

MAKAU WA MUTUA was educated at the University of Nairobi, the University of Dar-es-salaam, and Harvard Law School, where he obtained a doctorate in 1987. He is Professor of Law and Director of the Human Rights Center at the State University of New York at Buffalo School of Law. He teaches international law, human rights, and international business transactions. He has written extensively on human rights, international law, and African politics. He has been a visiting professor at Harvard Law School and the University of Puerto Rico School of Law. He has been a consultant for numerous United Nations and NGO projects on human rights. He is co-chair of the 2000 Annual Meeting of the American Society of International Law and chair of the Nairobi-based Kenya Human Rights Commission.

GEORG NOLTE is Professor of International Law at the University of Göttingen. From 1987 to 1999 he was a Fellow of the Max Planck Institute for Comparative Public Law and International Law. During this time he taught at the Universities of Leipzig (1990–1), New York University (1992), Saarbrücken (1998–9) and Regensburg (1999). He is the author of *Eingreifen auf Einladung* (*Intervention upon Invitation*) (Springer, 1999) as well as a number of articles on international law, comparative constitutional law, and comparative administrative law.

MARC PERRIN DE BRICHAMBAUT was educated at the Institut d'Etudes Politiques de Paris and the Ecole Normale d'Administration. He has served the government of France in numerous posts, including Special Assistant to the United Nations Under Secretary-General for International Economic and Social Affairs (1978–81); Adviser on development and economic issues to the Foreign Minister (1981–3); Chief of Staff to the Minister for European Affairs (1983–4); Chief of Staff to the Foreign Minister (1984–6); Cultural Counsellor at the French Embassy to the United States (1986–8); Principal Adviser to the Minister of Defence (1988–91); Ambassador and Representative of France to the CSCE/OSCE (1991–4); and now as Legal Adviser and Head of the Legal Division of the Foreign Ministry. He is a Conseiller d'Etat, has appeared on behalf of France before the International Court of Justice, and has published a number of articles on various issues of international relations and international law.

ANNE-MARIE SLAUGHTER is J. Sinclair Armstrong Professor of International, Foreign and Comparative Law and Director of Graduate and International Legal Studies at Harvard Law School. She has also taught at the University of Chicago. She holds doctoral degrees in both international law and international relations from Harvard and Oxford Universities and publishes widely in both disciplines, as well as being a leading contributor to the literature concerning the connections between international relations and international law.

BRIGITTE STERN was educated at the University of Strasbourg, Paris and New York University. She is Professor and Director of CEDIN-Paris 1, the Centre of International Law at the University of Paris I, Panthéon-Sorbonne. She has been a Visiting Professor at many law schools, among others Boston College, NYU Global Law School, Capetown University and San Paulo University. She is the Rapporteur of the International Law Association's Committee on State Succession, practises before the International Court of Justice, and publishes widely on subjects such as State succession, international legal theory, international arbitration, international economic law, international criminal law, and the extraterritorial application of law. She is the editor of *United Nations Peace-keeping Operations. A Guide to French Politics* (UNU Press, 1998) and the author of *20 ans de jurisprudence de la Cour internationale de justice* (Kluwer, 1998), and numerous articles.

STEPHEN TOOPE is Professor of Law at McGill University in Montreal. He completed his undergraduate education at Harvard University, holds two law degrees from McGill University, and has a Ph.D. in international law from the University of Cambridge. He served as a clerk to Chief Justice Brian Dickson of the Supreme Court of Canada. He is the author of *Mixed International Arbitration* (Cambridge University Press, 1990) and articles on family law, international environmental law, international arbitration, and human rights.

SIR ARTHUR WATTS KCMG QC read law at Downing College, Cambridge. He has been a barrister since 1957 and a Queen's Counsel since 1988. He joined the Foreign and Commonwealth Office in 1956 and served in various legal posts in London and abroad (Cairo, Bonn, Brussels). From 1987 to 1991 he was The Legal Adviser to the FCO. He is the author of numerous books and articles on international law, including (with Sir Robert Jennings QC) Volume I of the 9th edition of *Oppenheim's International Law*. He now practises at the Bar (20 Essex Street) and has appeared in several cases before the International Court of Justice. He is also the international mediator for Succession Issues in former Yugoslavia. From 1992 to 1998 he was President of the British Branch of the International Law Association; he now serves as Honorary President. He is a member of the Institut de droit international.

Introduction

MICHAEL BYERS

March the 24th 1999 might be considered one of the most important dates in the contemporary history of international law and international relations. On that day, the Judicial Appeals Committee of the House of Lords handed down its judgment in the *Pinochet Case*, holding that General Augusto Pinochet had no immunity for acts of torture allegedly committed while he was head of state in Chile during the 1970s and 1980s. For many international lawyers, this judgment by Britain's senior court was a pivotal moment, a highly public triumph of law over politics in the international arena. International law, long portrayed by sceptics as little more than a naïve delusion, had finally begun to bite—at the highest of levels and in the most visible of ways.

The euphoria, however, was short-lived. Just a few hours later, on that very same day, NATO cruise missiles and bombs began to rain down on the Federal Republic of Yugoslavia. In the eyes of most international lawyers, the attack was a clear violation of the United Nations Charter, the closest thing the international system has to a written constitution. The Charter not only prohibits the use of force without Security Council authorization in *all* circumstances except self-defence, it specifically requires that 'regional arrangements' obtain such authorization before they intervene in sovereign States.

To some lawyers, this deliberate violation of the most basic international obligation confirmed what they had long feared, that in the field of international peace and security, at least, law is a marginal consideration. The fact that most of the NATO States had long been among the staunchest supporters of an international rule of law only added insult to injury, as did the apparent sidelining of government legal advisers before, and during, the military campaign.

To other international lawyers, the air strikes were justified on a moral basis that was more important than traditional rules of international law. For them, the atrocities committed in Kosovo either justified an exceptional breach of the law, or compelled a re-evaluation of that law in light of developments in international politics and human rights such that the prohibition on the use of force would from now on be subject to a 'humanitarian' exception.

Coincidentally, 24 March 1999 was also the first day of the world's largest yearly gathering of academic international lawyers: the annual meeting of the American Society of International Law. Over one thousand experts had come together to discuss various aspects of the discipline, from human rights, to international trade, to the history and theory of international law. Appropriately, the meeting had explicitly been designed to explore the tensions that result from the influence of non-legal factors, of 'violence, money, power and culture', on the international legal system.

One could hardly imagine a more opportune moment, and a more suitable place, for a rigorous discussion of the fateful coincidence of these two momentous developments—Pinochet and Kosovo—and their implications for the future of international law.

Somewhat surprisingly, the convulsions experienced by the international legal system on that particular day were not debated in a sustained and public manner by those international lawyers gathered in Washington on 24 March 1999. True, there was a panel on the *Pinochet Case*, as well as a discussion designed around a hypothetical NATO intervention in an unnamed Balkan country. But it seems that the confluence of events in London and Kosovo was too unsettling, too momentous, too clearly the result of unresolved tensions between law, politics and morality, to be dealt with at that particular moment without a more lengthy consideration of their origins and consequences.

Many lawyers clearly feel that law should, and to a degree already does, play an important role in international affairs. This feeling is probably derived from some combination of experience, self-interest, and—in many cases—a morally based desire for a more stable and peaceful world. At the same time, most international lawyers concede that international law sometimes has a limited capacity to control political decisions. They readily admit that politics play a significant role in shaping legal structures and determining the content of rules, even if they often tend to shy away from considering how this actually occurs. All that said, to have expected a fuller discussion on the role of law in international politics on 24 March 1999 would have been like asking a geologist to theorize on plate tectonics while standing on the epicentre of a major earthquake.

Fortunately, a number of those present in Washington had considered many of these issues just less than one year earlier, at the annual conference of the British Branch of the International Law Association in Oxford on 24 and 25 April 1998. Without the pressure of momentous events weighing immediately upon them, 180 scholars and practitioners of international law and international relations had spent two full days discussing the relationship between their two areas, both generally and within a number of specific contexts. The result was a vigorous interdisciplinary exchange of ideas and insights that cast new light on the increasingly relevant issue of the role of law in international politics, as well as on subsequent developments such as the *Pinochet Case* and the Kosovo intervention. The papers delivered during those two days, and subsequently revised in light of the lengthy discussions that ensued, constitute the chapters of this book.

As the reader progresses through this volume, a number of themes will become apparent. These themes, which animated the Oxford conference, include the relationship between the disciplines of international law and international relations; the role of State and non-State actors in the ongoing development and application of the international legal system; the character of international norms, rules, and principles, and their effects—if any—on how States behave. All these themes are dealt with in sophisticated ways that reflect the maturity of academic thinking today on the relationship between international law and politics and that belie attempts to characterize such interdisciplinary contributions in simplistic terms, for example, as 'realist' versus 'legalist', or 'pragmatic' versus 'idealist'.

This volume also provides a rare window into another aspect of international law, namely the self-perception of international lawyers. How do international lawyers perceive their own role within the international political and legal systems? In the aftermath of the *Pinochet Case* and NATO's 'humanitarian war', it may now be appropriate to ask how conceptions of morality and justice affect what international lawyers do, for if those who advise and represent States in their international legal relations, and write about international law, are driven or at least influenced by their own conceptions of morality and justice, the influence of these conceptions on the content and application of that law may be significant indeed. The writings of the very same astute scholars who have contributed to this volume reflect an array of perspectives that are, in themselves, of interest to the attuned reader.

This book seeks to explore existing debates at the interface between international law and politics, and to add new voices and ideas to an already lively discussion. Perhaps most importantly, this book may well show that, while international lawyers recognize that international law and politics interact in highly complex ways, many international lawyers at the same time share a concern for peace and justice that motivates their efforts to promote, develop, and apply international law—both as it is, and as they believe it should be.

1

The Importance of International Law

SIR ARTHUR WATTS KCMG QC

'The importance of international law' is a beguilingly straightforward statement: bold, direct, positive, and confident. However, behind those apparent certainties lie the many uncertainties of the altogether more diffident questions: 'is international law important—and if so, how and why?'

One's sense of unease is sharpened by the thought that when considering our own national societies, we would not ask the equivalent question: 'is English law important?' And it may be instructive to ask why that should be so. There are perhaps three main reasons. We assume, rightly, that an effective legal system in our own countries *is* an important element in the fabric of society; we take it for granted that such a system, and the rule of law generally, do exist in practice; and we are generally confident that, given our democratic systems, the rules of law which go to make up those systems reflect a fair balance between the competing interests which exist within our own societies.

But at the international level there is a sufficient measure of doubt about each of these three elements to raise questions about the importance of international law. Each is therefore worthy of further consideration.

DO STATES ACCEPT THAT AN EFFECTIVE INTERNATIONAL LEGAL SYSTEM IS AN IMPORTANT ELEMENT IN THE FABRIC OF THE INTERNATIONAL COMMUNITY?

In principle, it would seem obvious that the importance of an effective international legal system is bound to be accepted at the international level. But the question still has to be posed: do States (as States are still the primary actors on the international stage) really want an effective international legal system? Do they assume its importance in international relations? The answer may well be a true lawyer's answer—'Yes' and 'No'.

The problem is grounded in the myth-begotten notion of State sovereignty. States, through their rulers or governments, think of themselves as sovereign. They do not, of course, always know what sovereignty means, but it is clearly worth having and keeping. Since from their perspective it probably includes something akin to a right to do whatever they want to do, the last thing that States are enthusiastic about admitting is the existence of something 'out there'—like a system of law—which tells them there are certain things they cannot do.

The instinctive attitude of many States is to do what they want, and legal considerations come well down the list of subsidiary matters to be taken into account.

Those with real international power seldom pay much attention to the law: for them, rather than international law being the framework which controls what they may do, it is their actions which shape the law. The constraints imposed by the law can be as unwelcome as they are sometimes unexpected. Indeed, to remind a politician active in international affairs of the relevance—and even of the very existence—of international law may sometimes be seen as an unfriendly act. But the fact remains that there are few, if any, aspects of international life which are without legal implications. Of course, the political aspects of many matters loom large, but this in no way deprives them of their legal aspects.[1] To assert the political quality of a State's international conduct cannot make international law irrelevant to the evaluation of that conduct. And while an international system of law may perhaps be thought to be an excellent thing for most of the time, at critical moments it can be rather a nuisance. Indeed, the more effective the international legal system is, the more of a nuisance for States it may become.

We have some experience of this in the United Kingdom. Successive generations of politicians have grown up comforted by the doctrine of the sovereignty of Parliament, and reassured that if they do not like the results of any particular state of legal affairs, Parliament can simply change the law. Part of the culture shock of joining the European Communities a quarter of a century ago was due to the slow dawning of an awareness that in an increasing number of fields there were external legal constraints upon what might be done, and that if those constraints were inconvenient, it was *not* simply a matter of Parliament removing the inconvenience. Experience with the processes of the European Convention on Human Rights and Fundamental Freedoms has been somewhat similar. In a very real sense the United Kingdom had become subject, as never before, to a written constitution impinging upon a significant portion of national life. But international law is not like that, is it? Internationally, we can still act in the way we think right, can't we? Well, actually, no, we cannot. There is this body of rules—international law—which, as well as conferring certain rights on States, also imposes certain obligations on them in the conduct of their international relations. It may therefore be time for another dose of culture shock. As Tolstoy put it in *War and Peace*, it is now 'necessary to renounce a freedom that does not exist, and to recognise a dependence of which we are not conscious'.

This body of international legal rules is obviously important in relation to the specific activities to which they apply—whether it be the use of force, rights on the high seas, the treatment of aliens, and so on. But even more important is what those specific rules imply at a much more general and abstract level. They are clear evidence of the existence of a climate of legality in international affairs, because unless States believe in the general notion of law as a basis for their behaviour, they would not seek to govern particular aspects of their behaviour by detailed rules.

---

[1] See the Advisory Opinion on *Legality of the Threat or Use of Nuclear Weapons* (1996) ICJ Reports, para. 13.

On the whole, States *do* acknowledge the importance of there being an effective international legal system. The rule of law in international affairs[2] involves the existence of a comprehensive system of law, certainty as to what the rules are, predictability as to the legal consequences of conduct, equality before the law, the absence of arbitrary power, and effective and impartial application of the law. The benefits of a state of affairs in which those elements are present are self-evident, and exert a powerful positive influence.

The rule of law represents a culture of order. In international affairs that culture has not yet been firmly established; nor, yet, has the international rule of law. But steady progress is being made. The rule of law is not something which can be established overnight either nationally, or internationally. Its benefits are long-term, not short-term: they are perceived not by the short-sighted, but by those with far-sight and insight. The rule of law involves accepting that international law is not an à la carte choice. It applies as a whole, and for all States including (and indeed especially) those with the physical and political power to marginalize the law if they so choose. The international community prospers when law and power are in partnership, not when they are in conflict.

Power carries responsibility, and even the short-sighted must see that the alternative to the rule of law is anarchy and disorder, even chaos. Except possibly in a short-term revolutionary context, the interests of *no* State can prosper in such circumstances. International trade and commerce, international finance, international communications—*all* are essential to the survival and well-being of States, and *all* require an international legal system to provide a stable framework within which they may function. The occasional constraints and disadvantages of the international legal system are overwhelmingly outweighed by the advantages which it confers on States.

It is, after all, the basis of their rights. More importantly, and more generally, it provides for stability in international relations. That stability is in turn the necessary basis for the pursuit by States of their national interests.

Thus, on the whole, one may be ready to conclude that States *do* regard an effective legal system as an important element in the functioning of the international community. They accept international law as an integral part of the international system of political order. State practice is replete with acknowledgements of the importance of international law as a system, and of the need to observe particular rules of the system. It is striking that virtually without exception States seek always to offer a legal justification for their actions, even in extreme circumstances where the action is manifestly contrary to international law—for example, Iraq's invasion of Kuwait in 1990. However valid or invalid the attempted justification may be, it is the very fact of advancing it which demonstrates the value attached by States to compliance with international law.

---

[2] See further A. Watts, 'The International Rule of Law' (1993) 36 German Yearbook of International Law 15.

However, one may legitimately ask why States behave in this way when, at least at first glance, the international legal system has sufficient weaknesses to tempt States, in the final analysis, simply to ignore it altogether. This is, of course, partly because States recognize, and reject, the alternatives of disorder and instability, and acknowledge that international law provides the only available framework for order and stability. But also it is partly because international law shares in the moral value which attaches to 'law' generally, and partly because of the weight attaching to considerations of reciprocity. It must also be said, even at the risk of seeming too cynical, that it is partly because States know that international law is imperfect, uncertain, and ineffective in important respects. There is room for the view that all that States need for the general purposes of conducting their international relations is to be able to advance a legal justification for their conduct which is not demonstrably rubbish. Thereafter, political factors can take over, and the international acceptability or otherwise of a State's conduct can be left to be determined by considerations of international policy rather than of international law. In this light, if politics is the art of the possible, then international law is merely the art of the plausible.

In effect, States' apparent acceptance of international law may be little more than high-sounding tokenism: they may feel that the importance of international law can be safely acknowledged precisely because, in the final analysis, it is weak and can be ignored.

This leads to the second main question which needs to be addressed.

DOES AN EFFECTIVE INTERNATIONAL SYSTEM OF LAW, INCORPORATING THE RULE OF LAW, IN FACT EXIST?

Looking at the day-to-day events of international life, the record is by and large good. Take the Eurostar train from London to Paris or Brussels—you can do so only because of an Anglo-French treaty about the Channel Tunnel; fly to Rome or New York—you can do so only because of air services agreements; try to sue a foreign diplomat, and discover that you cannot—again, because of rules about diplomatic immunity which are grounded in international law.

All of this we see as routine and we take for granted. Underlying these everyday activities is the wide range of international law issues embodied in such topics known to international lawyers as territorial sovereignty, freedom of the high seas, territorial waters, rights over aliens, and the application of treaties. For the most part, these routine aspects of international life seldom impinge upon the consciousness of the population at large, or even that of political élites.

But this is not always the case. Those who try to travel round the world by balloon, and omit to get clearance before they start from the various States whose territories they will overfly, quickly realize—as the Breitling Orbiter did in February 1998—that the Great Wall of China extends also around China's airspace. Air travel is *not* a right to be freely exercised world-wide by private persons! Even at the international inter-State level, air traffic agreements, although very technical, can also raise problems of very considerable commercial and political acuteness.

The general point, however, remains valid. For the most part, the day-to-day affairs of international intercourse run smoothly, and international law—which underpins them—plays its essential role without fanfare. The world gets on with its life safe in the (unstated) assumption that order exists in the international community. No doubt 95 per cent, perhaps more, of international life is like that.

However, the real systemic problems lie with the remaining 5 per cent of international life. The concern in respect of these areas is not for 'orderliness', but rather for 'order' in the sense of 'international public order'. *Who* ensures that international public order is maintained? Indeed, there is a prior question as to *whose* concept of international public order determines what it is that is to be maintained. And even if we know what 'public order' is to be maintained, and we know who is to maintain it, then there remains the further question as to *how* this should be achieved.

It is in these areas that the effectiveness of the international system of legal order comes under severe strain. It is tempting to see breakdowns in international order as affording some sort of analogy with murders at the national level. Murders certainly occur more often than we would wish. But no one seriously suggests that that means that the legal system as such has broken down: murder is accepted as an unfortunate occurrence *within* an ongoing legal system. However, this analogy provides only very limited comfort. The scale of the national and international legal systems is totally different, as is the magnitude of the consequences of such unfortunate occurrences. Murder usually involves a single victim, whereas war involves mass killing and maiming. Fortunately, inter-State wars of the traditional, formal type are no longer common (although it would be premature to assume their complete disappearance, as the outbreak of hostilities between Ethiopia and Eritrea in June 1998 sharply reminded us). But the balance of misfortune is restored by the more far-reaching international consequences which civil wars now have. These wars cannot be ring-fenced or quarantined, in the hope that the consequences will not spread. They spill over local boundaries, both in their hostilities (modern weapons are not boundary-sensitive) and their consequences (such as the refugee flows to which they give rise). They tempt participation, either openly or covertly, by outside States, which can lead *de facto* to inter-State wars, or to wars by proxy.

Armed conflicts clearly pose a threat to the international community as a whole, even if they are essentially civil wars, but of course even more so if they are truly international. Moreover, the international community has not yet found the proper response. Faced with situations where the unwillingness to tolerate forceful changes of international frontiers runs up against the emergence of stubbornly persistent factual situations of that kind, the principles of non-recognition serve a short-term purpose but can hardly offer a long-term solution. Similarly, attachment to the territorial integrity of States coexists uneasily with the principle of self-determination, and in most circumstances one or other, but never both, of these considerations is allowed to prevail. The confusion of the conflict is matched by the weakness and uncertainty of the response.

This is partly because some of the older certainties are being dismantled, without being effectively replaced. Two of the perceived underpinnings of the 'old' international community are disappearing before our eyes (if only we open them wide enough)—namely, sovereignty and territory. The modern world is no longer a fit place in which either of these two notions can prosper. The power which 'sovereignty' was thought to embody was probably always a myth and a label at the international level, but even if it once had real international significance, it has less and less now. It is being demoted to a symbol of emotional and nostalgic attachment to a fictitious past. As for territory, as the real expression of a State's exclusivity and the bedrock upon which stands every State's right to say 'this is mine' and 'Keep Out', it looks set to succumb to the globalization of the world's economy and communications. Globalization came upon States largely unnoticed, and now that they have noticed, they are finding that the traditional tools are no longer appropriate for the job. The consequences of globalization cannot be adequately regulated by reference to a legal order which is based on sovereignty and territory, the very concepts that are being outmoded by that same globalization.

Another major change involves the use of armed force. Unlike sovereignty and territory which, as useful basic concepts, are being outmoded by general developments in society at large, the international community sought itself to regulate the use of force. By voluntary choice, after looking around the world and seeing that the conflicts in it were bad, the international community cried 'Stop! Resort to force is prohibited'. But outlawing resort to force is like abolishing taxes—it sounds like a good idea at first, but the more one thinks about it, the more problems one foresees.

Perhaps the most serious problem with outlawing force is that sometimes resort to it is both necessary and desirable. It is often the only way to keep or restore order. To prohibit resort to force is to create a gap in the necessary mechanisms for the regulation of the international community which it has so far failed effectively to fill. There is a choice: the international community must either establish an international force to maintain order, or let States perform that function themselves. The framers of the United Nations Charter attempted the former, but their good intentions have never really been carried through. Although the emerging practice of national or multinational peacekeeping forces acting under *ad hoc* UN authority is a partial substitute, one is left in practice with self-appointed guardians of the peace. However, *that* cannot be a satisfactory basis on which to organize a legal order.

Nevertheless, such self-appointment is not necessarily a recipe for chaos or abuse. Of course, unilateral resort to armed force in blatant disregard of international law does tend in that direction, but unilateral action is still possible *within* the law rather than in breach of it.

First, resort to force is acceptable if undertaken pursuant to suitable international authorization, preferably from the Security Council. States accept this, provided they get the authorization they want. If they get it, and thereafter stay within it, the results fit readily within the formal requirements of the international community's legal order. However, the formal acceptability of authorized resort to armed force must not be allowed to conceal the frequently underlying reality. This is vividly illustrated in the Balkans, where the present century began and is now ending with extensive armed conflict. The Balkan Wars of 1911–13 were effectively settled by the mediation of the then Great Powers in 1913 and 1914. Those 'Powers' were Italy, Austria-Hungary, Germany, Great Britain, France, and Russia. More recently, the conflicts associated with the break-up of Yugoslavia are (hopefully) in the process of being settled by today's Great Powers. It is true that they have the general blessing of the Security Council and that they are no longer called the 'Great Powers' but rather act in some other nominal guise—such as Peace Implementation Council, Contact Group, or Steering Board. Nevertheless, in substance they are still the Great Powers: *plus ça change,* . . .

Those States determined to resort to armed force need not be deterred if they fail to get the international authorization which they seek (they may even refrain from seeking it, where circumstances are such that they are unlikely to attract sufficient supporting votes). There is a second lawful option open to them: they can invoke certain exceptions to the prohibition against the use of force. There are one and a half such exceptions.

The one clear exception is self-defence. That is, it is clear in the sense that self-defence is acknowledged to be an exception, but it is not at all clear what the content of that exception is. Given the need in practice to bring any resort to force which is not authorized by the Security Council within the scope of self-defence if it is to be considered lawful, the concept is being steadily distorted, so as to justify, or attempt to justify, a range of actions which no normal, traditional notion of self-defence would recognize as being comprised within it. However, this is not necessarily wrong. Self-defence probably has to be an inherently relative concept—relative to the times and circumstances in which it is invoked. Self-defence in the days of naval warfare, such as that at Trafalgar, is a very different thing from self-defence in the days of nuclear warfare, Exocet missiles, and the possibility of easy transport to almost any destination in the world of small packages of anthrax or nerve agents. All the same, there are limits to the burden which the concept of self-defence can safely, and legally, be called upon to bear. It is essentially a legal concept, and its application to any particular circumstances must be evaluated in accordance with international law. To stretch the concept to such an extent that it departs from the ordinary meaning of the term, as refined by judicial pronouncements, serves not only to undermine this particular branch of the law, but also to bring the law in general into disrepute.

The half-exception to the prohibition on the use of force is only just beginning to emerge. It is thus its merely emergent status which justifies it being regarded at present as only a half-exception. It is the use of force to meet overriding humanitarian concerns. At the time of the Gulf War, it was seen clearly in relation to the Kurds in northern Iraq. It has again been evident in many aspects of international action in former Yugoslavia, such as the establishment of so-called 'safe havens' in certain

towns in Bosnia and Herzegovina, and in concerns expressed in 1998 by the international community in relation to repressive action by Serb forces in the Yugoslav
province of Kosovo. And it is not only the occurrence of conflict which may bring
this exception into play. The intervention in response to the breakdown of all local
statal structures, with consequent overwhelming humanitarian consequences, that
occurred in Somalia in 1992–4, fell into this general category at least with regard to
its motivation, even though it was specifically authorized by the Security Council.
Whatever one may think of the individual incidents, the trend seems clear. The
world does have a social conscience: John Donne told us that we should 'ask not for
whom the bell tolls'—the answer ('It tolls for thee') is international as much as
personal. President Woodrow Wilson may be credited with some foresight when he
observed, in a speech at Pueblo in 1919, that 'you will see that international law is
revolutionized by putting morals into it'. There *is* an international social imperative
which cannot be ignored, whatever the letter of the law may say. Perhaps it represents a special kind of *ius cogens* which prevails even over Article 2.4 of the Charter
(bearing in mind that Article 103 of the Charter only refers to conflicts between the
Charter and other agreements; it does not expressly cover conflicts with other rules
of international law, let alone rules having the status of *ius cogens*, a concept which
was unknown in 1945).

This is perhaps all due in part to the decline of territory as an absolute in the
international community's legal order. Humanitarian action involves denying to a
State its exclusivity within its own territory. The plea that something is solely a
matter of a State's own internal affairs is a plea which, increasingly over the last fifty
years, has fallen on deaf ears. Increasingly, what happens within States can no longer
be treated as solely their concern. Human rights initiated the trend, the environment
followed suit and is in turn followed by conduct creating vast refugee flows and internal conflict which can nowadays so easily spill over and disrupt, if not destroy, whole
regions.

The situation in Kosovo, a part of the Federal Republic of Yugoslavia (FRY), in
1998 vividly illustrated these general considerations. The 90 per cent ethnic
Albanian population of Kosovo, who resent the rule of the Serb-dominated FRY of
which Kosovo forms part, sought first to regain the autonomy which Kosovo had
enjoyed until 1989, and then gradually resorted to armed struggle to gain independence from the FRY. Repression of these Kosovan movements by the armed forces
of the FRY took extreme forms which earned the strong condemnation of the international community in general—yet all States accepted that Kosovo was part of the
FRY. Indeed, the international community has been insistent that it did not agree to
independence as an acceptable goal for Kosovo. The territorial integrity of the FRY
has been given priority in this context, and remarkably little has been heard of the
principle of self-determination. Thus, the international community emphasized that
the matter was, essentially, a civil war and an internal matter for the FRY, for which
the latter was nevertheless internationally accountable.

It is necessary to try to shape concepts correctly, especially when they are first

emerging. And to assert an overriding international social imperative that gross violations of humanitarian standards cannot be permitted, one must ask whose standard
of social necessity determines the content of that imperative. The world is multicultural, and one region's standards are not necessarily better than another's. 'Different'
yes—but 'better'?

Even if one were to accept, with whatever qualifications are necessary, the enforcement of humanitarian standards as a possible exception to the general prohibition
against the use of force, alongside the more clearly established exceptions of self-
defence and international authorization, most internationally wrongful acts nevertheless remain beyond the realistic scope of forceful enforcement action. Generally
States have no lawful alternative but to rely on diplomatic remonstrations, and such
forms of unilateral pressure not involving force as they can bring to bear. These are
usually actions such as restricting or disrupting discretionary bilateral links, or
imposing various forms of economic or political sanctions, but they all lack compul-
sive authority. They are also relatively blunt instruments, which can damage others
than those against whom they are directed (even including the very States which have
invoked them). Although considerations of reciprocity, and the interdependence of
States, render such measures more effective than they might otherwise be if considered in isolation, they remain poor substitutes for what most societies accept as the
normal mechanism for enforcing the law and settling disputes, namely an effective
and comprehensive judicial system. However, at the international level, the reality is
that for the most part States can act without fear of effective legal control. Although
the International Court of Justice exists, it can only deal with an infinitesimally small
part of the whole range of international problems; and even then it can only deal
with them to the extent that the States concerned consent.

Much the same can be said of other international courts and tribunals.
Sometimes, of course, States get a shock and find themselves before a tribunal
through some earlier consent which they had overlooked or which had been given in
some other context but which, to their surprise, is held to cover also the instant case.
This is rare, however. Across the board, States can usually proceed without any practical fear of being called to account before an impartial judicial tribunal. The relative
weakness of the international judicial system inevitably reduces the effectiveness of
international law and thus its importance as a regulator of State behaviour.

It is, however, important not to overstate the weaknesses of the international judicial order, just as it is important not to equate the international judicial order with
the International Court of Justice alone. The network of international tribunals
functioning judicially has grown fast in the past fifty years, and looks set to continue
growing. In comparison with the situation 100 years ago, today's international judicial structures are impressively extensive.

None the less, the international judicial order suffers from one particular weakness, namely its consensual character. Even the so-called 'compulsory' jurisdiction of
the ICJ depends on the consent of States to participate in that part of the Court's
system. Unfortunately, it does not follow that where a State has accepted a Court's

jurisdiction it is ready to comply with the Court's judgments. This is illustrated by certain notorious cases,[3] and notwithstanding Article 94 of the United Nations Charter. Hitherto, international tribunals have been very solicitous of the interests of those who voluntarily accept their jurisdiction. Tribunals are indeed faced with a dilemma. On the one hand, the administration of justice may call for a tribunal to take a firm line with a State appearing in a case before it. On the other hand, if the tribunal takes too firm a line, the State concerned may walk away from the tribunal, and other States may be deterred from referring their problems to the hands of such a 'tough' tribunal. To seek to do justice in such a way that the curial mechanism for doing justice is undermined may not, in the long run, be the best way forward in the wider interests of international order.

There is room for the view that international tribunals could take a firmer line with those States appearing before them. It may be that the temper of the international community towards the international judicial system is becoming more rigorous—a kind of 'judicial climate change' may perhaps be detected. Looking at the International War Crimes Tribunal for former Yugoslavia (and even the less successful parallel Rwanda Tribunal), the prospective International Criminal Court, the former GATT panels, and now the WTO system of adjudication for trade disputes, the regional judicial structures such as the European Court of Human Rights, and so on, it may not be too fanciful to see in them not only a gradually greater willingness on the part of the international community to impose strong judicial structures on itself, but also a greater readiness on the part of States to accept that increased strength. It is, in fact, a measure of the international judicial system's authority how far it is willing to *impose* that authority on States. At the same time, the exercise of that authority may itself be expected to increase the esteem of the system, and thus render the rejection of that authority less likely. The circle becomes a virtuous upward spiral, not a vicious downward one.

Moreover, the need for international jurisdiction to be consensual may be showing some signs of erosion, in reality if not yet in theory. The closer integration of judicial structures into arrangements in which States have a strong interest in participating means that their acceptance of the judicial element becomes subsumed within their much greater need to accept the arrangement as a whole. While still a matter of consent, the attraction of the overall arrangement (e.g. in the field of international trade) is such that withholding that consent is not really an option. With that knowledge in the background, the integrated tribunal can afford to be robustly judicial without risking its authority being denied.

But, just as no tribunal can be robustly judicial if it fails, *qua* tribunal, to observe proper judicial standards, so too the authority it wields within the community

---

[3] Most recently in the *Case Concerning the Vienna Convention on Consular Relations (Paraguay v. USA)* (1998) ICJ Reports (Order of 9 Apr. 1998), in which, despite an Order from the ICJ requiring that the execution of a Paraguayan national be delayed pending consideration of the merits of the dispute, he was executed a few days after the Court made its Order.

reflects the extent to which the laws it applies command general respect. One must therefore ask a further question.

DO THE RULES OF INTERNATIONAL LAW REPRESENT A FAIR BALANCE BETWEEN THE COMPETING INTERESTS WITHIN THE INTERNATIONAL COMMUNITY?

The existence of competing interests is a normal feature of any society: international society is no different. But not all States are at the forefront of such competition: most just want order. However, some States seek to impose their own kind of order. Over the past fifty years there have been great conflicts of this kind. For example, the order of the old, imperial world was ranged against that of the newer, post-colonial world. The order of the economically developed world confronted that of the economically developing world. There was also the order of the communist world, pitted against that of the Western democratic world. That ideological struggle now seems to be over, but in the field of human rights a similar struggle still rages: is it *my* idea of human rights, or *yours* which is to prevail?

None of this is inimical to the existence or effectiveness of an international legal order. It is natural for social groups to struggle for what they see as their own best interests. Out of that struggle emerges a balance, which reflects the new order. The process is dynamic, not static: interests fade, existing interests change their emphasis, and new interests emerge. Moreover, the balance changes not just because of the changing interests of international society's component groupings, but also because of changing technologies which open up new areas in which balances have to be struck, and because of changes in the focus of States as they respond to world events.

As all these changes occur, the balances within the international community change too. International law, which can only be important to the international community if it reflects the balances within that community, must therefore change as well. An out-of-date law is an irrelevant law, and an irrelevant law cannot be an important law.

The processes of change in international law are, however, imperfect. Much of the law is customary international law, based on the general practice of States—a phenomenon which is as imprecise a source of law as it is a slow vehicle for change. Even if it is admitted that in applying the law courts may occasionally change it, judicial decisions can hardly be an appropriate way of securing methodical change. Judicial involvement with the law is in this context essentially haphazard, since it depends entirely on what particular matters States may choose to bring forward for judicial settlement. Moreover, a court will be concerned to decide the particular case brought before it, rather than formulate the whole branch of the law of which part may be in issue in the case. Treaties can generate general changes in the law, but only slowly, as part of a process involving the growth of new customary international law. For the most part treaties only bind the parties and do not, even when participation in them is widespread, approach the status of true law of general application. The reality is that the international legal system has no legislative process capable of producing instant and general change in the law.

An equal reality, however, is that international law *does* change. The processes of change may not be rapid, or reliable, or straightforward, but somehow the necessary changes occur. 'Muddling through' can be as effective in practice as it is unsatisfactory in principle. At least it shows that the international legal system does not suffer from so substantial an inability to change that the system itself is undermined. The problems lie more in the timeliness of change, and in securing the right direction for change.

CONCLUDING OBSERVATIONS

There seems no good reason to doubt that, across the board, international law *is* an important part of the structure of our international society. States accept it as such, and their record in observing it bears comparison with the level of law observance in many countries. It is, however, necessary to emphasize that it is 'part' of the structure, in two senses of the word. First, it is an integral part of it, and therefore not an optional extra; and second, it is but one part in the overall equation—important, but not to the exclusion of other parts.

Its importance is a function of its effectiveness and its ability to respond to change. Both, at the present time and for the most part, are adequate, but perhaps only just. Certainly, neither can be taken for granted. Both need attention and development within a framework of respect for the international rule of law, if a stable international order is to prevail.

2

Carl Schmitt, Hans Morgenthau, and the Image of Law in International Relations

MARTTI KOSKENNIEMI

Three themes cross the conventional boundary between international law and international relations today: (1) the end of the State; (2) liberal millenarianism; (3) a call from academia for interdisciplinary co-operation between international lawyers and international relations people. How might such themes relate to each other? We have been here before. I would like to sketch that story.

Once upon a time there was a young republic in Germany. Set up in 1919 it never had any real supporters but it did have a lot of enemies. The Constitution of Weimar stood only because it had been enacted; it was the formalist's dream of a pure law come true, with an ironic twist, valid without support from society or from a general sense of justness. Among its many critics Carl Schmitt—later named the crown jurist of the Third Reich, an indefatigable enemy of liberalism—stands out.[1] For him, it was clear that the Constitution's formal validity did not determine its success or failure, nor that of the political order it had set up. Their fate was, rather, dependent on the autonomous decision of the one who had the power to call in the police.[2] Weimar's official liberalism was incapable of putting up a meaningful resistance. It was a politics of anti-politics that allowed the capture of the State by special interests. The *Reichsrat* would not have decided to free either Christ or Barabbas but would have agreed to postpone the decision or to set up a Commission of Inquiry.

A realistic law is a reflection of the concrete order—*eine konkrete Ordnung*—not of formal validity. The same applies internationally. Different States were inhabited by nations that radiated different degrees of power and influence—of *Kultur*—over their neighbours. To ignore this was to condemn the law to irrelevance—look at the

---

[1] Among burgeoning secondary literature, see George Schwab, *The Challenge of the Exception: An Introduction to the Political Ideas of Carl Schmitt between 1921–1936* (New York: Greenwood Press, 1989), and Joseph W. Bendersky, *Carl Schmitt: Theorist for the Reich* (Princeton: Princeton University Press, 1983). For a recent review of the various sides in the Weimar debate, cf. David Dyzenhaus, *Legality and Legitimacy: Carl Schmitt, Hans Kelsen and Hermann Heller in Weimar* (Oxford: Clarendon Press, 1997). For Schmitt and international law, cf. Mathias Schmoeckel, *Die Grossraumtheorie. Ein Beitrag zur Geschichte der Völkerrechtswissenschaft im Dritten Reich, insbesondere der Kriegseit* (Berlin: Duncker and Humblot, 1994).

[2] That is to say, to decide on the institution of the state of exception (as well as, implicitly, of whether and under what conditions the 'normal situation' may be allowed to continue), cf. Carl Schmitt, *Political Theology: Four Chapters on the Concept of Sovereignty* (Cambridge, Mass.: MIT Press, 1985), 5, 13.

inability of the League to rectify the anachronisms of Versailles! A concrete law had to take such differences into account—as it sometimes did. The United States had had its Monroe doctrine; the British their Empire.[3] Let the Germans now have their *Grossraum.* Nothing less could be expected of a law that aspired to reflect the actual conditions of the society in which it existed.

In Coburg, Northern Bayern, in the Wilhelminian Empire a son was born in 1904 to an authoritarian father, a Jewish doctor and a German patriot, Ludwig Morgenthau. Later young Hans attended the Gymnasium Casimirianum. As the top student in his class, on 11 April 1922 he received the honour of being asked to deliver a speech to the graduates and lay a laurel on the statue of the Gymnasium's founder, Duke Johann Casimir. A photograph shows how, during the address, another Duke, Carl Eduard von Saxen-Coburg Gotha, sat in the front row holding his nose to show his contempt for the stinking Jew.[4] Here was the Weimar spirit.

Young Hans chose to study law—not, he tells, because he was interested in it but because his father would not let him study literature. Law was a second best as it 'appeared to make the least demands on special skills and emotional commitment'.[5] Having graduated from law school in 1927 Hans Morgenthau took up the position of assistant to the socialist lawyer Hugo Sinzheimer, a former participant in the Weimar Assembly, sometimes, from 1931, pleading on his behalf before the labour court. Morgenthau recounted of that experience:

What was decisive was not the merits of legal interpretation, but the distribution of political power. Most of the judges were passionately and sometimes openly hostile to the Republic and to the political parties and social structure supporting it.[6]

Or, in another context:

The judges were generally very conservative, if not reactionary, and they hated, first of all they hated Jews . . .[7]

Such experiences must have convinced Morgenthau about the futility of confidence in a formal Constitution, however rational its principles of organization or liberal its political ethos. Writing almost twenty years thereafter (1946), Morgenthau had not the slightest hesitation in characterizing Weimar, its ideal of the Rule of Law, and the liberal internationalism associated with the League of Nations, as forms of a *decadent* liberalism—in contrast to the 'heroic' liberalism of the nineteenth century—that lacked the courage to see the truth of human society as an unending struggle for power.[8]

---

[3] Carl Schmitt, *Völkerrechtliche Grossraumordnung. Mit Interventionsverbot für raumfremde Mächte* (Berlin: Deutscher Rechtsverlag, 1939), 46–64.

[4] The story is recounted in Christoph Frei, *Hans J. Morgenthau. Eine intellektuelle Biographie* (2nd edn., Berne: P. Haupt, 1994), 24–5, and in Kenneth W. Thompson, 'Hans J. Morgenthau: Principles of Political Realism', in id., *Masters of International Thought* (Baton Rouge, La.: Louisiana State University Press, 1980), 81.

[5] Hans Morgenthau, 'An Intellectual Autobiography' (Jan./Feb. 1978) 15 Society 63.

[6] Ibid. 65.   [7] Frei, *Morgenthau,* 41.

[8] Hans Morgenthau, *Scientific Man vs. Power Politics* (Chicago: University of Chicago Press, 1946), 41 *et seq.,* 68–71.

The latter part of the 1920s saw a relative calm in Weimar. But the crisis in German public law continued unabated. In his inaugural lecture in Geneva in 1932 on the topic *Der Kampf der deutschen Staatslehre um die Wirklichkeit des Staates*,[9] Morgenthau joined Schmitt and others in an attack against the formalism and conceptual abstractions of the old, neo-Kantian school of public law positivism associated with the names of Laband, Jellinek, and his future supporter, Kelsen. Morgenthau appreciated the way Schmitt founded his legal work on the centrality of the political, showing 'an uncommon spiritual intensity and certainty of instinct'. But he felt that Schmitt never succeeded in building more than a fragmentary set of proposals for a new public law; that Schmitt had gone only half-way, failing to see that at the heart of the political lies the unchanging psyche of the human being, his lust for power.[10]

Morgenthau first manifested his 'interdisciplinary' interest in the political in his dissertation in the Faculty of Law of Frankfurt am Main: *Die internationale Rechtspflege, ihr Wesen und ihre Grenzen* (1929).[11] This, he explained, was 'conceived partly as a reply to' Carl Schmitt's *Der Begriff des politischen*,[12] the first edition of which had been published two years earlier. The ostensible purpose of the thesis was to conduct an inquiry into the limits of the judicial and arbitral function in the international field—a rather standard object of scholarly interest in the 1920s. Behind the dogmatic surface, however, it is not difficult to detect a somewhat anxious attempt to come to grips with the relationship between law and politics in international life and, particularly, to develop an explanation for what it is that makes international law such a fragile structure.[13] For Morgenthau, the political and the legal were not mutually exclusive. To think otherwise would have abolished the judicial function altogether. For the political has no substance. It is a quality that may be attached to *any* object, describing the degree of intensity with which that object is linked to the State. Anything might be—and nothing is necessarily—political, including law.[14]

Accordingly, there are two kinds of international conflicts: 'disputes' (*Streitigkeiten*) that can be expressed in legal claims and 'tensions' (*Spannungen*) that cannot be so expressed because they seek a transformation of legal rights and

---

[9] [*The struggle within German public law doctrine concerning the reality of the State*]; cf. Frei, *Morgenthau*, 120–6.

[10] Ibid. 124. On Morgenthau's wish to inaugurate a psychological theory of the State, cf. ibid. 125, and on Freud's influence on Morgenthau, cf. Morgenthau, 'Autobiography', 67.

[11] [*International legal claims, their nature and their limits*].

[12] Morgenthau, 'Autobiography', 68. Schmitt's influential book has been translated as *The Concept of the Political* (translated with an introduction by George Schwab, with a new foreword by Tracy B. Strong, Chicago: University of Chicago Press, 1996).

[13] My reading has been much influenced by Pekka Korhonen, *Hans Morgenthau. Intellektuaalinen Historia* [in Finnish; *H.M. An Intellectual History*] (Jyväskylä: Myy Jyväskylän yliopisto, Valtio-opin laitos, 1983), 12–39.

[14] Hans Morgenthau, *Die internationale Rechspflege, ihr Wesen und ihre Grenzen* (Leipzig: Noste, 1929), 62–72. In fact, Morgenthau claims, the concept of the political and the concept of national 'honour' cover an identical space, ibid. 127–8.

duties.[15] To which class a conflict belongs cannot, however, be determined by pre-existing criteria. Moreover, the two kinds of conflict may also develop into, or include, each other, in whole or in part.[16] Everything depends on how the matter is subjectively viewed by the State—or the national community—itself.[17] Although 'tensions' cannot successfully be dealt with by formal dispute-settlement bodies, the legal system should none the less take account of them. The law should change from a static to a dynamic order.[18] It should be equipped with a (legislative) mechanism that would reflect the underlying political transformations and integrate new values and power relations into itself while at the same time limiting States' unilateral right to resort to war.[19]

Morgenthau's intention was not to defend increasingly frequent submissions of international disputes to third-party settlement. On the contrary, in his view the fact that disputes often contained or developed into political tensions frequently made them inappropriate for such settlement: the judges' (unconscious) bias would make them untrustworthy; or it would appear to the parties that a large issue was being decided by reference to its marginal aspects only.[20] In both cases, the essential precondition of justiciability in the subjective sense—namely trust in the settlement organ by the parties—could not be presumed. Trust, again, was conditioned on taking the interests of the parties adequately into account.[21] For Morgenthau, third-party settlement was not—as suggested by the 'Schiboleth of the arbitration movement' (*der Schiedsgerichtsbewegung*)—a precondition for the maintenance of peace but a consequence thereof.[22]

Like domestic society, international society was governed by a basic psychological drive: the desire for self-expression in and domination over community.[23] But while in domestic society there was a consensus on how the societal changes resulting from this drive were reflected in law, no such consensus existed at the international level. Here lay international law's special weakness. A shift in power would always be accompanied by threat of violence.[24]

It was not easy to see how, in the absence of formal legislation, law could 'take account' of the vicissitudes of politics without ceasing to be law. In an admiring memorial article on Gustav Stresemann, Germany's influential foreign minister from 1923 to 1929, Morgenthau made the point that Stresemann's success lay in his ability to conduct a genuinely German *Völkerrechtspolitik vis-à-vis* the Versailles settlement while at the same time strengthening the structures of international peace. The

---

[15] Morgenthau, *Die internationale Rechtspflege*, 73–84.

[16] Ibid. 80–3 and, for a slightly elaborated account, Hans Morgenthau, *La Notion du 'politique' et la théorie des différends internationaux* (Paris: Recueil Sirey, 1933), 72–85.

[17] Morgenthau, *Die internationale Rechtspflege*, 126–7.   [18] Ibid. 27.

[19] The integration of essential interests into the law meant, for instance, the exclusion from third-party settlement of disputes about *Lebensinteressen*. Interestingly, like Schmitt, Morgenthau applied this exclusion to the US Monroe Doctrine, ibid., for example, 107–9.   [20] Ibid. 84–97.

[21] Ibid. 84.   [22] Ibid. 95, 97.

[23] '. . . nach Selbsterhaltung und nach Geltung innerhalb der Gemeinschaft, kurz, von dem Triebe nach Erhaltung und Durchsetzung der Persönlichkeit', ibid. 74.

[24] Ibid. 77.

settlement—including the League of Nations—had been 'in seiner ursprünglichen geistigen und politischen Funktion dem deutschen Wesen fremd'.[25] By securing Germany's membership in the League, Stresemann was able to transform the nature and policy of the organization in accordance with the new European situation and to end Germany's spiritual isolation through means that did not involve the use of violence, indeed were opposed to it.[26]

This may have been a weak consolation, however, and certainly a doubtful argument for proving the law's importance. Later on, Morgenthau no longer saw the League as an example of a successful strategy for guaranteeing the realism of the law. Were Germany's (apparent) successes in Geneva not precisely proof of the weakness of international law which, as he argued in his dissertation that same year, lay in the fact that it was constantly penetrated by politics?

From that discovery there was but one step to the conclusion that what really mattered in relations among nations was not international law but international politics.[27]

A part of his second book *La Notion du 'politique' et la théorie des différends internationaux* (1933) repeats the discussion concerning the distinction between (legal) disputes and (political) tensions while another part is dedicated to a rather dogmatic critique of Schmitt's conception of the political.[28] None the less, the obsession with the political and its characterization as an intensity concept (i.e. a concept whose actualization was relative to the intensity with which the State regarded something as being in its interests) is shared by both; the critique seems more a sectarian struggle over orthodoxy than an important opposition. Here Morgenthau reveals his early infatuation with Nietzsche[29] by formulating his theory of the will to power (*volonté de puissance*) as the core of his sociology.[30] This was manifested internationally by the way all States sought to maintain, increase, or manifest power, pursuing thus either a politics of *status quo*, a politics of imperialism, or a politics of prestige.[31] Power was of no value in itself, however. Its value resided in the objects that it sought to attain.[32] Politics as the will to power always aimed at ensuring the widest possible sphere of influence within which the State could possess its desired objects.[33]

---

[25] ['in their original intellectual and political functions foreign to the German character'].

[26] Hans Morgenthau, 'Stresemann als Schöpfer der deutschen Völkerrechtspolitik' (1929) 5 Die Justiz 176.   [27] Morgenthau, 'Autobiography', 65.

[28] Morgenthau, *La Notion du 'politique'*, 46–61. Although Schmitt's definition of the political is different from Morgenthau's, linking it famously to the friend/enemy relationship, the sense of international politics as struggle is common to both. Morgenthau's later insistence on the non-rule-bound character of the prudence of the wise statesman is nothing more than Schmitt's famous decisionism dressed up in a language that could easily be adopted in American politics. Schmitt complimented Morgenthau on his dissertation—although their meeting shortly thereafter seems to have proved a disappointment to Morgenthau, who felt that Schmitt had modified the second edition of *The Concept of the Political* (1932) by incorporating Morgenthau's ideas—without openly acknowledging them. Morgenthau, 'Autobiography', 67–8.   [29] Cf. Frei, *Morgenthau*, 102–11.

[30] Morgenthau, *La Notion du 'politique'*, 42–3.   [31] Cf. ibid. 43, 61.

[32] '. . . le politique au sens spécifique consiste dans le degré particulier d'intensité du rapport que la volonté de puissance de l'Etat crée entre ses objets et l'Etat', ibid. 64.

[33] Ibid. 43, 71.

For Morgenthau, international law was not antithetical to but parallelly coexistent with politics. Its bias had, however, been with the politics of the *status quo*.[34] The mechanisms of change had been quite insufficiently developed, as demonstrated again by Versailles. But if law was on the side of *status quo* it became unrealistic if *status quo* powers were not winning. As the pressure for change increased, international law would break down. There was no magic formula for doing away with situations where States felt that the legal system did not adequately reflect their needs and power. True, sometimes a tension might successfully be converted into a (legal) dispute—the Alabama arbitration (1871) being an example. On the other hand, it was also possible that what was originally a (legal) dispute could change into (the symbol of) a (political) tension. Such cases could no longer be dealt with by reference to general rules or principles but now involved challenges to them.[35] At the end of his book, Morgenthau gave up the normative concerns that predominated his dissertation, saying that his task was now simply to create a scientific classification of disputes, not a formula for doing away with them, to point out that the characterization of 'political' disputes depended on the perspectives of the disputants themselves.[36] Clearly, by 1933 Morgenthau saw much less prospect for a 'dynamic' law than he had four years earlier.

Morgenthau's last legal book—his *Habilitationsschrift* in Geneva—*La Réalité des normes. En particulier des normes du droit international* (1934) was heavily influenced by Kelsen, though his attitude towards formalism remained unrepentantly Schmittian. Neo-Kantianism was:

l'expression fidèle de la décadence de la pensée philosophique universitaire dans l'Allemagne de la fin du siècle dernier.[37]

None the less, Morgenthau adopted from Kelsen a stress on 'validity' as the distinguishing property of legal (as against moral or social) norms.[38] For him, such validity was not, however, constituted by relations of systemic delegation (as in Kelsen) but by the norm's abstract ability to determine the content of someone's will. Normative relations were relations of will: the creator of the norm sought to impose its will on that of the addressee. The success of this effort was dependent on the existence of sanction. Morgenthau's anthropology was of a purely Hobbesian, mechanistic kind:

la volonté humaine ne peut être déterminée que par la perspective d'un plaisir ou la crainte d'un déplaisir.[39]

Instead of pure ought, Morgenthau wanted to examine the reality of the legal ought, the *Sein* of Kelsen's *Sollen*. Such *Sein* could only be psychological or physical,

---

[34] Morgenthau, *La Notion du 'politique'*, 65–71.   [35] Ibid. 79–85.
[36] Ibid. 86–90.
[37] Hans Morgenthau, *La Réalité des normes. En particulier des normes du droit international* (Paris: Alcan, 1934), p. xi.
[38] Ibid. 25–9. Also Kelsenian are his emphasis on the analytical distinction between 'le point de vue sociologique et le point de vue normatif' as well as the view of the State as the sphere of validity of State law, ibid. 214–16.   [39] Ibid. 46.

through sanctions it could be both. The fear of sanction was the psychological reality of norms that brought about conformity as the physical reality. If the expectation of sanction was missing, then the norm lacked reality:

Aujourd'hui, nous avons abouti à ce résultat que c'est dans la nature des sanctions qu'il convient de voir le problème essentiel.[40]

The essential question was whether someone could in fact send in the police. Schmitt again. And Weimar.

Morgenthau's views of human nature and motivation left no space for a law that would be anything but an instrument of causality whereby one will effectively determined the content of another. Such a (Nietzschean) outlook found no social reality for morality, or natural law, beyond this.[41] As Morgenthau put his moral subjectivism a few years later:

The appeal to moral principles in the international sphere has no universal meaning. It is either so vague as to have no concrete meaning that could provide rational guidance for political action, or it will be nothing but the reflection of the moral perceptions of a particular nation.[42]

An invocation of natural law threw an ideological veil over the relations of will thus justified. Such justification might be an indispensable element of social stability, or for overcoming constitutional crises.[43] But it was never the ultimate reason, or guarantor, of (the maintenance of) constitution. The guarantor was instead the executive body that had the power to put the sanctions into effect. Internationally, the executive power was constituted by the balance of power.

Morgenthau's analysis resembled the discussion between Kelsen and Schmitt over the 'ultimate validity' of the (Weimar) constitution, or the identity of its 'guardian' (*der Hüter der Verfassung*).[44] Morgenthau distinguished between the 'guardian' of the international legal system *in toto* and that of its individual norms. Since the former was the person holding executive power, Morgenthau came to the apparently inevitable, yet odd, suggestion that the international legal system was 'ultimately' guaranteed by the Heads of State of the members of the international

---

[40] Ibid. 242.

[41] Which is not to say, however, that Morgenthau would have joined Nieztsche in going 'beyond good and evil'. He seemed to acknowledge the existence of natural law but located it apparently beyond the grasp of political discourse. Morality's 'validity' is always relative to the individual's conscience, ibid. 53. If natural law can only express itself through voluntary law, it is relative to the community's view and the possibility of ideology or 'error' can never be excluded, ibid. 41–3.

[42] Hans Morgenthau, *American Foreign Policy* (New York: Knopf, 1951), 35.

[43] Morgenthau, *La Réalité des normes*, 43–4.

[44] Cf. Dyzenhaus, *Legality and Legitimacy*, 70–85, 108–23. In *Politics among Nations: The Struggle for Power and Peace* (New York: Knopf, 1948) the same theme is discussed in connection with sovereignty. Here Morgenthau moves from an initially Kelsenian conception that defines 'sovereignty' as 'supreme *legal* authority' (248, my emphasis) to a Schmittian notion under which such supremacy is a function of struggle between contending forces that normally lies dormant but asserts itself 'in times of crisis' (261).

community.[45] The sanction of the rest of international law was determined by the public opinion of individuals within those States:

l'ensemble des hommes appartenant aux Etats de la communauté internationale seront alors porteurs de la validité de la norme violée.[46]

Morgenthau's defence of international law's reality by reference to a system of sanctions administered by States and public opinion as agents of international law was at best half-hearted.[47] That his discussion remained—perhaps paradoxically— wholly conceptual and makes no reference to examples from international life emphasized the fragility of the argument. And he conceded that the fact that normative validity ('the abstract capacity of the norm to determine the will of a person') in international law was highly relative meant that the number of valid norms was significantly smaller than that exposed in standard treatises.[48]

In 1937, after a brief stay in Madrid, Morgenthau took refuge in the United States where he wrote his legal swan-song—the famous 1941 article that criticized the way international law was 'paying almost no attention to the psychological and sociological laws governing the actions of men in the international sphere'.[49] From his position of safety across the Atlantic he ridiculed the 'international law of Geneva'. The positivist formalism of the interwar had been an 'attempt to exorcise social evils by the indefatigable repetition of magic formulae'.[50] This was Weimar critique writ large. Like German public law positivists, international lawyers had been in the grips of an illusion. International law—like the Weimar Constitution— had nothing to do with 'rules of international law as they are actually applied'. Positivism's error lay in its dogmatic reliance on a notion of 'validity' that qualified as law those rules that were not actually applied, and failed to include all those that were.

The shift towards an interdisciplinary approach was clear. Although positivism had been blind to the relationship between law and ethics, law made constant reference to ethical and moral principles and 'the successful search for these principles is as essential for the scientific understanding of international law as of any legal system'.[51] Second, positivism failed to see the 'sociological context of economic interests, social tensions, and aspirations of power, which are the motivating forces

[45] Morgenthau, *La Réalité des normes*, 217–19, esp. 218: 'les Chefs des états particuliers sont donc à la fois les porteurs des ordres juridiques étatiques en question et d'ordre juridique international'. Morgenthau considered this situation analogous to the Middle Ages when the Emperor was the secular arm of the Church (222–3 n. 2). Under what seems to have been Kelsen's influence, Morgenthau describes States as merely groups of persons that have united in the name of the State and which, when carrying out sanctions, 'remplissent ici une fonction internationale déterminée' (233).

[46] Ibid. 220.

[47] The chapter on sanctions in international law is expressly written in the form of a defence against the 'deniers', cf. ibid. 223–4. For States as 'agents' of international law in this respect, cf. ibid. 231–8.

[48] Ibid. 227.

[49] Hans Morgenthau, 'Positivism, Functionalism and International Law' (1941) American Journal of International Law 283.   [50] Ibid. 260.   [51] Ibid. 268.

in the international field'.[52] Only a functional jurisprudence could remedy these errors, an interdisciplinary jurisprudence harking back to ethics and sociology.

But what would happen to law if the call for ethics or sociology were taken seriously? If in 1941 Morgenthau was vague about the ethics of statecraft, five years later he had formulated his Promethean view of statesmanship as the prudence of the wise individual:

The choice is not between legality and illegality but between political wisdom and political stupidity.[53]

This was in perfect harmony with his sociology of the international. In domestic society, situations were typical; in the international world, they were unique. Hence, 'only a strictly individualized rule of law will be adequate to it'.[54] Both Morgenthau's ethics and his sociology now pointed beyond law. They were not simple interdisciplinary additions to legal study, they were a substitute for or the antithesis of law—the *Ausnahme*, or the exception that Carl Schmitt always held them to be. Little wonder that Morgenthau stopped writing about law—beyond the *à la rigueur* invocation of law as the banal regulation of diplomatic status.[55]

Finally, in 1946 Morgenthau expressed his target clearly:

In no field of intellectual endeavor has the domestic experience of liberalism been so overwhelming as in this. The application of domestic legal experience to international law is really the main stock of trade of modern international thought.[56]

The analogy was false. No formal inter-State legislation lay behind international law. Instead, a 'competitive quest for power will determine the victorious social forces, and the change of the existing legal order will be decided, not through a legal procedure . . . but through a conflagration of conflicting social forces which challenge the legal order as a whole'.[57] What Morgenthau had to say about the League Assembly echoed what Schmitt said about the Weimar *Reichsrat*:

political problems were never solved but only tossed about and finally shelved according to the rules of the legal game.[58]

This approach was repeated in the UN as it sought to deal with the crises in Greece, Spain, Indonesia, and Iran:

These cases have provided opportunities for exercises in parliamentary procedure, but on no occasion has even an attempt been made of facing the political issues of which these situations are surface manifestations.[59]

In Morgenthau's call for the integration of the concrete context in law and his emphasis on the ethics of (political) prudence, we hear Schmitt's voice—*die Konkrete*

---

[52] Ibid. 269.   [53] Morgenthau, *Scientific Man*, 120.
[54] Morgenthau, 'Positivism', 271.
[55] Hans Morgenthau, *Politics Among Nations* (New York: Knopf, 1980), 255.
[56] Morgenthau, *Scientific Man*, 113.   [57] Morgenthau, 'Positivism', 276.
[58] Morgenthau, *Scientific Man*, 119.   [59] Ibid.

Ordnung and the authority of the effective decision. We hear it also in his view that (international) law did not emerge from formal legislation but from a struggle between social forces. Different States had different degrees of 'social force' and the sphere of their national interest was determined by how far their power reached—the basis for Morgenthau's subsequent critique of the United States presence in Vietnam. In other words, whatever international order may be attainable is:

predicated upon the existence of national communities capable of preserving order and real-
izing moral values within the limits of their power.[60]

Moreover, although 'social force' could lie within States, it could equally well lie with groups of States, or concentrations of ideological, economic, or military interest. Although Morgenthau saw this as a reason for moving towards a world federation, Schmitt was perhaps more consistent.

In 1939 Schmitt had asserted that, behind States, there were nations exercising their right to self-determination. These nations had high points when they some-times radiated influence over neighbouring territories. A realistic territorial order recognized this and, renouncing the nineteenth-century fiction of sovereign equality, granted to those nations—the *Reiche*—spheres of influence that extended beyond their formal boundaries.[61] This was the *Grossraum*; the large space of the nation that a dynamic international law needed to recognize, at the risk of falling into oblivion.

What is the image of law in international relations? The elements of an answer arise from the well-known fact that 'international relations' is a predominantly Anglo-American discipline whose origins lie in the academic activities of refugees—often with a legal background—from the German Reich in the United States during the early years of the Cold War.[62] The preceding pages have sketched the development of the ideas of Hans Morgenthau, whom Stanley Hoffmann has called, bluntly, 'the founder of the discipline',[63] and who was recently listed (with Hannah Arendt, Leo Strauss, and Herbert Marcuse) among 'the four most influential of [the] refugee intellectuals' in the development of political theory in the United States.[64] The image of law that emerges from his writings is one that was crafted within German public

[60] Hans Morgenthau, *American Foreign Policy* (New York: Knopf, 1951), 38, 117–21.

[61] Carl Schmitt, *Völkerrechtliche Grossraumordnung. Mit Interventionsverbot für raumfremde Mächte* (Berlin: Deutscher Rechtsverlag, 1939), 69–88.

[62] Cf. Alfons Söllner, *Vom Völkerrecht zum science of international relations. Vier typische Vertreter der politikwissenschaftlichen Emigration*, in Ilja Srubar (ed.), *Exil, Wissenschaft, Identität. Die Emigration deutscher Sozialwissenschafler 1933–1945* (Frankfurt-am-Main: Suhrkamp, 1988), 164–80 (discussing Kelsen, Morgenthau, John Herz, and Karl Deutsch as typical representatives of this emigration). Out of the at least sixty-four German social scientists who emigrated from Germany, more than half had a legal background and over 90 per cent took positions in American universities—in most cases in the field of international relations, ibid. 165.

[63] Stanley Hoffmann, 'An American Social Science: International Relations', in S. Hoffmann, *Janus and Minerva: Essays in the Theory and Practice of International Politics* (Boulder, Colo.: Westview Press, 1987), 6.

[64] Peter Graf Kielmansegg, 'Introduction', in P. G. Kielmansegg *et al.*, *German Emigrés and American Political Thought after World War II* (Cambridge: Cambridge University Press, 1995), 1.

law in the interwar era, whose central concern was the ability of the Weimar Constitution to withstand the challenges that were posed to it from the left and from the right. From this, Morgenthau extrapolated an analogous image of international law as the image of weakness, the image of a (pure) formalism or of moral illusion that are unable to maintain international order. He wrote about 'legalistic' exercises of foreign policy:

At best they have left the political issues where they found them; at worst, they have embittered international relations and thus made a peaceful settlement of the great political issues more difficult.[65]

To accompany that image, the German refugees also brought from Weimar a distinct sensibility about matters political, a sensibility which in Schmitt's case has been aptly described as an 'aesthetics of horror'[66] and which in Morgenthau's case gave rise to his pessimistic outlook on human nature and society. Both jurists, as well as the 'Realism' they inaugurated in the international relations academia, espoused a Hobbesian anthropology, were obsessed with the marginal situation, and shared a pervading sense of a spiritual and political 'crisis' in the (liberal) West[67] and constant concern over political collapse. Both believed that political order requires a powerful guardian who normally stands outside that order but who is ready to intervene if required. Both were led logically into a decisionism where it is either the *Führer* or the prudent statesman who finally gives formal legality its substance (legitimacy) and so unites the divergent political actors and parties into a firm political order.

The conditions of the Cold War—particularly the threat of a nuclear catastrophe—and the emerging global ambitions of the United States provided a uniquely suitable context for the cultivation of this spirit. So it was no wonder that there was, to quote Hoffmann again, 'a remarkable chronological convergence between [the needs of policy-makers in Washington] and the scholars' performances'.[68] An argument against isolationism and in favour of global involvement, intervention in the national interest, and the accumulation of power could not have been planted in a more fertile soil. After all, who else but the United States could think of itself as the 'guardian' of the international political order—and thus find a justification for bringing its force to bear if that seemed required. This was the ideological penchant that was so well expressed in the war policy of Presidents Wilson and Roosevelt:

what the moral law demanded was by a felicitous coincidence always identical with what the national interest seemed to require.[69]

---

[65] Morgenthau, *American Foreign Policy*, 102.

[66] Richard Wolin, 'Carl Schmitt: The Conservative Revolutionary Habitus and the Aesthetics of Horror' (1992) 20 Political Theory 424.

[67] Cf. Jürgen Gebhardt, 'Leo Strauss: The Quest for Truth in Times of Perplexity', in Kielmansegg *et al.*, *German Emigrés*, 84 (linking this attitude to the general outlook of the German academic élite—including the emigrés in the USA).   [68] Hoffmann, 'An American Social Science', 10.

[69] Morgenthau, *American Foreign Policy*, 19.

Morgenthau of course never advocated such a role for any single State (in fact, he favoured world government with an effective international police force[70]) and insisted on the ultimately moral justification for a limited national interest.[71] But it is significant that he felt himself a man with a mission and never shunned the opportunity to make normative statements, thus inaugurating the instrumentalist approach to international relations that still today sees scientific work justified most strongly if it ends up in policy proposals.

For the American Realists, international law was Weimar law writ large, law that was formalistic or moralistic and unable to reflect the dynamic nature of international relations. This is why George Kennan could write that the 'function of a system of international relationships is not to inhibit [the] process of change by imposing a legal strait jacket upon it'[72] and why the only references to 'laws' in Kenneth Waltz's influential *Theory of International Politics* are to the laws of logical relation and scientific explanation.[73]

Elsewhere, things have looked different. In France (with the exception of Raymond Aron) and many other European countries, international relations was, and continues to be, largely enmeshed with diplomatic history and the study of international organization. The image of law remains that of positive legal rules—especially treaties and the constitutions of international organizations—having a modest but none the less necessary role in structuring international life. Nor have the British (apart from, perhaps, E. H. Carr and F. H. Hinsley) discussed international law with the sense of impending doom that has been a part of the Weimar-Realist genre. Martin Wight saw international law as a historical tradition that, like theories about international relations, was divided into 'rationalist', 'realist', and 'revolutionist' streams, and confessed to having himself moved increasingly into the rationalist camp—with all the implications this had for the adoption of a Grotian legal morality.[74] Hedley Bull credited international law with a number of essential (albeit limited) 'functions' in relation to the international order[75] while his views on the practice of international law sound rather like those of Sir Gerald Fitzmaurice. According to this view, international law is—and should be—rules, and the role of the lawyer should be 'to state what the rules of international law are'.[76] In response to the interdisciplinary ambitions of the New Haven School he stated that thinking of international law as a 'process of authoritative decision . . . deprives international

---

[70] Cf. e.g. Hans Morgenthau, *Truth and Power: Essays of a Decade 1960–1970* (New York: Praeger, 1970), 306–14.

[71] For an early formulation, cf. Morgenthau, *American Foreign Policy*, 33–9 and *passim*.

[72] George Kennan, *American Diplomacy* (Chicago: University of Chicago Press, 1984), 98.

[73] Kenneth Waltz, *Theory of International Politics* (Reading, Mass.: Addison-Wesley Publishing Company, 1979).

[74] Martin Wight, *International Theory: The Three Traditions* (London: Leicester University Press for the Royal Institute of International Affairs, 1996), 233–58, 268.

[75] Hedley Bull, *The Anarchical Society: A Study of Order in World Politics* (New York: Columbia University Press, 1977), 140–5.   [76] Ibid. 150.

law of its essential focus and leads to its disappearance as a distinct branch of international studies'.[77]

By contrast, the image of international law in the United States has been—and continues to be—conceived from the perspective of a powerful nation, indeed a world power, whose leaders have 'options' and routinely choose among alternative 'strategies' in an ultimately hostile world. From that perspective, any conception of law as fixed 'rules' seems irrelevant to the extent that it is not backed by sanction and counterproductive inasmuch as it limits the choices available to those who do have the means to enforce them. The language of 'governance' (in contrast to government[78]), of the management of 'regimes', of ensuring 'compliance', is the language of a powerful and a confident actor with an enviable amount of resources to back up its policies.[79]

The historical circumstances of the Weimar Republic led Morgenthau to lose his faith in law as a significant professional or academic commitment. The call for dynamism, either in the form of 'taking account' of actual power relations or of having regard to the 'guiding ideas of justice and order' that prevailed in a society, constituted a slippery slope. As Max Weber—one of Morgenthau's spiritual fathers[80]—had shown, the call for 'realism' in law leads to a deformalized concept of the legal in which every administrative act becomes a (subjective) value judgement by the relevant decision-making authority. Although Morgenthau's focus on prudent statesmanship did resemble Weber's recourse to an ethic of responsibility as a substitute for the controlling force of general rules, Morgenthau's 'prudence' was directed inwards towards the national community (national interest) and could work as an argument about acceptable international order only by way of a further assumption about an invisible hand—an assumption that could not be sustained by his anthropological pessimism.[81]

I now look at the academic calls to integrate international law and international relations theory and wonder about the newly heroic liberalism from which they emanate. There is no doubt: this is an American crusade. By this, I do not mean only

---

[77] Ibid. 160.

[78] Anne-Marie Slaughter, Andrew Tulumello, and Stepan Wood, 'International Law and International Relations Theory: A New Generation of Interdisciplinary Scholarship' (1998) 92 American Journal of International Law 367 at 370–1.

[79] This, I guess, is the flip side of Oppenheim's *dictum* that respect for international law has been greatest in balance-of-power systems. If such balance is lacking, legal formalism gives way to the enforcement of the hegemon's morality. Cf. Stanley Hoffmann, 'International Systems and International Law', in Hoffmann *et al.*, *Essays*, 157–64.

[80] Morgenthau, 'Autobiography', 64; Frei, *Morgenthau*, 112–13.

[81] The tension between Morgenthau's theory of power and his faith in a controlling morality is highlighted in Jan Willem Honig, 'Totalitarianism and Realism: Hans Morgenthau's German Years', in Benjamin Frankel, *Roots of Realism* (London: Frank Cass, 1996), 307–10. For the argument that an application of the Weberian ethic of responsibility in international affairs requires a conception of moral community (of individuals and of States), cf. Daniel Warner, *An Ethic of Responsibility in International Relations* (Boulder, Colo.: Rienner, 1991), esp. 107–16.

that some of the crusaders have chosen to argue for an increasing recourse to United States principles of domestic legitimacy in justifying its external behaviour,[82] or that nearly all of the relevant literature comes from the United States.[83] (Indeed, an early review of legal responses to the 'realist challenge' found no significant examples beyond the universities of the American East.[84]) Nor, finally, am I relying on the fact that the concepts of 'liberalism' or 'democracy' in this literature refer back to an American (or should one say, 'United Statesian'?) understanding that links them with certain (Western) liberal institutions[85]—with deviating voices being neutralized under a convenient classification (such as, for example, 'Critical Legal Studies', 'constructivism', or 'postmodernism') that makes them seem readily welcome in American academia's homely embrace.[86]

What I want to say, instead, is that the particular combination of a call to increase 'collaboration' between international lawyers and international relations theorists, together with the sociology of the end-of-State (as we know it) and the political enthusiasm about the spread of 'liberalism', constitutes an academic project that cannot but buttress the justification of American hegemony in the world. This is not because of bad faith or conspiracy on anybody's part. It is the logic of an argument— the Weimar argument—that creates the image of law as an instrument for the values (or better, 'decisions') of the powerful that compels the conclusion.[87]

A recent review of interdisciplinary approaches identified three ways in which international lawyers 'use' international relations theory:

(1) to diagnose international policy problems and to formulate solutions to them; (2) to explain the function of particular international legal institutions; and (3) to examine and reconceptualise particular institutions of international law generally.[88]

The review argued that international lawyers had been able to contribute to international relations theory by examinations of the legal process as a causal mechanism, by showing how legal norms 'constructed' the international conceptual system, and by drawing attention to the effects of domestic and transnational law.[89] It then 'mapped a joint discipline' that would study the design of international regimes and processes, that would create specific analyses of the law's 'constructive' effects,

---

[82] Lea Brilmayer, *Justifying International Acts* (Ithaca, NY: Cornell University Press, 1989).

[83] Slaughter, Tulumello, and Wood, 'International Law', 393–7 (bibliography).

[84] That is to say, Yale (McDougal), Princeton (Falk), Harvard (Chayes), and Columbia (Henkin). The absence of NYU (Franck) must have been a simple oversight on the author's part. Anne-Marie Slaughter Burley, 'International Law and International Relations: A Dual Agenda' (1993) 87 American Journal of International Law 204 at 209–14.

[85] Susan Marks, 'The End of History? Reflexions on Some International Law Theses' (1997) 8 European Journal of International Law 449–77, esp. 471–5.

[86] Cf. Slaughter, Tulumello, and Wood, 'International Law', 373 and the bibliography at n. 83 above; Anthony Clark Arend, 'Do Legal Rules Matter? International Law and International Politics' (1998) 38 Virginia Journal of International Law 125–40.

[87] Cf. also Marks, 'End of History?', 467.

[88] Slaughter, Tulumello, and Wood, 'International Law', 373.

[89] Ibid. 379–83.

provide an account of structural transformations, and look into the disaggregation of States and the embeddedness of international institutions in domestic societies.[90]

Such an argument about 'collaboration' implies a thoroughly functionalist image of international law. The relevant literature is obsessed with questions such as: how and when do States use international institutions 'to manage interstate cooperation or conflict',[91] and when might it be useful for States to choose formal or informal agreements to realize their purposes?[92] Recently, Robert Keohane outlined two 'optics' for examining international law that could be used by lawyers and international relations theorists alike, namely instrumentalism and normativism.[93] These are Morgenthau's appeals for sociology and ethics, expressed in today's language. In none of these articles—nor in other writings within this genre—does there emerge an image of law that would be other than an idiosyncratic technique for studying either what works (instrumentalism) or what should work (normativism), in other words, a special kind of sociology or morality of the international.[94]

Since Kelsen, lawyers have tried to articulate their search for professional identity in terms of a middle ground between that which is sociological description (of what works) and that which is moral speculation (of what would be good). This is not because lawyers would have dismissed sociology or ethics as unworthy enterprises but because neither sociology nor ethics is able to answer the question that lawyers are called upon to answer; namely the question about (valid) law. Now there may be disagreement about the significance of that question—and some of the Weimar critics, including Schmitt and Morgenthau, certainly felt that it was uninteresting. Its significance depends on what view one takes of the proper place of formal law (including lawyers, courts, legal arguments, etc.) in society, a question that emerges—as it did in Weimar—especially in face of demands for increasing legislative intervention in the most varied of societal fields, to support particular interests or values.[95]

Sometimes there is a need for exceptional measures that cannot be encompassed within the general formulation of the formally valid rule. There may well be a time for revolution and the throwing off of valid law (and the profession that sustains it)

---

[90] Ibid. 384–93.

[91] Kenneth Abbott and Duncan Snidal, 'Why States Act through Formal International Organizations' (1998) 42 Journal of Conflict Resolution 8.

[92] Charles Lipson, 'Why are Some Agreements Informal?' (1991) 45 International Organization 495.

[93] Robert Keohane, 'International Relations and International Law: Two Optics' (1997) 38 Harvard International Law Journal 487.

[94] This is quite expressly stated in Keohane's article where he observes that causality (i.e. what works) cannot provide the sole perspective from which to look at international law and adds that 'the function of moral judgment' is 'fundamental', ibid. 488–9. No other alternative is considered. Law is either sociology or morality.

[95] For a famous argument about the dangers in the dilution of legal formality (and the emergence of a kind of 'Khadi justice') in complex modern society, cf. Max Weber, *On Law in Economy and Society* (edited with introduction and annotations by Max Rheinstein, Cambridge, Mass.: Harvard University Press, 1954), 305–15.

altogether. However, none of this detracts from the need to know about valid law. Rather, it is premissed upon our ability to know it. And that need cannot be satisfied by seeking to answer the causal or the moral question. On the contrary, these latter questions can only meaningfully be asked once we share an image of law as something that is—for want of a better word—'valid'. The absence of this image is a product of the Weimar heritage in American international relations theory.

Answers to the question about (valid) law are conditioned upon the criteria for validity that a legal system uses to define its substance. These criteria do refer to social facts and moral ideas but cannot be reduced to them without doing away with the legal question (by interpreting it as 'in fact' a question about what works, or what is good) and the profession that was assigned the task of answering it. Whatever one thinks of lawyers, or of a culture within which the question of 'validity' is a matter of professional concern and not of formalistic fiction, doing away with it has definite social consequences. Not least of these is the liberation of the executive from whatever constraints (valid) legal rules might exert over them.[96] The deformalization of law into a political or moral instrumentality by the use of general, evaluative clauses (such as 'democratic' or 'equitable', for instance) or of legislation targeted against or in favour of special interests transforms it into a means for that power that occupies or has control over the executive. In this process, benevolent jurisprudential intentions may be enlisted for dubious causes. The argument in favour of Weimar judges applying directly those social interests that lay 'behind' the law (Jhering) may have seemed a welcome reaction to the hair-splitting of Wilhelminian *Begriffsjurisprudenz*. None the less, Ernst Bloch comments:

In Germany, juridical liberalism was marked by progressive intentions, but the existing relations were not at all progressive. And so the Nazi as a judge, servile through and through, but free from juridical measures, demonstrated what he could do.[97]

As Schmitt and others criticized the false formality of general legislation in Weimar, an odd intellectual alliance was forged between Kelsenian formalists and the Marxian left, both of which insisted on the need to maintain the rule of law so as to prevent the executive enforcement of Nazi decrees.[98] Likewise, if what the 'dual agenda' achieves is a thoroughly function-dependent, non-autonomous law, it is simply another ingenious way of setting up a Hobbesian sovereign.

---

[96] It might be said in response that all talk of validity presumes that legal rules are determinate (or knowable) in a way that cannot be sustained. Regardless of what we think a plausible theory of legal determinacy, however, if law were completely indeterminate, any talk of collaboration would be pointless. The only conceivable interest international relations theorists might have in 'collaboration' lies in whatever it is that enables lawyers to produce determinate statements about the law. An indeterminate law cannot fulfil any 'functions'.

[97] Ernst Bloch, *Natural Law and Human Dignity* (trans. Dennis J. Schmidt, Cambridge, Mass.: MIT Press, 1986), 132, 149–52.

[98] For a recent review, cf. William E. Scheuerman, *Between the Norm and the Exception: The Frankfurt School and the Rule of Law* (Cambridge, Mass.: MIT Press, 1994), esp. 74–6, 93–6, 140–7, but also generally.

The other two themes—the end-of-State theory and liberal millenarianism—provide ready-made understandings of the substance of the sociology and ethics that international lawyers are supposed to learn through interdisciplinarity. Here is the political crux of the matter, for interdisciplinarity is not intended to transform lawyers into sociologists or moral theorists. How could it? Only so long as lawyers can look at these disciplines from the outside can they sustain a faith in the exotic that keeps them blind to the doubts, anomalies, and contradictions harboured within sociology and moral theory. Instead, the call is to accept as authoritative, and controlling, the styles of argument and substantive outcomes that international relations scholars have been able to scavenge from the battlefield. Behind the call for 'collaboration' is a strategy to use the international lawyer's 'Weimarian' insecurity in order to tempt him or her to accept the self-image of an underlabourer to the policy-agendas of international relations orthodoxy.

We have seen that Morgenthau's disillusionment about (pure) international law led, first, to a call for interdisciplinarity and then to an abandonment of international law altogether. This is only logical, for neither studying law as an instrument for external purposes (power) nor examining its legitimacy pull provides any significant room for the concept of validity. And inasmuch as *that* concept gets thrown away, nothing is left of law but a servile instrument for power (of what works) to realize its objectives (of what should work). In an agnostic world the 'normative optic' provides no more effective direction than do appeals for 'prudence', 'responsibility', or indeed 'legitimacy'.

Anne-Marie Slaughter has drawn a broad picture of (the real) new world order in which sovereign States are disaggregating while formal diplomacy and formal international organizations are being replaced by 'transgovernmental networks' (of courts, regulatory agencies, executives, even legislatures) within which judges, government officials, company executives, and members of governmental and non-governmental organizations and interest groups meet to co-ordinate their policies and enhance the enforcement of laws in a fashion which, by comparison to formal inter-State co-operation, is 'fast, flexible, and effective'.[99] Her version of the 'end-of-State' sociology is nuanced and moderate but still conceives of statehood and sovereign equality as formalistic obstacles to the realization of the dynamic embedded in 'real life'. An absolutely central aspect of this sociology is the fact that it is normatively tinged. Slaughter writes:

The most distinctive aspect of Liberal international relations theory is that it permits, indeed mandates, a distinction among different types of States, based on their domestic political structure and ideology.[100]

As sovereignty breaks down and globalization becomes the order of the day, the dynamic of a politically oriented law will no longer tolerate formalism:

[99] Anne-Marie Slaughter, 'The Real New World Order' (1997) 76 Foreign Affairs 193, 183–97.
[100] Anne-Marie Slaughter, 'International Law in a World of Liberal States' (1995) 6 European Journal of International Law 504.

The resulting behavioural distinctions between liberal democracies and other kinds of States, or more generally between liberal and non-liberal States, cannot be accommodated within the framework of classical international law.[101]

And further:

territorial boundaries become increasingly meaningless, so that situs analysis cedes its place to interest analysis.[102]

In other words, the interdisciplinary call cannot be divorced from the kinds of sociology and ethics that are being advocated. Interdisciplinarity does away with the image of valid law and thus leads lawyers to contemplate an agenda that is posed to them by an academic intelligentsia that has been thoroughly committed to smoothening the paths of the hegemon.

This is why I think that we have been here before. Carl Schmitt held that different nations radiated their *Kultur* differently on others, and that formal boundaries should not prevent the law from recognizing this. Morgenthau felt that the national interest, which for him was both a factual and a normative category, was a force that internationalists failed to take into account only at their peril. Both Schmitt and Morgenthau attacked formal validity as politically conservative and unable to live up to its ideal of neutrality. Both used the term 'dynamic' to characterize the new law that overrode a *status quo* gone stale. It is this dynamic that I hear in the pursuit of the dual agenda, the dynamic of a neo-liberal *Grossraum*.

---

[101] Ibid.

[102] Anne-Marie Slaughter, 'International Law and International Relations: A Dual Agenda' (1993) 87 American Journal of International Law 236.

3

How Do Norms Matter?

FRIEDRICH V. KRATOCHWIL

1. INTRODUCTION

The purpose of this chapter is to inquire into the possibilities of interdisciplinary research concerning the role of norms in social life in general, and in international politics in particular. Since we all know that the phenomena of the real world do not neatly coincide with disciplinary boundaries, interdisciplinary research usually enjoys considerable support, although its actual results are often disappointing. Often, all that is achieved are 'lists' of problems that result from some aggregation of disciplinary matrices. Sometimes the degree of conceptual integration seems higher, for example when a particular methodology is imported from one discipline into another, until one realizes that such efforts at colonization often amount to little more than the 'recasting' of some well-known problem in the new language or methodology. Thus, the heuristic value that is added is minimal if not non-existent, as such strategies also entail the danger of eradicating the specific contributions that different disciplines make to our understanding. For example, little is gained either for the discipline of international politics or for the discipline of international law when 'law' is simply equated with actual decision-making processes, or when 'politics' is eliminated by a discourse on 'human rights' or 'justice'.

Thus, disciplinary boundaries limit but also simultaneously provide the way in which we attain knowledge of a subject-matter. To that extent it seems wise—although contrary to the contemporary fashion—not to begin this inquiry by adopting a certain methodology but by probing the disciplinary boundaries which establish the respective fields of study, in our case 'law' and 'politics'. In this context, I shall argue, the modern concepts of 'politics' and 'law' as they emerged from the crisis of nineteenth-century philosophy and from the breakdown of the traditional order of the European State system in the First World War are of particular importance.[1] The formation of a discipline of international politics was not only a departure from old understandings of an exemplary history, or of history as 'progress', but it also created a totally implausible conception of politics and law that increasingly impoverished inquiries in both fields. Even more importantly, the anaemic conception of politics as 'power politics' was paralleled to a certain extent by the narrowing of the concerns of jurisprudence to issues of conceptual analysis and the strict demarcation of the legal system conceived as a hierarchy of norms. Oddly enough, the disciplinary

---

[1] See e.g. E. H. Carr, *The Twenty Years' Crisis* (New York: Harper and Row, 1964).

understandings were, if not directly complementary, at least in a certain way parasitic upon each other. It is therefore not surprising that the resulting interdisciplinary research which attempted to correct the respective myopias, for example into the 'political foundations' of law or into 'regimes', usually suffered from the reduced set of interesting puzzles which resulted from the respective disciplinary understandings.

It is my contention that continuing these attempts is not a very promising option and that a fundamental conceptual reorientation is therefore necessary. In short, if we are interested in how norms matter, we must begin with the problem of praxis and draw from there the implications for both political and legal analysis. Such an enterprise is clearly beyond the scope of a paper, or even a book, because it would necessitate the development of a new 'practical philosophy'.[2] However, I would like to investigate two conceptual problems that have played a decisive role in legal and political analysis: first, the conception of the indeterminacy of law and its corollary of extreme rule scepticism; and second, the idea that the influence of norms on actual choices requires the discovery of some 'causal mechanism'. Both positions, I shall argue, are the result of considerable conceptual befuddlement. In demonstrating this I also hope to make good a wider claim, namely that our conceptions of explanation and justification both in law and international relations analysis are unduly restrictive and that the alleged 'indeterminacy' of law as well as the inability of norms to 'cause' a certain behaviour in no way justify the conclusions which are usually drawn from such alleged failures of 'theory'. Rather, they call into question the adequacy of the notion of 'theory' itself, be it of law, or of international relations.

These claims are admittedly rather heady, and in order to support them I will take the following steps. In the next section, I investigate the defining moment of international relations analysis and assess the repercussions which resulted from the emphasis on power as a defining criterion of a field of study. I will try to show how the emerging discourse in a way impoverished both international relations analysis and international law. Section 3 is then devoted to the problem of rule scepticism in general and to the notion that, even if international law could be shown to be 'true' law, it could not avoid the weakness of all law, namely its aimless oscillation between 'apology and utopia'.[3] I approach this issue in two steps. First, I show that this position suffers from a semantic confusion about indeterminacy and second, I demonstrate that the far-reaching conclusions derived from this alleged failure are unjustified on logical as well as practical grounds. This argument in turn strengthens the normative pull of pluralism as a social ideal. Recognizing the implications of this value opportunism for the social order, however, also paves the way for a less doctrinal epistemology that mistakes practical choices for either logical propositions or simple causal relations in its explanatory accounts of actions.

---

[2] Such an attempt is made, e.g. by Joseph Raz (ed.), *Practical Reasoning* (Oxford: Oxford University Press, 1978); Frederick Schauer, *Playing by the Rules: A Philosophical Examination of Rule Based Decision Making in Law and in Life* (Oxford: Oxford University Press, 1991).

[3] See e.g. the argument in Martti Koskenniemi, *From Apology to Utopia* (Helsinki: Lakimiesliiton Kustannus, 1989).

Section 4 takes up the contemporary debate in international relations analysis concerning the status of norms as an explanatory variable. In particular, I examine the three dominant approaches, namely the rationalistic one, a more sociologically oriented one that partially coincides with constructivism, and the emerging 'liberal' theory of political action. In pointing to the respective strengths and weaknesses of these approaches, I prepare the way for a more principled discussion, in section 5, of the role of norms in explanatory schemes of social action. There I argue that our preoccupation with identifying the effective causes and 'mechanisms' by which norms are supposed to mould decisions has prevented us from recognizing that explanatory schemes for actions serve different purposes, and that adhering to an unrealizable logical ideal of uniqueness has therefore contributed to the derailment of social analysis. Similarly, given the constitutive interests which define practical problems, 'explanations' must satisfy different criteria and, on pain of irrelevance (i.e. that our explanations are then not to the point, even though they might be 'true' in some sense), we cannot pick one explanatory model and consider it standard. Far from suggesting, therefore, that 'anything goes', the upshot of this argument is that pragmatic criteria play a much greater role in social science explanations than is usually assumed.

2. THE STRANGE SYMBIOSIS OF REALISM AND LEGALISM

According to traditional thought, international relations emerged as a field of study when utopian hopes that, as a result of technical and economic progress, the rule of law would finally replace politics were disappointed in the blood baths of the First and Second World Wars. 'Utopian thinking' had been clearly identified by E. H. Carr,[4] the 'father' of the modern discipline of international relations, as the belief in the natural harmony of interest and the perfectibility of the social order through the progressive development of law and public opinion à la Bentham. The development of a new discipline of 'international relations' therefore required an independence from legal discourse and its concerns. Carr's cautious remarks on the impossibility of politics without a utopia, his rather measured assessment of the role of moral principles in the deliberations about, and in the conduct of, 'foreign' affairs, were subsequently largely cast to the wind. The need to legitimize the new discipline by claiming that it was a 'science' led to the rupture of the links that connected traditional prudential and pragmatic historical reflections with political praxis.

Morgenthau's work bears witness to the difficulties involved in making this radical break for the sake of 'science', because prudential considerations intrude at every turn.[5] However, the paradigmatic *homo politicus* as power maximizer analogous to

---

[4] See Carr, *The Twenty Years' Crisis*.
[5] Hans Morgenthau, *Politics among Nations* (4th edn., New York: Knopf, 1967), see particularly the contradiction between ch. 1 and chs. 31 and 32.

the *homo economicus* was now charged with establishing the autonomy of the discipline. Moreover, the effort to 'found' the discipline through the construction of the ideal type of a *homo politicus*[6] was strangely at odds with the 'greats' of the Realist tradition who emphasized the contingency of choice and moral luck and the close connection between the normative beliefs of a society and the possibility of political order.[7] Instead of contingency and historical variability, certainty is now emphasized. Instead of casuistic argument, a new secure maxim for all political actions provides the 'theorists' of international politics with an appropriate analytical tool. As in economics, the notion of different 'purposes' of actions can now be neglected because the means (money or power) have also become the ends of the activity in that sphere.

This is not the place to subject the fundamentally mistaken analogy between money and power to detailed criticism. For our purposes, it is sufficient to point to the attempt to establish a field of study by formal means, based on ideal types without any consideration of the realism of these assumptions. To that extent, the later fascination with methodological considerations becomes not only understandable— a tendency which Hedley Bull with his advocacy of a 'traditional approach' attempted to counteract[8]—it also explains a great deal of the curious mutual conditioning of the prevalent legal discourse and realism. As realism tried to cleanse itself of all normative conceptions (save power), so law largely attempted to free itself from all social and moral contingencies.[9] Rules of law were either to be distinguished by having a characteristic label attached, such as 'sanctioning rules', for example, or they had to be members of a 'system' and thus traceable back to some 'source' or 'rule of recognition'.[10] In this way, 'law' could establish its autonomy from morals or other social conventions, or from any unprincipled bargain.

There is no need here to rehearse the well-known arguments against such a conception of law, either in its Kelsenian version as a sanctioning order, or as a system of rules in which membership in the system establishes the character of the rule in question. What is interesting is the fact that, on the basis of largely methodological considerations, an entirely implausible conception of politics is paralleled by an equally problematic conception of law. The mutual conditioning of these conceptions has been aptly described by Judith Shklar.[11] In order to preserve the autonomy of politics, especially international politics, the 'national interest' in terms of power must never be confused with other goals. The lesson seems clear since war remains,

---

[6] See e.g. Morgenthau's remarks on his Sixth Principle of the 'Six Principles of Political Realism' in his *Politics among Nations*, 13 f.

[7] See e.g. not only Machiavelli's remarks on 'fortuna' in ch. 24 of his *Prince* but also his emphasis on 'virtu' and the constant need of a 'renaissance' which is necessary for maintaining a republican form of government in his *Discorsi* (Book III, 1–5; Book I, 16–18; Book II, 1–5).

[8] Hedley Bull, 'International Theory: The Case for a Classical Approach' (1966) 18 *World Politics* 361.

[9] See e.g. Hans Kelsen, *General Theory of Law and the State*, trans. A. Wedberg (Cambridge, Mass.: Harvard University Press, 1945).

[10] H. L. A. Hart, *The Concept of Law* (New York: Oxford University Press, 1961).

[11] Judith Shklar, *Legalism: Law, Morals, and Political Trials* (Cambridge, Mass.: Harvard University Press, 1986).

in Hobbesian terms, the ever-latent possibility. The core concern of international politics with power attains its predominance through the ever-latent potential of physical violence. However, quite aside from the fact that such 'theory' glosses over the important distinction between possibility and probability, the ideological character of this position becomes readily apparent:

What the 'national interest' can be except ideology is hard to say, but one thing is clear to realists—it must never be conceived in terms of moral or legalistic values. This was for instance, the great sin of Woodrow Wilson, the *bête noire* of realism . . . [Realism's] animus against Wilson goes well beyond a rejection of international law as the sole means to preserve peace. It is rather a direct dislike of liberal ideology, largely because the latter failed. The urge to debunk thus becomes a psychological response to disenchantment, a tough sneer at all 'cant'.[12]

Conversely, since the uncompromising character of justice, equated with the strict application of rules, militates against unprincipled forms of accommodation, all politics must either be assimilated to the paradigm of 'just action' or exorcized until the time finally comes when orderly processes of legal change prevail over violence or bargaining power. Law and politics are not one continuum in the realm of praxis, but radically different domains that must be kept separate.

David Kennedy has perceptively demonstrated how this belief characteristic of legalism survived the shock of the First World War. In at least one strand of narratives, the Versailles settlement represented the 'movement from war to peace as the capture of an unruly politics by law. The Peace Conference provides an analogy for the historical transition from war to peace, for it moves from the adduction of political positions to signature of a treaty'.[13] Thus it is not surprising that for adherents of this position the lesson of the First and Second World Wars was not that legalism failed because it relied on a non-viable social theory, but rather that its failure was due to the fact that the 'pre- and inter war doctrines concerning the "rule of law" had not gone far enough'.[14]

The strength of the impact of legalism on the analysis of practical problems is all the more surprising when this style of jurisprudential reflection is contrasted with the different methodological preoccupations and sensibilities, as well as with the differing visions of international politics and law, which had animated earlier writers in international law.[15] One is reminded that, for the 'fathers' of international law, 'war' was not only an accepted practice but also a subject on which they spent considerable time and effort.[16] Similarly, the speculation about the nature of man and his

---

[12] Ibid. 124.

[13] David Kennedy, 'The Move to Institutions' (1987) 8 Cardozo Law Review 841.

[14] See the well-taken critique by Martti Koskenniemi, 'The Politics of International Law' (1990) 4 European Journal of International Law 4.

[15] See for a sophisticated discussion of this point David Kennedy, 'Primitive Legal Scholarship' (1986) 27 Harvard International Law Journal 1.

[16] See e.g. Gentili's work *De Jure Belli* (1612), reprinted in *Classics of International Law* (Oxford: Oxford University Press, 1933); and Hugo Grotius, *De Jure Belli Ac Pacis Libri Tres* (1646) (reprinted New York: Oceana, 1964). For a brief assessment of these works see Peter Haggenmacher, 'Grotius and Gentili: A Reassessment of Thomas E. Holland's Inaugural Lecture' and G. I. A. D. Draper, 'Grotius' Place in the Development of Legal Ideas about War', both in H. Bull, B. Kingsbury, and A. Roberts (eds.), *Hugo Grotius and International Relations* (Oxford: Oxford University Press, 1992), chs. 4 and 5.

social character informed much of their discussions. Clearly, as soon as social and legal theory no longer placed this vision of the 'good life' at the centre, but defined justice formally in terms of conformity with rules, the nature of these rules, their characteristic label or pedigree, rather than any substantive ideal and its institutional implements, attained decisive importance.

Inherent in the notion of law as a system of rules is a vision that only principled choice can be just and that, therefore, the successful development of law provides the best prospects for a just and peaceful order. If one ignores that peace in the domestic arena has only partially to do with the 'rule of law', and a great deal more to do with the successful institutionalization of a political process, the peaceful resolution of conflict at home seems to provide the prescription for the international arena: codification and the further development of international law. As Oppenheim seemed to believe, the end of Machiavellianism was at hand because, although there would always be 'bad' men, States themselves had become more and more civilized.[17] Thus, law was not only independent of politics, it was also held to be superior to it. Politics could not be understood without some constitutional rules, while law was 'its own creation' and could freely generate new rules.

It requires only a moment's reflection to realize that a category mistake of considerable proportions was committed here. While rules might 'create' other rules in the sense that they validate them, it is clear that validation has little to do with historical creation or with the actual force these rules will have in moulding decisions. To believe that membership in the system alone creates the force which guides action is inaccurate for a number of reasons. First, the idea that law is a logically closed system is simply wrong, for higher order principles may be compatible with lower order rules that contradict each other.[18] 'Closure' occurs, if at all, only in the act of deciding a 'case', where a variety of factual as well as normative concerns play a role. Thus, not only do 'facts' count, but the weighing of different factual descriptions may play a more decisive role than the norms which are invoked in a decision.

Second, even explicitly formulated rules can do little until they are applied to concrete situations. Here, the difficulties quickly mount as soon as we realize how many implicit understandings must be invoked in order to establish the connection between the norms stated in the rule and the 'reality' it is supposed to govern. Consider in this context Simmonds's simple example of the injunction 'Dogs must be carried on the escalator'.[19] The prohibition seems clear and unambiguous, but only because it is embedded in a whole host of at first unarticulated shared understandings. Thus, knowing something about the potential dangers of moving stairs and the fears of animals and people seems as necessary to our 'correct' interpretation of the rule as being able to link the rule with entirely unarticulated legal norms which

---

[17] Lassa Oppenheim, *The Future of International Law* (Oxford: Clarendon Press, 1921), 54 f.

[18] This point has been powerfully made by Dworkin, criticizing the Hartian conception of law as a system of rules. See Ronald Dworkin, 'Is Law a System of Rules?', in id. (ed.), *The Philosophy of Law* (Oxford: Oxford University Press, 1977), ch. 2.

[19] Nigel Simmonds, 'Between Positivism and Idealism' (1991) 50 Cambridge Law Journal 308.

remain in the background. For example, can I argue that since this injunction only requires the picking up of *dogs* (plural!), I, with only my Fido on a leash, am at liberty to disregard it? If we object to this interpretation, pointing out that the 'obvious' meaning of dogs here is the generic form, new difficulties arise. Does this mean that my young mountain lion (clearly not a dog!) out on a walk 'falls under' this prohibition? Does it make a difference if the pet is my tabby Purzel?

Suppose further, as Simmonds suggests, that I, as an allegedly seditious person, am followed by the police's Basset hound Pluto which goes wherever I go. Do I have to pick him up and carry him on the escalator? We probably fall back on the 'understanding' that this injunction means only if the dog is *my* dog. But this again will not do, as I am clearly obliged to pick up a dog which does not belong to me but which I took out for a walk. Thus, an 'adequate interpretation of the rule requires that we locate it within a complex body of assumptions and shared understandings of the extent of individual responsibility (the point being that [the] Basset is not my *responsibility*). Such understandings form the background for our interpretations of the rule, while themselves being resistant to articulation in rule-like form.'[20]

The upshot of the above argument is that, to the extent that interpretation is an intrinsic part of a legal system, a theory of law which depicts law as a simple system of higher and lower order rules and which suggests that 'the law' only meets social reality in the former (in the *Grundnorm*, or in an extra-legal rule of recognition, for example) is simply incomplete. A rule approach cannot defend consistently the autonomy of law through the rigorous exclusion of considerations external to law, be they moral precepts, policy considerations, or contextual factors, since it is unable to account coherently for the differences among principles and rules, as well as for the different degrees of obligatory force of some rules—*jus cogens* as well as 'soft law' come to mind here.[21] It is therefore not surprising that modern legal theories have either radically challenged the notion of law as a system of rules, by emphasizing 'process' and 'policy', or have introduced the problem of interpretation as the central conceptual puzzle. A brief discussion is in order.

The radical denial of the importance of rules and the emphasis on policy, that in international relations is particularly characteristic of 'process approaches', is perhaps best exemplified by the McDougal inquiry.[22] Rules are devalued as they are only indicators for past trends that may or may no longer further present or future needs. Their binding force is a juristic illusion since their normative character derives from their effectiveness in furthering social goals, not from the validity conferred upon them by a source or other rule within a system. The objections to such a radical reformulation

---

[20] Ibid. 313 (emphasis in original).

[21] Ignaz Seidl Hohenfeldern, 'International Economic Soft Law' (1970) 163 Recueil des Cours 169; Prosper Weil, 'Towards Relative Normativity in International Law?' (1983) 77 American Journal of International Law 413.

[22] Myres McDougal, 'The Identification and Appraisal of Diverse Systems of Public Order', reprinted in Richard Falk and Saul Mendlovitz (eds.), *The Strategy of World Order*, ii. *International Law* (New York: World Law Fund, 1966).

of the legal *problématique* are legion and need not be rehearsed at length here. Above all, an approach that postulates a supreme 'goal value', as, for example, McDougal's 'human dignity', relies on a highly problematic naturalism which, together with the emphasis on the formative influence of the decision-making process on outcomes, is in constant danger of becoming just an apology for the policies and preferences of the most powerful.[23] To this extent, law is able neither to mediate between different conceptions of the good—a central tenet of liberal theory that is of obvious relevance to international law—nor to shape the political process in a distinct way, as it constitutes more or less the political process itself.

The other strategy for dealing with the ambiguities resulting from the rules approach is to make legal theory explicitly a theory of interpretation. Law is no longer viewed from the 'outside' as a system of rules, but from the 'inside' as an argumentative practice. What the law means is then no longer simply ascertainable by the formal status of rules, but by their use and the justifiability of the decisions arrived at. To this extent, Dworkin's remark that legal theory is 'the general part of adjudication' is an apt one. Legal theory is an interpretation of the practice of engaging in normative argument and arriving at justifiable positions. However, in contrast to morals, or to the process or policy perspective, this justifiability is firmly tied to the conception of the integrity of law. This means that rule-handlers—and judges in particular—are obliged to have regard to established practices and must not simply invent them. To this extent, earlier decisions constrain later ones and deviations or reversals have to be justified in terms of principled arguments, rather than by utility or policy considerations, particularly when rights are at stake.[24]

On the one hand, the emphasis of the 'internal aspect' of law preserves the autonomy of law and does not make it a 'function' of society, or of policy. On the other hand, the issue of the judge's 'discretion' looms large on the horizon and the justifiability of a decision depends almost entirely on whether this discretion was exercised within proper bounds. It is here that Dworkin attempts to show the virtually impossible: that even hard cases have, when all is said and done, one and only one 'right solution'. Fortunately for us, he charges a mythical figure (Hercules) with this task. Hercules,[25] although paradigmatic of the 'good' judge, is obviously not of this world and therefore need not concern us here, particularly since neither a constitutional text nor a doctrine of *stare decisis* apply in international law. For our purposes, two things are important: first, how this theory represents the latest attempt to uphold the tenets of legalism and thus reproduces once again the opposition and symbiosis of 'law' and 'politics'; and second, how this symbiosis is disturbed by the internal criticism this theory has engendered within the legal community itself. It is by way of

---

[23] See Francis Boyle, 'Ideals and Things: International Legal Scholarship and the Prison House of Language' (1985) 26 Harvard Journal of International Law 349.

[24] For a good exposition of these ideas, see e.g. the collection of essays by Ronald Dworkin, *A Matter of Principle* (Cambridge, Mass.: Harvard University Press, 1985).

[25] Ronald Dworkin, *Taking Rights Seriously* (Cambridge, Mass.: Harvard University Press, 1978), ch. 4.

the criticisms of this theory made by the Critical Legal Studies Movement[26] that I wish, in the next section, to approach the issue of rule guidance in legal contexts.

3. DISCRETION AND UNIQUENESS

The problem of the indeterminacy of rules has been one of the traditional chestnuts of jurisprudence. Legal realists had already pointed out that, due to the unclear boundaries of legal concepts, judicial decisions could not simply be derived from rules and, therefore, had to be largely the result of idiosyncratic factors. Dworkin's argument, that these problems could be circumvented and that the 'correct' solution could be found if the more general principles of a legal system were used in conjunction with the proper standards of interpretation, was therefore all the more important.[27] It is against this systemic conception of law that the Critical Legal Studies Movement directed its criticism. Originating in a critical assessment of contract law,[28] CLS soon branched out into constitutional law. Finally, in the field of international law, writers such as David Kennedy and Martti Koskenniemi have come closest to the CLS position.

For adherents of CLS, the existence of contradictions among rules and higher order principles make both the notion of one 'correct' judicial decision, and the idea of definite rule guidance for decisions in general, rather fanciful. Such contradictions arise systematically on three distinct levels of the legal order. The first level involves choices between specific rules and more general, and therefore vague, standards. The result of this contradiction is that, in adjudicating any concrete dispute, there remains the problem of how to justify the choice between strict rules and discretionary standards. The utilization of strict rules safeguards procedural uniformity; the invocation of discretionary standards results in more situation-sensitive decisions but does so on an *ad hoc* basis. Ambiguity also enters at a second level of doctrines designed to resolve first-level disputes. Doctrines, contrary to the hopes one might place in them, are only able to provide us with a list of counterpoised functional arguments for the applicability of rules and standards without, however, being able to provide a solution to the new dilemma. At a third level, underneath this doctrinal ambiguity lies a hidden ambivalence over substantive ideals, particularly in the standard liberal vision of adjudication. While rules express the ideals of self-reliance and individualism, standards favour substantive justice, and possibly altruism.

The differences between the CLS arguments and those of legal realism now become clear. By maintaining the autonomy of law but locating the indeterminacy

---

[26] For an introduction to CLS see Mark Kelman, *A Guide to Critical Legal Studies* (Cambridge, Mass.: Harvard University Press, 1987).

[27] For a criticism of this position see the collection of essays by Marshall Cohen (ed.), *Ronald Dworkin and Contemporary Jurisprudence* (Totowa, NJ: Rowman and Allanheld, 1984).

[28] See Duncan Kennedy, 'Form and Substance in Private Law Adjudication' (1976) 89 Harvard Law Review 1685.

deep within the legal system itself, the adherents of CLS cast considerable doubt on the availability of the simple cure which process adherents had advocated: the 'purposive' reading of legal prescriptions. In his trenchant criticism of the consequentialist yardstick used by the Law and Economics school, Duncan Kennedy pointed out that nothing in the principles of contract law is definite enough to allow a judge or legislator to calculate the costs which, for example, the insertion of implied warranties into contracts will impose on particular groups or interests. 'Since on Kennedy's analysis law is too indeterminate to be a bearer of economic interest, it follows that it cannot be used in an instrumental fashion.'[29] Thus, neither the 'economy' nor 'society' explains the development of law and its internal dynamic. Similarly, international legal arguments show the same structure, as Martti Koskenniemi suggests.[30] They too are based on differing conceptions of law (consent vs. justice) and differing doctrines, and have to deal with the same dilemma of rules vs. standards (concreteness vs. normativity). In criticizing the usual 'mainstream' solutions which, as strategies which involve 'middle of the road doctrines' or 'balancing' facts with legal rules (as in the case of the emergence and recognition of statehood), seem suspect and at odds with the notion of the rule of law, Koskenniemi remarks:

Mainstream doctrine retreats into general statements about the need to 'combine' concreteness and normativity, realism and idealism, which bear no consequence to its normative conclusion. It then advances, emphasizing the contextuality of each solution—thus undermining its own emphasis on the general and impartial character of its system.

A doctrine's own contradictions force it into an impoverished and unreflective pragmatism. On the one hand, the 'idealist' illusion is preserved that law can and does play a role in the organization of social life among states. On the other, the 'realist' criticisms have been accepted and the law is seen as distinctly secondary to power and politics. The style survives because we recognize in it the liberal doctrine within which we have been accustomed to press our political arguments.[31]

Here, the analysis is even more pessimistic. The autonomy of legal argument seems to have been emasculated even further and law seems little more than a common rhetorical style, to be used for political purposes but unable to provide any guidance for making choices or adjudicating controversies fairly in terms of its own criteria.

These are indeed serious dilemmas that could easily lead to nihilism and/or withdrawal, as no introduction of new values or purposes seems to be possible in order to resolve our quandary of the justifiability of our practical choices. True, there remains the position of 'existential' choice but by definition such choices have to be private, and it is unclear how any coherent understanding of social order and its requirements can be based on it. To this extent, the particular political agenda that many CLS members espouse seems even less justifiable than that which was

---

[29] David Jabbari, 'From Criticism to Construction in Modern Critical Legal Theory' (1992) 12 Oxford Journal of Legal Studies 507 at 525.
[30] Koskenniemi, *From Apology to Utopia.*
[31] Koskenniemi, 'The Politics of International Law', 12.

connected with the old liberal conceptions of law which CLS so vigorously criticized. Thus, a second dilemma arises: although we might now possess in law an at least powerful, rhetorical tool, the critical attitude seems to enjoin us from using it justifiably for public purposes, on pain of inconsistency with our professed theoretical stance. Our predicament seems to be circumscribed by the Scylla of blind and unjustifiable activism, and the Charybdis of existential withdrawal.

As with so many dilemmas, there is no solution as long as we accept the terms in which the dilemma is posed. Rather, a solution becomes possible only after we have 'deconstructed' the dilemma of law and reworked some of the crucial conceptual issues that led to the impasse. Only in this way can we hope to sidestep some of the pitfalls and perhaps perceive the entire problematic in a new way. The importance of such a *Gestalt* shift for social theory has been pointed out by Rorty and is familiar to every student of the history of political thought.[32] For example, the change from a conception of politics communicated by organic metaphors, such as the 'body politic', was supplanted in the seventeenth century largely by the metaphor of 'contract'. The important point in this context is that the new conceptualizations cannot be reached from the old vocabularies and their logic, nor can the process of producing a new set of concepts and puzzles be interpreted as hitting upon or approximating a 'correct' representation of reality. Rorty's method, called 'therapeutic re-description', provides us with the possibility of 'seeing' the old in a new way and in creating new opportunities for practices and experiences which sidestep the old vocabulary standing in the way:

Such creations are not the result of successfully fitting together pieces of a puzzle. They are not discoveries of a reality behind the appearances, of an undistorted view of the whole picture with which to replace myopic views of its parts. The proper analogy is with the invention of new tools to take the place of old tools. To come up with such a vocabulary is more like discarding the lever and the chock because one has envisaged the pulley.[33]

In other words, new ways of conceptualization presuppose two steps: one of 'unlearning' by deconstructing the problem, and one of construction by utilizing new conceptual tools in the analysis.

In applying these insights to our problem, we first have to clear up some fundamental misunderstandings concerning issues of 'indeterminacy' before we can examine various strategies for dealing with this problem. Implicit in our understanding of how norms mould decisions seems to be the idea that the conclusion must not only follow from the legal premiss (in conjunction with the 'facts' in the minor premiss) through the standard patterns of inference, but also that the solution has to be unique. To this extent, Dworkin's rather contorted argument about the availability of the 'right' decision is only the flip side of the argument that, in the absence of such determinacy, everything has to end up in 'relativism'. The idea that logical consistency requires convergence on a unique result, since both together constitute 'truth',

---

[32]   Richard Rorty, *Contingency, Irony, Solidarity* (Cambridge: Cambridge University Press, 1989).
[33]   Ibid. 12.

has, of course, great appeal. After all, a 'divergence' of results is usually interpreted as an 'error' or even as a refutation of the major premiss, which necessitates corrective steps.

As persuasive as such arguments appear, a moment's reflection shows that matters are a bit more complicated. Let us take up the prototypical case of 'determinacy', a mathematical problem in which the complexity of the 'real' world does not yet even play a part. Consequently, the 'solution' is entirely determined by logic. Nevertheless, we realize that 'uniqueness' does not necessarily follow. It seems that uniqueness is an additional criterion which does not always go hand in glove together with determinacy. One could not possibly argue that the solutions of quadratic equations, familiar from basic analytic geometry, are not 'determinate' because two values for x and y satisfy the equations. Similarly, the Folke theorem of game theory has shown that generally multiple equilibria exist for a whole range of interdependent choices. Thus determinacy and uniqueness are again not coincident. It seems rather problematic then to require 'uniqueness' as a criterion for judicial decisions, when it is frequently not available even in logic.

For whatever reasons we might believe that non-uniqueness condemns us to 'relativism', adhering to this ideal seems more like chasing a rainbow than a rational attitude in respect of practical problems. Furthermore, taking the particular features of the practical realm into account, Sir Isaiah Berlin identified that the 'right answer' thesis (uniqueness) and its flip side, 'relativism', depend on a utopian claim concerning the metaphysics of values and of normative justification. They assume that all questions in the domain have one answer, that this is knowable, and that all the answers in this entire realm are mutually compatible.[34] It requires no further elaboration to establish that such assumptions are not only inconsistent with our experiences (ranging from 'moral luck'[35] to 'tragic choices'[36]), but also misdiagnose the nature of practical arguments as concerning mainly cognitive issues. Besides, we all know from practical experience that without a certain value opportunism that allows us to make various trade-offs in different situations, 'life' would become pretty oppressive. Although consistency is certainly a virtue, in practical questions it might be the virtue of small minds and/or fanatics.

Far from drawing us into the vortex of 'relativism', the recognition of plural possibilities on the one hand, and the need to justify particular choices on the other is the basis for 'pluralism' and orderly change, which are the central goods a legal system is supposed to preserve. That these goals often conflict is hardly news. However, this conflict in no way implies the nihilistic or existential conclusion that anything goes and/or that because there is no single right answer, any answer is as good as another. Rather, what seems to be required is, first, an investigation of indeterminacy as it arises in legal reasoning, and second, how particular choices (out of several 'possible'

---

[34] Sir Isaiah Berlin, 'The Pursuit of the Ideal', in id., *The Crooked Timber of Humanity* (New York: Vintage, 1991).

[35] See Bernard Williams, 'Moral Luck', in id., *Moral Luck* (Cambridge: Cambridge University Press, 1981).   [36] Guido Calabresi, *Tragic Choices* (New York: Norton, 1978).

ones) can be justified on non-idiosyncratic grounds. Thus, the emphasis on justification brings into play pragmatic considerations that relieve us of the problems of semantic indeterminacy. To this extent, the solution adumbrated here is similar to that proposed by the late Wittgenstein. In his *Tractatus*, Wittgenstein tried to specify the rules of correspondence between a term and its object, its 'truth-conditions', but moved in his later work to a conception of language in which the meaning of a term was defined by its 'use'.[37] In other words, *criteria* now define the conditions for the assertability or justification for using a term, rather than the semantic 'content'.[38]

Without engaging in a comprehensive review of the sources of indeterminacy, some distinctions are in order. One type of indeterminacy concerns problems of *indifference* familiar both from deontological and utilitarian theories. Like Buridan's ass, there are certain situations in which not even explicit decision criteria such as 'utility' calculations (not to mention even general rules) can determine my choice because the alternatives are all the same to me. To resolve my quandary I have to resort to some additional choice mechanism, such as the flipping of a coin, or just do what I did last time. Whatever I do, one thing is clear, the original criterion for guiding my choice is unable to do so this time. Similarly, the function of rules in deontological theories consists largely in determining an area of freedom for individual choice by demarcating first the duties of an actor.[39] Since specific actions within the area of freedom are morally equivalent, we can say that the system of rules is *indeterminate* at the level of individual choice but *determinate* at the level of defining classes of actions. Thus, volunteering at a hospital is an act of charity, as is inviting a homeless person to Thanksgiving dinner or giving money to a UNICEF programme. Similarly, the legal system might provide tax deductions, in recognition of such charitable actions. It might even expand this class, for example, by making contributions to cultural institutions, such as opera companies or churches, tax deductible too.

Seen from this perspective, the notion that the main function of law is one of 'constraint' in order to arrive at determinate choices seems quaint indeed. If someone were to object to such indeterminacy and were committed to having things regulated once and for all, he would (and should) rightly be committed. This raises a more general point: large areas of law are therefore wrongly conceived as 'constraints', as the distinction between constitutive and regulative rules suggests. Constitutive rules are designed to enable actors to pursue their own plans. In so far as they are 'constraints' at all, it is only in the sense identified above, in that they allow us to characterize an action as falling within a certain class, such as the making of a contract. This means that the parties must observe certain formalities regulated by rules. However, these rules will not determine the particular substantive choices of

---

[37] See e.g. Ludwig Wittgenstein, *Philosophical Investigations*, trans. G. E. M. Anscombe (New York: Macmillan, 1953), § 43.

[38] See e.g. the discussion in the *Philosophical Investigations*, §§ 138–242.

[39] See Immanuel Kant, *The Metaphysics of Morals*, trans. Mary Gregor (Cambridge: Cambridge University Press, 1991), particularly 386–8.

the parties. The implications for international law are obvious: many if not most international legal norms (although not necessarily the ones which are most 'important', namely those which regulate the use of force) are of such a constitutive nature, such, for example, as the 'law of treaties'.

From this brief discussion we gather that only in very special circumstances will a rule lead to definite outcomes. It will be a small class of events (although it may contain quite a number of cases). As the above example of the rule of flipping a coin for decision-making showed, only a rule that solves a more or less pure problem of co-ordination will lead to definite outcomes. Its parasitic nature, i.e. its dependence on other rules establishing the class of permitted actions, as well as the necessity of *common interests* among the actors, should be obvious.[40] Technically speaking, we are dealing here with situations where a rule is supposed to resolve the problem of multiple equilibria. Examples from the international arena are easily found. Thus, no actor will care whether he transmits on any particular wavelength as long as he is allocated a specific spectrum that ensures that he can send his messages without undue interference. Although traditional thought on the 'self-enforcing' and unproblematic nature of these rules might be overly optimistic, as has been demonstrated by the hard bargaining on technical standards which has occurred in those organizations concerned with the telecommunications order,[41] it is true that these types of rules are closely tied to 'functional' co-operation in areas which are considered to be of a 'technical' nature.

Another type of indeterminacy arises when norms themselves conflict and make incompatible demands upon the actor. In extreme cases this amounts to tragic conflict, as the examples of Antigone or even Agamemnon show. Here the failure of normative guidance arises not out of equally possible and justifiable possibilities, but rather from the fact that, no matter what, one norm has to be violated. We react therefore not with indifference to such dilemmas, but with regret, or guilt. It is this type of conflict which is present not only in specific rules, but also in the underlying justifications and fundamental values, which CLS writers such as Kennedy have emphasized. Similarly, in the international arena, the 'ideal' of an international community militates against the conception of the basic liberty of states expressed in the *Lotus* rule. What aggravates the serious nature of such dilemmas in the international arena is the fact that some of the mitigating *political* practices of domestic orders are unavailable.

One way of dealing with the problem is, of course, the public/private distinction, which lessens the conflict by placing the pursuit of conflicting values in different domains. There is no such 'buffer' in the international public order. There is further-

---

[40] For a more extended discussion, see my *Rules, Norms, and Decisions* (Cambridge: Cambridge University Press, 1989), chs. 3 and 4.

[41] See the discussion of the role of governments, particularly the US, which pushed the proposals of its TNCs within the ITU, in William Drake, 'Policies for the National and Global Information Infrastructures', in id. (ed.), *The New Information Infrastructure* (New York: Twentieth Century Fund, 1995).

more no conception that the rudimentary international order is, as such, an expression of a collective identity and thus generative of certain interests and commitments. Finally, although normative conflict is inevitable in a pluralist society, the main mode of channelling conflict is through political means. Legislation, as the expression of the collective will and consensus at a particular time, can be unprincipled, although here again the raising of constitutional issues in domestic courts can easily trump political decisions. To this extent, the growth of 'judicial review' might lead to the atrophy of the political process and to a stalemated rather than a vibrant society, as the example of Germany seems to indicate. The idea of 'depoliticizing' questions by submitting them to constitutional courts might seem attractive at first, but might also engender significant costs further down the line, since the idea that a 'constitutional order' can resolve normative conflict by way of the 'right answer' thesis is one of the fantasies of legalism. In criticizing Dworkin, Christopher Kutz points out:

Dworkin's response misses the point: if values are genuinely plural, then there neither can nor should be a successful technique for resolving all conflicts between them, such as the reduction of normative deliberation to a monistic calculus (e.g. wealth maximization), or the stipulation of an overarching principle to order values. Normative conflicts will simply reemerge when we seek to justify that framework for deliberation or that of ordering values.[42]

While normative indeterminacy is usually held to be the most serious problem for the effectiveness of normative guidance for decisions, difficulties of a similarly serious nature arise out of the fact that rules have to be stated in ordinary language. Thus, a third source of indeterminacy is the eventually irreducible semantic ambiguity of most of the concepts in ordinary language. The examples above have already explained several of the puzzles of semantic indeterminacy. What the apparently clear statement 'No dogs on the escalator' meant in the example above was ambiguous in many senses and could be ascertained only by relying on contextual factors. Thus, pragmatics rather than semantics provided the key to deciding whether the instruction applied only to the plural, to any dog, to any pet, only to my dog, or to the animal in general for which I was responsible, etc. These terms only become more definite through the successive supply of a context by way of examples.

Even particles of rules such as the terms 'reckless', 'fair', 'big', or 'exact' create similar difficulties. Although we might assume that the difficulties stem from the existence of some normative standard, embodied in 'reckless' and 'fair' respectively, it is puzzling that we encounter the same problems when we use allegedly descriptive terms which are even susceptible to objective measurement, as in the case of 'big' or 'exact'. The problem is that in both cases the issue of interpretation does not depend on evidentiary matters. There is simply no 'fact of the matter', as the philosophers say, whether or not the term in question applies. As Aristotle reminded us, what is big or exact depends on circumstances and not primarily on

---

[42] Christopher Kutz, 'Just Disagreement: Indeterminacy and Rationality in the Rule of Law' (1994) 103 Yale Law Journal 997 at 1026.

measurement.[43] A deviation of 3 inches is not a problem for the architect of a five-storey house, but it is a big problem for a doctor who has to remove a 3-inch tumour from the brain, not to speak of the problem it poses for the micro-electronics engineer. What represents a reckless act can only be ascertained by taking the circumstances into account. Travelling at 10 miles per hour over the speed limit on an interstate highway in Kansas is not the same as transgressing the speed limit on a narrow mountain road in Scotland.

These are rather obvious observations. Although they introduce considerable uncertainty into practical reasoning—and here I treat law as a special form of practical reasoning—there is no point in belabouring the vagueness of such terms in pursuit of some mistaken semantic ideal. The only hope of sharpening the boundaries of the terms of everyday language consists precisely in the supply of a context and the successive elaboration of various implications by adding examples so as to probe the vague 'penumbras' of a term. If this sounds (to the semantic purist) like a pragmatic trick leading to *ad hoc* semantics, so be it.

After all, language itself cannot be restricted to consistency and purely tautological derivation. Here, semantics and syntax are supposed to specify the conditions for meaning, so that 'dog bites man' is not equivalent to 'man bites dog'. However, 'meaning' is also communicated by pragmatic understandings which we invoke to decode a message. Thus, 'I like her cooking' might, depending on the context, mean either the food or the activity. Furthermore, nobody could claim to have understood, if one mistook 'is Jim there?' on the phone as a genuine question, instead of a request. If one simply answers 'yes' and hangs up, one has certainly not understood. Apparently, communications about practical problems do not concern simple semantic issues.

We can see how mistaken the notion is that meaning can be reduced to issues of semantics if we imagine for a moment a world in which, finally, all terms have a clear referent in accordance with the semantic ideal. In a way, such a world would be that of a Hobbesian sovereign who, as the sole authoritative 'fixer' of signs, could prescribe everything. However, as Simmonds correctly points out, such a system of communication would nevertheless fail precisely because prescriptions need common understandings as a background for their interpretation:

For what understandings and apprehended concerns could possibly inform our interpretations, leading us to converge on a shared interpretation? . . .

The Hobbesian state of nature is not a chaos of subjectivity. Hobbes does indeed claim that there is no common rule of good and evil to be taken from the nature of the objects themselves. But this does not involve a denial of some degree of uniformity in the desires of men and women, such that many would concur in regarding the same objects as good or desirable. My argument is not intended to be a refutation of Hobbes. My object is simply to suggest that, in the chaos of subjectivity, a shared body of rules could not be created by a sovereign deliberately positing certain verbally formulated precepts. Shared rules require shared interpretations, but shared interpretations could not emerge in a chaos of subjectivity. When the

---

[43] Aristotle, *Nichomachean Ethics*, 1094 b13–1095 a7.

legal positivist solution to the problem of co-existence in a world of disagreement seems most necessary, it turns out to be *impossible*. Might it not be that when the solution is possible it could prove to be *unnecessary*?[44]

Thus, the upshot of this argument is that the lack of a 'hard edge' to our concepts and the dependency of their meaning upon context defeats the argument that only the insistence on authoritative texts and their semantic clarity can rescue us from the throes of uncertainty.

Finally, another more principled form of semantic indeterminacy arises out of the possibility that competing 'fact descriptions' are given for the same events or actions. This creates great difficulties in ethics and thus it is not surprising that similar problems are to be expected in law. Is my statement (to take Kant's famous example) that misleads an intruder in my house as to where my friend is hiding simply a lie (as Kant suggests), or is it a case of coercion where the characterization of lying is simply not apt (as Pufendorf would argue)? It is this difficulty that international lawyers are perhaps most familiar with: how am I to choose between describing some action as self-defence or aggression? Why are my freedom-fighters your terrorists or political criminals? Here, legal doctrine has sought over the years to develop distinctions between absolute and relative offences, and between different stages in the development of internal unrest, by attempting to impose certain responsibilities on the contending parties and their sympathizers and supporters. However, none of these typologies or casuistic methods can, of course, deny that we have to deal here with essentially contested concepts.[45] The problem with such concepts is that they are part of political struggles, not simply descriptions of them. It is obvious that courts of law become one of the arenas in which at least parts of these struggles occur. However, this does not prove the assertion that law is nothing but politics. After all, the style of reasoning is quite distinct when we engage in the political mode, and when we utilize legal arguments.[46] The use and admissibility of evidence, the way of structuring arguments, and, finally, the way in which norms are used will be quite different. The feature common to law and politics does not lie in the denial of their distinct styles within practical reasoning, but rather in their common concern with human action and the creation of the human (and hopefully humane) world.

4. THE ROLE OF NORMS: A SOCIAL SCIENCE PERSPECTIVE

The discussion above concerning the problems of a largely semantic theory of law pointed to the need for common understandings as a background to the interpretation

[44] Simmonds, 'Between Positivism and Idealism', 314.

[45] On 'essentially contested concepts' and their properties see W. B. Gallie, 'Essentially Contested Concepts', in *Proceedings of the Aristotelian Society*, 56 (London 1955/6), reprinted in Max Black (ed.), *The Importance of Language* (Englewood Cliffs, NJ: Prentice Hall, 1962), 121. For an elaboration in regard to political discourse, see William Connolly, *The Terms of Politics Discourse*, 2nd edn. (Princeton: Princeton University Press, 1983).

[46] See also Nigel Simmonds, 'Why Conventionalism does not collapse into Pragmatism' (1990) 49 *Cambridge Law Journal* 63.

of the rules and norms that are to govern our interactions. Such a stance rules out the possibility of radical rule scepticism as it emerged from a particular interpretation of Wittgenstein, § 198, in the *Philosophical Investigations*[47] and which has found its adherents in the legal community.[48] Since every rule must be interpreted and applied in specific contexts, Wittgenstein wonders how a rule can tell us what to do in any given situation: 'Whatever I do is compatible with some interpretation of the rule.'[49] In other words, rules cannot provide guidance.

This radical rule scepticism seems to result in a paradox. However, Wittgenstein himself suggested: 'The surprising, the paradox, is paradoxical only in a certain deficient environment. One has to complement this environment in such a way that what seemed to be paradoxical no longer appears to be paradoxical.'[50] Rule scepticism is as irrefutable on its own terms as Hume's paradox, and for Hume it was 'common sense' that protected us from despair. For Wittgenstein, the paradox dissolves as soon as we leave the atomistic world of the single speaker and take more seriously the notion that language is an intersubjective practice.[51] As a practice, a rule not only tells me how to proceed in a situation that I might never have faced before,[52] it is also governed by certain conventions of the community of which I am part. To this extent, my interpretations of a rule as well as my uses of words are monitored and reinforced by a group of competent speakers. Thus, while there are likely to be disagreements about the proper use of a term or the interpretation of a rule, purely idiosyncratic uses are excluded even if the use of the concepts remains contestable and contested. Again, a purely semantic analysis of language is rejected because it is the pragmatic dimension that provides the solution.

These remarks also have important implications for the status of norms as explanations of actions in international politics. Although regime analysis has over the last two decades flourished in international relations analysis by challenging the predominance of structural models, certain problems with this mode of analysis remain. Often, norms are little more than 'intervening variables' and the strategy of accepting explanations based ultimately on 'interest' and 'power' and reducing other approaches to the status of explaining only some of the remaining variances[53] biases

---

[47] Saul Kripke, *Wittgenstein on Rules and Private Language* (Cambridge, Mass.: Harvard University Press, 1982).

[48] For a collection of interesting essays addressing the problems of a Wittgensteinian conception of rules for legal theory, see the July 1998 issue of the Canadian Journal of Law and Jurisprudence with contributions by Bix, Schauer, Marmor, *et al.*

[49] Wittgenstein, *Philosophical Investigations*, § 198.

[50] Ludwig Wittgenstein, *Bemerkungen über die Grundlagen der Mathematik*, ed. G. E. M. Anscombe, Rush Rhees, and G. H. von Wright (Oxford: Basil Blackwell, 1978), 410.

[51] See Ulrich Volk, *Das Problem des Semantischen Skeptizismus: Saul Kripke's Wittgenstein-Interpretation* (Freiburg: Schäuble Verlag, 1988).

[52] See Wittgenstein, *Philosophical Investigations*, §§ 151 and 185.

[53] This is more or less Krasner's strategy in his 'Structural Causes and Regime Consequences: Regimes and Intervening Variables', in Stephen Krasner (ed.), *International Regimes* (Ithaca, NY: Cornell University Press, 1983), ch. 1.

the inquiry in more than one way. First, while 'interest' and 'power' seem somehow self-explanatory, norms, particularly in their constitutive function, are hardly perceived. This is all the more surprising given that the discourse on international politics could hardly have got off the ground in the absence of rules which informed us of who an actor is and how the 'poles' of the international system are supposed to be determined. Although the privileging of certain notions as an *explanans* might be understandable because of the predominance of realist and economic thinking, it is hardly justifiable if our goal is a better understanding of international politics.

Second, the debate about how we can prove that norms matter seems utterly confused since it is informed by incoherent notions concerning what constitutes a scientific explanation and how we can demonstrate the causal significance of norms. The former problem is largely connected with the uncritical and often incoherent acceptance of logical positivism as an epistemology that can provide foundational criteria for science. The latter points to the multiple meanings of 'cause' and to the difficulty of specifying context-independent criteria that would illustrate the significance of norms in determining choices. Both problems singly and in conjunction prevent us from developing more appropriate strategies for probing the role that rules and norms play in shaping international reality in general and decisions in particular. It is to these two problems that I now wish to turn. For this purpose, I shall briefly touch upon the regime debate and draw upon discussions of its three main schools: rationalism; the sociological approach (constructivism);[54] and the inchoate approach of liberal theory.[55]

Let us agree in a preliminary fashion that the criteria for ascertaining whether norms matter in international politics have something to do with the effectiveness and the robustness of a given regime. By choosing regimes as my focus, I argue that outcomes in the international arena are not the result of some fortuitous coincidence of choices but that these choices are in a way moulded by norms and common understandings which represent some form of governance.[56] In other words, we are not only observing certain patterns of interactions from the outside but also explaining these empirical regularities on the basis of an internal point of view, by taking rules and norms as an *explanans*. By *effectiveness* I accept the usual notion that regimes enable the participants to realize certain goals (which would otherwise have been impossible or difficult to reach) and that the rules and norms of regimes are defences against unilateral action and opportunism. *Robustness*, on the other hand, refers to the ability of regimes to withstand the challenges of change and their capacity to adjust to and provide orderly procedures for dealing with such 'environmental' shocks.[57]

[54] For a not quite accurate distinction of these two types of approaches that nevertheless has gained currency, see Robert Keohane, 'International Institutions: Two Approaches' (1988) 32 International Studies Quarterly 379.

[55] For a clear exposition of this approach, see Andrew Moravcik, 'Taking Preferences Seriously: A Liberal Theory of International Politics' (1997) 51 International Organization 513.

[56] See e.g. Oran Young, *International Governance* (Ithaca, NY: Cornell University Press, 1994).

[57] The definitions of effectiveness and robustness are taken from Robert Powell, 'Anarchy in International Relations Theory' (1994) 48 International Organization 313.

How do norms matter? The three schools mentioned above give quite different answers to this question. According to the predominant mode of analysis, norms matter because they express the 'interests' of the actors or the dominant hegemon. In the latter case regimes are little more than expressions of power. Meanwhile, the hegemonic stability debate has run its course but has contributed surprisingly little to the study of the effectiveness and robustness of regimes. Part of the reason for this has to do with the questionable characterization of regimes as collective goods, and part with the lack of empirical fit with the post-Second World War order. The multi-lateral institutions of the Bretton Woods regime developed much more 'stickiness' than was expected.[58] However, relying on a metaphor (stickiness) for an explanation is not tantamount to explaining the phenomenon. To this extent, the more general case of an interest-based explanation is more appropriate.[59] Thus, norms matter because regimes solve certain informational asymmetries that would otherwise inhibit co-operation. In other words, regimes have reputational effects[60] and persist because they represent sunk costs, which make it rational to play by the rules even in the face of certain dissatisfactions and opportunities for circumvention.[61]

Although each of these hypotheses makes an important point, they are not neces-sarily mutually compatible and therefore do not fit into a coherent 'theory'. The most obvious contradiction is the argument that regimes are crucial for actors' repu-tations by providing standards against which their behaviour can be assessed. While the latter is obviously true, for the rationalist approach it is true in a trivial sense only, in that it is still not clear what role reputation is supposed to play in explaining co-operation. If the main reason for the creation of a regime is transparency, as a result of which the participants can overcome information asymmetries, then it is not clear why reputation would be important. Since the actors have all the important infor-mation (or at least most of it), it is unclear why one actor would credit other actors with certain behavioural dispositions from which it could draw inferences about character (quite aside from the difficulties of such imputations in the case of corpo-rate actors). In short, as with the *homines economici* in the market, who are interested in prices and not the dispositional traits of other actors, it is not quite clear why repu-tation should matter to rational egotists. Indeed, reputations (acquired for whatever reasons) seem to take long to acquire and fade and thus are a highly problematic tool for solving information problems in particular situations.[62]

[58] See e.g. the discussion of John G. Ruggie, 'Multilateralism: The Anatomy of an Institution', in id. (ed.), *Multilateralism Matters* (New York: Columbia University Press, 1993), ch. 1.

[59] For a fundamental discussion of different approaches to regimes, see Andreas Hasenclever, Peter Mayer, and Volker Rittberger, *Theories of International Regimes* (Cambridge: Cambridge University Press, 1997).

[60] This point is made by Robert Keohane, *After Hegemony: Cooperation and Discord in the World Political Economy* (Princeton: Princeton University Press, 1984); see e.g. the discussion at 104–6.

[61] The 'sunk cost' argument is developed by Keohane in his article 'The Analysis of International Regimes: Towards a European-American Research Programme', in Volker Rittberger (ed.), *Regime Theory and International Relations* (Oxford: Oxford University Press, 1993), 23.

[62] For a fundamental discussion, see Jonathan Mercer, *Reputation and International Politics* (Ithaca, NY: Cornell University Press, 1996).

Besides, if reputation is important because transparency is insufficient, and thus reputation can actually significantly reduce the costs to others, it is not clear why it would be in the interest of any single actor to shoulder his part of what appears to be a collective action problem. Why take the trouble of disseminating information, particularly after being taken for a ride and in the face of possible retaliation by the actor who is being bad mouthed? We are all familiar with the phenomenon whereby some of the best recommendations are reserved for those whom we want to have leave. Besides, violations are seldom clear-cut, but are instead subject to different interpretations and rebuttals. Thus, unless we take this larger picture into account, there is often no way of even beginning to show what happened. True, *who* violated the rule may be more important to me than the fact that it *was* violated, as actors treat violations differently depending on whether they were committed by friend or foe. However, it is not clear how this phenomenon can be accommodated within a rationalist theory.[63] It leads to double standards and the devaluing of the necessary information, and it means that the 'framing' of the violation rather than the action itself seems to carry most weight in the explanation. The rationalist approach thus cuts itself off from important theoretical issues by systematically excluding issues of framing, and by neglecting possible excuses and rebuttals as part of the story.

Finally, the 'sunk costs' argument seems to be only a special case of the more general argument that regimes reduce transaction costs, but are at the same time, because of transaction costs, difficult to create. However, without specifying *ex ante* what counts as 'cost', it is again difficult to see how the demand for regimes can bring them into existence (since there are demonstrably many areas in which there is a demand but no regime) or why the existence of a regime should deter defections.[64] The regime would be self-enforcing and defection would be irrational only under the assumption that a 'self-destruct' mechanism would be triggered by any rule violation.[65] It is of course this fear that Hobbes plays upon in showing the irrationality of resistance to the sovereign, even if his particular actions are reprehensible. However, as we all know, no such mechanism exists either domestically or internationally and thus this 'explanation' fails. My cheating is usually unlikely to bring down the whole house of cards and therefore, *depending on how others interpret my defection*, it might or might not end the regime.[66] In other words, any outcome is compatible with the hypotheses of 'rationalist' theory.

The second school, which is much less unified in its general approach and

---

[63] Joann Gowa, 'Rational Hegemons, Excludable Goods, and Small Groups' (1989) 41 World Politics 307.

[64] The demand for regimes argument was made by Robert Keohane, 'The Demand for International Regimes', in Krasner (ed.), *International Regimes*, 141.

[65] This is suggested by Jon Elster, *The Cement of Society: A Study of Social Order* (Cambridge: Cambridge University Press, 1989), 44.

[66] This is, of course, the trouble with the universalization principle in ethics and the Kantian categorical imperative. For a further discussion, see my 'Vergeßt Kant' in Christine Chwazca and Wolfgang Kersting (eds.), *Politische Philosophie der Internationalen Beziehungen* (Frankfurt: Suhrkamp, 1998), 96.

methodological commitments,[67] shares as a common point of departure the notion that actors are never really in the state of nature and that social order cannot be derived systematically from individual maximizing choices. As corporate entities, the actors are themselves constituted by norms (social contract), but they are also much more deeply implicated in normative understandings than rationalists suggest. Hobbesian actors could never escape the state of war since their promises would not be binding and, in the absence of shared conventions, could not even determine what counts as a promise. Consequently, both international actors and the international system are constituted by norms. To this extent, the modern 'sociologists' share with the 'British school' of international relations a concern with the conventions that underlie every State system.

Although the international system might represent a strange form of 'sociality' in that neither a common notion of the *salus publica* nor a common identity is created—speculations concerning the regulative idea of a *civitas maxima* à la Wolf notwithstanding[68]—it is nevertheless a form of sociality. The actions of the participants are meaningfully oriented towards each other[69] and such meanings presuppose intersubjective understandings which are the preconditions, and thus antecedent to, any optimizing behaviour in which any actor might engage. To this extent, neither interests nor even power in terms of 'capabilities' are givens that can be used as unproblematic foundations. Both presuppose an understanding of the rules of the game that one wants to play by before issues of strategy or even resources arise. In the absence of such an understanding, neither the notion of 'winning' nor the notion of certain moves makes much sense. Rather strangely, even the question of what constitutes a resource remains unanswered. For example, strength and weight might be resources and provide an advantage to a player in a game of American football, but they will hardly help him in tennis or chess.

In contrast to rationalists who take 'regulative' rules as their only model of norms, theorists indebted to the sociological approach point to the importance of constitu-

---

[67] This school comprises 'sociologists' such as Oran Young, Martha Finnemore, and Andrew Hurrell as well as 'constructivists' of quite different orientations such as Peter Katzenstein, Harald Müller, Nicholas Onuf, Alex Wendt, and A. Klotz. See Oran Young, 'The Effectiveness of International Institutions: Hard Cases and Critical Variables', in James Rosenau and Ernst-Otto Czempiel (eds.), *Governance without Government: Order and Change in World Politics* (Cambridge: Cambridge University Press, 1992), 160; Martha Finnemore, 'Norms, Culture, and World Politics: Insights from Sociology's Institutionalism' (1996) 50 International Organization 349; Andrew Hurrell, 'International Society and Regimes', in Volker Rittberger (ed.), *Regime Theory and International Relations* (Oxford: Oxford University Press, 1993), ch. 3; Peter Katzenstein (ed.), *The Culture of National Security* (New York: Columbia University Press, 1996); Harald Müller, *Die Chance der Kooperation: Regime in den Internationalen Beziehungen* (Darmstadt: Wissenschaftliche Buchgemeinschaft, 1993); Nicholas Onuf, *The World of Our Making* (Columbia, SC: University of South Carolina Press, 1989), Alex Wendt, 'Anarchy is What the States Make of It' (1992) 46 International Organization 391.

[68] On this point see Nicholas Onuf, *The Republican Legacy in International Thought* (Cambridge: Cambridge University Press, 1998), especially ch. 4.

[69] This is Weber's definition of 'social' action, which represents the formal object for study in sociology. See his 'On the Concept of Sociology and the Meaning of Social Conduct', in H. P. Secher (ed.), *Basic Concepts in Sociology by Max Weber* (New York: Citadel, 1972), 58.

tive rules as well as to their enabling and constraining character in reproducing a system of action. Thus, even if rules and norms could be shown to 'derive' from some power, they function quite differently from a medium of exchange or some crude observational 'facts'.[70] Treating them merely as an epiphenomenon fundamentally misdiagnoses their function and significance for social life. In a way, it is as if we wanted to reduce the meaning of words to the number of different sounds from which they are formed instead of analysing their semantic, syntactic, and pragmatic functions. Norms are not simply instruments but have a logic of their own in that they characterize choice situations in terms of a 'logic of appropriateness' rather than one of consequences.[71]

To the extent that certain regimes result from some broader normative understandings, they reinforce co-operative solutions in the face of incentives to defect and leave in place a rather robust normative structure. International rules thus develop a compliance pull of their own. And, as Thomas Franck has argued persuasively, their legitimacy and thus their effectiveness and robustness is also enhanced by certain properties: their determinacy (textual clarity), coherence (compatibility with higher order norms which underlie the 'society of nations'), symbolic validation (rituals of recognition), and adherence (agreement with rules about application and interpretation).[72]

The effectiveness of a regime is therefore related to institutions and the role conception of the actors in a crucial way. Henkin's suggestion that the respect paid by actors to norms is the price of membership in international society and of interaction with other nations might be highly optimistic, in that it entirely discounts the possibility of 'cheating' as the 'best' of all possible worlds.[73] Nevertheless, he identifies an important source of normative pull. Yet though we may all share some 'transcendental interest' in the sanctity of property, or in the general presumption of veracity, for example, nobody would be so optimistic as to believe that this alone would be sufficient to guarantee adherence to the normative standard. We try to insure ourselves by a variety of means: small steps, third-party participation (escrow agreements), increase in transparency, etc., by which we seek to enhance the chances for compliance. Finally, as in the case of moral training, when we want to counteract the known temptations of lying or cheating by founding our arguments on more than just the basis of the obligatory character of rules transcending particular utility considerations, we also say to the child or person in question that such an action would not be fitting for a 'gentleman'. While such appeals might sound corny from our jaded perspective, appeals to roles and identities are known even in international

---

[70] On the distinction between observational, intentional, and institutional facts, see my 'Regimes, Interpretation and the "Science" of Politics' (1988) 17 Millennium 263.

[71] See James March and Johan Olsen, *Rediscovering Institutions* (New York: Free Press, 1989).

[72] Thomas Franck, *The Power of Legitimacy among Nations* (New York: Oxford University Press, 1990).

[73] Louis Henkin, *How Nations Behave* (New York: Praeger, 1968), 32 and 48; see a similar argument made by Franck, *Power of Legitimacy*, 106.

relations. There is some agreement on which are the 'outlaw' or 'pariah' States. Moreover, during the Cuban Missile Crisis, President Kennedy rejected seemingly effective forceful action because, as his brother, an influential member of the Excom group, remarked, an air-strike against Cuba would have placed the United States on the same level as Tojo, a comparison that compromised the United States' notion of role and self-understanding.[74]

Similarly, as Alex Wendt has pointed out, role conceptions and identities might change on the basis of continued and routine co-operation.[75] As a virtuous cycle begins, States might learn to establish more inclusive notions of identity which discourage free riding, increase diffuse reciprocity, and thus enhance the willingness to bear some costs for the 'us' or even the new 'we'. But it might be overly optimistic to expect a generally peaceful world on the basis of these observations. Both the existence of civil wars and the experiences with the emergence of new national identities have shown that conflicts might degenerate, and violence escalate, even in a well constituted society. On the other hand, even 'structural' certainties that seem immutable may, for better or for worse, dissolve rather quickly, as did those between the Soviet Union and the United States.[76] In short, making this point about the constructive possibilities of political actions (with all due respect to the possibility of misfires) frees us not only from overly deterministic modes of analysis, but also identifies possibilities for new beginnings.

It is strange, in this context, that one of the oldest and newest concerns seems rather underresearched, namely the role of institutions in the reinforcement of particular regimes or governmental structures. In a way, despite the dense network of treaties and regimes, the level of institutionalization at the international level might still be too low to create new identities. Even a successful example such as the European Union seems to suffer from a distinct lack of enthusiasm among its population, as recent debates about the Euro suggest. Despite the functionalist dynamics, even institutional structures which are well grounded in 'Community law' command much less respect than national institutions. Sociologists and constructivists in general have failed to analyse the different dimensions of this problem and to point out which trade-offs, and even possible spill-backs or breakdowns, are possible or likely to occur. Somehow our picture of the future always seems to be influenced by some dubious philosophy of history. We not only regard 'co-operation' as a consumption good, but also assume (against all historical evidence and practical experience) that the emergence of larger identities is somehow the wave of the future. To this extent, the robust-

---

[74] For the Tojo analogy see Graham Allison, *Essence of Decision* (Boston: Little Brown, 1971), 132, 197, and 203.

[75] Alex Wendt, 'Collective Identity Formation and the International State' (1994) 88 American Political Science Review 384.

[76] See Reynold Koslowski and Friedrich Kratochwil, 'Understanding Change in International Politics: The Soviet Empire's Demise and the International System' (1994) 48 International Organization 215. See also the general discussion and criticism by Ned Lebow, Janice Gross Stein, and Thomas Risse-Kappen in Ned Lebow and Thomas Risse-Kappen (eds.), *International Relations Theory and the End of the Cold War* (New York: Columbia University Press, 1995).

ness of those State structures (despite or perhaps because of all these changes) is as much of a puzzle to sociological as it is to rationalist explanations, since no clear pattern seems to be emerging. What we need is a more detailed understanding of why and when the pressures on the actors for reproduction are stronger than those for allowing or even favouring transformation. The rapidity with which the chances for a 'New World Order' appear to be slipping away from us seems worrying indeed, even though the turn of events has little to do with the systemic constraints of yesteryear.

But even if we are not prone to 'progressive' speculations, one of the important determinants of regime effectiveness and robustness is their institutional underpinning. Institutions are constituted by rules and have effect because they allow us to connect certain consequences with our actions. We make contracts or appoint and thereby empower people to take actions in certain areas, we demand, or even deter, and all of these actions are informed and constituted by institutional rules. Institutional rules are important for social life because they enable and constrain us at the same time as they systematically link the 'is' and the 'ought'. Since their intersubjective character is understood, institutions not only constitute a settled practice, they also make it possible to answer normative questions on the basis of seemingly factual observations. To this extent, they help us terminate otherwise endless arguments. If, for example, I can show you a document which has the word 'contract' and your signature on it, then I am entitled to conclude (save for limited possibilities of rebuttal) that you have an obligation. What you will do and whether you will discharge your obligation will, of course, depend upon a variety of factors, including the penalties associated with non-compliance. Nevertheless, one thing is clear: without such common understandings embedded in and reinforced by institutional rules, we would not be able to appraise the character of actions, speak of violations, make demands for information or restitution, or insist on our rights.

The third school, which is slowly emancipating itself from rationalist and realist presuppositions, shares certain assumptions with the other two approaches while emphasizing a distinct set of theoretical commitments.[77] The 'liberal' school remains radically individualistic and rejects the idea that the units of a system are all alike due to systemic constraints. Rather, constitutions matter and it is the character of the liberal, constitutional State which accounts for the observance of norms on the international level. To this extent, the liberal school, as carefully argued by Moravcik, objects to the so-called 'neo-liberal institutionalists' because the latter argue on the basis of a modified structural realist perspective that does not accept central tenets of the liberal approach.[78] However, liberals also differ significantly from sociologists,

[77] Here too belong the adherents of the 'democratic peace' argument, as well as attempts, such as that by Andrew Moravcik, to build a coherent theory on 'liberal' foundations. See on the 'democratic peace' e.g. Michael Doyle, 'Kant, Liberal Legacies and Foreign Affairs' (1983) 12 Philosophy and Public Affairs 205 and 323; Bruce Russett, *Grasping the Democratic Peace: Principles for a Post-Cold War World* (Princeton: Princeton University Press, 1993).

[78] See e.g. Robert Keohane, 'Neoliberal Institutionalism: A Perspective on World Politics', in id., *International Institutions and State Power: Essays in International Relations Theory* (Boulder, Colo.: Westview Press, 1989), 1.

who focus on the distinctly international character of the shared understandings in a society of States or nations. Instead, liberals view respect for law internationally as a function of the domestic structures of the individual States.[79] There is, so to speak, a spillover effect: when people are accustomed to perceiving themselves as autonomous self-governing persons, they then extend this self-respect to others, and to others' rights.[80] Allegedly, a 'live and let live' culture characterizes liberal regimes.

The cultural attributes find their structural expression in particular constitutional structures and their concomitant international means of implementation. For example, Anne-Marie Slaughter has pointed to the similarity in design that exists between the regulatory State and the institutions of the multilateral order that emerged after the First World War.[81] In short, the effectiveness of international regimes depends more on domestic political processes and the salience of international norms within these domestic political processes than it does on systemic factors. Similarly, the robustness of regimes is best explained by commitments to certain values and procedures that allow for a 'zone of overlapping consensus'[82] analogous to the new Rawlsian model of liberal politics.

In general, the similarities between the democratic peace argument and the liberal model are substantial and obviously not accidental. There exists considerable evidence that liberal States are more likely to live up to their international obligations by reinforcing international agreements with domestic implementing legislation.[83] This is all the more important since regimes address not only States and their subordinate structures, but also need the co-operation of powerful societal actors who often have a high degree of autonomy. Thus, environmental treaties and obligations are virtually useless unless States undertake to implement them by creating a domestic regulatory regime that requires scientific and technical judgement, harnesses bureaucratic capacities, and commits fiscal resources.[84] To this extent, liberals, like sociologists, emphasize the institutionalization of new processes domestically as well as internationally. Punitive sanctions are no longer considered to be the major element in securing compliance and making regimes both effective and robust, as the problem of compliance is multifaceted.[85] It involves not only the

---

[79] Thus, the 'openness' of particular electoral systems, which is often blamed for the ineffectiveness of policy-making in liberal democratic States, can actually serve as a signal to others that multilateral agreements will be kept. See Peter Cowhey, 'Elect Locally—Order Globally: Domestic Politics and Multilateral Cooperation', in Ruggie (ed.), *Multilateralism Matters*, ch. 5.

[80] This is the argument made by Russett, *Grasping the Democratic Peace*, 31.

[81] Anne-Marie Burley (now Slaughter), 'Regulating the World: Multilateralism, International Law, and the Projection of the New Deal Regulatory State', in Ruggie (ed.), *Multilateralism Matters*, ch. 4.

[82] This notion plays a decisive role in John Rawls's new attempt to provide a less abstract version of his social theory. See John Rawls, *Political Liberalism* (New York: Columbia University Press, 1993).

[83] See Abram Chayes and Antonia Handler-Chayes, 'On Compliance' (1993) 47 International Organization 175.

[84] Abram Chayes and Antonia Handler-Chayes, *The New Sovereignty: Compliance with International Regulatory Agreements* (Cambridge, Mass.: Harvard University Press, 1995), especially chs. 1 and 2.

[85] Fundamental for a broader analysis of the compliance problem was the pioneering study by Oran Young, *Compliance and Public Authority* (Baltimore: Johns Hopkins University Press, 1977).

means of discovering a violation, but also of ascertaining its significance, and justi-
ficatory arguments in which interested publics, international organizations,
national bureaucracies, and even 'private' parties interact and elaborate the concrete
measures which the norms require in a specific instance. Together, all of these
procedures resemble a management process more than they do a process of enforcement.

Nevertheless, liberal theories seem to equivocate on the role of common values.
On the one hand, for them it is not the 'we-ness', or any new identity, that enhances
the chances of co-operation and compliance with norms through a redefinition of
interests. Contrary to the charge that liberals are by nature 'cosmopolitans', some of
the most idealist liberals have argued that most people do not consider themselves to
be citizens of the world and that international institutions are therefore only effective when they correspond roughly to the prevailing State–society relations of domestic orders. Given the primacy of preferences of the societal actors in the liberal
scheme, these preferences have worked themselves through the domestic institutional framework to become State preferences. International co-operation is then
relatively easy: it occurs where interests converge, or are at least compatible. To this
extent, there is a strong 'functionalist' tinge to the liberal argument. However, in
contrast to functionalists, liberals do not necessarily believe in automatic progress
and unidirectional change. If the decisive obstacles to the formation of effective
regimes lie in the failures of domestic institutions to correct the rent-seeking behaviour of certain groups, or in their inability to abate market failures at home and
abroad, then a cautious attitude to international reform is in order. It seems that
international institutions can play a role only when social conditions in most of the
important States of an international system actually approximate those of liberal
theory.[86]

On the other hand, some liberals have also pointed to the changing nature of
transnational society and the emergence of a civil society on a world scale.[87] They
have also emphasized the commitment to certain values that is characteristic of the
liberal credo and leads to a choice of strategies that are 'value-rational' and not merely
instrumentally rational. In this respect, however, the liberal project itself seems to
become incoherent as substantive values rather than mere conceptions of procedural
fairness are suddenly invoked.[88] In general, there seem to be three fundamental

---

[86] These points are powerfully made by Moravcik, 'Taking Preferences Seriously', *passim.*

[87] On the concept of an emerging global civil society see e.g. Michael Walzer (ed.), *Toward a Global Civil Society* (Providence, RI: Berghan Books, 1995); Richard Falk, *Explorations at the Edge of Time* (Philadelphia: Temple University Press, 1992); Paul Wapner, 'Politics Beyond the State: Environmental Activism and World Civic Politics' (1995) 47 World Politics 311; Ronnie Lipshutz, *Global Civil Society and Global Environmental Governance* (Albany, NY: SUNY Press, 1996).

[88] This is, of course, a general problem with the liberal position, which we also encountered in Dworkin's theory. As Donald Regan pointed out: '. . . a central theme in Dworkin's theory of adjudication is a rather old fashioned idea of common law as a system of fundamental moral principles, accessible
to all, with only occasional and incidental reference to general social consequences' (Regan, 'Glosses on
Dworkin: Rights, Principles, and Policies', in Cohen (ed.), *Ronald Dworkin and Contemporary Jurisprudence*, ch. 6, p. 149).

issues that require further clarification. One concerns the problem of 'interest' which, although not fixed on the State level, seems to be simply assumed (fixed) on the individual level. Although the endogenization of preferences[89] can perhaps be neglected in games of co-ordination, we still require an approach to interests which casts the net wider. Only in this way can we hope to grasp the processes of persuasion and justification and the changes these procedures may induce in the preferences of actors.

The second problem concerns the rather indiscriminate aggregation of values and norms. Although both are, of course, part of the realm of 'ought', they function quite differently in guiding decisions. It does not seem to advance our understanding when these two distinct conceptual categories are again collapsed. Furthermore, considering the potential for conflict and the actual escalation which occurs when only values (and not more specific norms) are taken into account, one must wonder indeed whether the oft invoked 'value consensus' can carry the weight it is supposed to. In short, while values seem to be focal points for concern, their contribution to conflict seems as significant as their contribution to consensus. The most bitter fights occur precisely between people who profess the same values, as the conflicts among 'true believers' indicate. Perhaps it was not such a bad strategic choice for both legal and social theory to focus on norms and draw in values only in so far as they inform the normative discourse, rather than allowing the values to do most of the explaining.

The third problem, which is in a way connected with the second, arises in respect of attempts to explain either compliance or the lack thereof, i.e. the action-guiding function of norms. Here, the liberal approach seems rather vague and actually offers a straightforward answer only for situations resembling games of co-ordination. In other situations, as already pointed out, some indefinite respect for norms or even values in general is cited, but this respect is tempered by prudential reasons, for example when others are observed not to be complying. This is obviously insufficient and cries out for further conceptual development. One would expect a more explicit treatment of how norms influence actors' choices, particularly in a theory which has a strong commitment to methodological individualism, and usually also to the standard epistemological claims concerning causal explanations.

5. SOME COMMON PUZZLES: RULE GUIDANCE AND EXPLAINING WITH NORMS

With the last remarks, we have already re-entered the more general discussion of how we are to understand the way in which norms mould decisions. In this respect, the notion that explaining an action in terms of norms has to meet the criteria of logical positivism, the widely accepted epistemology in the social sciences, runs into heavy weather right from the start. First, taking the 'external point of view' on rules condemns us to focus on some 'behavioural regularities' (supposedly induced by

---

[89] See Wendt, 'Anarchy is What the States make of it', 391.

norms) and establish some correlations. However, quite aside from the fact that empirical generalizations do not exhibit the properties that are logically necessary for a subsumption model of explanation, three further, interrelated problems arise. The first problem is that 'tests' which are supposed to corroborate our 'theory' are hardly possible because a single case can no longer refute the general law. The second problem is that our confidence in this procedure that is prescribed by a scientific approach is not heightened when we realize that norms are counterfactually valid. For this reason, the idea of a test according to standard criteria seems futile indeed. Although we may observe a certain regularity that might be caused by some underlying norm, we have no clear idea how this hunch can be translated into a causal mechanism so that we can establish the actual aetiology between norms and resulting behaviour. This raises a third difficulty: since, as we have seen above, many norms do not prescribe anything in particular but rather serve only as determinants of a zone of permissibility, entire areas of human activity have to be neglected because otherwise our belief in causal connections becomes incoherent. Certainly such norms cannot be 'causes' in the same way as the causes we are accustomed to from the sciences. There, we think of x causing y when we perceive a constant conjunction between these two distinct phenomena.

The last remark seems debilitating even if we change the perspective and approach the matter from the actor's point of view. Again, the difficulties immediately mount even if we want to remain on a purely descriptive level. How can norms that belong to a different realm ever 'cause' anything? Not only does the concept of causality seem to lose its definite meaning, but we also become increasingly unsure what is involved in 'explaining' an action or even an event. All the familiar tools of analysis such as generalization, cause, action, and event have suddenly lost their edge and we seem hopelessly stuck in a conceptual morass in which, it seems, anything goes, but then, nothing can evade the charge of 'relativism'. Given this predicament (or conceptual morass), the best way out is to backtrack and see where the wrong path was taken. A brief discussion is in order.

Consider in this context Hart and Honore's observation: 'The statement that one person did something because another person threatened him, carries no implication or covert assertion that, if the circumstances were repeated, the same action would follow, nor does the statement require for its defence, as ordinary causal statements do, a generalization.'[90] Understanding the action and thus being able to explain it requires diagnosing it as a certain type without thereby relying on the semantic relationship which exists in the subsumption model between the single case and the general law. Similarly, as Dray has demonstrated, historical explanations do not depend on general laws which, even if they existed, would be trivial and would not do much of the explaining.[91] Rather, what carries the weight in those cases is the

[90] H. L. A. Hart and A. M. Honore, *Causation in the Law* (Oxford: Oxford University Press, 1959), 52.

[91] William Dray, *Laws and Explanation in History* (London: Oxford University Press, 1957). See also Arthur Danto, *Analytical Philosophy of History* (Cambridge: Cambridge University Press, 1965).

narrative context that assigns importance to certain factors and connects events and actions. Thus, contrary to Popper and the predominant epistemology, 'explaining' does not seem to involve simply the procedure of the 'subsuming' of a single case under a general law, but comprises a rather heterogeneous set of procedures by which we try to understand actions and events. Explaining often means providing a context, such as when we make a series of actions and events part of a wider narrative. However, explaining an action might also involve us in elaborations and justifications of the choices made, or of our reasons for choosing certain beginnings and ends. Counterfactual arguments are particularly important in this context, as are the specific interests that engender our questions.[92] Recalling some of the discussion above about the 'fact description', the framing of action, is helpful here.

If we are interested in establishing responsibility, factual descriptions will crucially influence our conclusions. One of their consequences is that the meaning of 'cause' changes. Consider the following example: some houses collapse during an earthquake but the entire area is not devastated. It is therefore not incorrect to call the earthquake the 'cause' of the collapse even if the same 'cause' did not result in a uniform 'effect'. However, we then notice that the houses that remain standing were all built according to code, while many, if not most of the collapsed houses were substandard. Here the obvious issue arises as to whether the contractor's failure to abide by the code should be called the 'cause', even if we find out that he can 'get away with it' since the new standards only came into force after this section of the development was built. Things become even more complicated when we realize that most of the collapsed houses were built along a recently completed tunnel that apparently weakened the foundations of the houses in question. Suppose that the tunnel was built according to a code but that it can be established that digging the tunnel in this particular geological configuration facilitated the transmission of shock waves. Would it make a difference for our causal assessment if the tunnel had also collapsed? If it had not been built to code? 'The cause' quickly becomes more and more complicated and our choice among the various options (or even their conjunction) is obviously not independent of whether we examine this issue as a geophysicist, a lawyer, a structural engineer, or a historian.

The above example dealt simply with an 'event'. Further complications arise when we inquire into the intentions that play a decisive role in distinguishing events from actions. Events can be explained by causes and contexts, but explaining actions usually involves more complicated operations. However, on the surface the explanations we give for events and actions seem parallel, because both require causal imputations. Events are caused by antecedent conditions, while intentions, motives, or purposes serve as causes in the explanatory scheme. To this extent, purposes or goals

[92] On the importance of counterfactual reasoning see James Fearon, 'Counterfactual and Hypothesis Testing in Political Science' (1991) 43 World Politics 169; Thomas Biersteker, 'Constructing Historical Counterfactuals to Assess the Consequences of International Regimes', in Rittberger (ed.), *Regime Theory and International Relations*, ch. 13; Philip Tetlock and Aaron Belkin, *Counterfactual Thought Experiments in World Politics* (Princeton: Princeton University Press, 1996).

do not seem to differ from causes, in that both provide the antecedent motive that makes the actor behave in a certain way. However, a moment's reflection shows that the two paradigmatic cases are not strictly analogous, since the causal mechanisms adduced for their explanation are rather different.

In the classical Humean account, the provision of a causal explanation means having two independent observations of the state of affairs at different times, as well as a 'constant conjunction' between the observed phenomena. Even if we argue that causality cannot be derived from observation, as this category is constitutive for and antecedent to every observation, the fact remains that, even in this version of a *synthetic* a priori, 'cause' means the antecedent condition which explains the subsequent phenomenon. A rather different picture emerges, however, when we explain an action in terms of purposes and intentions. Again, the goal of the action and the intention preceding the choice are conjoined, but it is clear that we no longer have independently defined observations since it is the 'goal' which also constitutes the antecedent 'motive' for the action.

This peculiarity of intentional accounts explains also why we do not necessarily reject an explanation when the predicted and observed results differ. For example, when we explain why a person is running by providing a motive for this action, in the absence of special circumstances we do not feel impelled to withdraw the proffered account when it turns out that this prediction failed. We simply say that the person 'missed' the train. Similarly, when we assert that one person wanted to obtain power over another, we know by analogy with a situation in which two bodies collide (and even if we were to incorporate factors of friction and elasticity) that there is no inherent necessity whereby the action will cause a definite reaction in accordance with Newton's law. Again, our ontology of social action prevents us from simply accepting the 'refuting evidence' which would oblige us to cast our explanations aside. Instead, we argue that the attempt to influence might simply have 'misfired', as the grammar of power also includes the notion of 'failure'. In order to revise our explanation we would need rather different reasons and alternative plausible accounts, instead of accepting a simple 'misfire' as a refutation.

Note that until now we have not even entered into the difficulties of using norms as the *explanans*. Although explanations using norms will obviously constitute a subcategory of intentional accounts, intentional explanations already violate the standard epistemological criteria of logical positivism, the canonical status of which is largely accepted in political science. Perhaps it is not surprising that realists who also usually pretend to be 'scientists' have such a hard time in trying to discover the role of norms in international relations. Equipped with a universal hammer, they try to catch some water by nailing it down, instead of changing the tool!

If we took the standard epistemology seriously, we ought to reject any type of intentional account because only antecedent or efficient causes have 'scientific' status. The fact that we continue to explain actions in terms of intentions or purposes seems to indicate that we recognize that this problem cannot be solved by epistemological fiat. The new interest in 'ideas' as explanatory factors, despite their epistemological problems, and the continuing relevance of the philosophical dilemmas which Albert Yee[93] details in his interesting treatment of data analysis among statisticians, reinforce this judgement. No matter how we twist or turn, a true causal account seems to escape us, because we do not seem to be able to visualize how ideas influence choices and actual behaviour (Descartes's 'solution' via the pituitary gland being no longer available to us![94]). Aside from the fact that here both the hoary mind–body problem and the freedom of will vs. determinism issue raise their ugly heads, part of our puzzlement might be explained by the unquestioned acceptance of, and thereby the misapplication of the metaphor of 'mechanism' to, the conjunction in question.

Showing the causal significance of one phenomenon for another demonstrates the existence of a connection. However, the nature of this connection need not be one of mechanics. Thus a connection is established if we think along the lines of 'building a bridge' which allows us to get from 'here' to 'there'. This is what we do when we provide an account in terms of purposes or goals, or when we cite the relevant rule that provides the missing element, showing us the reasons which motivated us to act in a certain way. No 'mechanism', no hammer hitting a lever, no springs, no billiard balls are involved here. This is what Weber meant when he talked about causal explanation in the social sciences.[95] We reconstruct a situation, view it from the perspective of the actor, and impute purposes and values based on evidence provided by the actor himself (although not necessarily limited to his own testimony). This, in turn, provides us with an intelligible account of the reasons for acting. Furthermore, such imputations have nothing to do with some mysterious empathy or the private mind of the actor (unless we try to discern some idiosyncrasies or pathologies). As in Wittgenstein's puzzle about the communication concerning pain, we do possess a language in which shared meanings make it possible to communicate, even if we never reach the 'actual' private sensations. Rather, the fuller characterization of the action that we are after is possible because the account we provide can be justified and defended in terms of intersubjectively shared 'reasons'. We might not know what actually transpired and competing explanations might persist. However, even in science all our accounts are subject to revision on the basis of new evidence or interpretations which seem to have a better 'fit' (as problematic as such an expression might be). Explanations have to end somewhere and in accounts of action, be they of social action or of law, pragmatic criteria are used to assess the justifiability of the interpretations rendered. As Wittgenstein put it: 'If I have exhausted the justifications, I have reached bedrock and my spade is turned. Then I am inclined to say: "This is simply what I do".'[96]

---

[93] Albert S. Yee, 'The Causal Effects of Ideas on Policies' (1996) 50 International Organization 69.

[94] For a short overview of the Cartesian explanations and mental causation, see Richard Montgomery, 'Non-Cartesian Explanations Meet the Problem of Mental Causation' (1995) 33 The Southern Journal of Philosophy 221.

[95] Max Weber, *Aufsätze zur Wissenschaftslehre*, ed. Johannes Winckelmann (3rd edn., Tübingen: J. C. B. Mohr, 1985), especially the controversies with Roscher and Knies, Stammler and Eduard Meyer.

[96] Wittgenstein, *Philosophical Investigations*, § 217.

As soon as we see the problem of explanation in this light, our puzzlement is relieved and we understand why and how the metaphor of a mechanism was misleading. We also begin to understand that the language game governing the use of the terms 'explanation' and 'cause' is not restricted to some mechanical paradigm or to the notion of efficient cause, to use Aristotle's parlance. As Wittgenstein suggested: 'Giving reasons for something one did or said means showing a way which leads to this action. In some cases it means telling the way which one has gone oneself; in others it means describing a way which leads there and is in accordance with certain accepted rules.'[97] Again, no reference need be made to private states of mind or internal occurrences since such a construction of the problematic is only the result of the 'mistaken addiction to Hobbist mechanism',[98] as Gilbert Ryle suggested a long time ago. To this extent, questions about the relations between a person and his mind, or between a person's body and his mind, are 'improper questions' in the same way as it does not make much sense to ask 'What transactions go on between the House of Commons and the British Constitution?'.[99]

But since we give 'explanations' in a variety of contexts, things might still be more complicated than this short passage indicates. In some contexts, our acceptance of accounts of action might resemble those of causes, while in others there is a fundamental difference. As R. S. Peters once pointed out, there is a difference between providing an explanation for the question 'What was his reason for doing it?' and asking 'What was the reason why he did it?' The former always requires an intentional account. The latter, although also concerned with 'reasons', comes close to a causal imputation. Usually, we find such an explanation satisfactory when issues of responsibility remain in the background, such as when something 'misfires' and we want to know what could have 'made' a person act in such a fashion. Such explanatory schemes will be particularly prominent in cases where the 'weakness of will' problem arises, where we want to explain the failure of an agent to act in a given situation.

The few examples provided above should not only have put the 'reasons/causes'[100] debate into perspective, but also have driven home the fact that explanations are not all of one and the same kind. What we accept as appropriate in a given case is thoroughly dependent on context and not reducible to some standard, logical, and automatically privileged form. Rather, providing explanations usually involves choosing between different possible versions, and justifying 'coming down on one side' rather than on another, by connecting and clarifying the account with the context within which an explanation is demanded. Thus, the point is not that no

---

[97] Ludwig Wittgenstein, *Preliminary Studies for the Philosophical Investigations: The Blue and Brown Books* (New York: Harper and Row, 1964), 14.

[98] A. J. Ayer, 'An Honest Ghost?', in Oscar Wood and George Pitcher (eds.), *Modern Studies in Philosophy: Ryle* (London: Macmillan, 1970), 53 at 54.

[99] Gilbert Ryle, *The Concept of Mind* (Chicago: University of Chicago Press, 1984), 167 f.

[100] See e.g. Donald Davidson, 'Action, Reasons and Causes' (1966) 63 Journal of Philosophy 685; see also the anthology by E. Sosa (ed.), *Causation and Conditionals* (London: Oxford University Press, 1975); Paul Humphreys, 'Causality in the Social Sciences: An Overview' (1986) 68 Synthese 1.

causal accounts of actions can be given. The rub is rather that our interests usually require a 'deeper', more dimensional version of an explanation, as all the analytical distinctions between the 'is' and the 'ought', between causes and reasons, are woven together in our grammar of explanation. In it are implicated our concepts of agency and responsibility, and the predicaments of choice as an existential condition rather than merely the result of incomplete information. Consequently, what 'serves' as an explanation cannot be decided once and for all. As in the example above where we could not determine what 'big' really meant, we cannot decide on the type of explanation and the standards of evidence unless we specify further the context. Given this predicament, the hope for an absolute point of view which would end all debates or dispense with the need to engage in often complicated justifications of one's decision, simply by subsuming it under some universally valid law or by hitting upon the single 'right' answer, is indeed as tempting as it is futile. It would be available to us only if we were no longer interested in all those things that are constitutive of law and politics.

4

The Concept of International Law

PHILIP ALLOTT

THE SOCIAL FUNCTION OF LAW

1. Law, including international law, has a threefold social function. (1) Law carries the structures and systems of society through time. (2) Law inserts the common interest of society into the behaviour of society-members. (3) Law establishes possible futures for society, in accordance with society's theories, values, and purposes.

2. Law is a presence of the social past. Law is an organizing of the social present. Law is a conditioning of the social future.

3. There are eight systematic implications of such an idea of the social function of law in general, and of international law in particular.

3.1. Law forms part of the *self-constituting* of a society. A society is a collective self-constituting of human beings as society-members, coexisting with their personal self-constituting as human individuals. International society is the collective self-constituting of all human beings, the society of all societies. International law is the law of international society.

3.2. The legal self-constituting of society (the *legal* constitution) coexists with other means of social self-constituting: self-constituting in the form of ideas (the *ideal* constitution) and self-constituting through the everyday willing and acting of society-members (the *real* constitution).

3.3. Law is generated, as a third thing with a *distinctive social form*, in the course of the ideal and real self-constituting of society, but law itself conditions those other forms of constituting.

3.4. Law is a *universalizing* system, reconceiving the infinite particularity of human willing and acting, in the light of the common interest of society.

3.5. Law is a *particularizing* system, disaggregating the common interest of society so that it may affect the infinite particularity of human willing and acting.

3.6. Law requires that society have adequate means for *determining the common interest* of society, in accordance with society's values and purposes. *Politics*, in the widest sense of the word, is the will-forming struggle in the ideal and real constitutions, the struggle to influence the determination of the common interest of society and to influence the making and application of law.

3.7. Law requires that society have *theories* which explain and justify law within social consciousness (the public mind) and within individual consciousness (the private mind, including the social consciousness of subordinate societies). Such theories reflect and condition society's values and purposes. They may be customary, religious, or philosophical theories: for example, theories of revealed transcendence, charismatic authority, natural law, sovereignty, constitutionalism, naturalism. They are generated and regenerated in the public mind of society in the course of its ideal and real self-constituting.

3.8. Law thus presupposes a *society* whose structures and systems make possible the mutual conditioning of the public mind and the private mind, and the mutual conditioning of the legal and the non-legal. These two reciprocating and reinforcing processes offer a limitless dynamic potentiality for human self-evolving through social self-constituting.

LAW AND SOCIAL PSYCHOLOGY

4. Society and law exist nowhere else than in the human mind. (1) They are products of and in the consciousness of actual human beings. But a society generates a social consciousness, a public mind, which is distinct from the private mind, distinct from the consciousness of actual human individuals. Social consciousness flows from and to individual consciousness, forming part of the self-consciousness of each society-member. The psychology of the public mind is a manifestation of the psychology of the private mind. The constitution of a society and the personality of a human person are both the product of human consciousness. (2) Social psychology is a form, but a modified form, of personal psychology. But social consciousness functions independently from the private consciousness of every society-member, and is retained in forms (the theories, structures, and systems of self-constituting society) which are an 'other' in relation to the 'self' of the self-constituting of any particular society-member. (3) Society wills and acts collectively, as the output of systems (including law-making systems) which aggregate the willing and acting of individual human beings. But the intervention of those systems creates a new mind-world, a new form of human reality, a new form of human world. The public mind is society's private mind. The public mind of international society is the private mind of the human species.

5. This peculiar relationship, separate but inseparable, between personal and social psychology means that all the systematic functions of personal psychology are present in social psychology, but functioning in a special way. For its own purposes and in its own way, society uses *emotion*, *memory*, *rationality*, and *morality*. And society's use of these functions affects their functioning in the psychology of individual society-members. Public emotion, especially the emotion of the crowd, flows from and to private emotion. Society's collective memory, its so-called history, flows from and to private memory. Society's collective deliberations, using the self-ordering functions of the human brain, including language and logic, flow from and to our private deliberating. Society's self-regulating in terms of its values and purposes flows from and to our private self-regulating in terms of duty. Beyond the systematic functions of individual

psychology, there is the power of unconscious consciousness, the residues of our biological inheritance and of our life-experience which do not function systematically but which intervene in every aspect of our personal self-constituting and must intervene in every aspect of the collective self-constituting of society. Social consciousness is also a collective unconscious.

6. For individual human beings, the integrating of the processes of the mind in the moment-to-moment self-constituting of personality is an unceasing struggle. The struggle of self-integrating can lead to crises which may be seen as pathological, in the sense that they threaten the survival or general well-being of the person concerned, or of other persons. Society-members contribute their psychic states to social consciousness, including pathological psychic states. Society-members with exceptional social power may even impose their own psycho-pathology on the society they dominate. So it is that a society may experience episodes of social psycho-pathology, when a society may be said, in crude terms, to go mad, may become alienated, with its potentiality of self-creating distorted by symptoms of self-wounding and self-destroying. Nowhere does social psycho-pathology reveal itself more clearly than in the society of societies, international society, where its symptoms can be human self-wounding and self-destroying on a massive scale.

7. Law, as a social phenomenon, corresponds to whatever is the ultimate self-integrating capacity of individual consciousness, that capacity which enables us to pursue our personal survival and prospering in our unique existential situation, in the moment and at the place where our own systematic functioning, as body and mind, intersects with the systematic functioning of all that is not us, that is to say, the natural world and the human world of other people as individuals and as society. I am, therefore I am a legal system for myself. A society also has a unique existential situation, the point in time and space at which it intersects with the existence of the natural world, the existence of other societies, and the existence of its society-members. To exist as a society is to have a legal system with a view to the survival and prospering of the society as a whole and of the human beings who are its members. International society has a legal system with a view to the survival and prospering of International society as a whole, that is to say, the survival and prospering of all subordinate human societies and of all human beings.

LAW AND JUSTICE

8. Law is purposive human activity, a particular species of willing and acting, so that it is necessarily action of moral significance, action which is subject to moral duty and gives rise to moral responsibility. Moral duty—the duty to do good and avoid evil—attaches to the participation of *individual human beings* in law-making, law-applying, law-enforcing, and law-abiding. The moral situation of *society* is more problematic, since society acts through systems whose aggregative systematic output—surplus social effect, as we may call it—is greater than the sum of the individual human

inputs, the surplus being the product, and the purpose, of the systematic process. Law is a surplus social effect of many systems within a society. The apparent consequence is that, since no human individual is responsible for the macro-product of social systems, there can be no moral responsibility for that product, including the macro-product known as law. Apparently, the social actual, and hence the legal actual, is necessarily right. This chain of reasoning, with its Machiavellian implications, has been especially characteristic of the conceiving of the relationship among those forms of society which came to be known as 'States'. So-called international relations seemed to be the more or less random aggregating of the aggregate output of the systems of those societies, so that the absence of potential moral responsibility was even more evidently the case between the States than within those States. It seemed also to follow that international law, even more than national law, was morally immune, since it was itself seen as a secondary surplus social effect of the morally immune relations between States, the content of those relations—so-called foreign policy—being itself the morally immune systematic product of the internal national systems.

9. *Cui bono?* In whose interest has it been to propagate such ideas? Machiavellism, the overriding of general moral duty by *raison d'état*, was well intentioned, in the sense that it was designed to define a special kind of moral duty (*virtù*) owed by 'the prince', by those with personal responsibility for government. Its paradoxical character, a morality of immorality, gave it a particular frisson, calculated to shock those with conventional moral ideas, especially the religiously conditioned. But it also gave an impulse of self-justification and self-assertion to those who would have power, not merely over this or that Italian city-state, but over the great centralizing monarchies, giving a veneer of moral necessity to the arrogance of their absolutism.

10. Machiavellism was also a calculated negation of a long tradition which conceived of values which transcend the power of even the holders of the highest forms of social power. Those ideas—especially ideas of justice and natural law, but also all those philosophies which speak of 'the good' or 'the good life'—were transcendental and aspirational and critical in character, that is to say, they were conceived of as an *ideal* which could not be overridden or even abridged by the merely *actual*, and in relation to which the actual should be oriented and would be judged. The idea of the ideal makes possible a morality of society. It makes possible the idea that society's systems, including the legal system, can have moral purpose at the systematic level, at the level of surplus social effect.

11. Within some national societies, an idea of the transcendental was actualized in the development of *constitutionalism*. It was found possible to conceive of a law-above-law which was nevertheless present within the same legal system. Appropriate *theories* were developed (especially social contract theory) to explain and justify the legal system, suggesting that the law itself had purposes, because the formation of society had purposes, and that the law had inherent limits—formal limits (the consent of the people through their representatives) and substantive limits (fundamental rights). In the national societies in question, Machiavellism was negated by constitutionalism, and law was conceived as being something other than merely a

manifestation of actual relations of social power. *Law* was made to coexist systematically with its ideal of *justice*. Constitutionalism accompanied, and made possible, the development of an idea of the *public realm*, that is to say, a part of the social process in which legal powers are to be exercised only in the public interest. The holders of public-realm powers are thus immediate and active agents of the common interest of society rather than, as in the case of private-realm power-holders, indirect agents who serve the common interest merely by conforming to the law.

12. International society, however, remained a constitution-free zone. On the contrary, the controllers of the national public realms found that they continued to be *ancien régime* free agents, constrained only by natural necessity and the force of the actual, in a form of coexistence which was clearly not a society, with only the most crude of organizing systems (diplomacy, war), and with a legal system which, fortunately, seemed to them, and their acolytes, to lack most of the essential characteristics of their national legal systems, not least a transcendental constitutional structure. And international unsociety was evidently also a morality-free zone, in which moral discourse had only a marginal rhetorical or tactical function, and the only recognized ethical imperative was self-judging Machiavellian princely virtue. For the controllers of the national public realms and their apologists, an international public realm without law or justice seemed to be a state of nature of the most exciting kind, in which the survival of the fittest is decided by an intoxicating mixture of urbane diplomacy and mass murder.

LAW AND THE COMMON INTEREST

13. Common interest is a society's self-interest, a self-interest which may conflict with the self-interest of society-members in their capacity as individual human beings, but which is in their interest in their capacity as society-members. Common interest is not merely an aggregation of particular interests. It is formed at the intersection between the ideal and the real, as society responds to its current and potential situation in the light of its continuing theories, values, and purposes. It is an idea of society's enlightened self-interest formed in a society's public mind. A given society may contain conflicting ideas of its theories, values, and purposes, conflicting ideas of its current and potential situation, and conflicting ideas about the relationship of the one to the other. Whether it is the whimsical will of a tyrant or direct consultation of the people or anything between, a society contains systematic means for resolving such conflicts, that is to say, *politics* in the widest sense of the word.

14. Other social systems are responsible for actualizing the common interest, including the dissemination of ideas and information with a view to the conditioning of social consciousness, educational systems with a view to conditioning the minds of the next social generation, action on the part of social institutions of all kinds in furtherance of the common interest. But it is, above all, a function of law to ensure that the willing and acting of society-members, including subordinate societies, serve the

common interest. The law is capable of performing this function with wonderful efficiency.

15. Law is not, as so often supposed, a system of legal rules. Law is a system of legal relations. A legal system is an infinite number of interlocking legal relations forming a network of infinite density. A legal relation (right, duty, power, freedom, liability, immunity, disability) is a pattern of potentiality into which actual persons and situations may be fitted. It is a *matrix* which identifies persons and situations in an abstract form. It is an *heuristic* which connects aspects of those persons and situations to each other in a particular way, in isolation from the rest of their reality and the rest of social reality. It is an *algorithm* which triggers the operation of other legal relations when actual persons and situations are found to fit its pattern of potentiality.

16. Such a network of legal relations constitutes a parallel *legal reality* in which every possible aspect of social reality has a second significance, in which language has a legal meaning, persons have a legal status, natural and human events have a legal character. Actual human beings may be more or less unaware of the legal relations to which they are potentially parties. They may abide by the law, or violate the law, without knowing that they are doing so. And the law itself can never be known for certain. The content of a legal relation is as imprecise as the language in which it is expressed, sharing in the necessary imprecision of all language or purposefully choosing limited precision (with such terms as 'reasonable', 'good faith', 'equal protection', 'due process'). And the abstract form of the content of a legal relation necessarily allows for a wide range of interpretations when the question arises of its application to actual persons and situations, interpretations which may alter with the identity of the interpreter and as a function of the time and context in which the interpretation occurs.

17. Notwithstanding the potential character of the legal relation and its limited certainty, and the ignorance of most people for most of the time as to the content of the law, the law gives to society a range of possible futures which society has chosen as being futures which would serve the common interest. When a person acts consciously or unconsciously in conformity with the law (exercises a power, claims a right, uses a freedom, carries out a duty . . .), that action, although it may involve a choice on the part of that person and a self-interested choice, actualizes society's determination of its common interest. The law-conforming action of all society-members is the self-constituting of a society through law.

THE INTERNATIONAL LEGAL SYSTEM

18. International law is the self-constituting of all humanity through law. It is the actualizing through law of the common interest of international society, the society of all societies. The legal relations of international law organize the potential willing and acting of all human beings and all human societies, including the forms of society conventionally known as 'States'.

19. The international legal system contains three systematic levels:

        (1) international constitutional law;

        (2) international public law;

        (3) the laws of the nations.

20. *International constitutional law* is what some older writers called the 'necessary' law of nations. It contains the structural legal relations which are intrinsic to the coexistence of all kinds of subordinate societies. It confers on artificial legal persons, including the State-societies, the capacity to act as parties to international legal relations. It determines the systematic relationship between levels (2) and (3), and the horizontal relationship among the many laws of the nations.

21. *International public law* is the law of the intergovernment of international society. It is that part of international law which regulates the interaction of the subordinate public realms within the international public realm. The principal participants in the legal relations of international public law are the 'States', represented by their 'governments', that is to say, by the controllers of their respective public realms. 'States' are considered to be those societies whose internal public realms are recognized as capable of participating in the international intergovernment. International constitutional law determines the conditions of that participation and also the participation of other persons, on the basis of legal relations to which they are made parties (for example, intergovernmental institutions, or individuals and non-governmental bodies participating in international public-law bodies).

22. *The laws of the nations* are an integral part of the international legal system.

22.1. It is international constitutional law which determines the participants in the international legal system (for example, making a particular society into a 'State'), and determines the conditions of their participation.

22.2. The geographical and material distribution of constitutional authority among subordinate legal systems cannot finally be determined by those legal systems themselves, but only by a superordinate legal system, namely international constitutional law.

22.3. The content of the law of the subordinate systems may be subject to legal relations arising under international constitutional and public law; and those legal relations prevail, as a matter of international constitutional law, over the law of the subordinate systems.

22.4. Legal transactions arising under the law of a subordinate system may take effect outside the sphere of the constitutional authority of that system and interact with transactions arising under the law of another system. That interaction may be legally regulated, in the first place, under private international law (itself also part of the international legal system), but always subject to any applicable international constitutional or public law. The so-called global economy, for example, is the aggregate product of the actualizing of legal relations arising under the laws of the nations (contract law, corporation law, securities law, etc.) and the actualizing of legal relations under international constitutional and public law.

23. It follows that international public law is a joint product of both international constitutional law and national constitutional law. International constitutional law determines the legal relationship of the subordinate public realms. National constitutional law determines the legal status and powers of each particular State-society and its government. It follows also that the three levels of the international legal system are a hierarchy, with international constitutional law having systematic supremacy, and with international public law dominating the exercise of legal powers within the national public realms, including the powers to make, apply, and enforce national law.

24. The international legal system, as a systematic totality, thus reconciles the respective common interests of all subordinate societies with the common interest of all human beings in the survival and prospering of the human species, one species among so many in a habitat shared by all.

THE MAKING OF INTERNATIONAL LAW: I. CUSTOMARY INTERNATIONAL LAW

25. International law has been made in the form of customary law. Customary law is a form of law which arises out of the ideal and real self-constituting of a society as a particular kind of residue of the past, rather than through a formal law-making process in the present. Society thereby makes law for itself through a tacit legislator which is society itself, universalizing its experience of self-ordering.

26. Customary law, including customary international law, is the product of a *dialectic of practice*, as opposed to legislation, including international treaty-law, which is the product of a *dialectic of ideas*. Society-members produce the conditions of their orderly social coexistence through the practice of orderly coexistence. Customary law is the presentation of those conditions in the form of law, that is to say, setting the terms of the future coexistence of society-members in the form of legal relations. It follows that the place of *consent* in the making of customary law is subtle. Clearly, it is not the specific consent of the subjects of the law. Customary law is not made by any specific act of will on the part of its subjects. Their assent to customary law (*opinio iuris*) is manifested, in the first place, in their participation in the society whose law it is. Secondly, it is manifested in their participation in the day-to-day struggle of social self-ordering, knowing that some aspect of that self-ordering may come to be universalized as law. Thirdly, it is manifested in their being party to, and relying on, the legal relations flowing from the existing state of customary law.

27. Customary law thus shares in the transcendental aspect of constitutionalism, discussed above, at least to the extent that it is systematically independent of the will of current society-members, especially current controllers of the public realm. Customary law may also be said to depend on a form of implicit 'social contract' theory, which finds the authority of the law in the hypothetical 'consent' of the subjects of the law, where consent is postulated as a corollary of their participation

in the society in question, including its law-making system. To borrow a Hobbesian play-on-words, society-members are the 'authors' of customary law because they are the source of its 'authority'. Society-members in a customary law system are also Kantian universal legislators, in the sense that they know that the governing principle of their own willing and acting is liable to be universalized as a governing principle of legal relations applying to all society-members.

28. It follows also that there is no merit in that trend in international legal theory which supposes that States, as the subjects of customary international law, consent to its formation as if by some specific act of will, as if their participation were a voluntary act. The abusive use of the ideas of the 'natural liberty' of States, and hence the need for their 'consent' to any abridgement of that liberty, are a cynical misappropriation of some part of the ethos of revolutionary democracy. For the controllers of the public realms of old- and new-regime States, it was good to learn from Vattel (*The Law of Nations*, 1758) that the States were all 'free, independent, and equal', fortunate inhabitants of a Lockian 'state of nature', so that the making, judging, and enforcement of the law was entirely in their hands. It might have been thought that such a voluntary theory of international law had reached its pitiful nadir in the decision of the Permanent Court of International Justice in the so-called *Lotus Case* (1927). But the intellectual decline has continued, reaching new low-points in such ideas as: (1) the idea that the formation of new rules of customary international law requires some actual assenting state of mind on the part of States, as if governments, let alone States, had determinable states of mind; (2) the idea that States might unilaterally exclude themselves from the application of a new rule of customary international law, or even, when they first become members of international society, from the application of pre-existing rules; (3) the idea that rules of international constitutional law about the limits on the treaty-making capacity of States (including so-called *ius cogens*) are the product of an expression of the *ad hoc* will of States (say, in the Vienna Convention on the Law of Treaties).

29. The dialectic of practice which makes customary law includes ideas, but ideas as a form of practice. At any particular time, society's struggle of self-ordering takes the form of both a struggle of willing and acting and a struggle about the theories, values, and purposes applicable to such willing and acting, including a struggle about what the law is and what it should be. It is possible to chart the development of international society over the last five centuries as a progressive self-ordering reflected in a corresponding development of customary international law. Each episode can be seen as a stage in a gradual process of international self-ordering at the level of *inter-government*, that is, the interaction of the controllers of the national public realms.

Public Order 1: The Possibility of Universal Law

Modern international law (from 1500) began with a dialectic of practice which produced a fragile notion of the potentiality of universal international order from profoundly disordering diversity (the New World, the disintegration of

Christendom), a dialectic in which powerful actors struggled using the weapons of powerful ideas (Christianity, civilization, law, reason, natural law, the law of nations, sovereignty, self-preservation, and self-interest).

Public Order 2: Diplomacy and War

In the sixteenth century, the centralizing monarchies and the multitude of other forms of polity became self-conscious participants in an evolutionary game of survival, in which diplomacy and war were the instruments of competition and coexistence, as each national realm began to identify itself in opposition to the many others, and as it came to seem necessary and possible to imagine a 'law of war and peace', as a compendium of the minimal conditions of coexistence.

Public Order 3: The Territorial Polity

Violent competition in the appropriation of overseas territories and in relation to the control of local and distant sea-areas focused the struggle of ideas on the question of the physical limits of State-power. Physical frontiers, which had been uncertain and unstable, became an integral part of the defining of the selfhood of the polities, and customary international law developed into an externalized feudal law of land-holding and the adjustment of relations between land-owners. The disintegration of Christianity meant that physical frontiers became mental frontiers (*Treaty of Augsburg*, 1555), and the dialectic of ideas within the dialectic of practice, which forms customary international law, came to be dominated by a dialectic of *reason of state*.

Public Order 4: The Two Realms

The idea of the intrinsic independence of the national and international realms was established before the period of seismic internal social change following the French Revolution. The dialectic of ideas soon freed itself from talk about 'natural law' as a universal quasi-legal and quasi-moral regime applying equally to both realms. The law of the coexistence of the 'States' came to be seen as a product of the mutual recognition of their right to determine the conditions of their internal self-ordering. With the development of the subjective identity of the 'nation', with its own personality and its own history, the international realm became derivative and residual in relation to the national realm, with the controllers of the national public realms (governments) now behaving not only as sole agents of the public realms of the States but also as sole representatives of national charisma in the inter-national struggle to survive and prosper, a struggle in which diplomacy and war were still the primary instruments of social control. (It was at the end of the eighteenth century that the word 'diplomacy' came to be used to apply to the conduct of the formal relations between States.) The 'law of nations' or 'international law' (a neologism dating from early in the nineteenth century) was still a secondary socializing phenomenon. It was seen as the rules of the game of the externalized public realms, a pale shadow of national public law. But it was a social phenomenon of growing intellectual and practical substance, developing in complexity and density in step with the development of national public law.

Public Order 5: The International Public Realm

From the latter part of the nineteenth century, there began to appear, in the international realm, *externalized forms of national public realm management*. International institutional processes proliferated as simulacra of national constitutional processes—deliberative, administrative, arbitral. They took on systematic integrity and organic life, each a social system with its own constitutional structure and process, but systematically linked to the national systems, with the social outputs of the external systems flowing back into the national systems as social inputs (leading to legislation and administration and judicial decisions giving effect to decisions of the international systems). In this way, national processes were *communalized externally* to form an informal and rudimentary international public realm of ever-increasing complexity (of organization) and density (of outputs), and national processes began to be *co-ordinated transnationally* with national decision making processes coming more and more to be conditioned by products of international decision-making processes. It began to be appropriate to see national public-realm systems as systematically integrated within an international public-realm system which had itself been formed from an external communalizing of the national systems. International constitutional law responded by acknowledging the capacity of international institutional systems to participate as such in international legal relations, legal relations with and in their own member-States and non-member-States (*ICJ Advisory Opinion on Reparation for Injuries*, 1948). International public law also expanded rapidly to include the law governing the intergovernmental public realm, including an international administrative law governing the internal and *inter se* functioning of the international public-realm systems.

Public Order 6: The Possibility of Universal Values

The management of a public realm of a society reflects the theories, values, and purposes of that society, given that it is itself an integral part not only of the real and legal self-constituting of society but also of its ideal self-constituting (para. 3.2 above). After 1945, the international public realm began to generate theories, values, and purposes appropriate to its general nature as a public realm and its particular nature as an international public realm. They are ideas which flow out from and into national social self-constituting, in such a way that it began to be appropriate to see an emerging process of ideal self-constituting even at the global level. As always, that process is inseparable from real self-constituting at the global level, as the controllers of national public realms bring vastly differing actual capacities to the dialectical struggle of idea-formation and law-making at the global level. The dialectical ideal struggle has been a struggle concerning the potential universality of particular ideas: human rights, the rule of law, public order, self-determination, distributive justice, global commons, environmental protection, democracy, public-realm crime. And it is also a struggle as to whether and how far such ideas are appropriate as the content of legal relations, both international public-law relations and legal relations under the laws of the nations as they are co-ordinated by international constitutional and public law. The reciprocating character of law as a social system (para. 3.8 above) means that the dialectic of idea-forming and the dialectic of law-making and the dialectic of real-world action have reinforced each other, together conditioning social consciousness (paras. 4–7 above), the social consciousness of all subordinate societies, and the social consciousness of international society itself.

30. The current self-ordering of international society is a palimpsest which includes all six layers of public order, in a cloudy confusion of atavism and progressivism. Customary international law is the legal form of the sedimentary self-ordering of a self-evolving international society.

THE MAKING OF INTERNATIONAL LAW: II. TREATY-LAW

31. Treaties are older than the idea of international law. Wherever polities have coexisted, the possibility of the inter-polity exchange of promises in ritualized form seems to have been present, even if, perhaps especially if, the promising parties do not regard each other as belonging to a single transcendental system of ideas, let alone of law. In the absence of a superordinate idea-system or legal system, the taboo-sanction for treaty-violation is determined by the respective idea-systems of the contracting parties—shame, ostracism, disrepute, reprisal, retorsion, purification, compensation. The social practice of treaty-making has continued from the days of the earliest recorded human history to the present day, more or less in isolation from the troubled development of international law in general. It is as if the controllers of the public realms of polities had treaty-making as an inherited and instinctive mode of behaviour, regardless of their attitude towards international law in general, and regardless of the familiar fact of human experience, that a treaty successfully regulates inter-polity interaction until the day when one or other party chooses otherwise.

32. Within the history of national societies, there came a time when the increasing complexity and density of social relations made necessary a transition from customary law to legislation, from slow-motion law-making to instant law-making. The hand of the invisible systemic legislator began to give way to the very visible hand of the institutional legislator. King, council, senate, parliament. Doom, decree, statute. Each society generated appropriate institutional forms. Lacking a legislative institution, international society has appropriated the hallowed institution of the treaty as its institutional legislator. As international society began to increase rapidly in

complexity and density from, say, 1815, treaties began to perform a social function closely analogous to legislation in national legal systems. (The *Règlement* on diplomatic representation of 19 March 1815 is a striking early example, but many of the other texts adopted at the Congress of Vienna are legislative in function.)

33. In legislation, the dialectic of ideas dominates the dialectic of practice. The dialectic of ideas which is concealed within the dialectic of practice of customary law becomes the dominant form of the dialectic of practice, in the sense that the act of legislating reflects a specific purposive choice of a possible future for the society in question (para. 1.3 above), a specific purposive actualizing of the common interest of the society (para. 1.2 above), in accordance with the society's theories and in implementation of its values and purposes (paras. 3.6 and 3.7 above). But legislated law is structurally the same as customary law, in the sense that it consists of legal relations, so that behaviour in conformity with legislated law is also necessarily behaviour which serves the common interest of society (para. 15 above).

34. The idea of the legislative function of treaties in international society necessarily raises two questions: (1) In what sense is the *common interest* of international society as a whole actualized in a treaty among particular members of international society? (2) In what sense is treaty-law subject to a will-forming process of *politics* in international society (para. 3.6 above)?

35. *Common interest.* A treaty is a disagreement reduced to writing (if one may be permitted to do such violence to the hallowed definition of a contract). But so is legislation. The eventual parties to a treaty enter into negotiation with different ideas of what they want to achieve. Negotiation is a process for finding a third thing which neither party wants but both parties can accept. The making of legislation, at least in a society with an active system of politics, is a similarly dialectical process, by which conflicts of ideas and interests are resolved into a legal form which then re-enters the general social process as a new datum. A treaty is not the end of a process, but the beginning of another process. And so is legislation. The treaty and the law become a datum in the general social process, but it is a datum with a life of its own. The parties to a treaty, like the parties interested in the making of a legislative act, no doubt have different ideas about what has been fixed in the treaty, and different interests in relation to its interpretation and its application to actual persons and events (its particularizing—para. 3.5 above). But their degree of control over their own social situation is limited by the social effectiveness of the treaty or the law. The treaty and the law create a micro-legal system within the general legal system from which they derive their legal effect, and within the society from which they derive their social effect.

36. There is a common interest of international society as a whole in the creation of micro-legal systems of treaties, just as there is a common interest of national societies in the creation of the micro-legal systems of legislation. They are an integral part of a society's legal self-constituting, its self-ordering through law. Treaties are a delegation of law-making power. The parties may make law for themselves, their legal capacity to do so deriving from international constitutional law, which may set

formal and substantial limitations on that capacity (for example: *ius cogens*, interaction with legal relations under other treaties). But the international legal system is a legal system which still contains a customary form of law, and treaties have a complex and subtle relationship to customary international law.

37. Treaty-law has three *meta-legislative effects*.

37.1. The first such effect is that treaties are an integral and important part of the *dialectic of practice* which generates customary international law. Within that dialectic, treaties may contribute to the formation of legal relations applying not only to their parties but also to non-parties.

37.2. The second meta-legislative effect is that treaties may create a *general legal situation* in which legal relations with non-parties are modified without their specific consent. This is the case where a treaty empowers a party to create a situation (say, a sea-area regime, or a regime of universal criminal jurisdiction, or an arms control regime, or a use-of-force regime, or an external trade regime) which cannot reasonably be applied on the basis of a discrimination between parties and non-parties. This is especially the case where the international regime falls to be applied within national legal systems, or where the international regime is an aspect of an indivisible conception of international public order. In such a case, the corresponding legal relations of customary international law must be understood as containing the power (of the party) and the liability (of the non-party) to create and to be affected by such a regime. It follows that the ruling of the International Court of Justice in the *Nicaragua Case* (1986), that the relevant customary international law coexists with the provisions of the UN Charter, can only be regarded as preposterous.

37.3. The general-legal-situation effect is a particular instance of a general effect of treaty-law. Treaty-law breaks the *network of mutuality* which underlies customary international law. A customary legal system is a permanent negotiating of a social contract, the forming and re-forming of a legal basis of social coexistence from day to day, with a necessary and inherent deep-structural mutuality of legal relationships. When, as in the international legal system, the surpassing of customary law by legislation is not a surpassing by and for all members of society, the relationship of the two sources of law cannot be conceived either in terms of a lazy analogy with contract law or by a one-to-one correspondence with their relationship in a national legal system. The existence of treaty-law modifies the legally protected expectations of all members of international society, including non-parties to particular treaties.

38. Within the history of national societies, the ever-greater complexity and density of social relations gave rise to the need for delegated legislation, and powers to make legislation are conferred, by legislative act, on persons or bodies other than the primary legislative institution, especially the executive branch of government. Nationally, the volume of delegated legislation soon came to exceed the volume of primary legislation. It is also important to understand that society delegates a law-making function to countless forms of subordinate society, especially industrial and commercial corporations, which are micro-systems of self-legislation and self-government. It is in the common interest of society that such micro-systems should pursue

their self-interest under and in conformity with the law of society which actualizes the common interest of society as a whole.

39. With the development of the international public realm (para. 29: Public Order 5, above), the need for delegated legislation has been met by conferring legislative powers on international institutional systems. The volume of treaty-law long since exceeded the volume of customary international law. The volume of international delegated legislation probably now rivals the volume of primary treaty-law. And international society, like national societies, includes the activity of countless subordinate societies, other than the State-societies, not least industrial and commercial corporations acting outside the place where they are incorporated. Such societies are systems of delegated self-legislation and self-government under and in conformity with international law and the laws of the nations in which their activities take place.

40. Within national systems, it also became necessary to develop forms of para-legislative acts (so-called *soft law*, such as codes of practice, administrative rules, etc.), whose function is to control specifically the law-interpreting and law-applying behaviour of public-realm persons and bodies. They do not give rise to direct legal relations to which the citizen is a party. Rather, they modify the application of pre-existing public-realm powers and duties in relation to the citizen. They have been held to give rise to 'legitimate expectations' on the part of the citizen that such powers and duties will be implemented in accordance with the soft-law provisions. Such a thing has now been found to be necessary also in the international public realm. Multilateral and unilateral declarations, resolutions, final acts, memoranda of understanding, statements of principles, programmes, action-plans—all such things have been developed organically to be something other than treaties, giving rise to legitimate expectations about the implementation of legal relations rather than themselves giving rise to legal relations. In those institutional systems where national public law and international public law are now functionally linked in the work of specialized international institutions, such para-legislative acts may especially affect the implementation of legal relations within national legal systems.

41. Within national societies, and now within international society, it became necessary also to confer a new kind of legal power on public-realm bodies. All legal powers include a double discretion (whether to exercise the power, what decision to take within the limits of the power). All legal powers include the potentiality of the modification of the legal situation of persons other than the power-holder. But what we may call *administrative-law powers* take these characteristics to a degree which almost gives rise to a difference of kind. Public-realm bodies take power-decisions within broad areas of discretion, sometimes formulated in the most general terms ('necessary in the public interest', 'with a view to the preservation of public order/international peace and security', 'in accordance with equitable principles', 'on a basis of non-discrimination', 'to give effect to the purposes of the present Act/treaty'). Although modern administrative law gives to courts a legal power to define and control the outer limits and the procedural aspects of such discretions, the generality of their scope and the scale of their effects (perhaps, the whole population or all

members of international society) give a sort of law-making power to public-realm bodies, including international institutions.

42. *Politics.* Politics seeks out public-realm power. Public-realm power seeks to negate politics. The social struggle to control and influence the exercise of public-realm power (para. 3.6 above) arises most powerfully in relation to the making of law. The exercise of public-realm power, especially the making of law, is a sustained effort to resolve the struggle of politics into an act which defines and enacts the common interest of society and transcends particular interests. Treaty-law, like all law-making, is a by-product of politics. Treaty-law negates the politics which produces it. In the case of treaty-law-making, however, the role of politics is obscure and complex.

43. There are three phases in the making of treaty-law.

43.1. *Projection.* The internal political process of each participant generates its input into the process of negotiation (sometimes referred to as 'instructions to the delegation') and then projects that input externally into the negotiation. The nature of the internal process is specific to each society and its constitutional structure. The process may itself involve complex interdepartmental negotiation within the public realm, and negotiation with parliamentary organs or relevant special interest-groups.

43.2. *Negotiation.* Negotiation is dominated by potential treaty-texts, most often prepared in advance, and the crux of the negotiation is a search for 'forms of words' acceptable to all, or the relevant, participants. The passionate and formless world of politics is re-born as a world of words. Matters of great practical consequence, perhaps involving life and death on a great scale, are concentrated into the tiny mass of a few words, in a sort of ritualized trench warfare, in which big victories are measured in small gains of verbal territory.

43.3. *Re-entry.* The treaty-text produced by negotiation is taken back into the internal political process of each participant. In constitutional systems where the executive branch of government and parliament are systematically integrated, the final acceptance of the treaty may be relatively straightforward, politically and legally. Elsewhere, most notoriously in the United States constitutional system, the re-entry stage is a resumption of the projection stage, and the fate of the treaty-text is as uncertain as that of any other executive-branch initiative.

44. The Wilsonian new-diplomacy ideal of 'open covenants openly arrived at' has not proved possible, even in the most apparently public of conference-settings. (Of the Paris Peace Conference itself, Harold Nicolson, a member of the British delegation, said: 'few negotiations in history have been so secret, or indeed so occult'.) The crux of a negotiation, as in the most traditional forms of diplomacy, is still located in confidential meetings of restricted groups of participants. A form of negotiation which has become common since 1945, and which may be entitled to be called a new form of diplomacy, is *parliamentary diplomacy*—large-scale conferences in which there is a projection of extra-parliamentary national politics, in the form of open-ended participation by persons and groups other than the representatives of the national and international public realms and where the rituals of diplomatic negotiation are overtaken by

free-ranging debate of a broad political character, about ends and means, values and purposes. But, even in this form of negotiation, the last word as to the content of the treaty-law and its re-entry into the national legal systems remains with the controllers of the public realms.

45. The making of treaty-law is accordingly anomalous in relation to national constitutional systems, in the sense that it brackets out of the national process a central part of the making of a form of law which is liable to become an important factor in national public-realm decision-making, or even to become part of the substance of national law. This bracketing-out means that normal national constitutional processes, including political accountability for executive-branch action, may apply in a disorderly way, if at all, to treaty-law-making. Treaty-law-making, a substantial and rapidly increasing part of the law-making of the international legal system, continues to share in the unreality of traditional diplomacy, a ghost-filled world of 'power' and 'national interest' and 'foreign policy', the world of war by other means. (It follows that nothing can be said in favour of the existence and the work of the International Law Commission which manages to combine the unreality of the academy with the unreality of traditional diplomacy.)

THE FUTURE OF THE INTERNATIONAL LEGAL SYSTEM

46. The *aggiornamento* of international society means purposively bringing international society into line with our best ideas and highest expectations about society in general. At the beginning of the twenty-first century, such a thing seems at last to be a reasonable enterprise. It is an enterprise of which the re-conceiving of the international legal system is an integral part. It is also an enterprise which faces a series of formidable obstacles which we must identify if we are to overcome them.

46.1. *The Degradation of Universal Values.* The emergence of potentially universal values after 1945 (para. 29 above) suffered a deformation as the emerging values were subjected to almost-instant rationalizing, legalizing, institutionalizing, and bureaucratizing. That is to say, they were corrupted before they could begin to act as transcendental, ideal, supra-societal, critical forces in relation to the emerging absolute statism of society, including 'democratic' society. They were also systematically corrupted before they could acquire a more clearly universal substance, so that they became vulnerable to charges of cultural relativism and hegemonism. And they were corrupted, finally, in the context of the so-called Cold War which was waged, at the ideal level, as a cynical disputation about general ideas, so that the 'winning' of the Cold War could be presented as a final validation of general ideas. It will not be easy to redeem the idea, the power, and the social function of transcendental values from such relentless degradation.

46.2. *The Hegemony of the Economic.* In democratic-capitalist societies, experience over the last two centuries of the relationship between the economic development of society and its socio-political development (including the development of the legal system) suggests that there is a definite correlation between the two, but no unequivocal correlation, either in point of time or in substance. Leading instances (the United Kingdom, the United States, Prussia, Japan, the European Union) show significant differences on the most critical of all points, namely, the post-Marxian questions of whether socio-political change is caused by economic development and whether the form of socio-political change is determined by the form of economic development. However, such questions have themselves been overtaken by a form of general social development which has led to the conceptual and practical dominance of economic phenomena over all other social phenomena.

46.2.1. The economy has become a virtual public realm. The 'economy' here means the socially organized transformation of natural and man-made resources through the application of physical and mental effort. In a capitalist society, private-interest economic activity is seen as activity also in the public interest. The primary function of management of the traditional public realm, where social power is exercised exclusively in the public interest, has gradually come to be, not the service of some common interest of well-being conceived in terms of general values (say, justice or solidarity or happiness or human flourishing), but the maintaining of the conditions required for the well-being of the economy, including, above all, the legal conditions.

46.2.2. The global economy is the limiting-case economy, as the transformatory activity of the whole human race comes to be socially organized under an international legal system which is, in this context, dominated by the laws of the nations (para. 22 above). Functional economic high values will dominate the development of the global economy, and hence presumably the further development of the international legal system, to an even greater extent than in national societies, so long as there is only a piecemeal international public realm and rudimentary international politics.

46.3. *The Poverty of Politics.* When politics is seen as a general social process for determining the common interest (para. 13 above), then it is possible to make judgements about the way in which politics makes such determinations in particular societies or at particular times. Since early in the nineteenth century, institutionalized politics has been public opinion led and ends oriented. There developed alongside such politics a public decision-making system ('government') which is rationality led and means oriented. The merit of a political system might be measured by the degree to which it allows for a rich debate about both ends and means and provides efficient systems for resolving the debate in the form of legal and other action.

46.3.1. Politics in the most socially developed national systems has recently degenerated into an impoverished debate within narrow dialectical limits, focused particularly on the manipulation of mass-opinion. At the same time, the professional controllers of the public realm (politicians and public servants) have acquired an unprecedented degree of de-politicized pragmatic power, corresponding to the urgency and complexity of the day-to-day problems of the internal and external management of such systems, especially the economic problems. It is the externalized form of this politics-free power that has been pooled in the intergovernmental institutions of the international public realm. And the controllers of the economic virtual public realm, often causing large-scale social effects by their private-interest decision-making, are not accountable through the general public-realm political and legal control-systems, but devote substantial resources to managing the outcomes of those systems. The development of the international system, including the international legal system, is likely to be determined by such national developments. It is not likely that international politics will be better than the best of national politics, even if it ever comes to be better than the worst.

46.4. *The Poverty of Philosophy.* Who killed philosophy? Was it democracy, with its capacity to process all questions of ends and means in the public forum? Or was it capitalism, with its own internalized high values, interpreted and applied in the market-place? The primary perpetrator was philosophy itself. While societies continued to embody the fruits of old-regime transcendental philosophy in the forms of their social organization, and continued to enact the fruits of old-regime philosophy in their self-understanding, their high values, and their purposes, a new-regime philosophy, strictly an unphilosophy or an anti-philosophy of terminal pragmatism, decreed that old-regime transcendental philosophy is impossible, an illusion, a fraud. It followed that the surpassing of old-regime philosophy on its own terms was impossible, and that the surpassing of existing forms of social organization and social consciousness was possible only to the extent that such surpassing arose within existing social processes. Democracy and capitalism have taken power over the possibility of their own negating, and hence over their own surpassing, and it is philosophy which has given a spurious charisma to their mental absolutism. Corrupted social consciousness fills the private minds of human beings everywhere with low values generated as systematic by-products of social systems which will soon be, if they are not already, beyond the redeeming power of higher values.

46.4.1. The reciprocating character of a legal system, formed by and forming the ideal and the real self-constituting of society (para. 3 above), means that a legal system cannot be better than the social consciousness that it enacts. If the role of philosophy in human self-surpassing and self-perfecting is not restored, perhaps with the assistance of non-Western participants in global social consciousness, then the development of the international legal system is condemned to be the impoverished product of an impoverished human consciousness.

46.5. *The Tyranny of the Actual.* The actual seems inevitable because, if it could have been otherwise, it would have been otherwise. From the necessity of the actual it is a short step to the rationality of the actual (Hegel), to believing that what is is right (Pope), in the best possible world (Leibniz). But the human actual, including the social actual, is the product of human choice, that is to say, moral choice. To rationalize or naturalize the human actual is to empty it of its moral content, to neutralize it. It has been an effect, if not the original purpose, of the 'human sciences', over the last century and a half, to rationalize and naturalize the human actual, and so to make the actual seem to be morally neutral. We seek to assign 'causes' to things in the human world, such as slavery or trench warfare or genocide, knowing that causation is our category for understanding the non-human world. Conversely, we assign personality to reified ideas of particular social systems ('nation' or 'state' or 'class'), so that actuality-making choice is isolated from any particular human moral agent or agents, and then we speak of the 'intention' of such a systematic process, knowing that a process cannot be morally responsible.

46.5.1. Nowhere has human de-moralizing been as relentlessly practised as in the international realm, the imaginary realm inhabited by 'States'. It is practised by those who act within that realm and by those who study it. The external aspect of government is still conducted in pursuit of what is still called 'foreign policy' through the means still known as 'diplomacy', old-regime games as anachronistic as real tennis or prize-fighting. And those who study such things still seek to uncover the rules of such games, as if they were studying the behaviour of alien life-forms, as if their bizarre ideas of the human actual were the hypothetical rationalizing of some part of the natural world.

46.5.2. The meaning and the measure of human progress are difficult to establish. A fair general judgement might be that material progress has not been matched by spiritual progress. It also seems right to say that such human progress as there has been, over the last several thousand years, has been due to three strange accidents of evolution, or gifts of God: rationality (the capacity to order our consciousness); morality (the capacity to take responsibility for our future); and imagination (the capacity to create a reality-for-ourselves). Using these capacities, we found within ourselves another capacity, the capacity to form the idea of the ideal—the idea of a better human future which we can choose to make actual. The ideal has been the anti-entropic and anti-inertial moving-force of human progress, of human self-surpassing and self-perfecting. To overcome the tyranny of the actual, to overcome the ignorant and infantile belief that the actual self-organizing of humanity is necessary and inevitable, we need only to recall and recover our extraordinary power constantly to reconceive the ideal, in order yet again to choose to make it actual.

THE NEW PARADIGM

47. The new paradigm of the international legal system is a new ideal of human self-constituting. It has three leading characteristics. (1) The international legal system is a system for disaggregating the common interest of all humanity, rather than merely a system for aggregating the self-determined interests of so-called States. (2) The international legal system contains all legal phenomena everywhere, overcoming the artificial separation of the national and the international realms, and removing the anomalous exclusion of non-governmental transnational events and transactions. (3) The international legal system, like any legal system, implies and requires an idea of a society whose legal system it is, a society with its own self-consciousness, with its own theories, values, and purposes, and with its own systems for choosing its future, including a system of politics.

48. The idea of international society, the society of the whole human race and the society of all societies, takes its place at last, centuries late, within human self-consciousness, and international law finds its place at last, centuries late, within the self-constituting of international society, that is to say, as an essential part of the self-creating and the self-perfecting of the human species.

5

Emerging Patterns of Governance and International Law

STEPHEN J. TOOPE[*]

International lawyers and international relations scholars are beginning to talk to one another. Just beginning—and as this volume indicates, we have much to learn from our rich, but surprisingly discrete, intellectual traditions. I leave it to others to canvass potential areas of fruitful collaboration. My purpose is not to argue why international law and international relations *should* share insights. But I do want to reflect briefly, from my perspective as an international lawyer, upon why the two disciplines *are* now reaching out to one another. I will attempt to answer this question with reference principally to developments in international environmental law and policy.

With hindsight, the previously entrenched cross-disciplinary lack of communication seems decidedly odd, for, as one reads the debates that have animated the two fields over the last forty or so years, one is struck by the mutual relevance of our work, though not of our dominant preoccupations. International lawyers asked questions about the power of norms in shaping international events and about the possible existence of an international community, or (more modestly) an international society. For much of the post-Second World War period, international relations experts emphasized the explanatory force of relative power and of State interests in predicting international behaviour. But with the failure of international relations theory to predict, or even explain, the end of the Cold War, new questions gained currency, questions more closely allied with the historical preoccupations of international law. Younger generations of international relations scholars investigate the constitution of actors and interests within the international system and evaluate the relative importance of actors and structures in shaping political events.

In addressing common issues, lawyers and political scientists have each gone back to shared sources of inspiration: Plato, Grotius, Pufendorf, Kant, Hegel, and Rousseau. But once these foundational thinkers have been re-examined, scholars of law and of politics have typically entered almost hermetically sealed chambers. In reading most international relations literature, one looks in vain for the musings of international lawyers—even those who adopted theoretical stances closely allied to methodologies of the other social sciences. The failure of most international relations specialists to assimilate the work of Lasswell and McDougal is particularly surprising.

* I would like to thank Jaye Ellis for her outstanding research assistance and critical insight, and Jutta Brunnée, Marty Finnemore, and Rene Provost for their helpful suggestions.

Yet the oversights are mutual. Modern international legal literature has paid almost no attention to the insights of international relations scholars. Even in the most sophisticated discussions of international law, one would search fruitlessly for a treatment of Hans Morgenthau or Hedley Bull.

International lawyers have traditionally emphasized the elaboration of explicit rules that are notionally binding upon States; we have built formal institutions to help shape and interpret those rules. But we have long been frustrated that at the moments of greatest tension and division in international life the rules often prove to lack the force we intended. Meanwhile, twentieth-century international relations scholars have, at least in the dominant realist tradition, sought principally to explain why States behave the way they do. Recent trends in international relations theory have opened up lines of inquiry distinct from the realist fixations upon State interest and relative State power, causing some scholars to discover the relevance of international law. Various schools have begun to explore the effect of formal and informal institutions in both shaping State identity and modifying State behaviour. In these discussions, the increasing role of State policy networks and of non-State actors has been highlighted.

These developments in international relations theory are mirrored in the changing preoccupations of international lawyers. In thinkers as diverse, even contradictory, as Philip Allott and Martti Koskenniemi, one discovers a common thread of concern to promote greater accountability of international actors. For generations, international law has been reified, treated as an abstract (and abstruse) set of rules governing the intercourse of sovereign States. More and more, international legal theorists recognize that international law is not simply about rules and formal 'participants' in the system—for ultimately the goals of international law are value laden and the true beneficiaries of the system are not States, but individuals and communities around the globe. Allott therefore calls for a reorientation of international law to highlight its social function: the identification and promotion of the international public interest.[1] From a seemingly contradictory starting-point, Koskenniemi passionately defends legal formalism and the role of the State as a means to promote democratic accountability and to resist the transfer of power to potentially oppressive transnational bureaucratic élites.[2]

This yearning for greater accountability is the golden thread of late twentieth-century international law, prompting an ever more intense focus upon questions of 'compliance with' or 'implementation of' international norms.[3] The new emphasis

---

[1] P. Allott, 'State Responsibility and the Unmaking of International Law' (1988) 29 Harvard International Law Journal 1 at 9 and 26; and P. Allott, *Eunomia: New Order for a New World* (Oxford: Oxford University Press, 1990), *passim*, but especially at 178 and 336 (hereinafter *Eunomia*).

[2] M. Koskenniemi, 'The Place of Law in Collective Security' (1996) 17 Michigan Journal of International Law 455 at 478; and M. Koskenniemi, *From Apology to Utopia: The Structure of International Legal Argument* (Helsinki: Lakimiesliiton Kustannus, 1989), at 35 and 487 (hereinafter *Apology*).

[3] Abram Chayes and Antonia Handler Chayes, *The New Sovereignty: Compliance with International Regulatory Agreements* (Cambridge, Mass., Harvard University Press, 1995), *passim*; Thomas Franck, *Fairness in International Law and Institutions* (Oxford: Clarendon Press, 1995), *passim*, but especially at

upon compliance or implementation—I eschew the term 'enforcement' for reasons discussed later—is the intellectual shift that forced international lawyers to open up inquiry into the work of international relations scholars.

Many international lawyers realize that we need better *explanatory* models for the evolution of binding norms, just as many international relations theorists understand that they need more nuanced *normative* models that differentiate amongst the various types of rules, norms, and principles which help to shape the performance of international actors. Within the international relations academy, various groupings of scholars have addressed this concern in differing ways. In this chapter, I explore primarily the work of neo-liberal institutionalists, constructivists, and promoters of the concept of 'governance'. Though I find the incessant self-labelling of international relations scholars somewhat precious, it is useful to identify the intellectual currents that inform the work of various thinkers. I relate this scholarship to the work of contemporary international law theorists, notably Allott, Koskenniemi, and Slaughter whose latest work is found elsewhere in this volume. I then trace out my own perspectives on the evolution of modern international law, testing my hypotheses in the specific issue-area of shared freshwater resources, the subject of a four-year research project I have undertaken with Jutta Brunnée.[4] This area of study is particularly fruitful, because environmental protection has served as a crucible for challenges to classical understandings of public international law.

I argue that regime theory and related discussions of governance amongst international relations scholars can provide dramatic insights for international lawyers into the formation of both conventional and customary law. Further, international lawyers should pay attention to the formation and nurturing of what Brunnée and I have called 'contextual regimes', nascent patterns of governance which have an independent value but which also serve as precursors to the crystallization of binding legal norms. In pointing to the importance of contextual regimes, I highlight the role played by international lawyers in the advocacy of substantive norms, and in the elaboration of procedural innovations which build confidence amongst relevant actors and prompt more co-operative behaviour.

23–4; Harold K. Jacobson and Edith Brown Weiss, 'Strengthening Compliance with International Environmental Accords: Preliminary Observations from a Collaborative Project' (1995) 1 Global Governance 119; S. Toope, 'Redefining Norms for the 21st Century' [1995] Proceedings Canadian Council of International Law 191; and John Setear, 'An Iterative Perspective on Treaties: A Synthesis of International Relations Theory and International Law' (1996) 37 Harvard International Law Journal 139. But see M. Byers, 'Taking the Law out of International Law: A Critique of the Iterative Perspective' (1997) 38 Harvard International Law Journal 201.

[4] See J. Brunnée and S. Toope, 'Environmental Security and Freshwater Resources: A Case for International Ecosystem Law' (1994) 5 Yearbook of International Environmental Law 41 (hereinafter 'Ecosystem Law'); J. Brunnée and S. Toope, 'Environmental Security and Freshwater Resources: Ecosystem Regime Building' (1997) 91 American Journal of International Law 26 (hereinafter 'Regime Building'); and S. Toope and J. Brunnée, 'Freshwater Regimes: The Mandate of the International Joint Commission' (1998) 15 Arizona Journal of International and Comparative Law 273 (hereinafter 'IJC').

INSIGHTS FROM INTERNATIONAL RELATIONS SCHOLARSHIP

I am spared the need to provide a comprehensive overview because two articles have appeared recently detailing contemporary debates amongst international relations scholars and their potential impact upon international law.[5] These articles outline the traditional dominance of realist interpretations of international intercourse, and survey the more recent explanatory challenges launched by neo-liberal institutional-ists[6] and constructivists.[7] I also explore a third cross-cutting intellectual current: the study of informal mechanisms of governance within the international arena.[8] All three scholarly agendas hold one intellectual goal in common, that is, to dispute the realist assertion that international behaviour is shaped entirely by the perceived self-interest of sovereign States, and that all interaction is determined by self-conscious calcula-tions of relative power. Where the approaches differ is on the processes through which

[5] Anthony Arend, 'Do Legal Rules Matter? International Law and International Politics' (1998) 38 Virginia Journal of International Law 107; and A.-M. Slaughter, A. S. Tulumello, and S. Wood, 'International Law and International Relations Theory: A New Generation of Interdisciplinary Scholarship' (1998) 92 American Journal of International Law 367. The fiftieth anniversary issue of the influential journal *International Organization* contains a comprehensive survey of contemporary intellec-tual debates in international political economy. The keynote contribution of Keohane, Krasner, and Katzenstein is magisterial, and sets out the various IR 'isms' with great clarity. See Robert O. Keohane, Stephen D. Krasner, and Peter Katzenstein, 'International Organization and the Study of World Politics' (1998) 52 International Organization 645. The remainder of the volume contains useful analyses of subdivisions of international relations theory, although the interplay between international relations and international law is not a predominant theme.

[6] See e.g. Robert O. Keohane, 'International Institutions: Two Approaches' (1988) 32 International Studies Quarterly 379; Robert O. Keohane, 'Neoliberal Institutionalism: A Perspective on World Politics', in id. (ed.), *International Institutions and State Power: Essays in International Relations Theory* (1989) 1; Stephen D. Krasner, 'Structural Causes and Regime Consequences: Regimes as Intervening Variables', in id. (ed.), *International Regimes* (1983), 1; Oran Young, *'International Cooperation: Building Regimes for Natural Resources and the Environment'* (Ithaca: Cornell University Press, 1989); and Oran Young, 'International Regimes: Toward a New Theory of Institutions' (1986) 39 World Politics 104.

[7] See e.g. Alexander Wendt, 'The Agent-Structure Problem in International Relations Theory' (1987) 41 International Organization 335; Alexander Wendt, 'Anarchy is What States Make Of It: The Social Construction of Power Politics' (1992) 46 International Organization 391 (hereinafter 'Anarchy'); Alexander Wendt, 'Collective Identity Formation and the International State' (1994) American Political Science Review 384 (hereinafter 'Identity'); Andrew Hurrell, 'International Society and the Study of Regimes: A Reflective Approach', in Volker Rittberger and Peter Mayer (eds.), *Regime Theory and International Relations* (Oxford: Clarendon Press, 1993), at 49; Nicholas Onuf, *World of Our Making: Rules and Rule in Social Theory and International Relations* (Columbia, SC: University of South Carolina Press, 1989); and John G. Ruggie, *Constructing the World Polity: Essays on International Institutionalization* (London: Routledge, 1998).

[8] The governance literature is closely linked to both the neo-liberal institutionalist and the construc-tivist schools. Various strains of governance discourse emphasize what Andrew Hurrell has called 'plural-ist' or 'coercive solidarist' visions of international society. By this he means coexistence with a diversity of legitimate aims (pluralism) versus the promotion of co-operation towards shared goals (coercive soli-darism). Andrew Hurrell, 'Sociedade Internacional e Governança Global,' (1999) 46 Lua Nova. Revista de Cultura e Política 55–75. See also Oran Young, *International Governance: Protecting the Environment in a Stateless Society* (Ithaca, NY: Cornell University Press, 1994); James Rosenau and Ernst-Otto Czempiel (eds.), *Governance Without Government: Order and Change in World Politics* (Cambridge: Cambridge University Press; 1992); and Gerry Stoker, 'Governance Theory: Five Propositions' (1998) 155 International Social Science Journal.

State behaviour is actually moulded and constrained. The neo-liberal institutionalists emphasize the importance of formal and informal institutions in the progressive 'enmeshment' of most, if not all, States in a world order premissed upon shared liberal values.[9] For constructivists, the international system is best viewed as a social structure wherein law plays a constitutive role through the implicit norms that underlie the entire system. The essential insight is that the participation of States in international regimes (formal and informal) shapes not only the perceived interests of States, but also their very identity.[10] The most comprehensive empirical data supporting this view are found in the ground-breaking study of UNESCO by Martha Finnemore.[11] Unlike the neo-liberal institutionalist model, the constructivist analysis does not assume the current existence, or even the ultimate creation, of a shared philosophical framework underlying the interactions of States in the international arena. The assertion is more careful: that some 'common meanings' may emerge through the interaction of various actors (including States) in bilateral and multilateral fora; these intersubjective meanings in turn allow for the evolution of legal rules.[12] In this sense, constructivism is a more cosmopolitan explanatory model than is neo-liberal institutionalism, which retains a strongly hegemonic flavour.[13]

[9] A nuanced version of this argument can be found in A.-M. Slaughter, 'International Law in a World of Liberal States' (1995) 6 European Journal of International Law 503; and A.-M. Slaughter, 'Liberal International Relations Theory and International Economic Law' (1995) 10 American Journal of International Law and Policy 717; a caricatured version in Francis Fukuyama, *The End of History and the Last Man* (New York: Fress Press, 1992). For the sake of narrative clarity, and because my principal goal here is to relate international legal scholarship to constructivist international relations theory, I am leaving aside a myriad of important debates amongst various categories of 'liberal' international relations theorists. For self-described neo-liberals such as Keohane, there is no analytical power in the concept of enmeshment in shared liberal values. Rather, the liberalism espoused is economic liberalism, and analysis is driven by microeconomic, especially game theoretical, models. It has been suggested that the central contemporary divide amongst American international relations scholars is between rational choice theorists, for whom all calculations of behaviour are utilitarian or consequentialist, and everyone else, including those people I have described as neo-liberal institutionalists and constructivists. See Keohane, Krasner, and Katzenstein, International Organization'.   [10] Wendt, 'Identity'

[11] Martha Finnemore, 'International Organizations as Teachers of Norms: The United Nations Education, Scientific and Cultural Organization and Science Policy' (1993) 47 International Organization 565. For Finnemore's extended theoretical argument and for case-studies drawn from the fields of security and development, see Martha Finnemore, *National Interests in International Society* (Ithaca, NY: Cornell University Press, 1996).

[12] See Wendt, 'Anarchy', at 397–9 and 413–14.

[13] Hurrell is right to point out that there are strains of liberalism, most notably in the work of Walzer and Rawls, that posit a 'pluralist' conception of the ends which States might legitimately pursue. But for the neo-liberal institutionalists, a strong commitment to shared liberal values has emerged, especially since the end of the Cold War. This commitment has prompted greater demands for the enforcement of norms reflecting liberal values. The constructivists, including Hurrell himself, challenge the legitimacy of 'the drive toward harder and more coercive forms of enforcement'. See Hurrell, 'Sociedade Internacional' at 67–71. Hurrell stresses that far from benignly 'enmeshing' outlier states through engagement in a common enterprise, the contemporary neo-liberal agenda is more accurately described as an attempt to force the adoption of a particular set of beliefs and values by all States. The 'force' employed is often the granting or withholding of membership in key formal and informal institutions ranging from the World Trade Organisation, to NATO, to the Group of Seven, to the Commonwealth. Andrew Hurrell and Ngaire Woods, 'Globalisation and Inequality' (1995) 24 Millennium: Journal of International Studies 447 (No. 3), at 457, and 460–2.

It is precisely this cosmopolitanism that connects the constructivist school with the governance debate. It was arguably Kant who first focused Western European attention on the problem of unconstrained State power; his vision of the *jus cosmopoliticum* as an alternative to the *jus gentium* evolved as a means to promote the emergence of international law as an effective restraining influence upon national power. But Kant went on to provide the foundation for an essentially liberal view of international society when he postulated that an international rule of law could only emerge if all States adopted a truly representative, in his words 'republican', form of government.[14] This argument is the source of much of the neo-liberal institutionalist agenda posited by proponents such as Slaughter.

Many contemporary thinkers on governance have attempted to distance themselves from the second limb of Kant's reasoning. Whilst embracing the need to understand international society as something more than a crucible for the resolution of competitive State interests, with law the mere handmaiden of power, some proponents of governance analysis have sought to uphold a truly cosmopolitan conception of the ends which might legitimately be pursued by international actors. Although this form of cosmopolitanism has not been typically apparent in the increasingly insistent and influential governance discourse of international financial institutions,[15] academic discourse has remained open to multiple understandings of the public good. Commonly, this cosmopolitanism is expressed through an emphasis upon the role of the private sector and civil society, especially non-governmental organizations, in articulating complex, and oftentimes conflicting, values which must be assimilated in international debate and negotiation.[16]

Like constructivists, writers on governance more generally have focused largely upon the processes through which the actions and inactions of States are shaped. It is the existence of formal and informal regimes that may alter the calculations of States. These regimes typically emerge through the interaction of governance networks. The concept of governance networks is broader than the notion of epistemic communities promoted by Peter Haas and Oran Young,[17] because such networks can be formed by members of government, international organizations, industry, and civil society. Their influence is not defined uniquely by superior knowledge, but also by commitment, defined interests, and access to decision-makers.[18] The influence of governance networks is not inevitably positive, nor even benign. Networks, like regimes, and regardless of their membership, are sites of power, and

---

[14] Anthony Pagden, 'The Genesis of "Governance" and Enlightenment Conceptions of the Cosmopolitan World Order' (1998) 155 International Social Science Journal 7, at 9–12.

[15] See Marie-Claude Smouts, 'The Proper Use of Governance in International Relations' (1998) 155 International Social Science Journal 81, at 83 and 88; Pagden, 'Genesis'.

[16] Rosenau and Czempiel (eds.), *Governance*, at 5; and Stoker, 'Governance Theory', at 17.

[17] Oran Young and Gail Osherenko, *Polar Politics: Creating International Environmental Regimes* (Ithaca, NY: Cornell University Press, 1993), at 245; and Peter Haas, 'Do Regimes Matter? Epistemic Communities and Mediterranean Pollution Control' (1989) 43 International Organization 377.

[18] See A.-M. Slaughter, 'The Real New World Order' [1997] Foreign Affairs 183 (Sept./Oct.); Stoker, 'Governance Theory', at 23; and Hurrell and Woods, 'Globalization and Inequality', at 450.

potentially of exclusion and inequality.[19] Like the various actors in the international arena, they are too often unaccountable. Indeed, as typically subterranean creatures, operating outside the realm of public scrutiny, governance networks may be even less accountable than some States. The only constraining influence is provided by the diversity of membership in the network; the need to accommodate industry, civil society, and government perspectives may prompt due attention to a form of the public good. But this form of accountability is not assured, since power differentials within the network may skew negotiated solutions, and there is no guarantee that all relevant interests will actually have a voice within the network.

The literature on governance betrays no common theoretical thread. It represents a loose amalgam of scholars interested in a fluid, almost undefined, concept of the 'regime'. Governance writing remains focused upon nascent and changing patterns of expectation, as it is not preoccupied with the consolidation of norms.[20] It also claims to explain less than constructivism because it does not deal with the issue of State identity. The academic discourse on governance merely attempts to reorient the scholarly viewpoint, but without positing specific normative implications. Its value, when linked to the insights of the constructivists, is to encourage attention to informal networks which influence international decision-making. But if one is ultimately to relate the discourse on governance to changing patterns of formal law, the constructivist explanation of State behaviour is crucial.

The key work linking constructivist insights to the evolution of international law has already been undertaken by Friedrich Kratochwil. As Kratochwil's views are represented in the first person in this volume, I will simply emphasize some central themes upon which I build my own argument.

For Kratochwil, the special vocation of law is not defined by formal institutions, nor by systems of hierarchical ordering principles. Law emerges in a continuing dialogue between norm and fact, and between means (process) and ends (substance).[21] International law, like all law, is best viewed as a form of practical reasoning, that is as 'rhetoric', in its rich and ancient sense.[22] Through the rhetoric of international law, international politics are shaped and some common meanings or understandings emerge.[23] These common meanings in turn serve to promote a

---

[19]   Ibid. at 467; and Wendt, 'Anarchy', at 399.

[20]   Smouts, 'Governance', at 86. Governance discourse therefore remains distinct from the notion of 'regime continuum', the movement from mere co-ordination of viewpoints to the possible hardening of sociological norms into legal rules, that I describe in this paper.

[21]   F. Kratochwil, *Rules, Norms and Decisions: On the Conditions of Practical and Legal Reasoning in International Relations and Domestic Affairs* (Cambridge: Cambridge University Press, 1989), at 181–211, especially 197; and at 240 (hereinafter, *Rules*).

[22]   As represented in the thought of Aristotle, *Rhetoric* (trans. E. S. Forster, 1966), as applied in a modern legal context by Chaim Perelman, *Logique juridique* (Paris: Dalloz, 1976).

[23]   Kratochwil, *Rules*, at 212–48, especially 218; and F. Kratochwil and J. Ruggie, 'International Organization: A State of the Art on the Art of the State' (1986) 40 International Organization 753, at 764. For a recent constructivist reading of one element of international law, see Thomas Risse and Kathryn Sikkink, 'The Socialization of International Human Rights Norms into Domestic Practices: Introduction', in Thomas Risse, Stephen Ropp, and Kathryn Sikkink, *The Power of Human Rights* (Cambridge: Cambridge University Press, 1999), 1.

greater coalescence of values which can help in the evolution of more far-reaching rules of international law. Law is rarely a direct cause of behaviour, but it can influence choice and can mould the self-definition of international actors, including States. Kratochwil has argued that '[a]ll norms and rules are problem-solving devices for dealing with conflict and cooperation'.[24] But there are differing 'rule-types' which correspond to differing social settings which then function differentially. Since following a rule involves argumentation (or rhetoric) and not mere blind obedience, 'it is through analyzing reasons specific to different rule-types that the inter-subjective validity of norms . . . can be established'.[25] The analysis of such reasons is not based purely upon the substantive content of the rule: one must ask whether the rule is logical in the context and whether it promotes inclusively supported outcomes or goals, but that is not enough. It is doubtful that law can be validated by reference to a common overarching teleology.[26] One must also address the processes through which the rule came into being; are these processes legitimate and authoritative? Kratochwil explains that '[t]his is why law is conveniently understood to be not only about providing guidance towards predetermined ends but also with the legitimation of means'.[27] Law then cannot be understood in purely instrumental terms.[28]

I would add that the legitimation of legal process is not value neutral. Common understandings of legitimate process do not relate merely to meeting formal 'constitutional' requirements, but typically require transparency, fairness, and accountability. Legal norms are both constitutive and directive. They mould processes of decision-making by establishing the vocabulary and parameters of argument (what counts as legally relevant) and by establishing rights of participation (who counts in debate). It is precisely these sorts of shared meanings that emerge within regimes constructed by actors who often begin the processes with diverse, even conflicting, goals. Legal authority arises from the perceived legitimacy of the processes of norm evolution, but it is also tested in processes of application and in a substantive evaluation of the norm itself. Law is therefore neither pure substance nor pure process, but a continuing interplay of legitimate means and legitimate ends. So the common meanings which arise in regimes do not depend upon one overarching philosophical goal such as the triumph of liberalism, but upon an incremental growth of shared perceptions fostered by participation in processes of norm evolution which are deemed to be fair and open.

A constructivist understanding of regime theory can help to identify sources of persuasive authority. International lawyers can also learn about the incremental evolution of norms—the behaviour of international actors is not 'determined' by the existence or non-existence of a legal rule, but by norms which *may* harden over time into binding obligations. The incremental approach to normativity also encourages

[24] F. Kratochwil, *Rules*, at 69.   [25] Ibid. 97.
[26] F. Kratochwil, 'The Force of Prescriptions' (1984) 38 International Organization 685, at 689; F. Kratochwil, 'On the Notion of "Interest" in International Relations' (1982) 36 International Organization 1, at 6; and Kratochwil, *Rules*, at 142.
[27] Kratochwil, *Rules*, at 197.   [28] Ibid. 198.

lawyers to imagine compliance in terms of *implementation* rather than *enforcement*. Enforcement of international law is too often made conceptually dependent upon the use of force or the threat of force. In a system of international law that is supposedly defined by the Charter of the United Nations in which the use or threat of force is severely restricted, this approach to normativity is incoherent. And I leave aside the practical problems inherent in a system of law that requires the application of a non-existent international police function; we have relearned since the heady days following the collapse of the Berlin Wall that States cannot be relied upon to 'enforce' international rules in any convincing or comprehensive manner. It is better to re-imagine what we are asking the international system of law to accomplish: the progressive, but incremental elaboration of norms which are implemented largely voluntarily. The central issue is how such voluntary adherence can be promoted. I believe that a careful reading of the constructivists, especially the work of Kratochwil, who addresses the purposes and functions of law most directly, can help international lawyers to develop more sophisticated understandings of their own role.

THE THEORETICAL CONTRIBUTIONS OF INTERNATIONAL LAWYERS

The new dialogue between international relations scholars and international lawyers presents opportunities for mutual learning. Despite the efforts of the constructivists, especially Kratochwil, Ruggie, and Wendt, international relations scholars often analyse State behaviour from an impoverished conception of normativity. Even the most creative and helpful regime theorists tend to treat all norms as mere sociological facts, and fail to distinguish amongst norms aimed at different functions (for example, constitutive versus declaratory norms). Most contemporary regime theorists stress the influence of norms in establishing 'negotiating frameworks', and in the co-ordination of the expectations of actors within the system.[29] From an international lawyer's perspective, this analysis implies that norms are nothing more than guides to action. But we lawyers react atavistically against such a generic conception of norms, and strive to identify distinctions amongst principles, norms of conduct, and legal rules (admittedly more or less solidly fixed).[30] International lawyers can help international relations scholars to address this complex topic in a more thoughtful fashion.

Unfortunately, twentieth-century international lawyers have until recently missed the opportunity to contribute to a debate with international relations thinkers because lawyers have typically adopted an inverse, and equally flawed, position

---

[29] See e.g. Krasner's influential definition of a regime, where he lumps together principles, norms, rules, and decision-making procedures and states that they all function as nodes 'around which actors' expectations converge'. Krasner, 'Structural Causes', at 2.

[30] For a full discussion, see Brunnée and Toope, 'Regime Building', at 30–7. See also M. Byers, *Custom, Power and the Power of Rules* (Cambridge: Cambridge University Press, 1999), *passim* (hereinafter *Custom*).

towards the role of norms in international society. For many international lawyers, the impetus has been towards the elaboration of ever-more precise 'rules', set out in explicit treaty commitments, and seemingly made effective by an emphasis upon formal mechanisms of enforcement. The aim to create binding and influential rules has often proved illusory in issue-areas as diverse as human rights, environmental law, and security. Why has this legal strategy failed?

First, an observation of *realpolitik*. Many States are perfectly willing to consent to explicit, formulaic rules which they have no intention of respecting in practice. The evident hypocrisy of scores of ratifications of international human rights instruments is testimony to this sad fact. The reasons for this fictitious consent are numerous, and need not detain us here.[31] The central question is how international lawyers may work strategically to promote the elaboration of regimes which do have real power to influence action. The most compelling attempt to answer this question was offered a generation ago by Myres McDougal and Harold Lasswell.[32] That team and their numerous intellectual progeny described law as a social process controlled through what they termed 'authoritative decision'. This authoritative decision emerged from 'common expectations concerning authority with a higher degree of corroboration in actual operation'.[33] The so-called New Haven School has been subjected to numerous pointed criticisms, including my own.[34] But their central insight was valuable in opening up the field of international law as an academic discipline with some explanatory validity: international law is not just about what States say in formal agreements; nor is it shaped only by State practice matched with formal and continuing consent. Law emerges through processes of interaction amongst various actors in international society, though primarily amongst States, and is solidified through a growing expectation of authority. Authority arises from processes which are seen to be legitimate, and is confirmed in the actual behaviour of relevant actors.

The essential flaw of the McDouglian paradigm is its raw instrumentalism.[35] Law serves an overarching social purpose: in the case of the New Haven School this is the promotion of 'human dignity'. But it seems to hold no internal morality, to adopt Lon Fuller's helpful terminology.[36] In McDougal's case, international law was the purveyor of immediate post-Second World War American idealism. Here we see a

---

[31] States may be seeking to satisfy internal political pressures, to establish a cheap rhetorical defence to international condemnation, or to create a more positive international image.

[32] See H. Lasswell and M. McDougal, *Jurisprudence for a Free Society* (New Haven: New Haven Press, 1992). For a comprehensive and jargon-free explanation of the McDouglian scheme, see Michael Reisman, 'The View from the New Haven School of International Law' (1992) 86 Proceedings of the American Society of International Law 118.

[33] M. McDougal and H. Lasswell, 'The Identification and Appraisal of Diverse Systems of Public Order', in Richard Falk and Saul Mendlovitz, *The Strategy of World Order* (New York: World Law Fund, 1966), 45, at 53.

[34] See S. Toope, 'Confronting Indeterminacy: Challenges to International Legal Theory' [1990] Proceedings of the Canadian Council on International Law 209, at 209–10; Byers, *Custom*, at 207–10; and Phillip Trimble, 'International Law, World Order, and Critical Studies' (1990) 42 Stanford Law Review 811.   [35] Kratochwil, *Rules*, at 196–8.

[36] L. Fuller, *The Morality of Law* (rev. edn., New Haven: Yale University Press, 1969).

strong link between the analysis of the New Haven School and the work of contemporary neo-liberal international relations scholars. They both assume that ultimately there will emerge a world-wide consensus on the moral superiority of liberal democracy. It simply needs to be actively promoted through the further enmeshment (or perhaps compulsion) of outliers in regimes which are posited on liberal values.

The neo-liberal and McDouglian institutionalist agendas assume the existence of a benevolent hegemon capable of moulding international relations. Although we may be living through a period of history quite similar to that of the immediate postwar era, in which a relatively enlightened sole hegemon does exist, the acceptance of a benevolent liberal enmeshment seems less widespread than some optimistic liberals may have hoped.[37] Consider the cosmopolitanism that runs hand in hand with globalization, a cosmopolitanism that seeks connections and linkages, but not commonality or integration. Hence the strong parallel trend towards wider applications of the principle of self-determination and nationalist cultural protection.[38]

At the conference from which this collection of papers emerged, we were presented with a dramatic opening session in which two leading international legal theorists articulated essentially opposing viewpoints. Philip Allott pleaded for a recognition of the social function of international law as the promotion of the common interest.[39] He bemoaned the essentially private and property-based understandings which dominate international legal discourse.[40] Martii Koskenniemi argued for an adherence to what can only be described as legal formalism, but not in support of State positivism. Rather, he warned that any attempt to promote global values, or legal cosmopolitanism, would be likely to result in new authoritarianism. His assumption was that States, for all their faults, are better positioned to uphold regional distinctiveness and to allow cultural pluralism to flourish.[41] Koskenniemi was decidedly uncomfortable with liberal triumphalism, seeing it—and here I extrapolate—as a mask for personal preferences which are shaped by hegemonic interests.

My own position on these fundamental questions draws upon cautionary notes from both Allott and Koskenniemi, but is grounded in Kratochwil's description of all law as an exercise in practical reasoning. While acknowledging that law cannot and should not be divorced from politics, I argue for the relative autonomy of inter-

---

[37] See e.g. Duncan Snidal, 'The Limits of Hegemonic Stability Theory' (1985) 39 International Organization 579; Brigitte Stern, this volume; Hurrell and Woods, 'Globalization and Inequality', at 461; and Smouts, 'Governance', at 88.

[38] See e.g. Oscar Schachter, 'The Decline of the Nation-State and its Implications for International Law' (1997) 36 Columbia Journal of Transnational Law 7, at 22; and S. Toope, 'State Sovereignty: The Challenge of a Changing World' [1992] Proceedings of the Canadian Council on International Law 294.

[39] Allott, this volume, p. 97; Allott, *Eunomia*, at 185 and 304.

[40] Ibid., at p. 97 and 326 (respectively).

[41] Koskenniemi, this volume, p. 45; M. Koskenniemi, 'The Police in the Temple, Order Justice and the UN: A Dialectical View' (1995) 6 European Journal of International Law 325; and Koskenniemi, *Apology*, at 35.

national law, and deny claims of an identity between law and raw power, which ultimately undermine the possibility of law, and between law and politics, which under-
cut law's legitimacy and authority. Law and power, and law and politics are not
opposites, but neither are they coextensive. I agree with Allott's suggestion that law
arises in the interaction between ideas (which may be political, philosophical, sociological, or other types of ideas) and practice, but that law becomes itself through
specific juridical processes that serve as part of its independent justification. Law
becomes a 'third thing'.[42] This analysis draws upon Lon Fuller's assertion that law
embodies both substantive and procedural values which provide it with independence from unmediated power and politics.[43]

As a result of my emphasis upon practical reasoning as the best analogy for the
creation of law, I do not agree with Koskenniemi that international law can be
understood only as an enduring, and irreconcilable, tension between antimonies
such as apology–utopia or normativity–order.[44] I concede that these opposites
exist—as does Kratochwil in his discussion of *topoi* or common meanings[45]—but I
believe that these opposites help to construct and shape arguments, not to render
discourse meaningless. Conceptual opposites exist, but each side of the conceptual
equation is more or less convincing, depending upon its congruence with other
applicable principles and norms, and upon the factual context. Here the work of the
constructivists is particularly helpful: politics exists to help construct common
understandings. These common understandings, which need not amount to broadly
shared values, provide fruitful terrain for the progressive elaboration of norms.

The rhetorical nature of international law, its form as practical reasoning, helps to
explain why international law so often relies upon the principle of good faith in shaping argument and assessing performance. It is our evaluation of the shorthand 'good
faith' which helps us to assess the convincing power of asserted norms. Not all arguments are equally convincing, and we judge legal arguments in part by their fidelity
to process values such as transparency, equality, justice, and fairness.

In invoking the role of values in the processes of practical reasoning, I further
distance myself from a central aspect of Koskenniemi's understanding of international law. He suggests that in an international context, reliance upon value-driven
understandings of legal normativity is imperialistic, even threatening. I agree to the
extent that one seeks to justify all of international law on the basis of one foundational value, such as the promotion of liberal democracy. But I have tried to suggest
that legal norms are value neutral neither in process nor in substance. They arise,
often in embryonic form, from intersubjective meanings which are generated within
formal and informal international regimes. Rules may progressively harden as these
common meanings become deeper and more inclusive, but this process is by no

---

[42] P. Allott, 'Remarks from the floor' at the conference 'The Role of Law in International Politics',
24–5 Apr. 1998, Rhodes House, Oxford (notes on file with the author).

[43] Fuller, *Morality of Law, passim*.

[44] Koskenniemi, *Apology*, at pp. xx, 40–1, and 449–50.

[45] Kratochwil, *Rules*, at 232.

means inevitable. Even modest common meanings have value, and international lawyers must resist the temptation to push a consensus which is not ripe, by seeking to define binding rules which are not actually desired or admitted in practice.

The role of values is not limited to the processes of law formation. In order that a norm, and ultimately a legal rule, be perceived as legitimate, the substantive content of the rule must be widely perceived as fair and just. Values help to shape regimes, and regimes come to affect the self-definition of international actors, which in turn modifies values. In any comprehensive analysis of international politics and international law, relative power, the interests of States and other actors, and values are all relevant variables. All three elements interact and affect normative evolution. In given contexts it is true that one or another of these variables may weigh more heavily in decision-making, but none should be ignored. Binding legal norms can arise only through a combination of legitimate process and value-laden substantive content.

My insistence upon the analytical importance of substantive, as well as procedural, values does not imply a belief in the existence of a global community. Here I distinguish my view from that of Allott, who has posited the emergence of a 'common human experience, an international consciousness'.[46] I doubt that the current 'interstatal unsociety'[47]—to adopt Allott's marvellous image, paraphrasing Kant—will soon be replaced by an 'intercultural or interpersonal society'. I share Kratochwil's emphasis upon the positive value of legal cosmopolitanism in mapping out spheres of freedom which may be experienced and practised differently.[48] I therefore find helpful Iris Young's postulation of the gift found in what she calls 'city life', the 'being together of strangers':

By 'city life' I mean a form of social relations which I define as the being together of strangers. In the city persons and groups interact within spaces and institutions they all experience them-selves as belonging to, but without those interactions dissolving into unity or commonness. City dwelling situates one's own identity and activity in relation to a horizon of a vast variety of other activity, and the awareness that this unknown, unfamiliar activity affects the condi-tions of one's own. . . . City dwellers are thus together, bound to one another, in what should be and sometimes is a single polity. Their being together entails some common problems and common interests, but they do not create a community of shared final ends, of mutual iden-tification and reciprocity.[49]

Although not intending it as such, Young presents a compelling definition of what the phenomenon of globalization means for international law and politics. My understanding of the possibilities of international normativity is predicated upon the view that there is no such thing as the 'international community', though genera-tions of UN Secretaries-General would have us believe otherwise. That said, there are

---

[46] Allott, *Eunomia*, at 293.   [47] Ibid. 244.

[48] F. Kratochwil, 'Remarks from the floor' at the conference 'The Role of Law in International Politics', 24–5 Apr. 1998, Rhodes House, Oxford (notes on file with the author); this volume, p. 63.

[49] I. Young, *Justice and the Politics of Difference* (Princeton: Princeton University Press, 1990), at 237–8.

creative possibilities in the construction and upholding of international regimes for the elaboration of some common meanings which may help us to live better together as strangers.

IMPLICATIONS FOR REGIMES GOVERNING SHARED FRESHWATER

While drawing upon the related insights of international relations and international legal theorists, I want to outline an approach to normative evolution within the issue-area of shared freshwater. Traditional approaches to international watercourse law have been flawed in two distinct respects. First, the preoccupation of the law has been with the allocation of water, from an entirely competitive and State-centred viewpoint. The result has been an almost entirely procedural approach to problem-solving, intended to enable parties to comply with the rule prohibiting significant harm to co-riparian States, and the rule of equitable utilization; hence, the focus upon prior notification and consultation. Second, the physical scope of the law's interest has been too narrow, at first being primarily sectoral (e.g. fishing rights or water abstraction rights), but later remaining interested only in the water resource *per se* rather than the ecosystem of which shared freshwater is but a part.[50]

This traditional approach has resulted in an undervaluing of the modest common meanings which have already emerged in principles and soft norms such as sustainable development, intergenerational equity, and precaution.[51] The ecosystem itself has not been treated as having inherent value. Current international law is simply incapable of promoting, much less ensuring, environmental security in the sense of a stable or improving quality of life for inhabitants of the planet (sometimes called 'ecological balance' or, more recently, 'ecological health'). Classical approaches to the creation of international law are not likely to improve this situation, being too often rooted in an unsophisticated command and enforcement paradigm. The elaboration of formal texts which contain seemingly binding rules will not result in changed behaviour without an underlying commitment on the part of States and other actors. Nor will detailed 'enforcement' and 'dispute settlement' mechanisms result in the modification of behaviour unless there is a political will to employ the new tools. Moreover, the search for more concrete, enforceable rules has undermined the adaptability of environmental law which, given our ever-changing scientific understandings of environmental cause and effect, is a *sine qua non* for a successful ecosystem regime.[52]

Regime theory, especially in its constructivist incarnation, helps to explain how binding legal norms may emerge from those patterns of expectation developed through the increasing co-ordination of discussions and actions amongst States. Common endeavour, even common debate, can give rise to shared meanings which

---

[50] For a detailed discussion, see Brunnée and Toope, 'Ecosystem Law', at 53–5.
[51] Ibid. 65–70.   [52] Ibid., *passim.*

crystallize into norms. States participating in such regimes 'learn', and the learning affects not only their appreciation of self-interest, but may even come to alter the self-perception and identification of the State. This process helps to explain the progressively more co-operative arrangements between the United States and Canada within the regime centred around the International Joint Commission.[53]

The constructivist insights are closely allied to arguments recently put forward by Brunnée and myself. We have postulated that regimes are not static structures, but that they can evolve along a continuum from dialogue and sharing of information, to more defined frameworks for co-operation, to binding rules in a precise, legal sense. Although the professional instinct of lawyers is to negotiate seemingly 'binding' agreements as soon as possible, the pre-legal or 'contextual' regime may actually be more effective in guiding the relations of international actors.

I value the 'third thing' which is law, and that is why I have argued for its relative autonomy from power and politics. To argue that formal legal regimes are best grounded in underlying contextual regimes where at least some common meanings have evolved, and where processes of norm evolution have emerged that are perceived to be legitimate by the relevant actors, is not to deny law, but to uphold it as something distinct and important. At the same time, I suggest that there is a crucial role for international lawyers during the evolution of contextual regimes, and before the hardening of binding rules, in the articulation and advocacy of substantive principles. Here I emphasize again that norms are not simply about process; their existence is also dependent upon an acceptance of the legitimacy (fairness and justice) of their substantive content.

How can international lawyers influence the substantive evolution of norms? Much is to be learned from the international relations literature. Neo-liberal, constructivist, and governance scholars have all undertaken important work in revealing the role of specialized interest groups in prompting normative change. Slaughter's project on government networks emphasizes the importance of informal gatherings of officials who are charged with similar mandates in the evolution of government policy and ultimately with the co-ordination of international expectations.[54] Haas and Young have studied the effect of 'epistemic communities', élite groupings of governmental and non-governmental scientists and technologists, upon State policies and legal constructs.[55] Most broadly, students of governance have posited the growing influence of informal transnational groupings of various characters (policy specialists, experts of every stripe, non-governmental organizations) upon the actual decision-making of governments. International lawyers can imagine themselves to be just such a 'governance network', especially if they continue to speak to other related experts such as political scientists.

The distinctive contributions of the international lawyer are most obviously in

---

[53] See Toope and Brunnée, 'IJC', *passim.*

[54] Slaughter, 'Real New World Order'. On 'principled issue networks', see also the important work of Risse and Sikkink, 'Socialization of International Human Rights Norms into Domestic Practices'.

[55] Young and Osherenko, *Polar Politics*; and Haas, 'Do Regimes Matter?'.

the design of processes of interaction and consultation (the 'constitution' in an informal sense) for the regime. But a second key role should not be neglected: the advocacy of evolving governing principles and soft law which might ultimately harden into rules. In the issue-area of shared freshwater, international lawyers can argue usefully for the application of principles borrowed from other domains of international environmental law: sustainable development, intergenerational equity, and precaution. Such advocacy, if pursued with rigour and determination, could break the sterile debates which have prevented the creative evolution of international watercourse law.[56] Indeed, such a meshing of institutional design skills and effective advocacy of new substantive principles has already allowed international lawyers to play an important role in the elaboration of modern freshwater treaties such as the ECE Convention on the Protection and Uses of Transboundary Watercourses and International Lakes,[57] and the Agreement on Great Lakes Water Quality, with its subsequent modifications.[58]

The argument for both a procedural and a substantive role for international lawyers in the development of contextual regimes implies an understanding of legal normativity that is value based. I have identified values inherent in the legal process that must be upheld by international lawyers, and I have suggested that to qualify as a binding rule, substantive outcomes must also meet an admittedly flexible test of fairness and justice. But this understanding of the role of international lawyers does not require a commitment to a universal goal or to an imagined global community. The argument is more modest: that lawyers can contribute to the construction of international regimes at every stage along the continuum of regime formation, in the early contextual days, and if and when the norms in a given regime are set to harden into legal rules. International lawyers are part of global governance networks, which can foster common meanings and help to alter the very identity of international actors, and particularly of States. Indeed, international lawyers may be very influential if their role perception is sophisticated enough. Part of a sophisticated role perception is to acknowledge and compose from the continuing, and inevitable, tension between self-interested, statist behaviour and common imperatives. For example, the principles promoted in what Brunnée and I have called international ecosystem law sometimes demand the elaboration of common, but differentiated obligations within societies and amongst States. Here I agree with Koskenniemi that the Montreal Protocol on Substances that Deplete the Ozone Layer serves as a useful model of new, and subtle, forms of environmental regulation.[59] Not only does the Protocol recognize differentiated obligations, but it adopts a positive and creative

---

[56] Brunnée and Toope, 'Regime Building', at 48–50; and Brunnee and Toope, 'Ecosystem Law', at 58–65.

[57] 17 Mar. 1992, reprinted in (1992) 31 International Legal Materials 1312.

[58] 15 Apr. 1972, US–Can., 23 UST 301; Agreement on Great Lakes Water Quality, 22 Nov. 1978, US–Can., 30 UST 1383; and Protocol Amending the Agreement Between the United States of America and Canada on Great Lakes Water Quality of 1978, 18 Nov. 1987, US–Can., TIAS No. 11, 551.

[59] M. Koskenniemi, 'Peaceful Settlement of Environmental Disputes' (1991) 60 Nordic Journal of International Law 73.

stance on the issue of compliance. The Implementation Committee created under the Protocol encourages and facilitates compliance, rather than defining compliance for the purpose of identifying a breach of obligations.[60] The goal of implementation is thus furthered whereas a model of static enforcement would have been likely to produce defections from the regime. A parallel approach was adopted in the Convention on Environmental Impact Assessment in a Transboundary Context,[61] where Inquiry Commissions are charged not with defining non-compliance, but with clarifying situations in which compliance may be required. These formal agreements were rooted in contextual regimes where a coalescence of common meanings had been allowed to mature. Even so, the formal codification of the regime retained a flexibility to encourage a continuing evolution of governance networks which may result in harder obligations in the future.

Five themes emerge from this analysis. First, ecosystem-oriented principles on the scope and content of regimes can play a significant role in shaping expectations in a given issue-area. International lawyers need to focus both on process and on the evolution of substantive content within regimes, and here my argument adds to the constructivist analysis, which tends to be almost wholly procedurally oriented. A dual emphasis upon process and content will be assisted if regimes are flexible enough to allow for the involvement of States other than those most directly affected by the regime, since the latter are more likely to contribute at the level of principle. Second, regime-building is a fluid process, which proceeds along a continuum from mere co-ordination of viewpoints to the hardening of binding rules, in some but not all cases. Third, regimes are more likely to be effective in shaping the behaviour of States if the regime has been allowed to develop organically, with increasing legitimacy and a growing body of intersubjective meanings. Premature efforts to harden the regime are likely to result in weakly rooted and ultimately irrelevant rules. Fourth, admitting the value base of a regime does not require an uncritical faith in commonality; differentiated obligations can accommodate real differences in perspectives, without sacrificing the integrity of the regime. Fifth, the type of regime formation I describe should cause international lawyers to limit their reliance upon 'enforcement', and prefer to build systems of implementation which will often require positive measures which further reinforce common meanings, in preference to sanctions which tend to marginalize international actors and prompt defections from regimes.

In his creative and provocative book *From Apology to Utopia*, Koskenniemi opined that 'by politicizing law and legalizing politics, an analysis of law's structure might point to alternative understandings of the relationship between law and its neighbouring discourses'.[62] I believe that working to understand the connections between international law and regime theory, while maintaining the relative autonomy of law, helps to promote just such 'alternative understandings'. Constructivist regime theory

---

[60]   16 Sept. 1987, reprinted in (1987) 26 International Legal Materials 1550.
[61]   25 Feb. 1991, reprinted in (1991) 30 International Legal Materials 800.
[62]   Koskenniemi, *Apology*, at p. xxiii.

helps international lawyers to ask questions about how norms evolve which can be truly influential in moulding the actions of States. It also helps us to appreciate the independent value of pre-legal normativity, and serves as a useful corrective to our tendency to declare rules and to demand enforcement of those rules in the absence of any real commitment on the part of States. In the issue-area of shared freshwater, international lawyers must work not only to promote procedural innovations, but to embrace our role as 'publicists', and engage in practical reasoning which has the rhetorical power to convince States to adopt new guiding principles. If those principles are increasingly ecosystem oriented, then international environmental law might find a vocation for environmental protection, and not simply resource allocation. Here is a challenge to our own accountability that is worth pursuing.

6

Domestic Politics and International Resources: What Role For International Law?

EYAL BENVENISTI

1. INTRODUCTION: THE RELATIONSHIP BETWEEN INTERNATIONAL LAW AND DOMESTIC POLITICS

When Hungarian activists formed the clandestine Danube Circle in 1984 and sought to prevent the damming of the Danube, they focused on mobilizing the Hungarian people against the massive project launched by the Communist government.[1] Their stunning success even brought about the downfall of the regime. But they ultimately failed in their quest: the project withstood their challenge because it was based on a treaty. As the International Court of Justice (ICJ) concluded in September 1997, the 1977 treaty between Hungary and Czechoslovakia on the construction of the Gabcikovo–Nagimaros system of dams survived all changes and challenges.[2] Without the other's consent, neither government could unilaterally revoke the treaty.

The consequences of this dispute highlight the often-neglected fact that international law plays a crucial role in domestic politics. It provides a useful tool for governments that wish to prevent future domestic challenges to their policies. Momentous internal political changes will not affect a State's international obligations. Treaties thus serve as trump cards in the domestic political game. A treaty is the ultimate guarantee for the durability of the deal struck between different domestic groups at the time of its ratification. It is often more effective than a protected constitutional clause because, unlike constitutional guarantees, no domestic majority can effect unilateral changes to a State's international obligations.[3] Domestic opposition to treaty-backed policies can succeed only through cross-boundary co-operation among domestic

---

[1] On the development of the internal environmental–political opposition in Hungary to the planned project on the Danube river see Fred Pearce, *Green Warriors* (London: Bodley Head, 1991), 107–16; Judit Galambos, 'Political Aspects of an Environmental Conflict: The Case of the Gabcikovo–Nagymaros Dam System', in Jyrki Käkönen (ed.), *Perspectives on Environmental Conflict and International Politics* (London: Pinter, 1992).

[2] Case concerning the Gabcikovo–Nagymaros Project (Hungary/Slovakia) (1997), http://www.icj-cij.org (1998) 37 International Legal Materials 167 (the declaration of Judge Rezek, the separate opinion of Judge Bedjaoui, and the dissenting opinions of Judges Herczegh and Ranjeva (all in French) do not appear in ILM).

[3] Compare William M. Landes and Richard A. Posner, 'The Independent Judiciary in an Interest-Group Perspective' (1975) 18 Journal of Law and Economics 875 (presenting constitutional guarantees as securing legislative deals among diverse interest groups).

interest groups that manage to press all involved governments to agree to modify their treaty. In retrospect, the failure of the Hungarian activists must be attributed to their inability to mobilize Slovak environmentalists in a simultaneous campaign against the bilateral treaty.

The role international law plays in domestic politics is a crucial one. This is especially true in respect of the management of internationally shared resources, where the attitudes of the States sharing the resource are determined by often intense domestic power struggles among the diverse interest groups. The dramatic effect treaties have on the domestic political scene, as demonstrated in the *Gabcikovo–Nagimaros Case*, is only one example of the influence international norms have on domestic politics. There are a number of other opportunities for international law to affect, even to shape, domestic politics. These opportunities invite us to consider policy choices. Was the norm adopted by the ICJ an appropriate one, viewed from the perspective of its potential influence on domestic politics? Do the other norms that carry domestic effects provide beneficial outcomes?

International law does not seem to be interested in these questions. Its 'constitutive norms'[4] are premissed on the perception of States as unitary actors that act solely through their governments. This law can be seen as reflecting an implicit historical pact between the world's governments to consolidate power domestically. However, this attitude is now outdated and requires reappraisal. The perception of States as unitary actors was perhaps plausible in the Cold War era, when national security was the paramount issue that overshadowed domestic conflicts of interest. But it is no longer valid in respect of many of the issues that currently divide States internally, especially issues concerning the allocation and management of shared resources. The understanding that States are actually heterogeneous actors and that domestic politics have crucial influence on a State's capability and willingness to undertake international commitments has been noted in recent years by international relations scholars.[5] This recognition and the further understanding that international co-operation requires resolution of problems inherent in States' internal political structures merit the attention of international law.

The Gabcikovo–Nagimaros decision, for example, raises questions regarding its effects on the future attitude of domestic interest groups contemplating whether to support the ratification of treaties. Domestic groups that dread long-term commitments could be discouraged by the finality of treaties and either try to lobby against their ratification altogether or seek to introduce more ambiguous terminology, more

    [4] See Louis Henkin, *International Law: Politics and Values* (Dordrecht: Martinus Nijhoff, 1995), 31–2 (referring to a 'number of assumptions and conceptions of axiomatic "constitutional" character' in international law). For Henkin's list of 'axioms of statehood' see ibid. 8–12.

    [5] See Robert D. Putnam, 'Diplomacy and Domestic Politics: The Logic of Two-Level Games' (1988) 42 International Organization 427; Helen V. Milner, *Interests, Institutions, and Information* (Princeton: Princeton University Press, 1997); George W. Downs and David M. Rocke, *Optimal Imperfection?* (Princeton: Princeton University Press, 1995). See also Peter B. Evans, Harold K. Jacobson, and Robert D. Putnam (eds.), *Double-Edge Diplomacy* (Berkeley: University of California Press, 1993) (an analysis of eleven cases of two-level bargaining).

escape clauses, or weaker enforcement mechanisms to offset the consequences of durable treaties.[6] Such attempts might in turn be interpreted negatively by foreign negotiators (and their domestic supporters) who could then opt to cease co-operation efforts. As a consequence, a norm that aims at securing co-operation may, when its domestic repercussions are examined, prove to be producing negative effects. These concerns require scrutiny. They should not be concealed behind the rhetoric of State sovereignty.[7]

This chapter evaluates the impact of international norms on domestic politics not from the point of view of constitutional theory (i.e. whether international law contributes to shaping the domestic political process) but from the point of view of collective action theory. It seeks to outline norms that are better shaped to promote an optimal and sustainable co-operation between heterogeneous States over internationally shared resources. Underlying collective action theory is the notion that co-operation among actors who share a common pool resource (CPR)—namely a resource that is shared by a number of actors but is excluded or excludable from other actors—can evolve endogenously and be backed by agreed-upon internal mechanisms, without the support of external enforcement agencies.[8]

Section 2 of this chapter attempts to justify the use of this focal point. It examines the applicability of collective action theory to international common pool resources (ICPRs), such as the Danube river. The fact that States are heterogeneous actors, each comprising several domestic interest groups as sub-actors, complicates the analysis. Being heterogeneous, States are strikingly different actors from the type of actors contemplated or observed in current CPR literature. Unitary actors who co-operate in the management of regular CPRs fully internalize the consequences of their actions, and this is indeed a precondition for the emergence of co-operation. But when an actor is heterogeneous, internalization becomes problematic and agency problems arise because the government which represents the polity in the international arena may adopt decisions which are at odds with the interests of significant parts of its population and its future generations. Therefore the possibility of co-operation among States in ICPR management hinges on the possibility of making governments internalize the diverse domestic consequences of their international acts.

Section 3 explores a number of norms that may potentially achieve this aim. My argument is that international law can be conducive to co-operation in ICPR management. Some of the current norms, including the one adopted by the ICJ in the *Gabcikovo–Nagimaros Case*, do provide the right incentives. But there are other

---

[6] See Downs and Rocke, *Optimal Imperfection?*; George W. Downs, 'Enforcement and the Evolution of Co-operation' (1998) 19 Michigan Journal of International Law 319 at 327.

[7] For a discussion of this issue, see section 3.4 below.

[8] Elinor Ostrom, *Governing the Commons* (Cambridge: Cambridge University Press, 1990); Gary D. Libecap, *Contracting for Property Rights* (Cambridge: Cambridge University Press, 1989); Todd Sandler, *Collective Action* (Ann Arbor: University of Michigan Press, 1992); Michael Taylor, *The Possibility of Co-operation* (Cambridge: Cambridge University Press, 1987).

norms, yet to gain full recognition, which could also contribute to providing the necessary legal background for the evolution of collective action in ICPR management.

2. GOVERNMENTS AS AGENTS OF DOMESTIC ACTORS

Robert Putnam has described the complex interactions between domestic and international politics as a 'two-level game',[9] a simultaneous game played by government representatives at the international level (Level I) with the representatives of foreign governments, and at the domestic level (Level II) with representatives of domestic interest groups and sub-State regions.[10] Domestic negotiations are necessary to secure domestic support for the international agreement negotiated at Level I. This is true not only in democratic countries where treaties must be approved by domestic ratification procedures. Non-democratic regimes must also secure informal ratification by the élites from which they draw support.[11] Although Putnam, and the literature following his article, focused on the two-level game of pre-agreement negotiations, the scope of the game is of course wider. The two-level game also goes on after successful negotiations culminate in a treaty. Once agreement is reached, claims concerning its further implementation, possible modification, or even breach are asserted from time to time, reflecting changes in the domestic support for the agreement. This continuous two-level game is particularly present in the context of ICPR management. Since collective action in the management of ICPR depends on co-operation of indefinite duration, the two-level game is in fact endless.

Governments' attitudes towards the possibility of international co-operation are influenced by the relative domestic strength of competing domestic interest groups.[12] Stronger domestic groups will try to steer their government's international position towards outcomes that impose externalities not only on other States but also (and on some occasions primarily) on relatively weaker domestic interest groups, or on future generations. This has often been the case in water-related projects such as the Gabcikovo–Nagimaros dispute.[13] Governments will usually comply with such efforts

---

[9] Putnam, 'Diplomacy and Domestic Politics'.					[10] Ibid. 436.

[11] See Peter B. Evans, 'Building an Integrative Approach to International and Domestic Politics', in *Double-Edged Diplomacy*, 397 at 415–16 (comparing domestic influence on international positions in democratic and non-democratic regimes); Kurt T. Gaubatz, 'Democratic States and Commitment in International Relations' (1996) 50 International Organization 108.

[12] This phenomenon of 'public choice' has been widely discussed in constitutional legal literature, drawing on the famed theorem by Kenneth Arrow. For a sample of the vast literature see: Daniel A. Farber and Philip P. Frickely, *Law and Public Choice* (Chicago: Chicago University Press, 1991); Patrick McAuslan, 'Public Law and Public Choice' (1988) 51 Modern Law Review 681; Cass Sunstein, 'Interest Groups in American Public Law' (1985) 38 Stanford Law Review 29.

[13] It has been suggested that one of Slovakia's reasons for going ahead with the Gabcikovo–Nagimaros project was the anti-Hungarian national sentiment, and the project's adverse effects on the Hungarian minority situated around the diversion canal. See 'Note: Flushing the Danube: the World Court's Decision Concerning the Gabcikovo Dam' (1998) 9 Colorado Journal of

and follow short-term domestic policies that help them stay in power. The consequences of such governmental proclivity are particularly disastrous for sustainable and optimal management of ICPRs. The negotiation and renegotiation of such treaties is often a source of conflicting domestic concerns and therefore especially prone to the agency problem of State negotiators. Any collective action must be based on the actors' shared long-term interest in indefinite future interaction. But when the 'shadow of the future'[14] is short, always limited by the next election, governments tend to discount the long-term national benefits of co-operation and prefer short-sighted gains.

A case in point is the recent reallocation of the waters of the Jordan river under the 1994 peace treaty between Israel and Jordan.[15] In May 1997, the Israeli government finally agreed to transfer a portion of water to Jordan.[16] This was in fact a forced transfer of revenues from one group, Israeli farmers located on the Israeli side of the Beit-Shean Valley, to another group, Jordanian landowners on the Jordanian side of the Valley. Due to this transfer, these landowners could continue to irrigate their lands without yielding their relatively large share to the thirsty domestic users in Jordan's cities. The Israeli farmers lost because they had less leverage under the Likud government than under the former Labour-led government (which in fact had balked from making the same concessions and stalled the negotiations for months).[17] At the same time, their Jordanian opposites were more effective in exerting domestic pressure on their King. These landowners, a very influential interest group in Jordan,[18] sought an increased share of the waters as a dividend for the

Environmental Law and Policy 401 at 412–13; Galambos, 'Environmental Conflict', at 85. For other water-related projects adversely affecting minorities see my 'Collective Action in the Utilization of Shared Freshwater: The Challenges of International Water Resources Law' (1996) 90 American Journal of International Law 384 at 404–5.

14   Robert Axelrod, *The Evolution of Co-operation* (New York: Basic Books, 1984), 126.

15   Israel–Jordan Treaty of Peace of 26 Oct. 1994, in (1995) 324 International Legal Materials 46.

16   The details on the agreement were reported to the Israeli government and made public only two weeks after its conclusion: 'Israel will Desalinate for Jordan 50 Million Cubic Meters Water per Year from the Springs of the Galilee Lake and the Gilbo'a Mountains' (15 May 1997) *Ha'aretz* (Israeli daily, in Hebrew). Apparently, the agreement comprises a letter from Israel's National Infrastructure Minister, Mr Ariel Sharon, to Jordan's Crown Prince Hassan from 20 May 1997, based on the Hussein–Netanyahu meeting from 8 May 1997: Zeev Schiff, 'An Awkward Agreement with Jordan', *Ha'aretz* (in Hebrew), 13 June 1997.

17   The agreement was linked to more general questions of peace and security supported by the larger Israeli public. Moreover, being politically associated with the Labour party in opposition, they could not threaten the stability of the Likud coalition. Apparently, the previous Labour government was more sensitive to the demands of the Israeli farmers and for that reason stalled the transfer.

18   These landowners, mostly residing in the capital Amman, have their lands tended by sharecroppers. See Rami G. Khouri, *The Jordan Valley: Life and Society below Sea Level* (London: Longman, 1981), 192–3. On this group's political influence see Tariq Tell and Toby Dodge, 'Peace and the Politics of Water in Jordan', in J. A. Allan (ed.), *Water, Peace and the Middle East* (London: Tauris Academic Studies, 1996), 169 at 182; Manuel Schiffler, 'Sustainable Development of Water Resources in Jordan: Ecological and Economic Aspects in a Long-Term Perspective', in J. A. Allen and Chibli Mallat (eds.), *Water in the Middle East* (London: I. B. Tauris Publishers, 1995), 239 at 243–5. There are of course indirect benefits to the greater Jordanian society, emphasized by officials, such as the prevention of desertification and of migration to the cities. See Munther Haddadin, 'Water Management: A Jordanian Viewpoint', in Allan (ed.), *Water, Peace and the Middle East*, 59 at 64 and 69 (explaining the reasons for not reallocating water from irrigation to domestic consumption and for subsidizing their costs).

support they had lent to the controversial peace with Israel. The Israeli farmers had to satisfy themselves with non-binding promises of future side-payments.[19] This forced exchange was clearly an outcome of negotiations between two governments seeking to further the partisan interests of domestic groups, in which the government that was more domestically vulnerable at a particular time won. No attempt at long-term planning was made and the population in Jordanian cities continued to suffer from insufficient water supply.[20]

The goal of promoting sustainable and optimal use of ICPRs therefore requires attention to potential conflicts of interest within both the international and the domestic spheres, and to the complex interactions between these two spheres. In particular, it poses a challenge to the law, both constitutional law and international law, in addressing the severe agency problem presented by the negotiating governments. International law must recognize that governments are agents of only a part of the communities they purport to represent at the international negotiating table. More specifically, it must recognize—as public choice literature has long recognized—that among the diverse domestic interest groups, governments are more likely to be influenced by those representing the interests of industry or agribusiness, namely, the potential polluters and heavy users. The law must counter these influences by creating conditions for governments that will prompt them, through inducements and constraints, to internalize and thus further the long-term national interests in international co-operation.

It should come as no surprise that the law, both international and constitutional, often fails to address these concerns in a satisfactory way. Instead, it is shaped by those same interest groups—seeking their own advantage.[21] It must therefore be recognized at the outset that the evolution of international norms addressing governments as agents is a difficult and perhaps prolonged process. The first step in this process has, of course, just been taken: the identification of the agency phenomenon and its influence on the law. The second step, taken in the next section of this chapter, is the assessment of the potentially relevant norms that address that phenomenon.

---

[19] Consisting of subsidies for research of potential intensification of uses of the reduced quotas. Schiff, 'Awkward Agreement'.

[20] United Press International, 'Jordan's water crisis unresolved' (3 Aug. 1998).

[21] Their interests are served, for example, by procedures for treaty ratification which involve the approval of the legislative branch (as opposed to ratification by the government which may be subject to a no-confidence vote). These legislative ratification procedures are often hailed as enhancing the government's international bargaining position, because the legislative body must be convinced to approve the treaty (see Putnam, 'Diplomacy and Domestic Politics', 448–50), but less attention is given to the fact that these ratification procedures increase the government's dependence on domestic interest groups and thus diminish the government's ability to further longer-term interests or the interests of non-dominant groups. Similarly, the tendency of national courts to defer to the government's international policies, although viewed as enhancing the government's international position, also contributes to the government's domestic vulnerability to the relatively stronger domestic groups, as the courts refuse to provide a forum to counter the stronger groups' policies. On this tendency of national courts see my 'Judicial Misgivings regarding the Application of International Norms: An Analysis of Attitudes of National Courts' (1993) 4 European Journal of International Law 159.

3. SUPPRESSING DOMESTIC MYOPICS THROUGH INTERNATIONAL LAW

This section examines a number of international norms that could create optimal incentives for, and constraints on, domestic political activity in respect of ICPR management. In general, the aim should be to reduce the possibility of groups influencing their governments into preferring short-sighted policies, while increasing the opportunities of these and other groups to influence outcomes at the international level through participation in the international decision-making and monitoring processes. The norms relate to the process of negotiating ICPR treaties and to the contents of such treaties. In addition, this section discusses the potential for relegating such treaties to lower-level undertakings among neighbouring sub-State entities such as provinces or towns. These norms provide tools for the public monitoring of governments and for making governments (or the domestic groups that support them) internalize the outcomes of their international policy choices.

3.1. Monitoring Against Defections: Governments' Duty to Provide Information to Counterparts and the Public

Any agreement on the allocation of shares in ICPR will be based on an analysis of all the available information regarding the States' supply of and demand for the resource. It is therefore expected that negotiators who pursue their State's long-term interest will have a strong incentive to provide their counterparts with as full and as accurate information as possible regarding their reliance on the shared resource. They could cheat, of course, but any short-term gains that might result from such a defection will be eclipsed by long-term losses, as governments are repeat players in the international negotiation game and retaliation is sure to follow. Anecdotal evidence supports this expectation.[22] Hence an international legal duty to provide accurate information may seem to be self-enforcing (and in other words, practically redundant).

However, this general expectation must be qualified due to three factors. First, there could be instances when local users of an ICPR who form a particularly influential interest group would insist that their government misinform the other governments, thereby externalizing the future costs of the defection (once they become known and retaliation takes place) to other domestic interest groups. A government will tend to cheat its partners if it values (or is led to value) immediate gains significantly more than it values potential future gains from co-operation. Second, governments may be tempted to promote narrow group interests by misinforming their general public, and even collude with their negotiating partners to misinform all

---

[22] State negotiators play a Prisoner's Dilemma game concerning the disclosure to their counterparts of their domestic constraints. However, when this game is repeated indefinitely, the incentive to co-operate conditionally often takes precedence. See Evans *et al.*, *Double-Edge Diplomacy*, 408–11 (survey found attempts to strategically manipulate external perceptions of what was ratifiable domestically, but not as often as expected and with much less success).

constituencies.[23] Without information, there will be little domestic awareness of lost opportunities.[24] Finally, it is quite possible that a government will be fed incorrect information by domestic interest groups, and hence inadvertently provide incorrect or incomplete information to its counterparts. There is indeed evidence that suggests that governments fail to realize their own political constraints and the possible prospects of ratification of a negotiated treaty, evidence that suggests clogged domestic information channels.[25]

Therefore the duty governments owe under international law to accumulate and provide 'the widest exchange of information'[26] on each State's current and expected supplies of, and demands from, a relevant ICPR is not always self-enforceable and is certainly not trivial, especially when it is complemented by a duty to disseminate that information to the general public. The dissemination of data will nurture domestic debate within all the participating countries regarding the range of options available to their governments, thereby increasing those governments' ability to assess public support, and at the same time constraining possible attempts by them to diverge from national interests.

The recognition of one government's duty to provide information to others could technically be based on the duty to co-operate in the utilization of shared resources,[27] or on the more general duty to negotiate resource-related agreements in good faith.[28] Since resource-sharing agreements focus on questions of management and allocation of the resource on the basis of the respective supplies and demands, withholding ample and accurate information on these two matters runs contrary to the duty to co-operate and does not constitute good faith.

A similar case could be made for recognizing a duty to employ and consult

---

[23] One example is the secretive 1997 agreement between Israel and Jordan, discussed in n. 16.

[24] See Downs and Rocke, *Optimal Imperfection?*, ch. 3 (negotiators are responsible, through the treaty-ratification process, for what they have agreed upon; they are rarely rebuked for their missed opportunities simply because those opportunities often remain unknown to the public).

[25] See Evans *et al.*, *Double-Edge Diplomacy*, 410; Putnam, 'Diplomacy and Domestic Politics', 452–3.

[26] Article 6 of the 1992 Helsinki Convention on the Protection and Use of Transboundary Watercourses and International Lakes (1992) 31 International Legal Materials 1312.

[27] See, with regard to shared freshwater, Article 8 of the United Nations Convention on the Law of the Non-Navigational Uses of International Watercourses (adopted on 21 May 1997) (1997) 36 International Legal Materials 700 ('the New-York Convention').

[28] See Article 3(5) of the New York Convention, mentioned in n. 27; Articles 6 and 7 of the Institute of International Law's Resolution on the Utilisation of Non-Maritime International Waters (Except for Navigation) adopted at its session at Salzburg (3–12 Sept. 1961) (1961) 49 (II) Annuaire de l'institut de droit international 370 (trans. in (1962) 66 American Journal of International Law 737). On the duty to negotiate in good faith see e.g. Julio A. Barberis, 'Bilan de recherches de la section de langue française du Centre d'étude et de recherche de l'Académie', in Centre for Studies and Research, *Rights and Duties of Riparian States of International Rivers* (The Hague: Peace Palace Library, 1990), 15 at 54–5; Janos Bruhacs, *The Law of Non-Navigational Uses of International Watercourses* (Dordrecht: Martinus Nijhoff, 1993), 176–8; Charles B. Bourne, 'Procedure in the Development of International Drainage Basins: The Duty to Consult and to Negotiate' (1972) 10 Canadian Yearbook of International Law 212 at 224–33; Dominique Alhertiere, 'Settlement of Public International Disputes on Shared Resources: Elements of a Comparative Study of International Instruments' (1985) 25 Natural Resources Journal 701.

experts. Scientists of various disciplines, identified recently as 'epistemic communities',[29] could suggest alternatives for reaching optimal solutions. Their contributions could realign politically skewed positions of domestic interest groups and hence of governments. Expert advice could also come from third parties, including NGOs. As the ICJ mentioned in its decision in the Gabcikovo–Nagimaros dispute, 'the readiness of the Parties to accept [third party] assistance would be evidence of the good faith with which they conduct bilateral negotiations'.[30]

The duty to disseminate the same information to the general public can be derived from the principle of freedom of information, a principle that is widely accepted in many democracies and imbedded in international human rights law. It also finds support in international instruments related to ICPRs. The 1992 Helsinki Convention on the Protection and Use of Transboundary Watercourses and International Lakes,[31] for example, requires riparians to 'ensure that information on the conditions of the transboundary waters, measures taken or planned to be taken to prevent, control or reduce transboundary impact, and the effectiveness of those measures, is made available to the public'.[32]

3.2. Increasing Public Participation

The duty to provide information among negotiators and to disseminate it to the public is not self-enforceable, and the opportunities for collusion between negotiators are numerous. *Post hoc* ratification procedures cannot ensure adequate public scrutiny of a government's behaviour in its dealings with foreign governments. The government-as-agent, enjoying the relative secrecy of international negotiations, may find it relatively easy to pursue partisan, short-term goals at the expense of its larger constituency. The necessity has therefore been felt to allow 'other voices' to be represented in the negotiation process, mainly NGOs who represent domestic voices but have failed to form strong domestic interest groups. For this reason, a right to be represented or consulted during such negotiations, or at the very least a right to be heard before agreements are signed, should be acknowledged—especially for those who may personally be affected adversely. Such an involvement would provide an opportunity for the representatives of less organized interest groups to present their concerns and have them examined, not only by governments, but also by the domestic interest groups of other States. The latter opportunity may lower the communication costs among environmentalists across national boundaries and thus increase

---

[29] See Peter M. Haas, 'Introduction: Epistemic Communities and International Policy Coordination' (1992) 46 International Organization 1.

[30] Paragraph 143 of the decision, discussed in n. 2. The Court was referring to the assistance and expertise offered by the Commission of the European Communities to settle the dispute.

[31] See n. 26.

[32] Article 16. See also Agenda 21, Chapter 18 (on freshwater resources), Principle 18.12(p) (concerning the dissemination of information as one of the means to improve integrated water management), reproduced in Nicholas A. Robinson (ed.), *Agenda 21 and the UNCED Proceedings* (New York: Oceana Publications, 1992), iv. 357 at 366.

their effectiveness. After an agreement has been ratified, public involvement in on-going decision-making processes of ICPR management institutions, through consultations, hearings, or even shared decision-making, is necessary for the same reasons.

The benefits of public participation have been recognized in recent international instruments. The 1992 Rio Declaration notes that '[e]nvironmental issues are best handled with the participation of all concerned citizens, *at the relevant level*'.[33] Chapter 18 of Agenda 21 calls for active public participation in shared freshwater management, which includes not only a right of hearing to oppose plans which could be detrimental to certain individuals or groups, but, more generally, requires States to aim at 'an approach of full public participation, including that of women, youth, indigenous people and local communities in water management policy-making and decision-making',[34] and suggests the '[d]evelopment of public partici-patory techniques and their implementation in decision-making'.[35] Although the New York Convention mentions neither of these ideas[36] and maintains the rigid separation between the international and domestic levels by providing only for State-to-State notification and consultation, there are scholars who find it possible to derive such participatory rights from more basic notions of civil and political rights,[37] and of general environmental law.[38]

3.3. Norms Regulating the Allocation of ICPRs

By regulating the process of allocating shares in the ICPR, the law requires governments to internalize interests that otherwise could be inundated by other voices in the domestic political process. Such a regulation involves both the inter-State determination of respective entitlements, and domestic allocation among local users.

A common stumbling-block to ICPR agreements is the demand that some States agree on reducing their share. Governments who face such a demand must resolve a domestic agency problem. Although such a reduction, in the context of a comprehensive regional agreement, may be in the country's best interest, it could jeopardize the interests of particularly influential sectors, typically agriculture or industry, who view their continuous use of the resource as vital. In fact, expecting such demands at

[33] Declaration of the UN Conference on Environment and Development, Rio de Janeiro, 3–14 June 1992, Principle 10 (emphasis added).

[34] Agenda 21, discussed in n. 32, Principle 18.9(c).

[35] Ibid., Principle 18.12(n). See also Ellen Hey, 'Sustainable Use of Shared Water Resources: The Need for a Paradigmatic Shift in International Watercourses Law', in Gerald H. Blake *et al.* (eds.), *The Peaceful Management of Transboundary Resources* (London: Graham and Trotman, 1995), 127 at 133.

[36] Ibid. 134–5.

[37] See Alan Boyle, 'The Role of International Human Rights in the Protection of the Environment', in A. Boyle and Michael Anderson (eds.), *Human Rights Approaches to Environmental Protection* (Oxford: Clarendon Press, 1996), 43 at 59.

[38] Ibid. 59–63; James Cameron and Ruth Mackenzie, 'Access to Environmental Justice and Procedural Rights in International Institutions', in Boyle and Anderson (eds.), *Human Rights Approaches*, 129 (esp. 134–5); Sionaidh Douglas-Scott, 'Environmental Rights in the European Union—Participatory Democracy or Democratic Deficit?', ibid. 109 at 112–20.

the outset, these sectors may even seek to block the commencement of negotiations. To reduce these difficulties to at least some extent, international law provides a vague standard governing the principles of reallocation, which gives conditional priority to existing beneficial uses. The prima-facie weight given to existing beneficial uses can encourage current users to support the commencement of negotiations and later to support the agreement.[39] The fact that this priority is only conditional leaves the door open for new users to demonstrate the merits of their claims. A strong claim for redistribution can be made when the existing allocation is grossly unequal, or if it is relatively inefficient, and therefore non-beneficial.

The law also has something meaningful to say with regard to the internal management of the national share of the ICPR. How States manage their respective shares of an ICPR affects the possibility of establishing regional co-operation in respect of it. This is because the domestic legal and institutional arrangements for the internal allocation and monitoring of the uses of the resource shape each State's ability to commit itself to international obligations, and to comply with them. They do so in a number of ways. First, the method for allocating shares among individual users, be it a relatively rigid system of inalienable property rights or a relatively flexible system of revocable permits, affects the government's ability to reduce its share of an ICPR. The existence of property rights to shares of the resource may tie the hands of State negotiators, either willingly or unwillingly, or increase enforcement costs through the litigation of expropriation cases. Second, different internal allocation methods shape the incentives of users to intervene in the political process in different ways. The more rigid the allocation system is, the higher the users' reliance on 'property rights', and hence the higher their incentive to obstruct the international agreement will be. Finally, poor administration and ineffective monitoring of uses and users by a government may add to the difficult task of implementing its international undertakings, or may be used as an excuse for failing to comply with them. Not surprisingly, powerful domestic groups are usually responsible for the existence of rigid allocations and for poor governmental controls.

International law could, through general customary law or a framework convention such as the New York Convention providing a set of principles, address these difficulties in a number of ways. First, it could stipulate that States must abstain from assigning inalienable property rights in shares of ICPRs and instead establish a more flexible system of revocable permits.[40] Although governments are usually empowered to requisition private property, this process, especially when protected by constitutional guarantees and judicial scrutiny, would be more complex and expensive than the termination or non-renewal of temporary permits. Second, the law—in this respect working in tandem with constitutional law— could lower the likelihood of skewed domestic allocation to powerful groups of

---

[39] See my 'Collective Action', 402.

[40] Eliminating the possibility of granting property rights does not preclude the option of establishing trade in ICPRs. The trade could be effected through market exchange of revocable permits, issued periodically by the institutions that manage these resources.

users by emphasizing the notions of equal access to national resources and individual rights to resources that sustain life, such as water and clean air.[41] Finally, the establishment of effective domestic institutions for the allocation of shares and the monitoring of uses, which could also provide procedural guarantees for transparency in decision-making, could lower the agency costs of both domestic resource management and international negotiations over the management of the ICPR. A duty to establish such effective institutions, included in a framework convention or considered as a general principle of international law, could thus promote collective action in ICPR management.

3.4. Insulating Treaties from Domestic Challenges

States parties to ICPR-sharing treaties may be tempted to invoke a number of legal doctrines escape their treaty obligations. In addition to the right to 'terminate' a treaty in response to another party's prior material breach,[42] the doctrine of *rebus sic stantibus* is also a potentially important and manipulable excuse,[43] as is the claim of a 'state of necessity'.[44] Lowering the threshold for any of these claims would increase the likelihood of domestic pressure being applied on governments to invoke them. Since long-term co-operation is the key to sustainable and optimal ICPR management, a high threshold for a unilateral right of exit is in the long-term interest of the participating States, and therefore appropriate. Other things being equal, the stricter the rules precluding a unilateral exit from treaty obligations are, the stronger a State party's commitments to long-term co-operation will be. Uncertainty as to possible future breaches will also be reduced.[45]

The recent ICJ decision in the *Gabcikovo–Nagimaros Case* clearly follows this logic and contributes to this effect. A project of huge proportions and with irreversible consequences, conceived by communist regimes of a past era, continues and will continue to constrain the decision-making power of current and future generations of leaders as well as communities within both countries, unless changed

---

[41] On the human right to the environment see nn. 37–8; on the human right to water see e.g. Stephen C. McCaffrey, 'A Human Right to Water: Domestic and International Implications' (1992) 5 Georgia International Environmental Law Review 1 at 12.

[42] Article 60 of the 1969 Vienna Convention on the Law of Treaties.

[43] Under Article 62(1) of the 1969 Vienna Convention on the Law of Treaties, a party may not unilaterally withdraw from its treaty obligations except under very strict conditions. This party must show, *inter alia*, that 'a fundamental change of circumstances has occurred with regard to those existing at the time of the conclusion of the treaty, and which was not foreseen by the parties'. (See also the Gabcikovo–Nagimaros decision, n. 2, at para. 104.) In most cases, the change in ICPR demand or supply would be incremental, quite foreseen by the parties to the agreement over the initial allocation.

[44] For a discussion of that claim which was raised by the Hungarian government, see the *Gabcikovo–Nagimaros Case*, n. 2, paras. 49–59.

[45] Note that treaties related to shared resources would be considered 'localized treaties' and therefore also survive State succession. See Article 12 of the 1978 Vienna Convention on Succession of States in Respect of Treaties, which was recognized by the ICJ as reflecting customary law and applied to the 1977 treaty in the *Gabcikovo–Nagimaros Case* (n. 2, at paras. 122–3).

through mutual consent.[46] To arrive at its decision the ICJ had to reject all unilateral moves by the two governments: Hungary's decision to suspend works at Nagimaros, the unilateral construction by Czechoslovakia of a diversion dam and bypass canal on Slovak territory,[47] and Hungary's subsequent purported termination of the treaty. The ICJ decided that the 1977 treaty survived the momentous political changes in both countries[48] and proclaimed that, under the treaty, both sides were obliged to negotiate in good faith the promotion of the objectives of the agreement, including the establishment of a 'joint regime'.[49] In reaching this conclusion the Court deliberately emphasized international undertakings at the expense of domestic pressures. It rejected Hungary's claim that a 'state of ecological necessity', if it existed, precluded the wrongfulness of the unilateral suspension of the project, and did so because Hungary could instead have recourse to negotiations to reduce the environmental risks.[50] It similarly rejected Hungary's claims to impossibility of performance, fundamental change of circumstances, and of a lawful response to Czechoslovakia's earlier material breach (namely, Slovakia's construction of the provisional diversion project).[51] The ICJ also found that Slovakia's diversion of the Danube waters breached its obligation towards Hungary to respect the right to an equitable and reasonable share of the river.[52] Despite its findings to the effect that both sides failed to comply with their obligations under the treaty, the ICJ concluded that 'this reciprocal wrongful conduct did not bring the Treaty to an end nor justify its termination'.[53] Finding the agreement flexible and therefore renegotiable, the ICJ held that the 1977 treaty continued to apply, requiring both sides to negotiate its implementation, taking into account current standards on environmental protection and sustainable development,[54] and to regard Slovakia's diversion dam and canal as a 'jointly operated unit' under the treaty regime.[55]

Without entering into the doctrinal aspects of the judgment,[56] it is revealing to examine its implications for the interface between domestic and international politics. The judgment clearly seeks to insulate international politics from the influence

---

[46] The agreement signed in 1977 between the Hungarian People's Republic and the Czechoslovak People's Republic provided for the construction and operation of a system of locks on the Danube river, between Gabcikovo (in Czechoslovak territory) and Nagymaros (in Hungarian territory), which would provide for diversion canals, and two hydroelectric power plants. The project was to be financed, constructed, and operated jointly, on an equal basis.

[47] The Court found that Czechoslovakia was entitled to proceed to its 'provisional solution', but not to put it into operation by damming the river.

[48] The court also rejected Hungary's notification of termination as having no legal effect.

[49] Ibid., at paras. 144–7.

[50] Ibid., at para. 57. (It found that Hungary did not prove an imminent peril, but made rather uncertain assumptions concerning long-term damage.)   [51] Ibid., at paras. 101–12.

[52] Ibid., at para. 78.   [53] Ibid., at para. 114.   [54] Ibid., at paras. 138–40.

[55] Ibid., at para. 146.

[56] The decision contains a number of important developments to the doctrine on international freshwater. These include, among others, the status of the New York Convention as declarative of customary law; the evolutionary interpretation of the 1977 treaty (see paras. 112 and 140); the duty to co-operate as inferring a duty to establish a joint regime (para. 147); as well as more general issues such as the conditions for recognizing changed circumstances, and the doctrine of necessity as a basis for terminating treaties.

of domestic politics.[57] Notwithstanding momentous internal political, economic, and social changes affecting both countries, and despite strong public pressure and even parliamentary resolutions, domestic options remain constrained by an international agreement entered into during a past era. Even when one government breaches its obligation to renegotiate in good faith, the other government cannot bow to internal public pressure and take unilateral action. It must exhaust all possible means, also through third parties, to persuade its counterpart to return to the negotiating table rather than act unilaterally. This is the cumulative message of the decision which, somewhat paradoxically, was shared by only a minority of six judges. The other nine judges approved the unilateral actions of one or another of the parties.[58] The message is captured in President Schwebel's declaration. Although he was 'not persuaded that Hungary's position as the Party initially at breach deprived it of a right to terminate the Treaty in response to Czechoslovakia's material breach', he joined the majority in imposing the resuscitated agreement on the parties.[59]

The Court stated clearly its preference for strong regional joint management institutions, institutions which 'reflect in an optimal way the concept of common utilisation of shared water resources'.[60] It certainly envisioned that in future disputes of this kind, governments, armed with this instruction from the ICJ, would be able to dodge domestic opposition to the international agreement simply because any alternative government would likewise be bound by the same obligations.

This outcome is not without its difficulties. Assuming that governments generally put their short-term interests first, existing agreements will tend to reflect the preferences of the strongest domestic actors at the time of signature. Often, these actors will be polluters and heavy users who would opt for lax control of their uses and impose externalities on third parties. Hence, other domestic interest groups that subsequently gain power will be constrained by what might be deemed an undesirable 'fatal embrace' of their predecessors. Indeed, the 1977 treaty serves as a prime example for such an agreement, the implementation of which may carry dire consequences for the shared environment. However, the ICJ addressed these concerns by reading into the treaty a degree of flexibility that opens the way to renegotiating its basic provisions in the light of new developments in international law, new understandings of environmental impacts, and new circumstances. Indeed, the Court upheld the 1977 treaty only after reading flexibility and mutuality into it, and after emphasizing the duty to achieve the object and purpose of the developing treaty relationship (an object and purpose that the Court in fact identified in the light of developing international law).[61] As this interpretation of the 1977 treaty indicates, any

---

[57] And perhaps also provide what the judges perceived as an appropriate *ad hoc* solution, having noticed the less than catastrophic outcomes of the 'provisional solution' as implemented by Czechoslovakia.

[58] Five judges approved Czechoslovakia's implementation of the provisional solution, whereas four other judges approved Hungary's termination of the treaty (para. 155).

[59] Ibid. (Declaration of President Schwebel).   [60] Ibid., para. 147.

[61] See n. 2, paras. 132–47. Judge Bedjaoui criticized this evolutionary interpretation: see his separate opinion, at http://www.icj-cij.org.

treaty on ICPR management must establish procedures that would provide for flexibility and mutuality, the prerequisites of long-term co-operation.[62]

Subsequent renegotiations of ICPR treaties should involve not only government officials, but also scientists and the general population, represented by various NGOs.[63] Thus, although these treaties remain beyond domestic challenge, domestic actors could be involved in renegotiations and present their demands for modifications in the international arena. Although the uses and allocations of ICPRs will be under constant reappraisal, renegotiations will be channelled into treaty bodies and away from potentially divisive domestic forums. Although there is always a risk that efforts to renegotiate problematic ICPR agreements will fail, this risk is significantly lower than the risks presented by unilateral abuses of any of the diverse 'escape doctrines' of the law of treaties.

3.5. Delegation of ICPR Management to Domestic Actors

The constitutional design of a government as a clearing-house for diverse and conflicting domestic interests is often responsible for failures to reach agreement on ICPR management. This design requires any sub-State actor wishing to co-operate across an international boundary with a neighbouring sub-State actor to invest resources in persuading her government to represent her *vis-à-vis* the other government. Each of the relevant governments may, however, have different interests, due to the influence of other domestic sectors or to linkages with other issues. In order to overcome this structural failure, it is necessary to develop the possibility of direct low-level interaction among such sub-State actors.

Numerous examples exist for sub-State co-operation in matters related to environmental protection and water utilization, particularly in Western Europe, but also between US States and Canadian provinces.[64] These examples suggest that it may be beneficial to resort at times to sub-State agreements negotiated by sub-State actors such as governors of provinces or mayors of neighbouring cities, in order to reduce the complexities involved with heterogeneous actors such as States.

Sub-State co-operation may be particularly necessary when national interests, such as security or trade, overshadow ICPR politics. A recent case in point is a 1996 agreement between two municipalities, the Regional Council of Emek-Hefer, located on the coastal plain of Israel, and the municipality of Tul-Karem, in the Palestinian-controlled area of the West Bank. These two municipalities share a small, severely polluted drainage basin, in which runoff from Palestinian towns and villages

---

[62] My 'Collective Action', at 409–11.   [63] See discussion in section 3.2.

[64] Maria Teresa Ponte Iglesias, 'Les Accords conclus par les autorités locales de différent États sur l'utilisation des eaux frontalières dans le cadre de la coopération transfrontalière' (1995(2)) Schweizerische Zeitschrift für internationales und europäisches Recht 103 at 129–30; Ulrich Beyerlin, 'Transfrontier Co-operation between Local or Regional Authorities', in *Encyclopedia of Public International Law*, vi. 350; Pierre-Marie Dupuy, 'La Coopération régionale transfrontalière et le droit international' (1977) 23 Annuaire française de droit international 837. See also the New York–Quebec Agreement on Acid Precipitation (1982), reproduced in (1982) 21 International Legal Materials 721.

as well as from Jewish settlements flows through a small stream across the Green Line into the Emek-Hefer area.[65] Since negotiations between the Israeli government and the Palestinian Council were blocked, the only avenue open to local administrators wishing to pursue a policy of rehabilitation was direct low-level negotiation, bypassing the deadlock at the national level. After having received implicit permission from both governments—the Israeli Ministry of the Environment and Chairman Arafat—the heads of the two municipalities met and signed an agreement outlining their commitment to co-operation.[66]

The promise of sub-State co-operation is also significant in the design of joint institutions for ICPR management. Instead of relying on the member states as the basic building blocks of such institutions, these institutions could be based on a system of smaller sub-units that co-ordinate the use of the resource in the different sub-components of the ICPR.[67] Thus, instead of a river commission headed by representatives of all participating national governments, for example, the system could be based on a cluster of sub-basin institutions, each comprising representatives of the local communities in each area. Public participation could be more effective and less costly in smaller-scale institutions, which are likely to be more sensitive to the concerns of those directly affected by the uses of the ICPR. The existence of a number of smaller institutions, each responsible for a single sub-basin, could facili-

---

[65] As a result, not only is the water unsuitable for drinking or irrigation, but bad smells and mosquitoes prevent the development of a beautiful landscape into a resort, and land developers cannot develop vast areas for the same reasons. The amount of pollutants is rising constantly, due to population increase.

[66] The originals are in both Arabic and Hebrew. My translation follows:

Letter of Intent

The District of Tul-Karem, the Municipality of Tul-Karem and Emek Hefer Regional Council recognize the acute necessity to promote and protect the environment, for the protection of the water we drink and the soil we cultivate. For the benefit of the inhabitants of Tul-Karem and environs, the Hefer Valley and environs.

It was therefore decided to establish a steering and planning committee that will be entrusted with supplying mutual expert solutions to resolve the problems in the short and immediate range and in the long range.

Those who stand at the helm will jointly work for obtaining funding and consent from international bodies, in an effort to realize the plans and to implement them.

The written text, in both languages, was prepared in advance by Mr Izkovic. He was escorted by Mr Abu-To'ama, a mayor of an Arab municipality in Israel, who made the initial contacts. Mr To'ama also signed the letter. The envisioned plans are rather ambitious and complex, and include sewage-treatment facilities to be constructed with international financing on West Bank territory, supplying treated water for Palestinian agricultural use.

[67] Negotiations over a similar sewage treatment facility are under way in another small catchment area further south, in which a few Israeli towns and the Palestinian-controlled town of Qalqilia are situated (*Ha'aretz*, 1 Mar. 1998). It seems that such a functional approach is nowhere more appropriate than in politically divided cities such as Jerusalem or Nicosia. Jerusalem remains the only major metropolitan area in Israel whose wastewater flows untreated, which is evidence of the immense political obstacles to a proper solution. Nicosia, however, although torn between the Greeks and the Turkish Cypriots, continues to benefit from the joint operation of a sewage system constructed before the division of the city. For options for low-key yet crucial joint ventures for Jerusalem, and a description of the Nicosian model, see Eran Feitelson and Qasem Hassan Abdul-Jaber, *Prospects for Israeli-Palestinian Co-operation in Wastewater Treatment and Re-Use in the Jerusalem Region* (Jerusalem: Jerusalem Institute for Israel Studies/Palestinian Hydrology Group, 1997).

tate efficient intra- and inter-basin trade in shares of the resource.[68] The central institution could serve as a forum for negotiations and even a clearing-house for transactions among sub-basin representatives.

These considerations of efficiency may be bolstered further by considerations of human rights and group rights. One can trace in international law an increasing recognition of the claims of minority groups, especially indigenous peoples, to a right to manage autonomously the natural resources in their vicinity as part of their claim to self-determination and cultural protection.[69] Delegating authority over ICPR management may therefore be beneficial not only economically, but also socially.

This idea of a special type of subsidiarity is not a panacea. There could be regions where cross-border co-operation is particularly difficult due to social and economic reasons and where co-operation at the national level would therefore be more effective. In multi-ethnic countries, central governments may worry that such cross-border co-operation might spur secessionist efforts by ethnic minorities situated in border areas. But these concerns do not rule out the potential of such agreements to provide positive results in some situations. International law should therefore offer normative frameworks to sustain such localized cross-boundary agreements and encourage their development.[70]

These normative frameworks must of course include rules concerning the law governing such sub-State agreements. When I asked the Mayor of the Emek-Hefer Regional Council, Mr Itzovicz, what he thought was the status of the inter-municipal agreement he had signed with the Governor of the Tul-Karem District, he did not have a clear answer. But he did say that they were both contemplating the establishment of an 'international corporation' to take over the design and implementation of the rehabilitation plans, and for that purpose were seeking legal advice on the appropriate steps that had to be taken.[71] Needless to say, the lack of clear legal infrastructure for such undertakings may very well undermine this joint venture.

International law has so far turned a blind eye to sub-State agreements, an omission

---

[68] See Eyal Brill, 'Applicability and Efficiency of Market Mechanisms for Allocation of Water with Bargaining' (Ph.D. dissertation, Hebrew University of Jerusalem, 1997) (in Hebrew), 102.

[69] The Draft United Nations Declaration on the Rights of Indigenous Peoples, adopted by the Sub-Commission on Prevention of Discrimination and Protection of Minorities, UN Commission on Human Rights, on 26 Aug. 1994 (reproduced in (1995) 34 International Legal Materials 541) recognizes the value of water resources to indigenous peoples' social structure, culture, and tradition (see the Preamble). The Draft Declaration sets out to ensure, *inter alia*, the indigenous peoples' right to maintain and strengthen their relationship with their land, territories, waters, and other resources (Article 25), to own and to manage these resources (Article 26), and their right to participate in decisions affecting these resources. See also Benedict Kingsbury, 'Claims by Non-State Groups in International Law' (1992) 25 Cornell International Law Journal 481.

[70] See Dupuy, 'La Coopération régionale', at 860 ('Moins que jamais, la frontière n'apparaît comme une ligne de partage brutale des compétences étatiques. Elle désigne au contraire une zone privilégiée de la collaboration des populations et des leurs représentants.'). See also Agenda 21, Chapter 18, Principle 18.12(o)(i) (recommending, 'as appropriate', to develop and strengthen mechanisms at all levels concerned, including 'at the lowest appropriate level' including 'the decentralization of government services to local authorities, private enterprises and communities').

[71] Personal interview with Mr Itzkovich, Emek Hefer Regional Council, 21 Jan. 1997.

that severely weakens their legal status and deters their very creation. Current doctrine seems to suggest that such agreements will not be governed by international law, but rather by one or a number of national laws. This doctrine is derived from two principles: first, the principle of unity of action of the State at the international level; and second, the lack of legal personality of sub-State entities in the international sphere.[72] Indeed, it is hardly surprising that national governments seek to maintain their monopoly as sole representatives of their people. As a result, international law, based and developed through State consent, reflects a cartel of power among national governments. But this doctrine may lead to inefficient outcomes by increasing the transaction costs of sub-State entities that negotiate with neighbouring communities across the border.[73] The negotiators will have to select the national law of one of the parties, or of a third party. The designation of one party's law as governing the agreement may be seen to indicate the dominance of that party, and thus may be resisted by the others. More importantly, such an assignment subjects the agreement to the possibility of unilateral modifications of the governing law of one of the States, and otherwise renders it vulnerable to one-sided changes of policy by the central government of that State. It also limits the possibility for 'evolutionary' interpretations of the parties' undertakings in light of developing norms of international law.[74] Being unable to designate international law as a set of default rules that could govern such agreements, sub-State entities must reinvent the wheel whenever they negotiate agreements. Often they are not even aware of the need to set their agreement in a valid international law framework, or lack the resources for doing so, and thus simply defer and possibly exacerbate the problem.[75]

As the examples above demonstrate, sub-State co-operation may often be less costly to establish and maintain than intergovernmental agreements. There is therefore good reason to develop rules to guide the contracting parties and provide authoritative assistance to them in cases of eventual breach. One such possibility is the conclusion of a framework convention. Just as the 1986 Vienna Convention on the Law of Treaties between States and International Organisations or between International Organisations[76] was a response to an emerging need to regulate an evolving phenomenon, a similar convention may be necessary in this context to address sub-State agreements. 'Soft law' approaches such as model rules may also prove helpful in guiding negotiators.

In 1980, the Council of Europe set an important precedent by adopting a frame-

---

[72] Ponte Iglesias, 'Les Accords', 122–4; Dupuy, 'La Coopération régionale', 852; Beyerlin, 'Transfrontier Co-operation', 64.

[73] See Joel P. Trachtman, 'L'Etat C'est Nous: Sovereignty, Economic Integration and Subsidiarity' (1992) 33 Harvard International Law Journal 459 at 472 (on the justification of the existence of political institutions as reducing transaction costs).

[74] For such an influence, see the *Gabcikovo–Nagimaros Case*, as discussed in n. 61 above.

[75] See Ulrich Beyerlin, 'Transfrontier Co-operation', 353 (about half of the agreements reviewed lacked any reference to a governing law).

[76] Concluded at Vienna on 21 Mar. 1986, UN Doc. A/CONF.129/15.

work convention to facilitate sub-State co-operation.[77] This convention requires State parties[78] to facilitate and foster such co-operation, to 'encourage any initiative by territorial communities or authorities', and to 'endeavour to resolve any legal, administrative or technical difficulties likely to hamper the development and the smooth running of transfrontier co-operation'.[79] The convention also provides two sets of outline agreements—one envisioning sub-State arrangements backed by the relevant national governments, and the other providing for agreements solely at the sub-State level—which local representatives may adopt and modify according to their specific requirements. Some of these agreements provide for default choice of law rules which refer to the law of the State of one of the parties, such as the law of the State whose local authority provides 'the principal service, or failing this, the local authority with the most important financial involvement',[80] or, in case a transfrontier private law association is established, the law of the country in which the headquarters are situated.[81] Other models provide (incomplete) arbitration machinery in case a dispute arises.[82] Further guidelines were prescribed in 1995 in an Additional Protocol to the Outline Convention.[83] A similar effort is now needed at the international level. In light of the previous discussion, this effort must clearly be aimed at subjecting such agreements to international law unless the parties choose otherwise.[84] Once approved by the internal legal processes such agreements must be considered binding upon the respective governments.

Until such a framework convention is operative, it may be possible to argue that,

---

[77] European Outline Convention on Transfrontier Co-operation between Territorial Communities or Authorities, ETS No. 106, Madrid, 21 May 1980, reproduced at http://www.coe.fr/eng/legaltxt/106e.htm.

[78] To date, twenty states have ratified it, and eight more have recently signed it.

[79] Articles 1, 3, 4 of the Convention.

[80] See Article 3 of Model Agreement no. 1.4 (Model Inter-State Agreement on Contractual Transfrontier Co-Operation Between Local Authorities).

[81] Model no. 2.11 (Model Agreement on the Creation and Management of Transfrontier Parks Between Private Law Associations, Article 1.2).

[82] See e.g. Model 2.4 (Outline Contract for the Provision of Supplies or Services Between Local Authorities in Frontier Areas), Article 5 (applicable law), and Article 7 (arbitration procedure which does not provide for cases where one of the parties refuses to appoint an arbitrator).

[83] ETS No. 159, adopted on 9 Nov. 1995, will enter into force on 1 Dec. 1998, after having been ratified by five States: http://www.coe.fr/tablconv/159t.htm.
Three salient principles are put forward by this Protocol:

1. States will recognize and respect such agreements provided they conform with national law and with the states' international commitments (Article 1.1). States' commitments will not be affected by the agreement which entails only the responsibilities of the contracting sub-State parties (Article 1.2);
2. Policies adopted under the agreement will have the status of measures taken under the national legal system of the entities involved (Article 2), and will be subject to the same supervision imposed by the law of each contracting State (Article 6.1);
3. The applicable law will be the national law of the State in which the headquarters of the joint body are located (Article 4.1 and 6.2).

[84] In general, it seems reasonable that similar norms to those governing international agreements should apply, *mutatis mutandis*, to these agreements. Of course, the relationships between international and sub-State agreements must expressly be spelled out, as must the question of responsibility for breach by non-parties.

absent evidence of the parties' express wish to the contrary, sub-State agreements are assumed to be governed by international law, both as the objective and the subjective law of the agreements. The determination that international law is the objective law of such agreements may be based on an express or implied delegation of powers from States to their lower level components. This delegation may be viewed as bestowing upon the sub-State actors, for the purpose of these agreements, the status of a subject of international law which is capable of undertaking international obligations.[85] Under this doctrine, the central government would be estopped, both under domestic constitutional law as well as under international law, from disregarding such agreements. In this sense, sub-State undertakings would constrain the respective governments *vis-à-vis* their domestic sub-State entities and *vis-à-vis* the other governments whose sub-State entities are the other party or parties to the agreement.

The promise of enhanced local cross-border interaction through sub-State co-operation suggests that the law on shared resources must not remain indifferent but rather complement its recognition of the validity of such agreements by endorsing them as potentially fruitful modes of co-operation. Such a positive signal could be embodied in a principle of subsidiarity, akin to the subsidiarity principle under European law,[86] which could be included as one of the factors that are considered in determining the equitable and reasonable allocation of ICPRs.[87]

4. CONCLUSION

The fact that State actors are agents representing heterogeneous constituencies and are subject to domestic pressures does not necessarily lower the prospects of beneficial international co-operation over the management of ICPRs. But it does refine the understanding of this potential by emphasizing the often neglected domestic facet of any international agreement. This facet has so far been neglected by international legal doctrine, which still views States as 'black boxes' and governments as the sole representatives of States' preferences and commitments.

This chapter has examined the influence that domestic politics have on States' policies in terms of co-operation in ICPR management, as well as the influence that

---

[85] Cf. Christoph Schreuer, 'The Waning of the Sovereign State: Towards a New Paradigm for International Law?' (1993) 4 European Journal of International Law 447 at 455–6 ('The logical outcome of these developments would be a general opening up of the treaty process for non-state actors to the extent that they have assumed the functions covered by the respective treaties.').

[86] Article 5 (formerly Article 3b) of the Consolidated Version of the Treaty Establishing the European Community (reproduced in http://ue.eu.int/Amsterdam/en/traiteco/en1.htm ('[. . .] In areas which do not fall within its exclusive competence, the Community shall take action, in accordance with the principle of subsidiarity, only if and insofar as the objectives of the proposed action cannot be sufficiently achieved by the Member States and can therefore, by reason of the scale or effects of the proposed action, be better achieved by the Community. [. . .]').

[87] See Article 6 of the New York Convention (on 'factors relevant to equitable and reasonable utilization' of freshwater).

some international norms have on domestic politics. The effort has been to discover appropriate international and national norms that would influence domestic politics in ways that could provide a solid legal and political basis for co-operation.

As suggested in this chapter, international norms can contribute to regional co-operation in a number of ways: by increasing the information available to all parties and their constituencies, by allowing for public participation in negotiations and decision-making, by regulating international and domestic allocations and reallocations of the ICPR, by strengthening existing agreements against domestic challenges, and by providing strong and clear bases for sub-State undertakings.

Governments may hesitate to accept such policies and implement them through general or specific treaties. After all, these policies do not assist the influential domestic interest groups to which many governments listen. NGOs, however, can be effective in raising awareness and mobilizing public opinion to support such initiatives. And ultimately the ICJ, which is somewhat removed from the immediate interests and domestic politics of national governments and considered by some to have 'a position of special trust and responsibility in relation to the principles of environmental law',[88] could take the lead towards such a development. In its recent decision concerning the Danube river, it certainly proved that it is able and willing to do so.

[88] Judge Weeramantry in Request for an Examination of the Situation in Accordance with Paragraph 63 of the Court's Judgment of 20 December 1974 in the Nuclear Tests (New Zealand v. France) Case (1995) ICJ Reports 288 at 345.

7

Human Rights and the Politics of Representation: Is There a Role For International Law?

CHRISTINE CHINKIN

1. INTRODUCTION

Social scientists have described in various terms the phenomenon of social movements that are 'conscious, collective, organised attempt[s] to bring about or resist large-scale change in the social order by non-institutionalised means'.[1] While definitions tend to emphasize the deliberate challenge presented to the established political, legal, or social order, there are divergent views as to the level of organization that occurs within a social movement itself. Thus for one author a social movement is 'unpredictable, irrational, unreasonable and disorganised', whereas another sees it as 'a group of people consciously attempting to build a radically new social order'.

In the 1990s international lawyers are becoming more aware of a number of social movements that are impinging directly upon their discipline and that are shaping an international society characterized by the participation of a broader range of actors than the sovereign States of the post-Westphalian era. Accordingly, it has been argued that international society is undergoing a paradigmatic shift from the era of geopolitics to one of geogovernance and that the starting-point for legal regulation of this 'radically new, inclusive social order' is not the positivist emphasis of the *Lotus Case*,[2] but instead a viewpoint that encompasses broader interests of social justice, such as the protection of human rights and of the environment. Richard Falk has noted that there are, however, two interlocking, and often clashing, trends that are instrumental in shaping this shift, which he terms 'globalisation from above' and 'globalisation from below'.[3] The former expression encapsulates the non-transparent, concealed movements of interests supporting economic globalization and capital flow. The latter embodies the apparently more democratic mobilization of what has been termed 'international civil society':[4] the formation of transnational networks of

---

[1] The definitions used in this paragraph were all cited by R. Cohen, 'Global Social Movements: Introductory Remarks', Social Movements Conference, University of Warwick, Mar. 1998 (paper in possession of author).

[2] *The Lotus Case (France v. Turkey)* (1927) PCIJ Series A, No. 10.

[3] R. Falk, 'The Nuclear Weapons Advisory Opinion and the New Jurisprudence of Global Civil Society' (1997) 7 Transnational Law and Contemporary Problems 333.

[4] See e.g. A. Arato and J. Cohen, *Civil Society and Political Theory* (Cambridge, Mass.: MIT Press, 1992).

peoples for the achievement of common goals,[5] drawn from diverse social movements, for example those of human rights, the 'green' movement, the international women's movement, and religious movements. In view of the anti-democratic tendencies of the former,[6] one study has concluded that 'the crucial role of civil society today is to advocate democracy' and to 'democratize global governance by harnessing the advantages that can come from globalization—such as new communications—while resisting its drawbacks, most specifically the centralization of economic power in the hands of TNCs [transnational corporations] and the international economic institutions—the WTO, the IMF and the World Bank'.[7] In both cases the pursuit of the preferred objectives has been transformed by the technological revolution that allows instantaneous communications between and across previously unimagined audiences.[8]

Both processes are fuelled by the claims and activities of a range of non-State actors that participate throughout the international legal order in diverse ways that cut across the established categories of international law.[9] They raise many questions about the international legal process at the end of the twentieth century. Does this 'paradigmatic shift' represent a social movement towards international democratization?[10] If so, is it new? Who are the key players? Who is represented within this wider participation and how is representation determined? Who remains excluded? What are the strategies engaged and in what arenas? Where are they successful in achieving their objectives and where do they fall short? How do they penetrate an international legal order formed by States to their own advantage, and with what effect? Are we witnessing a reallocation of international power, through a confrontation between those that previously held a monopoly of power (States) and those seeking to attain it, causing fragmentation, disruption, and chaos through the undermining of the stability of the State-centred system? Alternatively, is there a process of orderly accommodation and adaptation to the demands of these diverse players? Do these different globalizations represent a qualitative change in the international legal structure, or merely a quantitative one? Are they challenging the existing social order, or

---

[5] 'Networking' is understood as a regular exchange of information between persons who share common areas of concern through bypassing formal power structures; J. Barnard, *The Female World from a Global Perspective* (Bloomington, Ind.: Indiana University Press, 1987).

[6] It has been argued that while democracy and concepts of good governance 'are central to the ideology of the free market and are conditions imposed by donors and creditors, the reality is very different': M. Chossudovsky, *The Globalisation of Poverty Impacts of IMF and World Bank Reforms* (London: Zed Books, 1997), 36.

[7] R. Krut, *Globalization and Civil Society NGO Influence in International Decision-Making* (UN Research Institute for Social Development, 1997), 1.

[8] Compare J.-M. Guehenno: '[I]n the age of networks, the relationship of citizens to the body politic is in competition with the infinity of connections they establish outside it', cited in P. Spiro, 'New Actors on the International Stage' (1998) 2 Hofstra Law and Policy Symposium 101 at 103.

[9] For a discussion of the factors that have led to the consequent challenge to State authority see ibid., at 102.

[10] See J. Crawford, 'Democracy and International Law' (1993) 64 British Yearbook of International Law 113 for a discussion of the ways in which the current international legal order is non-democratic.

working effectively within it to achieve radical change, or merely to broaden the agenda and range of international concerns? What is the impact of such movements upon the questions of compliance and implementation of international obligations? Such questions evidently go to the heart of the relationship between international law and politics.

This chapter examines some of these questions in the limited context of the social movement for the more effective promotion and protection of international human rights, and even more specifically, the human rights of women. It seeks to show how this movement, one of the most powerful social forces since 1945, has been used by another social movement, the international women's movement, to create networks that confront the global subordination of women, and how this has challenged the boundaries, concepts, and structures of human rights law, and forced changes in the international legal regime.[11] It concludes that through this demand for representation, the presumed role for international law has been enhanced, but that nevertheless the legal regime for the protection of women's human rights remains a blunt instrument with which to combat the forces of globalization from above.

2. NGOS AND THE UN SYSTEM: TO ENGAGE OR TO STAND ALOOF?

During the 1990s the movement for the international recognition of women's human rights has achieved some notable success in penetrating the international legal order and has become a model for non-governmental organization (NGO) interventions.[12] Such success is indicated by a number of key events: the affirmation at the Vienna World Conference on Human Rights that the 'human rights of women and of the girl-child are an inalienable, integral and indivisible part of universal human rights';[13] the adoption by consensus in the United Nations General Assembly of the Declaration on the Elimination of Violence against Women;[14] the assertion at the Cairo Conference on Population and Development of the reproductive rights of women;[15] and the explicit inclusion of sexual crimes against women within the jurisdiction and indictments of the International War Crimes Tribunals for the Former

---

[11] Networking has become the prototypical women's strategy at local, regional, and international levels. See Barnard, *Female World*.

[12] For a fuller discussion of the work of NGOs in human rights see D. Weissbrodt, 'The Contribution of International Non-Governmental Organizations to the Protection of Human Rights', in T. Meron, *Human Rights in International Law: Legal and Policy Issues* (Oxford: Clarendon Press, 1984), 403. For the work of a particular human rights NGO see L. Wiseberg and H. Scoble, 'The International League for Human Rights. The Strategy of a Human Rights NGO' (1977) 7 Georgia Journal of International and Comparative Law 289.

[13] UN World Conference on Human Rights: Vienna Declaration and Programme of Action, 25 June 1993, reproduced in (1993) 32 International Legal Materials 1661.

[14] General Assembly Declaration on the Elimination of Violence against Women, GA Res. 48/103, 20 Dec. 1993.

[15] The International Conference on Population and Development, Cairo, 1994.

Yugoslavia and Rwanda[16] and the Rome Statute for the International Criminal Court[17] are perhaps the highlights. These advances are largely attributable to the campaigns engaged in, and co-ordinated by, women's international NGOs as they have sought representation within the global arenas.

The phenomenon of transnational action by non-State actors is not new.[18] Non-State agencies, whether they be committed people acting essentially alone or through transnational networks of NGOs, have long been instrumental in persuading States to foster human rights standards within international instruments and subsequently to comply with the obligations thus incurred.[19] NGOs are but one manifestation of the broader concept of international civil society[20] and it is debatable whether the explosion in the number, diverse activities, and membership of NGOs can of itself be accurately depicted as a social movement.[21] As seen above, social or popular movements are presented typically in terms of their radical agenda, unpredictability, irrationality, and fluidity, while by definition NGOs assume organization, formal membership, and internal mandates.[22] Further, since they are labelled in terms of what they are not, that is, non-governmental, the assumption of the primacy of the State, whether acting alone or through intergovernmental organizations, is not fundamentally opposed. Indeed, civil society is best able to function where the State retains a strong (in the sense of accountable and inclusive) government. It has therefore been argued that '[g]lobal civil society in parallel would rely on strong national

---

[16]   The Statute of the International Criminal Tribunal for Former Yugoslavia, SC Res. 827, 25 May 1993; Statute of the International Criminal Tribunal for Rwanda, SC Res. 955, 8 Nov. 1994.

[17]   Rome Statute for the International Criminal Court, 15 June–17 July 1998, UN Doc. A/Conf. 183/C.1/L.76.

[18]   This is especially true in respect of universalist issues such as the abolition of slavery, workers' rights, women's political rights, and the peace movement. See S. Charnovitz, 'Two Centuries of Participation: NGOs and International Governance' (1997) 18 Michigan Journal of International Law 183. For a full account of NGO activity before 1945 in many distinct fields including business and commerce, communications, agriculture, the press, and sport, see L. Cromwell White, *International Non-Governmental Organizations: Their Purposes, Methods and Accomplishments* (New Brunswick: Rutgers University Press, 1951).

[19]   Non-State actors in the form of employees and employers associations have long had formal representation within the International Labour Organisation, including in its standard setting activities. See V. Leary, 'Lessons from the Experience of the International Labour Organisation', in P. Alston (ed.), *The United Nations and Human Rights* (Oxford: Clarendon Press, 1992), 580.

[20]   Bianchi uses a functional analysis to distinguish between NGOs and other transnational networks, in particular professional networks; A. Bianchi, 'Globalization of Human Rights: The Role of Non-State Actors', in G. Teubner (ed.), *Global Law without a State* (Brookfield: Dartmouth, 1997), 179 at 192.

[21]   Secretary-General's Report, UN Doc. E/AC.70/1994/5, 15 June 1994, para. 9. The Report was prepared in accordance with ECOSOC Res. 1993/214; see also Arrangements and practices for the interaction of non-governmental organizations in all activities of the United Nations system, Report of the Secretary-General, UN Doc. A/53/170, 10 July 1998, para. 2.

[22]   For definitions of NGOs see H. H.-K. Rechenberg, 'International Relations and Legal Co-operation in General Diplomacy and Consular Relations', in R. Bernhardt (ed.), Encyclopedia of Public International Law, ix (Amsterdam: North-Holland, 1986), 276. The European Convention on Non-Governmental Organizations, Article 1, defines an NGO as having a non-profit-making aim of international utility; being established under the internal law of a Party; carrying on activities with effect in at least two States; and having its statutory office in one Party and central management and control in that Party, or another Party.

government and strong international governance from a reformulated United Nations'.[23]

Nevertheless, it has been due to the instrumentality of NGOs and the increasing accommodation of their demands that the concept of civil society has infiltrated the formal structures of the international legal system. The determination of NGO members at San Francisco resulted in the adoption of human rights articles within the UN Charter[24] and in the only Charter provision on NGOs, Article 71. This provides that the Economic and Social Council (ECOSOC) 'may make arrangements for consultation with non-governmental organizations which are concerned with matters within its competence'.

This rather unpromising starting-point has allowed the relationship between NGOs and the UN to develop, a relationship that was originally defined in terms of consultation, not representation. Nevertheless, the concept of accreditation has allowed NGO admission to international intergovernmental organizations (IGOs), and fuller participation therein than could have been envisaged by the drafters of Article 71. By 1998 over 1,350 NGOs have received some form of consultative status with ECOSOC,[25] which has resulted in access to the political human rights bodies of the UN such as the Human Rights Commission. Within these arenas NGOs are able to lobby, disseminate materials, and make presentations on matters of concern to them.

Inevitably, the evolution of the association between NGOs and States that has been largely played out within IGOs has produced tensions on all sides. For some States, the presence of NGOs in these intergovernmental arenas has been constraining and perceived as undermining State sovereignty. This was especially evident, for example, in the sometimes stormy relationship between NGOs and the Human Rights Commission over such issues as the naming of States responsible for gross violations of human rights and itemizing specific violations in reports.[26] States have had to come to terms with acceding to some NGO demands while attempting to preserve their privileged positions. In turn, individual NGOs have had to determine the extent of their participation in international arenas that have been moulded by States for their own purposes. Similarly, they have had to evaluate the benefits of seeking international law reform through the application of existing sources and other established channels against those of seeking radical change in, and of, these structures. The advantages for NGOs of collective, co-ordinated action through established State arenas may be offset by the risks of compromising their own independence through the implied legitimation of those structures, thus divorcing NGOs from the social movements that spawned them. The concepts of Apology and

---

[23] Krut, *Globalization*, at 3.
[24] Charter of the United Nations, Articles 1 (3), 55, and 56.
[25] See ECOSOC Res. 1296 (1968); ECOSOC Res. 1996/31; Secretary-General's Report (1998), at para. 2.
[26] P. Alston, 'The Commission on Human Rights', in Alston, *The United Nations*, 126 at 202.

Utopia[27] can be applied to the actions of non-State actors as well as to those of States: NGOs may seek a utopian world where the interests of social justice and human rights prevail, but too often must retreat apologetically into State-sponsored structures and the traditional machinery of international law to ensure legitimacy within those terms.

This dilemma is enhanced where the objective is the advancement of the international human rights of women. Feminists have long struggled with the quandary of using legal structures—themselves highly gendered—to combat women's subordination.[28] In the words of Peter Willets:

> The problem is that feminism . . . [is] hostile to the concept of organisation equating it with hierarchical patterns of authority. Nevertheless, networks, collectives and communities always have some organisational structure, even if it is non-hierarchical. If the movement is to cross country boundaries, then establishing effective communication channels, preparing the content of communications, transcending language barriers and meeting the associated costs all require a greater degree of bureaucracy rather than ad hoc informal communication.[29]

3. NGO ACCESS AND PARTICIPATION

3.1. Standard Setting

Despite such misgivings, the preferred response for many (but by no means all) NGOs has been to demand access to existing international institutions for the expression of their own agendas, while States have conceded to some of their demands. This has led to the consideration of NGO concerns both in the formulation of international human rights norms and in the application of those norms. In this way NGOs have become part of an international social movement for the inclusion of voices drawn from international civil society to influence State behaviour and to shape the discourse.

In the context of international standard setting NGOs have become sophisticated in co-ordinating their strategies to plug into available structures for the pursuit of their own objectives. A 'free space'[30] that has been exploited by women's NGOs in

---

[27] M. Koskenniemi, *From Apology to Utopia: The Structure of International Legal Argument* (Helsinki: Lakimiesliiton Kustannus, 1989).

[28] e.g. R. Graycar and J. Morgan, *The Hidden Gender of Law* (Sydney: Federation Press, 1990).

[29] P. Willetts, 'The Relationship between the Environmental Movement and the United Nations', paper given at Social Movements Conference, University of Warwick, Mar. 1998.

[30] This expression has been used by feminists to describe arenas in which women have been able to explore their commonalities. Arvonne Fraser describes how 'dedicated groups of women' used the Commission on the Status of Women and the Third Committee of ECOSOC for the drafting of the Convention on the Elimination of All Forms of Discrimination Against Women, 1979. See A. Fraser, 'The Convention on the Elimination of All Forms of Discrimination against Women (The Women's Convention)', in Anne Winslow (ed.), *Women, Politics, and the United Nations* (Westport, Conn.: Greenwood Press, 1995).

particular is the global summit meetings and parallel NGO fora that have dominated the international legal landscape during the 1990s. Although women's activism long predated the League of Nations,[31] the history of the incremental recognition of women's rights as international human rights can be traced through the parallel history of international institutionalism and global conferences.[32] Through the experience gained at successive summits, women's NGOs have developed ways of maximizing their impact upon diplomatic negotiations, either directly through the inclusion of their representatives in State delegations or indirectly through consciousness-raising activities, intensive and careful work on draft texts, campaigning at the national, regional, and international levels, and the formation of caucuses and international coalitions.[33] Some States have also realized the advantages of drawing upon NGO commitment and expertise, thereby reducing the resources allocated to the particular venture. A number of the final documents adopted by governments at such conferences have explicitly provided space for future consultative and advisory roles for NGOs,[34] thus ensuring the continuation of such inclusion. It is an important feature that attention has not been directed solely at institutions mandated to consider women's affairs. Instead there has been an insistence that all matters of global concern have a gendered dimension. The targeting of the Rio Conference on the Environment in 1992 for the articulation of a women's agenda in the achievement of a 'sustainable and equitable environment' was a crucial step in this process.[35] The Secretary-General's recognition of the need for mainstreaming gender throughout the totality of the UN's programmes is also significant in this cumulative process.[36]

3.2. Application and Implementation of Standards

There has been similar NGO intervention in seeking clarification of States' obligations and monitoring compliance with them. As is well known, the contentious jurisdiction of the International Court of Justice (ICJ) cannot be accessed by individuals

[31] J. Connors, 'NGOs and the Human Rights of Women at the United Nations', in P. Willetts (ed.), *'The Conscience of the World'· The Influence of Non-Governmental Organisations in the UN System* (Washington: Brookings Institution, 1996), 147.

[32] *The United Nations and the Advancement of Women 1945–1996* (New York: United Nations, 1995).

[33] The formation of a coalition of women's NGOs that worked throughout the process leading to the adoption of the Rome Statute for an International Criminal Court in July 1998 is a good example of this.

[34] e.g. Vienna Declaration and Programme of Action, I, para. 38; Beijing Platform for Action, para. 344.

[35] Agenda 21, Chapter 24. For a survey of some of the preparations taken by women to target UNCED see Recommendations for Relevant Meetings on Women in Environment and Development, Report of the Secretary-General, A/Conf.151/PC/114, notably including the NGO World Women's Congress for a Healthy Planet, Miami, Nov. 1991.

[36] The Question of Integrating the Human Rights of Women throughout the United Nations System, Report of the Secretary-General, E/CN.4/1998/49, 23 Mar. 1998.

or NGOs,[37] even for claims of human rights abuses or denial of rights owed *erga omnes* such as the right of self-determination.[38] This restriction can be variously perceived as either undermining the credibility of the ICJ by reducing its relevance to a range of non-State actors in contrast to other judicial bodies that do allow wider participation, or as confirming the Court's status as the principal judicial organ of the UN,[39] and as a sheltered domain for inter-State disputes.

NGO attention has turned to the advisory jurisdiction of the ICJ, the potential of which has been recommended as a means of enhancing the peaceful settlement of disputes.[40] A test case was the *Nuclear Weapons Advisory Opinion* which was formally first requested by the World Health Organisation[41] as a consequence of the mobilization of international civil society that was given expression through the World Court Project, an NGO initiative.[42] Subsequently, the General Assembly also requested an opinion in more general terms that were not limited to armed conflict.[43] The Court exercised its discretion to respond to the General Assembly's request, despite the argument that it should not do so because the original NGO involvement had rendered the questions political and that these unorthodox origins had in some sense tainted the request.[44] This argument ignored the fact that a majority of States were willing to succumb to NGO campaigns for the request of an advisory opinion. The Court considered that the political origins of the request did not detract from the central legal question posed. This history also shows that the interests of States cannot be simplistically categorized as confronting those of international civil society. Although the nuclear weapon States were opposed to seeking the Court's opinion, many others were not. The end of the Cold War has freed the expression of diverse interests among States and has allowed different groupings of States to emerge according to the particular subject-matter.[45] This in turn has freed NGOs from ideologically controlled agendas and has enabled them to seek support from targeted States on particular issues. Where NGOs have available to them resources that are outside the means of certain States, or where States seek alliances

---

[37] Statute of the International Court of Justice, Article 34.

[38] *Case Concerning East Timor (Portugal v. Australia)* (1995) ICJ Rep. 90.

[39] Charter of the United Nations, Article 7.

[40] An Agenda for Peace, Preventive Diplomacy, Peace making and Peacekeeping, Report of the Secretary-General pursuant to the Statement adopted by the Summit Meeting of the Security Council on 31 Jan. 1992, 17 June 1992, UN Doc. A/47/277; Supplement to An Agenda for Peace, 1 Jan. 1995, UN Doc. A/50/60–S/1995/1.

[41] *Legality of the Use by a State of Nuclear Weapons in Armed Conflict (Advisory Opinion)*, 8 July 1996, General List No. 93, <http://www.icj-cij.org>.

[42] Falk, 'Nuclear Weapons Advisory Opinion', at 340–2.

[43] *Legality of the Threat or Use of Nuclear Weapons (Advisory Opinion)*, 8 July 1996, General List No. 95, <http://www.icj-cij.org>, reproduced in (1996) 35 International Legal Materials 809.

[44] Judge Oda noted that the request for an advisory opinion 'originated in ideas developed by some NGOs' and that they had successfully lobbied non-aligned States. This constituted a reason why the Court should have declined to give an opinion. See ibid., at 845.

[45] An example is the alliance of 'like-minded States' for the negotiation of the Rome Statute for the International Criminal Court that eventually included permanent members of the Security Council and States from all regions of the world. In contrast, opponents to the Statute included the USA, China, and Qatar.

with NGOs, States themselves become the instruments through which NGOs can access State-controlled arenas. However, in its opinion on the legal question, the Court pursued a traditional State-oriented understanding of customary law as resting upon State practice and *opinio juris*. In assessing the normative value of relevant General Assembly Resolutions the majority discounted the voices of the broader body politic.[46]

Individuals and NGOs have had more immediate impact within the human rights bodies through their input in the State reporting system, their use of the individual complaints mechanisms, and advocacy.[47] Although only the Children's Convention provides formally for NGO participation in the State reporting process,[48] this has become an increasingly important site for intervention. National NGOs may mobilize around a State's requirement to report to the committees established by the human rights treaties.[49] International NGOs have facilitated this, for example by alerting local contacts of the reporting schedules, and have themselves supplied information to the respective committees.[50] The treaty bodies have responded favourably by providing greater opportunity for NGO participation.[51]

In contrast to reporting, which was designed as a State initiative, the complaint mechanism is by definition open to non-State actors. Not surprisingly, NGOs have explored its potential through identifying appropriate claims, supporting individual complainants, and submitting their own arguments. By initiating some complaints of human rights violations, NGOs have been able to ensure that cases have been presented in their terms and that States have been forced to respond rather than the other way round. Through the submission of arguments as *amici curiae*,[52] non-State actors have been able to extend the scope of argumentation before various tribunals. The indeterminate and imprecise language of human rights treaties has allowed innovative claims that have led to interpretations that encompass people and groups previously excluded in ways that were not necessarily envisaged when the treaties

---

[46] In contrast, Judge Weeramantry referred to the 'vast preponderance' of public opinion against nuclear weapons as shown by the millions of signatures on petitions addressed to the Court, and the broad range of groups (including women's organizations). See n. 41, at 879.

[47] The Beijing Platform for Action, para. 228, recognized the catalytic role played by NGOs, women's groups, and feminist activists in the promotion of women's human rights, including by networking and advocacy.

[48] Convention on the Rights of the Child, adopted GA Res. 44/736, 20 Nov. 1989, Article 45(a) allows the Committee on the Rights of the Child to invite 'competent bodies to provide expert advice on the implementation of the Convention'. NGOs played a significant role in the drafting of the Convention.

[49] e.g. at a Conference on the State reporting system at Cambridge University in 1997 Andrew Byrnes described the experience in Hong Kong in this respect.

[50] e.g. the work of the International Women's Rights Action Watch (IWRAW) in bringing information before the Committee on the Elimination of Discrimination Against Women is outlined in its Annual Reports of the Committee's work.

[51] The Committee on Economic, Social and Cultural Rights has been especially active, for example by inviting NGOs to pre-sessional meetings.

[52] The *ad hoc* War Crimes Tribunals for Former Yugoslavia and Rwanda have accepted, and indeed requested, *amicus* briefs from non-State bodies.

were first drafted.[53] The pioneering work of civil society has democratized the promise of human rights, but the dependence of such institutions on the vagaries of those who access them also allows for their appropriation by those already advantaged by the system.

4. STATES FIGHT BACK

Through these (and other) strategies, various non-State actors have achieved the inclusion of some of their political agendas within the fabric of international human rights law. The UN Convention on the Rights of the Child, the Draft Declaration on the Rights of Indigenous Peoples,[54] and the Landmines Convention[55] are just some examples of the direct political and legal consequences of their activities. Broader participation in the fora where legal standards of State behaviour are set accords with the rhetoric of the universality, indivisibility, inalienability, and interdependence of all human rights, but the reality should be treated with rather more caution. The picture is one of struggle, claim, and counter-claim. NGO access continues to be sought in arenas that are in some sense receptive, or where the political realities demand some formal recognition of their claims, or where the costs are low. Success has caused changed institutional and State practice, and thus contributed to evolving customary international law.[56] However, the drawbridges to IGO access may be resurrected by States through recourse to procedural and institutional formalism, negotiation ploys, alliance building, and a retreat to the sanctuary of State sovereignty.

Although NGOs have made significant inroads, States retain a tight grip on the formal law-making processes while apparently ceding ground. First, the choice of form of an instrument may be important. The soft law modalities of the final acts of the global summit meetings remain peripheral to the schema of the formal sources of international law: treaties and custom.[57] Despite the political and moral weight of Declarations and Programmes of Action, they lack the categorical force of treaties. Their deficiencies are enhanced by the typical refusal of States to agree high cost actions such as performance targets, compliance dates, or the commitment of

[53] e.g. inclusion of discrimination on the grounds of sexual preference within the provisions of the International Covenant on Civil and Political Rights, 16 Dec. 1966; *Toonen v. Australia* (1994) 1 International Human Rights Reports 97 (HRC); the inclusion of rape in custody within the prohibition of torture in the European Convention on Human Rights; *Aydin v. Turkey*, 3 Butterworths Human Rights Cases 300 (Judgment of 26 Aug. 1997).

[54] UN Doc. E/CN.4/Sub.2/1994/2/Add.1, 20 Apr. 1994.

[55] UN Convention on the Prohibition of the Use, Stockpiling, Production and Transfer of Anti-Personnel Mines and on their Destruction, Oslo, 18 Sept. 1997, reproduced in (1997) 36 International Legal Materials 1507.

[56] e.g. Amnesty International and other NGOs were instrumental in the articulation of the prohibition of torture. See N. Rodley, 'The Work of Non-governmental Organisations in the World-Wide Promotion and Protection of Human Rights' (1991) 90/1 UN Bulletin of Human Rights 84.

[57] Statute of the International Court of Justice, Article 38 (1).

resources.[58] Where the treaty form is agreed, NGOs may be excluded from crucial stages of negotiations[59] and the conclusion of the text.[60] The participation of NGOs in the preparatory stages and attendance by over 130 NGOs at the Diplomatic Conference on the Rome Treaty for the International Criminal Court did not prevent the final text being a compromise among States.

Another device is reliance upon soft measures of enforcement. For example, the World Bank (and other Development Banks) have responded to NGO pressure for greater accountability by the establishment of Inspection Panels,[61] which provide an avenue for participation, transparency, and inclusion that could not have been envisaged even a decade ago.[62] Nevertheless, the process is soft: the Inspection Panel can only make recommendations to the relevant Board, and such recommendations must be based on the Bank's compliance with its own policies and practices, and not upon the desirability of the project on other, objective criteria.

Second, States have utilized techniques of resisting NGO demands that have been honed by domestic élites to maintain their monopoly over agendas and knowledge. They retain control of access to arenas by the denial of accreditation to consultative status with ECOSOC,[63] and to attendance at particular NGO fora.[64] Other devices such as limited ticket allocations and speaking time (especially if scheduled for late at night after government delegates have departed) can also reduce the effectiveness of NGO attendance.[65] Control over the formal agendas is also jealously guarded. For example, despite the umbrella slogan of 'equality, development and peace' at the Fourth UN Conference on Women, participants were advised that this was not the appropriate forum for proposals in respect of macroeconomic issues, resources for development, peace, and disarmament issues. These 'important' matters were more appropriately reserved for elsewhere. In the words of a member of the Australian delegation, 'while women could negotiate on health, education, and other "social issues", it seems it is still not internationally legitimate for us to negotiate in these

[58] H. Charlesworth, 'Women as Sherpas: Are Global Summits Useful for Women?' (1996) 22 *Feminist Studies* 537.

[59] e.g. at the Rome Conference for the International Criminal Court it was reported that at the request of certain Arab States NGOs were excluded from crucial sessions on gender-related issues. See On the Record, ICC Conference, Rome 1998, Vol. 1, Issue 18, 4 (11 July).

[60] M. Posner and C. Whittome, 'The Status of Human Rights NGOs' (1994) 25 *Columbia Human Rights Law Review* 283.

[61] The establishment of the World Bank Inspection Panel was partly in response to criticisms expressed in B. Morse and T. Berger, *Report of the Independent Review, Sardar Sarovar* (Ottawa: Resources Futures International, 1992).

[62] I. Shihata, *The World Bank Inspection Panel* (Oxford: Clarendon Press, 1994). For details of the operation of the Panel see *The Inspection Panel International Bank for Reconstruction and Development Report August 1, 1994 to July 31, 1996* (Washington: World Bank, 1996).

[63] e.g. in 1994 the consultative status of the International Gay and Lesbian Association was withdrawn. See D. Otto, 'Non-governmental Organisations in the United Nations System: The Emerging Role of International Civil Society' (1996) 18 *Human Rights Quarterly* 107.

[64] Under pressure from the Chinese government certain NGOs, such as those with associations with Taiwan or Tibet, were denied accreditation for the Fourth World Conference on Women. See D. Otto, 'Holding up Half the Sky but for whose Benefit?' (1996) 6 *Australian Feminist Law Journal* 7.

[65] Posner and Whittome, 'Status of Human Rights NGOs'.

"tougher" areas'.[66] The campaigns in respect of violence against women that have led to some recognition of these issues within human rights discourse have also been confining and have detracted attention from the continued dominance of equality discourse and the denial of women's rights in other areas, especially those of economic and social rights.[67]

Third, even where obligations are concluded in treaty form, States retain the final word through accession and ratification procedures and the power to make reservations. The interplay of domestic and international politics may become crucial and open to manipulation by non-State actors. The demands by members of the US Congress threatened to derail the negotiations for establishing an International Criminal Court and may yet impede the entry into force of the adopted Statute. The force of American human rights NGOs supporting the process was insufficient to counter these pressures. Even when a State has formally accepted international standards, domestic imperatives may persuade it of the benefits of non-compliance or retraction from its obligations, especially at election time. An unusually explicit example is the aftermath of the *Shah Bano Case* in India which pitted women's rights to social justice and protection from destitution under the secular law against group claims for the application of religious-based personal laws.[68] Non-State actors campaigning for both views were active, but the politics of public disorder and greater bargaining power allowed the latter to prevail. When confronted by division between segments of civil society and with each segment seeking access to law to protect what they perceived as essential human rights, the bottom line was who wielded more real power in the domestic arena.

These realities prevent too ready an assumption that States have succumbed to the political demands of NGOs in the international law-making processes, or that their intrusions are welcomed. As Alston concludes:

Despite the fact that NGOs are indispensable to the effective functioning of the [Human Rights] Commission, their position will never be accepted more than grudgingly by the States that make up the Commission.[69]

5. GLOBALIZATION FROM BELOW: THE APPEARANCE OR REALITY OF DEMOCRACY?

There are also concerns as to whether NGO participation enhances democratic or representative decision-making. The *Shah Bano Case* illustrates that civil society cannot be regarded, even less than States, as monolithic. As Oscar Schachter

---

[66] J. Hunt, 'Reflections on Beijing' (1996) 6 Australian Feminist Law Journal 39.

[67] Yumi Lee, 'Violence against Women: Reflections on the Past and Strategies for the Future—an NGO Perspective' (1997) 19 Adelaide Law Review 45.

[68] For a discussion of the case and the segments of civil society activated by it see R. Coomaraswamy, ' "To Bellow Like a Cow": Women, Ethnicity and the Discourse of Rights', in R. Cook (ed.), *Human Rights of Women (National and International Perspectives)* (Pennsylvania: Pennsylvania University Press, 1994), at 39.

[69] Alston, 'Commission on Human Rights', at 203.

reminded the American Society of International Law at its 1998 Annual Meeting, there are 'good' and 'bad' NGOs and not necessarily consensus as to which are which. The different, often conflicting, interests of diverse groups who present themselves as human rights organizations foster the 'brokering and bartering' of human rights, which is at odds with the notion of inalienability of rights.[70] An example of this was the subjection of gay rights to negotiation at the Beijing Conference that allowed for the exclusion of sexual orientation in the Platform for Action.[71] A second example is the redefinition of gender in the Rome Statute for an International Criminal Court.[72]

Another concern is the appropriation by other non-State actors of the international space that has been opened up by non-profit-seeking NGOs, such as human rights organizations.[73] Krut notes the proliferation of TNCs within the UN and describes how their disproportionate financial power enables them to lobby more effectively than other NGOs,[74] in a fusion of globalization from below with globalization from above. Even within instruments such as the Beijing Platform for Action there is a failure to confront the premises of economic globalization or the interests of such multinational corporations. Inevitably, non-State actors with greater access to all forms of resources—whether business enterprises or non-profit NGOs—attract greater attention[75] and are likely to be accorded political and participatory space. This contributes to another dichotomy, that between 'insider' NGOs—those that work within the established processes and 'outsiders'—those that do not. States can claim greater legitimacy for their own actions where there has been consultation with the 'insider' bodies, but at the cost of further marginalizing the 'outsiders'. There is no guarantee of the representativeness of the views of high-profile NGOs, either generally, or even in respect of their claimed constituencies. NGOs are often non-democratic,[76] self-appointed, may consist of only a handful of people,[77] and determine their own agendas and priorities with a missionary-like[78] or élitist zeal. Their

---

[70] U. Baxi, 'Politics of Universality', Social Movements Conference, University of Warwick, Mar. 1998 (paper in possession of author).

[71] Otto, 'Holding up Half the Sky', at n. 25.

[72] Rome Statute for an International Criminal Court, Article 7(3).

[73] Again, the effectiveness of business-oriented NGOs is not new. White comments that '[w]ithin the field of business and finance some of the most powerful international non-governmental organizations . . . control and regulate vital segments of the world economy'. See White, 'International NGOs', at n. 19.

[74] *Transnational Corporations in the United Nations: Preventing Global Civil Governance (WEDO)*, cited in Krut, *Globalization*, at 20.

[75] There is the further issue of the sources of funding of NGOs and the concerns that the targets of NGO activity will mobilize 'to buy them off'. See P. Spiro, 'New Global Potentates: Nongovernmental Organizations and the "Unregulated" Marketplace' (1996) 18 Cardozo Law Review 957 at 966.

[76] Compare Spiro, ibid., at 963: 'Armed with the leverage of large memberships and knowing that those members are likely to be a docile herd, NGO leaders have emerged as a class of modern day, nonterritorial potentates, a position rather like that commanded by medieval bishops.'

[77] Krut comments that many NGOs are open to criticism for failing to put their own house in order in terms of equitable representation. See Krut, *Globalization*, at 15.

[78] This expression was used by Professor Thurer at the Kiel Symposium on Non-State Actors, Mar. 1998.

own decision-making processes may not be transparent and are often concealed behind a deluge of information. They do not have to address the full range of options that must be considered by State élites, but can limit themselves to their own concerns. The other side of the coin of representation is accountability. NGOs are acquiring a measure of international legal personality through procedural rights of access and standing, but their accountability has barely been addressed.

The wide diversity of organizations allows NGOs to claim inclusiveness and States to select from among their different viewpoints, while purporting to have sought the opinions of a wider audience. The representativeness of NGOs that appear before international institutions is also uncertain. The forming of coalitions may allow for a single, and therefore more forceful, NGO voice, but this may also conceal deep divisions among those within the coalition.[79] Dissenting voices might be silenced in order to maintain the appearance of unity. Women's NGOs in particular have frequently encountered unwillingness on the part of other NGOs to embrace gender issues.

There is also the risk that enhancing the role of international civil society might entrench the bias in favour of the agendas of NGOs from the North where civil society is vibrant and directed towards governmental action. In other societies an active civil society may be suppressed, not yet have emerged, or be ambivalent as to the role of the State as the protector of rights.[80] The 'paradigmatic shift' in international society towards geogovernance may in fact amount to little more than another means of validating essentially Northern assumptions and interests in a post-colonial, post-Cold War world. This viewpoint emerged in a survey of NGO attitudes in which over 70 per cent of those questioned expressed their concerns about the domination by larger, white, English-language NGOs.[81] One survey concluded that 'prejudices of racism, sexism and colonialism still endure'[82] despite the apparently more open texture of civil society. This particular allegation has become divisive in the discourse of women's human rights. Northern women have been decried for an essentialism that assumes a commonality in women's concerns without sufficient reference to contextual specificities. Localized histories of feminisms and women's movements in the South are easily overlooked as Northern conjectures about women's priorities are universalized.[83] Increased representation is justified in terms of the potential empow-

---

[79] *The Report of the Open-Ended Working Group on the Review of Arrangements for Consultation with Non-governmental Organisations*, UN Doc. A/49/215 (1994) para. 63 expressed concern that seeking consensus through NGO coalitions risked losing the range and diversity of opinions.

[80] Coomaraswamy, ' "To Bellow Like a Cow" '.

[81] *Democratic Global Governance, Report of the 1995 Benchmark Survey of NGOs*, cited in Krut, *Globalization*, at 13–16.

[82] Ibid., at 13. The Secretary-General addressed ways of capacity-building of NGOs from developing countries, and providing financial and other assistance. See Secretary-General's Report (1998), n. 21, at paras. 60–70.

[83] One often cited example is the Northern emphasis on freedom of reproductive choice without reference to the politics of forcible sterilization for poor (often minority) women within their own societies and in the South. See generally C. Romany, 'Black Women and Gender Equality in a New South Africa: Human Rights and the Intersection of Race and Gender' (1996) 21 Brooklyn Journal of

erment of those previously lacking power, but great care must be taken in identifying who is in fact benefiting from the process.

6. CONCLUSIONS

The focus of this chapter has been the targeting of States by NGOs within global human rights arenas. There remains an uncertainty as to the impact of the greater presence of NGO representatives within these arenas. There is a good deal of anecdotal evidence, but the need for empirical research to provide data for the assessment of these questions is very evident. Unfamiliarity with appropriate research methodologies tends to deter international lawyers from such investigations and is one of the (many) disadvantages of the little joint work undertaken with those working within international relations.[84]

State action is the focus of NGO activity because the discourse of human rights has been framed in terms of State responsibility for violations committed by public officials. Framing the agenda for the advancement of women in the language of human rights has been a useful conceptual tool that has also challenged some of the boundaries of that discourse. For example, the assertion of State responsibility for failure to exercise due diligence to prevent, or for acquiescence in, abuses committed by non-State actors, whether they be private individuals, para-military forces, multinational corporations or religious fundamentalists, extends the reach of human rights guarantees. So too does the move to make individual international criminal responsibility a reality by the agreement to establish a permanent International Criminal Court with jurisdiction over crimes against humanity. Bianchi has argued that diverse legal discourses, for example those of States, of corporate interests, of UN bureaucrats, of mainstream and women's NGOs, clash and converge in the evolution of a modern understanding of human rights law that is responsive to the needs of people across the globe. This process is far removed from the strait-jacket of legal positivism; by changing the information and environment in which State actors operate, non-State actors comprising civil society 'may alter human rights practices and eventually mandate new modalities in international law-making'.[85] Moving beyond international prescription to an examination of 'why States obey', Koh has emphasized the importance of the interaction of a broad range of non-State participants within the international human rights regime as a factor in promoting the

---

International Law 857; I. Gunning, 'Arrogant Perception, World Travelling and Multicultural Feminism: The Case of Female Genital Surgeries' (1992) 23 Columbia Human Rights Law Review 189; A. Wing, 'A Critical Race Feminist Conceptualization of Violence: South African and Palestinian Women' (1997) 60 Albany Law Review 943.

[84] A.-M. Slaughter, A. Tulumello, and S. Wood, 'International Law and International Relations Theory: A New Generation of Interdisciplinary Scholarship' (1998) 92 American Journal of International Law 367.

[85] Bianchi, 'Globalization of Human Rights', at 194.

political and legal internalization of norms within domestic systems.[86] Certainly the considerable financial and human resources that have been invested by such actors into strengthening the substance and procedures of human rights law suggests that there remains a strong belief in an international rule of law that reaches down to protect all individuals, including the most vulnerable.

However, State non-compliance with human rights norms continues in many instances while the assertion of State responsibility for violations by non-State actors rests upon assumptions of knowledge and control that in many cases States simply do not possess. Empowerment through representation must take account of the forces of globalization from above that are shifting the location of much crucial decision-making away from State agencies. Moreover, some intergovernmental institutions remain largely impervious to NGO demands for access. The restriction of NGO activity to matters within the competence of ECOSOC, that is, 'economic, social, cultural, educational, health and related matters' and the promotion of human rights,[87] has been a limiting factor as well as one of unimagined expansion. The extension of the social justice agenda of the General Assembly has facilitated ECOSOC accreditation for NGOs with diverse mandates, but the latitude accorded to NGOs within the human rights and environmental arenas has not translated into similar acceptance elsewhere. The primary responsibility of the Security Council for the maintenance of international peace and security has allowed that body to remain largely impenetrable. Similarly, NGOs have been less able to participate within the international bureaucracy controlling trade and financial matters, the IMF, World Bank, and WTO,[88] where questions of social justice and real equality between women and men are subordinated to economic ideology.[89]

These political truths undermine the role of international law in the protection of human rights. The inadequacy of international legal categorizations is also exposed when examined from the perspective of women's concerns which straddle the totality of life experiences. Proponents of women's advancement cannot restrict their attentions to the legal notions of State responsibility for the guarantee of rights, or to seeking more equal participation and representation within traditional arenas of governmental power. While broader participation would give the appearance of greater equity, it is the form and not the substance of inclusive democratic decision-making that would be addressed. Enhancing access to existing structures neither challenges their boundaries, nor guarantees greater gender awareness in decision-making or implementation of policy. Instead the gendered dimensions of trade, of global capital flows, of investment policies, of security issues, and of structural

---

[86] H. Koh, 'Why Do Nations Obey International Law?' (1997) 106 Yale Law Journal 2599.

[87] Charter of the United Nations, Article 62 (1) and (2).

[88] The Singapore Statement on NGO–WTO Relations urges WTO member States to undertake full consultations with NGOs to achieve a higher level of transparency. Reproduced in (1997) 27 Environmental Policy and Law 159. For a survey of relations between NGOs and funds, agencies and programmes within the UN system (including specialized agencies) see Secretary-General's Report (1998), n. 21, at paras. 16–31.

[89] Compare Krut, *Globalization*, at 31 and Chossudovsky, *Globalisation of Poverty*, at 16.

adjustment programmes, in short the entire global social and economic agenda, must be radically confronted. To achieve such a radical rethinking 'unity of purpose and worldwide co-ordination among diverse groups and social movements is crucial'.[90] Achievement of this goal will not be facilitated by ignoring and minimizing the divisions and fissures within international civil society. Rather, they must be addressed so that the strategies and expertise that have been gained can be further refined and directed towards providing alternative voices to those that currently dominate the discourse of economic globalization.

[90] Chossudovsky, ibid., at 27.

8

Politics And Human Rights:
An Essential Symbiosis

MAKAU WA MUTUA

1. INTRODUCTION

Since the Second World War, international human rights law has become one of the most pre-eminent doctrines of our time.[1] Diverse groups from sexual minorities to environmentalists now invoke the power of human rights language. But this universal reliance on the language of human rights has failed to create agreement on the scope and content of the human rights corpus. Debates rage over its cultural relevance, ideological and political orientation, and thematic incompleteness.[2] What these debates obscure is the fact that the human rights corpus is a political ideology, although its major authors present it as non-ideological. The originators of the discourse use a vocabulary that paints the human rights movement as both impartial and the quintessence of human goodness. They portray it as divorced from base materialism, self-interest, and 'ideology'.

This chapter examines the works of the major authors[3] of human rights discourse and argues that human rights and Western liberal democracy are close to a tautology. Although the two concepts seem different viewed from a distance, one is in fact the universalized version of the other, an attempt at the diffusion and

---

[1] In the wake of the Second World War, member States of the United Nations adopted, on 10 Dec. 1948, the Universal Declaration of Human Rights, G.A. Res. 217 A(III), UN Doc. A/810, at 71 (1948) (hereinafter UDHR). See Antonio Cassese, 'The General Assembly: Historical Perspective 1945–1989', in Philip Alston (ed.), *The United Nations and Human Rights: A Critical Appraisal* (Oxford: Clarendon Press, 1992), 25 at 31 fn. 22 (hereinafter United Nations and Human Rights). Now widely viewed as the 'gospel' of the human rights movement, the UDHR has been the predominant roadmap in the development and elaboration of a 'universal' jurisprudence of human rights.

[2] For different and conflicting cultural, historical, and intellectual bases and traditions in human rights, see Josiah A. M. Cobbah, 'African Values and the Human Rights Debate: An African Perspective' (1987) 9 Human Rights Quarterly 309; Jack Donnelly, 'Cultural Relativism and Universal Human Rights' (1984) 6 Human Rights Quarterly 400; Bilahari Kausikan, 'Asia's Different Standard' (1993) 92 Foreign Policy 24; Makau wa Mutua, 'The Banjul Charter and the African Cultural Fingerprint: An Evaluation of the Language of Duties' (1995) 35 Virginia Journal of International Law 339 (hereinafter Mutua, 'African Cultural Fingerprint'); Raimundo Pannikar, 'Is the Notion of Human Rights A Western Concept?' (1982) 120 Diogenes 75.

[3] The term 'authors' is here broadly used to describe all those individuals and entities which have exerted discernible influence in the normative development and practical enforcement of human rights law. These include the United Nations, regional intergovernmental organizations, non-governmental human rights organizations (NGOs), based almost exclusively in Western Europe and North America, and academic and other conceptual writers.

further development on the international level of the liberal political tradition. These processes have contributed to the re-examination and reconstruction of liberalism, and have in some respects refined and added to the liberal tradition. Although the concept of human rights is not unique to European societies, I argue here that the specific philosophy on which the current 'universal' and 'official'[4] human rights corpus is based is essentially European.[5] This exclusivity and cultural specificity necessarily deny the concept universality. The fact that human rights are violated in liberal democracies is of little consequence to my argument and does not distinguish the human rights corpus and the ideology of Western liberalism; rather, it emphasizes the contradictions and imperfections of liberalism.

Since the Second World War, the United Nations, non-governmental organizations, and scholarly writers have created a thicket of norms, processes, and institutions which purport to promote and protect human rights. Working with the so-called 'International Bill of Rights' as their basis,[6] this key, but diverse, collection of organizations and scholars has tended to agree on an irreducible human rights core.[7] This core, though stated in human rights terms, is now being formulated into the emergent norm of democratic governance in international law.[8] The routes different authors have taken to arrive at these conclusions are, of course, varied. Nevertheless, I have identified the four defining approaches or schools of thought into which I believe all the paramount voices writing and acting in the human rights idiom fall.[9] It is argued in this chapter that these voices express the

---

[4] I use the term 'official' to describe the 'mainstream' and popular conceptions of the human rights movement, that is, as norms and codes of conduct developed and promoted by Westerners after the Second World War for the purposes of limiting the abuse of individuals by their governments. This version of human rights has been largely authenticated and mediated through the United Nations. See e.g. UDHR; the International Covenant on Economic, Social and Cultural Rights, UNGA Res. 2200 (XXI), UN GAOR, 21st Sess., Supp. No. 16, at 49, UN Doc. A/6316 (1966) (entered into force 3 Jan. 1976) (hereinafter ICESCR); the International Covenant on Civil and Political Rights, UNGA Res. 2200 (XXI), UN GAOR, 21st Sess., Supp. No. 16, at 52, UN Doc. A/6316 (1966) (entered into force 3 Jan. 1976) (hereinafter ICCPR); the Optional Protocol to the International Covenant on Civil and Political Rights, UNGA Res. 2200 (XXI), UN GAOR, 21st Sess., Supp. No. 16, at 59, UN Doc. A/6316 (1966) (entered into force 23 Mar. 1976) (hereinafter Optional Protocol).
[5] See Jack Donnelly, 'Human Rights and Western Liberalism', in Abdullahi Ahmed An-Na'im and Francis M. Deng (eds.), *Human Rights in Africa: Cross-Cultural Perspectives* (Washington: Brookings Institution, 1990), 31 (hereinafter *Cross-Cultural Perspectives*).
[6] The International Bill of Rights is comprised of: (i) the UDHR; (ii) the ICCPR; (iii) the ICESCR; and (iv) the Optional Protocol.
[7] This core is comprised of personal security rights, rights that implicate State power. In conventional jargon, they are negative, 'hands off' rights which individuals enjoy *vis-à-vis* the State.
[8] For discussion of the norm of democratic governance in international law, see Gregory H. Fox, 'The Right to Political Participation in International Law' (1992) 17 Yale Journal of International Law 539; Thomas M. Franck, 'The Emerging Right to Democratic Governance' (1992) 86 American Journal of International Law 46.
[9] There are, of course, other major voices, such as Martti Koskenniemi, whose work has focused on the deconstruction of human rights discourse and the unveiling of the interests, struggles, and politics that are hidden behind the rhetoric of international law and human rights. But when I speak of the paramount voices in the movement, I do not mean Koskenniemi or those with similar approaches; I speak primarily of the originators, the conceptualizers of the movement, those who are responsible for its construction. See e.g. M. Koskenniemi, 'The Politics of International Law' (1990) 1 European Journal of International Law 4.

close synonymy and fit of the human rights regime with its parent, Western liberalism.

The proponents of and adherents to the four dominant schools of thought may be classified as (i) conventional doctrinalists, (ii) constitutionalists or conceptualizers, (iii) cultural agnostics or multiculturalists, and (iv) political strategists or instrumentalists. Although most of these voices differ, in some instances radically, over the content of human rights and whether or how they should be ranked, they are none the less united by the belief that there are basic human rights. They also believe that these human rights should be promoted and where possible protected by the State, the basic obligor of human rights law. These different schools disagree, however, on the political orientation of human rights, the weight accorded to certain rights, and strategies and tactics for the enforcement of the human rights movement's norms. These disagreements reflect the different visions and trajectories of liberalism and the types of society intended by advocates of the human rights regime, and the different purposes to which they feel the discourse should be put.

This chapter argues that the human rights corpus, as a statement of ideals and values, and particularly the positive law of human rights, requires the reconstruction of States to reflect the structures and values of governance which derive from Western liberalism, especially the contemporary variations of liberal democracy practised in Western democracies. While these democracies differ in the content of the rights they guarantee and the organizational structures they take, they are nevertheless based on the same idea of constitutionalism.

The first two approaches, which are espoused by conventional doctrinalists and conceptualizers or constitutionalists, are closest in ideological orientation. Admittedly, there is a wide and, often contradictory, contrasting diversity of attitudes towards the human rights corpus within the two schools. While the doctrinalists tend to be statisticians of violence, conceptualizers are essentially systematizers of the human rights corpus. For the latter, human rights norms arise out of the liberal tradition and their application should lead to a type of system generally referred to as constitutionalism. Such a system generally has the following characteristics, although the weight accorded to each of them differs from one State to the next. First, political society is based on the concept of popular sovereignty. Second, the State is constitutionally required to be popularly accountable through various processes such as periodic, genuine, multi-party elections. Third, government is controlled and limited in its powers through checks and balances and the separation of powers, a central tenet of the liberal tradition. Fourth, the judiciary is independent and safeguards legality and the rule of law, and finally, the formal declaration of individual civil and political rights is an indispensable facet of the State.[10]

While conceptualizers are more critical of the corpus, many of the doctrinalists see it in almost religious dimensions. Nevertheless, many of the voices in the two

---

[10] See Henry J. Steiner and Philip Alston, *International Human Rights in Context: Law, Politics, Morals* (Oxford: Clarendon Press, 1996), 710–25.

schools see themselves in a variety of guises: as inheritors of the Western historical tradition pitting individual rights against the State, as guardians of human rights law, or as founders, conceptualizers, and elaborators of the human rights corpus. The two schools constitute what I call the human rights 'orchestra', in which their proponents are the composers and conductors of the discourse. They 'control' the content and map the margins of the discourse. Conventional doctrinalists are characterized by their heavy, and virtually exclusive, reliance on positive law in treaties, custom, and other sources of international law as the basis for their activist advocacy or scholarly inquiry. The vast majority of doctrinalists 'who matter' operate in the context of human rights NGOs in the West, although a number of academics also write in this mould. In contrast, constitutionalists are usually prominent in the realm of theory.

Both schools enjoy a spirited supporting cast in the non-Western world. Over the last several decades, national human rights NGOs and human rights academics have mushroomed in the South. In virtually all cases, they reproduce intellectual patterns and strategies for advocacy similar to those in the West. Although there are some significant differences on the emphasis placed on certain rights, there has been little originality as the corpus has conquered new territory outside the West.

Substantively, doctrinalists stress the primacy of civil and political rights over all other classes of rights. Thus, only a small number of 'traditional' civil and political rights comprise the heart of the human rights regime. Moreover, they seek immediate and 'blind' application of these rights without regard to any historical, cultural, or evolutionary differences between States and societies. Many constitutionalists, on the other hand, recognize the supremacy of these 'core' rights but point out that the list could or should be expanded. They see the difficulties of 'immediate' implementation and prefer a more nuanced approach, staggered to take into account variables of culture, history, and other cleavages. Although many who adopt this approach are positivist, some are critical thinkers who subject the human rights regime to a probing critique. I call them constitutionalists because they believe that, as a whole, human rights law is or should be a constitutional regime *and* a philosophy—which is constitutive of a liberal democratic society along a spectrum that stretches from a bare republican State to the social democratic State. In the republican 'minimum' State, namely the archetypal nineteenth-century liberal State, the government protects the privileges of the few against the poor masses, women, and ethnic, racial, religious, and sexual minorities. In the twentieth century, however, the liberal tradition is developed and constructs the social welfare State, where the government progressively and affirmatively seeks to give substance to formal equality.

Cultural agnostics are generally outsiders who visualize the universality or convergence of some human rights norms with certain non-Western norms and as a result partially embrace the human rights corpus. Many of them are scholars and policymakers of multicultural heritage or orientation who, though familiar and sometimes even comfortable with Western culture, regard cross-cultural referencing as the most critical variable in the creation of a universal corpus of human rights. They criticize the human rights corpus as culturally exclusive in some respects and therefore view parts of it as illegitimate or, at the very least, irrelevant in non-Western societies. Some, such as this author, have called for a multicultural approach to reform the human rights regime and to make it more universal.

Many proponents of the first two schools, who regard themselves as universalists, have labelled many cultural agnostics as cultural relativists. This form of typecasting or human rights name-calling has generally had the effect of stigmatizing those who resist the Eurocentric formulation of human rights. But these so-called 'universalists' are in fact cultural relativists themselves because they operate within a specific cultural space and distinct historical tradition. Cultural agnostics are not sympathetic to cynical élites who deliberately manipulate cultural images to justify despotic rule. Rather, by cultural agnostics I refer to academics and policy-makers who see the potential dynamism of the human rights corpus as an opportunity for the creation of a multicultural corpus of human rights.

The fourth school, that of political strategists or instrumentalists, abounds with governments and institutions that selectively and inconsistently deploy human rights discourse for strategic and political ends. While all States—socialist or capitalist, developed or underdeveloped—are generally cynical in their deployment of human rights norms, my focus here is not on all States. If it were, I would discuss the hypocrisies of the Zairian State under Mobutu Sese Seko, the former Soviet Union, and many others across the political spectrum who professed allegiance to human rights but violated them as official policy. However, my concern here is not with the claims of States in respect of their internal application of human rights norms. Rather, I am only interested in Western democracies and their institutions which alone rhetorically champion the 'universalization' of human rights. Such institutions include the World Bank and the North Atlantic Treaty Organization (NATO), whose primary purposes are related to the preservation and enhancement of liberalism and free markets. Increasingly, they have invoked human rights when these two goals have been endangered to an allegedly unacceptable degree. Examples of such unacceptable dangers include civil war or regional conflicts that threaten 'vital' Western interests, such as access to strategic resources. In the view of international financial institutions, donor agencies and donor countries, such a risk could engender autocratic forms of governance which encourage intolerable levels of corruption and economic mismanagement and negatively affect the growth or functioning of markets and international trade. In the past responses to such risks, including military responses, have often been couched in human rights terminology.[11] Obviously, human rights issues cannot be the only factors which determine foreign policy choices, nor should they be. Other 'vital' interests such as trade could trump human rights in the calculus of geopolitics because States have 'many fish to fry'. But it is precisely this 'necessity' to balance competing objectives that makes States unreliable, unprincipled, and manipulative proponents of the human rights corpus.

---

[11] See e.g. Diane Bartz, 'Amnesty International Scores Washington for Hypocrisy in Human Rights', UPI, 9 July 1991, available in LEXIS-NEXIS, News Library, ARCNWS File.

The second section of this chapter briefly discusses the basic notions and requirements of liberal democracy and relates them to the central tenets of the human rights
corpus. Section 3 focuses on the first school, that of the abolitionists or doctrinal
conventionalists. Section 4 explores the assumptions and views of constitutionalists.
Section 5 examines the dilemmas of cultural agnostics. Section 6 looks at political
strategists. In all these cases, I analyse the schools of thought and action and demonstrate how their development may be traced back to liberal democracy. The conclusion attempts to respond to the challenges and questions posed to the human rights
corpus by these typologies. In particular, it revisits questions of universality and legitimacy and considers the possibility of a new internationality in human rights, and
the potential implications this might have for post-liberal society.

2. FROM LIBERALISM TO DEMOCRACY AND HUMAN RIGHTS

Liberalism is distinguished from other traditions by its commitment to formal
autonomy and abstract equality. It is a tradition that, in its contemporary expression,
requires a constitutional State with limited powers, a State that is moreover accountable to the broad public. These aspirations are the basis for the development and
elaboration of liberal democracy and, as this chapter contends, the construction and
universalization of the jurisprudence of human rights. In the historical continuum,
therefore, liberalism gave birth to democracy, which, in turn, now seeks to present
itself internationally as the ideology of human rights. This section briefly explores the
relationships among liberalism, political democracy, and human rights norms.

Notwithstanding the abundance of definitions of Western liberal democracy, the
most prominent define it in procedural, not substantive, terms. Huntington, for
example, emphasizes the Schumpeterian[12] tradition and defines democracy in purely
procedural language.[13] For Huntington, the democratic method involves two basic
dimensions: contestation and participation, where the 'most powerful collective decision-makers are selected through fair, honest, and periodic elections in which candi-
dates freely compete for votes and in which virtually all the adult population is
eligible to vote'.[14] Contestation and participation, according to Huntington, also
imply certain civil and political freedoms which are necessary for free and fair elections: the right to speak, publish, assemble, and organize.[15]

There is virtual agreement that the early formulation and codification of human
rights standards was dominated by Western cultural and political norms. This was
particularly true of the formulation and adoption of the Universal Declaration on
Human Rights, the 'spiritual parent of and inspiration for many human rights

[12] Joseph Schumpeter, *Capitalism, Socialism, and Democracy* (3rd edn., New York: Harper, 1950).
[13] Samuel Huntington, *The Third Wave: Democratization in the Late Twentieth Century* (Norman,
Okla.: University of Oklahoma Press, 1991), 6. [14] Ibid. 7.
[15] Ibid. 7. These rights are central features of the human rights corpus. See e.g. UDHR, Articles
19–21; ICCPR, Articles 19–22.

treaties'.[16] As one author has remarked, the West was able to 'impose' its philosophy of human rights on the rest of the world because in 1948 it dominated the United Nations.[17] The minority socialist bloc abstained, having put up ineffectual resistance on the grounds that economic, social, and cultural rights were downgraded.[18] More importantly, non-Western views were largely unrepresented because the so-called Third World at the United Nations was composed mainly of Latin American countries, whose dominant world-view was European.[19] In 1948, most African and Asian States were absent from the United Nations because they were European colonies.[20]

A closer examination of the rights listed in both the UDHR and the ICCPR leaves no doubt that both documents—which are regarded as the two most important human rights instruments[21]—are attempts to universalize those civil and political rights that are accepted or aspired to in Western liberal democracies. Many articles in the UDHR echo or reproduce many provisions of the United States Constitution and the jurisprudence of Western European States such as France and the United Kingdom. The UDHR prohibits 'cruel, inhuman or degrading treatment or punishment',[22] the US Constitution prohibits the infliction of 'cruel and unusual punishments'.[23] Other parallels include due process protections,[24] rights of speech,[25] and privacy.[26]

3. CONVENTIONAL DOCTRINALISTS

Perhaps no other school in human rights has been more influential in the promotion of the 'universalization' of human rights norms than that of the conventional doctrinalists, although the formal creation of human rights law is carried out by collections of States—the so-called international community—acting both in concert and separately within and outside the ambit of the United Nations. It is generally accepted that a serious attempt to universalize human rights ideals was not made until after the Nazi atrocities of half a century ago, although the development of human rights norms and ideals preceded the Holocaust.

The most active element in the internationalization of the human rights movement has been the so-called international non-governmental organization

---

[16] Henry Steiner, 'Political Participation as a Human Right' (1988) 1 Harvard Human Rights Year Book 77 at 79.   [17] See Cassese, 'The General Assembly', at 31–2.

[18] Ibid. 31.   [19] Ibid. 32.

[20] The UDHR was drafted by people who were from 'Western Europe or the Americas or were non-Europeans educated in the West' (Virginia A. Leary, 'The Effect of Western Perspectives on International Human Rights', in An-Na'im and Deng (eds.), *Cross-Cultural Perspectives*, 15 at 20).

[21] The ICESCR has been relegated to the backwater of human rights discourse.

[22] UDHR, Article 5.   [23] US Constitution, amendment VIII.

[24] US Constitution, amendments V, VI; UDHR, Articles 7–11.

[25] US Constitution, amendment I; UDHR, Article 19.

[26] US Constitution, amendment IV; UDHR, Article 12.

(INGO).[27] The most prominent INGOs in this regard are based in the West and seek to enforce the application of human rights norms internationally, particularly towards repressive states in the South. They are ideological copycats, both in theory and in method, of the traditional civil rights organizations in the West which preceded them. The American Civil Liberties Union (ACLU), one of the most influential civil rights organizations in the United States, is the classic example of the Western civil rights organization.[28] Two other equally important domestic civil rights organizations are the National Association for the Advancement of Colored People (NAACP)[29] and the NAACP Legal Defense and Educational Fund (LDF).[30] Although these organizations are called civil rights groups by Americans, they are in reality human rights organizations. The historical origin of the distinction between a 'civil rights' group and a 'human rights' group in the United States remains unclear. The primary difference is that Western human rights groups focus on abusive practices and traditions in what they regard as relatively repressive, 'backward', foreign countries and cultures, while the agenda of civil rights groups concentrates on domestic issues. Thus, although human rights groups such as Human Rights Watch publish reports on human rights abuses in the US, the focus of their activity is upon the human rights 'problems' or 'abuses' of other countries.[31]

At any rate, the half-dozen leading human rights organizations, the prototypical conventional doctrinalists, have arisen in the West over the last half-century with the express intent of promoting certain basic Western liberal values—now dubbed human rights—throughout the world, and especially the non-Western world. These INGOs were the brainchildren of prominent Western civil rights advocates, lawyers, and private citizens. The International League for the Rights of Man, now the International League for Human Rights (ILHR), is the oldest such organization, founded in New York in 1942.[32] At various times, it has focused on victims of torture, religious intolerance, the rights of human rights monitors at its affiliates abroad, the reunification of Eastern Europeans with relatives in the West during the Cold War, and the human rights treaty State reporting system within the United Nations.[33] Roger Baldwin, the founder of the ACLU, also founded the ILHR.[34]

---

[27] INGOs may be contrasted with non-governmental organizations (NGOs). This term, although used to refer to private, non-governmental groups as well, is often used to describe 'domestic' or national organizations.

[28] Initially founded in 1920 to advocate the rights of conscientious objectors, the ACLU sees itself as the 'guardian of the Bill of Rights which guarantees fundamental civil liberties to all of us'. See Laurie S. Wiseberg and Hazel Sirett (eds.), *North American Human Rights Directory* (Garrett Park, Md.: Garrett Park Press, 1984), 19 (hereinafter *North American Directory*).

[29] The NAACP, the United States' oldest civil rights organization, was founded in 1909 to seek equal treatment for African-Americans through peaceful reform. Ibid., at 161.

[30] The LDF was founded in 1939 as the legal arm of the NAACP. It has initiated legal action in courts to challenge discrimination and promote equality in schools, jobs, the electoral system, land use, and other services and areas. Ibid. 159.

[31] See e.g. Human Rights Watch, *Questions and Answers* (undated), 3: 'We examine both how the U.S. government promoted human rights abroad and how it respects human rights at home.'

[32] See Wiseberg and Sirett (eds.), *North American Directory*, at 135.   [33] Ibid.

[34] See Rita McWilliams, 'Who Watched Americas Watch' (1990) 19 National Interest 45 at 53.

The ILHR itself was responsible for establishing in 1975 in New York the Lawyers Committee for International Human Rights, now known as the Lawyers Committee for Human Rights (LCHR), another of the more important Western INGOs. The LCHR promotes the human rights standards contained in the International Bill of Rights. The New York-based Human Rights Watch (HRW) was founded in 1978[35] and has developed into the most dominant American INGO, working to expose violations of basic liberal freedoms.[36] The founder of HRW is Aryeh Neier, a former national executive director of the ACLU.[37]

The two other leading INGOs are located in Europe, in the United Kingdom and Switzerland. The Geneva-based International Commission of Jurists (ICJ) was 'founded in 1952 to promote the "rule of law" throughout the world'.[38] The ICJ was accused of being a tool of the West in the Cold War, spending considerable resources on exposing the failures of Soviet bloc and one-party States.[39] Today, however, it is regarded as a bona fide INGO, concerned with rule of law questions in the South.

Finally, the London-based Amnesty International (AI), the most powerful human rights INGO, is synonymous today with the human rights movement and has inspired the creation of many similar human rights groups around the world. It was launched by an article written by Peter Benenson, a British lawyer, in the 28 May 1961 issues of the *Observer* and *Le Monde*.[40] Benenson's article, 'Forgotten Prisoners', urged moral outrage and appeals for amnesty for individuals who were imprisoned, tortured, or executed because of their political opinions or religion.[41] The recipient of the 1977 Nobel Peace Prize, AI says that its object is 'to contribute to the observance throughout the world of human rights as set out in the Universal Declaration of Human Rights'[42] through campaigns to free prisoners of conscience.[43] Thus, it seeks to ensure fair trials within a reasonable time[44] for political prisoners, to abol-

---

[35] Human Rights Watch began in 1978 with the founding of the Helsinki Watch.

[36] See Human Rights Watch, *Human Rights Watch World Report 1995: Events of 1994* (New York: Human Rights Watch, 1995), p. vii.

[37] See Aryeh Neier, 'Political Consequences of the United States Ratification of the International Covenant on Civil and Political Rights' (1993) 42 DePaul Law Review 1233.

[38] Laurie Wiseberg and Hazel Sirett (eds.), *Human Rights Directory: Western Europe* (Garrett Park, Md.: Garrett Park Press, 1982), 216.

[39] See Issa G. Shivji, *The Concept of Human Rights in Africa* (London: Codesria Book Series, 1989), 34. See also Claude E. Welch, Jr., *Protecting Human Rights in Africa: Roles and Strategies of Non-Governmental Organizations* (Philadelphia: University of Pennsylvania Press, 1995), 163.

[40] See Wiseberg and Sirett (eds.), *Western Europe Directory*, at 265.

[41] See Ian Martin, 'Lecture by the Edward A. Smith Visiting Fellow presented by the Harvard Law School Human Rights Program' (14 Apr. 1993), in *The New World Order: Opportunity or Threat for Human Rights?* (1993), 4–5 (hereinafter *New World Order*). From 1986–92, Martin was the Secretary General of Amnesty International.

[42] 'Statute of Amnesty International', Articles 1 and 2, reprinted in Amnesty International, *Amnesty International Report* (London: Amnesty International, 1994), appendix II, at 332.

[43] Prisoners of conscience are individuals detained anywhere for their belief or because of their ethnic origin, sex, colour, or language—who have not used or advocated violence. Ibid., at 333. For a discussion of AI's narrow mandate, see Peter R. Baehr, 'Amnesty International and Its Self-Imposed Limited Mandate' (1994) Netherlands Human Rights Quarterly 5.

[44] 'Statute of Amnesty International', 332.

ish the death penalty, torture, and other cruel treatment of prisoners,[45] and to end extra-judicial executions and disappearances.[46]

Substantively, conventional doctrinalists insist upon a narrow range of civil and political rights, as the mandates of leading INGOs such as Amnesty International and Human Rights Watch reflect. Throughout the Cold War, INGOs concentrated their attention on the exposure of violations of what they deemed 'core' rights in Soviet bloc countries, Africa, Asia, and Latin America. In a reflection of this ideological bias, INGOs mirrored the position of the industrial democracies and generally assumed an unsympathetic, and at times hostile, stance towards calls for the expansion of their mandates to include economic and social rights.[47]

Traditionally, the work of INGOs has typically involved investigation,[48] reporting,[49] and advocacy.[50] Investigation usually takes place in a 'Third World' country while reporting and advocacy aim at reforming the policies of industrial democracies and intergovernmental agencies in order to trigger bilateral and multilateral action against the repressive State. Some INGOs now go beyond this denunciatory framework and work to foster and strengthen the processes and institutions—rule of law, laws and constitutions, judiciaries, legislatures, electoral machineries—which ensure the protection of civil and political rights.[51] Although the ideological commitment of these INGOs seems clear through their mandates and work, they none the less present themselves as non-ideological. They perceive themselves to be politically neutral modern-day abolitionists whose only purpose is to identify 'evil' and root it out.

Thus, although INGOs are 'political' organizations working to vindicate political and moral principles that shape the basic characteristics of a State, they consciously present themselves as disinterested in the political character of a State. When HRW asserts that it 'addresses the human rights practices of governments of all political stripes, of all geopolitical alignments, and of all ethnic and religious persuasions',[52] it is anticipating charges that it is pro-Western, pro-capitalist, and unsympathetic to Islamic and other non-Western religious and political traditions. The first two charges could have been fatal to a group's credibility at the height of the Cold War. In reality, however, INGOs have been highly partial: their work has concentrated

---

[45] 'Statute of Amnesty International', 332–3.   [46] Ibid. 333.

[47] See Aryeh Neier, 'Human Rights', in Joel Krieger *et al.* (eds.), *The Oxford Companion to Politics of the World* (New York: Oxford University Press, 1993), 401 at 403.

[48] An investigation, known as a human rights fact-finding mission, is conducted by the staffs of INGOs who typically spend anywhere from several days to a number of weeks in a 'Third World'. See generally Diane F. Orentlicher, 'Bearing Witness: The Art and Science of Human Rights Fact-Finding' (1990) 3 Harvard Human Rights Journal 83.

[49] Reporting involves compiling data and information from the fact-finding mission and correlating them to human rights standards to bring out discrepancies and disseminating the result through reports or other media. This method is also called 'shaming' because it spotlights the offending State to the international community.

[50] This includes lobbying governments and international institutions to use their leverage to alleviate violations.   [51] 'Statute of Amnesty International', appendix II, 333.

[52] See *World Report 1995*, p. vii.

historically on those countries that have not attained the stable and functioning democracies of the West, the standard for liberal democracy. Target States have included the Soviet bloc and virtually the entire South, where undemocratic or repressive one-party States and military dictatorships have thrived.

The content of the work of INGOs reveals their partiality as well. The typical INGO report is a catalogue of abuses committed by a government against liberal values. Steiner notes that:

Given the ideological commitments of these NGOs, their investigative work naturally concentrates on matters such as governmental abuses of rights to personal security, discrimination, and basic political rights. By habit or established practice, NGOs' reports stress the nature and number of violations, rather than explore the socioeconomic and other factors that underlie them.[53]

Reports further document the abridgement of the freedoms of speech and association, violations of due process, and various forms of discrimination. Many INGOs fear that explaining why abuses occur may serve to justify those abuses or give credence to the claims of some governments that civil and political rights violations take place because of underdevelopment. If accepted, such an argument would destroy the abolitionists' mission by delaying, perhaps indefinitely, the otherwise urgent need to comply with human rights standards. This argument, they fear, would allow governments to continue repressive policies while escaping their obligations under human rights law. Thus INGOs demand the immediate protection and respect of civil and political rights regardless of the level of development of the offending State. By taking cover behind the international human rights instruments, INGOs are able to fight for liberal values without appearing 'partisan', 'biased', or 'ideological'.

Conventional doctrinalists also perpetuate the appearance of objectivity by explicitly distinguishing themselves from agencies, communities, and government programmes that promote democracy and democratization. The 'democracy' and 'human rights' communities regard themselves as distinct from one another.[54] The former is made up of individuals and institutions[55] devoted to 'democracy assistance programs' abroad, while the latter is composed primarily of INGOs. The human rights community has created a law-versus-politics dichotomy through which it presents itself as the guardian of international law, in this case human rights law, rather than the promoter of the more elusive concept of democracy, which it considers a political ideology.[56]

---

[53] Henry J. Steiner, *Diverse Partners: Non-Governmental Organizations in the Human Rights Movement* (Cambridge, Mass.: Harvard Law School Human Rights Program, 1991), 19.

[54] For a comprehensive journalistic account of the differences between the two communities, see Thomas Carothers, 'Democracy and Human Rights: Policy Allies or Rivals?' (Summer 1994) Washington Quarterly 109.

[55] These include governmental agencies such as USAID or their European and Canadian equivalents, quasi-governmental and non-governmental organizations, programmes at major Western universities, policy institutes, foundations, and academic and policy specialists. Ibid. 110.

[56] Ibid. 111.

4. THE CONCEPTUALIZERS: HUMAN RIGHTS AND CONSTITUTIONALISM

Conceptualizers regard, or would like to regard, the human rights corpus as a constitutional framework: a set of norms, ideals, and principles—moral, philosophical, legal, even cultural—which cohere to determine the fundamental character of a State and its society. They do not openly distinguish or distance themselves from doctrinalists, whom they see as the human rights movement's critical core, its foot soldiers, those on whom the practical advocacy, proselytization, and universalization of its creed depend. Rather, constitutionalists are the 'thinking' corps of the movement; as its ideologues, they provide intellectual direction and rigour. They explore and explain issues relating to the movement's origin, its philosophical and historical bases, its normative content, and the connections among social, political, and cultural structures and values, as well as the questions which arise from the enforcement and internationalization of human rights norms. When constitutionalists criticize the human rights corpus and its movement, it is in language that is internal and 'friendly' to the discourse. They seek to sharpen the movement's focus and expand its influence by exploring moral and political dilemmas, normative conflicts within the corpus, the scope of the movement, and differences in the strategies deployed in the vindication of the movement's values. Constitutionalists were among the founders of INGOs and many serve on their boards.[57]

In this section, I will explore the works of a number of leading constitutionalists and both bring out and underline the basic messages and themes they advance in order to create and crystallize what I refer to as the 'defining' character of the human rights movement. Prominent among the constitutionalists has been Louis Henkin.[58] Perhaps more than any other proponent in this school, Henkin has combined extensive and authoritative scholarship with active association with the nerve centre of the American human rights community in New York. Among others in this school, I will also briefly explore the works of Henry Steiner[59] and Thomas Franck.[60] I contend here that while these thinkers do not completely agree on the content or even the normative importance of different human rights, nevertheless they are united generally in their vision of the political society intended by the human rights corpus.

In the preface to the *Age of Rights*, a collection of essays that crystallizes his ideas

[57] Examples include Professor Louis Henkin, who serves on the board of directors of the Lawyers Committee for Human Rights and Professor Norman Dorsen, who chairs the Lawyers Committee board of directors.

[58] Some of Henkin's human rights works include: *The Age of Rights* (New York: Columbia University Press, 1990) (hereinafter Henkin, *Age of Rights*); Henkin, *The Rights of Man Today* (Boulder, Colo.: Westview Press, 1978); *Human Rights: An Agenda for the Next Century* (Washington: American Society of International Law, 1994) (edited with John L. Hargrove).

[59] Steiner's writings include: *Diverse Partners* and 'Political Participation' (cited in nn. 53 and 16); 'Ideals and Counter-Ideals in the Struggle Over Autonomy Regimes for Minorities' (1991) 66 Notre Dame Law Review 1539 (hereinafter Steiner, 'Autonomy Regimes'); 'The Youth of Rights' (1991) 104 Harvard Law Review 917 (reviewing Henkin, *Age of Rights*) (hereinafter Steiner, 'Youth of Rights').

[60] See Franck, 'The Emerging Right' (cited in n. 8).

on human rights, Henkin underlines his belief in the omnipotence of human rights by elevating them to a near-mythical, almost biblical plateau. For him, the universality of the acceptance of the idea of human rights sets it apart from all other ideas and gives it a most distinctive position in modern times. He boldly states that:

Ours is the age of rights. Human rights is the idea of our time, the only political-moral idea that has received universal acceptance. The Universal Declaration of Human Rights, adopted by the United Nations General Assembly in 1948, has been approved by virtually all governments representing all societies. Human rights are enshrined in the constitutions of virtually every one of today's 170 states—old states and new; religious, secular, and atheist; Western and Eastern; democratic, authoritarian, and totalitarian; market economy, socialist, and mixed; rich and poor, developed, developing, and less developed. Human rights is the subject of numerous international agreements, the daily grist of the mills of international politics, and a bone of continuing contention among superpowers.[61]

This celebratory and triumphant passage uses a quantitative approach—that is, the idea's dissemination and the diffusion of the idea to most corners of the earth—as the linchpin for determining the superiority of human rights over other ideas. But the quantitative approach, while persuasive, has its own problems. Based on this criterion, another plausible argument might be that ideas about free markets being the engine of economic development are equally, if not more universally, accepted than human rights. Furthermore, depending on how universal acceptance is calibrated, and who the participants are, might it not have been possible to argue at the close of the last century that colonialism enjoyed a similar status?

In any case, it seems highly doubtful that many of the States which constitute the international community are representative of their societies and cultures. It is certainly possible that the homage such States pay to human rights is part of a cynically manipulative strategy to be seen 'to belong' among the 'civilized' members of the international community. Universality obtained at the expense of genuine understanding and commitment cheapens and devalues the idea of human rights. Ultimately, such universality is of little normative value in the reconstruction of societies.

Like other Western pioneers of the concept of human rights, Henkin rejects claims of 'cultural relativism' or a multicultural approach to the construction of human rights.[62] He accuses those who advocate cultural and ideological diversity in the creation of the human rights corpus of desiring a vague, broad, ambiguous, and general text of human rights.[63] He sees such an approach as fatal because it would allow different societies to read into human rights texts what they will. Instead, he turns to the Universal Declaration of Human Rights, which he sees as the bedrock, and constitution, of human rights.[64] Although Henkin insists that human rights are

---

[61] Henkin, *Age of Rights*, p. ix.   [62] Ibid. p. x.   [63] Ibid.

[64] The UDHR, Henkin says, reflects a 'general commitment to ideas . . . that have become part of our zeitgeist' (ibid.). The framers of the international human rights texts, Henkin writes, did not seek to build an 'umbrella large enough to encompass everyone, but rather to respond to a sensed common moral intuition and to identify a small core of common values' (ibid.).

universal, he does not offer any non-Western political or moral underpinnings for them. Rather, he emphasizes that human rights are derived from 'natural rights theories and systems, harking back through English, American, and French constitutionalism to John Locke'.[65] Yet it would appear that the reason human rights instruments did not articulate the Western philosophical basis for the corpus was the need to present the image of universality and not simply, as Henkin suggests, because the framers were politicians and citizens as opposed to philosophers.[66]

Henkin draws many parallels between human rights and American or Western constitutionalism but, surprisingly, concludes that the human rights corpus does not require a particular political ideology. This conclusion, with which this chapter disagrees, has been popular among the pioneers of the human rights movement for a number of reasons, including their basic assertion that human rights are distinct from politics, defined here as a particular ideology, and can be achieved in different political traditions such as socialist, religious, or free-market systems. A further examination of the views of Henkin and other constitutionalists indicates just the opposite: that taken as a whole, their philosophy of human rights leads to the construction of liberal democratic States.

Henkin outlines and uses the basic precepts of American constitutionalism to argue that they are not required by the human rights corpus. He identifies these precepts as: 'original individual autonomy translated into popular sovereignty', a social contract requiring self-government 'through accountable representatives; . . . limited government for limited purposes', and basic individual rights.[67] He argues that the human rights regime 'reflect[s] no comprehensive political theory'[68] about how the individual should relate to the State and vice versa, that a State's failure to respect individual rights does not trigger the right of revolution, although the corpus gives a 'nod to popular sovereignty'[69] and requires the State to be more active because of the ideas of socialism and the welfare state.[70] Henkin concedes that human rights instruments point to particular principles, but quickly denies that such principles imply a particular political theory:

> Necessarily, however, the idea of rights reflected in the instruments, the particular rights recognized, and the consequent responsibilities for political societies, imply particular political ideas and moral principles. International human rights does not hint at any theory of social contract, but it is committed to popular sovereignty. 'The will of the people shall be the basis of the authority of government' and is to 'be expressed in periodic elections which shall be by universal and equal suffrage.' It is not required that government based on the will of the people take any particular form.[71]

---

65 Henkin, *Age of Rights*, 6.
66 Ibid. Henkin has suggested that the diversity of cultures and political traditions has caused the human rights movement to eschew inquiries into the philosophical origins and justifications for the human rights corpus, fearing that such inquiry would prove 'disruptive and unhelpful'. Steiner, 'Youth of Rights', 919.   67 Henkin, *Age of Rights*, 6.   68 Ibid.
69 Ibid.   70 Ibid.
71 Ibid. 7 (footnote omitted) (quoting UDHR, Article 21(3)).

In addition to the Universal Declaration on Human Rights, the International Covenant on Civil and Political Rights gives citizens the right to political participation through elections and the guarantee of the right to assemble, associate, and disseminate their ideas.[72] These, along with the rights to equality and a fair trial, imply a society with the following structure: a regularly elected government, with real competition for political office, and the separation and independence of powers among the branches of government. The protection of the individual, his autonomy, and property are among the key goals of such a society. The human rights regime does not dictate the particular variant of liberal society or the colour of democracy it envisions. But the rights it guarantees, the ones which Henkin champions as the corner-stone of the human rights regime, seem to require a Western liberal democracy.

Henkin seeks to distinguish human rights from American constitutionalism according to the bases on which government is instituted. He argues that while 'American rights' originally required a government for limited purposes, human rights, born after socialism and the welfare state, 'imply a government that is activist, intervening, [and] committed to economic-social planning' to meet the needs of the individual.[73] This distinction, which relies on the traditional bifurcation of the responsibilities of government—either as the hands-off, negative instrumentalist or the regulating, positive interventionist—is more fictitious than real. The social democratic strand of liberalism, which Donnelly credits with the welfare state,[74] has deep roots in liberalism and has historically challenged the individualist formulations of American constitutionalism. As Henkin himself acknowledges, the United States is not a welfare state by constitutional compulsion, but it is a welfare state nevertheless.[75] The political struggles of working Americans and particularly of historically excluded groups such as African-Americans and women have transformed 'original American rights' and explicitly imposed interventionist commitments on the American State to alleviate economic and social disparities. Thus the distance between 'American rights' and human rights that Henkin creates is somewhat exaggerated.

Henry Steiner, another constitutionalist whose writing has concentrated on the content of human rights norms and the structure of the human rights regime, is more inclined to the view that human rights norms are best accomplished, and in most cases only accomplished, within liberal democracy. There is no suggestion that a theocracy or a military regime could accomplish human rights. Although he does not state it explicitly, a number of his writings suggest this conclusion.[76] In his first major article on human rights, for example, Steiner chose to explore the question of political participation, a foundational norm in liberal democracies, from a human

---

[72] On assembly, see ICCPR, Articles 21 and 22; the right to political participation is contained in Article 25; the right to expression in Article 19; the rights of free speech in Article 18.
[73] Henkin, *Age of Rights*, 145.   [74] Donnelly, 'Human Rights', 54–5.
[75] Henkin, *Age of Rights*, 153.
[76] See e.g. Steiner and Alston, *International Human Rights in Context*.

rights perspective.[77] Drawing primarily on the UDHR and the ICCPR, which Steiner terms the 'two most significant' human rights instruments,[78] the article side-steps any discussion about the philosophical and historical origins or justifications for human rights.[79]

Steiner realizes the complex character of the norm of political participation and even argues that different political systems could meet its standard as formulated in Article 25. He nevertheless pushes for an understanding of it that comes closer to a liberal pluralist formulation. Such an understanding would reject hereditary, non-competitive, one-party, or ritualistic 'yes-or-no' electoral systems where the citizens vote to evaluate a single candidate only as inadequate. When seen as part of the gamut of the other four categories of rights which Steiner identifies, an interpretation of Article 25 brings the norm of political participation closer to liberal political democracy.

Moreover, although Steiner seems to agree with Henkin that association and participation rights do not impose a particular government or political ideology, he identifies liberal democratic systems such as parliamentary or presidential systems, unicameral or bicameral legislatures, proportional representation or the 'first past the post' system as permissible under human rights standards.[80] At the same time, he notes that dictatorships, inherited leadership, and many forms of one-party States would probably violate associational rights.[81]

Elsewhere, Steiner is more explicit about the association of human rights norms with liberalism and the political structures of liberal democracy. In an article on autonomy regimes for minorities, Steiner imagines the application of norms and ideals which are essential to liberalism.[82] He argues for a political regime that recognizes the rights of ethnic, racial, and religious minorities to cultural survival and freedom from violence and repression by the majority. He notes that repressive and authoritarian governments preclude an effective voice for minorities, as would majority democracies where the political structures give the 'minority no effective electoral power or political leverage'.[83] He further notes that minorities can use the ICCPR to argue for the 'kind of fair or equitable political participation that article 25 [ICCPR] should be interpreted to require'.[84] He locates the basis for the protection of the rights of minorities in the human rights regime's insistence upon and promotion of difference and diversity.[85]

Steiner emphasizes that the norm of equal protection—'perhaps the preeminent

---

[77] Steiner, 'Political Participation', 177.

[78] Ibid. 79. Steiner calls the UDHR the 'spiritual parent' of many human rights treaties; the ICCPR's importance hinges on its acceptance by most of the world's States in all regions and ideological blocs. These facts give the two instruments 'universal scope' (ibid.).

[79] Continuing the theme of universality, he notes, however, that 'rights may be understood to be rooted in natural law or positive enactment. They may be justified by liberal postulates or by the imperative of socialist construction' (ibid. 80).   [80] Steiner, 'Youth of Rights', 930.

[81] Ibid. 930–1.   [82] See Steiner, 'Autonomy Regimes', 1539.

[83] Ibid. 1546.   [84] Ibid.   [85] Ibid. 1547–8.

human rights norm'[86]—plays a key role in the protection and encouragement of diversity. He cites the freedoms of association, assembly, and expression as the vital complement to the project of equal protection.[87] In my view, the following passage sums up Steiner's 'philosophy' of human rights and reveals his biases, although in most of his writings he seems studiously to avoid identifying human rights law with any one ideological orientation:

The aspirations of the human rights movement reach beyond the goal of preventing disasters. The movement also has a 'utopian' dimension that envisions a vibrant and broadly based political community. Such a vision underscores the potential of the human rights movement for conflict with regimes all over the world. *A society honoring the full range of contemporary human rights would be hospitable to many types of pluralism and skeptical about any one final truth, at least to the point of allowing and protecting difference. It would not stop at the protection of negative rights but would encourage citizens to exercise their right to political participation, one path toward enabling peoples to realize the right to self-determination. It would ensure room for dissent and alternative visions of social and political life by keeping open and protecting access to the roads toward change.*[88]

Thomas Franck is the first prominent constitutionalist to argue that democratic governance[89] has evolved from moral prescription into an international legal obligation.[90] Franck regards three recent occurrences as the unmistakable signs of the emergent right to governance: first, the failure of the August 1991 coup in the Soviet Union; second, the unanimous October 1991 resolution by the UN General Assembly to restore Jean-Bertrand Aristide, the then-ousted Haitian president; and third, the proliferation of States committed to competitive elections.[91] In celebratory fashion, Franck highlights the rejection of the 'dictatorship of the proletariat',[92] 'people's democracy',[93] and the dictatorships of Africa and Asia by 'people almost everywhere'[94] who 'now demand that government be validated by western-style parliamentary, multiparty democratic process'.[95] He emphasizes that '[o]nly a few, usually military or theocratic, regimes still resist the trend'.[96]

After exploring the involvement of regional and international organizations and governments in activities which enhance the right to democratic governance—such as sanctions systems and election monitoring—Franck lists the human rights instruments that constitute 'the large normative canon'[97] which promotes democratic entitlement. These instruments recognize individual rights and require equal protection. Franck here uses human rights law to underpin the right to democratic governance.

While the majority of constitutionalists are reluctant to make explicit connections

---

[86] Ibid. 1548.   [87] Ibid.
[88] Steiner, 'The Youth of Rights', 931 (emphasis added).
[89] He uses the term to describe a legal and practical commitment to 'open, multiparty, secret-ballot elections with a universal franchise' (Franck, 'The Emerging Right', 47).
[90] Ibid.   [91] Ibid. 46–7.   [92] Ibid. 48.   [93] Ibid. 47.
[94] Ibid. 49.   [95] Ibid.
[96] Ibid. He adds that '[v]ery few argue that parliamentary democracy is a western illusion and a neocolonialist trap for unwary Third World peoples' (ibid.).   [97] Ibid. 79.

between the human rights corpus and political democracy, they generally use typically Western conceptions of rights to explain the content and implications of human rights law. Although many make references to the influence of different types of socialism on the making of human rights, such references are scattered and carry minor significance in these analyses. Constitutionalists virtually never explore non-Western ideals and notions of rights or duties in an inclusive manner. However, there is no paucity of references to non-Western ideas, practices, and political and social structures that contradict human rights norms.

5. THE AGNOSTIC CHALLENGE TO HUMAN RIGHTS

One of the most probing critiques of the human rights corpus has come from non-Western thinkers who, though educated in the West or in Western-oriented educational systems, pose philosophical, moral, and cultural questions about the distinctly Eurocentric formulation of human rights discourse. They have difficulties accepting the specific cultural and historical experiences of the West as the standard for all humanity. As outsider-insiders,[98] cultural agnostics understand and accept certain contributions of Western (largely European) civilization to the human rights movement, but reject the wholesale adoption or imposition of Western ideas and concepts of human rights. Instead, they present external critiques of human rights discourse, while generally applying language internal to that discourse. By agnostics, I do not refer to external critics who think that as a Western project the human rights system is irredeemable and cannot rearrange its priorities or be transformed by other cultural milieux to reflect a genuinely universal character and consensus. Rather, I mean those who advocate a multicultural approach in the reconstruction of the entire edifice of human rights. They could also be termed human rights pluralists.

There is no dispute about the European origins of the philosophy of the human rights movement, even Westerners who advocate its universality accept this basic fact. Refuge from this disturbing reality is taken in the large number of States, from all cultural blocs, who have indicated their acceptance of the regime by becoming parties to the principal human rights instruments.[99] Others argue that as more non-Western States have become significant members of the international community, their influence on international law-making has corrected the initial lopsidedness of the enterprise and allowed other historical heritages to exert themselves.

This positivist approach has some value but it does not answer the agnostic challenge or endow the human rights corpus with multicultural universality. There are fundamental defects in presenting the State as the reservoir of cultural heritage.

---

[98] I use the term 'outsider-insiders' to bunch together Africans, Asians, Latin Americans, non-mainstream Western scholars, and certain members of racial and cultural minorities in the West, such as African-Americans and Asian-Americans.

[99] As of Oct. 1997, 138 States had ratified, acceded, or succeeded to the ICCPR. See 1997 Report of the Human Rights Committee, GAOR Supp. No. 40 (A/52/40).

Many States have been alien to their populations and it is questionable whether they represent those populations or whether they are little more than internationally recognized cartels organized for the sake of maintaining power and access to resources.[100] It is difficult to identify the motivations, for example, which led the abusive Zairian State of Mobutu Sese Seko to ratify the major human rights instruments.[101] Respect for international standards could not have been high among them. Many States seem to ratify human rights instruments to blunt criticism and because as a general rule the cost to their sovereignty is nominal.

Agnostics look beyond the positive law and explore the historical and cultural imperatives that are essential for the creation of a legitimate corpus. Some point, for example, to the celebration of the individual egoist in human rights law as a demonstration of its limited application. As I have noted elsewhere:

The argument by current reformers that Africa merely needs a liberal democratic, rule-of-law state to be freed from despotism is mistaken. The transplantation of the narrow formulation of Western liberalism cannot adequately respond to the historical reality and the political and social needs of Africa. The sacralization of the individual and the supremacy of the jurisprudence of individual rights in organized political and social society is not a natural, 'transhistorical', or universal phenomenon, applicable to all societies, without regard to time and place.[102]

Thus, some agnostics resist the unremitting emphasis on the individual. In particular, some African scholars have been uncomfortable with this emphasis. Okere notes, for example, that '[t]he African conception of man is not that of an isolated and abstract individual, but an integral member of a group animated by a spirit of solidarity'.[103] Individuals are not atomistic units 'locked in a constant struggle against society for the redemption of their rights'.[104] The concept of the group-centred individual in Africa delicately entwines rights and duties, and harmonizes the individual with the society. Such a conception does not necessarily consider society—whether organized as the community or the State—as the individual's primary antagonist.[105] Nor does it permit the overindulgence of the individual at the expense

---

[100] I have argued elsewhere that the State in Africa was organized for the purposes of colonial exploitation, it was decolonized as a tool of the international State system and the Cold War, and it has survived without internal legitimacy or coherence because of external support. See Makau wa Mutua, 'Why Redraw the Map of Africa: A Moral and Legal Inquiry' (1995) 16 Michigan Journal of International Law 1113.

[101] See Makau wa Mutua and Peter Rosenblum, *Zaire: Repression As Policy* (Lawyers Committee for Human Rights, 1990) (documenting the abuses of the Zairian State against its own citizens).

[102] Mutua, 'African Cultural Fingerprint', 341.

[103] B. Obinna Okere, 'The Protection of Human Rights in Africa and the African Charter on Human and Peoples' Rights: A Comparative Analysis with the European and American Systems' (1984) 6 Human Rights Quarterly 141 at 148. John Mbiti has argued that in Africa the individual's rights, needs, sorrows, and duties are woven in a tapestry that denies runaway individualism. 'I am because we are; and since we are, therefore I am' (Mbiti, *African Religions and Philosophy* (New York: Praeger, 1969), 141).

[104] Richard N. Kiwanuka, 'The Meaning of "People" in the African Charter on Human and Peoples' Rights' (1988) 82 American Journal of International Law 80 at 82.

[105] See Mutua, 'African Cultural Fingerprint', 363.

of the society.[106] This conception resists casting the individual as the centre of the moral universe; instead, both the community and the individual exist on an equally hallowed plane.

In the context of Asia, a number of writers have also cast doubt on the individualist conception of rights and its emphasis on negative rights.[107] Although many of these commentators are connected to governments in the region, and therefore have an interest in defending certain policy and development approaches, it would be unwise to dismiss them out of hand. Such dismissals, which the INGO community issues with haste and without much thought as to the cultural character of the human rights corpus, have aggravated differences between the West and certain Asian countries over the interpretation of human rights.[108] Yash Ghai of the University of Hong Kong powerfully criticizes the cynical distortion of Asian conceptions of community, culture, and religion, as well as the use of the State apparatus to crush dissent. He argues that political élites manipulate cultural imagery to further economic development and retain power.[109] But that critique does not elaborate upon the cultural and philosophical differences between different Asian and Western traditions nor how those differences might manifest themselves in the construction of human rights norms.

Cultural agnostics do not reject the Western conception of human rights in its entirety, nor even deny that a universal corpus may ultimately yield societal typologies and structures similar to those imagined by the present human rights regime. What they hold dear is the opportunity for all major cultural blocs to negotiate the normative content of human rights law and the purposes for which the discourse should legitimately be deployed. Many African agnostics and some Africanists, for example, have demonstrated the similarity of human rights norms in Western States to those in precolonial African States and societies. These included due (fair) process protections,[110]

---

[106] Dunstan Wai argues that African conceptions of human rights guaranteed a 'modicum of social justice and values concerned with individual and collective rights' (Wai, 'Human Rights in Sub-Saharan Africa', in Adamantia Pollis and Peter Schwab (eds.), *Human Rights: Cultural and Ideological Perspectives* (New York: Praeger, 1979), 115 at 116). Asmarom Legesse notes the importance of this balance between the individual and the society so that 'individuals do not deviate so far from the norm that they can overwhelm the society' (Legesse, 'Human Rights in African Political Culture', in Kenneth W. Thompson (ed.), *The Moral Imperatives of Human Rights: A World Survey* (Lanham, Md.: University Press of America, 1980), 123 at 125).

[107] A vocal advocate of the Asian conception of human rights has argued, for instance, that many East and South-east Asians 'prefer a situation in which distinctions between the individual, society, and state are less clear-cut, or at least less adversarial' (Kausikan, 'Asia's Different Standard', 36). For a forceful repudiation of Kausikan, see Aryeh Neier, 'Asia's Unacceptable Standard' (1993) 92 Foreign Policy 42.

[108] Human Rights Watch has rejected the so-called Asian concept of human rights. See *World Report 1995*, p. xiv.

[109] See Yash Ghai, 'Human Rights and Governance: The Asian Debate' (1994) 15 Australian Yearbook of International Law 1 at 20.

[110] Kwasi Wiredu, for example, contends that the principle of innocence until proven guilty was an essential part of Akan (West African peoples') consciousness (Wiredu, 'An Akan Perspective on Human Rights', in An-Na'im and Deng (eds.), *Cross-Cultural Perspectives*, 243 at 252). Timothy Fernyhough notes Africa's respect for the right to life and procedural due process (Fernyhough, 'Human Rights and Precolonial Africa', in Ronald Cohen *et al.* (eds.), *Human Rights and Governance in Africa* (Gainesville,

the right to political participation,[111] and the rights to welfare, limited government, free speech, conscience, and association.[112] These rights, however, were enjoyed neither as an end in themselves nor with the sole intent of fulfilling the self only. Among the major human rights instruments, the African Charter on Human and Peoples' Rights alone attempts the comprehensive unification of these conflicting notions of community, individual rights, and duties to the family, the community, and the State.[113]

Agnostics agree that many of the human rights in the current corpus are valid as human rights, their Western origin notwithstanding. The difficulty lies in the emphasis placed on certain rights, their ranking within the corpus, and ultimately the political character of the State required or implied by that conception of rights. Although African agnostics, for example, bitterly oppose the violations of civil and political rights by the post-colonial State, they see little redemption in a campaign or world-view that seeks merely to transplant Western notions of political democracy and 'negative' rights to African States. The contrived nature of the African State and its inability to claim the loyalties of its citizens have been compounded by the delegitimation of cultural and philosophical identities by European values and practices. Africa appears to have lost its pre-colonial moral compass and fallen prey to the machinations of bands of élites who exist in cultural suspension, being neither African nor foreign.

The dilemma of the agnostic is therefore not that he sees an 'evil' in the Eurocentric formulation of the human rights corpus; although he sees a lot of good in it, he does not agree with its zealous Western construction and its close identification with liberal democracy. Ultimately, of course, the major bone of contention is the cultural legitimacy of the corpus in non-Western settings.

6. POLITICAL INSTRUMENTALISM IN HUMAN RIGHTS

Of all the four typologies explored here, the school of political strategists is the least principled and the most open-textured in the manner and purposes for which it deploys human rights discourse. Apart from the United Nations, whose Office of the High Commissioner for Human Rights is responsible for human rights matters, Western governments, and particularly the United States, have been the principal advocates for the use of human rights as an instrument of policy against other States. In this respect, human rights standards have been viewed as norms with

Fla.: University Press of Florida, 1993), 39 at 56). He notes, further, that 'in the Tio kingdom north of modern Brazzaville, . . . as elsewhere in Africa, a strong tradition of jurisprudence existed, with specific rulings for penalties cited as precedents, such as levels of fines for adultery' (ibid. 62).

[111] See Wiredu, 'An Akan Perspective', 248–9.

[112] For example, Wiredu notes that Akan thought recognized the right of children to be nursed and educated, the right of an adult to land, and the rights to expression and political participation (ibid. 257). See also Mutua, 'African Cultural Fingerprint', 346–7.

[113] African Charter on Human and Peoples' Rights, 27 June 1981, OAU Doc. CAB/LEG/67/3/Rev.5 (1981), reprinted in (1982) 21 International Legal Materials 59.

which non-Western, non-democratic States must comply. From the birth of the movement half a century ago, the United States viewed human rights 'as designed to improve the condition of human rights in countries other than the United States (and a very few like-minded liberal states)'.[114] Henkin thinks that because individual rights 'dominate its [American] constitutional jurisprudence, and are the pride of its people, their banner to the world',[115] such a view is natural. Western European industrial democracies hold similar viewpoints, as evidenced by their trade and aid policies towards each other and non-Western states.[116] International financial institutions—Western institutions such as the World Bank and the IMF—have followed the lead of these major powers and started to link some of their activities to human rights concerns.[117]

The United States was a principal player in the drafting of the major international human rights instruments, although it has been reluctant to become a party to most of them.[118] It was not until the 1970s that the United States started institutionalizing human rights within its foreign policy bureaucracy.[119] Policy upheavals triggered by US intervention in Vietnam, American support for repressive regimes in Latin America, and the crises of the Nixon presidency precipitated a more systematic evaluation of human rights concerns in American foreign policy.[120] As a result, some laws were amended to restrict assistance to countries with particular levels of human rights abuses.[121] In 1977, President Jimmy Carter elevated the head of the Human Rights Bureau[122] within the Department of State to the rank of Assistant Secretary of State for Human Rights and Humanitarian Affairs.[123] Perhaps Carter's lasting achievement will be the rhetorical prominence that his administration gave human rights within American foreign policy.

---

[114] Henkin, *Age of Rights*, 74.   [115] Ibid. 65.

[116] See Demetrios James Marantis, 'Human Rights, Democracy, and Development: The European Community Model' (1994) 7 Harvard Human Rights Journal 1.

[117] See F. L. Osunsade, *IMF Support for African Adjustment Programs: Questions and Answers* (Washington: IMF, 1993), 8; cf. Balakrishnan Rajagopal, 'Crossing the Rubicon: Synthesizing the Soft International Law of the IMF and Human Rights' (1993) 11 Boston University International Law Journal 81.

[118] The United States has only recently ratified two important human rights instruments: the 1949 Convention on the Prevention and Punishment of Genocide, ratified by the US in 1988; and the ICCPR, ratified by the US in 1992. Among others, the US has still not ratified the ICESCR, the Convention on the Elimination of All Forms of Racial Discrimination, the Convention for the Elimination of All Forms of Discrimination Against Women, and the American Convention on Human Rights. See Henkin, *Age of Rights*, 74–5.

[119] See American Association for the International Commission of Jurists, *Human Rights and US Foreign Policy: The First Decade 1973–1983* (New York: American Association for the International Commission of Jurists, 1984), 6 (hereinafter *US Foreign Policy*).

[120] Ibid. 9.

[121] See Foreign Assistance Act, Pub. L. No. 93–559, § 46, 88 Stat. 1795, 1815 (1974); International Development and Food Assistance Act, Pub. L. 94–161, title III, § 310, 89 Stat. 849, 860 (1975). The amendments made human rights a 'principal goal' of US foreign policy.

[122] Congress mandated the establishment of this office and instructed it to report annually on the human rights conditions in every country in the world.

[123] *US Foreign Policy*, 17.

The Carter legacy has not achieved continued support or consistency in the application of human rights to foreign policy. There have always been glaring gaps between declared US policy and actual practice towards foreign countries. Under Carter, inconsistent attempts were made to link support for particular countries to their human rights records, a task that was made increasingly difficult by the logic of the Cold War. As a general rule, pro-Western but despotic States such as the Shah's Iran, Zaire, South Korea, and Indonesia continued to receive US military assistance.[124] The Reagan administration continued American support for abusive client States by enlisting human rights as a key ally in the greater struggle against communism.[125]

This reasoning eventually led the administration to solidify its human rights policy around the promotion of democracy. This policy was outlined as the promotion of 'democratic processes in order to help build a world environment more favorable to respect for human rights'.[126] It was billed as a dual policy that opposed human rights violations while strengthening democracy. The policy was aimed singularly at the promotion of democracy 'as *the* human right, rejecting in principle not only the military "juntas" but the many one-party states of Africa and Asia'.[127] In reality, of course, the administration supported right-wing dictatorships and oppressive pro-Western regimes, including apartheid South Africa. Since the end of the Cold War, however, political conditionality has frequently been used to push one-party States towards the creation of more open, democratic political structures.[128]

The Bush administration did not dramatically depart from the substance of the Reagan policy, although it withdrew knee-jerk support for some pro-Western regimes, primarily as a result of the collapse of communism.[129] Despite its rhetorical defence of human rights, the Clinton administration has been more concerned with the promotion of democratic initiatives and trade opportunities than with the principled application of human rights norms.[130] The United States has frequently used human rights as a weapon of its foreign policy, but that use has rarely been principled. The invocation of human rights has been used in various ways to justify access

---

[124] Ibid. 21 (quoting Secretary of State Cyrus Vance: ' "In each case", the Secretary explained, "we must balance a political concern for human rights against economic and security goals".').

[125] Henkin, *Age of Rights*, 71.

[126] Department of State, *Country Reports for Human Rights Practices for 1985* (Washington: US Government Printers, 1986), 3.

[127] Henkin, *Age of Rights*, 72.

[128] See Lawyers Committee for Human Rights, *The World Bank: Governance and Human Rights* (New York: Lawyers Committee for Human Rights, 1993). See also Jane Perlez, 'On Eve of Talks with Aid Donors, Kenya is under Pressure to Democratize', *New York Times*, 25 Nov. 1991, A9.

[129] See generally Human Rights Watch, *Human Rights Watch World Report 1992: Events of 1991* (New York: Human Rights Watch, 1992), 1–2.

[130] In Oct. 1994, for example, the Clinton administration forced the restoration to power of the democratically elected Haitian government of President Aristide. See *World Report 1995*, 99. However, in May of that same year, it also ended the linkage of China's Most Favoured Nation status to human rights conditions (ibid. 146–7).

to markets or resources vital to the United States, as was the case with the US-led military defeat of Iraq in 1991. The support and promotion of popularly elected regimes has, however, been privileged by the Clinton administration as the more effective method for advancing what it regards as the three inseparable goals of democracy, human rights, and, most importantly, free markets.[131]

International financial institutions and donor agencies also constitute an increasingly important component of the political strategy approach. Groups of donors led by the World Bank, which keep many States in the South from total economic collapse, have used human rights conditionalities to force economic liberalization, a measure of public accountability, and political pluralism. But the World Bank's concern with 'good governance' has not been altruistic. That change in attitude came after the Bank's utter failure to reverse economic decline in Africa. Overlooking its own role in exacerbating Africa's underdevelopment, the Bank concluded in 1989 that 'underlying the litany of Africa's development problems is a crisis of governance'.[132] In what amounted to a prescription for liberal democracy, it defined governance in the following familiar language:

By governance is meant the exercise of political power to manage a nation's affairs. Because countervailing power has been lacking, state officials in many countries have served their own interests without fear of being called to account. . . . The leadership assumes broad discretionary authority and loses its legitimacy. Information is controlled, and many voluntary organizations are co-opted or disbanded. This environment cannot readily support a dynamic economy. At worst the state becomes coercive and arbitrary. These trends, however, can be resisted. . . . It requires a systematic effort to build a pluralistic institutional structure, a determination to respect the rule of law, and vigorous protection of the freedom of the press and human rights.[133]

The Bank has used its forbidding political and economic muscle to stare a few States down and push for political reform. Through its consultative groups (CGs)—the collection of donors—it pressed for political change in Kenya and Malawi in the early 1990s, although it did not heed its own message in continuing support for China, Zaire, Morocco, and Indonesia, to name just a few undemocratic States with serious human rights problems.[134] INGOs have seized this opening to seek a more systematic application of human rights norms by multilateral donors.[135] The significance of the Bank's general attitude lies in its conclusions: economic liberalization and free markets are less likely to occur in undemocratic regimes that abuse basic liberal freedoms.[136] The trademark of political strategists is their unabashed deploy-

---

[131] As a demonstration of the view that human rights, democracy, and free markets are intrinsically linked, the Assistant Secretary of State for Human Rights and Humanitarian Affairs has been renamed the 'Assistant Secretary of State for Democracy, Human Rights, and Labor'. See 22 USC § 2151n(c) (1994).

[132] World Bank, *Sub-Saharan Africa: From Crisis to Sustainable Growth, a Long-Term Prospective Study* (Washington: World Bank, 1989), 60.   [133] Ibid. 60–1.

[134] See Lawyers Committee for Human Rights, *The World Bank*, 37–42.

[135] Ibid.

[136] World Bank, 'The Challenge for Development', in *World Development Report 1991* (1991), 133, cited in Lawyers Committee for Human Rights, *The World Bank*, 41–2.

ment of human rights and democracy as interchangeable in order to advance a variety of interests: strategic, tactical, geopolitical, security, 'vital', economic, and political. Not one of the preceding three schools of thought manages to equal their cynicism.

7. CONCLUDING REMARKS

This chapter has attempted to make a more explicit link between human rights norms and the fundamental characteristics of liberal democracy as practised in the West, and to question the mythical elevation of the human rights corpus beyond politics and political ideology. In the past, the main authors of the human rights discourse were reluctant to make this connection either, I suspect, because they sincerely did not believe that an honest inquiry could pin the human rights movement down to a specific political structure, or because it would have been an admission against interest in the context of the Cold War, amidst States only too eager to exploit cultural and political excuses to justify or continue repressive policies and practices. Now that the end of the Cold War has lifted at least part of that injunction, it seems imperative that probing inquiries about the philosophical and political *raison d'être* of the human rights regime be encouraged and welcomed.

While I do not suppose that the human rights movement is a conspiracy to strengthen the West's cultural stranglehold over the globe, I do believe that its abstraction and apoliticization obscure the political character of the norms that it seeks to universalize. As I see it, that universe is at once in its core and, within its many details, both liberal and European. The continued reluctance to identify liberal democracy with human rights delays the reformation, reconstruction, and the multiculturization of those rights. Defining those who seek to reopen or continue the debate about the cultural nature and the raw political purposes of the human rights regime as 'outsiders' or even 'enemies' of the movement is the greatest impediment to the achievement of true universalization.

Half a century after the Universal Declaration of Human Rights laid the foundation for the human rights movement, its ideas have been embraced by diverse peoples across the earth. That fact is undeniable. But it is only half the story. Those same people who have embraced the corpus also seek to contribute to it, sometimes by radically reformulating it, sometimes tinkering at the margins. The human rights movement must therefore not be closed to the idea of change or believe that it is the 'final' answer. This belief, which is religious in the evangelical sense, invites 'end of history'-type conclusions and leaves humanity stuck at the doors of liberalism, unable to go forward or even imagine a post-liberal society. As the assertion of a final truth, it must be rejected.

From the perspective of this chapter, the human rights corpus is a philosophy that seeks the diffusion of liberalism and its primacy around the globe. It is, ironically, favourable to political and cultural homogenization and hostile to difference and diversity, the two variables that are at the heart of the vitality of the world today. Yet, strangely, many human rights instruments explicitly encourage diversity through the norm of equal protection.

The paradox of the corpus is that it seeks to foster diversity and difference but does so only under the rubric of Western political democracy. In other words, it says that diversity is good so long as it is exercised within the liberal paradigm, a construct that for the purposes of the corpus is not negotiable. The doors of difference appear open while in reality being shut. This inelasticity and cultural parochialism of the human rights corpus requires urgent revision so that the ideals of difference and diversity can realize their true meaning. The long-term interests of the human rights movement are not likely to be served by the pious and righteous advocacy of human rights norms as frozen and fixed principles whose content and cultural relevance is unquestionable.

Based on this premiss, the human rights movement needs to alter its orientation, away from its moral, political, and legal certitude. There needs to be a realization that the movement is young, and that its youth gives it an experimental status, not that of a final truth. The major authors of the human rights discourse seem to believe that all the most important human rights standards and norms have been set and that what remains of the project is elaboration and implementation. This attitude is at the heart of the push prematurely to cut off debate about the political and philosophical roots, nature, and relevance of the human rights corpus.

The failure of most universalists, particularly the conventional doctrinalists, to engage positively in this debate unnecessarily antagonizes cultural agnostics and may engender legitimate charges of cultural imperialism. This is particularly the case if the human rights corpus is seen purely as a liberal project whose overriding goal, though not explicitly stated, is the imposition of a Western-style liberal democracy. The forceful rejection of dialogue also leads to the inevitable conclusion that there is a hierarchy of cultures, an assumption that is not only detrimental to the human rights project but is also inconsistent with the human rights corpus's commitment to equality, diversity, and difference. Ultimately, the unrelenting universalist push seeks to destroy difference by creating the rationale for various forms of intervention and penetration of other cultures with the intent of transforming them into the liberal model. This view legitimizes intervention and leaves open to choice only the mode of that intervention, that is, whether it is to be imposed by military action, through sanction systems, bilaterally or multilaterally, as a cultural package bound in one or another form of exchange, or through trade and aid.

It is important that conversations about human rights should not be singularly obsessed with the universalization of one or another cultural model. On the contrary, the overriding objective of actors in this discourse should be the conceptualization of norms and political models whose experimental purpose is the reduction—if not the elimination—of conditions which foster human indignity, violence, poverty, and powerlessness. For that to be possible and to resonate in different corners of the earth, societies have to participate at their grass roots in the construction of principles and structures which enhance the human dignity of all, be they big or small, male or female, believer or unbeliever, of different races or different communities. But those principles and structures must be grown at home, and must utilize the cultural tools familiar to those people at the grass roots. Even if they turn out to resemble the ideas and institutions of political democracy, or to borrow from it, they will belong to the people. What the human rights movement must not do is to close all doors, turn away other cultures, and impose itself in its current form and structure upon the world. A post-liberal society, whatsoever form that takes, cannot be constructed by freezing liberalism in time.

9

Governing the Global Economy through Government Networks

ANNE-MARIE SLAUGHTER

How can States regulate an increasingly global economy? The litany of threats to State sovereignty is familiar: global financial flows, global corporations, global television, global computing, and global transportation networks. The generally accepted account of how such threats render State borders increasingly permeable and thus State power increasingly feeble conceives of sovereignty itself as a curiously static attribute, as if State power depended on maintaining territory as a hermetically sealed sphere. However, as Abram and Antonia Chayes point out, sovereignty in the post-Cold War and even the post-Second World War world is increasingly defined not by the power to insulate but by the power to participate—in international institutions of all kinds.[1] As globalization literally turns the world inside-out, nationalizing international law and internationalizing national law, the opportunities for such participation expand exponentially. What is new is that the resulting institutions are as likely to be transgovernmental as they are international or supranational. The result is indeed a 'power shift', but more within the State than away from it.[2]

Traditional conceptions of international law and international relations assume that States are the primary actors on the international stage and that States themselves are unitary, opaque, and capable of rational calculation. This is the image that gives rise to familiar metaphors such as billiard balls and black boxes; it is the assumption that feeds critical attacks on the liberal projection of the unitary individual onto the international system. As a unitary actor, the State speaks with one voice through the mouth of the head of state or chief executive. The assumption is not that the chief executive speaks only on his or her own account; on the contrary, he or she may be but a spokesperson for an outcome reached as the result of a complex interplay of domestic institutions and interests. Nevertheless, it is the head of state who is the embodiment and representative of the State in the international system, the gatekeeper for all interactions, both domestic and international.

Furthermore, it follows from this conception of the international system and of States as the primary actors within it that the rules governing international life must be a product of either State practice or negotiation. The resulting rules and institutions are described as being by States, for States, and of States. The paradigm is the multilateral international convention, negotiated over many years in various inter-

---

[1] Abram and Antonia Chayes, *The New Sovereignty* (Cambridge, Mass.: Harvard University Press, 1996). [2] See Jessica T. Mathews, 'Power Shift' (1997) 1 Foreign Affairs 76.

national watering holes, signed and ratified with attendant flourish and formality, and given continuing life through the efforts of an international secretariat whose members prod and assist ongoing rounds of negotiation aimed at securing compliance with obligations already undertaken and at expanding the scope and precision of existing rules. The rules and institutions described by the traditional conceptions of international law are indeed important for the regulation of international conflict and the facilitation of international co-operation. In short, they are important for the creation and maintenance of international order. However, they apply to part only, and arguably a diminishing part, of the rules and institutions that are generated outside any one national legal system but that directly regulate individuals and groups in both their domestic and foreign interactions.

The conventional debate over globalization and the attendant decline of State power is handicapped by this traditional conception of States and State institutions. In fact, the State is not disappearing; it is disaggregating into its component institutions. The primary State actors in the international realm are no longer foreign ministries and heads of state, but the same government institutions that dominate domestic politics: administrative agencies, courts, and legislatures. The traditional actors continue to play a role, but they are joined by fellow government officials pursuing quasi-autonomous policy agendas. The disaggregated State, as opposed to the mythical unitary State, is thus hydra-headed, represented and governed by multiple institutions in complex interaction with one another abroad as well as at home.

The corollary of the disaggregation of the State in foreign relations is the rise of government networks. Courts, administrative agencies, legislators, and heads of State are all networking with their foreign counterparts. Each of these institutions has the capacity not only to represent 'the national interest' in interactions with its foreign counterparts, but also to act on a subset of interests arising from its particular domestic function that are likely to be shared by its foreign counterparts. The resulting networks take a variety of forms and perform a variety of functions, some of which will be elaborated in the rest of this chapter. But they are all the tangible manifestation of a new era of transgovernmental regulatory co-operation. More broadly still, they define transgovernmentalism as a distinctive mode of global governance: horizontal rather than vertical, composed of national government officials rather than international bureaucrats, decentralized and informal rather than organized and rigid.

Against this backdrop, it is worth returning to the question posed at the beginning of this chapter: how can States regulate an increasingly global economy? The answer is through government networks. When President Clinton called for a co-ordinated institutional response to the burgeoning global economic crisis, he immediately deployed not his Secretary of State, but the Secretary of the Treasury and the Chairman of the Federal Reserve to contact their foreign counterparts and co-ordinate a global interest rate cut. International networks of these officials are already well established. Indeed, in many cases they have formed their own organizations, which bear little resemblance to traditional international organizations. Steadily growing economic interdependence, at both the macro and micro levels, has forced economic regulators to work with one another transnationally in order to perform their domestic jobs more effectively. They are thus at the forefront of transgovernmental initiatives.

This chapter will focus on two particular types of government networks among financial regulators: central bankers, securities regulators, insurance commissioners, and antitrust officials. The first type are the relatively more formal transgovernmental regulatory organizations (TROs). The members of these organizations are domestic agencies, or even subnational agencies such as provincial or State regulators, in contrast to conventional international organizations, which are comprised primarily, or solely, of nation-States. These transgovernmental organizations tend to operate with a minimum of physical and legal infrastructure. Most lack a foundational treaty, and operate under only a few agreed objectives or by-laws. Nothing they do purports to be legally binding on their members and mechanisms for formal enforcement or implementation are rare. Instead, these functions are left to the members themselves. But despite this informal structure and loose organization, these organizations have had an important influence on international financial regulatory co-operation.

The second type of government network consists of agreements between the domestic regulatory agencies of two or more States. The last few decades have witnessed the emergence of a vast network of such agreements, which effectively institutionalize channels of regulatory co-operation between specific countries. These agreements embrace principles that can be implemented by the regulators themselves. Widespread use of Memoranda of Understanding (MOUs) and even less formal initiatives has sped the growth of governmental networks. Further, while these agreements are most commonly bilateral arrangements, they may also evolve into plurilateral arrangements, offering greater flexibility with less formality than traditional international organizations.

Government networks have many advantages. They are fast, flexible, cheap, and potentially more effective, accountable, and inclusive than existing international institutions. They can spring up virtually overnight, address a host of issues, and form 'mega-networks' that link existing networks. As international actors from non-governmental organizations (NGOs) to corporations have already recognized, globalization and the information technology revolution make networking the organizational form of choice for a rapidly changing and varied environment. In comparison, formal international organizations increasingly resemble slow-moving dinosaurs. Government networks also offer more scope for experimentation. For example, they facilitate the development of potential solutions by small groups of countries, which can then be tested before being adopted more generally in a more traditional multilateral form.

In addition, government networks are comprised of national government officials rather than international officials, which avoids any need for two-level adoption or implementation of international rules. The actors who make the rules or formulate the principles guiding government networks are the same actors who have the power to enforce them. This attribute of government networks can work to enhance both effectiveness and accountability. Regarding effectiveness, the nature of international regulation increasingly requires States to assume obligations that involve commitments concerning the way in which, and the degree to which, they enforce their own national laws. Implementation of international agreements will thus become increasingly difficult unless the relevant national officials are involved from the beginning. Government networks bypass a great deal of cumbersome and formal international negotiating procedure.

Regarding accountability, government networks certainly pose problems, but are likely to emerge as the lesser of two evils. As domestic political resistance to globalization in many countries triggers a backlash against both existing international institutions and the prospect of new ones, transgovernmental activity by elected or even appointed national officials will seem less threatening than a burgeoning supranational bureaucracy. In Robert Kuttner's dark formulation: '[i]f the Federal Reserve operates domestically at one remove from democratic accountability, the IMF and the World Bank operate at two removes'.[3] More optimistically, government networks tend to be functionally oriented and easy to expand, meaning that they can include any actors who perform similar functions, whether private or public, national or supranational, regional or local. The result is a vast array of opportunities for participation in rule-making by an eclectic mix of actors.

These are rosy scenarios. Government networks also have disadvantages and worrisome features. Most of these fall under the heading of accountability, both domestic and international. First is the concern that government networks reflect technocracy more than democracy, that their purported effectiveness rests on shared functional values rather than on responsiveness to underlying social and political issues. Such concerns spawn a need to build mechanisms for accountability to domestic constituencies in countries participating in government networks. Second, however, is a set of concerns about global accountability: concerns about the politics of insulation and the politics of imposition. On the one hand, many developing countries are likely to see government networks as simply the latest effort to insulate the decisions of the powerful from the input of the weak. On the other hand, other countries, both developed and developing, may see government networks as a device whereby the most powerful countries penetrate the defences of national sovereignty to impose their policy templates on everyone else.

In addition to concerns about accountability, critics of government networks have also charged them with reflecting if not encouraging a minimalist global agenda and displacing traditional international organizations. Both of these claims are overblown and overlook the extent to which government networks can and do coexist with international organizations. The agenda pursued by government networks is generally a transnational regulatory agenda rather than a more traditional agenda devoted to providing global public goods, but they are hardly a *cause* of the asserted decline

---

[3] Robert Kuttner, 'Globalism Bites Back' (Mar.–Apr. 1998) 6 The American Prospect 7.

in resources allocated to combating global poverty, to human rights, and health care. Moreover, to the extent that they are displacing traditional international organizations, it is either because those organizations have proved relatively ineffective or, more frequently, because government networks are better adapted to a host of contemporary tasks and the technology available to accomplish them. Finally, government networks may be particularly well suited to the exercise of 'soft power', a form of influence and persuasion that requires States genuinely to interact with and learn from each other in a non-hierarchical setting.

Section 1 of this chapter describes the evolution of a number of the most important transgovernmental regulatory organizations in the global economic and financial arena. Section 2 explores the development of less formal bilateral and plurilateral ties, largely between the United States and other countries. Section 3 canvasses problems with existing government networks and sketches their implications for the larger project of global governance.

1. AGENCIES ACROSS BORDERS: TRANSGOVERNMENTAL REGULATORY ORGANIZATIONS

The key identifying feature of government networks is the interaction across borders of government institutions with similar functions and facing similar problems. This interaction is more highly developed in the financial regulatory area than in any other, leading one scholar to coin the term 'international financial regulatory organizations' (IFROs).[4] David Zaring has analysed the common features of these organizations among central bankers, securities regulators, and insurance commissioners and described their evolution and impact.[5] This part of this chapter summarizes his work and elaborates upon it in the general context of more formalized government networks. From this perspective, international financial regulatory organizations are more accurately described as a category of transgovernmental regulatory organizations.

1.1. The Basle Committee on Banking Supervision

Established in 1975 under the Bank for International Settlements (BIS), the Basle Committee is a standing group of the Central Bank Governors of the G-10 countries, Switzerland, and Luxembourg.[6] The Basle Committee exists without a formal

---

[4] David Zaring, 'International Law by Other Means: The Twilight Existence of International Financial Regulatory Organizations' (1998) 33 Texas International Law Journal 281.

[5] Ibid.

[6] Peter Cooke, 'Bank Capital Adequacy' (1991), excerpted in Hal S. Scott and Philip A. Wellons, *International Finance: Transactions, Policy, and Regulation* (2nd edn., Westbury, NY: Foundation Press, 1995) at 232; Joseph J. Norton, 'Trends in International Bank Supervision and the Basle Committee on Banking Supervision' (1994) 48 Consumer Finance Law Quarterly, 415, 417.

constitution or by-laws, and operates without its own staff or facilities. Its founding mandate was a press communiqué, issued by the Bank Governors through the BIS. The BIS itself is a private bank, located in Basle, Switzerland, that is mostly owned by the central banks of twenty-nine countries.[7] It was founded in the interwar period to 'promote the co-operation of central banks and provide additional facilities for international financial operations'.[8] Although the charter membership of the BIS and the Basle Committee overlaps, the BIS does not formally participate in the Committee. None the less, the small staff of the BIS serves as the Basle Committee's secretariat, and the Committee meets four times a year in Basle at the BIS.

The Basle Committee is not an open organization. Membership is strictly limited to the world's most powerful banking States and will likely remain so.[9] Conducting its business in secret, the Committee makes every effort to maintain a low profile. As former chairman Huib Muller observed: 'We don't like publicity. We prefer, I might say, our hidden secret world of the supervisory continent.'[10]

The stated objectives of the Basle Committee are very broad. It describes itself as a 'forum for ongoing cooperation among member countries on banking supervisory matters' that aims to 'strengthen international cooperation, improve the overall quality of banking supervision worldwide, and ensure that no foreign banking establishment escapes supervision'.[11] In practice, the Committee only makes consensus-based 'recommendations', which are then left for the Governors to implement within their own national systems. Even though the Committee derives its formal authority solely from the support of the Central Bank Governors, its recommendations have been implemented by member and non-member countries alike.[12]

The Basle Committee's recommendation-making process exemplifies the distinctive nature of transgovernmental regulatory co-operation. The Committee's 1988 Capital Accord, setting minimum capitalization standards for international banks under the regulatory power of the Central Bank Governors, provides an instructive example. Following several secret meetings, the Basle Committee announced that agreement on a proposal had been reached. A six-month period followed, during which time the Committee accepted comments from private bankers and other interested parties. The final version of the Accord appeared in the summer of 1988, after which time the Governors of the member banks implemented the agreed standards.

---

[7] *The Bank for International Settlements: A Profile of an International Institution* (Basle: Bank for International Settlements, 1991), at 2.

[8] Statute of the Bank for International Settlements, 20 Jan. 1930, reprinted in *Bank for International Settlements, Basic Texts* (Basle: Bank for International Settlements, 1987), 11.

[9] General Accounting Office, Report to Congressional Committees, 'International Banking— Strengthening the Framework for Supervising International Banks' (Mar. 1994), at 37.

[10] Huib J. Muller, 'Address to the 5th International Conference of Banking Supervisors' (16 May 1988), quoted in Tony Porter, *States, Markets, and Regimes in Global Finance* (New York: St Martin's Press, 1993), 66.

[11] Basle Committee on Banking Supervision, *Annexure C* (1995), para. 3.

[12] For example, Brazil's Central Bank adopted the Basle Accord in Aug. 1994. Scott and Wellons, *International Finance*, at 249.

The drafters of the Accord used simple language in writing the agreement, deliberately avoiding legalese. The use of more informal language is not unusual; the products of Committee agreements are usually short, generally worded documents which, as Peter Cooke has stated, 'do not have, and were never intended to have, legal force'.[13] Furthermore, unlike most treaties or other legal agreements, the 1988 Accord has been subject to frequent amendments since its promulgation and is intended to evolve over time.

Despite their informality and professed lack of authority, Basle Committee members consider the agreements binding, even if they do not 'approach the legal status of treaty'.[14] Given the lack of an independent mechanism for monitoring non-compliance, enforcement is left to the members of the Committee themselves, with pressure from their colleagues. Specific meetings review the implementation and consistency of the agreements. As all member countries have implemented the 1988 Accord's capital adequacy requirements, and countries not party to the original agreement continue to join,[15] the Basle Committee's system of enforcement, however informal, appears to be quite effective. In fact, the adoption of the capital adequacy standards has been so effective that governments did not withdraw their support of the Accord even when many scholars argued that the resulting deceleration in bank lending intensified the recession of the early 1990s in the United States and other industrialized countries.[16] Some members of the United States Congress proposed that the Accord should be scrapped or amended, since it was obviously 'harming' the domestic economy.[17] However, no action was taken on these proposals, demonstrating the degree of autonomy and influence over domestic government that the Basle Committee has achieved.

Why does this system function as effectively as it does? The primary reason for success seems to be the Basle Committee's facilitation of close personal contacts among the Central Bank Governors. The Committee itself acknowledges the importance of its role in this regard, declaring that 'the development of close personal contacts between supervisors in different countries has greatly helped in the handling and resolution of problems affecting individual banks ... [t]his is an important, though necessarily unpublicised element in the Committee's regular work'.[18] The Basle Committee also seeks to organize and facilitate networking among the rest of the world's central bankers and other financial regulators. The Committee supported the formation of, among others, the Offshore Supervisors Group, the Southeast Asia,

---

[13] Peter Cooke, Chair of the Basle Committee, quoted in Joseph Jude Norton, *Devising International Bank Supervisory Standards* (London: Graham and Trotman, 1995), 177.

[14] According to Charles Freeland, a member of the Committee. See Freeland, 'The Work of the Basle Committee', in Robert C. Effros (ed.), *Current Legal Issues Affecting Central Banks* (Washington: International Monetary Fund, 1992), 232.

[15] See Scott and Wellons, *International Finance* (3rd edn., 1996), at 249.

[16] See e.g. Robert Litan, 'Nightmare in Basle' (Nov./Dec. 1992) The International Economy 7.

[17] Scott and Wellons, *International Finance*, at 251.

[18] Bank of International Settlements, *Compendium of Documents Produced by the Basle Committee on Banking Supervision* (Apr. 1995), 14.

New Zealand and Australia Forum of Banking Supervisors, and the Caribbean Banking Supervisors Group. Furthermore, the Basle Committee has established links with regulators from other financial sectors through groups such as the Joint Forum, which is discussed below.

The Basle Committee is recognized as a significant player in international financial regulation. It has effectively promulgated binding international standards, even though such standards have at times proved expensive and burdensome for member States. Moreover, it has proved itself competent in developing new principles of banking supervision, such as the 'consolidated supervision' standard adopted in the Basle Concordat, which expands the regulatory responsibilities of member governors beyond territorial borders as a matter of first principle. Most recently, after close consultation with bank supervisors from sixteen developing countries, it has developed and promulgated a set of principles designed to codify the basic 'elements of a sound supervisory system'.[19] It is a key player in the regulation of the global economy. But it is a government network, with few or none of the trappings of a formal international organization. Its attributes as a government network are likely to prove both its strength and its weakness.

1.2. The International Organisation of Securities Commissioners

The International Organisation of Securities Commissioners (IOSCO) is a global network of securities regulators.[20] It has over 150 members, divided among 'ordinary members' comprised of national securities commissions or self-regulatory organizations such as stock exchanges from countries with no official government regulatory agency; 'associate members' comprised of provincial or regional securities regulators when the national regulatory agency is already a member; and 'affiliate members' comprised of international or regional organizations charged with the regulation or development of capital or other organizations recommended by the Executive Committee.[21] Unlike the Basle Committee, membership in IOSCO has not been limited to regulators from prosperous countries, and even includes non-governmental regulators such as private stock exchanges. IOSCO has no charter or founding treaty. It maintains an evolving set of by-laws and has established a permanent secretariat in Montreal.[22] According to its Secretary-General, Paul Guy, IOSCO's goal is to improve the harmonization of securities and futures regulations on the international level.[23] Guy further explains that according to IOSCO, harmonization does

---

[19]   Press Statement, 22 Sep. 1997, http://www.bis.org/press/p970922.htm. The principles themselves can be found at http://www.bis.ord.

[20]   See Paul Guy, 'Regulatory Harmonization to Achieve Effective International Competition', in F . R. Edwards and H. T. Patrick (eds.), *Regulating International Financial Markets: Issues and Policies* (Boston: Kluwer, 1992), 291. For an in-depth look at the organization and functioning of the IOSCO, see David Zaring, 'International Law', at 20–31.

[21]   For a list of IOSCO members, see http://www.iosco.org/index 4.html.

[22]   See Zaring, 'International Law'.

[23]   See Guy, 'Regulatory Harmonization', at 291.

not necessarily mean that regulations must be identical;[24] rather, it ensures that the organization has employed a cautious, consensus-based approach. IOSCO monitors members' compliance with agreed standards through informal methods of self-reporting. Like the Basle Committee, membership in IOSCO leads to an element of moral suasion in implementing common standards.[25]

IOSCO has made some notable contributions in the areas of information sharing and enforcement agreements. The 'ancestor' of all reciprocal information-sharing MOUs was issued by IOSCO in 1986 as a 'Resolution on Reciprocal Assistance',[26] and has been signed by forty agencies.[27] The Organisation also created widely used 'Principles for Memoranda of Understanding', which lay down basic guidelines for creating enforcement MOUs for securities law violations.[28] In 1989, IOSCO proposed a resolution calling for members to enter into information-sharing MOUs and adopted a set of principles for the negotiation and implementation of such memoranda.[29] As discussed below, this groundwork, along with a combination of other factors, has led to a whole network of bilateral MOUs that regulate insider trading and information exchange.

However, IOSCO has not achieved the success of the Basle Committee in implementing global standards for securities regulators. Indeed, IOSCO's attempt to develop capital adequacy standards for securities firms failed in 1992, and its efforts in this regard have been abandoned. In addition, many resolutions passed by IOSCO are not implemented at the domestic level. These failures highlight the inability of government networks to exercise any coercive power over their members. They may also reflect wide disparities in the domestic power actually exercised by IOSCO members, some of whom have far more authority to take autonomous domestic action than others. As section 2 of this chapter explains, MOUs concluded between the United States Securities and Exchange Commission (SEC) and its counterparts in other countries frequently stipulate that the foreign agency must have a certain degree of independence from the national legislature.

1.3. The International Association of Insurance Supervisors

The International Association of Insurance Supervisors (IAIS), founded in 1994, is the leading transgovernmental regulatory organization for State agencies that supervise and regulate the insurance industry.[30] It serves primarily as a means for regulators to come together, share experiences, and consider global standards for the

---

[24] See ibid., at 296.　　　　　　　　　　[25] See Zaring, 'International Law', at 27.

[26] IOSCO Annual Report 1990.

[27] See Michael D. Mann and Lise A. Lustgarten, 'Internationalization of Insider Trading Enforcement: A Guide to Regulation and Cooperation' (1993) 7 PLI/Corp 798.

[28] See generally Michael D. Mann *et al.*, 'The Establishment of International Mechanisms for Enforcing Provisional Orders and Final Judgements Arising From Securities Law Violations' (1992) 55 Law & Contemporary Problems 303.

[29] These MOUs are discussed in detail in Mann and Lustgarten, 'Internationalization'.

[30] See IAIS, 1994 Annual Report; see generally Zaring, 'International Law', at 31–9.

insurance industry. Regulators from sixty-seven countries and seventeen American States belong to the IAIS. The organization works from a governing set of by-laws which cover only eight pages and which 'do not impose legal obligations on members . . .'[31] Its goals, or 'wishes', include 'engender[ing] awareness of common interests' and 'encourag[ing] wide international personal and official contacts'.[32] Similar to IOSCO and the Basle Committee, the IAIS maintains only a tiny centralized bureaucracy, and has subcontracted the role of its general secretariat to the American National Association of Insurance Commissioners.[33]

Since its inception, the IAIS has held two general meetings, both in conjunction with the American National Association of Insurance Commissioners meetings. The IAIS does not yet have the power to promote minimum standards or multinational regulations. It has, however, approved an information-sharing 'recommendation', which has been signed by fifty-one members.[34] Despite its brevity—one half-page in length—it has received acclaim by some insurance regulators. To date, however, the IAIS's main role seems to be the interpersonal one described by David Walsh, an American insurance regulator: '[The IAIS] is a very good vehicle for regulators to get to know one another and develop the kind of relationship where you just pick up the phone and say, "What's going on here?" '[35]

The IAIS is likely to strike many observers as more of a 'talking shop' than a genuine government network. Certainly it does not appear to exercise any kind of power that could be described as 'governmental'. Its value lies in providing regular channels for communication and cross-fertilization among national regulators often seeking to regulate the same entities across national lines, or simply facing the same problems within their national jurisdictions. Within a spectrum of government networks, the Basle Committee would fall at one end and the IAIS at the other. Nevertheless, the IAIS is likely to evolve in ways that will give it more influence over its members and thus eventually power. In the meantime, as this chapter describes below, it at least provides insurance regulators around the world with the possibility of being a 'node' in a more important network.

1.4. Networked Networks

At least in the financial arena, government networks proliferate by joining together in networks of networks. This organizational form is so flexible, cheap, and easy to establish that 'mega-networks' are a natural development. Two prominent examples are the Joint Forum on Financial Conglomerates and the Year 2000 Network.

---

[31] See International Association of Insurance Supervisors By-Laws.

[32] Ibid. at Preamble.

[33] According to David Zaring, the National Association of Insurance Commissioners in turn delegated the job to an employee, a recent law school graduate. See Zaring, 'International Law', at 35.

[34] See IAIS, 'Recommendation Concerning Mutual Assistance, Cooperation, and Sharing of Information', reprinted in (Summer 1995) IAIS Newsletter 5.

[35] Thomas Ressler, 'International Regulators Hold First Meeting' (4 Apr. 1994) The Insurance Regulator 8.

The Joint Forum was established in 1996 under the auspices of the Basle Committee, IOSCO, and IAIS. It is comprised of senior bank, insurance, and securities supervisors from thirteen countries, with the EU Commission attending in an observer capacity.[36] In a prior, even less formal, incarnation as the 'Tripartite Group', it issued a discussion paper in 1995 on the supervision of financial conglomerates, which urges the development of uniform standards and information exchange, and underscores the need for 'intensive cooperation between supervisors' and their 'right to exchange prudential information'.[37] It has subsequently prepared a number of papers for consideration by its three parent organizations on subjects such as capital adequacy principles and a framework and principles for supervisory information sharing.[38]

Another more specialized example is the creation of the Joint Year 2000 Council by the Basle Committee, the BIS Committee on Payment and Settlement Systems (CPSS), IOSCO, and IAIS. The formation of the Council was welcomed by the G-7 Finance Ministers; its Secretariat is provided by the BIS. Its mission is to encourage the development of co-ordinated national strategies to address the Year 2000 problem, including the development of a global databank of contacts in individual countries covering a wide range of actors in both the private and public sectors; the publication of policy papers on specific Year 2000 issues; and the provision of supervisory guidance on assessing Year 2000 preparations by financial institutions. It acknowledges and welcomes efforts by the World Bank and other international institutions to help address the Year 2000 problem, but is focusing its attention directly on both private and public actors in the global financial supervisory community.[39]

The members of the Year 2000 Council are senior members of the sponsoring networks, including chief financial regulators from Belgium, Chile, Italy, Saudi Arabia, South Africa, Canada, Australia, Finland, France, the United States, Japan, and Malaysia. A member of the Board of Governors of the United States Federal Reserve chairs the Council; the chairmen of the Basle Committee, CPSS, IOSCO, and IAIS are *ex officio* members.[40] The Council has formed an External Consultative Committee that includes representatives from international financial services providers, international financial market associations (International Federation of Stock Exchanges, International Federation of Accountants, International Chamber of Commerce), international organizations (the IMF, the World Bank), financial rating agencies (Moody's, Standard and Poor's), and a number of other international industry associations. The purpose of the External Consultative Committee is to enhance global information sharing about measures being taken to address the Year 2000 problem and to 'coordinate as far as possible actions taken by the public and

---

[36] See http://www.bis.org/publ/bcbs34.htm. The members of the Joint Forum are Australia, Belgium, Canada, France, Germany, Italy, Japan, The Netherlands, Spain, Sweden, Switzerland, the United Kingdom, and the United States.

[37] 'US Objections Prompt Limited Global Pact on Financial Services' (21 Aug. 1995) 14 (16) Banking Policy Reporter 17.   [38] See http://www.bis.org/publ/bcbs34.htm.

[39] Press Release, Joint Year 2000 Council, http://www.bis.org/press/p980706.htm.

[40] Joint Year 2000 Council Fact Sheet, http://www.bis.org/ongoing/y2kintro.htm.

private sectors'.[41] Finally, the Council has contacted individual countries and collected information from their 'financial infrastructure operators' on the preparation of their systems for the Year 2000 date change, information that is then published in the form of 'country pages' with contact information for regulatory authorities and system operators in each country.[42]

What is absolutely striking about this Council is the speed and sophistication with which it has organized itself. It is a functional network, which addresses itself to the solution of a specific but very important problem. It exercises no actual authority; its principal functions are co-ordination and information sharing. Nevertheless, it has been able to marshal key figures world-wide to create synergies and enhance their individual capacity to address the problem. It offers recommendations to national authorities and provides them with the information necessary to act on those recommendations. And all of this within the time-span of barely six months.[43] It is difficult to imagine the global community doing anything so fast or so effectively through the traditional machinery of international negotiations or even through traditional international institutions.

1.5. Common Features of Transgovernmental Regulatory Organizations

The transgovernmental regulatory organizations described above share a number of common features. Zaring emphasizes their informal charters and by-laws, flexible internal organization, relative secrecy, and status as 'substate actors', meaning that they are composed of State institutions rather than of 'member States'.[44] Their creation is generally *ad hoc*, and they tend to have only minimal structural components such as founding treaties, by-laws, and staff. The extremely limited budgets of these organizations inhibit the development of a strong central or supranational character,[45] and ensure that each retains a highly flexible internal organization.[46]

Members of TROs emphasize the voluntary nature of participation; the agreements reached are generally phrased in non-legal (although sometimes technical) language and are largely the product of consensus. Importantly, the members insist that the agreements reached by these kinds of transgovernmental organizations are non-binding.[47] The resolutions, MOUs, or communiqués agreed on by these orga-

---

[41] External Consultative Committee, http://www.bis.org/ongoing/ecclist.htm.

[42] Year 2000 Country Pages, http://www.bis.org/ongoing/cpage.htm.

[43] The sponsoring committees of the Council began by organizing a Round Table on the Year 2000 at the Bank for International Settlements on 8 Apr. 1998. The decision to organize the Council was taken at that meeting; all the efforts described in the text were underway by Oct. 1998. Introduction, http://www.bis.org/ongoing/y2kintro.htm.

[44] See Zaring, 'International Law', at 39.

[45] In fact, IOSCO's annual revenues do not amount to $US 750,000; IAIS did not exceed $US 125,000 in 1994; and while the Basle Committee does not disclose its dues, 'since it does not support a secretariat, they are presumably also minimal'. See ibid., at 43.

[46] See ibid., at 40.

[47] See e.g. Interview with Paul Leder, Deputy Director, Office of International Affairs, SEC, 11 Jan. 1996; as quoted ibid., at 43.

nizations are rarely, if ever, elevated to treaty status by the members of the organization. More often the domestic actors themselves implement agreements, avoiding the need for domestic legislation or ratification. A final, complementary, feature is a general lack of formal mechanisms to monitor compliance—at best the members themselves tend to exercise informal oversight.

Notwithstanding their apparent *ad hoc* formation and self-proclaimed lack of legal force, the members of TROs regard them as generally effective in performing their self-appointed functions. The regulatory agreements they negotiate are pledges of good faith that are self-enforcing, in the sense that each State will be better able to enforce its national law by implementing the agreement if other States do likewise. Zaring notes that the organizations maintain strong 'connections with one another, and have created an interlocking web of financial regulators'.[48]

An important dimension of TRO effectiveness is the 'nationalization of international law'. TROs do not aspire to exercise power in the international system independent of their members. Indeed, the main purpose of TROs is to help national regulators to apprehend those who would harm the interests of their citizens, or otherwise to enhance the enforcement of national laws by co-ordinating efforts across borders or promulgating common solutions to problems which each State already faces within its own borders. The result is an international rule-making process that directly engages national officials and national promulgation and enforcement mechanisms, without formal translation and implementation mechanisms from the international to the national.

2. AGENCIES ACROSS BORDERS: BILATERAL AND PLURILATERAL REGULATORY CO-OPERATION

National regulatory agencies also reach out to their counterparts across borders and co-operate in developing joint, harmonized, or co-ordinated policies and agendas outside TROs. These bilateral and plurilateral agreements between domestic agencies, ranging from highly formalized treaties to completely informal initiatives, comprise a second type of government network dedicated to transnational regulatory co-operation. The impulse to engage in *ad hoc* negotiations or discussions on policy has occurred primarily between bilateral partners, although the success of bilateral agreements encourages bilateral partners to consult additional parties, resulting in plurilateral co-operation. As with TROs, bilateral and plurilateral regulatory co-operation is particularly strong in the financial arena.

2.1. MOUs and MLATs

At the centre of the spectrum of agreements lies the standard building block of the informal international order, the MOU. Transnational regulators sign MOUs as

---

[48] Zaring, 'International Law', at 45.

non-binding statements of their intent to co-operate in order to address specific regulatory problems. Should concrete ideas or policies result from the negotiations, the regulatory authorities themselves are charged with implementing the decisions in their respective countries. MOUs have proliferated in recent decades, steadily gaining in popularity as a mode of conducting transgovernmental regulatory business.

The comparison between the process of creating MOUs and more formal agreements such as Mutual Legal Assistance Treaties (MLATs) is instructive.[49] Both MOUs and MLATs are, in essence, agreements between regulators in specific and discrete subject areas. The formal distinction is that MLATs are actual treaties; they create legally binding obligations whereas MOUs do not create legal burdens. As a result, creating a MLAT typically involves all the traditional organs of the unitary State model: diplomatic negotiation among State officials, precise and contested drafting of a treaty, and a formal domestic implementation process, such as Senate ratification in the United States, or passage of implementing legislation elsewhere.

The process by which the United States reached the MLAT with Switzerland during the 1970s shows how onerous the bilateral treaty process can be, even for technical matters.[50] Negotiations began in 1967, having previously failed in 1922, 1925, 1938, and 1962. On the American side, several domestic agencies, including the SEC and the State, Justice, and Treasury Departments, initiated the effort. However, the actual negotiations were conducted by high level officials, up to and including the respective ambassadors. After a long and tumultuous process, the accord was signed in 1977, a full decade after the negotiations began. Finally, and to the further frustration of the Justice Department, many of the concessions gained by the negotiators were undermined by the Swiss implementing legislation. It was not until the end of the 1980s that substantial problems with the Swiss MLAT were overcome, in part through a series of MOUs.

Thus, where possible, domestic agencies have sought to avoid the delay and burden of treaty negotiations in favour of quick, less formal, and purportedly non-binding MOUs. Unlike MLATs or other treaties, MOUs are agreed by the regulators themselves, if possible without the involvement of traditional diplomatic actors. MOU agreements are often brief, and drafted in non-legal language. And, perhaps most importantly, MOUs are fast—both in the negotiation process, and in the implementation process, which typically is performed directly by the agency itself, without any involvement of the domestic legislature or other domestic actors.

The growth of MOUs may reflect increased recognition of the general advantages of informal over formal agreements, at least among like-minded regulatory agencies.

---

[49] See generally Note, 'International Securities Law Enforcement: Recent Advances in Assistance and Cooperation' (1994) 27 Vanderbilt Journal of Transnational Law 635; Charles Vaughn Baltic III, Note, 'The Next Step in Insider Trading Regulation: Internal Cooperative Efforts in the Global Securities Market' (1991–2) 2 Law and Policy in International Business 167.

[50] Ethan A. Nadelmann, *Cops Across Borders: The Internationalization of U.S. Criminal Law Enforcement* (University Parle, Pa.: Pennsylvania State University Press, 1993), 321–41; Lionel Frei and Stefan Treschel, 'Origins and Applications of the United States–Switzerland Treaty on Mutual Assistance in Criminal Matters' (1991) Harvard International Law Journal 31.

Formal obligations to co-operate on matters traditionally considered to be at the heart of domestic authority raise prickly issues of sovereignty and public policy. It will often be better simply to agree on a general framework for co-operation and to let the pursuit of common functions and purposes, and deepening interpersonal relationships, take care of the rest. No obligations devolve upon the State as a whole, only upon specific regulatory entities participating in horizontal governance networks.

Examples of areas in which regulators have taken the MOU route include securities regulation,[51] commodities regulation,[52] antitrust,[53] environmental regulation,[54] and health policy.[55] In some cases the development of MOU-networks has been explicitly supported by national legislation. For example, in the 1980s, the SEC proposed legislation authorizing it to investigate suspected violations of United States securities laws in foreign countries, while permitting foreign securities officials to do the same in the United States.[56] One purpose of this legislation was to promote the exchange of information through MOUs.

Of course, use of one or the other type of bilateral agreement is not limited to particular subject-matters; MOUs and MLATs may be used interchangeably and are also often used together. For example, after the Swiss MLAT was signed in 1977, the

---

[51] See Brad Begin, 'A Proposed Blueprint for Achieving Cooperation in Policing Transborder Securities Fraud' (1986) 27 Vanderbilt Journal of International Law 65; Paula Jimenez, 'Comment, International Securities Enforcement Cooperation Act and Memoranda of Understanding' (1990) 31 Harvard International Law Journal 295. See also Mark S. Klock, 'Comment, A Comparative Analysis of Recent Accords Which Facilitate Transnational SEC Investigations of Insider Trading' (1987) 11 Maryland Journal of International Law and Trade 243.

[52] In June 1995 the US Commodities Future Trading Commission and Italy's Commissione Nazionale per la Società à la Borsa signed a mutual assistance agreement entitled 'Memorandum of Understanding on Consultation and Mutual Assistance for the Exchange of Information'. The MOU authorizes US and Italian regulators to request and obtain accessed information contained in each other's files, take statements from persons subject to each other's jurisdiction, and obtain documents regarding futures trading (Aug. 1995) 11 International Enforcement Law Reporter 318. In May 1995 the Mexican National Banking and Securities Commission and the USCFTC negotiated a MOU to facilitate the exchange of information and improve the enforcement of laws and regulations related to the futures and options markets in the United States and Mexico.

[53] See Nina Hachigian, 'Essential Mutual Assistance in International Antitrust Enforcement' (1995) 29 International Lawyer 117, 138.

[54] See James D. Vieregg et al., 'Cross-Border Environmental Law Enforcement' (20 Oct. 1994) ALI-ABA Course of Study: Criminal Enforcement of Environmental Laws, C964 ALI-ABA 455.

[55] For example, in Nov. 1991 the US Food & Drug Administration participated in an International Conference on Harmonisation, which included drug regulators and pharmaceutical manufacturers from the EC, Japan, and USA (the countries which account for the vast majority of drug production, research, and development). The FDA agreed to accept data collected in foreign clinical tests and explored the possibility of developing common standards. David W. Jordan, 'Note, International Regulatory Harmonization: A New Era in Prescription Drug Approval' (1992) 25 Vanderbilt Journal of Transnational Law 471; see also Rosemarie Kanusky, 'Comment, Pharmaceutical Harmonization: Standardizing Regulations Among the United States, the European Economic Community, and Japan' (1994) 16 Houston Journal of International Law 665.

[56] The International Securities Enforcement Cooperation Act, S. 2544, 100th Cong., 2d Sess. (1988). On 19 Nov. 1988, Congress adopted a less comprehensive version of S. 2544, the Insider Trading and Securities Fraud Enforcement Act of 1988, 15 U.S.C. § 78 (1988).

United States and Swiss securities agencies negotiated a separate MOU to share information regarding insider trading investigations. The additional agreement was necessary because insider trading was not a criminal violation under the Swiss Penal Code, even after conclusion of the formal treaty, and thus insider trading fell outside the scope of the MLAT.

2.2. Informal Initiatives

Informal initiatives lie at the opposite end of the bilateral agreement spectrum from MLATs. The joint survey of the internal management and financial controls of several international securities firms undertaken jointly by the SEC and the British Securities and Investments Board in July 1995 provides one example of such an initiative. The two regulatory agencies sought to co-operate to improve the supervision of securities firms' foreign affiliates in the light of problems recently experienced by Baring's Bank. It was the first joint initiative to assess the global activities of international securities firms, although the SEC and SIB agreed on a joint statement for the supervision of derivatives activities in March 1994.[57] This joint exercise of investigatory authority creates a kind of voluntary horizontal governance, linking two agencies that exercise the requisite hierarchical authority over the individuals and groups within their territorial and extra-territorial jurisdiction, but not forming a supranational source of coercion. Such initiatives differ from MOUs more in degree than in kind; they are likely to be *ad hoc* and addressed to a specific problem. However, they reflect a deep level of trust and comfort in working together on the part of the participating agencies.

In another informal initiative, the SEC has created an international institute for securities market development. The institute 'is part of [the SEC's] continuing effort to assist foreign countries with developing capital markets that are critical to a dynamic free enterprise system. The SEC has been particularly generous in supplying technical help to many Eastern European countries.'[58] Such efforts may represent a distinctive and new form of foreign aid, perhaps partially compensating for the steep decline in more traditional forms of aid. Allowing national agencies to administer aid on a functional regulatory basis further contributes to their autonomy in transnational relations.

Another example of an informal initiative arises in the area of derivatives regulation. The SEC, the CFTC, and the UK's Securities and Investments Board have established a joint statement of co-operation on derivatives,[59] consisting of a seven-point programme that includes information sharing and creation of more uniform

---

[57] 'U.S.–U.K. Initiate Assessment of Supervision of Foreign Affiliates' (Aug. 1995) 11 International Enforcement Law Report 319.

[58] Stewart J. Kaswell, 'SEC Chair Breeden Underscores the Importance of the Rule of Law' (Summer 1992) ABA International Law News 5.

[59] 'SEC, CFTC, UK Regulators Issue Statement on OTC Derivatives Oversight' (16 Mar. 1994) International Business & Finance Daily, D9.

standards.[60] This initiative coexists with more formal initiatives by the Basle Committee and IOSCO, both of which have issued guidelines for derivatives users that encourage companies to implement standards of internal risk management rather than external, SEC-style regulation.[61] At least one observer argues that such transnational co-operation promises more effective regulation than would Congressional action rooted in the extraterritorial application of strict derivatives oversight.[62] From a process point of view, what is striking is the plethora of different ways in which government networks can be used to achieve a particular regulatory goal.

3. REGULATING THE GLOBAL ECONOMY THROUGH GOVERNMENT NETWORKS: IMPLICATIONS AND PROBLEMS

What are the implications of government networks? At the most general level, they offer a new vision of global governance: horizontal rather than vertical, decentralized rather than centralized, and composed of national government officials rather than a supranational bureaucracy. They are *potentially* both more effective and more accountable than traditional international institutions, at least for some purposes. They simultaneously strengthen the power of the State and equip State actors to interact meaningfully and innovatively with a host of other actors. These include public actors at the supranational, subnational, and regional levels, private actors such as corporations and NGOs, and 'mixed' actors that are privately organized but increasingly perform public functions. Further, government networks are optimally adapted to the technology of the Information Age, existing more in virtual than real space. Finally, as the form of governance changes, function is likely to follow suit, enabling government networks to deploy resources away from command and control regulation and towards a variety of catalysing and supporting roles.[63]

Yet government networks trigger both suspicion and anxiety. The suspicion is of a burgeoning global technocracy, insensitive to political choices driven by more than functional considerations and unresponsive to existing mechanisms of democratic governance at the national or international levels. The anxiety is a function of many of the same network attributes that are positively evaluated above. As any feminist who has battled 'the old boy network' will quickly recognize, the informality, flexibility, and decentralization of networks means that it is very difficult to establish

---

[60] See Thomas C. Singher, 'Regulating Derivatives: Does Transnational Regulatory Cooperation Offer a Viable Alternative to Congressional Action?' (1995) 18 Fordam International Law Journal 1397, 1465–8.   [61] Ibid.   [62] Ibid.

[63] The public management section of the OECD (called PUMA) has launched a major regulatory reform initiative that operates through a 'regulatory management and reform network'. A major focus of reform efforts is the shift away from 'command and control regulations' to a wide range of alternative instruments, many of them market-based or relying on self-regulation incentives. For an overview of this programme, see the PUMA website at http://www.oecd.org/puma/regref/work.htm. In the United States similar work has been done under Vice President Al Gore's 'Reinventing Government' initiative.

precisely who is acting and when. Influence is subtle and hard to track; important decisions may be made in very informal settings. As Martti Koskenniemi argues in his contribution to this volume, giving up form and validity is ceding fundamental constraints on power.[64]

At this stage, systematic empirical observations of government networks are so limited that both camps can see what they want to see, or at least what they are primed to look for. Existing networks differ in many ways, both within and across issue areas; even where the literature is fairly extensive, as in the documentation of new forms of financial regulation, it is often quite technical and silent on questions such as accountability. Further, different government networks have different relationships with existing international or supranational organizations. Similarly, their members have a range of different relationships with various national supervisory bodies such as legislative committees. Both international lawyers and political scientists could usefully engage in case studies and systematic research across issue areas.

At this stage of the analysis, a review of some of the principal criticisms of government networks that have been advanced in print and in public audiences, together with some tentative responses, may help guide future research agendas. This section distils three such criticisms: lack of accountability; promotion of a minimalist and exclusionary policy agenda; and marginalization and displacement of traditional international organizations. After reviewing each critique, I set forth some initial responses, many of which will also pose questions for further study.

3.1. A New Technocratic Élite

The sharpest criticisms of government networks emphasize their lack of accountability. According to Philip Alston, if [Slaughter's] analysis 'is correct . . . , [i]t implies the marginalisation of governments as such and their replacement by special interest groups . . . It suggests a move away from arenas of relative transparency into the back rooms . . . and the bypassing of the national political arenas to which the United States and other proponents of the importance of healthy democratic institutions attach so much importance'.[65] Antonio Perez, identifying a related argument about networks among national and international bureaucrats in Abram and Antonia Chayes's *The New Sovereignty*, accuses them of adopting 'Platonic Guardianship as a mode of transnational governance', an open 'move toward technocratic elitism'.[66] And Sol Picciotto, who also chronicles the rise of government networks but from a more explicitly critical perspective, argues: 'A chronic lack of legitimacy plagues direct international contacts at the sub-State level among national officials and

---

[64] Koskenniemi, chapter 3.

[65] Philip Alston, 'The Myopia of the Handmaidens: International Lawyers and Globalisation' (1997) 8 European Journal of International Law 435, 441.

[66] Antonio Perez, 'Who Killed Sovereignty? Or: Changing Norms Concerning Sovereignty In International Law' (1996) 14 Wisconsin International Law Journal 463, 476.

administrators'.[67] He attributes this lack of legitimacy to their informality and confidentiality, precisely the attributes that make them so attractive to the participants.[68]

Such charges are much easier to make than to prove. To begin with, concerns about accountability assume that government networks are developing and implementing substantive policies in ways that differ significantly from outcomes that would be reached as the result of purely national processes or of negotiations within traditional international institutions. Although reasons exist to accept this premiss with regard to policy initiatives such as the 1988 Capital Accord adopted by the Basle Committee,[69] it is less clear regarding other networks, even within the financial arena. Network initiatives are theoretically subject to the normal political constraints on domestic policy-making processes once they have been introduced at the domestic level. Arguments that they circumvent these constraints rest on the presumed ability of national officials in the same issue area to collude with one another in ways that strengthen their respective positions *vis-à-vis* bureaucratic rivals or legislative overseers back home. This presumption is often contested by experts in the different fields of financial regulation and requires further research on a case by case basis.

More generally, many government networks remain primarily talking shops, dedicated to the sharing of information, the cross-fertilization of new ideas, and the development of common principles based on the respective experiences of participating members. The power of information is soft power, persuasive rather than coercive.[70] It is 'the ability to get desired outcomes because others want what you want'.[71] Specific government institutions may still enjoy a substantial advantage over others due to the quality, quantity, and credibility of the information they have to exchange.[72] But in giving and receiving this information, even in ways that may significantly affect their thinking, government officials are not exercising power in the traditional ways which polities find it necessary to hold them accountable for. We may need to develop new metrics or even new conceptions of accountability geared towards the distinctive features of power in the Information Age.

A second and related response raises the question whether and when direct accountability is necessary for legitimate government. Some domestic institutions, such as courts and central banks, are deemed to act legitimately without direct accountability. Legitimacy may be conferred or attained independent of mechanisms of direct accountability—performance may be measured by outcomes as much as by process. Insulated institutions are designed to counter the voters' changing will and

---

[67] Sol Picciotto, 'Networks in International Economic Integration: Fragmented States and the Dilemmas of Neo-Liberalism' (1996–7) 17 Northwestern Journal of International Law and Business 1014, 1047. [68] Ibid., at 1049.

[69] Ethan B. Kapstein, *Supervising International Banks: Origins and Implications of the Basle Accord* (Princeton: Department of Economics, Princeton University, 1991).

[70] Robert O. Keohane and Joseph S. Nye Jr., 'Power and Interdependence in the Information Age' (1998) 77 Foreign Affairs 81, 86. [71] Ibid.

[72] See ibid., at 89–92 (discussing 'the politics of credibility').

whim, in order to garner the benefits of expertise and stability and to protect minorities. Many of the policy arenas in which government networks are likely to be most active are those in which domestic polities have agreed that a degree of insulation and expertise is desirable. Thus, it is not automatically clear that the transgovernmental extension of these domestic activities poses legitimacy problems.

A third response is: 'accountable compared to what?' The presumed accountability or lack thereof of government networks must be contrasted with the accountability of international organizations on the one hand and NGOs on the other. International organizations are widely perceived as being accountable only to diplomats and international lawyers, which helps explain their relative disrepute in many countries. And accountable to whom? The United Nations suffers from the perennial perception that it is answerable primarily to its own bureaucracy; the International Monetary Fund and, to a lesser extent, the World Bank are widely seen as fronts for the United States; European Union institutions have been in crisis over a purported 'democracy deficit' for much of this decade; the World Trade Organisation draws populist fire for privileging free trade, and hence the large corporate interests best positioned to benefit from free trade, over the employment, welfare, environmental, and cultural interests of large numbers of voters.[73]

NGOs hardly fare better. Although they must routinely sing for their supper and thus depend on their ability to persuade individual and institutional contributors of the worth of their activities, many, if not most, are single issue groups who target a particular demographic and political segment of society and may well wield power quite disproportionate to the number of their supporters. Further, their contributors rarely have any direct control over policy decisions once the contribution has been made, or, equally important, any means of ensuring how their contribution was spent.

In this context, government networks have a number of potential advantages. First, they are composed of the same officials who make and implement regulations domestically. To the extent that these networks do actually make policy, and to the extent that the policies made and subsequently adopted at the national level differ significantly from the outcome of a purely domestic regulatory process, it is reasonable to expect that other domestic political institutions—legislators, courts, or other branches of the bureaucracy—will extend their normal oversight functions to transgovernmental as well as domestic activities. Alston rejects this claim as excessively optimistic, arguing that all the organs of the State have been significantly weakened

---

[73] Consider the following passage from political scientist Henry Nau, which sounds virtually the same themes as Alston's critique of government networks: 'Whose political interests [are] being served by international institutions? Realists said State interests, but the major States today are democracies and consist of many societal and special interests that do not reflect a single government, let alone national interest. Critics of international institutions suspect that these special interests, especially corporate and bureaucratic élites with stakes in globalization, now dominate international organizations and use them to circumvent democratic accountability.' Nau, 'Institutional Skepticism', Letter to the Editor (Summer 1998) 111 Foreign Policy 168.

by globalization and the neo-liberal economic agenda that has accompanied it.[74] That, however, is a separate argument, which is considered separately below. It is also an argument with far broader implications: if the State is really so weakened, then the prospects of enhancing the accountability of any of the important actors in international life are slim indeed.

A promising development that suggests that State institutions with a more directly representative mandate are not yet dead is the growth of legislative networks: links among those national officials who are most directly responsible for ensuring bureaucratic accountability. In some areas, national legislation has been used to facilitate the growth of government networks.[75] In others, such as human rights and the environment, national legislators are increasingly recognizing that they have common interests. In the European Union, governments are increasingly having to submit their European policies to special parliamentary committees, who are themselves networking.[76] The result, according to German international relations scholar Karl Kaiser, is the 'reparliamentarization' of national policy.[77] In addition, legislative networks can be used to strengthen national legislative institutions. For example, the Association of African Election Authorities was founded in 1997. It is composed both of government officials and leaders of NGOs directly involved in monitoring and assisting elections.

Other examples include legislative networks contained within international organizations, as discussed further below. These networks allow the regulators or parliaments of weak States to participate in global governance, and thereby serve the functions both of setting a good example for fragile institutions and of lending their strength and status to the organization in question. The OSCE Parliamentary Assembly, for example, has played an important role in legitimizing Eastern European parliaments by monitoring elections and including parliamentarians in all OSCE deliberations. The controversy surrounding the OSCE's rejection of a Belarussian delegation in July 1997 demonstrates that membership in the Assembly has become a symbol of governmental legitimacy.[78]

A final response to the accountability critique is that the critics are missing a more significant point about the changing nature of power itself. Government networks are far better suited to exercising 'soft power' than 'hard power'—that is, the power flowing from an ability to convince others that they want what you want rather than an ability to compel them to forgo their preferences by using either threats or rewards.[79] Soft power rests much more on persuasive than coercive authority, a base

---

[74] Alston, 'Myopia of the Handmaidens', at 442.

[75] MOUs between the SEC and its foreign counterparts, for example, have been directly encouraged and facilitated by several United States statutes passed expressly for the purpose. Faith T. Teo, 'Memoranda of Understanding among Securities Regulators: Frameworks for Cooperation, Implications for Governance' (1998), 29–43 (ms on file with author, Harvard Law School).

[76] Shirley Williams, 'Sovereignty and Accountability in the European Union', in Robert Keohane and Stanley Hoffman (eds.), *The New European Community* (Boulder, Colo.: Westview Press, 1991).

[77] Karl Kaiser, 'Globalisierung als Problem der Demokratie' (Apr 1998) *Internationale Politik* 3.

[78] Aleksandr Potemkin, *Session of OSCE Parliamentary Assembly ends in Moscow*, ITAR-TASS News Agency, 9 July 1997.   [79] Keohane and Nye, 'Power and Interdependence', at 86.

that may in turn require a capacity for genuine engagement and dialogue with others. To the extent that government officials seek to persuade but then find that they must in turn allow themselves to be persuaded in their interactions with their foreign counterparts, what should mechanisms of accountability be designed to accomplish?

If a judge, or a regulator, or even a legislator, learns about alternative approaches to a problem facing him or her in the process of disseminating his or her own country's solution, and views that solution more critically thereafter, is there an accountability problem? The answer is likely to be that an accountable government does not seek to constrain the sources of knowledge brought to bear on a particular governance problem, but rather the ways in which that knowledge is acted upon. Fair enough, but many government officials will think and act differently as a result of their participation in transgovernmental networks in ways that we cannot, and arguably should not, control.

3.2. A Minimalist Global Agenda

A second major critique of government networks is that they instantiate a radically scaled-back global policy agenda. Alston observes that the formulation of the transgovernmental policy agenda focuses on issues that are essentially spillovers from the domestic policy agendas of the industrialized world, leaving out global poverty, malnutrition, human rights, refugees, the persecution of minority groups, and disease.[80] On a superficial level, he is right. The formulation of the policy agenda in my own previous writing on transgovernmentalism and in an article by Michael Reisman[81] who makes a number of similar points does focus more on the extension of a national regulatory agenda than on more traditional international issues. In this sense the 'real new world order', to quote from my own work, is more about the globalization of national regulatory problems and solutions than the extension of traditional international institutions that was apparently initially envisaged by George Bush.

But that is a rhetorical flourish, a point advanced as provocatively as possible. Alston is making a more important point, arguing that the transgovernmental regulatory agenda is *displacing* the traditional internationalist agenda of providing public goods to solve international collective action problems. That is a much more serious charge, but it confuses the symptoms with the disease. How can the emergence of transgovernmental regulatory networks addressing domestic policy issues that have become globalized be adduced as a *cause* of declining interest in an older but perennial set of international problems? Frustration with international bureaucracy, doubt about the value received for money already spent, neo-liberal economics as a (dubi-

---

[80]   Alston, 'Myopia of the Handmaidens', at 439.

[81]   Michael Reisman, 'Designing and Managing the Future of the State' (1997) 8 European Journal of International Law 409.

ous) domestic solution that in many countries is projected on to the national sphere, the converse crisis of the social democratic (liberal, in the United States) welfare State—surely these are the real culprits. The resulting issues demand introspection and innovation, on all our parts.

More generally, the problems Alston identifies are best addressed at the level of changing domestic State preferences. It is national officials who must be motivated to renew their commitment to the global public issues he identifies. They must also be convinced that at least partial solutions to problems such as poverty, disease, famine, human rights abuses (including women's and children's rights) are achievable and worth pursuing on a global rather than a purely national scale. Focusing on networks of national government officials, many of whom are grappling with these problems within their own countries, is a sensible strategy for pursuing this agenda, and possibly the optimal strategy. Even if traditional international institutions are the best mechanisms for implementing a revived maximalist global agenda, a question addressed in the next section, it is States and thus government officials who must set and fund that agenda.

3.3. Displacing International Institutions

The third critique of government networks is that they are displacing international institutions. Alston makes this charge by again equating government networks with the values of globalization and then lamenting the impact of those values on international organizations.[82] However, a broader critique along the same lines emerges not only from the contrast that I and others have drawn between traditional liberal internationalism and transgovernmentalism, but also from the perception that government networks offer some States a way of escaping or circumventing undesirable aspects of international organizations. In particular, government networks can be seen as a way of avoiding the universality of international organizations and the cumbersome formality of their procedures that is typically designed to ensure some measure of equality of participation. Members of a government network can pick and choose new members, establish tiers of membership, or simply design procedures that ensure that power is concentrated among some members. Networks that fit this description fuel fears that their members are engaging in a politics of insulation from the global community.

These are genuine and potentially serious concerns that may well be warranted in respect of some government networks at least some of the time. But at this level, the debate is too general to have much bite. The charges of insulating powerful States at the expense of weaker States will have to be demonstrated and rebutted in the context of specific networks. The much larger point, however, is that the apparent opposition between government networks and international organizations is likely to prove a false dichotomy. Transgovernmentalism represents an alternative paradigm of

---

[82] Alston, 'Myopia of the Handmaidens', at 444.

global governance, but, like all paradigms, its purity is quickly stained in practice. Further, continuing to frame the debate in these terms will obscure an extraordinary set of opportunities to design new hybrid forms of governance that build on network concepts as well as on more traditional modes of organization.

In some issue areas, a real choice is emerging between regulation through government networks and through either existing or new international organizations. In international antitrust regulation, for example, the United States is actively pushing for transgovernmental co-operation, albeit under the auspices of the Organisation for Economic Co-operation and Development, rather than intergovernmental harmonization through an organization like the World Trade Organisation or the United Nations or a new international antitrust authority.[83] In such cases the claim that government networks will displace international organizations carries weight, although the international organization risking displacement will not be a promoter of the global agenda that champions of traditional international organizations appear to have in mind. Nevertheless, the outcome of such debates will depend on the relative merit not only of the institutional values fostered by competing institutional forms (speed, flexibility, and policy autonomy versus universality, formality, and deliberation), but also by the substantive regulatory outcomes each form is supposed to promote in the issue area in question (mutual recognition versus harmonization).

In many other issue areas, however, government networks will exist alongside or even within international institutions and are very likely to complement their functions. The NAFTA environmental enforcement network, for instance, is an example of a 'nested network', in which a government network implements the agenda of an international organization that is at least semi-traditional. Networks of national officials operating within the World Intellectual Property Organisation, at least for the purposes of negotiating new approaches to international intellectual property regulation, offer another example. The real research questions will ultimately involve efforts to determine which organizational forms are best suited to which governance functions. It may even be possible to develop a principle of global subsidiarity, designed to facilitate the allocation of functions between international organizations and national officials operating within government networks, or some combination of the two.[84] In the meantime, the threat of competition from government networks

---

[83] According to Spencer Weber Waller, '[Transgovernmental] [c]ooperation is currently in vogue because it *increases* national power. Substantive harmonization and true international antitrust law, in contrast, promise the diminution of both national lawmaking and enforcement power. Not surprisingly, the United States, although the current leader in pushing for cooperation, is the most reluctant harmonizer on the international scene.' 'The Internationalization of Antitrust Enforcement' (1997) 77 Boston University Law Review 343, 378.

[84] As a starting-point, one might argue that co-operative networks of national regulatory officials can and should focus on the issues which they are best equipped to address—the extension of their domestic policy briefs. International institutions should address those issues which either no one State is adequately equipped to address or which fail to be addressed at all at the national level, either as a result of collective action problems, or because of other reasons for resistance.

will add the spur of competition to salutary efforts to reform existing international organizations.

A final critique of government networks implicates an idea, and perhaps an ideal, of internationalism: a distinction between international and domestic politics that is embodied in and protected by a conception of national sovereignty. However much their agendas now address issues once of purely domestic concern, international organizations still operate in a self-consciously international space. They employ independent international bureaucrats, whose loyalty is supposed to shift away from their national governments. And when they convene meetings of relevant national officials, as they frequently do, those officials are at the very least wearing dual hats, formally representing their governments in external affairs. As a result, the resolutions or even rules adopted can be resisted at the national level as being external and imposed.

One of the major advantages of government networks, at least from the perspective of those who are often frustrated by the difficulty of ensuring compliance with international rules and norms, is that they directly engage the national officials who have the power to implement domestic policy changes. As a result, the policies they adopt, implement, or at least promote are much harder to combat on grounds of national sovereignty. From a theoretical perspective, government networks straddle and ultimately erase the domestic/international divide. But from the perspective of some governments, such as the Mexican environmental officials participating in the North American Free Trade Agreement (NAFTA) 'environmental enforcement network', the result is a politics of imposition that is but the latest face of imperialism, or at least hegemony.

This critique must also be contextualized. In many international issue areas, such as human rights or environmental regulation, or even many types of financial regulation, the point is precisely to penetrate national sovereignty. The policy decisions that are the subject of international concern are being made at the domestic level. Conversely, rules and principles being adopted in the international or transgovernmental sphere are supposed to shape governments' relations with their own systems. Further, these goals are often shared by many domestic actors. Thus, to say that government networks are particularly effective at penetrating the face of national sovereignty and defusing opposition based on the 'imposition' of foreign or international rules and institutions is as likely to be praise as censure.

3.4. Advantages of Government Networks: Bringing the (Disaggregated) State Back In

The danger in responding to specific criticisms is always that of losing sight of the forest. In this case, much of the critique of transgovernmentalism betrays reflexive hostility and poverty of imagination—a defensive attachment to a liberal internationalist agenda that champions international organizations either as ends in themselves or as the only means to achieve transcendent policy goals. For many, even those who share the underlying policy goals, this agenda is nothing more than yesterday's *status quo*: the welfare State at home, international bureaucracy abroad. Transgovernmentalism may in some cases be associated with other policy agendas, such as neo-liberal economics. But it also reflects the rise of an organizational form as a mode of adaptation to a host of factors, from technology to the decline of inter-State conflict, that cannot be wished or argued away. It is a choice, of course, whether to celebrate or lament this development. But here again, the choice even to frame transgovernmentalism as an issue offers numerous advantages that its critics apparently have not stopped to ponder.

First, and most important, transgovernmentalism is all about bringing the State back in as an important international actor. As emerges repeatedly in Alston's analysis, his underlying concern is the decline of State power. He argues: 'Several parallel developments are working to reduce the powers of the state, of national legislatures, and of international organisations, while private power (that of corporations rather than NGOs) is taking up even more of the slack left by the emergence of the minimalist state.'[85] This has certainly been the conventional wisdom for much of the past decade. But a new consensus is emerging on the importance of a strong State. Gerard Helman and Steven Ratner began by pointing out the terrible consequences of 'failed States', an argument that was reviled for its neo-colonial overtones in suggesting international substitutes for domestic State power, but that can be read equally as highlighting the importance of a well-functioning State.[86] Stephen Holmes has followed suit with his diagnosis of the disasters flowing from 'weak-State liberalism' in the former Soviet Union.[87] And as Alston himself acknowledges, even the World Bank is recognizing 'that the backlash against the state . . . has gone too far'.[88]

The point of presenting transgovernmentalism as a 'new world order', in contrast to the claims of liberal internationalists who seek to devolve power ever upward to international organizations and 'new medievalists' who predict or even call for the demise of the Westphalian system, was to argue that State power was disaggregating rather than disappearing. State actors are exercising their power by different means and through different channels. Alston is quite right to claim that this is a partial image—'one . . . layer out of a much more complex set of strata'.[89] But singling out this layer is a reminder that the State is not standing still. Further, thinking about global policy issues—in all areas—in terms of networks of State actors that compete with, complement, and even bridge the gap to networks of supranational, subnational, and private actors opens the door to a host of new ways in which State actors can address global problems.

A final example is in order. The arrest and requested extradition of General Augusto Pinochet from Britain to Spain to stand trial for crimes against humanity

---

[85] Alston, 'Myopia of the Handmaidens', at 442.

[86] See e.g. Gerald Helman and Steven Ratner, 'Saving Failed States' (1992–3) 89 Foreign Policy 3.

[87] Stephen Holmes, 'What Russia Teaches Us Now' (July–Aug. 1997) American Prospect 30; see also Grigory Yavlinsky, 'Russia's Phoney Capitalism' (May/June 1998) Foreign Affairs 67.

[88] Alston, 'Myopia of the Handmaidens', at 444.   [89] Ibid., at 441.

committed in Chile illustrates the impact of transnational judicial networks. A Spanish judge not only requests the British government to proceed with arrest and extradition under applicable British and European law, but specifically addresses arguments to his British counterparts by tailoring his extradition request to take account of objections raised in an initial judgment blocking extradition by a lower British court. Furthermore, other European magistrates—from France, Switzerland, Belgium, Luxembourg, and Sweden—all quickly voiced their support of the Spanish position by announcing potential extradition requests of their own. Judges in each country have been reinforced in their interpretation of international and domestic law by an awareness of their counterparts abroad, lending substance to the idea of a global community of law. The substance of their achievement in helping to bring a notorious human rights violator to justice might be even greater with the added assistance of an international institution such as the projected international criminal court. But disaggregated State actors, interacting with the political branches but maintaining their own autonomy, have not done so badly.

A second major advantage of government networks concerns the ways in which they can be used to strengthen individual State institutions without labelling the State as a whole as 'weak', 'failed', 'illiberal', or anything else. Networks target specific institutions, imposing particular conditions or at least goals regarding the level and quality of their functioning and often providing direct information and even material aid. The SEC, for example, distributes considerable technical assistance through its network of MOUs with other securities regulation agencies.[90] The criteria for participation have little to do with the political system as a whole and a great deal to do with technical or professional competence. While it may seem odd to praise the act of turning a blind eye to abuses and worse elsewhere in a national political system, the concept of a disaggregated State recognizes that wholesale labels are likely to be misleading and/or counter-productive. States are not unitary actors inside or out; absent revolution, they are likely to evolve and change in complex institutional patterns. Government networks may be exclusionary in various ways, but they are also inclusive in ways that some international organizations cannot afford to be.

On a more theoretical level, Abram and Antonia Chayes argue that 'the new sovereignty' is actually 'status—the vindication of the state's existence in the international system'.[91] They demonstrate that in contemporary international relations, sovereignty has been redefined to mean 'membership . . . in the regimes that make up the substance of international life'.[92] Disaggregating the State makes it possible to disaggregate sovereignty as well, helping specific State institutions derive strength and status from participation in a transgovernmental order. The net cost or benefit of this development will depend on the values transmitted through any particular government network, but no values are inherent in the organizational form itself.

[90] Teo, 'Memoranda', at 23–4.   [91] Chayes and Chayes, *The New Sovereignty*, at 27.
[92] Ibid.

However, the potential to be gained from piercing the sovereign veil and targeting specific institutions is enormous.

4. CONCLUSION

Many international lawyers will not like the message of this chapter. It seems an assault on all that internationalists have laboured so painstakingly to build in the twentieth century. It offers a horizontal rather than a vertical model of global governance, an informal and frequently selective set of institutions in place of formal and highly scripted fora in which each State is accorded an equal voice. Alternatively, government networks may appear trendy but inconsequential—talking shops at best and opportunities for foreign junkets at worst. After all, international institutions have proliferated over the past decades and seem sufficiently robust that at least one noted political scientist has posed the question 'why do they never die?'[93]

In fact, government networks are here to stay and will assume increasing importance in all areas of international life. They are the optimal form of organization for the Information Age. Note the responses to the East Asian financial crisis; amid calls for a new Bretton Woods agreement to craft and implement a new international architecture, the real forum for policy innovation and implementation is the G22. Governmental networks are less likely to displace international organizations than to infiltrate and complement them; they will also be the ideal fora for pioneering initiatives and pilot projects among smaller groups of States. In economic regulation in particular, they develop easily as they are based on shared technical expertise among regulators and the escalating demands of a globalized economy among both the richest States and the most promising emerging markets.

The provenance of current government networks should not limit their applicability, however. They offer an important governance alternative to both traditional international institutions and 'new medievalist' networks of non-State, regional, local, and supranational actors. It is an alternative that can be promoted and used in imaginative ways, from bolstering legislative and judicial networks to 'nesting networks' within existing international institutions and creating standing links between government networks and NGO networks. Such initiatives will simultaneously have to address rising questions of the accountability of transgovernmental actors: how to define it and how to implement it.

Perhaps the sharpest challenge that proponents of and participants in government networks will have to surmount comes from those who see them as the newest blind for the projection of United States power. In its crudest form, the claim is that as international institutions have become too constraining, the United States has moved away from its traditional liberal internationalist agenda and begun promot-

---

[93] Susan Strange, 'Why Do International Organizations Never Die?', in B. Reinalda and V. Verbeek (eds.), *Autonomous Policy Making by International Organizations* (London: Routledge, 1998), 213.

ing more informal co-operation through government networks which allow individual United States government institutions to play a dominant role. From this perspective, networks are an optimal organizational form only in so far as a United States institution remains the central node.

In contrast to this critique, however, United States policy-makers are beginning to find that in some areas networks create their own demands. In the areas of data privacy and cultural policy, for example, the United States is being excluded from transgovernmental co-operation because it does not have domestic government institutions concerned with these issues. Participation in a transgovernmental network requires a national node, but creation of such a node carries its own implications, and dangers, from the perspective of those who oppose such policy altogether. Thus, just as United States securities regulators encourage the creation of at least quasi-autonomous securities commissions in emerging markets as the price of entry into both bilateral and plurilateral network relations, the United States executive and legislature is facing a similar choice in policy areas more foreign to United States traditions.

Finally, different organizational forms have their own impact on the ways in which power is most effectively exercised. The informality and flexibility of government networks privileges the expertise and superior resources of United States government institutions in many ways. At the same time, however, the absence of formal voting rules or even of established institutional protocols prevents the United States or any other powerful State from actually imposing its will. The dominant currency is engagement and persuasion, built on long-term relationships and trust. United States government officials from regulators to judges to legislators are likely to find themselves enmeshed in networks even as they try to engineer them.

Every age needs its own idealistic vision: the Information Age will celebrate the exchange of ideas over the imposition of ideology. Networks are the medium for that exchange, a medium that, like others before it, will itself become the message. The result will be the effective adaptation of national governments to the growth of networks among the private and semi-public actors they supposedly govern. The State will thus be able to retain its position as a primary locus of political, economic, and even social power in the international system, but shifts in both the organization and the nature of that power will ultimately transform the State itself.

10

The Politics of Law-Making: Are the Method and Character of Norm Creation Changing?

VAUGHAN LOWE

My contribution to this volume is concerned with the sources of public international law and the methods of law creation. I shall refer to both under the rubric of 'sources doctrine'. There are several different purposes served by sources doctrine, and the failure to distinguish between them is the cause of some confusion. For example, sometimes doctrine is concerned to explain *who* has the power to make law (and, more important, who does not). Sometimes it seeks to determine *when* binding norms emerge; and sometimes to explain *where* rules apply—what is the geographical ambit of their normativity, which States are bound by them? Again, sometimes sources doctrine tries to explain *how*—in what manner—rules of international law bind: how, for example, rules of law differ from rules of 'soft law'. Sometimes the aim is to explain *how*—by what process—rules acquire their binding force. Here I shall address one of the more general questions subsumed within sources doctrine: in what manner are the most significant norms of international law likely to emerge during the next generation? This contains elements of several of the above questions: but I shall attempt to give a primarily descriptive explanation of one particular aspect of what is going on within international law and of how the processes of norm creation are changing.

The chapter falls into two parts. In the first, I consider what changes might be expected in the method and character of norm creation in international law. In the second, I briefly suggest a model of the development of normative systems, which, I believe, casts some light on the ways in which these changes occur.

THE PREMISS: THE PRACTICAL COMPLETENESS OF INTERNATIONAL LAW

The obvious starting place for an answer to the question, how are the method and character of norm creation in international law changing?, is to consider how the international legal system stands at present. My premiss is that the basic architecture of the international legal system is already established: that most of the fundamental rules, principles, and institutions of public international law are already in place.

Every legal system has at its heart a relatively small number of principles, doctrines, institutions, and so on that combine in various ways to make up the fabric of the law. That is why so many textbooks carry titles such as *Principles of the Law of* . . . something or other. In criminal law, for example, the elements would include the principles defining intention and foresight, the defences of incapacity and involuntary conduct and agency, the concept of causation, and rights of property and personal integrity, and the notion of interference with such rights. Once those elements are established, they may be applied in endless combinations and concrete applications in order to create particular crimes. One substantive crime more or less is immaterial to the nature of the criminal law system; but the removal of the concept of intention or of property would effect a dramatic change in the character of that system.

When the elements of a legal system can be combined to build up a normative structure adequate for the needs of the society to which it applies, we may think of the legal system as being complete. In practice, we are more likely to think of the converse. Completeness attracts little attention; but if a system is incomplete, this may readily become apparent. For instance, in a celebrated postwar arbitration, the contract underlying the dispute between Petroleum Development Ltd and the Sheikh of Abu Dhabi would prima facie have been governed by the law of Abu Dhabi. But the arbitrator, Lord Asquith, rather patronizingly observed that:

[N]o such law can reasonably be said to exist. The Sheikh administers a purely discretionary justice with the assistance of the Koran; and it would be fanciful to suggest that within this very primitive region there is any settled body of legal principles applicable to the construction of modern commercial instruments.[1]

Incompleteness is rare. We might say of a national legal system that its laws on banking or employment, for example, need to be modified or developed to accommodate technological and social changes; but we would not describe the system as being radically incomplete in the way that Lord Asquith thought the law of Abu Dhabi to be incomplete. As long as the fundamental legal institutions and principles that are the building blocks, the elements, of the system are in place, the system can modify itself to cope with the need for change and development. We would, on the other hand, describe a legal system that had no concept of corporate personality as radically incomplete in the context of the modern world of international commerce. My premiss is that international law has moved beyond the stage of radical incompleteness, and in that sense is a 'complete' (but, of course, continuously developing) legal system.

In international law there are basic elements such as the rules on law creation (customary law and treaties), the concepts of statehood and international personality, of territorial sovereignty and jurisdiction, and the notion of State responsibility. From these elements more specific rules and regimes are built up. International environmental law, for example, could scarcely be claimed to have existed fifty years ago. It has, it is true, its own 'flavour', its own vocabulary, its own characteristic approach to problems which differs from that found in other parts of international law; but

---

[1] *Petroleum Development Ltd v. Sheikh of Abu Dhabi* (1951) 18 International Law Reports 144 at 149.

contemporary international environmental law contains no fundamental legal principles or institutions that were not in existence fifty years ago. It is not, in that sense, new.

It is in this sense that I think that the system of international law has reached the stage of completeness—or is at least very close to it. This is a qualitative judgement and a matter of appreciation, and there is no precise moment at which the system becomes complete. The number of individual rules will of course continue to grow (no matter how one defines individual rules—the *normatons* or whatever the normative equivalent of fundamental physical particles might be[2]). These new rules will regulate more and more aspects of international life, and in increasing detail. Nor am I making the trivial point that the rules necessary for the existence of a theoretically complete, self-sustaining legal system are in place. That would be true if the system contained rules for making new norms and displacing old norms and a closure rule that permitted all that was not expressly prohibited. Rather, I mean that, given the manner in which the international political order is structured, and given the distribution of powers and functions between States, organizations, individuals, and other social groups, international law provides a normative framework that is adequate to accommodate most international transactions that in fact take place at present.

True, international law lacks as yet satisfactory mechanisms for dealing with community interests, such as the sea and airspace beyond national jurisdiction, and for dealing with group rights (a limitation that it shares with most national laws). International law is also poorly equipped to deal with circumstances where causes or effects, or both, of injurious activities are widely dispersed, no one actor having a major standing in this respect. This, too, is a problem that it has in common with most national legal systems. But these do not amount to radical incompleteness. International law constitutes a system within which dealings between States can be conducted with much the same ease and predictability that national legal systems secure for the dealings of individuals and corporations. Further, it provides a stable and predictable international context within which legal relations can be established in turn by national legal systems. In short, it can support the present international society of States and State laws.

The important point is that there is in place a *system* of international law. The system has emerged as a result of a series of phases of development. First, questions as to 'proper' courses of international conduct have arisen in the day-to-day dealings of States, and solutions to the questions have been consciously adopted, with the consciousness or intention that the solutions should carry, as it were, a normative charge. Further, the solutions have been recorded. At first the problem and solution are recorded together, in memory or in an oral tradition, and then in writing. At a later stage the solution is detached from the problem and recorded separately—the rule is stated without the facts of the precedents. And then a third stage is reached,

---

[2] If, indeed, it even makes sense to speak of an individual rule. See Joseph Raz, *The Concept of a Legal System* (Oxford: Clarendon Press, 1980), ch. 4.

in which the solutions are brought into order and coherence, and the relations between the rules clarified and systematized. Finally, and crucially, there is the stage at which the ordered solutions are *recognized* as constituting a legal system. That is to say, it is recognized that the system of ordered solutions—the system of rules—is capable of generating solutions to questions of kinds that have not previously arisen. The norms have a force that reaches beyond the scope of the problems that gave rise to them. At this stage there is an active, self-generating system of norms, not simply a copybook of precedents.[3] There is, in Maine's words, 'a complete, coherent, symmetrical body of . . . law, of an amplitude sufficient to furnish principles which would apply to any conceivable combination of circumstances'.[4]

The fundamental principles of the international legal system have completed this process. I repeat that this does not mean that the system now covers all aspects of international life. The scope of the system is a separate question. There may, for example, be systematic solutions which generate rules covering most areas of international life but not matters such as the exploitation by States of their own resources, or the use of radio frequencies. In other words, there may not be a *comprehensive* code. But comprehensiveness is a more difficult concept than it may at first seem. We regard English law as comprehensive, but there is no civil or criminal remedy against, or control on, the publication or broadcasting of junk. That is regarded as unregulated, or as a liberty or freedom; and the fact that it is unregulated is not regarded as undermining in any way the comprehensiveness of the English legal system.

The point that is being made here is closely paralleled by the difference of perception represented by the concepts of *non liquet* and non-justiciability.[5] *Non liquet* is an acknowledgement that the matter should be regulated by the law, but that there is no identifiable rule that can be applied to the facts before the tribunal. Non-justiciability is an acknowledgement that the matter may be regulated by law but that it is inappropriate for the tribunal to apply the relevant rule. *Non liquet* is a declaration of incompetence; non-justiciability is a posture of abstention. The shift from *non liquet* to non-justiciability depends upon the acceptance of a particular role for, and confi-

---

[3] These stages find echoes both in Maine's account of the development of legal systems and in Cassirer's account of the development of language: see Sir Henry Maine, *Ancient Law* (1861), chs. 1 and 2; Ernst Cassirer, *Language and Myth* (trans. Suzanne K. Langer, 1946), chs. 4, 6, and *passim*.

[4] *Ancient Law* (1861) (Everyman Edition, 1917, 19). The point is unaffected by the fact that Maine believed this stage of completeness to be a legal fiction, concealing the legislative power of the judges. A legal system is complete when it enables judges (and other decision-makers) to act as if it were complete.

[5] To my surprise, the argument for the practical completeness of international law was regarded at the Oxford conference as controversial. For a good exposition of a similar position see Sir Hersch Lauterpacht, 'Some Observations on the Prohibition of "Non Liquet" and the Completeness of International Law', in *Symbolae Verzijl* (The Hague: Martinus Nijhoff, 1958), 196. See also the rejoinder (and consideration of the opposing argument of Professor Stone in *Legal Controls of International Conflict* (2nd edn., London: Stevens, 1959), 153) by Sir Gerald Fitzmaurice, 'The Problem of Non-Liquet: Prolegomena to a Restatement', in *Mélanges offerts à Charles Rousseau* (Paris: Pedone, 1974), 89. In my view, Fitzmaurice gives insufficient weight to the necessity for decision by analogy in practical reasoning.

dence in, the legal system and its decision-makers (courts, in centralized legal systems, and also other processes in decentralized systems such as international law). *Non liquet* can be abandoned only when the completeness of the legal system is recognized.

International law had arguably reached the stage of practical completeness by the time that the Permanent Court of International Justice (PCIJ) was established in 1920. A reflection of this can be seen if one compares the approach to dispute settlement in the 1899/1907 Hague Convention on the Pacific Settlement of International Disputes with that in the Statute of the PCIJ.[6] The 1899/1907 Convention provided for the establishment of the Permanent Court of Arbitration 'with the object of facilitating immediate recourse to arbitration for international differences, which it has not been possible to settle by diplomacy'.[7] An adjudicatory tribunal was to be established *by the parties* for each individual dispute. The parties decided to take the dispute before the arbitrators whom they had empowered to settle the matter. By contrast, the PCIJ was a standing court. States could, under article 36 of its Statute, agree on an *ad hoc* basis to put cases before it. They could also subscribe to the so-called Optional Clause in article 36, declaring that 'they recognize as compulsory *ipso facto* and without special agreement, in relation to any other Member or State accepting the same obligation, the jurisdiction of the Court . . .' Instead of States choosing to put disputes before a tribunal, the Optional Clause permitted States to be obliged to appear before the Court to defend their actions.

The distinction reflects two different conceptions of the function of arbitral or judicial settlement. One conception treats it as an extension of bilateral diplomacy between the disputing parties, the other as a judicial procedure for prescribing a solution to disputes according to law.[8] The shift from the one to the other was possible because the PCIJ could *always* give an answer to a legal dispute, precisely because international law was regarded as always providing an answer. The capacity of the PCIJ to apply rules to each and every dispute that came before it was a consequence of the character of the law that it applied, rather than a result of the authority given to it in each case by the parties. It was, in other words, the fact that the international legal system was considered by those acting on behalf of States to be 'complete' that made it possible to invite the submission of any dispute whatsoever to the PCIJ. This is, of course, no more than a change in attitude. There is no reason why any dispute that could have been put before the PCIJ and adjudicated upon by it could not have been put before an *ad hoc* arbitral tribunal and adjudicated upon by that tribunal.

[6] Cf. Michael Dunne, *The United States and the World Court 1920–1935* (London: Pinter, 1988), chs. 1 and 2.

[7] Article 41 of the 1907 Convention (UKTS 1971, No. 6; Cmnd. 4575; 100 BFSP 298), which derives from article 20 of the 1899 text.

[8] See the Report of Georges Scelle to the International Law Commission on Arbitral Procedure, UN Doc. A/CN.4/113 (1958), *Yearbook of the International Law Commission, 1958*, ii. 1 at 2. For an example of the problems that can arise from divergent expectations of the nature of arbitration, see the *Buraimi Oasis* arbitration, J. G. Wetter, *The International Arbitral Process* (Dobbs Ferry, NY: Oceana Publications, 1979), iii. 357.

But the framing of the PCIJ Statute was undoubtedly a very significant step in the development of the international legal system.

Since 1920 some further elemental building blocks of the international legal system have been created: the concepts of the continental shelf and the exclusive economic zone, and of Permanent Sovereignty over natural resources, and of the Common Heritage of Mankind are all prominent examples. These have arisen by the 'normal' processes for the validation of putative norms and institutions: by treaty, or by the combination of State practice and *opinio juris* that generates customary international law. I do not claim that this phase is now over and that no new elemental concepts will be added to the catalogue of international law.[9] But I do believe that this process is slowing down markedly and that the emphasis is shifting towards other forms of development of the international legal system.

Some readers may find the claims for the practical completeness of the basic architecture of the international legal system unconvincing. To them I offer an alternative and uncontroversial starting-point: that in the next few decades many of the most interesting developments in international law are likely to arise in the area of the regulation of the relationship between existing norms and institutions of international law, rather than in the creation of entirely novel norms and institutions.

INTERSTITIAL NORMS AS THE ENGINE OF CHANGE IN INTERNATIONAL LAW

What forms of development are characteristic of contemporary international law? First, and most obviously, there is much activity in the field of detailed rule-making in fields such as environmental, trade, and maritime law. This has great practical, but little theoretical, interest. It is a reflection of the fact that national bureaucracies operate increasingly on the international plane, particularly in relation to the setting of technical standards and regulatory requirements where divergences can give significant economic advantages to States. Rule-making of this kind is closer to the bureaucratic implementation of policy than to law-making. It does not in itself lead to the development of fundamentally new legal principles and institutions. It may lead to innovations of other kinds. For example, requirements of compliance with internationally agreed standards may be made a condition of IMF support, or of World Bank or national development funding. The extension of the normative force of international standards by the device of conditionality is an important characteristic of contemporary international law. But it is with the development of novel concepts that I am concerned, and I will put rule-making to one side.

There is a second process by which international law is being developed. It does not focus upon what one might call the 'primary' norms of international law: that is,

---

[9] Exceptional cases may be readily foreseen. Most probable are new norms on the global commons, group rights, and 'widely distributed harm', noted above.

the rules that mandate or forbid or permit certain activities, and the legal institutions, such as States and continental shelves, through or upon which those primary norms operate. Rather, the development is taking the form of the emergence of normative concepts operating in the interstices between those primary norms. These emergent concepts we may call 'interstitial norms' or 'modifying norms' or 'meta-principles', because they do not themselves have a normative force of the traditional kind but instead operate by modifying the normative effect of other, primary norms of international law.

These modifying norms arise because in all legal systems there is the possibility that rules and principles may overlap. An overlap may arise in one of two very closely related ways. First, it may arise from problems of characterization. Abstract norms have no necessary relationship with concrete facts. No set of factual circumstances[10] *of itself* entails the application of a particular rule or principle. The application of the norm is a process of juristic evaluation. The jurist considers the facts, characterizes them in a particular manner, and determines which rules or principles apply as a result of that characterization. It is the act of characterization, rather than the existence of the facts themselves, that entails the application of particular norms. Now, because it may be possible to characterize any given set of factual circumstances in a number of different ways, it follows that it may be possible to determine that a number of different rules and principles are applicable to them, perhaps leading to different legal outcomes.

For example, take a case where a new revolutionary government in a State appoints 'managers' of foreign-owned businesses whose original managers have fled in the face of the revolutionary upheavals, in order to ensure that the business continues to operate.[11] Is that a step towards the possibly unlawful expropriation of the foreign property, or a step in fulfilment of the legal obligation to take reasonable steps to protect foreign property in the State? Again, take a case where a company incorporated in State A buys, in good faith and for a fair price, from the government of State B property that the government had, some years previously, expropriated without compensation from a national of State C. If State C takes the property from the State A company, without compensation, is that itself an unlawful taking of alien property, or is it a lawful measure of self help in response to the initial violation of the rights of the State C national?[12] Or, to take another example, is the entry of armed police into diplomatic premises from which shots have been fired, killing

---

[10] This rather windy phrase is more accurate than 'set of facts'. The identification and articulation of a 'set of facts' itself presupposes a characterization of the circumstances. The point is well recognized: 'norms are seldom explicitly referred to in Soga disputes: instead, argument and decision-making proceed through reference to facts, the choice of which implies reliance upon a norm that is mutually understood'. Roger M. Keesing, *Cultural Anthropology* (2nd edn., New York: Holt, Rinehart, and Winston, 1981), 327, quoting J. L. Comaroff and S. A. Roberts.

[11] Cf. *Starrett Housing Corp. v. Iran* (1983) 4 Iran–US CTR 122, 85 International Law Reports 349.

[12] Cf. the controversy over the US Helms–Burton legislation (1997) 46 International and Comparative Law Quarterly 378.

someone in the street outside, a violation of diplomatic immunity and inviolability or is it a lawful measure of internal policing or of self-defence?[13]

Second, overlaps and conflicts may arise from the fact that norms and principles have no clear boundaries.[14] Even where the basic legal characterization of a given set of factual circumstances is clear and uncontroversial, it may be unclear whether or not a particular rule applies. For example, does the rule on the inviolability of the diplomatic bag preclude its exposure to sniffer dogs trained to search out drugs or explosives? Do oil rigs have a right of innocent passage? Is the conduct of military exercises in the exclusive economic zone of a foreign State a lawful exercise of third State rights in that zone? In each case, if the answer is no, the circumstances fall outside the scope of one rule and become subject to another rule. Clearly, this is very similar to the situation of competing characterizations of factual circumstances.

In each of these examples there are two (and perhaps more) possible legal characterizations of the factual circumstances. The judges (or others concerned to ascribe legal characterizations to factual circumstances) are faced with a choice as to the way in which they will characterize the facts, or as to whether to determine that a particular rule does or does not apply to the facts in question. That choice cannot be determined by syllogistic reasoning. In the context of the analogical reasoning that is a necessary part of the process of applying abstract norms to concrete factual situations, there is no way in which it can be determined that a given norm necessarily applies (or necessarily does not apply) to a particular case. There will be a range of possible decisions or characterizations, none of which can be logically proven to be 'the right answer' or, indeed, to be a wrong answer.

So far I have referred to the choice in terms of the coexistence of a number of possible legal norms that might be applied to the facts in question. It would be more exact to say that the choice is essentially a matter of determining the relationship between the legal norms that are potentially applicable. That relationship is often described by the misleading metaphor of the 'boundaries' of the rule, implying that there can be a one-to-one mapping of facts to laws. But there is no such simple relationship. The relationship is structured in an altogether more complex and subtle fashion. Given the absence of clear boundaries for norms, it is clearly probable that particular pairs or groups of norms, appropriate for application to particular kinds of factual situations, will tend to arise together as competing approaches to the analysis of those situations.[15] For instance, it is likely that in many cases arising from the environmental impact of industrial projects the facts can be viewed from the perspective either of a right to development or of a duty to protect the environment. Indeed,

---

[13] Cf. the *Libyan People's Bureau* incident (1984): Cameron (1985) 34 International and Comparative Law Quarterly 610; Rosalyn Higgins, 'The Abuse of Diplomatic Privileges and Immunities: Recent United Kingdom Experience' (1985) 79 American Journal of International Law 641.

[14] See J. Raz, *The Authority of Law* (Oxford: Clarendon Press, 1979), 72–4.

[15] See Julius Stone, *Legal System and Lawyers' Reasonings* (London: Stevens, 1964), ch. 8.

that was the precise phenomenon addressed by the International Court of Justice in the *Gabcikovo Case*, which illustrates the point well.[16]

The *Gabcikovo Case* arose out of a dispute between Hungary and Czechoslovakia (as it then was) concerning hydroelectric and navigational and flood control works on the Danube. Reflecting the conflict of values at the heart of the dispute, the majority judgment in the ICJ referred to the 'need to reconcile economic development with protection of the environment'. The concepts of economic development and the protection of the environment were treated as legal principles, and their reconciliation was, in the words of the Court, 'aptly expressed in the concept of sustainable development'. Judge Weeramantry, in the elaborate discussion of sustainable development in his Separate Opinion, refers to it as 'more than a mere concept, [it is] . . . a principle with normative value'. Noting that the right to development and the need to protect the environment may collide, he asserts that '[t]he law necessarily contains within itself the principle of reconciliation. That principle is the principle of sustainable development.'

There are two steps taken in Judge Weeramantry's argument. First, it is asserted that there must be a reconciliation of the conflicting principles. Second, it is said that the relevant 'principle of reconciliation' is the principle of sustainable development. I will take each step in turn.

Clearly, faced with conflicting principles whose application would lead to incompatible decisions, courts and tribunals[17] must choose which to apply. The choice could be made on a case-by-case basis. It could be said that this rule does not extend to these circumstances, that those circumstances fall within the ambit of that rule, and so on. But the persuasiveness of the decision and the goals of certainty and predictability within the legal system are advanced if there is a consistent principle that motivates the individual instances of resolutions of conflicts between the principles.[18] In any event, it would almost certainly be possible to infer consistent principles from collections of individual decisions. Consistency serves the ends of justice, the identification of similarities and differences between cases making it possible to demonstrate that like cases have indeed been treated alike. And the gradual refinement of a consistent principle, tested in the crucible of a succession of concrete cases, makes possible the distillation of the detailed, carefully considered analyses spread throughout the mass of individual decisions. This is a continuing process. Legal principles are never static. They may be constantly adjusted to changes in material and social circumstances, and in this way offer the prospect of maintaining a principle suited to the exigencies of modern life.

Principles for the resolution of conflicts between the primary norms of international law—the 'do this', 'don't do that', 'you may do this' rules generated by the

---

[16] (1982) 37 International Legal Materials 162; http://www.icj-cij.org.

[17] I make the point in the judicial context, where it is clearest. But it applies whenever anyone has to make a legal characterization of a given set of factual circumstances.

[18] See Robert Alexy, *A Theory of Legal Argumentation* (Oxford: Clarendon Press, 1989), 226–30 and *passim*.

traditional process of State practice plus *opinio juris*—are desirable. The content of
such principles, however, is *ex hypothesi* drawn from sources other than the primary
rules themselves. The choice is made by the judge not on the basis of the internal
logic of the primary norms, but on the basis of extraneous factors. Those factors are
many and varied. Two are obvious, and likely to carry great weight. The first is the
consistency of the preferred outcome with what is thought, on broad moral and
political grounds, to be 'desirable'—a kind of broad equity.[19] The second factor is
the general cohesion of the preferred outcome with the existing norms of the legal
system, which is in itself one of the *desiderata* of judicial decision-making. These
factors are often, but not always, made explicit in the reasoning of the tribunal which
is offered in justification of the decision.

Judge Weeramantry argues that international law needs coherent principles of this
kind for the resolution of its internal conflicts and tensions; and he argues that, in
the case of the conflict between the right to development and the protection of the
environment, sustainable development is such a principle.

I have argued elsewhere that there is no adequate basis on which it can be said
that sustainable development has emerged as a norm of customary international law
by the traditional processes described by the ICJ in the *North Sea Continental Shelf*
and *Nicaragua Cases*.[20] There is not the State practice and *opinio juris* to support it.
Indeed, in my view it does not even have the potential to be a primary norm of international law. There is no coherent formulation of a free-standing duty to develop
sustainably, or even not to develop unsustainably, that could be given normative
force by the usual combination of State practice and *opinio juris*. It is rather an interstitial principle, acting upon other, primary legal rules and principles—in this case,
acting upon what the International Court took to be the legal principles of economic
development and protection of the environment. It exercises an interstitial normativity by establishing the relationship between the neighbouring primary norms
when they threaten to overlap or conflict with each other.

This is how interstitial norms operate. They have no independent normative
charge of their own. They do not instruct persons subject to the legal system to do
or abstain from doing anything, or confer powers, in the way that primary norms do.
They direct the manner in which competing or conflicting norms that do have their
own normativity should interact in practice. The dependence of interstitial norms
upon true primary norms is reflected in the fact that some of the interstitial norms
will sit between several pairs or sets of primary norms. Perhaps the most obvious
example of such a versatile concept is 'reasonableness'. It comes into play in a host of
contexts: for example, in municipal law it is familiar as a standard of care in tort and
in criminal law, and of propriety in administrative decision-making. In international

---

[19] I return to this point below, arguing that it permits (indeed, requires) the shaping of legal decisions by a wide range of extra-legal factors. See also Vaughan Lowe, 'The Role of Equity in International
Law' (1992) 12 Australian Yearbook of International Law 54.

[20] The following section of this chapter is a summary of the argument in my paper written for the
Festschrift for Professor Patricia Birnie.

law it is employed in contexts such as reasonable notice of the termination of agreements, the existence of reasonable grounds for suspicion when suspected pirate ships are intercepted, and the duties of reasonable care owed by a State to aliens within its territory. And like all good interstitial principles, the concept of reasonableness is capable, no matter how precisely its application is pinned down in any individual case, of being redefined with infinite flexibility in order to accommodate social change.

These interstitial or modifying norms are simply concepts. If the tribunal chooses to adopt the concept, the very *idea* of sustainable development is enough to point the tribunal towards a coherent approach to a decision in cases where development and environment conflict. There is absolutely no need for the concept to have been embodied in State practice coupled with the associated *opinio juris*. Its employment does not depend upon it having normative force of the kind held by primary norms of international law. Tribunals employ interstitial norms not because those norms are obligatory as a matter of law, but because they are necessary in order that legal reasoning should proceed. All that is needed to enable the norms to perform this role is that they be clearly and coherently articulated.

Once they have been articulated, they operate as modifying norms, bearing upon the primary norms that surround them. But they have a broader significance. If, for example, sustainable development is declared to be the reconciling principle that establishes the relationship between development and environment, it is highly unlikely that any other principle will be employed to effect that reconciliation, at least until sustainable development is displaced. The concept effectively 'occupies the field', to borrow a phrase from European Community law. Further, any shifts in emphasis that may be necessitated by the accidents of case law will be tested for their coherence with sustainable development. In these senses, the principle exercises an immense gravitational pull.

These interstitial norms can exercise a very great influence on the system. For instance, the importance of sustainable development in reconciling the conflicting demands of development and the environment can scarcely be overstated. Consider, for example, the possible alternatives. The international community could have rested with the 'polluter pays' principle that was so popular in the 1970s, relying on market mechanisms to control pollution. Or it could have affirmed the primacy of States' rights to develop their economies. Either of these solutions would have led to very different approaches to the development/environment conflict.

The *Gabcikovo Case* was used as an example of the use of the concept of sustainable development; but, as has been remarked already, the point is by no means confined to judicial tribunals. If a politician wishes to protest against pollution emanating from a neighbouring State, which defends its action on the basis of a claimed right to development, both the politician and the polluting State are very likely to resort to the language and the concept of sustainable development in order to support their respective positions. Similarly, those negotiating treaties, or development loans, or environmental controls, at the national or the international level, are likely to approach that task within the context of the concept of sustainable development. The concept colours the whole approach to this area of international law.

The metaphor of colour is, indeed, a powerful one. The effect of interstitial norms is to set the tone of the approach of international law to contemporary problems, bringing subtlety and depth to the relatively crude, black-and-white quality of primary norms. I have used one example; but I expect there to be many others in the coming decades, during a phase in the development of international law analogous to the development of equity in English law. For example, it is likely that international law will begin to develop its own concepts of unjust enrichment and other restitutionary remedies, across a whole range of contexts from the determination of compensation in cases of expropriation and injury to alien property to remedies for breaches of treaty obligations. The concept of *abus de droit*, already established in the approach of civil lawyers to international law, is likely to achieve much greater prominence as a check upon exercises of legal power by States. Through the influence of these principles, the whole character of international law and its relation to the most pressing problems of fairness and justice can be materially altered. And, to make the point once more, this is done by principles that owe none of their normative force to the traditional 'State practice plus *opinio juris*' or to treaty law processes for the creation of binding legal norms. I expect the method and character of the creation of the most important and influential norms of international law in the next generation to be markedly different from that which has obtained in the past.

Some may doubt whether the main developments in international law will indeed occur in this way. The suggestion that the main change may be in the techniques for giving effect to existing norms, for example by extending the use of the device of conditionality, has already been noted. Another candidate for the title of 'most significant change' is the possibility of a paradigm shift in the conception of the basic nature of international law. Philip Allott has remarked in his work on the persistence of the private law model of international law, according to which treaties are, perhaps subconsciously, approached as if they were contracts, and the rules of customary international law as if they were rules of the law of tort or obligations.[21] Why should we not effect a paradigm shift, and approach the regulation of State power on the basis of the public law model? Why not require States to conform to public law standards of reasonableness, rationality, and proportionality? Why not permit the international review of the 'constitutionality' of national action? It may well be that there is a movement in this direction, and that the early stirrings of it can be seen in developments such as the scrutiny of internal State policies effected by the UN Human Rights Committee and the demands for the judicial review of Security Council action in the *Lockerbie Case*. Indeed, I believe that those who call for or predict such a move are right: that is the direction in which international society must move; and

---

[21] And see the excellent study by E. Raftopoulos, *The Inadequacy of the Contractual Analogy in the Law of Treaties* (Athens: Hellenic Institute of International and Foreign Law, 1990).

I think that the development of interstitial norms will represent a major contribution to this process. But I do not expect there to be a sudden paradigm shift within the next generation, which is the horizon within which this chapter is confined.

THE SIGNIFICANCE OF INTERSTITIAL NORMS

Whether or not the development of interstitial principles becomes the dominant mode of change in international law within the next two or three decades, it will certainly be *an* important mode of change. The method and character of creating interstitial norms have a number of features that give that process a particular significance.

First, interstitial norms are not generated by the same processes as the traditional 'primary' norms of international law. They have no 'authors', in the sense that it might be said that the UN Security Council is the author of certain resolutions creating binding obligations under the UN Charter, or that States are the authors of treaties and of customary international law. They simply 'emerge' from within the international legal system. Of course, they do not emerge unaided. They are drawn out. If the validity of the norm is questioned, that which in the case of a primary norm is a question of the authoritativeness of the authorship becomes in the case of these interstitial norms an inquiry into the validity of the drawing out of the norm. This is in part a question as to the authority of the drawer. If the ICJ articulates the interstitial norm, the validity of the norm will usually be generally recognized. It would be less persuasive if Greenpeace, rather than the Court, were to announce, for example, that sustainable development is the norm that resolves conflicts between a right to development and a duty to protect the environment. The validity of the norm is also in part a question as to the persuasiveness of the interstitial principle itself, regardless of the 'authorship' of the argument (as might be expected where norms are essentially authorless). The argument for using sustainable development in this way either is or is not attractive and persuasive; and I suspect that the aesthetic and affective aspects of the matter are of at least as much importance in the process of acceptance as is rational analysis.

Second, it follows from this that it is possible for participation in the development of international law to become much more widely diffused. Following a conservative approach to international law, one would say that States and States alone are capable of generating legal obligations by the making of treaties and customary international law. But, since interstitial norms do not derive their force from the processes of treaty or customary law formation, there is no reason why only States should participate in their generation. For example, Greenpeace may study and explain the content of the concept of sustainable development. If that explanation is persuasive, in the sense that a rhetorical, topical argument addressed to the invisible college of international lawyers may be persuasive, it is likely to take root. There is, in principle, no limit to the category of persons who may contribute to the development of interstitial norms.

A tribunal, or anyone else deciding on the legal characterization of factual circumstances, may draw on any articulations and discussions of the norm, regardless of their authorship.

Third, there is a further consequence. This diffusion of participation in the development of interstitial norms, because it is essentially driven by rhetorical argument and may involve a very wide range of contributors, depends much more than does the development of traditional, State-authored legal norms upon consonance with the 'spirit of the age'. A much wider range of concepts and social pressures come to shape these interstitial norms than is ordinarily the case in international law.

The concept of sustainable development, to stay with that example, was framed by the Bruntland Commission,[22] and then refined as it was taken up and discussed, and continues to be discussed, by other bodies and individuals.[23] In that process its implications have been considered by economists and biologists, by chemists and moral philosophers, by specialists in development and specialists in ecology, and by many others upon whose work or interests the concept impinges. Discoveries in science and shifts in the prevailing wisdom in politics or economics can feed *directly* into the continuous process of refining the concept. Perhaps more importantly, the broad themes of history and popular culture will exercise a powerful underlying influence on the direction of that process.

Whenever legal norms compete for application and some principle of reconciliation is sought there occurs a process similar to that described as 'the back and forth movement between the "if-then" idiom of general precept, however expressed, and the "as-therefore" one of the concrete case, however argued'.[24] The question is whether the putative principle of reconciliation 'fits' or 'feels right'. This principle is initially conceived as a hypothesis, but, like the course set by a driver approaching a narrow opening, as the moment of decision draws closer small changes of direction are made to bring the course in line with what experience suggests is best. The 'fit' or 'feeling' about principles of reconciliation is not a matter of compliance with legal norms. It is a matter of harmony with what, for want of a better word, one might term experience and common sense.[25] This experience and common sense is an unsystematized complex of moral, cultural, aesthetic, and other values and experiences. But for all its vagueness (or the vagueness of my description of it), it exercises immense power.

A student of twentieth-century intellectual history, looking back in years to come on the development of a legal concept such as humanitarian intervention, would have great difficulty understanding it in relation to the work of Hart or Kelsen or

---

[22] Report of the World Commission on Environment and Development (the 'Bruntland Report'), *Our Common Future* (Oxford: Oxford University Press, 1987).

[23] Following the familiar route of the *grande idée*: see Clifford Geertz, *The Interpretation of Cultures* (1973; London: Fontana, 1993), 3–4.

[24] Clifford Geertz, *Local Knowledge* (New York: Basic Books, 1983), 174, citing F. von Benda-Beckmann, *Property in Social Continuity* (The Hague: Martinus Nijhoff, 1979).

[25] See Clifford Geertz, 'Common Sense as a Cultural System', in *Local Knowledge*, 73.

McDougal. It makes little more sense against the background of the primary norms of international law. But it makes perfect sense against the background of John Ford and John Wayne movies. The myth of the US Seventh Cavalry, riding in to sweep the innocent victims to safety, is one of the most potent images of moral action in the present century, echoed in each Galahad, Indiana Jones, and Superman of popular culture. The same is true of the dogged detective tracking the wicked suspect to the ends of the earth: the road from the *French Connection* to the International Criminal Court may be tortuous, but it can clearly be traced.

I make this point in all seriousness. In a system where the plausibility of analogical reasoning and the persuasiveness of topical, rhetorical argument lie at the root of the perception of legitimacy, the influence of such extra-legal factors is of central importance. This holds still truer in the realm of State action where extra-legal conceptions are undeniably a more immediate influence on foreign policy than are abstract legal norms. Legal concepts and norms are important. But the matrix in which they are set is not a normative system of pure juridical reason. No one—statesman, judge, or whatever—can switch his or her brain into a purely legal or purely non-legal mode. Brains are brains. The same brain functions as the judge judges, reads newspapers and novels, watches films and television, and does everything else. It is inevitable that reasoning, in whatever context, proceeds against an inarticulate and perhaps irrational backcloth of concepts, linkages, suppositions, and prejudices built up from the general experience of life. And it is because interstitial norms operate in precisely those areas where primary legal norms do not dictate clear legal solutions that they are the most likely to be heavily (I would say overwhelmingly) influenced by non-legal factors. Interstitial norms are the points where general culture obtrudes most clearly into the processes of legal reasoning.

THE SECULARIZATION OF INTERNATIONAL LAW

This leads me to my final point. International law is, in my view, undergoing a process comparable to the secularization of religion. I do not claim that there is some Toynbean law of history bearing down on international law; but neither is the comparison (which I employ merely as a heuristic tool) fanciful. Indeed, it would be remarkable if there were no parallels between the developments of law and religion, given that both are social institutions that claim to prescribe comprehensive normative codes which, taken together with the residual freedoms that they permit, govern the whole of life. The parallels are sufficiently striking for a comparison of the two systems to yield some valuable insights.

The parallel between the great text-based theistic religions and international law is particularly striking, which again should not be surprising, given the structural similarities of the two normative systems. The key characteristic of classical public international law as a social institution is that it is an institution in which a more or less closed and self-perpetuating band of experts—people acting in roles as international judges, and as international lawyers in government, universities, and private practice—infer norms from the supposed will and acts of an abstract, immaterial entity (the State), whose real existence is posited as the foundation of the entire institution and, indeed, of an entire way of understanding the world. The parallel with that species of text-based theistic religion exemplified by the 'People of the Book'—Judaism, Christianity, and Islam—is clear. There, norms of conduct are derived by a more or less closed and self-perpetuating priesthood from the postulated existence and supposed will and acts of an abstract, immaterial entity, God, whose existence underpins the system and an entire way of understanding the world.

Given the intellectual debt of modern international law to writers such as Francisco Victoria, Professor of Sacred Theology in the University of Salamanca, and Francisco Suarez SJ, it is only to be expected that there should be stylistic similarities between international law and religion. These are evident both in the manner in which the prescriptions are presented in the two systems and in the manner in which the prescriptions come to exercise their normative influence within society at large.

There is an early strand within most religions in which teaching is communicated through narratives. This is obvious in the creation myths which exist all around the world, and which present an account of the natural order of the world.[26] It is also, and more pertinently, true of the narratives specifically intended to communicate norms of social conduct. The earliest books of the Old Testament chronicle the history of the people of Israel. Those chronicles, which constitute essentially the diplomatic history of Israel, are represented as the bearers of a normative message. The people flourished or floundered, depending on whether they did right or wrong. The precedents exemplify the norms implicit within the chronicled experiences.

The same use of the chronicle as the medium of normative message is clearly evident in the writings of the second generation of early international lawyers, which succeeded those, such as Victoria, who had adopted an essentially theological approach to the subject. Indeed, it was this recourse to 'the illumination of history' that Grotius singled out as the mark of learning.[27] So, for example, when Balthazar Ayala asserted that 'Ambassadors were safe and inviolable among all peoples. This was provided by the law of nations', he supported the assertion with passages such as this:

The Romans, accordingly, made ruthless war on the people of Fidenae for slaying the Roman ambassadors at the bidding of Tolumnius, King of Veii, to whom they had defected; and also on the people of Illyria in return for the beheading of the Roman ambassadors. David, too, made war on the king of the Ammonites in return for the outrage upon his ambassadors.[28]

---

[26] See Barbara C. Sproul, *Primal Myths* (London: Ricler, 1980).

[27] See his prolegomena to *De Jure Belli et Pacis*, conveniently reprinted in Robert J. Beck, Anthony Clark Arend, and Robert D. Vander Lugt (eds.), *International Rules: Approaches from International Law and International Relations* (New York: Oxford University Press, 1996), 34 at 47. Grotius proceeds, none the less, to a lengthy discussion of Aristotle and the Old and New Testaments.

[28] Balthazar Ayala, *Three Books, on the Law of War, And on the Duties Connected with War, And on Military Discipline* (1597) (trans. John Pawley Bate, 1912), 88.

The incident embodies the norm. Diplomatic history is, one might say, the Old Testament of international law.[29] It chronicles the acts of States in a way that discloses the norms considered, at least in retrospect, to be immanent in State conduct. Customary international law is the harvest gathered in from the field of State practice.

This narrative phase is superseded[30] by a second phase, in which direct acts of prophecy are the medium for transmission of the normative message. The law is now deliberately stated, not by recording historical actions but by directly announcing the principles which previously would have been exemplified by those actions. This is a phase through which the text-based religions passed. It is represented by the later Old Testament prophets, by the New Testament, and by the Koran. Its international legal parallel is reflected in the great diplomatic conferences, from the 1899 Hague conference onwards, at which States sought to generate pure legal norms independently of State practice in concrete instances. At those conferences States sought not merely to negotiate a treaty bargain, but to reach an international consensus on the outlines of an international legal order. The 1899 Hague Convention, the League Covenant, and the UN Charter are the clearest examples. This phase, however, is also manifest in international law in circumstances where the existence of norms is asserted on the basis of what appears to be regarded as their self-evident correctness.[31] It also appears as naked prophecy as to how the world should be, of the kind in which President Truman engaged when he 'proclaimed' that the resources of the continental shelf adjacent to the United States appertained to the United States.[32] That proclamation, like all prophecy, depended upon a degree of acceptance for its survival.

The direct, prophetic announcement of norms is a dangerous activity. Who counts as a true prophet? Which norms are valid? It is natural that this phase should be accompanied by a concern to control the process and to preserve the purity of the wells from which the norms flow. In the religious context this takes the form of action to preserve the canonicity of the religious code. It is exemplified by the work of the councils of the early Church, such as the Council that generated in 382 the Gelasian decree defining the canon of scripture. In the context of international law this process is exemplified by the work of the International Law Commission, acting in its codification (rather than its progressive development) mode. It is epitomized by the proceedings of the UN General Assembly in drafting its great declaratory resolutions such as the Declaration on Principles of International Law Concerning

---

[29] A point not lost on historians of international law: see T. A. Walker, *A History of the Law of Nations*, i. (1899), Part I, ch. I.

[30] In written texts, compiled after the event, the two phases often coexist, as do the diplomatic histories and the Mosaic and Deuteronomic codes in the Old Testament.

[31] e.g. the reference in the *Corfu Channel Case* to 'elementary considerations of humanity': (1949) ICJ Reports 4 at 22.

[32] See M. M. Whiteman, *Digest of International Law* (Washington: US Government Printers, 1963–74), iv. 756. The early assertions of the existence of a right of humanitarian intervention might also be regarded as an example in this category.

Friendly Relations and Co-operation Among States.[33] This is also the role of Article 38(1) of the Statute of the International Court of Justice. The same process occurs in the trial of the arguments made before the International Court of Justice and other tribunals, as the adversarial process seeks to root out heresy and misconceived argument—the legal equivalent of the *autos-da-fé*.

It is the phase of identifying and fixing primary principles that in my view is now winding down. The basic principles of the normative canon having been set, two further processes follow. The first has been the subject of the first part of this chapter. It is the glossing of the basic norms and the adaptation of the central tenets to the changing social and political demands of the day. In the religious context, it is the stage represented by the development of the Sunna in Islam, the Talmud in Judaism, and the writings of the early Church Fathers in Christianity, as well as by the continuing process of elaboration of the religious code within the canon itself. In international law, it is represented by the stage of the development of interstitial norms as well as by the continuing refinement of the primary rules of international law.

The second process may be referred to as secularization, in which the basic principles, structures, and processes of the normative system are transferred out of the system itself and into other areas of life. This transfer was a major element of the Renaissance, when humanism and secularization sat side by side with the Church and religion. The theoretical basis of political philosophy became disengaged from theology, but the concepts—sovereignty, citizenship, authority, and so on—remained much the same, as one would expect where the concern was to provide a new interpretation of existing reality. In their new, secular ground these concepts flourished with a vitality that enabled them to survive the decline of the world-view that had generated them. This transfer of concepts is exemplified by the great debates between Las Casas and Sepúlveda, which generated the Spanish texts which lie at the base of much of the present system of international law.[34] Those debates both influenced the secular political order in the Spanish Americas, and constituted the first steps towards the disengagement of international law from theology. The modern, secular system of international law ultimately broke out of this common origin and purported to offer a standard, independent of religion, against which the behaviour of States could be measured.

There is a similar process of diffusion currently taking place in relation to international law. In the same way that the early writers on international law (and it begs the question to describe them as international lawyers) adopted the norms and the reasoning processes of theology, so the norms and processes of classical inter-State public international law are being adopted outside the classical inter-State domain. The techniques and principles of public international law are being borrowed most

---

[33] UN GA Res. 2625(XXV), 24 Oct. 1970. My point would have been clearer if the General Assembly had entitled the resolution the Declaration *of* Principles of International Law, rather than the Declaration *on* Principles: but the point stands.

[34] See D. A. Brading, *The First America: The Spanish Monarchy, Creole Patriots and the Liberal State 1492–1867* (Cambridge: Cambridge University Press, 1993), ch. 4 and *passim*.

obviously and applied in the dealings and legal relations of private companies and non-governmental organizations and, more generally, in the internal legal orders of States. This is very obvious in cases where States and corporations make agreements that are practically indistinguishable from treaties, and over which they may litigate on an equal footing in tribunals set up *ad hoc* or under the auspices of the International Centre for the Settlement of Investment Disputes or some other body.[35] It is evident, too, in cases where national courts, even though under no national or international legal *obligation* to do so, construe State powers in the light of human rights law.[36] And it is evident in the accords reached between international corporations, and the increasing penetration of corporations and NGOs into the work of intergovernmental conferences and organizations.

It is a commonplace that States (or rather, individuals acting in the name of States) are becoming relatively less important as the power and influence of other institutions increases. The shift is gradual. States still possess greater power, broadly speaking, than other social institutions. States control most of the money supplies and most of the guns, and as a result their views are commonly thought to be more important than those of others. But in terms of the actions and policies that have the most immediate impact upon the daily lives of most people, the acts and policies of private corporations are of primary importance. They dominate the private sphere of individuals' lives. To the extent that individuals are truly engaged by and participate in affairs of State and public life, the manner of that engagement and participation is shaped by corporations. Corporations control communications (a term whose meaning is greatly extended in a world of electronic commerce), transportation, prices and technical standards for the supply of goods and services, and much else of modern life. Although 'the State' may have the power to *intervene* and to control their activities, it is the activities of the corporations that impinge most directly upon individuals. For most people, most of the time, it is the personal, the private, and the parochial that matters, not the civic, public sphere. Where banking, teaching packages, the purchase of food, clothes, houses, holidays, and practically anything else can all be conducted under the auspices of AOL or Microsoft, the actions of those companies—their policies on free speech, conditions of supply, and so on—may come to be of more immediate importance than many State policies. It is the concepts and norms of international law as they permeate the world *outside* the classical, State-centred world of international law that are likely to be of increasing significance to most people, most of the time, in the future. The conceptual framework of international law is likely to become diffused throughout the vast web of non-State international dealings. This simple process, that mirrors the similar process through which originally religious norms and concepts were diffused throughout the secular sphere, is all that I mean by secularization.

---

[35] See e.g. *Texaco v. Libya* (1977) 53 International Law Reports 389; *Asian Agricultural Products v. Sri Lanka* (1990) 30 International Legal Materials 577.

[36] See e.g. the discussion in *R. v. Secretary of State for the Home Department, ex parte Brind* [1991] 2 Weekly Law Reports 588; [1991] 1 All England Reports 720.

This secularization is, in effect, the mirror image of the phenomenon described in the first part of this chapter. There I sought to draw a picture of the non-legal world intruding into the reserved sphere of classical inter-State international law. Here I argue for the protrusion of international law beyond that reserved sphere into the non-international law world. Those, then, are my themes: first, that the major developments in international law in the next generation will occur not in traditional primary norms, but in other kinds of normativity that are overwhelmingly influenced by the contemporary cultural milieu; and second, that international law is beginning a process of migration into areas of 'private' life analogous to the secularization of religion.

11

Regulating the International Economy: What Role for the State?

EDWARD KWAKWA[*]

1. INTRODUCTION

Development—economic, social, and sustainable—without an effective state is impossible. It is increasingly recognised that an effective state—not a minimal one— is central to economic and social development, but more as partner and facilitator than as director.

World Development Report 1997: The State in a Changing World

(World Bank, 1997)

The international economy is going through what could be described as a revolution in terms of the pace of change in technology, in regulation, in growth, and in adjustment. The major challenge of this trend may lie in finding an international regulatory framework, which draws a judicious balance between the sometimes divergent interests and concerns of different entities in the international economic system. Adjustments to the new reality of the international economy are taking place at a number of levels, including the private sector, the State, intergovernmental, and non-governmental organizations.

In this chapter, I discuss the role of the State in regulating the international economy.[1] I focus on the particular concerns and issues affecting 'less developed' or 'developing' countries (LDCs). The focus on LDCs is for four reasons. First, and least important, is the fact that I am from an LDC. Second, and more importantly, sufficient literature exists on the role of 'developed' countries (DCs) in regulating the international economy. In so far as DCs and LDCs do not possess equal bargaining strength or influence the process of regulating the international economy in identical fashion, the two should be separated. The third reason for focusing on LDCs is the difference in the role of the State in those countries. The role of the State in a DC is, by definition, more limited than in an LDC. It is well known that the priva-

[*] The views expressed here are my personal ones and are not necessarily shared by WIPO or the United Nations. I am grateful to Kathleen Lawand, Kwame Kessie, and H. Kwasi Prempeh for providing very helpful comments on an earlier draft.

[1] I understand the topic to refer to the role of the State in providing an appropriate environment or framework for a market-oriented global economy. In this context, 'State' is all-inclusive and is intended to encompass the whole array of institutions and agencies which possess and exercise a legitimate means of coercion over a defined territory and population. The term 'State' in this chapter is therefore coterminous with the term 'government'.

tization drive is not as deeply rooted in LDCs as it is in DCs. In several LDCs, there continue to exist monopolies in certain sensitive sectors, such as telecommunications and financial services. To the extent that several State-owned businesses remain in LDCs, this raises the question of how efficiently the State can regulate itself internally, not to mention how it may help to regulate the international economy. Finally, there has been a tremendous expansion and growth of the world economy. The benefits of this expansion, however, have not been evenly distributed. A number of LDCs, in particular the least-developed ones among them, have been marginalized in the process. The focus of most policy-makers and international institutions is thus how best to assist these LDCs to reverse this trend and to help them to integrate themselves better into the global economy and to secure a share in growth in international trade commensurate with the needs of their economic development. In this regard, it is clear that appropriate policy responses have to be adopted at both the national and international levels. My focus on the LDCs is aimed at discussing the role of the State in furthering this process.

The chapter is presented in six sections. Section 2 discusses the present *context in which the international economy is regulated*. In particular, it describes the inevitable trend of globalization and its impact on States. Section 3 describes some of the reasons *why the international economy is regulated*. In section 4, the discussion focuses on *how the international economy is regulated*, or *who sets the rules by which the international economy is regulated*. I argue that the rules by which the international economy is regulated are, in large measure, set by 'paradigm-setting States' (P-SSs), and that the 'paradigm-receiving States' (P-RSs) have no real choice but to play by the rules of the game.[2] Section 4 also provides examples of the role of politics in international law, as well as of the role of law in international politics. Section 5 discusses the desirable responses of P-RSs and the role that they should play in regulating the international economy. I argue that, rather than resulting in the end of the State as we know it, globalization and efforts to regulate the international economy will in fact enhance some of the important functions of the State. I also conclude that the far-reaching repercussions of the Asian financial crisis amply demonstrate why the role of the State in the international economy is so important. Section 6 presents some final observations.

2. THE CONTEXT IN WHICH THE INTERNATIONAL ECONOMY IS REGULATED

The effects of globalization are hardly recondite. They include a much greater liberalization of the world trading system, increased mobility of labour and capital, the establishment of regional trading blocs, and the world-wide availability of new technologies. Perhaps the most important indicium of globalization is the shift from a system of distinct national economies to an international economy in which produc-

---

[2] The terms 'paradigm-setting States' and 'paradigm-receiving States' are defined in section 4.

tion is internationalized and financial capital flows instantly and almost unhindered between countries. It bears emphasis that while globalization *per se* is a phenomenon with historical antecedents, the effects or implications of its contemporary manifestation are significantly different from what they have been in the past. In this regard, globalization today is changing lives in ways scarcely imagined a few years ago.

The globalization of companies and markets has also undermined national regulators and, in certain instances, led to policy conflicts between and among various national jurisdictions. The international private sector (represented in large part by transnational companies (TNCs)) is playing an ever-increasing role in the global economy. To be sure, TNCs, which are widely perceived to be among the main channels for trade, finance, and technology, are now major, even dominant, global actors. They are responsible for a significant proportion of world trade and investment. But while the importance of the State appears to be dwindling in favour of the TNCs, it is also worth noting that the industrialized countries, as the 'home' of most TNCs, have taken to championing the interests of TNCs at the international bargaining table.

Due to the inevitable trend of globalization, several dire predictions have been made on the decline of the State.[3] The view that globalization makes it more difficult for governments to perform their traditional tasks now seems to be widely accepted.

As a result of the virtual erosion of borders, governments now find it more difficult to control such practices as pornography and the importation of computer software. Information technology has virtually eliminated the capacity of States to isolate themselves from the outside world. The monetary and fiscal policies of governments have not been spared from the effects of globalization. During the recent Asian financial crisis, for example, the currency in several Asian countries came under pressure as investors, fearing that their assets would erode in value, converted their holdings mainly into United States dollars. It is not uncommon these days for a government to state categorically that its programmes are drawn up according to the dictates of the global market, rather than what the government itself would have liked to do. As rightly pointed out by Richard Blackhurst, however, governments are

---

[3] See e.g. Oscar Schachter, 'The Decline of the Nation-State and its Implications for International Law' (1997) 36 Columbia Journal of Transnational Law 7; Arthur Schlesinger, Jr., 'Has Democracy a Future?' (1997) 76(5) Foreign Affairs 2 at 12 ('Nation-states will continue to decline as effective power units: too small for the big problems, as the sociologist Daniel Bell has said, and too big for the small problems.'); Susan Strange, 'The Erosion of the State' (Nov. 1997) Current History 365; Anne-Marie Slaughter, 'The Real New World Order' (1997) 76(5) Foreign Affairs 183 at 192 ('Globalisation implies the erosion of national boundaries. Consequently, regulators' power to implement national regulations within those boundaries declines both because people can easily flee their jurisdiction and because the flows of capital, pollution, pathogens, and weapons are too great and sudden for any one regulator to control.'). Compare Michael Reisman, 'Designing and Managing the Future of the State' (1997) 8(3) European Journal of International Law 409 at 419 (concluding that '[t]he international system in the next century will find not only that it must continue to live with the state, but that one of its systemic objectives will continue to be the improvement of the functions of the state in specific decision sectors.').

to blame in certain cases for adopting bad policies which may exacerbate the baneful effects of globalization.[4]

It is worth noting that globalization is not without its critics. In developed countries, for example, some critics claim that the greater flow of imports from the more advanced developing countries, as well as the flow of foreign direct investment (FDI) to those countries, have resulted in increasing income inequality, job losses, and stagnant or lower wages for less-skilled workers in the developed countries. Indeed, it is generally believed that the rejection of legislation that would have granted the United States President 'fast-track' authority to negotiate trade arrangements that the Congress could not amend, but could only vote up or down, may be an example of the strength of the backlash against globalization.[5] Similarly, in some East Asian countries, critics claim that the openness of those economies to trade and FDI flows and, in particular, to the international capital markets was largely responsible for the financial crisis in those countries. And in the developing world in general, it is argued by some that, in addition to creating massive pressure for adjustment and restructuring, globalization serves to legitimate the international pressures for the LDCs to accept the hegemony of international capital within their borders.[6] Others, including Prime Minister Mahathir Mohammed of Malaysia, have gone so far as to call for international regulation of short-term capital flows and the activities of speculators.

An obvious effect of globalization, in the context of our discussion, is the growing recognition that there are certain areas that governments simply cannot regulate alone. Due to the virtual elimination of borders and rapid changes in technology, the repercussions of inadequate or flawed regulation are more likely to affect other countries. A quintessential example of such an area is the Internet. It is well known that the Internet is now an important medium for electronic commerce.[7] The fact that this medium of commerce has clear inter-jurisdictional implications suggests the need for concerted international responses to some of the policy challenges posed by it. Another example of an area that governments cannot regulate alone is that of corruption. As I explain in section 5 of this chapter, the transnational effects of corruption pose a threat, not only to the development and governance of States, but also to the rule of law in the international system. Part of the problem lies in the fact

---

[4] Blackhurst has argued that: 'To a large extent, governments have only themselves to blame for the backlash. Part of the problem is their frequent lack of candour regarding the fact that even though globalisation clearly benefits the country as a whole, some groups in the economy will lose. . . . More important is their reluctance to publicly acknowledge that while globalisation creates tremendous opportunities, it also raises the cost of bad policies—such as labour market rigidities, over-regulation, sub-standard schools and educational policies, tax policies that discourage job creation, and chronic budget deficits that reduce investment by reducing national savings.' See Richard Blackhurst, 'The WTO and the Global Economy' (Aug. 1997) 20 (5) The World Economy 527 at 531.

[5] See Richard Haas and Robert Litan, 'Globalisation and its Discontents' (May/June 1998) 77 (3) Foreign Affairs 2 at 3.

[6] See Ray Bush and Morris Szeftel, 'Globalisation and the Regulation of Africa' (June 1998) 76 Review of African Political Economy 173 at 176.

[7] For a detailed account of the history and economics of the Internet, see generally *Electronic Commerce and the Role of the WTO* (Geneva: Special Studies 2, World Trade Organisation, 1998).

that globalization is further increasing the number of international business transactions in which bribes may be changing hands, and thus further weakening the prospects for dealing with the problem by internal regulation alone.

Other areas or shared challenges where the interests of individual States can only be protected by collective action include those of combating environmental degradation and enhancing the global financial system. In short, increased globalization increases the need for a framework of rules and institutions to structure and regulate international economic relations. The section below discusses other reasons why the international economy must be regulated.

3. WHY DO WE NEED TO REGULATE THE INTERNATIONAL ECONOMY?

There are various reasons why the international economy must be regulated. Primarily, it is regulated for reasons of economic efficiency. In simple terms, it is necessary to have in place a multilateral system which promotes international efficiency. It is widely agreed that the recent boom in international trade is in part attributable to efforts to regulate the international economy. To the extent that international co-operation leads to increased trade and financial stability, all countries benefit from the orderliness, transparency, and predictability which are produced by a rules-based global economic system.[8]

Secondly, the international economy may be regulated through various forms of international co-operation, as a way of channelling resources to, or away from, particular sectors of the economy. An example of this is the efforts made by multilateral institutions, including the United Nations Conference on Trade and Development (UNCTAD) and the World Trade Organisation (WTO), to encourage greater FDI in LDCs. Another example would be the imposition of trade sanctions, for political reasons, on a particular country. This has the effect of restricting the flow of goods and services to that country.

In the view of most economic commentators, the absence of an effective regulatory framework results in chaos in the international economic order. This largely explains the decline of the international trading order, the disruption of international trading relationships, and the massive outbreak of 'beggar-thy-neighbour' policies in the 1920s, including severe trade restrictions which led to the collapse of many domestic economies as well as the world economy at large.[9] Thus, the goal of the forty-four countries which met at the United Nations Monetary and Financial

[8] Other issues relating to regulation and economic efficiency include deregulation of access to the market, liberalization and internationalization, promoting automation, enhancing transparency of over-the-counter markets, and creating or boosting new markets, for example through privatization.

[9] See generally Michael Trebilcock and Robert Howse, *The Regulation of International Trade* (London: Routledge, 1995), 1–24. According to the authors, 'the most notorious of such attempts [at adopting extreme forms of trade protectionism] was the enactment by the US Congress of the Smoot-Hawley Tariff in 1930, which raised duties on imports to an average of 60%, and quickly provoked similar retaliatory measures by most of the USA's major trading partners.' Ibid., at 20.

Conference in Bretton Woods, New Hampshire, in 1944 was to rebuild the international economic system. The International Bank for Reconstruction and Development (the World Bank), for example, was established with the conviction that economic depression and other disasters could be averted through international co-operation for mutual benefit and, in particular, through full participation in the international economy by all States. To this end, the World Bank was one of the institutions created to facilitate private and official foreign financial flows to developing countries. Similarly, the International Monetary Fund (IMF) and the General Agreement on Tariffs and Trade (GATT) were designed to promote long-term prosperity through stable exchange rates and open trade.

A third reason for regulating the international economy is the need to protect the investor. The international economy today relies on the market, which, in turn, cannot function properly without adequate safeguards to protect the investor. In this respect, it may be recalled that the WTO's General Agreement on Trade in Services (GATS) explicitly recognizes, not only the right of all governments to regulate financial markets, but also their absolute freedom to take whatever prudential measures are necessary to safeguard the integrity of those markets.[10]

Against this background of reasons as to why the international economy is regulated, how are the rules formulated?

4. WHO SETS THE RULES?

There are two broad sets of 'State' players in the international economy—we could refer to them as the 'paradigm-setting States' (P-SSs) and the 'paradigm-receiving States' (P-RSs).[11] The P-SSs, exemplified by the United States and other highly industrialized economies, are those that largely determine the content of the rules by which the international economy must operate. The second set, the P-RSs, by virtue of their inadequate economic-human-capital resources and their historical incorporation into the international economy as colonies or dependent territories, have much less input in determining the content of the rules of the game they inevitably must play. This second set invariably includes countries that, in United Nations terminology, are either LDCs or 'least-developed countries'.[12] It is possible that a few

---

[10] See the Annex on Financial Services, General Agreement on Trade in Services, in *The Results of the Uruguay Round of Multilateral Trade Negotiations: The Legal Texts* (Geneva: WTO, 1995), 327.

[11] I am grateful to Mr H. Kwasi Prempeh, Associate, Cleary, Gottlieb, Steen and Hamilton, Washington, DC, for suggesting the use of these terms.

[12] The United Nations currently regards a group of forty-eight countries as 'least developed'. They are: Afghanistan, Angola, Bangladesh, Benin, Bhutan, Burkina Faso, Burundi, Cambodia, Cape Verde, Central African Republic, Chad, Comoros, Democratic Republic of Congo, Djibouti, Equatorial Guinea, Eritrea, Ethiopia, Gambia, Guinea, Guinea-Bissau, Haiti, Kiribati, Laos, Lesotho, Liberia, Madagascar, Malawi, Maldives, Mali, Mauritania, Mozambique, Myanmar, Nepal, Niger, Rwanda, Samoa, Sao Tome and Principe, Sierra Leone, Solomon Islands, Somalia, Sudan, Togo, Tuvalu, Uganda, United Republic of Tanzania, Vanuatu, Yemen, and Zambia.

countries may be both P-SSs and P-RSs. Likely examples are Mexico and the Republic of Korea. While these two countries are included in the UN list of LDCs, they are also members of the Organisation for Economic Co-operation and Development (OECD), which is the quintessential example of a club representing the interests and concerns of P-SSs.[13]

The system by which the international economy is regulated is not necessarily skewed against the P-RSs, nor do the P-RSs lack a forum where they could potentially influence the system. As I argue later, the WTO in fact presents them with a reasonably good forum. The problem, however, is that the P-RSs simply do not have the means or the ability to influence the process. In a paper prepared for a commemorative volume on the first fifty years of the multilateral trading system, Ademola Oyejide identifies 'three significant disabilities which made more active participation in the GATT process virtually impossible for the low-income developing countries'.[14] As a result of these and other reasons which I explain below, the P-RSs face considerable difficulties in participating in policy formulation and the implementation of obligations under the multilateral economic system. There are several reasons for this. I will use the Geneva-based international organizations with which I am familiar to illustrate my point.

First, the P-RSs normally do not have enough experienced personnel to cover the issues. At the WTO, for example, only a few P-RSs, such as Brazil and India, are active participants in the discussions and negotiations which take place there.

The second reason for the lack of influence of the P-RSs is low or inadequate representation. There are several P-RSs which do not even have Permanent Missions to the United Nations Office in Geneva. Such countries normally cover the issues at the WTO or elsewhere in Geneva by occasionally sending a representative from some nearby Mission. It is common knowledge, for example, that a few African countries frequently send their representatives based in Brussels to Geneva for meetings.

For those countries that have Permanent Missions in Geneva, the problem is sometimes insufficiency in numbers. Some countries may have a single trade attaché covering trade issues at the WTO, who also covers intellectual property discussions at the

---

[13] The OECD Members are: Australia, Austria, Belgium, Canada, Czech Republic, Denmark, Finland, France, Germany, Greece, Hungary, Iceland, Ireland, Italy, Japan, Korea, Luxembourg, Mexico, The Netherlands, New Zealand, Norway, Poland, Portugal, Spain, Sweden, Switzerland, Turkey, United Kingdom, and United States. It will be noticed that countries such as Mexico, the Czech Republic, Poland, and Hungary also fall within the United Nations' rubric of LDCs or countries in transition towards a market economy.

[14] See A. Oyejide, 'Low-Income Developing Countries in the GATT/WTO Framework: The First Fifty Years and Beyond' (Paper presented at Symposium on the World Trading System, Geneva, 30 Apr. 1998), at 4–5: 'First, since they were not "principal suppliers" with respect to any of the trade sectors in which the developed countries chose to negotiate, the low-income developing countries lacked the "right" to negotiate. Second, they also lacked the "power" or leverage to negotiate since they were usually not major markets, individually or collectively, of significant developed country exports. Third, the low-income developing countries lacked the human and institutional capacity to participate effectively in the GATT process, both in terms of the capability in state capitals to articulate their trade interests and in terms of adequate permanent representation at the GATT to assert their membership rights and negotiate those interests.'

World Intellectual Property Organisation (WIPO) as well as trying to follow discussions at UNCTAD. This contrasts significantly with some of the P-SSs, which have a special Ambassador to the WTO (separate from those countries' Ambassadors to the United Nations Office in Geneva) and sometimes twenty or more officers covering the WTO exclusively. The United States, for example, frequently has thirteen officers covering negotiations at the WTO, while Japan sometimes has as many as twenty-two, each covering a separate agreement in the WTO framework of agreements.

The problem is closely related to a lack of financial resources. The international organizations sometimes have to fund the participation of P-RS officials in important meetings and discussions. Those countries that cannot afford to pay for their representatives to attend such meetings risk being excluded from the decision-making process if the budget of the organization does not allow for the funding of such meetings.

Where the P-RSs have been able to surmount all the obstacles outlined above, they are sometimes faced with the problem of being unable to effect a change in rules which may have been promulgated before they joined the club. The Articles of Agreement of the International Monetary Fund (IMF), for example, use a system of weighted voting to arrive at decisions, including amendments to the Agreement. The original members of the IMF apparently decided that the IMF would function more efficiently and responsibly by relating members' voting power directly to the amount of money they contributed to the institution through a quota system. As a result, the more a country contributes to the IMF, the stronger the country's voice in determining IMF policies.[15] The same rule applies in respect of the constituent instruments of the World Bank and some other international institutions.[16] Although the WTO has a one-country, one-vote system rather than a voting system based on the amount of money contributed, a vote is conducted only where a decision cannot be arrived at by consensus. The consensus rule makes it very difficult to change certain provisions of the WTO Agreement.[17]

It is evident from the above that the P-SSs play a much greater role than the P-RSs in setting the rules by which the international economy is regulated. The position in which the P-RSs find themselves may be equated with a contract of adhesion or some variant of a Hobson's choice, which they must either accept as it is, or refuse to accept, with no other feasible options.

I will use some recent and ongoing examples to illustrate my argument that the rules by which the international economy is regulated are largely determined by P-SSs. The

---

[15] See Articles of Agreement of the International Monetary Fund, Article XII, Section 5.

[16] See e.g. Articles of Agreement of the International Bank for Reconstruction and Development, Article V, Section 3(a) ('Each member shall have two hundred fifty votes plus one additional vote for each share of stock held'); and Articles of Agreement of the International Finance Corporation, Article IV, Section 3(a) (identical language).

[17] See Articles IX and X of the Marrakech Agreement Establishing the World Trade Organisation, in *The Results of the Uruguay Round of Multilateral Trade Negotiations*, at 6. See also Mary Footer, 'The Role of Consensus in GATT/WTO Decision-Making' (1996/7) 17(2 and 3) Northwestern Journal of International Law & Business 653.

first example is the Multilateral Agreement on Investment (MAI). This is an attempt to provide the same liberal environment for international investment that exists for international trade and services.[18] It is being negotiated at the OECD.[19] In general, the drive for stronger protection of foreign investments is spearheaded by businesses based in developed countries, which find bilateral investment protection agreements unsatisfactory or inadequate.

The MAI is not without its critics. Some claim that the MAI is nothing less than a global economic constitution which will give TNCs the power to sue governments before domestic and international courts and overturn or modify laws protecting the environment and workers' health. In particular, the MAI would prevent governments from restricting certain types of foreign investments and could be misused to attack the regulatory powers of governments in areas which have little or nothing to do with investment.[20]

While the MAI is being negotiated by P-SSs, I would suggest that the P-RSs are more in need of such an agreement. First, most of the OECD countries already have in place functioning legal systems which do not discriminate unreasonably against foreign investors. It can hardly be denied that the P-RSs have more significant barriers to foreign investment than the P-SSs. Thus, at least one critic has concluded that 'the contents of the OECD MAI seem in the main to be directed at developing rather than developed countries' investment regimes'.[21] Secondly, the OECD countries alone account for 85 per cent of FDI outflows and 60 per cent of FDI inflows. This would seem to suggest that the non-OECD countries have more at stake in seeking to attract a bigger chunk of the 85 per cent of FDI that originates in the developed countries. For the foreign investor, a country which has signed a MAI guaranteeing certain protections to the investor would naturally be a better haven than one which had not signed such an agreement or had not provided for such guarantees in its domestic laws. Thirdly, the importance of FDI for the economic development of LDCs is no longer in doubt. For the host country, FDI normally brings the transfer of much needed capital, new technology, and know how. It can also provide a stimulus to competition, innovation, savings, and capital formation, all of which can result in job creation.[22]

---

[18] It must be noted, however, that there are several international agreements and institutions which aim at regulating FDI. Indeed, as argued by Rosalind Thomas, 'attempts to regulate FDI can be traced back to the beginning of the General Agreement on Tariffs and Trade (GATT) in 1947 and to the aborted International Trade Organisation (ITO)'. See R. Thomas, 'The Need for a Southern African Development Community Response to Proposals for a Multilateral Agreement on Investment' (June 1998) 21(4) World Competition: Law and Economics Review 84 at 87.

[19] Five non-OECD countries are also participating as 'observers' in the negotiations on the MAI: Argentina, Brazil, Chile, Hong Kong (China), and Slovakia.

[20] See generally Pranay Gupte, 'New Rules, Old Results: A Pact on Foreign Investors' Rights has the Developing World Worried' (30 Mar. 1998) Newsweek at 21.

[21] See Thomas, 'Development Community Response', at 93.

[22] See generally *World Investment Report 1997: Transnational Corporations, Market Structure and Competition Policy* (New York: UNCTAD, 1997); *World Trade Organisation Annual Report 1996* (Geneva: WTO, 1996), 44–78; and Robert Pritchard (ed.), *Economic Development, Foreign Investment and the Law* (Boston: Kluwer International Bar Association, 1996).

Discussions on the MAI were put on hold for a period of six months as of May 1998. There is reason to believe that those discussions have now been suspended indefinitely, as far as the OECD is concerned.[23] My guess is that those discussions will end up eventually at the WTO, where discussions on a MAI would be more acceptable in the sense that they would include a much wider spectrum of countries. While the OECD is an organization of twenty-nine of the world's most advanced economies, the WTO comprises 134 countries, 80 per cent of which are LDCs and economies in transition towards a market-based economy. The logic of moving negotiations on the MAI to the WTO does not seem hard to grasp. To the extent that it is negotiated only by OECD countries, it is evident that the MAI will have an OECD bias *vis-à-vis* the P-RSs. In order to avoid this risk, it is imperative that the P-RSs be allowed to play a more active role and become a part of the process by which efforts are being made to regulate FDI flows. I should mention, however, that some critics have already expressed concern at efforts to move the MAI process to the WTO.[24]

A second example of the pre-eminence of P-SSs in regulating the international economy is the United States' Africa Growth and Opportunity Act.[25] Under this Act, those African countries that make progress towards establishing a market-based economy are eligible to participate in programmes, projects, or activities, or to receive assistance or other benefits under the Act. This may well be domestic United States legislation, but the underlying message seems to be that African countries need to play by the rules of the game, as established by the United States, in order to receive certain benefits. The proposed United States legislation has therefore been criticized by certain African countries as being tantamount to the imposition of conditions on the receipt of assistance.

A third example of P-SS predominance is the Electronic Commerce Agreement. Under a United States proposal, countries would make a commitment to exempt from customs duty those transactions that are conducted through the electronic

---

[23] Discussions on the MAI were put in jeopardy when France, and later Australia, pulled out, arguing, among other reasons, that the proposed treaty gave too much power to corporations at the expense of governments, and excluded emerging economies. The discussions were also suspended partly as a result of stiff opposition from environmental and labour advocates in the OECD countries. See Bloomberg News, 'OECD Suspends Talks on Investment Treaty', *International Herald Tribune*, 5–6 Dec. 1998, at 13, col. 2.

[24] The fear has been expressed that 'shifting the investment issue to the WTO will place great pressure on developing countries to negotiate and eventually join an agreement that would have disastrous effects on their development prospects. Moreover, promises to include environmental and social concerns are likely to be only an eyewash to co-opt the public to accept the basic tenets of the MAI. The strong enforcement capability of the WTO through its dispute settlement system will also mean that all countries, especially developing countries, will be forced to comply'. See 'Trade: NGOs Call for End to Investment Talks at OECD & WTO' (8 June 1998) South-North Development Monitor at 4.

[25] The Africa Growth and Opportunity Act was before the 105th Congress of the United States of America. For a summary and status of the Bill, see http://thomas.loc.gov/cgi-bin/bdquery/z?d105:SN00778. Although the legislation died in October when it became encumbered with other items, President Bill Clinton remains committed to the passage of the Africa Growth and Opportunity Act. See Victor Mallet, 'US Warns on Southern Africa Barriers', *Financial Times*, 2 Dec. 1998, at 7, col. 4.

medium. Although no country currently imposes duties on trading or transmissions by electronic means, some WTO Member States are wary of making a binding commitment to this effect at this time. Opponents of this arrangement argue that P-RSs would gain nothing, but lose a great deal. In particular, they argue that the exporters of electronic commerce are generally the P-SSs, and that the P-RSs, the general importers, stand to lose by relinquishing the option of levying an import tax on such transactions. Opponents further contend that the zero-duty proposal, to the extent that it constitutes a discipline on a particular mode of transaction, and not on goods and services *per se*, would open a new chapter in international trade relations, with systemic implications at the WTO.[26]

Having given examples of what may be seen as the role of international politics in law, I will now turn to the role of law in international politics. For this, I will again use the WTO to illustrate my point.

Several of the P-RSs remained passive bystanders in the early rounds of multilateral trade negotiations conducted under GATT auspices. In general, many P-RSs viewed the GATT as an exclusive rich-country club. In the Uruguay Round, however, the eighth, and by far the largest, round of trade negotiations (which also resulted in the creation of the WTO), the LDCs played a more active role than they had done in earlier Rounds.[27] While the GATT began with fewer than twenty-five members, most of which were developed countries, its successor, the WTO, currently has 134 members, the majority of which are developing countries.

The accomplishments of the Uruguay Round are too well known to need recounting. For the purposes of this chapter, it is enough to recall that the Round brought about a 'Single Undertaking', with common or uniform rules and obligations for all WTO Members.[28] The establishment of the WTO resulted in an extension of the regulatory system to new areas not covered by the GATT, such as intellectual property rights, services, and investment measures. It also resulted in a much stronger procedure for settling disputes and a mechanism for reviewing individual country policies.[29]

[26] See generally Bhagirath Lal Das, 'Trade: Electronic Commerce in the WTO' (5 May 1998) South-North Development Monitor, at 5 (referring to the proposal on electronic commerce as 'a peculiar proposal in the contractual context of the GATT/WTO' and 'an example of the special and differential treatment in reverse'). Another example of the pre-eminence of P-SSs in regulating the economy is the Information Technology Agreement (ITA). The ITA arose from the Ministerial Declaration on Trade in Information Technology Products, which was signed on 13 Dec. 1996 in Singapore by twenty-eight governments at the conclusion of the first WTO Ministerial Conference. It provides for the elimination of customs duties and other charges on information technology products through equal annual reductions. While this Agreement was negotiated initially by P-SSs, its implementation was made possible only after other countries, including several P-RSs, signed on to an already-agreed text, thus raising the Agreement's coverage to over 90 per cent of world trade in information technology products.

[27] On the participation of the LDCs during the Uruguay Round, see generally Gilbert Winham, 'Explanations of Developing Country Behaviour in the GATT Uruguay Round Negotiations' (1998) 21(3) World Competition: Law and Economics Review 109.

[28] The exception to this uniformity of obligations is the various transitional periods provided for LDCs and least-developed countries.

[29] On the achievements of the Uruguay Round of Trade Negotiations, see generally John Croone, *Reshaping the World Trading System: A History of the Uruguay Round* (Geneva: WTO, 1995).

As is well known, accession to the WTO Agreement reduces the ability of a country to adopt 'autonomous' measures which conflict with the multilateral trading system. For example, the WTO Subsidies Agreement disciplines the use of subsidies and regulates the actions which a State can take to counter the effects of subsidies.[30] In addition to providing a specific definition of a subsidy, the Agreement provides that certain subsidies can, in certain circumstances, be challenged without the requirement that those subsidies be proved to have produced adverse effects on trade. In short, the Agreement circumscribes the actions which a State can take in respect of subsidies.[31]

In my view, the WTO could serve to put States on a more equal footing. Under the prevailing system at the WTO, the P-RSs have a forum within which to attack those policies of P-SSs that may be at variance with the rules of the world trading system. For example, before the WTO came into being DCs accounted for 95 per cent of the dispute-settlement cases brought under GATT. Since the WTO came into being, however, that figure has shrunk to about 70 per cent, with the LDCs now initiating and defending about 30 per cent of the cases.

The dispute-settlement mechanism is one of the hallmarks of the WTO that distinguish it from other international organizations. To help illustrate my point, it is appropriate to refer to a statement by the Director-General of the WTO:

No review of the achievements of the WTO would be complete without mentioning the Dispute Settlement system, in many ways the central pillar of the multilateral trading system and the WTO's most individual contribution to the stability of the global economy. The new WTO system is at once stronger, more automatic and more credible than its GATT predecessor. This is reflected in the increased diversity of countries using it and in the tendency to resolve cases 'out of court' before they get to the final decision . . . The system is working as intended—as a means above all for conciliation and for encouraging resolution of disputes, rather than just for making judgements. By reducing the scope for unilateral actions, it is also an important guarantee of fair trade for [less powerful countries].[32]

The dispute-settlement system has thus been described as the 'most important element of the WTO—the jewel in the crown'.[33] That system is now more rules based and less power based than was the case under the GATT. It has more specific time limits, is faster, and has a greater degree of automatic procedures. Thus, it is

---

[30] See Agreement on Subsidies and Countervailing Measures, in *The Results of the Uruguay Round of Multilateral Trade Negotiations*, at 264.

[31] In recognition of the fact that subsidies may play an important role in the economies of LDCs, the Agreement exempts LDCs (including the least-developed ones among them) with less than $1,000 per capita GNP from disciplines on prohibited export subsidies and provides to least-developed countries a grace period up to 2003, by which time they must eliminate subsidies designed to help domestic production and avoid importing.

[32] Statement by Renato Ruggiero, 17 Apr. 1997, in WTO, *Trading Into the Future* (Geneva: WTO, 1997), at 3.4.

[33] See Sylvia Ostry, 'Looking Back to Look Forward: The Multilateral Trading System After 50 Years' (Paper presented at Symposium on the World Trading System, Geneva, 30 Apr. 1998), at 16.

much more difficult to block the findings of dispute-settlement panels—and their implementation.[34] At the second Ministerial Meeting of the WTO, held on 18 and 20 May 1998, in Geneva, several LDCs stated that, despite its inadequacies, relatively small countries could rely on the WTO's dispute-settlement system as the most effective tool with which to compete fairly and effectively in the growing and increasingly complex global market.[35] It may be recalled that powerful Member States sometimes ignored GATT rulings with impunity. The European Union, for example, brushed aside two GATT panel decisions which called for changes to its banana import regime. In 1997, in a third case concerning bananas, the WTO ruled against the EU's regime, just as the GATT had ruled on two previous occasions.[36] This time, however, the EU indicated that it would implement the WTO Panel's decision. Although this is not in the interest of the banana-producing P-RSs in the African, Caribbean, and Pacific regions, it nevertheless bodes well for other P-RSs in the Latin American region.[37]

It may be recalled also that one of the very first cases submitted to the Dispute Settlement Body of WTO was initiated by two P-RSs, Venezuela and Brazil, against the quintessential P-SS, the United States. The WTO Appellate Body held in April 1996 that a United States regulation on 'reformulated' gasoline violated the national treatment guarantee enshrined in Article III: 4 of GATT. This was because Venezuelan and Brazilian refiners were subject to a methodology that imposed more stringent emissions reduction requirements on them than on United States refiners.[38] The United States has since complied with the decision. Indeed, all the losing parties in the dispute-settlement panels have indicated that they intend to comply with the results of decisions against them. As rightly pointed out by John Jackson, so far, 'there seems to be no exception to this spirit

---

[34] On the WTO dispute-settlement mechanism in general, see Ernst-Ulrich Petersmann, *The GATT/WTO Dispute Settlement System: International Law, International Organisations and Dispute Settlement* (London: Kluwer, 1997); Debra Steger, 'WTO Dispute Settlement: Revitalisation of Multilateralism After the Uruguay Round' (1996) 9 Leiden Journal of International Law 319.

[35] See e.g. Statement Circulated by José Miguel Insulza, Minister for Foreign Affairs of Chile, WTO Doc. WT/MIN(98)/ST/35.

[36] See *European Communities—Regime for the Importation, Sale and Distribution of Bananas,* WTO Doc. WT/DS27. The period for implementation of this decision was set by arbitration at fifteen months and one week from the date of the adoption of the reports, i.e. it expired on 1 Jan. 1999.

[37] The disenchantment of the ACP countries with the decision was summed up in a statement at the second Ministerial Meeting of the WTO. See Statement by Edison C. James, Prime Minister of Dominica, WTO Doc. WT/FIFTY/H/ST/9 (19 May 1998) (arguing that the WTO Panel's decision 'has had an adverse impact on trade with our trading partners and undermined confidence in the WTO process', and that '[t]he so-called "systemic" complaints raised by a major trading partner, not only run the risk of upsetting the balance of rights and obligations, but also undermining the balance of benefits to developing countries, laboriously negotiated during the Uruguay Round').

[38] See WTO Appellate Body, *United States-Standards for Reformulated and Conventional Gasoline,* WTO Doc. WT/DS2/AB/R (29 Apr. 1996), in (1996) 35 International Legal Materials 603. For a summary and brief analysis of the Appellate Body decision, see Maury Shenk, 'United States-Standards for Reformulated and Conventional Gasoline' (1996) 90(4) American Journal of International Law 669. The earlier panel decision is reproduced in (1996) 35 International Legal Materials 274.

of compliance, although the question of what is appropriate "compliance" is controverted from time to time'.[39]

The discussion above suggests that, in the process by which the international economy is regulated, there is a role for law as well as for politics. Indeed, the examples provided above illustrate the role of politics in international law as well as the role of law in international politics. In light of this discussion, then, what are appropriate responses for the P-RSs? What should be the role of these States in regulating the international economy? There will be a wide range of views on this matter, and the suggestions I provide below are not intended to be exhaustive. I hope, however, that they will be sufficient to stimulate thought and discussion.

5. WHAT ROLE FOR THE STATE?

I agree with the theoretical possibility that the role of the State may be diminished by the impact of globalization and increased efforts to regulate the international economy. Indeed, to the extent that sovereignty is defined as the ability to exercise control without outside interference, then the sovereignty of States is clearly declining.

In my view, however, predictions of the end of the State fly in the face of reality. As the text quoted at the beginning of this chapter suggests, after more than a decade of fighting against statism and its concomitant bureaucracy, the World Bank is now touting the virtues of the State. Admittedly, the Bank's sudden enchantment is with the State as facilitator for private economic initiative.[40] This raises issues relating to privatization, deregulation, the eradication of corruption, and the promotion of the rule of law, all of which are discussed in this chapter. The fact remains, however, that international institutions such as the World Bank see an increased, and not a decreased, role for the State in facilitating the process by which the international economy is regulated.

A recent survey by *The Economist* also points out that public spending as a percentage of national income in developed countries is higher today than it was in 1990, and that the increase in the economic role of the State has been especially rapid since 1960.[41] While government spending alone is not synonymous with control of the economy, such expenditure certainly affects the global economy.

It is a truism that more and more governments are submitting themselves to various kinds of international monitoring and control. Examples of such developments include the Organisation for the Prohibition of Chemical Weapons, which monitors

---

[39] See John Jackson, 'Emerging Problems of the WTO Constitution: Dispute Settlement and Decision-Making in the Jurisprudence of the WTO' (Paper presented at Symposium on the World Trading System, Geneva, 30 Apr. 1998), at 10.

[40] See generally The World Bank, *World Development Report 1996: From Plan to Market* (New York: Oxford University Press, 1996).

[41] See 'Schools Brief: Bearing the Weight of the Market' (6 Dec. 1997) *The Economist* 90.

compliance with the Chemical Weapons Convention through on-site verification, and certain environmental treaties requiring States to report on their emissions of pollutants to a monitoring body.[42] The process of multilateral treaty-making has undergone a prodigious expansion in recent years. When more States join international organizations, regional groupings, and other intergovernmental entities, those entities are granted increased powers of legislation and various forms of monitoring or powers of control. Ultimately, however, it is the States involved which will do the necessary implementation. And the extent of implementation depends on the will of the State. In other words, nothing has changed. The State is still sovereign, and may implement its obligations at will. It may be recalled, however, that non-implementation may entail heavy costs for the State, including the imposition of sanctions or intervention by the international community, and damage to the State's reputation.

The continuing relevance of the State applies with equal force in the international economy. I would argue that, for P-RSs, retreat to a minimalist existence is not a viable option for survival in an increasingly competitive international economy. To be sure, the international economic system has a set of 'carrots and sticks'—a system of rewards and penalties—for eliciting the co-operation of P-RSs. These include aid flows, trade flows, capital investment, technology transfer, immigration policy, and the like. As with all clubs, the benefits which are mutually accorded by members presuppose compliance with the rules of the club. The P-RSs are therefore expected to comply with the rules of the game, as a minimum, in order to receive the benefits that come with membership. For example, the Generalised System of Preferences (GSP) schemes of some P-SSs grant greater preferences to LDCs which respect core labour rights and environmental standards.

The State can, and should, play a crucial role in regulating the international economy. Various measures, whether autonomous, bilateral, or multilateral, can help to ensure this. At the national level, States are expected to lay a firm rule-of-law foundation for markets to operate freely, and for property rights to be protected. This accounts for the increasing emphasis on legal and judicial reform in P-RSs.[43] In effect, *P-RSs must have the institutional capacity to enforce internally the rules of the game promulgated internationally*. In particular, P-RSs will have to take certain affirmative steps, examples of which are provided below, to improve their competitiveness in the international economy. An essential first step towards more competitive markets is to eliminate monopolistic structures by, for example, privatizing huge and inefficient State enterprises.

The P-RSs do not possess effective mechanisms by which they can articulate the views and concerns of their private sector or industry groups at negotiating confer-

---

[42] See generally Phillip Saunders, 'Development Cooperation and Compliance with International Environmental Law' (1996) 90 Proceedings of the American Society of International Law 359.

[43] For a comprehensive discussion of issues relating to governance, legal and judicial reform as well as the policies and practices of the World Bank *vis-à-vis* P-RSs, see Ibrahim Shihata, *Complementary Reform: Essays on Legal, Judicial and Other Institutional Reforms Supported by the World Bank* (Boston: Kluwer, 1997).

ences and other multilateral fora. In this regard, it is imperative that they strengthen the relationship between government and the private sector. This would enable the government more adequately to represent the interests and positions of the private sector in the P-RSs at the international level.

The P-RSs have a responsibility to ensure financial discipline within their economies, while at the same time fostering competition. It is vital that they develop strong, transparent, and accountable institutions to support and effectively implement sound economic policies. Similarly, P-RSs should adopt domestic policies which will enable them to take advantage of the benefits of the multilateral trading system. The P-RSs must address market imperfections and other sources of market failure. They should, for example, promote inward and outward information flows, as well as ensure transparency in providing such information. This should ultimately minimize sources of economic rent and thus reduce corruption.

With regard to corruption, there currently exist several multilateral instruments indicating the opprobrium that attaches to corruption.[44] These multilateral instruments are all part of a larger trend towards greater international regulation of corruption in international business transactions. In the particular context of P-RSs, corruption discourages foreign investment and ultimately impoverishes the bulk of the population, distorts policy-making, raises transaction costs, and increases inefficient economic outcomes. Thus it ultimately undermines the legitimacy of the State. It is a truism that capital flows to more predictable environments. A society with endemic corruption is therefore less likely to receive investment than a relatively uncorrupt society. The role of governments in this area is to promote ethical and legal behaviour on the part of companies and individuals within those governments' jurisdictions. Fighting corruption will require strengthening the rule of law, for example, by providing clear legislation, and ensuring effective enforcement and an independent judiciary.[45] In the absence of a generally accepted multilateral convention on combating corruption, an interesting question is the role that a government could, or should, play in trying to combat corruption in other countries where that corruption has direct effects on its own business community. For example, does the government of country A have the right to insulate businesses in country A from the effects of corruption in country B? This question is more than academic, given the

---

[44]   Prominent examples are: (i) the OAS Inter-American Convention against Corruption, adopted on 29 Mar. 1996, in (1996) 35 International Legal Materials 724; (ii) the OECD Convention on Combating Bribery of Foreign Public Officials in International Business Transactions, adopted on 21 Nov. 1997, in (1998) 37 International Legal Materials 1; and (iii) the United Nations Declaration against Corruption and Bribery in International Commercial Transactions, adopted on 16 Dec. 1996, in (1997) 36 International Legal Materials 1043.

[45]   For a comprehensive account of the role a State could play in combating corruption, see generally Susan Rose-Ackerman, 'Redesigning the State to Fight Corruption' (World Bank: Note No. 75, Apr. 1996); *Helping Countries Combat Corruption: The Role of the World Bank* (World Bank: Sept. 1997). For a more general discussion on the costs and effects of corruption, as well as proposed solutions, see Jeremy Pope, 'Containing Corruption in International Transactions—The Challenge of the 1990s', in The Commission on Global Governance, *Issues In Global Governance* (London: Kluwer, 1995), 67.

history behind the United States' Foreign Corrupt Practices Act and the WTO Agreement on Government Procurement.

Another effective response on the part of P-RSs would be to form regional economic groupings, although in an era of globalization the rationale behind regionalism may be difficult to grasp. While regional trading blocs may result in increased trade among countries in the region, there is an inherent danger of discrimination against third countries. Critics also argue that, even if regionalism could provide an important complement to the multilateral system, it is not a substitute and, in any event, it cannot provide the same efficiency as equal access under a multilateral trading system. Moreover, or so the argument goes, regional trading groups, and in particular those in which LDCs are involved, traditionally have a high failure rate.

The arguments against regionalism are clear. The force of the counter-arguments, however, is formidable.

Regional economic integration is an increasingly attractive way for P-RSs to enhance their collective bargaining power in the formulation of the rules of the international game. The Association of South-East Asian Nations (ASEAN)[46] and the Common Market of the South (MERCOSUR)[47] are two examples of such groupings. Open regional economic groupings can facilitate the often difficult integration of LDCs into the global economy. Moreover, regional groupings may offer countries an opportunity to start resolving issues which would be more difficult to resolve in the wider multilateral context.[48] Such regional groups also promote the efficient allocation of resources within the region. If companies are competitive regionally, they may become so internationally. Indeed, it is instructive that virtually all of the 134 WTO Member States belong to at least one or the other regional economic grouping.

Of course, regional trade blocs which do not serve the broader cause of global free trade will end up doing more harm than good, as explained above. To this extent, there should be coherence among the various regional groupings in an effort to protect the viability of the multilateral trading system. The rules relating to such arrangements should be clear and precise, and should ensure also that market access is not denied or reduced for third countries.

In connection with regional trade groupings, I should also mention that there are economic groupings which are not necessarily based on regions. A prominent example is the Group of Fifteen (G-15).[49] The G-15 was established to promote greater,

---

[46] The members of ASEAN are: Brunei Darussalam, Indonesia, Laos, Malaysia, Myanmar (Burma), Philippines, Singapore, Thailand, and Vietnam.

[47] The members of MERCOSUR are: Argentina, Brazil, Paraguay, and Uruguay. On the performance of MERCOSUR to date, see generally Alexander Yeats, 'Does Mercosur's Trade Performance Raise Concerns about the Effects of Regional Arrangements?' (1998) 12 (1) The World Bank Economic Review 1.

[48] See also The Commission on Global Governance, *Our Global Neighbourhood* (New York: Oxford University Press, 1995), 151 (arguing that '[r]egional economic groups can also contribute to burying historic enmities through developing closer economic and political linkages, realising economies of scale, developing common infrastructure, and pioneering new methods for deepening integration in advance of progress at the global level').

[49] Members of the G-15 are: Algeria, Argentina, Brazil, Chile, Egypt, India, Indonesia, Jamaica, Kenya, Malaysia, Mexico, Nigeria, Peru, Senegal, Venezuela, and Zimbabwe.

mutually beneficial co-operation among LDCs, especially in the areas of investment, trade, and technology. By acting as a catalyst for greater South–South co-operation, the Group aims at facilitating national efforts for development and economic progress. Groups of this kind are essential, not only because they can increase the collective bargaining strength of LDCs, but also because there are very few economic groupings of LDCs which are transregional in scope.

The State has to ensure that it adheres to its international obligations. As is well known, the State is indispensable in the effective functioning of international agreements, whether in the area of trade, intellectual property, or banking and financial services. To this extent, the State should strive to adopt a policy environment which is in line with international agreements while renewing its commitment to international organizations. Thus, for example, the WTO should be strengthened to provide a common institutional framework for the conduct of trade relations, the WIPO should be strengthened to promote the protection of intellectual property world-wide, and the ILO should be strengthened to ensure respect for core labour rights. These are all tasks that can only be achieved by the Member States of the respective organizations.

The scenario I have described above may seem to have the trappings of a new imperialism of P-SSs over P-RSs. It is true that the 'hold-out' States—those P-RSs that fail to align their economies with the international economic order—would be even further marginalized from the international rule-making process. However, those P-RSs that redefined their internal roles to be consistent with the rules of the game would, in the long run, develop the capacity, the competitive strength, and the influence to make their voices heard in the process by which the international economy is regulated.

Today, the P-RSs that cannot be ignored in determining rule-content are those that have already developed their internal capacity to compete internationally, such as Singapore and Hong Kong. It is instructive that Singapore and Hong Kong were again ranked the first and second most competitive economies by the World Economic Forum's Global Competitiveness Report 1998.[50]

Having mentioned Singapore and Hong Kong, it is appropriate to refer to the Asian financial crisis, even if only to give a brief description of the role of government in that crisis. First, it should be stressed that the problems in Asia revolved around private debt, not public debt. It is, however, widely acknowledged that the crisis was caused in part by too little or too ineffective government regulation in some areas, and too many administrative controls in others. The lack of adequate financial regulation allowed banks to make excessively risky loans without adequate monitoring. In a sense, this mistake resulted from the lack of transparency. In the absence of reliable information, banks had difficulty distinguishing good from bad

---

[50] The World Economic Forum's Global Competitiveness Report 1998 ranks countries according to their openness, government, finance, infrastructure, technology, management, labour, and institutions. See The Associated Press, 'Singapore is Most Competitive', *International Herald Tribune*, 6–7 June 1998, at 13, col. 3.

firms.[51] This crisis and, in particular, the effects produced around the world goes to show that the actions or inaction of a government may have potentially far-reaching repercussions for the international economy.[52]

6. CONCLUSION

Regulating the economy in the international arena obviously differs from regulating a domestic economy, and issues which may be relevant in the international context may not necessarily apply at the domestic level. This is evidenced, for example, in the dispute between the United States and the European Union on the Helms–Burton legislation, which is discussed by Brigitte Stern in her contribution to this volume.[53] As the world economy becomes increasingly integrated, the scope for conflict between national jurisdictions or regulatory systems also increases.[54] To this extent, national regulations will have to be co-ordinated through increased co-operation between national authorities. States must find innovative ways of reconciling their disparate regulatory frameworks and interests, in light of the fact that there is likely to be a greater need for more effective regulation as economic pressure on States increases.

Although this chapter has discussed the predominant role of P-SSs in regulating the international economy, it has not focused on the concerns as such of those States, nor has it suggested ways in which P-SSs could play a more effective role in regulating the international economy. Any meaningful role for P-SSs would include extending existing preference schemes for LDCs, opening up new market access opportunities for LDC exports, and generally helping to improve the capacity of LDCs to integrate into the international economic system.

The agenda I have sketched for P-RSs is a challenging one, but these are challenging times. It is imperative, however, that governments undertake only what they can do well within their resource constraints. In view of the risks as well as the

---

[51] For a more detailed account of the Asian crisis, including its causes and suggested solutions, see generally James Wolfensohn, 'Transcript of Address to the National Press Club' (Address by the President of the World Bank to the National Press Club, Washington, DC, 25 Mar. 1998), at http://www.worldbank.org/html/extdr/extme/jdwsp032598.htm.

[52] The effects of the Asian financial crisis seem too well known to be described in detail here. The most dramatic of the repercussions was the near-collapse of the banking systems in South-east Asia, which adversely affected the commodities markets world-wide and resulted in the collapse of several copper plants. For a more recent review of the Asian financial crisis, see generally Robert Wade, 'The Asian Crisis and the Global Economy: Causes, Consequences and Cure' (Nov. 1998) Current History 361; and John Gray, *False Dawn: The Delusions of Global Capitalism* (London: Granta Books, 1998), at 218–26.

[53] See also 'International Symposium on the Cuban Liberty and Democratic Solidarity (Libertad) Act of 1996' (1996–7) 30(2 and 3) George Washington Journal of International Law and Economics 201.

[54] Sylvia Ostry has provided us with potent examples of what she refers to as 'system friction'. For example, to what extent can governments differentiate in their regulation of foreign and domestic capital? Do differing labour-market regulations constitute a non-tariff barrier? See S. Ostry, 'New Dimensions of Market Access: Challenges for the Trading System', in *New Dimensions of Market Access in a Globalising World Economy* (Paris: OECD, 1995).

opportunities presented by globalization, the role of the State becomes even more indispensable, both in regulating the international economy and in helping enterprises to exploit the opportunities presented by the global market-place. It is palpably clear that globalization is an omnipresent fact of life that cannot be ignored or rolled back. To this extent, the discussion should focus on how best to manage it in order to minimize the costs while maximizing the benefits. Given the breadth and complexity of globalization, P-RSs need to be part of the system by which the international economy is regulated. To be sure, there does not seem to be any alternative to the multilateral trading system for global economic development. The challenge for P-RSs is to try and influence international rule-making; the only way for them effectively to do this is to reaffirm the primacy of, and to participate more meaningfully and deliberately in, the international economic system. The role of law in international politics should go a long way in helping P-RSs to meet this challenge.

12

How to Regulate Globalization?

BRIGITTE STERN

It is quite common today to speak of globalization and the crisis of the nation-State as being two interwoven phenomena that characterize the recent evolution of the world community. In the words of one contemporary author, there exists a 're-composition of space by the universalization of the economy'.[1] Thus, globalization would appear to be the new dominant paradigm for international politics.

It is therefore necessary to try first to understand what the concept of globalization means, before presenting some reflections on the concept of the nation-State as a provider of legal norms. Once these two concepts have been clarified, a few remarks can be made on the interaction of law and politics.

THE THEORETICAL FRAMEWORK

The Concept of Globalization

Globalization appears to have two main dimensions. First, it implies that we are dealing with a universal phenomenon. Second, it implies that we are dealing with a one-dimensional phenomenon.

Globalization as a 'universal phenomenon'

The process which we refer to today as the world economy, globalization, or, in French, *mondialisation*, began in the middle of the nineteenth century—when the first transatlantic telegraph cable was laid in 1858. The process of creating a world economy continues today, although it has already reached a high level of achievement. It is thus possible to say that the economy has become universal.

To speak of globalization is to insist on the fact that there are increased economic exchanges and intercourse between States and that, as a result, these States have become increasingly interdependent. Robert Dahl has expressed this quite clearly: 'A country's economic life, physical environment, national security and survival are highly, and probably increasingly, dependent on actors and actions that are outside the country's boundaries and not directly subject to its government.'[2]

Economic globalization has three main aspects: the internationalization of

---

[1] '[L]a recomposition de l'espace par la mondialisation de l'économie', Bertrand Badie, *La fin des territoires. Essai sur le désordre international et sur l'utilité sociale du respect* (Paris: Fayard, 1995), 181.

[2] Robert Dahl, *Democracy and its Critics* (New Haven: Yale University Press, 1989), 319.

economic exchanges of goods, in other words, the internationalization of trade; the globalization of companies which all tend to become 'world companies' through mergers and acquisitions; and the globalization of flows of capital through the international financial system.[3]

It has long been recognized that *trade* has an inherent tendency to escape from a State's territory. At the beginning of this century, Hauriou was already able to write: '[l]e commerce des échanges a une tendance invincible à s'extravaser, il ne s'enferme pas à l'intérieur d'une nation donnée, il est essentiellement international: il a lui aussi des sphères territoriales, mais elles ne se confondent pas avec les frontières politiques; cela s'appelle des marchés.'[4] It is worth emphasizing that, in the last fifty years, international trade has developed twice as quickly as the production of goods. Renato Ruggieri, the Director-General of the World Trade Organisation, has recently declared that, by the end of the century, 60 per cent of world trade will be achieved without any customs barriers.[5] This tendency can raise serious non-economic problems in respect of certain types of trade, like the arms trade and drugs traffic.

Moreover, *transnational firms* are major actors in contemporary international relations, their importance being comparable to the economic weight of many States. As an example, it may be recalled that the annual turnover of ITT was higher than the Gross National Product of Chile at the time President Allende was overthrown, and that it has been contended that ITT contributed to that event. Even when such an extreme outcome does not occur, it is quite clear that the power of multinational corporations competes with the power of States and can hamper, if not their political sovereignty, at least their economic sovereignty over their natural resources and economic wealth.

One of the sectors in which globalization is particularly far advanced involves international transfers of funds, that is *financial markets*. This may be because financial markets deal with immaterial goods which cross State borders more easily than other goods. According to the World Bank (International Bank for Reconstruction and Development), the amount of money involved in international financial transactions is fifty times greater than that involved in the international trade of goods and services.

In summary, globalization is a reality in relation to economic exchanges of goods, financial flows, and the strategies of multinational corporations. But an attempt to extend its reach by negotiating a Multilateral Agreement on Investment (MAI) within the context of the Organisation for Economic Co-operation and Development (OECD) may be less successful. Referred to in French as the AMI (thus allowing the former French Minister of Culture, Jack Lang, to make a play on

---

[3] This is in line with the definition given by the International Monetary Fund: globalization is 'the rapid integration of economies worldwide through trade, financial flows, technology spillovers, information networks, and cross-cultural currents'. IMF, *World Economic Outlook—May 1997* (http://www.imf.org/external/pubs/weomay), ch. 1.

[4] Maurice Hauriou, *Principes de droit public* (Paris: Sirey, 1910), 181.

[5] Babette Stern, 'AMI et NTM, les mauvais chemins de la mondialisation', *Le Monde*, 27 Mar. 1998, 15.

words in saying 'L'AMI, c'est l'ennemi'),[6] the MAI would allow total liberalization, not only for international trade which transcends the State's frontiers by itself, but also for investment and therefore production, an activity rooted within the State's territory. This, then, ultimately constitutes an attack against the State's territorial sovereignty, and for this reason has met with very negative reactions from the majority of European countries, and an even greater majority of developing countries. For example, during the annual OECD ministerial meeting in Paris on 27–28 April 1998, France repeated its opposition to the MAI and asked that 'la libéralisation des investissements soit limitée au nom du respect de l'"exception culturelle", de la préférence communautaire, et du respect des normes sociales et environnementales'.[7] In other words, States should be able to set their own hierarchy of values and not be forced to tolerate the outcomes of liberalization without question. Finally, in November 1998 negotiations were stopped, and the MAI is for the time being dead.

However, and as we all know, globalization is not confined to the economic sphere. It has a tendency to appear in many fields of human activity, especially the field of *information and communication*. New techniques of information and communication no longer pay any attention to State frontiers. One of the most striking examples of this is 'television without frontiers'. Technology based on radiodiffusion satellites, instead of telecommunication satellites, allows television broadcasts to be received by private persons with parabolic antennae anywhere in the world. This restricts the possibility of State control to the complete interdiction of parabolic antennae, as has been decided in Iran. But of course, all new means of communication—fax, e-mail, and the Internet, which can be termed one of the revolutionary developments of this century—transcend State frontiers and create a new world community in which State sovereignty loses part of its meaning.

Globalization as a 'one-dimensional phenomenon'

Despite its expansion into other fields, the fact that globalization originated in the economic field implies that the privileged approach to any problem today is an economic approach, that is, an approach based on economic costs and economic benefits. In other words, globalization entails the *merchandising* of every aspect of social life, as well as *liberalization* as the only regulatory device of human relations.

To an increasing extent, everything is analysed now in purely economic terms. It is well known that the labour force has to be considered as a 'factor of production' to be taken into account in every economic endeavour, and that the merchandising of human capital has always existed to a certain degree. However, it seems to me that this phenomenon is being aggravated. One may resent humans being analysed solely with regard to their economic capability, which might be one of the main problems of twenty-first-century civilization. I cannot help but be troubled, for example, when I read the following analysis: 'Indeed the message that open markets lead to gains in

---

6 *Le Monde*, 10 Feb. 1998, 15.
7 'La France réitère son opposition à l'AMI', *Le Monde*, 28 Apr. 1998, 4.

aggregate welfare . . . does not fit well with analysis suggesting that the earnings of workers in new jobs do not quickly regain their previous level, especially when a change of industry is required and *existing stocks of human capital become obsolete.*'[8]

The same holds true of the World Trade Organisation approach to liberalization, where everything is considered to be merchandise, including cultural production. The recent conflict over the 'cultural exception', led by France, is a reaction towards this unilateralism of economic thinking, towards this mercantile globalization.

In its present state, globalization rests merely on regulation through the mechanism of the free market, which implies that 'liberalization' is the key word, i.e. no barriers to free trade, and especially no State barriers.

Since the time of Ricardo, nobody contests the fact that liberalization brings about economic growth. According to the principle of comparative advantage, it is recognized that nation-States should concentrate on those things which they can produce more efficiently than other nation-States, considering their endowments in factors of production—natural resources, labour, and capital. Economic growth will be higher, on the national as well as international levels, if the international division of labour is based on the theory of comparative advantage rather than on autarkic theories.

However, while there seems to be a general agreement on the positive 'global' aspects of liberalization with regard to economic relations between States, two schools of thought have emerged in respect of the analysis of liberalization.

For some, this global economic efficiency of liberalization and deregulation is enough to justify its total acceptance, its absolute reign over all aspects of human behaviour.

For others, it is not enough to look at global efficiency, one must also consider the distribution of the gains of liberal globalization. In doing so, it becomes apparent that these gains are distributed unevenly between different States, as well as inside them. This thus requires corrective action, which explains why the Trade Director of the OECD has declared that 'this is why politics and the exercise of leadership at both the national and the international level continue to matter greatly'.[9] To complete the picture, it could be added that 'this is why law at both the national and the international level continue to matter greatly'. International economic relations are shaped by law and power, with power being able to take the form of politics, economic power, or force.

This chapter focuses on this interaction between law and power politics in the international economic field. However, it is necessary first to address the question of the definition and role of the State in international economic relations.

The Concept of the State, and the Legal Order

States are still the main actors in international relations, even if their role has been reduced by 'globalization'.

[8] Pierre Sauvé, 'Open Markets Matter' (June 1998) 21 World Competition 70, emphasis added.
[9] Ibid. 18.

The State is a different type of social entity from any other social group because only the State is endowed with the monopoly of organized armed force within its territory, and thus with the monopoly of issuing and determining law, above all *national law*. By its very nature, national law is deemed to apply to the State, and not to the whole world.

If, on the national level, a State can issue legal rules unilaterally, on the international level a State can only do so in co-ordination with other States. *International law* is thus a product of States, as is national law. More precisely, if the State's acceptance of a rule of international law is a necessary condition for that rule to come into existence, it is not a sufficient condition. For a rule of international law to emerge there must be a meeting of consents, or at least of assents or non-dissents.[10] These consents can be given tacitly, as in the case of a rule of customary international law, or expressly, as in the case of a treaty. They might also be given by States through the channel of an international organization, as, under certain conditions, in the case of a resolution. Traditionally, however, according to Article 38 of the Statute of the International Court of Justice, custom and treaty are the main sources of international law, while resolutions of international organizations have no binding force.

Although the issue of whether the method and character of norm creation are changing is dealt with elsewhere in this volume, a few comments on it are called for here, especially since legal norms always have to be appraised in their political context, taking into account the balance of power they reflect.

Even if the resolutions of international organizations have no binding value, this does not mean that they have no legal effect. In practice, the role played by resolutions of international organizations in the creation of new rules or principles of international law is very complex. Resolutions can, of course, be a contributory element in a customary process, but they can also have an effect by themselves if conditions are such as to give them a 'legal efficiency' whereby they approach the legal value of an international treaty. The factors to be taken into account are the conditions of adoption of the resolution, its content, and the existence of a control.[11] As I explained some years ago,

much will depend, of course, on the conditions of adoption: the more representative of all groups composing the international community, the majority, the closer the resolution will be to being regarded as an instrument of binding force . . . Likewise, the more precise the content of the resolution, the more likely it is to have legal consequences . . . Also, the means of enforcement, which are specified, tell much about the probable translation of the resolution into legal reality. . . . Besides, the mechanism of control is also quite relevant: its existence gives more chances to the resolution to be enforced than its absence . . . It must be noticed here that the type of dialectical analysis . . . made in order to appraise the legal value of a resolution, can

---

[10] See, on this question of the precise role of *opinio juris*, Brigitte Stern, 'La coutume au cœur du droit international', in *Mélanges offerts à Paul Reuter, Le droit international: unité et diversité* (Paris: Pedone, 1981), 479.

[11] These conditions were enumerated by René-Jean Dupuy in the *Texaco Case* (1978) 17 International Legal Materials 1.

also, and must also, be made for international conventions. Although the treaty is formally binding, and the resolution formally recommendatory, it is necessary to go beyond this formal analysis to assess their ultimate legal signification. The treaty will often remain a dead letter, when the very same conditions, whose presence give the resolution a quasi-binding force, are absent. Thus, the conditions of adoption can show that the treaty is a true agreement, or on the contrary, hides very diverging views, its content can be so vague as to be almost unenforceable, it can provide for measures of control or not.[12]

The identification of these variables provides a partial answer to questions about the legal value or legal efficiency of the numerous resolutions that have been adopted on economic questions, environmental matters, and other fields of recent concern. It also indicates that the formal approach to law is insufficient and that law must always be read in the light of existing political conditions.

The Relationship between Law and Politics

As stated by Martti Koskenniemi,

The relations between law, economics and politics are notoriously complex. Still, it is perhaps not so much this complexity, but recurrent attempts to do away with it, that account for popular skepticism about international law. For to suggest that there is a linear causal relationship between the three is either to dismiss law as a passive reflexion of economic and political forces or to create inflated, and thus inevitably failing, expectations on it as an instrument of economic and political change. Both strategies share the same mistake of assuming that the three can be distinguished from each other so as to create simple networks of causal relations.[13]

Far from trying to identify simple relationships between international law and international politics, I too would like to underline the dialectical complexity of their interrelationship. In fact, I would like to emphasize that, if law is dependent on power, it also influences power relations in society. There is definitely a fallacy in opposing law and politics. Politics is included in the process of law creation, and the use of law or, at least, the reference to law is one of the elements of politics.

The dialectic relationship between law and society

It is uncontested that law is to a certain extent the product of the society that it is deemed to regulate. This has been recalled by Adam Roberts, who has said that 'law reflects the balance of forces and changes in ethics in society'.[14] Depending on the specific balance of powers within a society, whether national or international, law

---

[12] Brigitte Bollecker-Stern, 'The Legal Character of Emerging Norms Relating to the New International Economic Order: Some Comments', in Kamal Hossain (ed.), *Legal Aspects of the New International Economic Order* (London: Pinter, 1980), 71.

[13] Martii Koskenniemi and Marja Letho, 'The Privilege of Universality. International Law, Economic Ideology and Seabed Resources' (1996) 65 Nordic Journal of International Law 533.

[14] A. Roberts, 'Remarks from the floor' at the conference 'The Role of Law in International Politics,' 24–5 Apr. 1998, Rhodes House, Oxford (notes on file with the author).

will play a different role in that society's evolution. In other words, I consider law to be an element that results either in reinforcing the existing reality, ignoring it, or modifying it.[15] This, of course, does not constitute a free choice for the social system, but is determined by the structure of the system itself.

If law reinforces reality with all its existing inequalities, this means that the inequalities in the society are such that those who benefit from them can impose their power without hindrance. In this case, law reinforces the existing power inequality with parallel legal inequalities: the veto power in the United Nations Security Council or, in the economic field, the weighted votes in the International Monetary Fund or World Bank are all examples of such types of rules.

If law ignores reality with all its existing inequalities, this means that the victims of existing inequalities begin to acquire sufficient power and influence in society to ensure that at least formal satisfactions are granted to them. In this case, law pretends to be neutral, to establish the same rules for all, whatever their power. However, it is plainly apparent that when all the actors are treated in the same way, power relations can not only function without hindrance, but with the legitimization that is brought by the legal system. The recurrent emphasis on the sovereign equality of States in international relations exemplifies this type of rule.

If law modifies reality with all its existing inequalities, this means that the victims of existing inequalities begin to acquire sufficient power and influence in that society to obtain real changes in their situations. In this case, law embodies rules that are meant to correct the existing inequalities, in order to grant the same opportunities to all. This situation is clearly illustrated by the claim for what have come to be known as 'compensatory inequalities'. In international relations, the General System of Preferences is made up of rules of this type, as were the rules developed in the 1970s to foster the emergence of a New International Economic Order.

Of course, in the same way as the content of law is to a certain extent dependent on the balance of power in each society, rules, when adopted, become part of social reality and in turn have an influence on the social relations they are deemed to regulate.

Thus if law depends on society, society also depends on law.

The need for law in every society

It is sometimes stated that the economy has its own inherent rules of regulation which render law unnecessary. Is what is called 'deregulation' a real challenge to the rule of law? The answer must be negative, both on the national and international levels.

It is quite simplistic to oppose law and economy. Law, with its procedures guaranteeing security in economic dealings, has been one of the key factors in the devel-

---

[15] For developments of this idea, of which only a summary is provided here, see Brigitte Stern, 'Le droit international du développement, un droit de finalité?', in *La formation des normes en droit international du développement* (Paris and Algiers: CNRS and OPU, 1984), 43.

opment of liberalism. One author has underlined this aspect by writing: 'le souci de précision et d'unification du droit indispensable à la fixation des règles du jeu libéral ont été les principaux outils juridiques de développement de l'échange marchand et du système de libre concurrence'[16] or, to put it more poetically, 'l'économie ne se développe pas durablement sans un supplément d'âme juridique'.[17]

The same is true of the global world. It is true that all economic aspects that transcend the frontiers of a State—trade, the economic strategies of transnational firms, financial markets—tend to expand to become universal and merely appear to be regulated by the 'invisible hand' of market forces.

It can seem that neither national law nor international law is capable of dealing with the manifold aspects of globalization. At the same time, a need for regulation is apparent. As Sir Arthur Watts states elsewhere in this volume, 'the interests of no State can prosper if there is anarchy'.[18] It is increasingly evident that 'savage liberalism' cannot bring prosperity and justice to the people of the world. This is not a statement of a dreaming professor nor of a dangerous leftist. It is a fact recognized by serious economic authorities such as Jacques de Larosière, President of the European Bank for Reconstruction and Development, and Michel Camdessus, Director-General of the International Monetary Fund. Larosière warns against the global dangers that necessarily appear in a global world:

Dans un monde globalisé, les dangers aussi sont globaux: ceux de la pollution de l'atmosphère, ceux des épidémies, ceux des dévaluations compétitives, etc. Ce monde requiert donc des règles et une surveillance effective qui s'applique aux forts comme aux faibles. Tel est le défi du XXIe siècle . . . Il en va de la paix, il en va aussi de nos nations, qui, malgré les contraintes et les chances offertes par la mondialisation, doivent absolument conserver leur culture, leurs traditions et leur identité, conditions même de leur survie.[19]

Camdessus, for his part, insists that there are two principal risks that stem from globalization. He writes:

[Q]ui dit nouvelles chances, dit aussi nouveaux risques . . . Je me contenterai d'en signaler deux parmi les plus préoccupants. Le premier est le risque d'instabilité financière . . . Le second risque est celui de la marginalisation . . . Le fait est que les pays qui ne sont pas capables de participer à l'expansion du commerce mondial ou d'attirer un volume significatif d'investissements privés sont en passe de devenir les laissés-pour-compte de l'économie mondiale . . . La communauté internationale ne peut pas se résigner à cette dérive.[20]

Several kinds of attempts are being or could be made to answer this *need for law*. Some are based on mere assertions of power, even when they pretend to use the channel of law: this is the case when a State tries to impose a *world-wide extension of its*

---

[16] Mohamed Salah Mohamed Mahmoud, 'Mondialisation et souveraineté de l'Etat' (1993) 3 Journal du droit international 615.   [17] Ibid. 646.   [18] See p. 35.

[19] Jacques de Larosière, 'Implications de la mondialisation', in *Rapport moral sur l'argent dans le monde. 1997. L'éthique financière face à la mondialisation* (Paris: Montchrestien, 1997), 36.

[20] Michel Camdessus, 'Les conditions d'une mondialisation réussie', in *Rapport moral sur l'argent dans le monde. 1997. L'éthique financière face à la mondialisation* (Paris: Montchrestien, 1997), 38.

national legal system. Others are clearly attempts by entities or individuals to create regulatory systems which are not territorially confined like states' legal orders and which are neither national law nor international law: this is the case of the *creation of non-statal regulatory systems.* None of these attempts at the regulation of globalization seems to prove satisfactory, because they all have what I would call 'a legal deficit'. The only way to regulate the global economy and the global world is to improve the efficiency of international law, both in respect of its content and its institutional framework: in other words, there is no solution apart from the *creation of a truly world-wide international law system of regulation.*

ATTEMPTS AT REGULATING GLOBALIZATION

Unilateral Regulation by a State: The World-Wide Extraterritorial Extension of National Law

Considering, as has been explained above, that the economy is globalized, and the legal field fragmented into multiple national legal orders, one practical device to regulate the global order would be to extend to that global order, the national legal order of a dominant State. This has been, and still is, attempted by the United States. However, such an imperial imposition of a national legal order while it may prove efficient to some degree in international economic relations because of the existing balance of power, contradicts the basic structure of the international community of States and violates the existing rules of international law.

Extraterritorial application of US law for political purposes: the Helms–Burton and D'Amato Acts[21]

In 1996 the United States Congress adopted two laws of an extraterritorial character which have been denounced almost unanimously. However, the principal goal was not to regulate international economic relations, but rather to use international economic relations as a tool to foster American politics. Nonetheless, the result is that the United States attempted to set rules of economic conduct for the world as a whole, and to punish non-compliance through economic sanctions according to the provisions of those extraterritorial laws.

---

[21] For an analysis of those laws, see Brigitte Stern, 'Can the United States set Rules for the World? A French View' (Aug. 1998) 31 Journal of World Trade 5. See also Brigitte Stern, 'Note d'actualité, Vers la mondialisation juridique? Les lois Helms-Burton et D'Amato-Kennedy' (1996) 100(4) Revue générale de droit international public 8/9. For a political science perspective, see Brigitte Stern, 'Einsitige Wirtschaftssanktionen. Helms-Burton, D'Amato und die Europeär' (1997) 4 Internationale Politik 7 (this article has been translated in the Russian issue of Internationale Politik). For the European Union reaction, see Brigitte Stern, 'De simples "Commentaires" à une "action commune": la naissance d'une politique juridique communautaire en matière d'extraterritorialité' (1997) 2 Europe 8–9. See also Brigitte Stern, 'Les Etats-Unis et le droit impérialiste', *Le Monde*, 12 Sept. 1996, and Brigitte Stern, 'Helms-Burton and D'Amato Flout International Law', at http//www.AdeToqueville.com.

The goal of the Cuban Liberty and Democratic Solidarity Act (LIBERTAD), adopted on 12 March 1996 and better known as the Helms–Burton Act,[22] is political, namely the overthrow of Castro's regime. To that purpose, the law sets *rules* of conduct for *any person* in the world. No physical or legal person anywhere is authorized to 'traffic' in property that belonged to Americans (or Cubans who later became Americans) and was expropriated by Cuba some forty years ago.

If such persons disregard the rules of conduct set by the United States, they are exposed to *sanctions*. The two most contested forms of sanction are set out in Titles III and IV of the Act. Title III creates a right of action in United States courts for Americans whose property was expropriated against any person convicted of 'trafficking', while Title IV excludes such 'traffickers' and their spouses and minor children from United States territory.

The Iran and Libya Sanctions Act of 1996, adopted on 5 August 1996 and better known as the D'Amato Act,[23] also has a political objective. It seeks to deprive Libya and Iran, which are considered 'rogue States' or 'pariah States', of the financial means to foster international terrorism and develop their arms industries. To that purpose, the law also sets *rules* of conduct for *any person* anywhere in the world who invests more than forty million dollars in either of those two countries' oil industries.

If anyone disregards these rules, he is exposed to *sanctions*, some of which consist of a deprivation of certain economic advantages, and others of a prohibition on importing goods sold by a person who violated this extraterritorial rule into the United States.

In other words, in these two laws, the United States seeks to legislate for all persons everywhere, whatever their nationality, which is definitely one way of regulating the entire world.

One may also recall that, in the Siberian pipeline dispute, the United States asserted jurisdiction over all 'goods of United States origin', that is to say, all goods including American technology.

Through this kind of world-wide extraterritorial legislation, the United States purports to regulate globalization in accordance with its own national interests.

The two extraterritorial acts violate international law

It is well known that a State cannot set rules for the whole world, but only for persons, property, and acts having a certain link with that State. This was recalled recently by Lionel Jospin, the French Prime Minister, when he stated in respect of these American extraterritorial laws: 'Les lois américaines sont faites pour s'appliquer aux Américains, pas pour s'appliquer aux Français.'

More precisely, the international rules[24] governing State jurisdiction have been

---

[22] Public law 104th–114, 12 Mar. 1996, 110 Stat. 785.

[23] House of Representatives, HR, 3107.

[24] For the general development of international law and extraterritoriality, see, for a comparative approach, Brigitte Stern (ed.), *L'Application extraterritoriale du droit économique* (Paris: Montchrestien, 1987) (Cahiers du CEDIN, no. 3); for a very general theoretical approach to the topic of extraterritoriality,

clearly established since the *Lotus Case*[25] and may be summarized as follows: juris-diction to enforce is strictly territorial and can never, therefore, be extraterritorial. This means that enforcement by one State's authorities on the territory of another State is forbidden by international law in all circumstances. Jurisdiction to prescribe—and jurisdiction to adjudicate—can both be extraterritorial, as long as the prescribing or adjudicating State respects the limitations placed on such exercises of jurisdiction by international law. The adoption of an extraterritorial rule or decision is not always contrary to international law, it is only contrary to international law *when it does not have a reasonable link* with the State enacting such a rule or making such a decision. The links which are recognized by international law as allowing a State to set rules of law are the territorial principle, the nationality principle, the protective principle, and the universality principle.

The *principle of territoriality* means that according to international law a State has jurisdiction to set rules or take decisions for persons or property on its territory or events taking place on its territory. In order for a State to have jurisdiction over an act, it is enough that one constitutive element of that act has been consummated on the territory of the State. One speaks of 'objective territoriality' when an act has been initiated abroad but is consummated in the territory, and of 'subjective territoriality' when an act has been initiated in the territory but is consummated abroad. The United States extends this territorial principle by the so-called 'effects doctrine', according to which it has jurisdiction over an act as soon as that act has a substantial effect in United States territory.

The *principle of nationality* means that a State is entitled to exercise jurisdiction over its nationals, which can become extraterritorial when a national is outside its territory. However, this does not allow it to regulate all the activities of its nationals all over the world. For example, it is quite clear that the United States cannot set rules concerning the acquisition or sale by an American citizen of property situated in Cuba. Moreover, this does not allow the United States to expand the definition of the national link beyond the accepted international definition. For example, no rule of international law allows the United States to exercise jurisdiction over corporations that are not incorporated under its laws. In fact, the United States considers that, when it is substantially in the national interest, the 'persons subject to the jurisdiction of the United States' include the foreign subsidiaries of American corporations or even foreign corporations 'controlled' by Americans,[26] when American corporations are the main clients of the foreign corporations. This is clearly against international law.

Brigitte Stern, 'Quelques observations sur les règles internationales relatives à l'application extraterritoriale du droit' (1986) Annuaire français de droit international 7, Brigitte Stern, 'L'Extraterritorialité revisitée. Où il est question des affaires Alvarez-Machain, Pâte de bois et de quelques autres . . .' (1992) Annuaire français de droit international 239, and Brigitte Stern, 'Droit international public et sanctions unilatérales', in H. Gherari and S. Szurek (eds.), *Sanctions unilatérales, mondialisation du commerce et ordre juridique international* (Paris: Montchrestien, 1998) (Cahiers du CEDIN, no. 14), 185.

[25] *S.S. Lotus* (1927) Permanent Court of International Justice Reports, Series A, no. 10, 18–19.

[26] See Foreign Assets Control Regulations, 31 C.F.R. § 500.329 and Cuban Assets Control Regulations, 31 C.F.R. § 515.329.

The *protective principle* means that a State can assert extraterritorial jurisdiction over acts done abroad which affect fundamental aspects of its existence and security.

The *universality principle* means that a State is entitled to assert extraterritorial jurisdiction to punish on its territory certain acts committed abroad which are considered to be international crimes, such as piracy, terrorism, or crimes against humanity.

None of these bases of jurisdiction exists, for example, in the Helms–Burton Act. The acts giving rise to sanctions did not take place on United States territory, nor did they have any direct or indirect effect on it. These acts could have been committed by any person in the world, with no link of nationality to the United States, even in the most extensive American interpretation. Yet the sale of sugar produced by a French corporation for a German corporation on a property nationalized forty years ago could not put the existence or security of the world's largest power into jeopardy, nor were the economic operations involved so contrary to the basic rules of humanity as to justify universal jurisdiction. In other words, according to the existing rules of international law, this extraterritorial law is clearly illegal, as is the D'Amato Act.

The two extraterritorial acts can be effective in international economic relations

Despite its demonstrated illegality, the Helms–Burton Act might well succeed in having some effects, even if not the furthering of United States policy towards Cuba. This is mainly because the sanctions applied are territorial. On the face of it, such legislation is an exercise of extraterritorial jurisdiction to prescribe, even if the sanctions seem to be more or less related to United States territory. The abstract scheme of 'extraterritorial laws' may be summarized as follows:

A rule is enacted which applies to a person having neither a territorial nor a personal link with the enacting State. This is called 'extraterritorial prescription'.

Two possible types of sanctions can be provided for violations of this rule. First, sanctions can be enacted as part of the territorial jurisdiction of the State. A good example of such a 'territorial sanction' is the interruption of commercial relations with the sanctioned person, because each State has territorial jurisdiction to impose rules for the entry of merchandise or persons into its territory. Second, sanctions can be enacted that are not part of the territorial jurisdiction of the State. An example of such an 'extraterritorial sanction' occurs when a State recovers a fine outside its territory, which has been imposed by one of its courts.

Thus, when a State adopts illegal extraterritorial legislation, it seeks generally to impose sanctions on its own territory for violations of it. However, the fact that the enforcement is territorial does not conceal or erase the fact that the prescription is extraterritorial, and thus the entire law remains illegal. Sir Robert Jennings pointed this out as far back as 1964: '[T]he excessive devotion to legalism has often blinded us to the fact that the exercise of straight territorial jurisdiction over a person present in the territory may—albeit indirectly—be in fact the most effective way of exercising the state's power extraterritorially.'[27]

---

[27] 'Extraterritorial Application of Trade Legislation', in *Report of the 51st Conference of the International Law Association, Tokyo* (1964), 311.

However, there are very few ways of opposing the application of such sanctions, because each State has exclusive enforcement jurisdiction within its own territory. If a United States court applies Title III of the Helms–Burton Act to a foreign corporation that has assets in the United States, nothing will prevent a seizure of those assets according to a court order.

Moreover, this type of legislation, when adopted by a State as powerful as the United States, does not even need territorial enforcement to be effective. In fact, quite a few international projects have been abandoned for fear of United States sanctions which would be applied within the United States under internationally illegal legislation. For example, it has been reported that, as a result of the Helms–Burton and D'Amato Acts, some Japanese companies renounced investments in Iran, the Mexican corporation Cemex withdrew from Cuba, and the Australian corporation Broken Hill Proprietary abandoned a project for the construction of a 1,000-mile-long pipeline between Iran and Pakistan.[28] This demonstrates the importance of power and territorial effectiveness in international relations.

Could the effectiveness of United States extraterritorial legislation create a new rule of international law?

It is well known that customary international law is 'a general practice accepted as law'[29] and thus, that it is by way of custom that 'that which "is" becomes that which "must be" '.[30]

The question must therefore be raised as to whether the United States' action could generate a new rule of customary international law. Some authors have contended that it could, and that, even if the actions of the United States are in violation of existing rules of international law, it should maintain this practice in order to promote a new rule of international law which would deal more effectively with globalization than the present rules setting limits on the extraterritorial reach of national legal systems. However, such reasoning is seriously flawed, in that practice is not sufficient to create a rule of customary international law, not even if it is the practice of the most interested or powerful States, or a general practice, or even a unanimous practice. Practice can only be transformed into custom if it is accompanied by *opinio juris*, by the acceptance of States that this practice is imposed by law.

The extraterritorial legislation of the United States has not only not been accepted, it has been denounced vigorously all over the world, by numerous States and international organizations.[31] As was explained above, international law is the

---

[28] 'US Sanctions Law Begins to Take Toll', *Asia Times*, 7 Aug. 1996.

[29] For a theoretical approach to customary international law, see Brigitte Stern, 'La coutume au cœur du droit international. Quelques reflexions'.

[30] *Right of Passage Case*, Individual Opinion of Judge Armand Hugon (1960) International Court of Justice Reports 82.

[31] For the main reactions, see Brigitte Stern, 'Vers la mondialisation juridique? Les lois Helms-Burton et D'Amato-Kennedy'.

common creation of all States. No State, not even the most powerful, can create a new rule of customary international law through its unilateral practice. In other words, the unilateral practice of the United States cannot create international law on its own because it is not accompanied by *opinio juris*, neither on the part of the generality of States, nor even on the part of the United States. The State Department itself readily admitted that the United States is acting consciously in complete disregard of international law.[32]

Could this extraterritoriality be justified by a principle of subsidiarity?

The idea advanced by the United States is that, in an international system which is not sufficiently effective in so far as its enforcement powers are concerned, States can, if they so desire, take on the role of enforcement agents for international law. Ironically, this type of reasoning has been advanced in Section 301 of the Helms–Burton Act. Faced with the confiscation of American property by the Cuban regime, the United States asserts that 'the international judicial system, as currently structured, lacks fully effective remedies for the wrongful confiscation of property'. The United States must therefore do justice unto itself: 'The United States Government has an obligation to its citizens to provide protection against wrongful confiscations by foreign nations . . .'

Of course, the United States can enforce national law and international law, but only—and this caveat is of the utmost importance—when the illegal act has a connection to it. However, as I have explained elsewhere, due to the fact that each State has this privilege within its own territory, it cannot—either directly or indirectly—impose sanctions in order to enforce national or international law outside its territory. If such sanctions were possible, this would be the end of international law.

No government is in charge of the enactment of international law all over the world. This is true even when the violation of the principle of the non-use of force has triggered the adoption of compulsory sanctions under Chapter VII of the United Nations Charter. As an example, one may recall the precise wording of Security Council Resolution 748, which was adopted against Libya, and by which States were asked to prohibit certain actions—such as the selling of arms to Libya or the provision of certain types of technical assistance—'*by their nationals or from their territory*'.[33] The Security Council has never considered asking States to exceed their international granted powers when implementing sanctions, not even in respect of the collective sanctions directed at preventing international terrorism and compelling Libya to surrender two Libyan agents charged with responsibility for the bombing of Pan Am Flight 103.

The deficiencies of international law are no excuse for its violation. In the *Corfu*

---

[32] Legal Considerations on Title III of LIBERTAD Act, reimpression 141, Congressional Record, S 15106–8, 12 Oct. 1995: 'The LIBERTAD Bill would be very difficult to defend under international law . . . The civil remedy created by the LIBERTAD Bill would represent an unprecedented extraterritorial application of U.S. law . . . The principles behind Title III are not consistent with the traditions of the international system.'   [33] 31 Mar. 1992, S/RES/748 (1992).

Channel Case the International Court of Justice warned States against the kind of reasoning according to which a State could be 'justified' in disregarding the limitations on its powers, because of the existing failures of international law. In that case the United Kingdom sought to justify its entering into Albanian territorial waters on the basis that nobody else would act, in much the same high-handed manner as the United States behaved with regard to the two Acts discussed above. The Court held that this was not an admissible legal justification:

The Court cannot accept this line of defence. The Court can only regard the alleged right of intervention as a policy of force, such as has, in the past, given rise to the most serious abuses and such as cannot, *whatever be the present defects in international organisation,* find a place in international law. Intervention is perhaps still less admissible in the particular form it would take here, for, from the nature of things, it would be reserved to the most powerful states . . .[34]

It is true that international law is not perfectly enforced, but neither is national law. However, this does not allow for 'private justice', either on the national or international level.[35] Whatever the good intentions behind United States policy towards Cuba, such intentions provide no justification whatsoever for disregarding the rule of law.

Of course the globalization of the economy highlights the fact that States are not always well equipped with the legal means to deal with actions, especially those of multinational corporations, having world-wide repercussions. However, this is not a reason for one State to proclaim itself the ruler of the world. On the contrary, collective ways and means must be sought *to improve the legal approach to economic globalization.* The solution has to be found in improving the effectiveness of international law. Some, however, are not prepared to wait for such evolution and have started to create their own systems of regulation, one which is totally disconnected with States and thus disconnected from both national and international law.

Multilateral Regulation by Private Powers: Non-State Regulatory Systems

Law, as a creation of States, has to compete with other, private means of regulation. As a result of globalization, many non-State actors tend to refer only to the global world as their playing ground. This is of course the case with multinational corporations. However, it is also true of other emerging actors in international relations, such as non-governmental organizations (NGOs), or even private individuals using the Internet.

The normative contribution of NGOs

It is interesting to note that NGOs do not purport to create a new system of regulation. They consider their role to be that of enhancing the existing system, of helping

---

[34] (1949) International Court of Justice Reports 35, emphasis added.
[35] See Brigitte Stern, 'Can the United States set Rules for the World? *A French View*', 21–3.

to modify existing rules of international law so that those rules take better account of some of the values for which they fight.[36]

They do not purport to negate international law, nor to replace it. Instead, they wish to improve the existing system.

NGOs use several methods in seeking to achieve this goal. Obviously, they engage in political lobbying and international campaigns directed at world public opinion. However, they also participate in legal drafting processes within international organizations, when they are recognized as having observer status in one or another such international organization.

In other words, NGOs, which themselves represent political interests—in the broad sense of the Greek term *polis*—can be seen to participate, at least to a certain degree, in the creation of rules of international law for the regulation of the contemporary global system.

Private systems of regulation: lex mercatoria

The existence of globalization raises the problem of what is referred to as the *lex mercatoria*, the 'law' of international merchants. What kind of 'law' is this? Quite often, the usages of multinational corporations that have been qualified as rules merely embody the power relations that exist between the different private actors in international economic relations. An example of such analysis may be found in an article by Paul Lagarde, in which he writes:

[C]ombien de fois, les opérateurs du commerce international et leurs conseils n'ont-ils pas . . . appelé à s'affranchir du 'carcan' des législations nationales pour se soumettre à des règles mieux adaptées, qu'ils se donneraient eux-mêmes, 'spontanément' et combien de fois, en retour, cette tentative n'a-t-elle pas été frappée du soupçon de dissimuler un 'droit des faits' imposé par les entreprises puissantes aux plus faibles, voire une 'appréhension' de 'l'espace' juridique transnational par les pouvoirs économiques privés?[37]

If it is true that rules of behaviour have emerged from the usages of international commercial relations and are applied in international arbitration, then it is also true that they have developed with the tolerance of States. These rules depend on States for their creation and enforcement, and thus the *lex mercatoria* exists only to complement the international law created by States. After all, the law of merchants is based on the autonomy of will in the choice of law, which is recognized in most legal systems in respect of contracts involving international commercial interests. For example, in the French decree of 12 May 1981 regulating international arbitration, it is stated in Article 1496: 'The arbitrator shall decide the dispute according to the rules chosen by the parties; in the absence of such a choice, he shall decide according to the rules he deems appropriate. In all cases, he shall take into account trade usages.'

It must be emphasized that these rules are ultimately subordinate to State law, in

---

[36] For a subtle analysis of the role of NGOs, see Christine Chinkin's contribution to this volume, p. 159.

[37] 'Approche critique de la lex mercatoria', in *Mélanges Goldman. Le droit des relations économiques internationales* (Paris: LITEC, 1982), 125.

so far as they are not spontaneously enforced. This subordination results from the hierarchy of powers, in that the State monopolizes enforcement jurisdiction. But, interestingly enough, it has also been explained by Philippe Kahn as resulting from what he calls a hierarchy of goals, such that the *lex mercatoria*, which is also some- times called transnational law, is based solely on economic interests, while the State legal order is based on a broader solidarity of interests.[38]

It can therefore be concluded that the *lex mercatoria* is included within legal systems because it is both recognized and enforced by States, in the same way as the rights and obligations created by contracts between private persons.

Self-contained systems of regulation: lex internautica

Today, the same type of autonomous regulation can be found among the 'internauts'. Like the merchants, they live in their own global system—the world-wide web— which seems completely detached from any State. Codes of conduct are adopted by the participants in the system, in order to avoid some of the inevitable excesses of absolute freedom.

This has been underlined in a recent report by a French Senator, René Trégouët, presented to the Prime Minister on 8 April 1998. Trégouët describes this phenomenon quite distinctly: 'Il y a sur Internet une sorte de surveillance mutuelle et d'automaticité du droit de réponse, par la possibilité de débats contradictoires, qui équivault à une certaine forme d'autorégulation, sans doute insuffisante, mais néanmoins réelle.'[39]

For example, as music of a quality approaching that of a CD can now be sold on the Internet, difficult questions of copyright and protection of intellectual property are raised and a system has to be developed to prevent piracy. Some forerunners appear to have organized a system in which a CD obtained over the Internet can only be copied once.[40] However, there is still a long way to go and the articulation of self- regulatory rules and legal rules—whether national or international—will certainly raise innumerable problems in the years to come.

Nevertheless, and in the same way as the 'law of merchants', the 'law of inter- nauts' will ultimately require the enforcement powers of States when conflicts arise as to the interpretation or application of these self-regulatory norms.

Multilateral Regulation by States: Towards the Creation of a World-Wide International Legal System of Regulation

The international global system needs the globalization of legal rules, and thus of legal control, as no system can work in the long term without rules and control. As was stated recently by Boutros Boutros Ghali:

[38] 'Droit international économique, droit du développement, lex mercatoria: concept unique ou pluralisme d'ordres juridiques', in *Mélanges Goldman*, 99.

[39] See *Le Monde*, 9 Apr. 1998, 22.

[40] Yves Eudes, 'Premières tentatives de réglementation convaincantes sur Internet', *Le Monde*, 29–30 Mar. 1998, 24.

[L]'imbrication des phénomènes est désormais si grande, que ce soit pour le terrorisme, le trafic de drogue, etc., qu'il sera difficile de trouver des solutions à l'échelon continental, régional ou sous-régional. Certains problèmes pourront être résolus à ces niveaux, mais les véritables problèmes qui vont dominer la planète sont des problèmes qui ne pourront être réglés qu'à l'échelle planétaire.[41]

Some international legal responses to globalization can already be seen at work in international economic relations.

One response is the development of *agreements between States*, by equipping the traditional means of creating rules of international law with new characteristics which are adapted to the challenges posed by the specialization of international law in manifold economic fields. Elsewhere in this volume, Anne-Marie Slaughter explains how tight *government networks* have been created, involving all kinds of economic organs and agencies of the State, or para-statal institutions such as the Central Banks. These government networks present certain advantages, such as adaptability and technical pertinence, but also some disadvantages, such as secrecy and the absence of democratic control.

Another response to the discrepancy between restricted national legal orders and the global economy is the development of institutional frameworks for regulatory purposes. This may occur at intermediary levels, for example, through the creation of *regional organizations* such as the European Union. It may also occur through the development of a *world-wide economic institution* entrusted with the task of creating a global legal order for the regulation of economic relations. The matrix of such an institution might be seen in the creation of the World Trade Organisation.

A regional legal order: the European Union

Many people today insist that the nation-State is in decline,[42] and one reason[43] that is sometimes advanced in order to explain this phenomenon is the transfer of sovereign powers or duties from States to multilateral supranational entities. However, there is a great difference between the decline in sovereignty which is *imposed* on States against their will by the *facts* of modern life—the globalization of the economy, the development of new communications technologies, or the diversification of the actors in international relations—and the decline in sovereignty which is *accepted* and even welcomed by them in the name of global solidarity, which appears in the form of supranational *norms*. The development of regional organizations contributes to this second trend, the implications of which are quite different from those of the first. Faced with economic globalization, States have sought to act collectively. The best example of this is the slow but steady creation of what were first the European Economic Communities and is now the European Union. European States have

---

[41] 'Un dialogue à l'Unesco pour imaginer le XXIe siècle', *Le Monde*, 28 Apr. 1998, 16.

[42] See, for example, Oscar Schachter, 'The Decline of the Nation-State and its Implications for International Law' (1997) 35 Columbia Journal of Transnational Law 7.

[43] I deal here only with 'attacks' on the nation-State from 'above', not with 'attacks' from 'below' through nationalistic or religious claims.

sought to act collectively to promote development and establish a common legal order to master economic relations between them, and to a certain extent with the rest of the world. As a result of the Treaty of Rome of 1959, the Single European Act of 1986 which unified the European Economic Community, the Steel and Coal Community, and Euratom into the European Community and created a single European market with no internal customs or barriers, the Treaty of Maastricht of 1992 which created the European Union and established that this new entity would have a common currency (the Euro), and the Treaty of Amsterdam which widened the political aspects of the European Union, Europe has developed a relatively effective new legal order. The effectiveness of the new communitarian legal order was certainly strengthened by, and is arguably the result of, the jurisprudence of the European Court of Justice in Luxembourg. First there was the *Van Gend en Loos Case*,[44] in which the 'direct effect' of European rules—the rules in the Treaties as well as the rules adopted by the European organs, the so-called *droit dérivé*—was asserted. Then there was the *Costa Case*,[45] in which the superiority of the European legal order over national orders was averred, that superiority resulting from the 'definitive limitation of the sovereign rights of States'. However, this limitation was agreed by the States themselves, in order to deal better with globalization.

Many other economic regional international organizations seek to respond to challenges of globalization—Mercosur, NAFTA, APEC, and so on—but none has really given birth to a true legal order of its own, like the European Union.

How should the NTM, the New Transatlantic Market, be analysed in this context? It seems to be an attempt to erase any intermediary level of regulation that could appear as a fragmentation of globalization. But in my view, it would, if adopted, dilute the European Union within a broader framework and nullify its special characteristics.

A world organization for the regulation of the global economy: the World Trade Organisation

It is well known that, after the Second World War, the United States was reluctant to accept the creation of the International Trade Organisation because, according to its liberal *credo*, it did not wish trade to be regulated. As a result, only the IMF and the IBRD came into existence.

Only one chapter of the Havana Charter was saved; this was the origin of GATT, which has now been transformed into a real international organization, the World Trade Organisation, by the Marrakech Agreements.

The WTO is a world in itself, one which it is not my purpose to explain at any length here, apart from observing that the philosophy of the WTO is undoubtedly liberal, and that the WTO does not seem to constitute a major threat to unhampered economic globalization.

---

[44] Case 26/62, [1963] European Court Reports 1.
[45] Case 6/64, [1964] European Court Reports 1141.

However, I would like to emphasize one aspect of the changes brought about by the WTO, as compared to GATT, namely the 'juridictionalization' of the dispute settlement procedure. In particular, the creation of the Dispute Settlement Mechanism and in particular the Appellate Body, which can review the decisions of the panels, introduces a kind of jurisdictional procedure which is characteristic of well established legal systems. Moreover, the new procedure which leads to the adoption of the panel decision or the Appellate Body decision by the Council, which is a political organ, shows *a retreat of politics and an advancement of law*. Under the GATT system, a panel decision could only be adopted unanimously, which meant that the losing party was always free to refuse to accept it, and could be said to hold a real power of veto. Under the present WTO system, a panel decision or a decision of the Appellate Body can only be rejected if there is unanimity in favour of rejection. This means that the losing party, even if it is a very powerful State, will not be able to prevent the decision being adopted. Of course, this system, which is referred to as the 'reverse veto', does not guarantee that the State which has been declared to be in violation of the rules will abide practically with the decision, but it can still be regarded as an improvement in comparison with the situation which existed anterior to the Marrakech Agreements.

Of course, much could be said about the specific rules which this Dispute Settlement Mechanism applies, but this would exceed the framework of this contribution. It should, however, be mentioned that one of the consequences of economic globalization seems to be a 'downward' unification of social, environmental, and other standards for the protection of individuals. The rules governing trade, which are currently united almost solely by the single slogan of trade liberalization, should take other dimensions into account.

A last point might be added, which is linked to the preceding remark. In order for all different human interests and values to be taken into account, and not just economic values, all States—and possibly other actors in international relations— should enjoy a fair representation in all international organizations. Michel Camdessus addresses the point in the form of a question: 'Comment, au moment où la mondialisation avance si vite, trouver les structures mondiales adaptées, où chacun serait équitablement représenté, et qui permettraient de parvenir à une meilleure formulation de stratégies globales au niveau de l'économie mondiale?'[46] This is evidently an issue for imaginative institutional thinking on the part of international lawyers.

CONCLUSION: WHAT ROLE FOR THE STATE?

Saying that international law should be developed in order to be able to regulate globalization does not imply the end of States, but the contrary.

International law is created by States. Thus, for international law to have legiti-

---

[46] Camdessus, 'Les conditions d'une mondialisation réussie', 46.

macy and strength, States must exist and be effective. As long as there is no world army or police force, States remain the *unique vectors of law creation and enforcement*. This is true for the creation and enforcement of national law, for the enforcement of all other non-State systems of regulation, and even for the creation and enforcement of international law, with the reservation that each State can only enforce international law against its own people and within its own territory.

However, there are other reasons why States should not disappear from the international arena. Even if international law becomes capable of dealing more effectively with globalization, not everything can—or at least not everything should—be dealt with at the global level. Some diversity is a richness of our earthly world. It is of utmost importance to preserve diversity: ideological, political, linguistic, cultural, and legal. States therefore have some functions to fulfil, which cannot be fulfilled globally.

States must play the role of *arbitrators between market and society*. This idea has also been expressed by Oscar Schachter, who wrote: 'States alone have provided the structures of authority needed to cope with the incessant claims of competing societal groups and to provide public justice essential to social order and responsibility.'[47]

States have a function as *guardians of non-mercantile values*, including cultural values as well as, more generally, the values of democracy and human rights. In this respect, the dialectic between globalization, as for example experienced with the Internet, and States can bring about a positive evolution in States, and not their destruction. René Trégouët, in the report mentioned above, highlights the challenge to States, as vertical, hierarchical structures of power, which is posed by a system like the Internet, itself a horizontal, egalitarian network of knowledge.

States also have a function as *organs of solidarity*. Only a State can correct the negative consequences of globalization for the community of individuals living on its territory. We all know that the process of globalization brings with it far-reaching changes in almost every aspect of human life: in technology, working conditions, employment, competition, consumption habits, etc. Only States, entrusted with their mission, and trusted by their citizens, can ensure a minimum of social sharing of wealth and national solidarity. In the words of Oscar Schachter, 'the weak and vulnerable are, on the whole, more likely to obtain protection and benefits through their territorial state than through free markets or the non-governmental associations that lack effective authority'.[48] Or as Monique Chemillier Gendreau has aptly commented, 'les futurs citoyens ne pourront se passer ni d'ancrage territorial ni de niches humaines de solidarités intermédiaires entre l'un de l'individu et le tout de l'espèce. L'Etat-nation peut encore trouver là une grande utilité.'[49]

---

[47] Schachter, 'The Decline of the Nation-State', 22. [48] Ibid. 23.
[49] *Humanité et souverainetés. Essai sur la fonction du droit international* (Paris: Edition de la Découverte, 1995), 28.

Finally, only States can play the role of *mirrors of identity*. As we approach the third millennium we may feel that we are, more and more, citizens of the world. However, I believe that identification with a community 'à échelle humaine' is absolutely necessary, if the individual—whose well-being and happiness should be the ultimate goal of any society—is not to be totally crushed by globalization.

13

The Role of the United Nations Security Council in the International Legal System

MARC PERRIN DE BRICHAMBAUT*

INTRODUCTION

Is the United Nations Security Council a law-creating organ? There are two reasons why the question deserves to be raised. First, when one refers to the Security Council, one generally tends to refer to its political role and not to its influence on the international legal system. Second, there has recently been a late but intense increase in Security Council activity, although this increase is now probably past its peak.

I will begin with a few simple propositions:

1. No international organ is invested with legislative power unless States have specifically entrusted it with this role. It is a fact that the United Nations Charter does not entrust such a role to the Security Council.
2. A resolution may be considered to be a norm. Since the Security Council adopts resolutions, one can therefore assume that it is involved in the creation of norms within the institutional framework that is defined by the Charter. However, this does not mean that Security Council resolutions can be considered as being among the sources of international law set out in Article 38(1) of the Statute of the International Court of Justice. It only means that the Security Council can create rights and obligations for member States of the United Nations.

THE POWERS OF THE SECURITY COUNCIL

The Security Council is a political organ that produces resolutions having legal consequences. The competence granted to the Council by the Charter, and in particular by Chapter VII, is a normative one.

Article 39 of the Charter provides the Security Council with a quasi-discretionary power to determine whether a situation constitutes a breach of international peace and security.[1] This power extends to determining whether a situation constitutes a

---

* The views expressed here are those of the author and not necessarily those of the French government.

[1] Article 39 reads: 'The Security Council shall determine the existence of any threat to the peace, breach of the peace, or act of aggression and shall make recommendations, or decide what measures shall be taken in accordance with Articles 41 and 42, to maintain or restore international peace and security.'

threat to international peace and security, a notion for which there is no definition to be found either in the Charter or in the actual practice of the United Nations since its creation in 1945. This conceptual imprecision provides a broad scope of manœuvre to the Council in assessing whether a situation constitutes a threat to peace, a breach of the peace, or an act of aggression.

Article 40 of the Charter gives the Security Council the right to give legally binding orders to States.[2] More importantly still, Articles 41 and 42 give it decisional power.[3] As the International Court of Justice explained in its 1971 Advisory Opinion on Namibia,

the language of a resolution of the Security Council should be carefully analysed before a conclusion can be made as to its binding effect. In view of the nature of the powers invested in article 25, the question whether they have been in fact exercised is to be determined in each case, having regard to the terms of the resolution to be interpreted, the discussions leading to it, the Charter provisions invoked and in general, all circumstances that might assist in determining the legal consequences of the resolution of the Security Council.[4]

The Security Council can also create subsidiary organs that it deems necessary for the performance of its functions (Article 29 of the Charter).

When making use of these powers, the Security Council acts as an organ that implements the Charter and not as an organ that creates legal norms.

SECURITY COUNCIL RESOLUTIONS AS A SOURCE OF RIGHTS AND OBLIGATIONS

It is my view that Security Council resolutions are essentially only a source of rights and obligations for member States of the United Nations. This is true whether one interprets the Charter traditionally in accordance with the practice of the United Nations during the Cold War, or constructively with reference to more recent practice. Three examples serve to illustrate the point:

---

[2] Article 40 reads: 'In order to prevent an aggravation of the situation, the Security Council may, before making the recommendations or deciding upon the measures provided for in Article 39, call upon the parties concerned to comply with such provisional measures as it deems necessary or desirable. Such provisional measures shall be without prejudice to the rights, claims, or position of the parties concerned. The Security Council shall duly take account of failure to comply with such provisional measures.'

[3] Article 41 reads: 'The Security Council may decide what measures not involving the use of armed force are to be employed to give effect to its decisions, and it may call upon the Members of the United Nations to apply such measures. These may include complete or partial interruption of economic relations and of rail, sea, air, postal, telegraphic, radio, and other means of communication, and the severance of diplomatic relations.'

Article 42 reads: 'Should the Security Council consider that measures provided for in Article 41 would be inadequate or have proved to be inadequate, it may take such action by air, sea, or land forces as may be necessary to maintain or restore international peace and security. Such action may include demonstration, blockade, or other operations by air, sea, or land forces of Members of the United Nations.'

[4] (1971) ICJ Rep. 41.

Terrorism

Security Council Resolution 731 of 21 January 1992, which concerned the bombing of Pan Am Flight 103 over Lockerbie, Scotland, stressed in its preamble that:

[T]he world wide persistence of acts of international terrorism in all its forms, including those in which states are involved directly or indirectly, which endanger or take innocent lives, have a deleterious effect on international relations and jeopardise the security of states.[5]

The Security Council recalled the right of all States, in conformity with the Charter and the principles of international law, to protect their nationals from acts of terrorism which constitute 'a threat to international peace and security'.

Similarly, Resolution 748 of 31 March 1992 stressed in its preamble that 'the suppression of acts of international terrorism, including those in which states are directly or indirectly involved, is essential for the maintenance of international peace and security'. An identical position was adopted in Resolution 883 of 11 November 1993. Thus, the Security Council has been careful, in all its resolutions concerning terrorism, to assert a link with the preservation of international peace and security.

In these resolutions the Security Council imposed different obligations on different States. In Resolution 731 it imposed an obligation on Libya to extradite its two accused nationals, and an obligation on other States to encourage Libya to respect this resolution.

By way of Resolution 748, it imposed a selective embargo on Libya, and in doing so created rights as well as obligations. Thus, all States had an obligation to engage in the embargo, and all States had the right to ignore existing contracts previously signed with Libya.

It should also be noted in this context that Article 40(2)(c) of the current version of the International Law Commission's Draft Articles on State Responsibility confirms that Security Council resolutions can confer rights on States. It reads:

2. In particular, 'injured State' means:

. . .

c. if the right infringed by the act of a State arises from a binding decision of an international organ other than an international court or tribunal, the State or States which, in accordance with the constituent instrument of the international organisation concerned, are entitled to the benefit of that right; . . .[6]

International Criminal Justice

By way of Security Council Resolutions 827 of 25 May 1993 and 955 of 8 November 1994, two international criminal tribunals were created in order to prosecute and try individuals who were alleged to be responsible for grave violations of international

---

[5] For Security Council resolutions generally, see http://www.un.org/Docs/sc.htm.

[6] See Report of the ILC on the work of its forty-eighth session, 6 May–26 July 1996, http://www.un.org/law/ilc.

humanitarian law in the former Yugoslavia and Rwanda, respectively. These tribunals constitute subsidiary organs of the Security Council.

In creating these tribunals on the basis of Chapter VII of the United Nations Charter, the Security Council was interpreting the Charter in a very innovative way. However, it was perfectly allowed to do so. If the Council believes that the lack of punishment for individuals who are responsible for violations of international humanitarian law represents a threat to international peace and security, nothing prevents it from using Article 29 of the Charter to create a subsidiary organ in order to try those persons. This is an appropriate interpretation and implementation of the Charter.

These subsidiary organs, which were created according to the existing law of the Charter, themselves apply existing law, namely international humanitarian law, which is referred to in their statutes. They do not create new law.

Security Guarantees for Non-Nuclear States

Resolution 984 of 11 April 1995 provides the third example, which touches upon the security guarantees provided by nuclear powers. The wording of Paragraph 3, which refers to the positive guarantees provided by those States which possess nuclear weapons, to those States which do not possess nuclear weapons *and* are parties to the Treaty on the Non-Proliferation of Nuclear Weapons, appears to have legal consequences.[7] The Security Council clearly admits that, when a non-nuclear party to the Non-Proliferation Treaty suffers or is threatened with aggression, any State can request that the Security Council give its immediate attention to the situation so that appropriate action can be taken and assistance provided to the victim State. Such a commitment does seem to create an obligation to behave in a certain way, on the part of those nuclear States which are permanent members of the Security Council.

Thus, those acts which are frequently referred to as new forms of Security Council intervention turn out, in practice, to fit within the Council's traditional role of preserving international peace and security. They cannot be described as involving an assertion of jurisdiction over new areas.

SECURITY COUNCIL INNOVATIONS IN THE LEGAL DOMAIN

There is no question that the Security Council has been fairly innovative in qualifying some acts as illegal under international law. For example, in Resolution 674 of

---

[7] Paragraph 3 of Res. 984 (1995) reads: '*The Security Council . . . recognizes further* that, in case of aggression with nuclear weapons or the threat of such aggression against a non-nuclear-weapon State Party to the Treaty on the Non-Proliferation of Nuclear Weapons, any State may bring the matter immediately to the attention of the Security Council to enable the Council to take urgent action to provide assistance, in accordance with the Charter, to the State victim of an act of, or object of a threat of, such aggression; and *recognizes also* that the nuclear-weapon State permanent members of the Security Council will bring the matter immediately to the attention of the Council and seek Council action to provide, in accordance with the Charter, the necessary assistance to the State victim.'

29 October 1990 the Council clearly indicated that Iraq's invasion of Kuwait was illegal. This qualification was made by reference to existing law. The Council emphasized that Iraq's actions were contrary to Council resolutions, to the Charter of the United Nations, to the fourth Geneva Convention of 1949, to the 1961 Vienna Convention on Diplomatic Relations, and to the 1963 Vienna Convention on Consular Relations, as well as to customary international law. The Council drew a number of consequences for international responsibility from this qualification. In Resolutions 705 of 15 August 1991 and 715 of 11 October 1991 it established the conditions for the fulfilment of Iraq's legal responsibility, and thereby went so far as to grant itself quasi-judicial powers. This was a major innovation because an evaluation by the Security Council on the basis of Article 39 of the Charter normally has no consequences in terms of State responsibility. Indeed, Article 39 only mentions situations which may affect international peace and security.

The Security Council was equally innovative in its settlement of the border dispute between Iraq and Kuwait, which it accomplished in Resolution 773 of 26 August 1992. This, along with the other resolutions concerning Iraq mentioned above, is probably the furthest it has reached in stretching its powers within the legal domain.

SECURITY COUNCIL RESOLUTIONS AND CUSTOMARY INTERNATIONAL LAW

If the Security Council is able to create rights and obligations within the institutional framework of the United Nations, is it conceivable that its resolutions could also contribute to the formation of international law—in the same way that they contribute to the interpretation of existing international law? In 1985, in the *Libya/Malta Continental Shelf Case*, the International Court of Justice explained that the substance of customary international law should be sought, in the first instance, in the effective practice and *opinio juris* of States.[8] Several sources provide evidence of *opinio juris*, the psychological element of customary international law. The subject-matter of some United Nations General Assembly resolutions may reflect the *opinio juris* of States. For example, this would seem to have been true of Resolution 2625 (XXV) of 24 October 1970, which included as an annex the Declaration on Friendly Relations between States. Security Council resolutions may be similarly relevant, provided that their subject-matter is not restricted to particular circumstances. If their subject-matter is too closely linked to particular circumstances, it becomes difficult for them to contribute to general international law.

It should also be recalled, as the International Court of Justice indicated in the 1969 *North Sea Continental Shelf Cases*, that effective and general practice, the

---

[8] (1985) ICJ Reports 29–30.

material element of customary international law, plays a crucial role in the creation of customary rules.[9]

TREATIES AND SECURITY COUNCIL RESOLUTIONS

The rights and obligations created by Security Council resolutions override those derived from treaties. Article 103 of the Charter of the United Nations states:

In the event of a conflict between the obligations of the Members of the United Nations under the present Charter and their obligations under any other international agreement, their obligations under the present Charter shall prevail.

Rights and obligations that derive from Security Council resolutions can thus supplant rights and obligations derived from treaties and conventions. However, the International Court of Justice is currently concerned with this issue in the *Lockerbie Case*,[10] and for this reason I will not elaborate further on it, but await the Court's decision on the merits with great interest.

SECURITY COUNCIL RESOLUTIONS, OBLIGATIONS *ERGA OMNES*,
AND PENAL RESPONSIBILITY

In its judgment of 29 October 1997 in the *Blaskic Case*, the Appeals Chamber of the International Criminal Tribunal for the former Yugoslavia determined that obligations derived from Article 29 of the Tribunal's Statute are obligations *erga omnes*.[11] The reasoning followed by the Appeals Chamber seems to imply that any member of the United Nations has a legal interest in respect of Article 29. The Appeals Chamber took the position that any member of the United Nations can request any other State which is not respecting its obligations under that Article to comply with it. It even suggested that in such a situation the requesting State may take unilateral

---

[9]   (1969) ICJ Reports 43.
[10]   For the 27 Feb. 1998 judgment on preliminary objections, see http://www.icj-cij.org/icj002.htm.
[11]   Judgment on the request of the Republic of Croatia for review of the decision of Trial Chamber II of 18 July 1997, http://www.un.org/icty/blaskic, para. 26. Article 29, which concerns co-operation and judicial assistance, reads:

1. States shall co-operate with the International Tribunal in the investigation and prosecution of persons accused of committing serious violations of international humanitarian law.
2. States shall comply without undue delay with any request for assistance or an order issued by a Trial Chamber, including, but not limited to:
(a) the identification and location of persons;
(b) the taking of testimony and the production of evidence;
(c) the service of documents;
(d) the arrest or detention of persons;
(e) the surrender or the transfer of the accused to the International Tribunal.

action against the recalcitrant State. This is clearly a new and interesting develop-ment that needs to be handled with some care.

That said, the Security Council is definitely not a judicial organ. It cannot take measures that would have a penal character. This point needs to be stressed because a degree of confusion exists in some quarters concerning the nature of sanctions applied by the Security Council. It has been suggested that these sanctions have a penal character, which then implies that the Security Council itself might have a penal function. This is clearly not the case. The United Nations can in no way question the penal responsibility of States. In the context of Security Council reso-lutions, therefore, one should avoid using words drawn from the vocabulary of criminal law.

Finally, there is the question of the legal consequences of Security Council reso-lutions in the domestic legal framework of United Nations member States. The implementation of Security Council resolutions is not always easy. Recently, Resolution 1127 of 28 August 1997, which imposes a number of sanctions on the Uniao Nacional para a Independencia Total de Angola (UNITA), raised some seri-ous difficulties in France. On 29 December 1997, the Conseil d'Etat took a signifi-cant decision in respect of the implementation of this resolution, ruling that any regulation taken to implement a Security Council resolution is an 'act of govern-ment' and therefore not subject to any judicial control.

CONCLUSIONS

John Foster Dulles once claimed that the Security Council not only implements the law, but is the law.[12] This goes a bit too far. The Security Council does play a signif-icant role in the international legal system. It does so, not so much as an original source of law, but as an organ in charge of implementing the law, and more precisely the Charter of the United Nations. Although the Security Council does not have the power to create law, it does have the power to create rights and obligations for the member States of the United Nations. It does so on the basis of the Charter it inter-prets and implements. Security Council resolutions can therefore have a certain impact on the international legal order. Moreover, these new rights and obligations will sometimes supplant pre-existing rights and obligations.

When interpreting the Charter, the Security Council does so for its own purposes only. It does not do so in an abstract or context-neutral way, but rather selects the interpretation that is most appropriate for the circumstances with which it is confronted.

The Security Council, therefore, is not, properly speaking, an organ that creates law. Instead, it simply interprets and applies existing law, and in particular Chapter

---

[12] J. F. Dulles, *War or Peace* (New York: Macmillan, 1950), 194–5, cited by Mohammed Bedjaoui, *Nouvel ordre mondial et contrôle de la légalité des actes de la Sécurité* (Brussels: Bruylant, 1994), 11.

VII of the United Nations Charter. Although some people have argued that the Security Council exercises a creeping jurisdiction over a growing number of problems, a more accurate assessment is, I believe, that the end of the Cold War has permitted the progressive *realization* of those aspects of Article 1 of the Charter which concern international peace and security.[13] It remains to be seen whether this trend will continue.

[13] Article 1 reads, *inter alia*: 'The purposes of the United Nations are: 1. To maintain international peace and security, and to that end: to take effective collective measures for the prevention and removal of threats to the peace, and for the suppression of acts of aggression or other breaches of the peace, and to bring about by peaceful means, and in conformity with the principles of justice and international law, adjustment or settlement of international disputes or situations which might lead to a breach of the peace; . . .'

14

The Functions of the United Nations Security Council in the International Legal System

VERA GOWLLAND-DEBBAS

1. INTRODUCTION

The question of what functions are fulfilled by the Security Council in the international legal system is doubtless open to debate. I propose to approach the question in terms of the use which has been made of the Council's collective and institutionalized mechanisms for the enforcement of international legal norms—in other words, by focusing on its legal sanctioning function. The mechanisms instituted under Chapter VII of the United Nations Charter grant extensive, discretionary powers to an élitist, political organ whose primary responsibility is the maintenance of a political conception of international ordering—i.e. the maintenance of international peace and security. It is interesting to see how these mechanisms have become increasingly central to collective responses to violations of fundamental legal norms, and thus to diffused and largely unsystematic efforts directed at the forging of what some have termed an 'international public policy' or 'public order' of the international community.

Conceptions of the International Legal System and its Interaction with the Social Environment

What is meant by the international legal system, and how does it interact with its social environment? The international legal system may be conceived in a formalist sense as a kind of self-contained black box, a mix of mental and empirical construct, containing a coherently ordered set of structural and normative arrangements whose interacting parts cannot be envisaged in isolation, for '[t]he idea of a single legal norm has no meaning'.[1] In this sense, it has been said that international law is not

---

[1] François Ewald, 'The Law of Law', in Gunther Teubner (ed.), *Autopoietic Law: A New Approach to Law and Society* (Berlin: Walter de Gruyter, 1988), 36–50 at 36. See also Hans Kelsen, *General Theory of Law and State* (Cambridge, Mass.: Harvard University Press, 1945), 3: 'It is impossible to grasp the nature of law if we limit our attention to the single isolated rule. The relations which link together the particular rules of a legal order are also essential to the nature of law.'

just formed of bric-à-brac, a hotchpotch of legal norms, institutions, and acts, but actually constitutes a system.[2]

This systemic character—the manner in which legal norms are produced, generated, and articulated with each other—has been envisaged in different ways. From a Kelsenian perspective, the legal system is a strictly linear and hierarchical or pyramidal structure. Within this structure, the validity of a norm results purely from its conformity to a superior norm, ending with the norm of norms, or 'grundnorm', the unity of the system deriving here from this formal method of norm creation.[3] For Herbert Hart, it is the union of primary and secondary rules which lies at the centre of a legal system.[4] Alternatively, theories of legal autopoesis, in a kind of neo-Kelsenian revival, while adapting from methods borrowed from outside the discipline, have viewed the legal system in terms of circularity. The system thus produces and reproduces its own elements, whether these are considered legal acts or communications, as well as its organization and structures through the recursive interaction of its elements, while providing for its unity by specifying its boundaries. In this vision, it is not the system's adaptation to its environment, but its own behaviour that leads to its diversification and increasing complexity.[5]

From all these perspectives, the legal system can be regarded as a unity that is self-generating and self-regulating.[6] This triumph of rationalized form over content is said to guarantee the law's autonomy and shield it from its ambient environment. In a 'pure theory of law' approach, ethical or political considerations remain outside the

----

[2] See Jean Combacau, 'Le Droit international: bric-à-brac ou système?', in *Archives de philosophie du droit: Le système juridique* (Paris: Sirey, 1986), xxxi. 85–105 at 86, who describes a 'système' as 'un ensemble dont les éléments ne s'agrègent pas au hasard mais constituent un "ordre" en ce qu'ils sont reliés les uns aux autres et à l'ensemble lui-même par des liens tels qu'on ne peut envisager l'un de ces éléments isolé de son entourage sans l'analyser faussement.'

[3] Hans Kelsen, *Pure Theory of Law* (trans. by Max Knight) (Berkeley: University of California Press, 1978), 21: 'An "order" is a system of norms whose unity is constituted by the fact that they all have the same reason for their validity; and the reason for the validity of a normative order is a basic norm . . . from which the validity of all norms of the order are derived.' Again, on p. 221: 'The legal order is not a system of co-ordinated norms of equal level, but a hierarchy of different levels of legal norms.' See Francois Ost, 'Between Order and Disorder: The Game of Law', in Teuber (ed.), *Autopoietic Law*, 70–96 at 78.

[4] Herbert Hart, *The Concept of Law* (Oxford: Clarendon Press, 1961), 96. In Hart's view, we can only speak of a legal system in relation to a society possessing both primary rules (i.e. those which require certain actions or abstentions) and secondary rules (those which provide for the validation of primary rules, their production, extinction, or modification, and the adjudication and sanctioning of their breaches); otherwise, we would only be in the presence of a block of separate standards lacking any common identifying mark.

[5] See Gunther Teubner, 'Introduction to Autopoietic Law', in id. (ed.), *Autopoietic Law*, 1–11 at 1: 'The message is that circularity is not a flaw in legal thinking which ought to be avoided, but rather that the reality of law consists of a multitude of circular processes . . . In the autopoietic perspective . . . [t]he whole legal system is seen as a dynamic cyclical reproduction of legal elements embedded in hypercyclical relations of legal structures and processes.' In biology, the autopoietic paradigm was formulated by H. Maturana and F. Varela; its transposition to the legal system is owed in particular to Niklas Luhmann and G. Teubner. For a critical discussion, see Ost, ibid. 70–9. Though autopoiesis has been termed a neo-Kelsenian revival, Kelsen may not have approved of this 'methodological syncretism' (see *Pure Theory of Law*, 1).

[6] 'The peculiarity of the law [is] that it regulates its own creation' (ibid. 221).

ken of the international jurist. Only the application or interpretation of the norm is inspired by extra-legal considerations, with the fundamental norm serving as a boundary between the legal system and its extra-systemic social environment.[7] In an autopoietic perspective, the external environment at best constitutes 'off-stage noise'.[8]

At the other extreme, however, lie 'open systems' views in which the international legal system is open-ended, empirically and sociologically based on an *a posteriori* finding of what rules are actually applied (by the judge or the policy-maker) and respected, i.e. validated from below through recognition by social norms. In this way, law interrelates with other social disciplines—politics, ethics, etc.—and with social reality itself. Such views are also concerned with adapting the law to social change, approaching international law as instrumental, there to promote the finalities and underlying values and interests of social actors. The legal system becomes synonymous with the notion of legal order,[9] in the sense of a particular *substantive* content, surfacing at a particular time, and hence dynamic in its responses to the changing configuration and requirements of international society.

It would seem that the former view is more likely to remain unchallenged at a time of great social stability, while the latter is more likely to find its *raison d'être* when there is growing divergence between social mores and legal institutions.[10] Yet, did not Kelsen's insistence on the strict autonomy of the law take place in reaction to the brutal transformations of the social order of his time, and in some way constitute an attempt to save the law from destruction through its instrumentalization for political purposes?[11]

In considering the international legal system, theories seem therefore to oscillate between the extremes of vacuous form and amorphous content, 'between the rigidity of metal and the decomposition of smoke'.[12] Yet it has been held that the boundaries of law, the way in which the legal system distinguishes itself from other social phenomena, can be maintained on the basis of the autopoietic paradox of combining 'normative closure and cognitive openness', of a compromise between the 'demand for continuous adjustment of law to social development while maintaining

---

[7] See ibid. 198 and 353.

[8] Gunther Teubner: 'The legal system is forced by the uproar outside, by the "noise" of the economic actors, to vary its internal "order" until relative quiet returns . . .' Quoted in Jean-Pierre Dupuy, 'On the Supposed Closure of Normative Systems', in Teubner (ed.), *Autopoietic Law*, 51–69 at 55–6.

[9] For some authors, legal system and legal order are synonymous in any event. See e.g. Kelsen, *Pure Theory of Law*. See also Michel Troper, 'Système juridique et Etat', in *Archives de philosophie du droit*, xxxi. 29–44 at 30.

[10] See Michel van Kerchove and François Ost, *Le Système juridique entre ordre et désordre* (Paris: Presses universitaires de France, 1988), 131.

[11] Kelsen (*General Theory of Law and State*, p. xvii), however, in his search for a science of law, was at the same time well aware of the dilemma created by his postulate of the complete separation of jurisprudence from politics: 'This is especially true in our time, which indeed "is out of joint" when the foundations of social life have been shaken to the depths by two World Wars. The ideal of an objective science of law and State, free from all political ideologies, has a better chance for recognition in a period of social equilibrium. It seems, therefore, that a pure theory of law is untimely today . . .'

[12] See Henri Atlan, *Entre le cristal et la fumée* (Paris: Seuil, 1979), 5—quoted in Ost, 'Between Order and Disorder', 81.

the regenerative capacity of normativity'.[13] The paradoxes here are not seen as cracks in the edifice, but as an inherent part of it.

This process of adjustment, however, is a complex one, for the international legal system does not transform any reality into law. Consequently, the relationship between, say, law and politics can neither be disposed of altogether, nor analysed simply in terms of the impact of the one on the other in the manner of traditional input/output systems theories. Distanced from the indeterminate mass of social phenomena, law preserves its detachment from the disturbance emanating from its social environment, or rather transforms the noise (or 'music' as Teubner would have it[14]) into order meaningful to itself. Rather than consider that the more the environment influences law, the less autonomous law becomes, these random external perturbations are transformed 'into an organizing factor which generates increased complexity' and strengthens the law's autonomy.[15]

The legal system ingests only that part of social reality that it considers relevant, laying down the conditions that determine which legally relevant facts are to be attributed legal consequences. It defines the threshold of normativity that must be crossed, providing its own means of validation, bestowing legally normative quality on its elements through its sources or rules of recognition, regulating the relationship between fact and law, and sanctioning violations of its binding norms on the basis of a binary code: legal/illegal. This threshold may be determined rigidly through adherence to the formal sources of law, or in terms of soft law-making processes, by penetrating that infra-red band that surrounds the formal international law system. This zone of exchange between law and non-law, which has been referred to variously as *droit sauvage*, *droit vulgaire*, or guerrilla rules, clamours for legal recognition.[16] But the legal system determines substance in addition to form, regulating not only the formal validity of the rule (Dworkin's pedigree test), its enactment pursuant to intra-systemic criteria, but also its substantive validity based on empirical, teleological, and axiological criteria (notions of effectiveness or legitimacy, finalities, essential values), incorporated as underlying or implicit rules of the formal legal system.[17]

---

[13]   See Niklas Luhmann, 'The Unity of the Legal System', in Teubner (ed.), *Autopoietic Law*, 12–35 at 20–1. One of the most challenging theses of autopoietic theory, according to Teubner ('Introduction', in *Autopoietic Law*, 2), is that '[T]he more the legal system gains in operational closure and autonomy, the more it gains in openness towards social facts, political demands, social science theories and human needs.'

[14]   See Gunther Teubner, 'The Two Faces of Janus: Rethinking Legal Pluralism' (1992) 13 Cardozo Law Review 1443 at 1447.

[15]   Ost, 'Between Order and Disorder', 81. See also Kerchove and Ost, *Système juridique*, 17: 'Loin d'apparaître comme l'antithèse de l'ordre, ou à tout le moins comme son image déchue, le désordre opère plutôt comme condition de l'ordre; d'un ordre "autre", d'un sens nouveau qui garantirait l'indispensable adaptation du système. D'autant que le désordre pourrait bien n'être, après tout, que la figure d'émergence d'une rationalité qui, si elle nous échappe encore aujourd'hui, pourrait bien s'éclairer demain.'

[16]   On this 'dégradé normatif', see Alain Pellet, 'Le "bon droit" et l'ivraie—plaidoyer pour l'ivraie. Remarques sur quelques problèmes de méthode en droit international du développement', in *Mélanges offerts à Charles Chaumont* (Paris: Pedone, 1984), 465–93 at 488.

[17]   Ost, in 'Between Order and Disorder', 91–2. It is pointed out that in interpreting the law the judge does not only have recourse to the formal validity of the rules but, in having to choose between different rules, will apply such implicit rules as the need to maintain the logical or ideological coherence of the legal order (Kerchove and Ost, *Système juridique*, 137–40).

The legal system, in constructing its own legal reality, also establishes its own language or meaning. This means that interdisciplinary theory-building that attempts to overcome the academic compartmentalization of disciplines has to cope with terminological barriers as well. One can think of the different connotations in law and politics of terms of art such as 'normative' or 'responsibility', or differences in vocabulary which partly cover the same object, such as 'regime theory' on the one hand, and 'treaty' or 'international organization' on the other.

The relations which law entertains with social reality have been likened to those between maps and spatial reality, a 'misreading' which is not chaotic but which 'occurs through determinate and determinable mechanisms'.[18] In short, it has been said that law has the paradoxical position of being both open, because without society it is nothing, and closed, because society—and with it its teleology and value content—is reinterpreted or 'misread' in a legal context according to a specifically legal matrix.

The Concept of International Public Policy

The international legal system has mirrored the contradictory pulls of centrifugal and globalizing forces in international society, by paradoxical legal processes: fragmentation and compartmentalization of particular fields of international law, verging on legal pluralism, as well as increasing technicality on the one hand, and the construction of unifying, universalizing, and generalizing elements on the other.[19] The latter process has resulted, *inter alia*, in the creation and expansion of a domain of general or public interest and the development of what can broadly be viewed, along the lines of some domestic legal systems, as an international public policy or *ordre public*.

The concept of public policy or *ordre public* is to be distinguished from the notion of public order (in the sense of the maintenance of law and order), although the latter may form part of the content of the former. Found in most national systems of law, it is based on the principle that the will of individual subjects is limited by the need to protect overriding community values and interests, although both the notion and its content vary over time and place.[20] The transposition of the concept

[18] See Boaventura De Sousa Santos, 'Law: A Map of Misreading. Toward a Postmodern Conception of Law' (1987) 14 Journal of Law and Society 279 at 281–2: '[L]aw, like poems, must misread or distort reality and for similar reasons. Poems misread in order to establish their originality, while laws misread in order to establish their exclusivity.'

[19] On the survival of universal principles and concepts in a multicultural world, see Michel Virally, 'Le rôle du droit dans un conflit de civilisations: le cas Iran-U.S.A.' (1988) Revue des sciences morales et politiques 37.

[20] On the elusive nature of the very concept of public policy in municipal law and on its relation with public law, see *Case concerning the Application of the Convention of 1902 governing the Guardianship of Infants* (1958) ICJ Rep., Separate Opinion of Judge Sir Percy Spender, 122, where he states: 'Public policy in every country is in a constant state of flux. It is always evolving. It is impossible to ascertain any absolute criterion. It cannot be determined within a formula. It is a conception.' See also *Case concerning the Payment of Various Serbian Loans Issued in France* (1929) PCIJ Rep., Series A, No. 20, 46, where the

to the sphere of international law is a novel, and as yet undefined and contested, development. Yet there is undoubtedly an emerging trend that juxtaposes alongside the traditional conceptual legal framework based largely on a network of bilateral and contractual relations between atomistic States, one that is based on objective community interests.[21]

The concept of international community in this context may not necessarily correspond to the Weberian conception of a society tending towards a higher degree of integration, with shared values and a feeling of solidarity.[22] However, it is a very real legal construct, if not a legal fiction,[23] by which a social grouping is attributed rights and obligations, and one which points to a novel development in the legal system. Paid lip service to by States over and above claims of cultural relativism (interestingly, it is those countries which insist on the universality of human rights law which have, at some point in time, been ardent opponents of such concepts as *jus cogens* or international crimes), it has been referred to in treaties and discoursed upon by international courts. The expression 'international community', although

Court referred to public policy as 'a conception the definition of which in any particular country is largely dependent on the opinion prevailing at any given time in such country itself'. See as well Erik Suy, 'The Concept of Jus Cogens in Public International Law', in *The Concept of Jus Cogens in Public International Law. Papers and Proceedings of the Lagonissi Conference* (Geneva: Carnegie Endowment for International Peace, 1967), 17–77; Marie-José Domestici-Met, 'Recherches sur le concept d'ordre public en droit international public' (unpublished thesis, University of Nice, 1979).

[21] Hermann Mosler, *The International Society As a Legal Community* (Alphen aan den Rijn: Sijthoff & Noordhoff, 1980), 17–19, used the term 'public order of the international community' which '. . . consists of principles and rules the enforcement of which is of such vital importance to the international community as a whole that any unilateral action or any agreement which contravenes these principles can have no legal force. The reason for this follows simply from logic: the law cannot recognise any act either of one member or of several members in concert, as being legally valid if it is directed against the very foundation of law'; though 'not generally accepted as a term of art, the reality behind the term is not disputed'. See also the comments of Sir Hersch Lauterpacht ('Report on the law of treaties' (1953 II) Yearbook of the International Law Commission 155) in relation to the draft article on *jus cogens*, who referred to 'overriding principles of international law which may be regarded as constituting principles of international public policy (*ordre international public*). These principles need not necessarily have crystallized in a clearly accepted rule of law . . . They may be expressive of rules of international morality so cogent that an international tribunal would consider them as forming part of those principles of law generally recognized by civilized nations . . .'; and of Sir Humphrey Waldock ('Second report on the law of treaties' (1963 II) Yearbook of the International Law Commission 52): 'Imperfect though international legal order may be, the view that in the last analysis there is no international public order—no rule from which States cannot of their own free will contract out—has become increasingly difficult to sustain.' The concept has since been widened to embrace more than just *jus cogens*. See Juan-Antonio Carrillo-Salcedo, 'Droit international et souveraineté des Etats. Cours général de droit international public' (1996) 257 Recueil des Cours 35 at 132–46; Jonathan Charney, 'Universal International Law' (1993) 87 American Journal of International Law 529; Bruno Simma, 'From Bilateralism to Community Interest in International Law' (1994) 250 Recueil des Cours 221; Christian Tomuschat, 'Obligations Arising for States Without or Against Their Will' (1993) 241 Recueil des Cours 197 at 211.

[22] For a discussion of the relation between society and community, see World Society Research Group, 'In Search of World Society' (1996) 53/54 Law and State 17.

[23] See Monique Chemillier-Gendreau, 'Origine et rôle de la fiction en droit international public' (1987) 32 Archives de philosophie du droit: le droit international 153 at 156.

attributed different meanings, has thus served to galvanize the concept of funda-mental obligations owed to it.[24]

These norms have been assigned different purposes: the maintenance of interna-tional public order (rules relating to the non-use of force); the transformation of that order based on notions of justice (the right to self-determination); the incorporation into law of a certain universal moral or ethical foundation (the core principles of human rights or humanitarian law); the physical protection or survival of mankind (emerging norms relating to the global commons or the protection of the natural environment). These form the content of a variety of umbrella concepts operating in different fields of international law and having different purposes and legal effects (e.g. treaty law, the law of claims, State responsibility, and individual criminal responsibility), although they have differing degrees of 'positivity' and some remain highly controversial. To the familiar triptych of international lawyers—*jus cogens*, obligations *erga omnes*, international crimes of State—one should add the emerging concept of 'the most serious crimes of concern to the international community as a whole' giving rise to individual criminal responsibility under international law.[25]

---

[24] See Article 53 of the 1969 Vienna Convention on the Law of Treaties; Article 19 of the International Law Commission's Draft Articles on State Responsibility; and the various references by the ICJ or individual judges attesting to the existence of fundamental norms owed to the 'international community as a whole', a concept usually but not always equated to the community of States (*International Status of South-West Africa* (1950) ICJ Rep. 132–3, 176; *South-West Africa Cases (Preliminary Objections)* (1962) ICJ Rep. 343; *Barcelona Traction Case* (1970) ICJ Rep. 32; more recently, *East Timor Case* (1995) ICJ Rep. 102; *Genocide Convention Case (Preliminary Objections)* (1996) ICJ Rep. 616). However, Christian Tomuschat states: '[I]t would be wrong to assume that States as a mere juxta-position of individual units constitute the international community. Rather, the concept denotes an over-arching system which embodies a common interest of all States and, indirectly, of mankind' ('Obligations Arising for States', 227). While questioning the place of Article 19 in the Draft Articles and the appro-priateness of introducing two distinct regimes of responsibility arising from the distinction between inter-national crimes and international delicts, James Crawford, the new Special Rapporteur, nevertheless recognizes that '[j]udicial decisions since 1976 certainly support the idea that international law contains different kinds of norms, and is not limited to the "classical" idea of bilateral norms' His first report also confirms the view 'that within the field of general international law there is some hierarchy of norms, and that the importance of at least a few basic substantive norms is recognized as involving a difference not merely of degree but of kind. Such a difference would be expected to have its consequences in the field of State responsibility' (though within the framework of a single generic conception) (First Report on State Responsibility, ILC 50th sess., 1998, A/CN.4/490/Add. 2, pp. 3, 8–9). See also René-Jean Dupuy, *La Communauté internationale entre le mythe et l'histoire* (Paris: UNESCO, 1986), 13–14; Roberto Ago, 'Obligations *erga omnes* and the International Community', in Joseph Weiler, Antonio Cassese, and Marina Spinedi (eds.), *International Crimes of State: A Critical Analysis of the ILC's Draft Article 19 on State Responsibility* (Berlin: Walter de Gruyter, 1989), 237–9 at 238.

[25] See the Preamble and Article 5 of the recently adopted Rome Statute of the International Criminal Court ((1998) 37 International Legal Materials 999). The operation in the field of treaty law of the concept of *jus cogens* (Articles 53 and 64 of the 1969 Vienna Convention) serves to remove from States their traditional right to derogate by a treaty (however trivial) from a norm of international law (however important), on pain of nullity of the treaty. From the law of claims there has emerged the concept of oblig-ations *erga omnes*, which widens the circle of States able to invoke the illegality beyond that State which is directly injured (see e.g. Article 40(3) of the ILC Draft Articles on State Responsibility: 'In addition, "injured State" means, if the internationally wrongful act constitutes an international crime, all other States.'). In the realm of State responsibility, the concept of international crimes of States introduced in Article 19 of the ILC Draft Articles, which depends on the subject-matter of the international obligation

What has amounted to a hierarchization, or fragmentation, of the monolithic framework of international law norms has paradoxically promoted a view, based on its unity or universality, which has opposed its centrifugal forces. For Prosper Weil, who at one time had expressed his concern with this process, this has led to an emphasis on what unifies rather than on what divides.[26]

The Concept of Sanctions and its Evolution

The juxtaposition of community interests alongside inter-State interests has had an impact on basic premisses of international law, particularly on those of State sovereignty and consent in the formation and application of international law. A tension between consensualism and community interests has been produced by the notion that the freedom of States to conduct their legal relations within a bilateral framework based on subjective State interests is limited by the need to protect essential communal values and interests prevailing at a given time. This has recently been well illustrated by the International Court of Justice's Advisory Opinion on Nuclear Weapons, in which it applied bilateral mechanisms based on voluntarist '*Lotus* principles' to fundamental community interests.[27]

It has also had an impact on the evolution of the concept of sanctions. Sanctions are clearly linked to the general problem of compliance inherent in the prescriptive nature of any legal order. However, the concept of sanctions has also been at the core of traditional debates on the nature and function of international law—do sanctions constitute the essence or characteristic of the legal norm or legal system?[28] Moreover,

---

breached, has led to efforts to formulate a distinct regime of State responsibility, while in the field of individual criminal responsibility under international law, efforts have been made to circumscribe the crimes of crimes, including in the ILC Draft Articles on the Draft Code of Crimes against the Peace and Security of Mankind. See, for a general discussion in relation to the jurisprudence of the Court: V. Gowlland-Debbas, 'Judicial Insights into Fundamental Values and Interests of the International Community', in A. S. Muller, D. Raic, and J. M. Thuranszky (eds.), *The International Court of Justice: Its Future Role after Fifty Years* (The Hague: Martinus Nijhoff, 1997), 327–66.

[26] See Prosper Weil, 'Le Droit international en quête de son identité. Cours général de droit international public' (1992) 237 Recueil des Cours 9 at 309: 'Quelle que soit la connotation que l'on entend lui conférer, la référence à la communauté internationale tend à substituer à la société international atomisée et fractionnée . . . la vision d'une communauté unie et solidaire. La société des Etats, telle que la connaissait le droit international classique, privilégiait l'Etat et sa souveraineté; la communauté internationale, telle que l'affectionne le droit international moderne, met l'accent sur ce qui rassemble plutôt que sur ce qui sépare. La référence à la communauté internationale dépasse l'effet de style et de mode: derrière le glissement sémantique se profile une évolution même du système international.'

[27] *Legality of the Threat or Use of Nuclear Weapons*, Advisory Opinion of 8 July 1996 ((1996) ICJ Rep. 226). See V. Gowlland-Debbas, 'The Right to Life and Genocide: The Court and an International Public Policy', in Laurence Boisson de Chazournes and Philippe Sands, *International Law, the World Court and Nuclear Weapons* (Cambridge: Cambridge University Press, 1999). This interpretation of the *Lotus Case*, however, is not uncontroversial.

[28] In the Austinian conception of law as the command of the sovereign, it was the power to inflict punishment, or the sanction, which converted an expression of a wish into a command and hence into law. For Kelsen, 'Law is the primary norm, which stipulates the sanction' (*General Theory of Law and State*, 61), and 'Law is, by its very nature, a coercive order. A coercive order is a system of rules prescribing certain patterns of behaviour by providing coercive measures, as sanctions, to be taken in case of contrary

ιn a system in which the obligations of one State are opposed to the rights of another, reactions to violations of international law have traditionally been unilateral and based on subjective interpretations of rules of law and the conduct of States. They have also taken decentralized and unpredictable forms, such as counter-measures or reprisals—hence the debate over whether centrally organized sanctions constitute the hallmark of a developed legal system.

The imposition of sanctions has now, in the International Law Commission's Draft Articles, been made part and parcel of the law of State responsibility—the latter being defined as *all* the legal consequences of a violation of international law and not just the duty to make reparations.[29] Moreover, the term 'sanctions', as a term of art, has been reserved by the ILC to centralized mechanisms.[30] And while many of these hierarchically superior norms remain undefined and open-textured, it is through lip service—not State practice—that they have been given substance, and this largely through the attachment of more serious consequences resulting from their violation, such as nullity, aggravated State responsibility, or individual criminal responsibility.

If the international legal system is indeed moving towards the recognition of community interests, the question is whether it is, or should be, also moving towards the creation of international institutional responses to violations of such core norms. It is at least in this way that Roberto Ago, who, as Special Rapporteur on State responsibility, fathered the concept of State crimes embedded in Article 19, had envisaged the legal consequences of such crimes.[31]

To insist, however, that the international legal system does not contain institutions that mirror the role of public authorities endowed with a monopoly of physi-

---

behaviour' (*The Law of the United Nations: A Critical Analysis of its Fundamental Problems* (London: Stevens & Sons, 1950), 706). For a discussion of the view that sanctions are part of the legal system rather than a constituent part of the legal norm, see Georges Abi-Saab, 'Cours général de droit international public' (1987) 207 Recueil des Cours 9 at 116–18.

[29] The ILC intended to cover 'every kind of new relations which may arise, in international law, from the internationally wrongful act of a State, whether such relations are limited to the offending State and the directly injured State or extend also to other subjects of international law, and whether they are centred on the duty of the guilty State to restore the injured State in its rights and repair the damage caused, or whether they also give the injured State itself or other subjects of international law the right to impose on the offending State a sanction admitted by international law' ((1973 II) Yearbook of the International Law Commission 175).

[30] See commentary of Roberto Ago on Article 30 of Part I of the Draft Articles on the term countermeasures, in (1979 II) Yearbook of the International Law Commission (Part One), 39–66, and ibid., vol. II (Part Two), 115–22; and Gaetano Arangio-Ruiz, 'Third Report on State responsibility', A/CN.4/440, 13.

[31] 'It is understandable, therefore, that a community such as the international community, in seeking a more structured organization, even if only an incipient "institutionalization", should have turned in another direction, namely toward a system vesting in international institutions other than States the exclusive responsibility, first, for determining the existence of a breach of an obligation of basic importance to the international community as a whole, and thereafter, for deciding what measures should be taken in response and how they should be implemented' ((1979 II) Yearbook of the International Law Commission (Part One), 43; ibid., vol. II (Part Two), 118–19).

cal force within the analogy of domestic law is to close one's eyes to the actual functions performed at the international level.[32]

The role which the Security Council, as a political organ, plays in the international legal system provides an interesting illustration of this process. Although it has no parallel in domestic law, the Security Council has played a role in international law enforcement and, more specifically, has sometimes provided the impetus for the development of the content of an international public policy through its collective responses to violations of fundamental norms, considered by it to be component parts of the security fabric. The link between the measures adopted by the Security Council in recent years and the concept of legal sanctions, more particularly the way in which Chapter VII mechanisms have been incorporated into the process of institutionalizing both State and individual criminal responsibility in international law, is examined below. This is followed by a brief review of some general international law issues arising from these operations of the Security Council, including those relating to the law/politics debate and to the question of accountability.

2. THE USE OF CHAPTER VII MECHANISMS AS LEGAL SANCTIONS

Characteristics as Legal Sanctions

The link between the Charter mechanisms for peace maintenance and the concept of legal sanction may appear to be tenuous. The purpose of enforcement action, we have classically been told, 'is not: to maintain or restore the law, but to maintain, or restore peace, which is not necessarily identical with the law'.[33] The term sanctions appears nowhere in the Charter, although it has crept into the vocabulary of Security Council resolutions and the practice of member States.

---

[32] Bruno Simma has expressed concern 'about new conceptions being grafted upon universal international law without support through, and serious attempts at, adequate institution building. It is therefore quite legitimate to ask what would happen if the concept of legal obligations in the common or public interest, which in domestic systems are being implemented through the intervention of public authority endowed with a monopoly of physical force, is left to the play of individual auto-determination of duties and self-enforcement of rights' ('Bilateralism to Community Interest', 249).

[33] See Kelsen, *Law of the United Nations*, 294; and Hans Kelsen, 'Collective Security and Collective Self-Defense under the Charter of the United Nations' (1948) 42 American Journal of International Law 783 at 788, where he stated: 'That means that the Security Council has the power to take enforcement actions even in case no obligation expressly imposed on the members has been violated, provided that the Security Council considers such action necessary for the maintenance of international peace and security.' But Kelsen advanced an alternative theory, considering that, since a forcible interference in the sphere of interests of a State—the case in respect of Articles 41 and 42—could only be permitted as a reaction against a violation of the law, then such a measure would have to be interpreted as a sanction if the Charter were to be deemed in conformity with international law. In that case any conduct to which the Council is authorized to react with enforcement action has to have the character of illegal conduct (*Law of the United Nations*, 735–7). The original draft drawn up at Dumbarton Oaks provided that enforcement action would be applied solely against a State which did not conform to a Security Council decision prescribing measures to be taken to restore international peace, and hence was in breach of a conventional obligation (Chapter VIII, B(2) and B(3)).

The mandatory decisions of the Security Council under Chapter VII, which are triggered by a determination under Article 39 that there is either a threat to or breach of the peace, or an act of aggression, are the outcome of political considerations, not legal reasoning, and nor are its proceedings subject to judicial procedures.[34] That its reactions to events can be neither automatic nor impartial is an intended result of the way its competence and powers are delimited in the Charter.

The Council was deliberately given wide discretionary powers in:

1. its determination of what constitutes a threat to the peace (which is nowhere defined). The Security Council's Summit Declaration of 31 January 1991 even acknowledged that threats to international peace and security can come from '. . . sources of instability in the economic, social, humanitarian and ecological field',[35] and a recent Security Council resolution in reaction to India and Pakistan's nuclear tests (Resolution 1172 of 1998) reiterated that 'the proliferation of all weapons of mass destruction constitutes a threat to international peace and security';

2. its choice of responses following a determination under Article 39. The Charter does not require the Security Council to match the gravity of the situation—threat to the peace, breach of the peace, or act of aggression—to a rising scale of severity of the response, since it is not *explicitly* required to adopt the measures provided for under Chapter VII in any order (these range from total inaction through recommendations, calls for provisional measures, mandatory non-forcible measures, to military force).

As a result of this selective and to a large extent arbitrary process (it may be noted that Article 1(1) of the Charter associates justice with the peaceful settlement of disputes and not with peace maintenance), the Security Council has been much under fire for going too far—as during the period immediately after the Gulf War—and for being ineffectual—as in the more depressing stages of the Bosnian conflict or of Israeli occupation of Palestinian territory.

However, a legal construction can be made of the Council's discretionary determinations under Article 39, and its resulting actions—in other words, of what are in fact random and discretionary exercises of police powers. This construction serves to illustrate the way in which law operates in the selection and transformation of political decisions into legally significant elements or acts with definitive and far-reaching legal consequences, which escape the ambit of political processes and in turn set new constraints on political action.

For it is the existence of legal mechanisms—the operation of a treaty, its formal and substantive content, its interpretation by judicial organs exercising an element of

---

[34] It does not have to insist on the production of evidence, cross-examine witnesses, or examine legal considerations in any depth, although to be fair, it has resorted to or called for fact-finding (e.g. in the case of Iraq (Res. 674 (1990)), Yugoslavia (Res. 780 (1992)), and Rwanda (Res. 935 (1994)), and, under Article 32 of the Charter, must invite States parties to the dispute if these are not members of the Council.

[35] UN Doc. S/24111 (1992).

judicial discretion (e.g. through the application of the doctrine of implied powers), and the broader legal environment within which it exists (e.g. the relation of the treaty to general international law, including imperative norms)—which encapsulates political action within a legal framework, and bestows legal authority on a political organ and normative quality on its decisions, including the attribution of legal significance to its practice (as both legal interpretation and legal development).[36]

Although the Council is not *required* to react to violations of international law, its practice—in the form of contingency decisions which are the outcomes of political activity—produces recognizable legal patterns which change the legal positions not only of States, but also of individuals, engendering legal consequences and making possible new normative expectations. In short, perturbations from outside the legal system are transformed into orderly structures that are *meaningful* to the system.

The Security Council and the Responsibility of States

A number of the Security Council resolutions adopted under Chapter VII contain all the legal elements which are familiar to international lawyers when they deal with the responsibility of States for breaches of international law: the finding of a prior breach, imputability, and the application of legal sanctions.[37]

The finding of a breach of international law and its imputability

First, the mandatory measures adopted by the Security Council under Article 41 have been, with some exceptions,[38] based not only on a finding of fact but also on one of law.[39] Determinations under Article 39 have thus been linked to alleged breaches of international law and imputed to particular legal entities, with the violation becoming a constituent element of the threat to or breach of the peace (a determination of an act of aggression being a matter of international law in any event, to which the Council so far has never resorted).

[36] See e.g. the legal significance attributed to the practice of the permanent members of the Security Council, in the matter of abstentions, by the ICJ in its *Namibia Advisory Opinion* (1971) ICJ Rep. 22. See also Eli Lauterpacht, 'The Development of the Law of International Organization by the Decisions of International Tribunals' (1976) 152 Receuil des Cours 377.

[37] For a more detailed treatment of the link between Security Council resolutions and State responsibility issues, see V. Gowlland-Debbas, *Collective Responses to Illegal Acts in International Law* (Dordrecht: Martinus Nijhoff, 1990); and V. Gowlland-Debbas, 'Security Council Enforcement Action and Issues of State Responsibility' (1994) 43 International and Comparative Law Quarterly 55.

[38] The cases of Liberia and Haiti, for example, are not so conclusive in this respect (see Res. 788 (1992) and Res. 841 (1993), respectively). Res. 1132 (1997), on the situation in Sierra Leone, is concerned with the violence, loss of life, and deteriorating humanitarian conditions following the military coup of 25 May 1997, and its objective is the restoration of the democratically elected government and a return to constitutional order.

[39] In this sense they may be said to be '[r]eactive measures applied by virtue of a decision taken by an international organization following a breach of an international obligation having serious consequences for the international community as a whole, and in particular . . . certain measures which the United Nations is empowered to adopt, under the system established by the Charter, with a view to the maintenance of international peace and security' ((1979 II) Yearbook of the International Law Commission (Part Two), 121).

Moreover, beginning with the case of Southern Rhodesia in 1966, the Council has singled out breaches of those norms that are now considered to be fundamental. The concept of international peace and security has thus acquired a meaning that extends far beyond that of collective security (envisaged as an all-out collective response to armed attack), one in which ethnic cleansing, genocide, and other gross violations of human rights, including the right to self-determination, as well as grave breaches of humanitarian law, including those encompassed within a State's own borders, are considered component parts of the security fabric. In sum, what was once relegated to the realm of peace-building (the longer-term development of conditions conducive to peace) and therefore made secondary to the Charter's main goal, such as human rights, or, again, deliberately kept outside the ambit of the Charter, such as the law of armed conflict, has now shifted in priority and forms part of the peace maintenance (and peace enforcement) function itself.

In this way, the Council's determination that the invasion and occupation of Kuwait was contrary to Iraq's obligations under the Charter was followed by a series of resolutions which referred to Iraq's additional violations of international law—ranging over human rights and humanitarian law, diplomatic immunities, environmental damage, and the depletion of natural resources—although the initial illegal act, i.e. the unlawful invasion and occupation of Kuwait, continued to serve as the basis for State responsibility in Resolution 687 of 1991.[40]

In relation to the conflict in former Yugoslavia, the Security Council reaffirmed that any taking of territory by force was unlawful and unacceptable, called on 'all parties and others concerned to respect strictly the territorial integrity of the Republic of Bosnia and Herzegovina', and affirmed 'that any entities unilaterally declared or arrangements imposed in contravention thereof will not be accepted'. Council resolutions were also punctuated by condemnations of the massive and systematic violations of human rights and fundamental freedoms, including those of ethnic minorities, and of the grave breaches of international humanitarian law, including the practice of 'ethnic cleansing' and the deliberate impeding of deliveries of food and medical supplies to the civilian population.[41]

In the Somali and Rwandan crises, both of which were clearly internal conflicts, the Council strongly condemned 'violations of international humanitarian law'. It also used the word genocide for the first time—in connection with the massacres in Rwanda.[42] As for the conflict in Kosovo, although Council concern has been triggered by the instability created in the region and the threat of intervention by neighbouring

---

[40] See e.g. SC Res. 664, 667 and 670 (1990), and 687 (1991). These refer to the 1961 and 1963 Vienna Conventions on Diplomatic and Consular Relations, condemn Iraqi treatment of third State and Kuwaiti nationals, including acts of violence, the taking of hostages, the unlawful destruction and seizure of public and private property, and other human rights violations and cite for the first time under Chapter VII, the Fourth Geneva Convention.

[41] See, *inter alia*, Res. 713, 752, 757, 770, and 787 (1992), 819, 820, and 836 (1993).

[42] See e.g. Res. 794 (1992) and 837 (1992) on Somalia, 925 and 935 (1994) on Rwanda.

States—a major security concern[43]—considerations relating to violations of fundamental principles of international law also lie at the heart of the crisis. Although the
Council stresses respect for the territorial integrity and sovereignty of the Federal
Republic of Yugoslavia, far from regarding the internal crisis as falling within that
State's domestic jurisdiction, it expresses grave concern in respect of Yugoslavia's 'excessive and indiscriminate use of force', as well as condemning acts of violence tantamount
to 'terrorism in pursuit of political goals'. It also emphasizes the 'increasing violations
of human rights and of international humanitarian law, and . . . the need to ensure that
the rights of all inhabitants of Kosovo are respected'—in short, the need to respect
minority rights—as well as reaffirming the right to return of refugees and displaced
persons.

The Council has also imputed or attributed such violations not only to State
entities (the latest being the Federal Republic of Yugoslavia for its actions in Kosovo),
but also to non-State entities, such as the white minority in Rhodesia, UNITA in
Angola, and the Bosnian Serbs. In the case of Kosovo, it '*(i)nsists* that the Kosovo
Albanian leadership condemn all terrorist action' and pursue their goals by peaceful
means only. In one curious case—that of Libya—the Council appears to make the
leap from individual to State responsibility for international terrorism (which, in
Resolution 748 of 1992, is brought within the ambit of the Charter by being linked
to Article 2(4) relating to the prohibition of the threat or use of force), through a
simple reference to a set of document numbers to which Libya is required to give a
'full and effective response'. From this may be inferred that the Council is implicitly
endorsing the position of two of its permanent members who had imputed the
actions of two Libyan suspects to Libya, in requiring Libya to accept responsibility
for the actions of what are designated as 'Libyan officials', to surrender these persons
and pay appropriate compensation.[44]

---

[43] In Res. 1160 (1998) the Council purports to act under Chapter VII, but does so in the absence
of a preliminary finding of a threat to international peace and security, contrary to an established and
consistent practice beginning with the case of Southern Rhodesia. It later makes up for this, however, in
Res. 1199 (1998).

[44] Res. 748 (1992), which refers to the institution of sanctions against Libya under Chapter VII in
case of non-compliance, states: '*Determining*, . . . that the failure by the Libyan Government to demonstrate by concrete actions its renunciation of terrorism and in particular its continued failure to respond
fully and effectively to the requests in resolution 731 (1992) constitute a threat to international peace and
security . . .' *decides* 'that the Libyan Government must now comply without any further delay with paragraph 3 of resolution 731 (1992) regarding the requests contained in documents S/23306, S/23308 and
S/23309'. Although it is clear that any accusations of Libyan responsibility would have to presume the
guilt of two individuals who had not yet been brought to trial, the United States has tried to argue that
the Council was not making such a legal judgment but acting within a larger framework, and that in any
event the public declarations of Libyan responsibility which had been made by the United States would
not be admissible before a court (see *Lockerbie Case (Preliminary Objections)*, Public sitting, 15 Oct. 1997,
CR 97/19, 18–20). For arguments that the Council's resolutions were not requiring Libya to surrender its
nationals to the US or the UK, see ibid., Professor Erik Suy, Counsel for Libya, Public sitting, 17 Oct.
1997, CR 97/21, 20–7. It should be noted that Res. 748 differs from Res. 1044 and 1054 (1996) regarding the Sudan, in which compliance with an existing extradition treaty was in issue.

Legal consequences which ensue for the sanctioned State

The measures based on the mandatory provisions of Chapter VII which follow this qualification of State and non-State acts have the effects of legal sanctions, in the sense that they deny all legal effects of the illegal acts of the State against which they are applied, and also result in the forcible temporary suspension of its subjective legal rights.

(*i*) *The sanction of nullity and non-recognition.* The Council denied statehood to the Southern Rhodesian white minority in 1965, thereby treating its evident effectiveness as irrelevant. It decided that the 'annexation of Kuwait by Iraq under any form and whatever pretext has no legal validity, and is considered null and void'. On various occasions, it has declared 'null and void' domestic acts of States, such as Decree No. 377 of the Revolution Command Council of Iraq of 16 September 1990, and even private acts of individuals, such as all property transactions made under duress in Bosnia. It has imposed a duty of collective non-recognition on States, even calling on them to ensure that their courts do not apply the laws or acts of the sanctioned entity, and to deny rights inherent in governmental status, such as the right to sue or to State immunity. This has also included, for example in the case of the Federal Republic of Yugoslavia, exclusion from international organizations or suspension from the work of certain UN organs. The Council pronounced 'that the State formerly known as the Socialist Federal Republic of Yugoslavia has ceased to exist'.[45]

These are all operations of law. They constitute legal determinations, which have what the Court has called 'operational design' in the sense of entailing definitive and far-reaching legal effects, and are aimed at the denial of legal effects to illegal acts.[46]

(*ii*) *Economic and financial measures.* The wide range of economic measures taken by the Council under Article 41—restrictions on commodities and products (including general or selective embargoes, such as on petroleum, arms, or aircraft), the freez-

---

[45] See, *inter alia*, for Southern Rhodesia: Res. 216, 217 (1965), 277 (1970), and 423 (1978); for Iraq: Res. 662, 670 (1990), 706, and 712 (1991) (in connection with petroleum and petroleum products under Iraqi title); for former Yugoslavia: Res. 777 (1992), 820, and 821 (1993). It is interesting to note in relation to the latter that the Council's endorsement of 'the principle that all statements or commitments made under duress, particularly those relating to land and property, are wholly null and void' is reflected in Annex 7 of the Dayton Peace Agreement relating to the Agreement on Refugees and Displaced Persons which, with reference to restitution of property, declares invalid 'any illegal property transaction, including any transfer that was made under duress, in exchange for exit permission or documents, or that was otherwise in connection with ethnic cleansing'.

[46] See *Namibia Advisory Opinion*, 50. In his Separate Opinion, Judge Onyeama emphasized the essentially declaratory and hence not legislative determination of the Council: 'The declaration of the illegality of the continued presence of South Africa in Namibia did not itself make such presence illegal; it was . . . a statement of the Security Council's assessment of the legal quality of the situation created by South Africa's failure to comply with the General Assembly's resolution . . . it was in fact a judicial determination' (ibid. 147). The Court also maintained that such determinations could not remain without effect under general international law, and 'were opposable to all States in the sense of barring *erga omnes* the legality of a situation which is maintained in violation of international law'. It added: 'A binding determination made by a competent organ of the United Nations to the effect that a situation is illegal cannot remain without consequence. . . . This decision entails a legal consequence, namely that of putting an end to an illegal situation.' (ibid. 56 and 54).

ing of funds, the prohibition of financial and other services, the severance of means of communication on land or sea, the banning of transhipments of commodities and products, and the seizure of modes of transport, to name a few—also constitute encroachments on State rights to engage in international trade and communications, that are normally protected under international law.[47]

Directed against abstract entities, these measures also have far-reaching effects on the populations of sanctioned States, despite the problematic Security Council practice of including so-called humanitarian exceptions (exempting, for example, medical supplies and foodstuffs 'in humanitarian circumstances').

(iii) Object and termination of sanctions. Since such findings of illegality have formed in practice a constituent part of Council determinations, it is evident that peace could not be restored without putting an end to the violation. Council resolutions have therefore included calls for the cessation of the acts in question, such as withdrawal from occupied territory, an end to violations of human rights or humanitarian law, or the renunciation of terrorism. This has resulted, however, in the creation of certain ambiguities, since the definition of a return to legality and hence the conditions for restoration of international peace have proved to be elastic. This is most evident in the case of Iraq, where a second set of objectives were grafted on to the initial objective, defined in Resolution 660 of 1990, of unconditional withdrawal of all Iraqi forces from Kuwait. This second set of objectives called for compliance with all Council resolutions, including the demands laid down in Resolution 687 of 1991.[48]

In the case of Iraq, the Council has also called for reparations. Following a determination of Iraqi liability 'for any direct loss, damage, including environmental damage and the depletion of any natural resources, or injury to foreign Governments, nationals and corporations as a result of Iraq's unlawful invasion and occupation of Kuwait' (Resolution 687 of 1991), the Council for the first time established a compensation mechanism. This mechanism serves as a comprehensive framework for dealing with Iraqi liability. It includes the creation of a fund to be financed out of a determined percentage of Iraqi oil export revenues (Resolutions 705 and 706 of 1991) and the establishment of a Compensation Commission to administer this fund.[49] This constitutes an interesting example of the institutionalization of an international mechanism for compensation which goes beyond a strictly

---

[47] For select sanctions resolutions, see Iraq: Res. 661, 670 (1990), and 1137 (1997); Yugoslavia: Res. 713 (1991), 757, 787 (1992), 820, and 942 (1993), 1160 (1998); Somalia: Res. 733 (1992); Libya: Res. 748 (1992) and 883 (1993); Liberia: Res. 788 (1992); Haiti: Res. 841 (1993); Rwanda: Res. 918 (1994); Sudan: Res. 1054 (1996); Sierra Leone: Res. 1132 (1997).

[48] See also the case of Libya, where the Security Council has periodically refused to lift sanctions on the basis of that State's refusal to conform with Council resolutions, despite Libya's numerous alternative proposals for the trial of its two nationals, including by a tribunal in The Hague. This situation may finally be in the process of being resolved (see Res. 1192 (1998)).

[49] However, unlike other claims tribunals, in which responsibility has first to be determined, the issues here are only the damage suffered by the claimant and the causal connection between this damage and the invasion and occupation of Kuwait. Res. 986 (1995), 1111, and 1129 (1997) authorize States to permit the import of specified amounts of Iraqi petroleum and petroleum products:

bilateral relationship, is defined by a political and not a judicial body,[50] and effectively amounts to the sequestration of the natural resources of a country.[51]

Security Council resolutions have also included what can only be described, in State responsibility terms, as guarantees of non-repetition—which in certain cases go beyond pre-existing legal obligations, as illustrated by the submission of Iraq, under Resolution 687, to the destruction, removal, or rendering harmless of its nuclear, chemical, and biological weapons, the 'technical' demarcation of its boundary with Kuwait, and the establishment of a demilitarized zone.

Legal consequences which ensue for implementing States

Security Council mandatory decisions, which are regulated by Article 25 of the Charter, also create duties for all member States (and arguably non-member States), thereby creating a 'vertical' relationship between these States and the organization. They thus differ from unilateral countermeasures, which are based on a right and create a 'horizontal' relationship between the States applying the countermeasures and the violating State. Moreover, they also infringe upon the subjective rights of implementing States.

Council decisions override pleas of *force majeure* or necessity from States, including the neighbours or significant trading partners of the target State, which may, as a result of sanctions, suffer disruptions to trading patterns which are far greater than those faced by the targeted State itself. The only recourse available to such States is a right to consult the Council under Article 50 of the Charter.

Council decisions—assimilated to (non-self-executing) treaty obligations—have a significant impact on domestic law. They entail complex problems of implementation, including the adaptation of legislation and even constitutions, which in some cases is made more complex by the interposition of regional organizations such as the European Union. Council decisions therefore introduce a new complexity into the traditional relationship between domestic and international law. They have extensive effects on private contractual rights since they are to be applied 'notwithstanding any contract entered into or any licence granted before the date of the resolution'. They require the exercise of control over the activities of private parties, even extraterritorially, which raises major problems today in view of the non-territorial nature of financial and other transactions. They pose problems of compatibility between domestic and international law, which may be exacerbated by conflicts of interpretation between sanctions committees and domestic courts.[52]

---

[50] P.-M. Dupuy, 'Après la guerre du golfe . . .' (1992) 96 Revue générale de droit international public 621 at 637.

[51] Michael Reisman, 'The Constitutional Crisis in the United Nations' (1993) 87 American Journal of International Law 83 at 88–9.

[52] See e.g. the decision of the Irish High Court in *Bosphorus Hava v. Minister for Transport* ((1994) 2 ILRM 551), relating to the impounding by the Irish authorities of an aircraft registered in Turkey but leased by a wholly owned Turkish company from Yugoslav Airlines. The Court, in reaching the conclusion that the Irish authorities were not empowered to impound the aircraft in the circumstances, and summarily dismissing the Sanctions Committee decision that the aircraft fell within the terms of Res. 820

Finally, sanctions resolutions affect the relationship between Charter law and other rules of international law, for they have the effect of suspending prior treaty obligations, which may be seen as amounting to a dispensation for implementing States from the performance of their obligations under other international agreements. The operation of Article 103 of the Charter, which states that: 'In the event of a conflict between the obligations of the Members of the United Nations under the present Charter and their obligations under any other international agreement, their obligations under the present Charter shall prevail', has had concrete results, such as the suspension of international agreements relating to civil aviation and trade, and the denial by the International Court of Justice of interim measures of protection to Libya.[53]

Security Council measures have also, on the basis of authorizations to States, resulted in the temporary suspension of (non-imperative) rules of customary international law.[54] Such measures as the interception, forcible search, and even arrest of third-party ships on the high seas were once characterized by a Security Council representative as 'one of the gravest and most far-reaching proposals that has been made to this Council . . . we are asked . . . to put our sanction upon what will be a rule of international law—that when this Council acts vessels on the high seas can be arrested and detained in the interest of the international law which we will be making here today . . .'. Another stated: 'Without the authority of the Security Council . . . our government has to face defiance of the United Nations with its hands tied.' The first statement was made by Arthur Goldberg, the second by Lord Caradon, both speaking in April 1966 during the debate preceding the adoption of the so-called 'Beira Resolution' (Resolution 221).[55]

(1993), stated: '[I]t is clear that the regulations are not intended to punish or penalise peoples or countries who have not in any way caused or contributed to these tragic events.' In contrast, the Court of Justice of the European Communities relied on a different teleology. It considered that the implementation by the EC of Security Council sanctions was in the pursuit of a particularly fundamental general interest of the international community, namely the ending of a state of war and of the massive violations of human rights and humanitarian law in Bosnia-Herzegovina (see Opinion of Advocate General F. V. Jacobs, delivered on 30 Apr. 1996 and Judgment of 30 July 1996, Court of Justice of the European Communities, Case C-84/95: *Bosphorus*, Reports of Cases before the Court of Justice and the Court of First Instance, Part I, Court of Justice, 1996–7, paras. 2 and 64–9. See also Judgment of 27 Feb. 1997, Case C-177/95: *Ebony Maritime*).

[53] In the *Lockerbie Case (Provisional Measures)* (Orders of 14 Apr. 1992) (1992) ICJ Rep. 1 and 113, the Court acted on the basis that the adoption of Res. 748 had had the effect of removing the object of protection—namely Libya's rights under the Montreal Convention. However, in its decision of 27 Feb. 1998 on Preliminary Objections, the Court upheld neither objections to its jurisdiction nor objections to the admissibility of the Libyan application, on the bases that: a dispute existed between the parties on the question of the interpretation and application of the Montreal Convention; the critical date for establishing both its jurisdiction and the admissibility of the Libyan application predated Res. 748; and the objection according to which the Libyan claims had been rendered without object as a result of the adoption of Res. 748 was not one of an exclusively preliminary character and would be dealt with in the merits.

[54] See e.g.: Res. 221 (1966) for Rhodesia; 665 (1990) for Iraq; 787 (1992) for Yugoslavia; 841 (1993) for Haiti.

[55] Security Council Official Records, 21st year, 1276th meeting, paras. 21, 68, and 69, respectively.

The Security Council and Individual Criminal Responsibility

The link between individual crimes and international peace and security

Security Council action under Chapter VII has also had an impact on the process of institutionalizing individual criminal responsibility. Although certain of its resolutions had earlier referred to the liability of individuals under humanitarian law,[56] this impetus has largely been due to the unprecedented creation of the two *ad hoc* international criminal tribunals for Yugoslavia and Rwanda as subsidiary organs of the Council.[57]

A link was thus established between threats to international peace and security and the core crimes giving rise to individual criminal responsibility under international law. In countering the argument that the Security Council could not create criminal liability or prosecute physical persons, the Appeals Chamber of the Yugoslavia Tribunal, in the *Tadic Case*,[58] upheld the view that the legality of its creation rested on Article 41 of the UN Charter—its establishment thus constituting one measure the Security Council could itself impose under Chapter VII (as opposed to those measures it called on member States to carry out). Justice has therefore been seen as one means of contributing to the restoration and maintenance of peace in the former Yugoslavia. The Statute of the International Criminal Court adopted in Rome in July 1998 sustains this view, stating in its preamble 'that such grave crimes threaten the peace, security and wellbeing of the world'.[59]

The relationship between the Security Council and the ICC

The Rome Statute further engages the Security Council in this process, for though it will have its own treaty basis the ICC will nevertheless have a formal relationship with the United Nations. The Statute avoids the original pitfalls and potentially wide-reaching implications for criminal law enforcement of Article 23 of the International Law Commission's Draft Statute, which had initially defined the relationship between the Security Council and the Court.[60] Nevertheless, it likewise

---

[56]   See e.g. Res. 670 and 674 (1990) on Iraq; and Res. 794 and 837 (1992) on Somalia.

[57]   Res. 808, 827 (1993), and 955 (1994), respectively.

[58]   See International Tribunal for the Prosecution of Persons Responsible for Serious Violations of International Humanitarian Law Committed in the Territory of Former Yugoslavia since 1991, *The Prosecutor v. Dusko Tadic a/k/a 'Dule'*, Decision on the Defence Motion for Interlocutory Appeal on Jurisdiction, 2 Oct. 1995, paras. 32–6.

[59]   See Rome Statute of the International Criminal Court (1998) 37 International Legal Materials 999.

[60]   Draft Statute for an International Criminal Court (1994) 33 International Legal Materials 253. Article 23, one of the most controversial, went through considerable mutations within the meetings of the Preparatory Committee established in 1995 by the General Assembly to draft a consolidated text of a convention. During the fourth session of the Preparatory Committee in Aug. 1997, several States supported alternative language for what then became Article 10 (see Preparatory Committee on the Establishment of an International Criminal Court, 16 Mar.–3 Apr. 1998, Report of the Inter-Sessional Meeting from 19 to 30 Jan. 1998 in Zutphen, The Netherlands (UN Doc.A/AC.249/1998/L.13)). See also V. Gowlland-Debbas, 'The Relationship between the Security Council and the International Criminal Court' (1998) 3 Journal of Armed Conflict Law 97.

embeds the Council's discretionary determinations under Article 39 within the Court's procedures, with potentially important implications for the legal position of individuals.

The functions of the ICC and the Council are certainly complementary. The four crimes over which the Court will now assume jurisdiction—genocide, crimes against humanity, war crimes, and aggression (Article 5(1))—are the ones which, as has been seen, are the most likely to be viewed by the Council as constituting threats to international peace and security and hence falling within its primary responsibility under the Charter. Moreover, under the Rome Statute, the Council has been given powers of referral and deferral as well as a potential role in the determination of the crime of aggression.

With regard to powers of referral, the Rome Statute retains the provision of former Article 23(1) under which the Council had the possibility of triggering the Court's exercise of jurisdiction. Under Article 13(b) of the new Statute, the Council can, acting under Chapter VII, refer to the Prosecutor 'a situation in which one or more of such crimes appears to have been committed'. In terms of the institutionalization of individual criminal responsibility, this serves to introduce a collective triggering mechanism parallel to those exercised unilaterally by States parties (Article 13(a)) or by the Prosecutor (Article 13(c)) and is intended to avoid the establishment of *ad hoc* tribunals by the Council.

It also has important implications for State consent. For in a case thus referred to the Prosecutor by the Security Council, the preconditions for the exercise of jurisdiction by the Court under Article 12, which stop short of conferring universal jurisdiction on the ICC, do not apply.[61] This allows the Council to initiate a process leading to the prosecution of individuals who have committed a crime on the territory of, or who are nationals of, States which are not parties to the Statute, in the absence of those States' consent and notwithstanding the rules on admissibility (formerly 'complementarity') which relate to investigation or prosecution under domestic law.[62] As all international lawyers know, this is a form of compulsory jurisdiction unfamiliar to international law and at variance with Chapter VI of the Charter (under which the Council can only recommend that States submit their disputes to judicial settlement by the ICJ (Article 36(3)) or other forms of settlement). Moreover, in stipulating only that the Council is acting under Chapter VII, the Statute also leaves room for a referral of a situation to the Court on the basis of a non-binding decision of the Council. This would provide an interesting Kelsenian transformation of a non-binding resolution into one having mandatory effect.

---

[61] Under the new Statute the Court has inherent jurisdiction over all of the crimes, not just genocide as was previously the case. The original State consent regime or opting-in procedure has been dropped. However, the preconditions for the exercise of jurisdiction in Article 12 stipulate that for the Court to exercise jurisdiction in a particular case, *either* the State on the territory of which the crime was committed *or* the State of which the person accused of the crime is a national must be a party to the Statute. States which are not parties to the Statute may, by means of a declaration, accept jurisdiction in respect of a particular case.   [62] See Articles 17 and 18.

Finally, it also implies that non-parties to the Statute, acting through the Security Council, could nevertheless engineer the referral of cases to it.

Seen from a voluntarist perspective, the original source of consent in the treaty-making process therefore becomes increasingly remote and complex, which makes Sir Elihu Lauterpacht's comments regarding quasi-judicial decisions of the Security Council, in his earlier inquiry into the administration of international justice, even more fitting:

[W]here do we find the consent of those affected by a quasi-judicial decision of the Security Council to the exercise by that organ of such a jurisdiction? . . . [W]e either have to identify a more remote act of consent or conclude that we are in the presence of a usurped power. Either way, it will be seen, the significance of consent—in the sense in which it has been relied upon by the ICJ and other international tribunals—is much reduced.[63]

As for the Council's power to defer investigation or prosecution, while this has been circumscribed in the Rome Statute, it nevertheless retains its potency. If adopted, Article 23(3) of the ILC Draft Statute would have constituted the most extensive reach of the Council's creeping jurisdiction in the field of international criminal law by allowing the Council, in a situation being dealt with under Chapter VII as a threat to or breach of the peace, to bar the commencement of a prosecution by the Court until the Council decided to allow it to proceed. In practice, this implied the potential power of a permanent member of the Council to obstruct the Court without temporal limitation, as the open-ended nature of the sanctions adopted against Iraq well illustrate, and in respect of any of the crimes within the Court's jurisdiction, since any of these have been or could be linked to Council determinations under Article 39. Yet while there is a certain logic to the veto power for enforcement action under the Charter, for such action could not realistically be launched against one of the permanent members, the same logic applied to the prosecution of individuals would have seriously called into question the principle of equality of individuals before the law—a fundamental principle of criminal justice — by serving to shield certain individuals from the administration of justice by the Court.

However, this provision has substantially been altered as a result of a proposal by Singapore, combined with a Canadian amendment. Article 16 of the Rome Statute states: 'No investigation or prosecution may be commenced or proceeded with under this Statute for a period of 12 months after the Security Council, in a resolution adopted under Chapter VII of the Charter of the United Nations, has requested the Court to that effect; that request may be renewed by the Council under the same conditions.' The situation has therefore been reversed, for now the Security Council must act affirmatively on the basis of a resolution requesting the Court to defer its investigation, which would mean having to obtain the consensus of all five permanent

---

[63] Eli Lauterpacht, *Aspects of the Administration of International Justice* (Cambridge: Grotius, 1991), 46. This concern was also expressed by States during the Rome Conference. See e.g. the explanation of vote by the Indian representative following the adoption of the Statute on 17 July 1998 (www.un.org/icc).

members of the Council in any effort to block the Court. Moreover, the temporal time limit—although subject to renewal—acts as an additional safeguard. Since the resolution is one adopted under Chapter VII, there must presumably be a prior determination under Article 39, the prerequisite for any action. This leads to speculation as to what would then have to constitute the threat to or breach of the peace—the situation itself or the Court's commencement of an investigation into the commission of a crime? Could justice be seen here as undermining security?

These safeguards have attenuated some of the concerns expressed in Rome, that the previous provisions considerably undermined the independence of the Court by allowing for extensive control by a political organ. Yet as was clearly stated by several delegations on a number of occasions, the Statute itself cannot affect the powers of the Council under the Charter,[64] which include the power to override the Statute. The Council, were it to adopt a mandatory resolution under Chapter VII, could still, by virtue of the operation of Article 103 of the Charter, bypass existing treaty mechanisms for the prosecution of individuals.

The ILC Draft Statute would also have required the prior determination by the Security Council, acting under Article 39 of the Charter, of an act of aggression by a *State*, before a complaint regarding an individual act of aggression could be brought before the Court (Article 23(2)). At the Rome conference, the controversy surrounding the crime of aggression was finally resolved by means of a compromise (Article 5(2)). Aggression continues to figure as a core crime, but this is dependent on a legal definition being subsequently incorporated into the Statute, along the same lines as the other Statute crimes and setting out the conditions for the exercise of the Court's jurisdiction in respect of it. Such a provision is to be adopted through an amendment process seven years after the entry into force of the treaty.[65] Article 5(2) does not refer to the Security Council but does state that '[s]uch a provision shall be consistent with the relevant provisions of the Charter of the United Nations'.

In an explanation of vote, the United States expressed the view that the Statute must recognize the role of the Security Council in determining that aggression has been committed, and that no State party could derogate from the powers of the Security Council, under the Charter, in respect of the maintenance of international peace and security. The United Kingdom also declared that Article 5(2) would be interpreted as meaning that the Security Council should make a prior determination of aggression.[66] But if the term 'relevant provisions of the Charter' were interpreted in this way, as granting exclusive responsibility to the Council in making such a determination, this would not avoid the serious problems raised in the original Draft Statute because there is no watertight division between State and individual responsi-

---

[64] This is not the same thing as saying, as the United States has done, that the Statute cannot purport to set temporal limitations on Security Council resolutions. The treaty parties are at liberty to agree on the conditions for the deferral of the exercise of the Court's jurisdiction; they are not thereby imposing conditions on the Council itself. So long as the Council does not meet these conditions—which it obviously is at liberty to do—the Court is not constrained in its exercise of jurisdiction.

[65] See Articles 121 and 123.

[66] See explanations of vote following the adoption of the Statute (www.un.org/icc).

bility. Were the Council to have exclusive responsibility to determine that a State had committed an act of aggression and were this finding to be authoritative for, and non-reviewable by, the Court, this could have the effect, for instance, of depriving a head of State or other high official of the presumption of innocence or a legal defence such as a claim of self-defence. Security Council determinations under Article 39 of the Charter would therefore have a serious impact on the legal position of an individual brought before the Court. Moreover, through this exclusive prerogative, the Council would effectively control access to the Court in so far as aggression was concerned.

In practice, however, the Security Council has not yet made a finding of an act of aggression (not even in respect of the Iraqi invasion of Kuwait). Moreover, when it has on occasion expressed concern over acts of States which it has qualified as aggressive, it has not done so as part of a formal determination under Article 39 which could serve as a clear-cut basis for ICC action. For example, it branded as aggressive only the acts of violence against diplomatic missions and their personnel in Kuwait (Resolution 667 of 1990) and simply stated that 'the *acts of aggression* of the Southern Rhodesian illegal regime against neighbouring independent States constituted *a threat to international peace and security*' (italics added) (Resolution 445 of 1979). This ambiguous language would make it very difficult for the Court to rely on such a finding.[67]

Moreover, the reference to 'the relevant provisions of the Charter' in Article 5(2) of the Rome Statute clearly must be interpreted in the light of United Nations practice. It is true that the Security Council has a certain priority under the UN Charter in respect of the qualification of aggression and its consequences.[68] However, as the International Court of Justice has classically stated, primary does not mean exclusive responsibility in matters of international peace and security. The General Assembly has itself assumed the competence to define aggression (admittedly without author-itative force), and the ICJ, another principal organ of the United Nations, has not considered itself debarred from a case in which aggression was alleged, which means that it can also reach its own separate qualification of such acts, even after a deter-mination has been reached by the Council under Article 39.[69]

---

[67] This has led the judges on the Yugoslavia Tribunal, consulted on the ILC Draft Statute, to state: 'It does not seem necessary to provide that the court defer to the Security Council on the subject of aggres-sion, the effect of which would be to give the Security Council, and in particular the permanent members, exclusive rights of definition over the term "aggression", making it the "mouth of the oracle" for this cate-gory of crimes. The Tribunal's judges respectfully suggest that this would be an undesirable outcome.' (See Ad Hoc Committee on the Establishment of an International Criminal Court, 3–13 Apr. 1995, Comments received pursuant to paragraph 4 of General Assembly Resolution 49/53 on the Establishment of an International Criminal Court, Report of the Secretary-General (UN Doc. A/AC.244/1, 20 Mar. 1995), 30.)

[68] See the ILC's commentaries to Articles 20(b) and 23(c) of its Draft Statute ((1994 II) Yearbook of the International Law Commission (Part Two), 38–9 and 44–5), and Article 16 of the Draft Code of Crimes against the Peace and Security of Mankind (General Assembly Official Records, 48th Sess., suppl. no. 10 (A/51/10, pp. 83–5)).

[69] See *Nicaragua Case (Jurisdiction & Admissibility)* (1984) ICJ Rep. 432, and Dissenting Opinion of Judge Schwebel, *Nicaragua Case (Merits)* (1986) ICJ Rep. 287–93, who pointed out that nothing in the Charter or *travaux préparatoires* supports the view that it was the intent of the drafters of the Charter to vest the determination of acts of aggression exclusively in the Security Council.

The Security Council and the Development of the Content of an International Public Policy

It is important to underline that the Council's resolutions are not legislative in the sense of applying outside the framework of particular cases of restoration of international peace and security. Moreover, they cannot—by analogy with General Assembly resolutions—be said to reflect either *opinio juris*, that subjective element said to be essential as evidence for the existence of customary international law, nor the generality of the requisite State practice. Yet it is undeniable that the cumulative actions of the Security Council under Chapter VII—the reflection of post-Cold War political jostling and readjustment in the pursuit of particular interests—in instituting collective responses to situations involving breaches of fundamental norms of international law have nevertheless had an impact on the shaping of an international public policy.

While it is not possible to give an in-depth exposé of this development within the context of this chapter, it is evident that core norms of human rights, humanitarian law, and international criminal law have been affected through the impetus provided by Security Council activities.[70] Council condemnation, *inter alia*, of violations of the right to self-determination, of ethnic cleansing or genocide, and of grave breaches of the Geneva Conventions, as well as the legal consequences which have ensued, have served to underline, if not to reinforce, the existing minimum content of an international public policy.

However, the Council's resolutions in the field of international peace and security have also promoted the progressive development of international law. The establishment of judicial tribunals by this political organ has had important implications for the international legal system, leading through the operation of a judicial process (which includes the interpretation of rules in the light of underlying or implicit axiological or teleological criteria) to the development not only of the procedural aspects of international criminal law, but also of its content. The Yugoslavia Tribunal's pronouncements in the *Tadic Case* regarding the extension to internal armed conflicts of the general rules and principles applicable to international conflicts, the violations of which entail criminal responsibility, served to crystallize the development of customary international law in this field.[71] Such a legal process, along with condemnations by the Security Council of, *inter alia*, attacks on UN personnel in time of armed conflict (followed by the adoption by the General Assembly of the 1994 Convention on the Safety of United Nations and Associated Personnel), or the

---

[70] See e.g. Laurence Boisson de Chazournes, 'Les Résolutions des organes des Nations Unies, et en particulier celles du Conseil de sécurité, en tant que source du droit international humanitaire', in Luigi Condorelli, Anne-Marie la Rosa, and Sylvie Scherrer (eds.), *Les Nations Unies et le droit international humanitaire/The United Nations and International Humanitarian Law* (Paris: Pedone, 1996), 149–73.

[71] *Tadic Case*, paras. 96–136.

affirmation that rape is a crime against humanity falling within the jurisdiction of the two *ad hoc* tribunals, subsequently fed into the Rome Statute of the ICC as part of the content of core crimes.[72]

There are, needless to say, many risks involved in developing international law through a process that includes the *ad hoc* and piecemeal reactions of a political organ to particular crises, particularly in respect of the coherence of international law. Yet is this any different from the process by which law ingests the haphazard practice of States, giving it legal relevance only under certain conditions defined by the legal system?

3. THE LEGAL CONSTRAINTS TO POLITICAL ACTION AND THE QUESTION OF ACCOUNTABILITY

It was asserted at the beginning of this chapter that the emergence of the concept of community interests logically calls for the development, within the international legal system, of centralized, institutional mechanisms to ensure that responses to violations of obligations owed to the international community as a whole are collective, coherent, and operate across the board.

However, in the process of drawing legal consequences from the distinction between delict and crime, the recent work of the International Law Commission has drifted away from Ago's initial conception. Since the Draft Articles cannot purport to affect the centralized machinery of the UN Charter, they have centred on the *entitlement* of the injured State (and this extends, in accordance with Article 40(3), to every single State of the international community) to react *uti singuli* to the commission of crimes. Moreover, such entitlement covers not only all the allowable reactions to violations of delicts but, in addition, is not subject to certain of the limitations imposed on claims for reparation (restitution and satisfaction).[73] In short, in the words of James Crawford, the current Special Rapporteur, they '[a]llow

---

[72] See Rome Statute of the International Criminal Court, Articles 7(1)(g) (on rape as a crime against humanity); 8(2)(biii and eiii) and 8(2)(bxxii and evi) (on attacks against UN and associated personnel and the commission of rape, respectively, as war crimes both in international and internal armed conflicts).

[73] In accordance with Article 52(a), the entitlement of injured States in the case of an international crime to restitution is not subject to the limitations of Articles 43(c) and (d) relating to proportionality and to the political independence or economic stability of the State, while Article 52(b) removes the limitations under Article 45(3) in regard to demands for satisfaction which would impair the dignity of the State which has committed the internationally wrongful act. As to the possibility of taking countermeasures under Articles 47–50, no distinction is drawn between States injured by crimes and other injured States. As Crawford points out, the ILC had previously rejected '[t]his "least common denominator" approach to international crimes . . . the "delicts plus" approach . . .'. For Crawford, however, 'It is not the case that responses to the most serious breaches are the exclusive prerogative of international organisations, in particular the Security Council. States, acting in solidarity with those most directly injured, also have a role.' See First Report on State Responsibility, ILC 50th sess., 1998, A/CN.4/490/Add.3, 10.

for reactions by individual States acting without regard to the position of the international community as a whole'.[74]

It should be said in passing that addressing this issue would not inexorably require killing Article 19, and it would be inconceivable for the Draft Articles not to reflect this emerging hierarchy among primary norms. However, while not excluding unilateral measures as the consequences of such crimes, it would seem that the Draft Articles should emphasize the obligations, rather than the entitlements, of all States to react within strictly defined limits, and in complement with collective measures, to such breaches.[75] At the same time, it is clear that the development of centralized responses to violations of norms of concern to the international community as a whole can only lie outside an eventual treaty on State responsibility.

The use made of collective mechanisms in the institutionalization of such responses within the international legal system brings us back to our initial discussion on the relationship between legal and political systems. This does not only include the process whereby the international legal system selects and transforms random political 'noise' into normative order, as was seen in relation to the Security Council's role in the unsystematic and diffused efforts to forge an international public policy. It also includes the process of legally constraining political activity within a binary system that operates by qualifying acts as 'legal' or 'illegal'. Seen in our context, this raises the problem of the application of principles of accountability and legal responsibility to the activities of a political organ of the United Nations. Indeed, following its recent heavy-handed sanctions policy, the Security Council has been the focus of a major controversy over its legitimacy and the outer limits of its powers and competence. Two major issues have been debated, the first of which relates to the existence of legal constraints on Security Council action, and the second to that of third-party scrutiny of its activities.

The Normative Constraints

Effectiveness and legitimacy

The operations of the Security Council serve to illustrate the broader debate on the interplay between political and legal systems, including the relationship between fact and law. This raises that classical problem which Sir Hersch Lauterpacht once evoked in terms of the perennial tension between 'effectiveness' and 'legitimacy'.[76]

Viewed from a political perspective, the composition and procedural voting requirements of the Council, as embedded in the Charter, reflect the realities of the

---

[74]   Ibid., A/CN.4/490/Add.1, 9.

[75]   These minimum obligations of States in all cases of international crimes are spelled out in Article 53(a–d). It will be recalled that the ICJ has underlined not a right, but a *duty*, of third States under customary international law to react to breaches of certain fundamental obligations. See *Namibia Advisory Opinion*, 55–6, and *Nicaragua Case (Merits)*, 114.

[76]   Sir Hersch Lauterpacht, *Recognition in International Law* (London: Cambridge University Press, 1947), 426–7, 431.

postwar world of 1945. Within that machinery, one of the permanent members has come, in the immediate post-Cold War world, to play a dominant—though recently not entirely decisive—role in the Council's decision-making. Seen from the perspective of the international legal system, however, a particular institutionalization of power relations engenders far-reaching legal consequences for State and individual rights. Far from negating the normative quality of international law, this constitutes part of its normal operation: the incorporation of State political will or other manifestations of effectiveness, such as reprisals or military occupation, into legal processes. In short, what may be viewed as power or effectiveness from one systemic perspective may, when viewed from another perspective, paradoxically be seen to contribute to the reaffirmation of legal norms and the strengthening of a legal edifice. For this reception of fact into law (though not of any fact, since the legal system resists the incorporation of certain facts) encapsulates fact in a legal straitjacket, conditions it, and leads to the generation of new law, thereby adding to the increasing complexity and sophistication of the system. This process may be seen to operate in several ways.

First, it is not unusual to incorporate security concerns into international legal instruments, that is, to give normative meaning—however vague—to *political* perceptions of threats, such as the determination of a threat to, or breach of, the peace under Article 39 of the Charter. Human rights instruments contain similar provisions, such as references to 'reasonable grounds for regarding as a danger to the security of the country concerned', to 'public order', or to a 'public emergency threatening the life of the nation'. Such provisions grant a broad margin of discretion to political authorities—the fact continuing to buzz within the law, so to speak.[77]

However, that this so-called 'margin of appreciation' of States in evaluating threats to security or public order is, nevertheless, conditioned has been frequently reiterated. The European Court of Human Rights, while recognizing that the European Convention of Human Rights leaves the contracting parties a degree of discretion, has stated with reference to the emergency powers of States:

It falls in the first place to each Contracting State, with its responsibility for 'the life of [its] nation', to determine whether that life is threatened by a 'public emergency' and, if so, how far it is necessary to go in attempting to overcome the emergency. By reason of their direct and continuous contact with the pressing needs of the moment, the national authorities are in principle in a better position than the international judge to decide both on the presence of such an emergency and on the nature and scope of derogations necessary to avert it . . . Nevertheless, the States do not enjoy an unlimited power in this respect. The Court . . . is empowered to rule on whether the States have gone beyond the 'extent strictly required by the

---

[77] See Kerchove and Ost, *Système juridique*, 161: 'Ce qui, du point de vue du droit, apparaît comme désordre extérieur, n'est que partiellement ordonné par le biais de la qualification (l'encodage) et le traitement juridiques: le fait continue à "vrombir" au sein de la machinerie juridique, lui assurant cet élément de désordre dont il a besoin pour survivre et progresser.'

exigencies' of the crisis . . . The domestic margin of appreciation is thus accompanied by a European supervision.[78]

Second, discretionary policy, once institutionalized, is no longer subject to discretionary change, as the Uniting for Peace mechanism once illustrated. More recently, this has been clearly demonstrated by the fact that not even the United States was able to terminate the Security Council's mandatory arms embargo against Bosnia, in the face of the lack of requisite consensus. For similar reasons, the United States was unable to use the Council's machinery for institutionalized reactions to Iraq's refusal to allow inspection of its sites, and felt compelled to resort to unilateral measures, in other words, to act outside the system.

Third, the law may, however, also refuse to acknowledge the facts. This may of course create a fictional gap between fact and law—for example the refusal to recognize entities or situations despite their evident effectiveness, or the creation of symbolic tribunals with the obvious incapacity to override sovereign barriers. However, it is precisely through the creation of such fictions that the legal system, by rejecting or refusing to give effect to effectiveness, or by providing alternatives to those offered by the international environment, contributes to its own autonomy and hence effectiveness. On occasion, this has also served to erode the effectiveness of the factual situation itself. For law has a variety of purposes, some of which may be instrumental, and some of which may be purely symbolic.[79]

The legal limits to the political activities of the Security Council

Seen from the perspective of the legal system, the Security Council's authority emanates from the Charter. It is by virtue of an operation of law, not of fact, that the member States agree to carry out the Council's decisions and to subject their international agreements to the overriding effects of the Charter. But as a result, the political activities of the Council, as well as those of its members, also remain subject to that treaty's legal constraints. As the International Court of Justice once stated, the 'political character of an organ cannot release it from the observance of the treaty provisions established by the Charter when they constitute limitations on its powers or criteria for its judgment'.[80] The Charter sets limits not only on the Council's margin of discretion in qualifying a situation, but also on its decision on the measures to be applied.

It has consistently been reiterated that the Charter stipulates both the procedural

---

[78] *Case of Ireland v. The United Kingdom*, ECHR, Series A, Vol. 25, para. 207. See also Michael Bothe, 'Les Limites des pouvoirs du Conseil de sécurité', in *The Development of the Role of the Security Council* (Dordrecht: Martinus Nijhoff, 1993), 67–81 at 70.

[79] See Kerchove and Ost, *Système juridique*, 163. It was undoubtedly the duty of collective nonrecognition imposed by the Security Council which, by refusing to acknowledge the evident effectiveness of the situation created by the unilateral declaration of independence of Southern Rhodesia, served to undermine that very effectiveness and bring Southern Rhodesia closer to a solution than otherwise would have been possible had it been admitted to UN membership under white minority domination in 1965.

[80] *Admission of a State to Membership in the United Nations (Advisory Opinion)* (1948) ICJ Reports 64.

(e.g. the voting provisions of Article 27) and substantive limits on the Council's action (e.g. Articles 24(2) and 25), i.e. the organization's purposes and principles. Articles 1(1) and 2 of the Charter reflect the underlying ideological strata as it existed in 1945. But by virtue of a dynamic interpretation carried out by a judicial operation, these purposes may now be read within the framework of the contemporary legal system, including its contemporary ideological content. The purposes of the UN thus not only underline the primary goal of peace maintenance, but also reflect human rights, humanitarian, economic, and social concerns—as they exist today. The human rights component, for example, includes recently emphasized economic, social, and cultural rights, such as the right to food, to health, and to a decent standard of living.

It is in this sense that General Comment No. 8, adopted by the Committee on Economic, Social and Cultural Rights in 1997, reminds the permanent members of the Security Council of their joint and several responsibilities, by contending that the provisions of the Covenant remain applicable even if a decision has been taken to impose sanctions:

7. . . . Just as the international community insists that any targeted State must respect the civil and political rights of its citizens, so too must that State and the international community itself do everything possible to protect at least the core content of the economic, social and cultural rights of the affected peoples of that State . . .
8. While this obligation of every State is derived from the commitment in the United Nations Charter to promote respect for all human rights, it should also be recalled that every Permanent Member of the Security Council has signed the Covenant, although two (China and the United States) have yet to ratify it . . .

However, as a matter of treaty law, UN member States are not necessarily barred from doing collectively, on the basis of a Security Council decision, what they are prohibited from doing as parties to a treaty. It can be argued that Article 103 of the Charter serves to override the provisions of any international agreement, including human rights treaties (and hence even the non derogable rights contained therein), with the exception of those that have attained the status of *jus cogens*, as well as to exonerate implementing States from responsibility for treaty breaches. This results from the normal operation of the law of treaties, and possibly State responsibility.[81] However, to the extent that such human rights treaties have been acknowledged as having a special status in international law inasmuch as they embody an objective and common purpose, or because core human rights may be said to give effect to the broad purposes of the United Nations or contribute to the content of an international public policy, then they do effectively set teleological limits on Council action.

Moreover, the rules governing treaty law also govern the Charter's relationship with rules of customary international law, including peremptory norms from which

---

[81] See Article 30(1) of the 1969 Vienna Convention on the Law of Treaties, and (1979 II) Yearbook of the International Law Commission (Part Two), 119; ibid., vol. II (Part One), 43–4.

treaties may not derogate, as well as its relationship with general principles of law such as the concept of abuse of rights or the principle of good faith.

The proliferation of sanctions measures adopted by the Security Council has resulted in numerous proposals and pressures from diverse sources. The General Assembly has renewed efforts to render the Council accountable and has initiated discussion within subsidiary organs, including the Special Committee on the Charter of the United Nations and the Sixth Committee, on particular issues of concern arising from the application of sanctions.[82] The Committee on Economic, Social and Cultural Rights has made a number of proposals in its General Comment No. 8 for ensuring that such rights are taken fully into account when designing sanctions regimes. Other subsidiary organs, such as UNICEF, specialized agencies such as WHO, or non-governmental organizations such as the International Committee of the Red Cross, have also underlined the limits set by the human rights and humanitarian law framework.[83]

The Articulation of the Relationship between Political and Judicial Organs

It may be inferred from the discussion above that the Security Council remains legally responsible for overstepping these constraints, for legal obligations suppose legal accountability. In the *Lockerbie Case (Preliminary Objections)*, Judge *ad hoc* Sir

[82] See e.g. GA Res. 51/193 in which it '[e]ncourages the Security Council to provide special reports in accordance with Articles 15 and 24 of the Charter', and GA Res. 49/58, 50/51, 50/58E, and 51/208, inviting an examination of the special economic problems confronting States in carrying out sanctions, under Article 50 of the Charter. This has led to a series of reports, such as from the Secretary-General and Special Committee on the Charter of the United Nations and on the Strengthening of the Role of the Organization, on means of improving the mechanisms and criteria concerning the implementation and lifting of sanctions (see e.g. A/50/361, A/50/423, and A/51/356).

[83] See studies and reports by the following agencies: United Nations Department on Humanitarian Affairs: Report by Claudia von Braunmühl and Manfred Kulessa, *The Impact of UN Sanctions on Humanitarian Assistance Activities* (Berlin, Dec. 1995); World Health Organisation: *The Health Conditions of the Population in Iraq Since the Gulf Crisis* (WHO/EHA/96.1, Mar. 1996); UNICEF: *Impact of Reduction in Food Ration on the Most Vulnerable Children and Women* (Baghdad, Oct. 1994); *Iraq Country Situation Report* (Baghdad, Sept. 1996); Erik Hoskins, *A Study of UNICEF's Perspective on Sanctions*, 1997. See also the work of the Inter-Agency Standing Committee on the Humanitarian Impact of Sanctions established pursuant to General Assembly Resolution 46/182 and which includes representatives of United Nations organizations and intergovernmental and non-governmental organizations active in humanitarian assistance operations (e.g. its Statement to the Security Council on the humanitarian impact of sanctions (S/1998/147, 23 Feb. 1998)).

It is also interesting to note that, apparently under pressure from the ICRC, Res. 666 (1990), in singling out the need to pay particular attention to the more vulnerable categories of civilians, i.e. children under 15 years of age, expectant mothers, maternity cases, the sick and the elderly, brought the earlier Res. 661 imposing sanctions on Iraq into line with the 1949 Geneva Conventions. The Human Rights Commission, however, has been reluctant to consider the implications for human rights of United Nations actions, deciding 'to avoid making judgements on issues that are within the responsibility of other United Nations' bodies . . .' (Decision 1995/107, 3 Mar. 1995, Commission on Human Rights, Report on the Fifty-First Session, 291) (see Claire Palley, 'Legal Issues Arising from Conflicts between UN Humanitarian and Political Mandates—a Survey', in V. Gowlland-Debbas (ed.), *The Problem of Refugees in the Light of Contemporary International Law Issues* (The Hague: Martinus Nijhoff, 1996), 145–68.

Robert Jennings, who dissented strongly from the rest of the Court's conclusions concerning jurisdiction and admissibility, nevertheless stated:

The first principle of the applicable law is this: that all discretionary powers of lawful decision-making are necessarily derived from the law, and are therefore governed and qualified by the law. This must be so if only because the sole authority of such decisions flows itself from the law. It is not logically possible to claim to represent the power and authority of the law, and at the same time, claim to be above the law . . . I therefore wholly agree with the Libyan argument that the Security Council decisions and actions should in no wise be regarded as enjoying some sort of 'immunity' from the jurisdiction of the principal judicial organ of the United Nations; though I ought perhaps to add that the United Kingdom argument made no such claim.

It remains the case that the existence of legal constraints on the activities of political organs is independent of the question as to whether there is third-party review of such activities. Although it may eventually (though traditionally not necessarily) be open for the judge or arbitrator to challenge a State's qualification of another State's act as illegal as a prior condition for the application of countermeasures, as well as the measures adopted in response,[84] the question of whether the Security Council as a political organ is subject to judicial review has been hotly debated. While none of the parties in the *Lockerbie Case (Preliminary Objections)* denied that the powers of the Security Council were defined and limited by law, it was the extent of the ICJ's competence to inquire into Council resolutions that was at issue.

The search for applicable constitutional and legal restraints on the Security Council also involves, therefore, an examination of the relationship between political and judicial organs. How, indeed, can the relationship between the Security Council and the ICJ, or, for that matter, the *ad hoc* criminal tribunals, be articulated?

One approach taken in numerous cases by the ICJ in rejecting contentions that certain disputes are inherently political, and that it therefore cannot assume concurrent jurisdiction over a matter currently before the Security Council, has been to state: 'The Council has functions of a political nature assigned to it, whereas the Court exercises purely judicial functions. Both organs can therefore perform their separate but complementary functions with respect to the same events.'[85]

However, this view that there is a clear division of functions between the Court and the Council along the lines of a political/legal dichotomy is not really tenable. As we have already seen, in the majority of cases in which it has acted under the mandatory provisions of Chapter VII, the Council has clearly been operating not

---

[84] Judicial settlement procedures in relation to *unilateral* countermeasures by States may be invoked as an alternative to such measures or as a means of pre-empting them (Libya's intention in the *Lockerbie Case*), in parallel (*Hostages Case*), or after the event in order to assess the legality of measures taken (*Corfu Channel Case*). See G. Arangio-Ruiz, 'Fifth Report on State Responsibility' (A/CN.4/453 and Add. 1). The adoption of countermeasures has been linked to dispute-settlement mechanisms in the Draft Articles on State Responsibility (see Article 48 and section 3).

[85] *Lockerbie Case (Provisional Measures)*, Declaration of Judge Ni at 22 and 134, citing *Nicaragua Case (Jurisdiction & Admissibility)*, 434–5, para. 95.

within a political, but a legal framework. It has linked its determinations under Article 39 to a finding that a State (or non-State entity in some cases) has breached a fundamental international obligation. Such determinations have been followed by measures which have temporarily divested States and individuals of legal rights, with definitive legal effect and extensive legal consequences.

The distinction between Court and Council, therefore, is not a distinction between judicial and political bodies, but between two distinct instrumental processes offered by the *legal* system for attaining much the same ends, i.e. a return to a situation of legality through peaceful settlement procedures on the one hand, and institutionalized sanctions on the other. At the same time, the Council, in reacting to violations of fundamental norms of international law, is not acting as an impartial arbitrator or third party (i.e. as a court would act) but in lieu and place of the injured States in matters which affect the interests of the international community as a whole.

This means, on the one hand, that the Council's decisions may come to have a direct legal impact on the judicial outcome in a particular case over which both bodies have concurrent jurisdiction, even at times rendering impossible a judicial solution on the part of the Court—as was pointed out in the *Lockerbie Case*.[86] On the other hand, it does also indicate that there is and has to be room for third-party control of the Council's legal activities.

I have discussed elsewhere the question of judicial review and will not go through the arguments here.[87] It is clear that the Charter does not provide for judicial review of the acts of political organs, in the sense of an automatic and established procedure similar to the ones we find in some legal systems. The ICJ itself has quite clearly stated:

In the legal systems of States, there is often some procedure for determining the validity of even a legislative or governmental act, but no analogous procedure is to be found in the structure of the United Nations. Proposals made during the drafting of the Charter to place the *ultimate authority* to interpret the Charter in the International Court of Justice were not accepted.[88]

However, this has not prevented challenges to the exercise of the Council's broad powers being brought incidentally before judicial organs. Moreover, although judicial review as an automatic procedure was rejected at San Francisco, this was not considered as debarring member States from bringing questions involving Charter interpretation, as with any other treaty, before the ICJ.[89]

---

[86]   Ibid., and Dissenting Opinion of Judge Bedjaoui, 44 and 154.

[87]   V. Gowlland-Debbas, 'The Relationship between the International Court of Justice and the Security Council in the Light of the *Lockerbie* Case' (1994) 88 American Journal of International Law 643.

[88]   *Expenses Case* (1962) ICJ Rep. 168 (emphasis added). See ibid. 661–73.

[89]   'If two member States are at variance concerning the correct interpretation of the Charter, they are of course free to submit the dispute to the International Court of Justice as in the case of any other treaty' (UNCIO, Doc. 933, IV/2/42 (2) of 12 June 1945, *Documents*, xiii. 709).

The relationship between the Council and one of its own creations—the Yugoslavia Tribunal—was questioned in the *Tadic Case*, while that between the Council and the ICJ lies at the heart of the *Lockerbie Case*.[90] So far, neither tribunal has challenged the Security Council's innovative use of its powers. The ICJ rejected Libya's application for provisional measures to protect its rights under the Montreal Convention on the basis that these could no longer be regarded as 'appropriate for protection' following the adoption of a mandatory Chapter VII resolution (Resolution 748 of 1992) and as a result of the operation of Article 103 of the Charter. The Appeals Chamber of the Yugoslavia Tribunal justified its own creation on the basis of the implied powers of the Security Council, under Article 41, to create a judicial body in the exercise of its primary responsibility for maintaining international peace and security.

Yet neither Tribunal rejected its own competence to inquire into the validity of Security Council resolutions. The Yugoslavia Tribunal, drawing on its inherent judicial powers, refused to regard itself exclusively as a 'subsidiary organ' of the Security Council—'a "creation" totally fashioned to the smallest detail by its "creator" and remaining totally in its power and at its mercy'.[91]

As for the ICJ in its decision in the *Lockerbie Case (Preliminary Objections)*, it has asserted its jurisdiction to try the case on its merits. Its task as guardian of UN legality appears to have been acknowledged by all the parties concerned, for, as Judge *ad hoc* Sir Robert Jennings reminds us, its task must involve 'declaring, interpreting, applying and protecting the law of the United Nations'. This must surely imply that it is not debarred from scrutinizing the resolutions of the political organs in order to ascertain whether they are in conformity with the Charter.

What appears to be more controversial is whether the Court may question the discretionary competence of the Council, under Article 39, to decide that a threat to the peace exists, as well as the measures to be followed. It has been argued that such discretionary decisions are similar to an act of State, that they arise from a political decision that is not justiciable. Oscar Schachter, Counsel for the United States in the *Lockerbie Case*, in distinguishing between interpretation and application of a legal rule by the Court, on the one hand, and assertions of a power of judicial control that would annul Security Council decisions, on the other, stated:

However, such exercise of the Court's judicial role is critically different from the claim made by Libya in this case—a claim directed against the Council's exercise of its discretionary authority to determine that a situation is a threat to the peace and that enforcement measures under Chapter VII should be imposed. The non-reviewable authority of the Council in this

---

[90] *Tadic Case* and *Lockerbie Case (Provisional Measures)* and *(Preliminary Objections)*. The decision of the Court on the merits is now pending.

[91] *Tadic Case*, 7–9. It is true, of course, as the Tribunal goes on to say, that such inherent judicial powers as the principle of 'compétence de la compétence' can be limited by an express (though not inferred) provision in the Tribunal's constitutive instrument. However, it was the view of the Tribunal that 'the latter possibility is controversial, particularly where the limitation risks undermining the judicial character or the independence of the Tribunal'.

case is not against or outside of the law. It is grounded in the Charter itself and the obligations based on the Charter . . . we submit that in this case the Court would furnish a legal solution by applying the governing rule of law—namely the mandatory effect of the Security Council decision taken under Chapter VII. Surely there is no impairment of the judicial function or disregard of the rule of law in the Court's determining that the law of the Charter applies to the Council's decision. The Court would then be fulfilling its judicial function consonant with the rule of law.[92]

However, though it may be true that the qualification in itself cannot be questioned *as a basis for the Council's actions under Chapter VII in the fulfilment of its own functions*, there is no reason to suppose that the ICJ could not exercise its right to protect the law of the Charter should the finding itself or the choice of measures be patently contrary to the procedural or substantive requirements of the Charter, to the principle of good faith, or to peremptory norms. Moreover, to the extent that such qualifications have been linked to findings of breaches of fundamental norms, then these secondary findings can only be declaratory and not constitutive of the legal situation. Finally, a determination of an act of aggression is clearly a matter of international law and, as was explained above, the ICJ has not considered itself debarred from making such a finding. It is therefore difficult to maintain the view that these legal findings fall exclusively within the discretion of the Council. It would seem that here, again, there is nothing to prevent judicial organs from coming to a different conclusion in regard to the legal responsibilities of States, of individuals, or of the Security Council itself, in the normal judicial process of applying general and conventional rules of international law to particular cases.

There have been concerns that judicial scrutiny of the activities of a political organ that is entrusted with primary responsibility for policing emergency situations would only serve to erode its effectiveness. This is why, it has been pointed out, the Council cannot be concerned with justice when it is exercising such a function. Eric Suy, Counsel for Libya in the *Lockerbie Case*, argued that this reasoning does not hold where the Council is, under the guise of Chapter VII, deciding on the merits of a dispute.[93] We can go even further in stating that, in view of the extensive role the Security Council is presently playing in the formulation and enforcement of norms considered fundamental to the international community as a whole (a role which goes far beyond its traditional policing role), and in view of the serious, long-term impact its decisions have on the rights of States, populations, and individuals, as well as on the development of the legal system as a whole, the notion that its powers cannot be subjected to some form of third-party scrutiny, whether judicial or political, would be totally inimical to the legal system's implicit rules and future development.

The diffuse and unsystematic efforts that are being made to shape a role for the Security Council in the new international legal system must, therefore, go hand in

---

[92] *Lockerbie Case (Preliminary Objections)*, Public sitting, 15 Oct. 1997, CR 97/19, 29.
[93] Ibid., 17 Oct. 1977, CR 97/21, 28–9.

hand with efforts to delineate the constitutional and general international law limits to its powers, as well as to devise a means of control.

4. CONCLUSION

This chapter does not purport to reach overarching conclusions, or to suggest that there is only one theoretical approach to the interaction between law and society. Theories of the international legal system, whether indigenous or borrowed from other disciplines, are useful in casting new light on traditional problems. They do not help us to transcend our inevitable position of the visually impaired groping around the elephant—if indeed an elephant there is—in our efforts to define the absolute from hermetic perspectives.

If emphasis has been placed on the role of the Security Council in international law enforcement, this is not meant to obscure its numerous other functions which have expressly (such as the peaceful settlement of disputes) or through implication (such as peacekeeping) been bestowed upon that political organ by the Charter in the fulfilment of its primary function, or to intimate that its sanctioning function is of overriding significance.

This focus has only served to illustrate some interesting mechanisms of interaction between the international legal system and its environment and to underline that the reception of politics into law or the role played by law in politics is not a simple matter of the effects of the one on the other. The way these mechanisms operate counters simplistic assertions that manifestations of power in the political arena are transported unmodified into the legal system, thus serving to weaken its autonomy. The negotiations in Rome which resulted in the adoption of the Statute of the International Criminal Court showed how a process originating from the dominant role played by some permanent members within the Security Council could develop a momentum of its own once initiated into the legal system, and have a final result which could not be foreseen or forestalled even by the Council's most prominent member. The transformation of random 'disturbance' emanating from the political environment can thus, through the operation of legal mechanisms, contribute to increasing the coherence and complexity of the international legal system—in other words, produce order from disorder. Moreover, the law can also resist and refuse to give effect to certain facts.

Focusing on the practice of the Security Council in law enforcement (as scholars once focused on Assembly resolutions in law development) also illustrates how a political organ can contribute to the evolution of the international legal system, albeit in an unsystematic and largely unconscious fashion. This evolution points to the gradual emergence of what may be called an 'international public policy'. But it also raises the question of the part which sanctions should play within this development, for there is no intimation here that sanctions are the *essence* of either legal norm or legal system, or that the law's effectiveness can only be achieved through law enforcement.

On the one hand, the development of the concept of fundamental community norms logically calls for centralized and institutionalized mechanisms to ensure their respect and enforcement. This logic comes not from the application of domestic analogies, but from the need, in a heterogeneous world, to avoid unilateral decisions regarding community interests. Moreover, in view of the pivotal role given to the Security Council in recent times, not only under the Charter but also under certain multilateral treaties, it would appear to be impractical to deny the Council any role at all in the forging of a future public policy. To argue that in the absence of third-party judicial mechanisms there can be no centralization of the international legal system is to transfer domestic concepts to the international plane through a process of analogy which first, perceives international law from a negative perspective—all that it is not—and second, fails to see the process that is actually there.

On the other hand, this does raise essential questions concerning the sanctioning mechanism itself. In his *Agenda for Peace*, Boutros Boutros-Ghali, the former Secretary-General of the United Nations, declared: 'Sanctions, as is generally recognized, are a blunt instrument. They raise the ethical question of whether suffering inflicted on vulnerable groups in the target country is a legitimate means of exerting pressure on political leaders whose behavior is unlikely to be affected by the plight of their subjects.' This has led to a number of debates in various fora over targeting and 'fine-tuning' sanctions, and even over whether prolonged economic sanctions are not a greater evil than the use of military force (with euphemisms such as 'surgical strikes' and 'collateral damage' thrown into the debate for good measure).

Beyond the question of substantive limits to sanctions measures, however, is that of conditioning resort to sanctions, as well as that of accountability. The trend in international law has been to limit and condition the exercise of unilateral counter-measures; similar efforts should now be directed to formulating the outer boundaries of collective responses, particularly in view of their far-reaching effects, and to the acceptance of some form of third-party scrutiny. It would not be in keeping with contemporary developments for States to escape the conditions imposed on unilateral measures by hiding behind the corporate veil. Moreover, if the Security Council's actions can in part be contained within the legal system, its authority must also derive from that system. Authority is, unlike power, derived from notions of legitimacy, so that legitimacy may also be said to be an important part of its effectiveness.

Developments in international law enforcement have also taken off in another direction, in moving towards the institutionalization of individual criminal responsibility. This pierces another corporate veil: the fiction of the monolithic State and the traditional position that it is responsible for all acts committed within its territory. This is a development that, in certain cases, may well be preferable to holding entire populations accountable for the acts of their leaders, as the International Military Tribunal at Nuremberg recognized some time ago.

But in the final analysis, no legal system can depend on coercion alone. Sanctions, therefore, have to be seen within the context of the international legal system as a whole. As Georges Abi-Saab envisions, sanctions as coercion should only be the final resort of a legal system, while the concept of sanctions in its broader meaning, as an attribute of the system (and not the norm), 'recouvrirait l'ensemble des garanties et moyens dont dispose le système juridique pour assurer sa cohérence et son intégrité normatives, c'est-à-dire la conformité du comportement social avec ses règles'.[94]

Sanctions constitute one of the *formal* functions of the legal system, part of the secondary rules that Hart has evoked. But as was stated at the beginning of this chapter, the legal system is not just form but also substance, containing underlying teleological and axiological rules. While I have not evoked the relationship between legal and moral or ethical systems, the notion of justice in its different forms and manifestations—whether formal or distributive—has been received into the legal system itself, and, whether as part of the underlying implicit rules or in its expressed manifestations in legal instruments, has been used to temper the application of rules or as an aid in choosing between conflicting norms. Although references to justice within the Charter were kept separate from the peace maintenance function, the Council's enforcement of norms which can be termed humanitarian (in the broad sense) as well as ethical have resulted, in the longer term, not only in modifications of the legal position of States, but also in changed legal expectations. As a result, the Council's actions cannot, without falling into contradictions, continue to be based on the premiss that security concerns must prevail over longer-term considerations of justice, or encroach on the very values that its practice has served to promote. Moreover, the shift from longer-term so-called 'peace building' to day-to-day 'peace maintenance', from participation by a representative organ in the development of international law to that of an élitist organ in the enforcement of international law, must not obscure the fact that the development of an international public policy requires the participation of, and recognition by, that essential legal construct called 'the international community as a whole'.

---

[94] Abi-Saab, 'Cour général de droit international public', 276–7.

15

The Limits of the Security Council's Powers and its Functions in the International Legal System: Some Reflections

GEORG NOLTE*

1. INTRODUCTION

Once upon a time a nation was led to believe that its own qualities were superior to those of all other nations. It therefore felt justified in attempting to occupy other nations. These other nations, however, allied together and defeated the aggressor. Then, in order to prevent such a disturbance reoccurring, the allied nations created an institution and endowed it with the necessary powers. The largest of the allied nations was particularly concerned about the preservation of world peace. It was convinced that *its* qualities, if adopted by all the others, would guarantee peace and security in the world. It therefore put pressure on the other allies to use the powers of the institution to that end. One of the allies, however, objected. Its Minister of Foreign Affairs said:

In this Alliance, as in all other human arrangements, nothing is more likely to impair, or even destroy its real utility, than any attempt to push its duties and its obligations beyond the sphere which its original conception and understood principles will warrant. It was a Union for the re-conquest and liberation of a great proportion of the continent of Europe from . . . military dominion ; and having subdued the conqueror, it took the state of possession, as estab lished by the peace, under the protection of the Alliance. It never was, however, intended as a Union for the government of the World, or for the Superintendence of the Internal Affairs of other States.

This statement was not made after the Second World War, nor even after the First World War. It is contained in the famous note of the British Foreign Minister Lord Castlereagh, of May 1820, in which he objected to the practice and claims of the Holy Alliance.[1] It can perhaps serve as a useful reminder today, because the practice

* I wish to thank Eyal Benvenisti and Nico Krisch for helpful comments. All mistakes are my own.
[1] Georg Friedrich von Martens, *Supplément au Recueil des Principaux Traités* (Goettingen, 1828), x. 177 f.: 'Dans cette alliance, comme dans tous les autres arrangements humains, rien n'est plus propre à altérer, ou même à détruire son utilité réelle que toute tendance pour étendre ses devoirs et ses obligations au delà de la sphère marquée par les idées et les principes bien connus qui ont présidé à sa formation. Ce fut une union pour reconquérir et délivrer une grande partie du continent de l'Europe de la domination militaire de la France: après avoir abattu le conquérant elle mit l'état de choses établie par la paix sous la protection de l'alliance; mais on entendit jamais en faire une autorité suprème pour le gouvernement du monde, ou pour la surintendance des affaires intérieures des autres états . . .'

of the Security Council since about 1990 raises not only the question of the nature of the Council's functions in the international legal system, but also whether that system sets any limits on its actions.

2. THE POWERS OF THE COUNCIL AND THE LIMITS OF SUCH POWERS

The Security Council has, since 1990, interpreted its powers under the UN Charter very broadly.[2] It is an ominous sign that the Council, in Resolution 1160 of 31 March 1998 concerning Kosovo, for the first time dispensed with declaring that the application of its powers under Chapter VII was based on a determination that the specific situation constituted a threat to the peace. The British government was conscientious enough to insist, in a statement before the Council, that such a determination was implied in the Resolution.[3] However, one permanent member, the Russian Federation, while voting in favour of the resolution under Chapter VII, declared that the situation under consideration did not constitute a threat to the peace.[4] It is submitted that if a majority of the Council's members expressed such a view before passing a Chapter VII resolution, that resolution would be a clear example of an *ultra vires* act.

Most commentators today agree that the Council 'must, in the first place at least',[5] determine its own jurisdiction and that it possesses a wide, but not unlimited, margin of appreciation in determining whether a situation constitutes a threat to the peace.[6] The International Court of Justice has been careful *not* to declare that the Council is the authentic or exclusive interpreter of its own powers,[7] while the Appeals Chamber of the International Criminal Tribunal for the Former Yugoslavia insisted, in the *Tadic Case*, that 'the Security Council is an organ of an international organization, established by a treaty which serves as a constitutional framework for that organization' and that 'the Security Council is thus subjected to certain constitutional limitations, however broad its powers under the constitution may be'.[8]

Since language is a social construct an 'authentic' interpreter may attribute any

---

[2] See e.g. Thomas M. Franck, *Fairness in International Law and Institutions* (Oxford: Clarendon, 1995), 218 ff.; Martti Koskenniemi, 'The Police in the Temple—Order, Justice and the UN: A Dialectical View' (1995) 6 European Journal of International Law 325–48.

[3] UN Doc. S/PV.3868, at 12.   [4] UN Doc. S/PV.3868, at 10.

[5] *Certain Expenses of the United Nations (Advisory Opinion)* (1962) ICJ Rep. 151 at 168.

[6] Matthias Herdegen, *Die Befugnisse des UN-Sicherheitsrates—Aufgeklärter Absolutismus im Völkerrecht?* (Heidelberg: Müller, 1998), at 9 f.

[7] *Case Concerning Questions of Interpretation and Application of the 1971 Montreal Convention Arising from the Aerial Incident at Lockerbie (Libyan Arab Jamahiriya v. United Kingdom) (Libyan Arab Jamahiriya v. United States)*, Judgment of 27 Feb. 1998 (Preliminary Objections), (1998) ICJ Rep. 115, http://www.icj-cij.org; *Certain Expenses of the United Nations (Advisory Opinion)* (1962) ICJ Rep. 151 at 162 f.

[8] *Prosecutor v. Dusko Tadic a/k/a 'Dule'*, Decision of 2 Oct. 1995 on the Defence Motion for Interlocutory Appeal on Jurisdiction, ICTY, Judicial Reports 1994–1995, vol. I (The Hague: Kluwer, 1999), 381, at no. 28, http://www.un.org/icty.

meaning to any particular combination of letters. Despite suggestions to the contrary in the early days of the Charter,[9] it seems to be agreed today that the Security Council cannot legitimately supplant all other decision-making competences on the basis of a Kelsenian positivism or, if you will, 'decisionism'. Words are supposed to carry meaning and meaning is ultimately determined by 'shared understandings',[10] that is, on the basis of a discussion by the community as a whole. This elementary principle is confirmed in the requirement of Article 24 of the Charter, according to which the Security Council shall act in accordance with the Purposes and Principles of the United Nations.[11]

Marc Perrin de Brichambaut appears to share this view. He acknowledges that there are limits to the powers of the Council.[12] However, his statement that, 'if the Council believes that ... [the lack of punishment] represents a threat to international peace and security, nothing prevents it from using' Article 29 of the Charter[13] suggests that he considers those limits to be of mere theoretical and not much practical significance. The same is true of his distinction between 'law' or 'sources of law' on the one hand (which the Security Council cannot create), and 'norms' or 'rights and obligations' on the other (which the Security Council can create).[14] At first glance, this appears to leave international law in place as the framework for Security Council action. But this distinction can also be interpreted as a careful reiteration of Kelsen's position, according to which the Council would be empowered to pursue justice if it considered the existing law to be unsatisfactory, and thus to enforce a decision which it considered to be just even if it was not in conformity with existing law.[15] The adoption of this approach by an influential legal practitioner is prudently ambiguous, but leads me to add a few reflections on the limits of Security Council's powers and its functions in the international legal system.

3. JUDICIAL DETERMINATION

If words like 'threat to the peace' or 'principles and purposes of the United Nations' do have meaning and if the Security Council cannot in all cases finally and exclusively determine this meaning, then who can? The *Lockerbie Case*[16] provoked international lawyers into evaluating the proposition that the International Court of

---

[9] United Nations Conference on International Organization (London/New York, 1945), xii. 505: 'The Committee ... decided ... to leave to the Council the entire discretion as to what constitutes a threat to the peace, a breach of the peace or an act of aggression.'

[10] See Friedrich Kratochwil, p. 68; Michael Byers, *Custom, Power and the Power of Rules* (Cambridge: Cambridge University Press, 1999).   [11] See *Tadic Case*, at no. 28.

[12] Perrin de Brichambaut, pp. 297 and 303.   [13] Ibid. 300.

[14] Ibid. 297 and 302.

[15] Hans Kelsen, *The Law of the United Nations* (London: Stevens & Sons, 1950), 295.

[16] See n. 7.

Justice could or should be the 'ultimate guardian of UN legality'.[17] Although the *Lockerbie Case* certainly raises a point of great significance, it is nevertheless a secondary issue from the perspective of the international legal and political system as a whole. For the foreseeable future, the question whether the International Court of Justice can exercise (incidental) jurisdiction over a given dispute must remain fortuitous. It is even possible that a judgment by the Court declaring a Security Council resolution *ultra vires* would be disregarded by the Council. Such disregard would put the international system into far greater jeopardy than if the question of the lawfulness of Security Council action remained unresolved. This is true of both preventive and retroactive exercises of jurisdiction. More attention, therefore, should be paid to the role of individual UN member States, acting alone or within a representative group of other member States, as the possible ultimate interpreters of the legality of Security Council action.

4. DETERMINATION BY STATES

If the Security Council is not the exclusive interpreter of its own powers (and if there is no competent judicial organ), a residual power to determine the legality of Security Council action rests with the international community and individual member States of the UN.[18] The question, therefore, is not *whether* States may challenge the validity or legality of Security Council action, but under what circumstances they may do so. It may even be possible to reach agreement on an abstract formula such as a requirement that there be a 'manifest contradiction with the Principles and Purposes of the Charter'.[19] Of course, such a formula cannot prevent disagreement about what constitutes a 'manifest contradiction' in a particular situation and what the legal consequences of such a determination would be.[20] Such disagreement, however, cannot be excluded once it is admitted that the powers of the Security Council are not absolute or exclusively a matter for the Council itself to determine.

It is possible that a set of criteria will be developed from State practice. In this process much will depend on the perception States hold of the development of the international system, the given demands for security, self-determination, and other fundamental international values. I assume, however, that one important factor in this process will be the correlation between the degree of questioning which occurs

---

[17] See, *inter alia*, Thomas M. Franck, 'The "Powers of Appreciation": Who is the Ultimate Guardian of UN Legality?' (1992) 86 American Journal of International Law 519; Mohammed Bedjaoui, *Nouvel Ordre mondial et contrôle de la légalité des actes du conseil de sécurité* (Brussels: Bruylant, 1994); Matthias Herdegen, 'The "Constitutionalization" of the UN Security System' (1994) 27 Vanderbilt Journal of International Law 135; Jose E. Alvarez, 'Judging the Security Council' (1996) 90 American Journal of International Law 1; Peter H. F. Bekker, 'Case note concerning the decision of the International Court of Justice, 27 February 1998, (Libyan Arab Jamahiriya v. United Kingdom and Libyan Arab Jamahiriya v. United States)' (1998) 92 American Journal of International Law 503.

[18] Herdegen, 'Constitutionalization', 158 f.   [19] *Tadic Case*, at no. 22.
[20] Herdegen, 'Constitutionalization', at 149.

of the validity or legality of Security Council action on the one hand, and the frequency of unilateral interpretations of Security Council action on the other.[21] The question whether Resolution 678 provides a basis for the use of force against Iraq in response to violations of Resolution 687 must, in the absence of another decision by the Council, be determined by the traditional means of dialogue within the community of member States.[22] A similar kind of question can be said to arise when a *bona fide* case is made that the Security Council has manifestly overstepped its wide 'scope of manœuvre'.[23] From a formal point of view, both questions raise the issue whether a particular act (bombing of Iraq, Security Council action) is in conformity with the applicable legal rule (Security Council resolution(s), UN Charter). It is true that the first case concerns only the interpretation of a Security Council resolution whereas the second also concerns its legality or validity. This difference, however, is not crucial if the yardstick is conformity of actions with the Charter (regardless of whether they are determined by different standards of review). A possible objection to this formalistic view is that the danger to the integrity of the UN system of collective security is much greater if the legality or validity of Security Council action is questioned by individual States than if there are mere differences over the interpretation of such action. This objection, however, is itself rather formalistic. It probably underestimates the disintegrative effect of unilateral invocations of Security Council resolutions for the purpose of legitimizing the unilateral use of force and overstates the dangers of a legal argument that is tailored to exclude the possibility of its abuse ('manifest contradiction with the Principles and Purposes of the Charter'). Therefore, in both cases much depends on the preservation of 'shared understandings', i.e. how a representative group of States interprets the Charter and individual Security Council resolutions.

Originally, it may have been inconceivable that a group of States challenging the legality or validity of a particular Security Council action could arguably be more representative of the community of all member States than a group supporting a Security Council resolution. Such a situation is no longer inconceivable. The longer a resolution is in force, the greater the likelihood that a representative group of States will challenge its legality or validity. For example, the longer the arms embargo against the Bosnian Muslims was maintained, the greater the possibility that challenges to the legality or validity of that Security Council action would be brought by a group of States which was, arguably, more representative than the group which continued to stand behind the Security Council resolution.[24] The Iraq crises of February/March and November/December 1998 have shown that sometimes only a small minority of States seriously continues to assert

---

[21] See Jochen A. Frowein, 'Unilateral Interpretation of Security Council Resolutions—A Threat to Collective Security?', in Volkmar Götz, Peter Selmer, and Rüdiger Wolfrum (eds.), *Liber amicorum Günther Jaenicke* (Berlin: Springer, 1998), 97.
[22] See Christian Tomuschat, 'Using Force Against Iraq' (1997) 73 Friedenswarte 75.
[23] Brichambaut, p. 298.
[24] See GA Res. 48/88 of 20 Dec. 1993, at paras. 17 and 18.

that a long-standing authorization under Chapter VII has remained valid or been 'revived'.[25]

Challenges to the legality or validity of Security Council decisions do not necessarily emanate from the political branches of government alone. They can also emanate from national courts, since not every judiciary accepts the domestic implementation of Security Council resolutions as determinative 'actes du gouvernement'.[26] The German Constitutional Court, for example, has held that the application of European Community legislation that is manifestly *ultra vires* would be unconstitutional and might therefore be declared inoperative in Germany.[27] This judgment can be criticized as violating EC law which possesses its own system of judicial review.[28] National courts should not, however, have difficulty applying a similar reasoning to measures designed to implement Security Council resolutions which 'manifestly contradict' the principles and purposes of the Charter. The same is true of international courts such as the European Court of Human Rights which must ensure that member States of the Council of Europe do not support or participate in violations of fundamental human rights (which may, for example, be caused by economic embargoes leading to mass starvation).[29]

5. INHERENT LIMITS OF THE COUNCIL'S FUNCTIONS

To insist that the Security Council is not the ultimate and exclusive interpreter of its powers is not to deny the important role that the Council plays in the international legal system. Indeed, there can be no doubt that the Council is a law-making body in so far as its decisions are binding. Those decisions are only binding, however, if the Security Council has acted within its powers. There are two types of possible limits to Council action, one being substantive, the other formal.

5.1. Substantive Limits

Matthias Herdegen has recently suggested a number of substantive limits to Security Council action.[30] He asserts that the Council may only act to counter threats to very important international values, in particular to the physical integrity of persons, but

---

[25] Statements by the USA and UK in the Security Council on 16 Dec. 1998, S/PV.3955, at 7 and 10.   [26] Brichambaut, p. 303.

[27] BVerfGE 89, 155 at 188 (Maastricht) (English translation in (1994) 98 International Law Reports 196).

[28] Jochen A. Frowein, 'Das Maastricht-Urteil und die Grenzen der Verfassungsgerichtsbarkeit' (1994) 54 Zeitschrift für ausländisches öffentliches Recht und Völkerrecht 1 at 8 seq.; Wolfgang Graf Vitzthum, 'Gemeinschaftsgericht und Verfassungsgericht—rechtsvergleichende Aspekte' (1998) 53(4) Juristenzeitung 161.

[29] See, *mutatis mutandis*, ECHR Ser. A, no. 161, Judgment of 7 July 1989 (*Soering v. United Kingdom*), at paras. 86–91.

[30] Herdegen, *Befugnisse*, 15 and 'Constitutionalization', 156 f.

not, for example, to protect the proper functioning of a democratic system. He accepts that the Council may take measures against violations of basic human rights occurring during an internal conflict but insists that, in the absence of such aggravating factors, it may not prohibit a government from suppressing an insurrection. Finally, he contends that the Council must itself respect the *ius in bello* and the principle of proportionality and that it may not order a State to defer to the higher interests of world peace. Vera Gowlland-Debbas has also drawn up a list of rules and principles which the Council may not violate.[31] Both authors suggest a balance is needed between the powers of the Security Council to undertake an 'authoritative concretization' of its own powers and the most basic rights of States and individuals.[32] I have doubts whether substantive approaches at this level of abstraction can lead very far and whether they will stand the test of time. In any specific instance, there may be a number of reasons why the suppression of an insurrection (one that does not involve human rights violations and does not threaten to spill over international borders) may nevertheless constitute a 'threat to the peace' or why it is necessary for the preservation of international peace to obey, for example, a domestic rule of democratic succession. Abstract categorization is helpful for a prima-facie assessment of the issues at stake but it cannot preclude the Council correctly determining in specific instances that a 'threat to the peace' is present. Therefore, the point at which an excessive use by the Security Council of its powers becomes manifest[33] must be determined by reference to all the factors of the specific case—with the possible exception of the authorization of measures which on the face of it constitute violations of international humanitarian law.

5.2. Formal Limits

It may be more fruitful to concentrate on the formal limits to Security Council action. It is true that domestic concepts of separation of powers cannot and should not easily be projected into the United Nations system.[34] Nevertheless, however far one goes towards accepting that the Council has a power of 'authoritative concretization', it may not, I submit, overstep two limits that are inherent in its function: Security Council law must remain preliminary[35] and situation specific. Even Kelsen only went so far as to assert that a Council decision might create new law for a concrete case.[36] For example, the Council could one day be confronted with demands to enact, under Chapter VII, general rules concerning weapons of mass destruction or the protection of the environment.[37] Such demands might seek justification in the International

---

[31] Vera Gowlland-Debbas.   [32] Herdegen, *Befugnisse*, 23.
[33] Herdegen, 'Constitutionalization', 158.
[34] W. Michael Riesman, 'The Constitutional Crisis in the United Nations' (1993) 87 American Journal of International Law 83 at 83 f.; Herdegen, *Befugnisse*, 25.
[35] See section 6 below.   [36] Kelsen, *Law of the United Nations*, 259.
[37] Christian Tomuschat, 'Obligations Arising for States Without or Against Their Will' (1993 IV) Recueil de Cours 195 at 344–6.

Court's *Namibia Advisory Opinion* according to which the binding force of Security Council resolutions is not restricted to measures taken under Chapter VII.[38] If this argument were accepted, however, the Security Council could then establish itself as a world legislator, a role for which it was not designed.[39]

This is not to say that the International Criminal Tribunals for the Former Yugoslavia and Rwanda or the United Nations Compensation Commission could not have been created because their decisions are final. Instead, the point is that the Security Council could not have acted itself as a criminal court[40] or compensation commission. It is, however, accepted in international law that some organs can create technically subsidiary organs having the power to perform tasks which the delegating organ would not have the power to perform itself.[41] Such exceptions to the classical maxim that no organ can transfer powers it does not itself possess can be justified if the particular subsidiary organ is endowed with a minimum degree of independence and if it operates with the necessary procedural safeguards. The creation of such subsidiary organs has become an important function of the Security Council. However, it must remain limited by the requirement that the work of a subsidiary organ be related to a specific case or situation. The demarcation of the border between Kuwait and Iraq is arguably the most questionable case of this kind, since the Security Council there achieved a result which traditionally would have been a matter for inter-State negotiations or international legal or adjudicatory procedures. In that case, however, the Council did not purport to change the boundary: it asserted only the power to determine facts by means of a subsidiary organ operating according to regular procedures.[42] Ultimately, therefore, the Boundary Commission has exercised essentially the same kind of powers as are exercised by other subsidiary organs.

6. DETERMINATION OF RESPONSIBILITY

Vera Gowlland-Debbas suggests that the Council performs a useful and accepted task in imputing responsibility to States and other actors. It is true that the Council

---

[38] (1971) ICJ Rep. 12, at 52 f. (paras. 110 and 114); Rosalyn Higgins, 'The Advisory Opinion on Namibia: Which UN Resolutions are Binding Under Article 25 of the Charter?' (1972) 21 International and Comparative Law Quarterly 270 at 286; Bernd Martenczuk, *Rechtsbindung und Rechtskontrolle des Weltsicherheitsrats* (Berlin: Duncker and Humblot, 1996) at 38 n. 44.

[39] Brichambaut, p. 297.

[40] The US Senate exercises its (quasi-)judicial power of impeachment on the basis of an express authorization contained in the United States Constitution.

[41] Danesh Sarooshi, 'The Legal Framework Governing United Nations Subsidiary Organs' (1996) 57 British Yearbook of International Law 413 at 425 f. with reference to the *Administrative Tribunal Case* (1954) ICJ Rep. 47.

[42] See UN Doc. S/25811 of 21 May 1993 (Final Report on the Demarcation of the International Boundary Between the Republic of Iraq and the State of Kuwait by the United Nations Iraq–Kuwait Boundary Demarcation Commission) (reproduced in Richard Schofield, *The Iraq-Kuwait Dispute: 1830–1994* (Slough: Archive Editions, 1994), 839).

has the power to impute responsibility, but again, this is limited to the extent that it is necessary for the exercise of its other powers. Even domestic police forces (which have far lesser powers 'to conclusively attribute responsibility') have the power and the duty to make a prima-facie evaluation of the legal situation and to act on the basis of that evaluation. Domestic police forces also make preliminary determinations regardless of the relative importance of the legal values at stake in a given situation. And even domestic police forces must give reasons for their actions taken to protect a particular legal interest. It should not therefore come as a surprise if the Security Council determines, for example, that a particular State is an aggressor and that measures are to be taken against it. However, it is quite another question whether the Council may determine that a particular State or person has committed the crime of aggression (or genocide) for the purposes of a criminal conviction or the final adjudication of damages. In the preparatory work leading up to the adoption of the Rome Statute for a Permanent International Criminal Court the United States proposed that 'the determination of the Security Council that a State has committed an act of aggression shall be binding on the deliberation of the Court in respect of a complaint, the subject matter of which is the act of aggression'.[43] It is difficult to imagine a clearer case of an assumption of the final decision-making power that compromises the judicial function. On the other hand, a power on the part of the Security Council to initiate or block a prosecution for aggression constitutes a traditional executive function in which considerations of public order play a legitimate role, and the allocation of such a power under the Rome Statute should satisfy both American and British concerns.[44]

Regardless of whether the Council has the power to attribute responsibility for purposes which lie beyond its own (preliminary) function, one should be careful not to infer too great an intention on its part conclusively to attribute responsibility in any of its decisions. When the Council states, for example, that violations of humanitarian law or excessive or indiscriminate uses of force have occurred, this is not necessarily a statement that is meant to be determinative for any type of legal proceedings. It is more reasonable to assume that such wording merely serves to justify why the Council took action. When the Council determines that Iraq shall not pay more than 30 per cent of the annual value of its exports of petroleum and petroleum products as compensation, this does not constitute a final determination of the amount of compensation due.[45] When the Council determines the conditions of the inspection regime with which Iraq must comply, it neither attributes international legal responsibility in the classical sense nor grants itself quasi-judicial powers.[46] Rather, it merely imposes an innovative coercive measure to restore international peace and security.

Nevertheless, there remain cases where the Council expressly declares an activity

---

[43] Art. 10(23), A/AC.249/1998/CRP.8 of 2 Apr. 1998, at 25.
[44] Gowlland-Debbas, p. 323.   [45] But see ibid. 320.
[46] But see Brichambaut, p. 301.

or situation to be 'illegal' or 'null and void', or where it obliges States not to recognize such a situation. In these cases the Council seems to do more than just impose a temporary settlement. Rather than simply dealing with the matter, it seems to consider that its determination is final. A closer look, however, reveals that what the Council is doing in such cases is merely asserting what the situation is under general international law and invoking the binding effect of that law, while at the same time imposing a (temporary) sanction. True, this operation is hard to distinguish from a regular attribution of responsibility. The difference, however, is that the invocation of general international law may be erroneous and that an international tribunal or a group of States may assert correctly that the Security Council erred in its decision. To some, this conclusion may appear too 'binary' or simplistic.[47] However, Vera Gowlland-Debbas's distinction between 'declaratory' determinations by the Council, on the one hand, and 'constitutive' determinations by tribunals, on the other,[48] may incur the misunderstanding that both kinds of determinations can legally coexist even if they engender different conclusions. The same misunderstanding can arise from her view that the distinction between the Court and the Council is (merely) that between two 'processes offered by the legal system for attaining much the same ends, i.e. a return to a situation of legality through peaceful settlement procedures on the one hand, and institutionalized sanctions on the other'.[49] These processes are not equivalent: one is preliminary, the other is final.

7. THE ROLE OF THE COUNCIL IN LAW CREATION AND INTERPRETATION

The law-making role of the Security Council is not limited to the exercise of its powers under Chapter VII. In principle, the Council can, like the General Assembly, contribute to the process of law creation within the community of States. The Council can thereby influence the process of customary international law and the process of subsequent authentic interpretation of the Charter. Vera Gowlland-Debbas provides examples where the Council has contributed to the development of customary international law, especially in the field of humanitarian law.[50] It is true that the Council does not influence this development in any 'legislative' sense but by 'cumulative actions' which reflect changes in the *opinio iuris* of the community of States. It should be borne in mind, however, that the members of the Security Council usually act under time constraints and are preoccupied with specific situations. These are not merely incidental and factual constraints on the contributions of the Council to the development of international law. Security Council action is linked, by definition, to concrete circumstances and the presumption is that it does not purport to influence the existing law beyond the scope of these circumstances. I would not, therefore, adopt Marc Perrin de Brichambaut's formulation that Security

---

[47] Gowlland-Debbas, p. 335.   [48] Ibid. 336.   [49] Ibid. 336.
[50] Ibid. 316.

Council resolutions can have an effect that is similar to that of the General Assembly's Friendly Relations Declaration 'provided that their subject-matter is not restricted to particular circumstances'.[51] Given the limited number of its members, even a unanimous resolution of the Council must receive more explicit acceptance as law than a unanimous resolution of the General Assembly.

An essential difference is whether one asserts that the Council may, as an authentic interpreter of its own powers, declare certain situations to be a threat to the peace, or whether, by declaring such situations to be a threat to the peace, it has submitted an 'innovative' interpretation of its own powers to the community of States which has in turn accepted or acquiesced in this new understanding of the Charter. So far, the Council's assertion of its expanded powers has met with little determined resistance and much official approval. There are signs, however, that this trend may not continue. If this is the case, the community of States is not reduced to the role of the sorcerer's apprentice who lost control of what he had brought to life.

The role of the Security Council in the process of customary international law is not, however, limited to giving impulses to the evolution of rules through its decisions. The Council also absorbs possible impulses by States. The use of force in 1998 by Nigerian and ECOWAS troops in Sierra Leone, by which a military coup was reversed and the democratically elected government reinstated, serves as an example in support of this proposition. There was no prior Security Council authorization for Nigeria or ECOWAS. However, after the operation the Council, in a Presidential Statement, commended the ECOWAS States for their efforts in achieving a peaceful resolution of the crisis.[52] What does this case stand as a precedent for? I submit that the Council could not and did not formally authorize the use of force after the event.[53] Thus, the Presidential Statement was, at best, an opinion as to the legality of the ECOWAS action. It could simply have constituted applause for the result, it could also have signalled approval of the means used. But if it constituted approval, on what grounds did the members of the Security Council consider the action justified? Did they recognize a right to restore democratically elected regimes, did they recognize a right to conduct humanitarian interventions, or did they just accept the invitation by the deposed government as the sole justification?[54]

If the Security Council were not expected to act or comment in such situations, States would probably formulate more clearly and openly their own respective positions as to the legality of such uses of force. One of the effects of Security Council activity is therefore to absorb—or diminish the intensity of—debates among States as to the legality of certain uses of force. This makes it more difficult for international

---

[51] Brichambaudt. [52] S/PRST/1998/5, 26 Feb. 1998.

[53] But see Christian Walter, *Vereinte Nationen und Regionalorganisationen* (Berlin: Springer, 1996), at 291 f.

[54] Georg Nolte, *Eingreifen auf Finladung (Intervention upon Invitation)—Zur volkerrechtlichen Zulässigkeit des Einsatzes fremder Truppen im internen Konflikt auf Einladung der Regierung (Use of Force by Foreign Troops in Internal Conflicts at the Invitation of a Government under International Law) (English Summary)* (Berlin: Springer, 1999), 425.

lawyers to assess State practice and expressions of *opinio iuris* in certain areas of customary or Charter law. From a political perspective, however, this effect of Security Council activity should not be deplored. After all, it must be desirable for an institution to work as a catalyst to create agreement and to make fruitless debates about the legality of certain actions unnecessary. However, if it is no longer clear what the participants in the discussion have agreed (or disagreed) upon, general international law is in danger of becoming either blurred or ossified.

8. CONCLUSION

For centuries the defining feature of international law has been the lack of central and comprehensive law creation, enforcement, and judicial mechanisms. International lawyers, in particular, have longed to see the development of such mechanisms. However, they should not prematurely—and *faute de mieux*—jump at the possibility of entrusting the Security Council with all those tasks that precede and follow the peace enforcement function, that is, law creation and judicial settlement. The boundaries between these different functions may not always be clear. What seems clear, however, is that if their separate existence is not properly acknowledged the system may disintegrate from lack of acceptance. Those who are confident that their current position of power and influence will guarantee that the Council can sustain law-making and judicial functions should bear in mind Lord Castlereagh's objection to the Holy Alliance. The political life span of the Holy Alliance was short, not least due to Britain's disagreement. It lasted about ten years— the same length of time that has elapsed between the Iraqi invasion of Kuwait and today.

Conclusion

International Law and the Changing Constitution of International Society

ANDREW HURRELL

This concluding chapter addresses two questions:

1. What have we learnt about the relationship between international law and international politics?
2. How have the changes associated with the concept of globalization affected the international legal order?

The scope of these questions is, of course, immense, as is the diversity of views and approaches debated in the preceding chapters. It is clear, then, that no definitive answers can be given within the compass of one brief chapter. Nevertheless, returning to these central issues provides a framework for drawing together some of the main arguments that have run through this volume and for isolating some of the principal points of divergence and debate.

1. THE RELATIONSHIP BETWEEN INTERNATIONAL LAW AND INTERNATIONAL POLITICS

There is a long tradition of viewing international politics and international law as separate arenas of social activity. Friedrich Kratochwil's chapter traces the way in which the development of the academic disciplines of both international relations and international politics have reinforced this division. He notes how political realism distanced itself from legal discourse and from a belief in the political importance of law; and the extent to which this was paralleled by developments within international law. As he puts it: 'Even more importantly, the anaemic conception of politics as "power politics" was paralleled to a certain extent by the narrowing of the concerns of jurisprudence to issues of conceptual analysis and the strict demarcation of the legal system conceived as a hierarchy of norms'.[1] Or again: 'As realism tried to cleanse itself of all normative conceptions (save power), so law largely attempted to free itself from all social and moral contingencies.'[2]

Martti Koskenniemi's chapter provides a fascinating picture of how this attitude towards law evolved within the work of the most influential political realist, Hans Morgenthau. There is an ongoing tension in Morgenthau's work between the

---

[1] See p. 63.   [2] See p. 66.

emphasis on the autonomy of the political ('Intellectually, the political realist maintains the autonomy of the political sphere, as the economist, the lawyer, the moralist maintain theirs'); and the detailed attention that he actually gave to the role of law and institutions—in striking contrast both to contemporary neo-realists and to the stylized textbook accounts of his own position.[3]

Nevertheless, Morgenthau's deeply pessimistic conclusions, established by the mid-1940s, exercised a profound effect on subsequent understandings of law within the fast-expanding discipline of international relations (above all in the United States): the belief in the special weakness of the international legal order; the perceived tendency of law to engage in futile efforts to uphold the *status quo* as power shifted towards revisionist States; the extent to which an appeal to universal values disguised the interests and particular values of the strongest; the belief that formalist positivist law had nothing to do with the 'rules of international law as they are actually applied'; and, above all, the endlessly repeated assertion that power and material forces would always determine political outcomes: 'a competitive quest for power will determine the victorious social forces, and the change of the existing legal order will be decided, not through a legal procedure . . . but through a conflagration of conflicting social forces which challenge the legal order as a whole'.[4]

Yet this notion of wholly separate realms or spheres of social activity is deeply misleading. The attempt to bring international law and international relations closer together has in large measure revolved around different ways of challenging this excessively stark divide. The most important feature of this convergence has been to build on the notion of interest and the degree to which law reflects the reality of common interests. States co-operate because, however different their values and however problematic their power relations, they see the possibility of gain. Rules, laws, and conventions can, and often do, emerge without an overarching authority and are of mutual benefit because they help shape expectations, increase the predictability of international life, and thereby reduce the costs and dangers of uncertainty and insecurity.

Several of the essays in this collection reflect the long-standing awareness amongst international lawyers that law and interest are by no means antithetical and that the legal order relies on the imperatives of long-term self-interest and on the cement of reciprocity and reputation. As Arthur Watts puts it in his chapter: 'The benefits of a state of affairs in which those elements [of the rule of law] are present are self-evident, and exert a powerful positive influence.'[5] The legal order depends not on the power or coercion but on the co-ordination of interests and on patterned expectations. On this classical view, law codifies the basic rules of social coexistence and establishes a society of States as the basic organizing principle of world politics; it regulates international co-operation and places constraints on international conflict;

---

[3] See Hans J. Morgenthau, *Politics Among Nations: The Struggle for Power and Peace* (New York: Alfred Knopf, 1959), 10 and chs. 18 and 19.
[4] As cited in Koskenniemi's chapter, p. 53.
[5] See p. 35.

and it helps to promote a co-operative international political culture and develop a shared normative discourse.

To political scientists rediscovering institutions in the 1980s after the brutal simplifications of the neo-realist revival, interest-based explanations for law, norms, and institutions provided the critical point of entry. Institutionalist analysis (certainly in its dominant rationalist form) has been concerned with ways in which institutions make it rational for States to co-operate out of self-interest. Norms and institutions are viewed as purposively generated solutions to different kinds of collective action problems. They are negotiated and contracted in the process of social interaction, rather than being the 'givens' of the society to which individual actors or groups belong. The tenor of this overwhelmingly rationalist style of analysis is well described by James Coleman: 'Social norms . . . specify what actions are regarded by a set of persons as proper or correct, or improper or incorrect. They are purposively generated, in that those persons who initiate or help maintain a norm see themselves as benefitting from its being observed or harmed by its being violated.'[6] Kratochwil's chapter explores this kind of utilitarian and interest based explanations of norms with its characteristic language of information, transparency, transaction costs, and iterated game playing.

The essays in this volume also reflect convergence on some of the important areas for ongoing research. There have been, for example, calls in both disciplines for work on linkages between international law and domestic politics. Eyal Benvenisti takes up this issue in his chapter and stresses the importance of two-way linkage: on the one hand, the importance of domestic politics for understanding international agreements; on the other, the impact of international norms on domestic politics. His chapter also adopts the most overtly 'political science' approach of all the contributors. The disaggregation of the State and the blurring of the division between the domestic and the international is also central to the analysis in Anne-Marie Slaughter's chapter. A related common theme has been the development of the concept of governance and of the role of different sets of networks within an expanded range of governance mechanisms and institutions—which is discussed most fully in the chapter by Stephen Toope.

The rhetoric of interests, of regimes, of governance mechanisms has therefore been crucial to increased dialogue between international relations and international law. But to a significant extent this has been to the detriment of the equally important links between law and power. It is certainly the case that many of the chapters in this volume reflect the common reaction against the idea of law as a closed normative order. The chapters by Stern and Gowlland-Debbas, for example, underline the need to see law in terms of a broader social process and an ever-widening range of public policy concerns. Stern speaks unequivocally of the 'fallacy in opposing law and politics'.[7] Kratochwil elegantly highlights the difficulty of defending consistently

---

[6] James S. Coleman, *Foundations of Social Theory* (Cambridge, Mass.: Belknap/Harvard University Press, 1990), 242. [7] See p. 280.

the autonomy of law and of excluding moral precepts, policy considerations, and contextual factors. And several chapters refer to the insights and ongoing relevance of the New Haven School. And yet, at least on the evidence of this volume, there must remain some doubt as to how far, or how systematically, international lawyers are willing to examine the problematic and often destabilizing linkages between law and power.

The neglect of the links between power and law within international relations is perhaps more surprising. On the one hand, even hard-headed liberals tend to shy away from power, to see politics essentially in terms of problems of collective action, and to stress the ways in which either institutions or domestic reform may help over-come such problems. On the other, neo-realists fail to appreciate the importance of norms and of law to the analysis of power. They mistakenly view norms, rules, insti-tutions, and values as mere reflections of material forces. Power remains central to the analysis of international relations, but power is a social attribute. To understand power we must place it side by side with other quintessentially social concepts such as prestige, authority, legitimacy, and legality. Indeed, it is one of the great paradoxes that, because it so resolutely neglects the social dimensions of power, realism is unable to give a full or convincing account of its own proclaimed central category.

To believe in the importance of a common framework of rules and social norms does not imply that power and conflict do not play a major, even at times dominant, role in international relations. Norms are just as central to the functioning of the balance of power or the changing character of war as they are to understanding the more obviously co-operative aspects of world politics. Conflict and war, certainly at the inter-State level, have generally taken place within a highly institutionalized set of normative structures—legal, moral, and political. International relations is consti-tuted by the interaction of material forces and norms and institutions. The State system, and global society more generally, are only comprehensible when material forces are set against the norms and institutions that have shaped how States have understood their interests and structured their power relations. This does not imply that norms somehow control the actions of States, acting upon them from outside. But it does mean that they shape the game of politics, the nature and identity of the actors, the purposes for which power is deployed, and the ways in which actors have justified and legitimized their actions.

As is clear from Kratochwil's discussion of constructivist approaches to interna-tional law, social order cannot be systematically derived from individual maximizing choices and the role of constitutive norms is crucial. But constructivism does not imply that norms are necessarily nice and liberal. Nor does it suggest that, because international life is socially constructed, progress can easily be achieved. In other words, the notion of a divide between law and politics can still be challenged even if one holds a reasonably pessimistic view of international society.

Legal rules and relations are important, then, in so far as they constitute the game of power politics. But they are also important more directly in stabilizing and legit-imizing the power of particular actors. To a much greater extent than realists acknowledge, States need international law and institutions both to share the material and political costs of protecting their interests and to gain the authority and legitimacy that the possession of crude power can never on its own secure. Law and legal institutions do indeed reflect power, but there is much more to this than the idea of 'mere reflection' might suggest. It is therefore a mistake to view 'law' as something that is, or can be, wholly separated from 'power' or 'power-political interest'.

And yet, whilst the notion of separate spheres is misleading, the idea of a specificity to law cannot be totally avoided. Indeed, the stress on the relative autonomy of the legal order comes across powerfully in most of the contributions to this volume. Thus Stephen Toope argues for the 'relative autonomy of international law'. Vera Gowlland-Debbas recognizes the need for law to adjust to social developments but argues that it must still retain its 'normative capacity'. International law remains highly selective in identifying which parts of reality are deemed to be legally relevant. As she puts it: 'The legal system ingests only that part of social reality that it considers relevant, laying down conditions that determine which legally relevant facts are to be attributed legal consequences.'[8]

International law represents a particular form of practice, of reasoning, and of argumentation that is socially contrived and historically constructed, but it is based on a remarkably broad consensus and is relatively well institutionalized. The relative autonomy of law as a distinct arena of politics involves the creation of a shared interpretative community of lawyers who inhabit a more or less unified conceptual universe. It is by dint of this that questions related to the determinacy of rules or the meaning of contested concepts can be rationally debated, even if never fully resolved. The nature of the relation to both politics and morality varies enormously and is, of course, endlessly debated. For Philip Allott, the legal order is a human construct within which an objective set of moral purposes can be rationally constituted, reflecting the purposes and values of international society as a whole. For others, law functions as a more or less autonomous institution on the back of a good deal of historical contingency and pragmatic acceptance and adaptation. And yet, even those who are most inclined to stress the theoretical insecurities of the international legal space nevertheless uphold the idea of a normative order within which the concept of legal validity remains meaningful. For Koskenniemi, the insistence on the importance of valid law becomes more important as the specifically legal space is challenged, in the real world, by the special claims of the hegemon and by the universalizing pretensions of Western liberalism and, in the academic world, by the calls of interdisciplinary collaboration. As he puts it:

Answers to the question about (valid) law are conditioned upon the criteria for validity that a legal system uses to define its substance. These criteria do refer to social facts and moral ideas but cannot be reduced to them without doing away with the legal question (by interpreting it as 'in fact' a question about what works, or what is good) and the profession that was assigned the task of answering it.[9]

[8] See p. 308.   [9] See p. 60.

Lawyers, then, cannot escape from the idea of law as a distinct social institution. But neither can political scientists interested in the political roles of law. The great contribution of international relations has been to develop a theoretically sophisticated account of norms and institutions and to be willing to face up to the difficult questions that lawyers have all too often skirted around: exactly how does law make a difference? under what conditions is it likely to prove effective? how might we explain variance in patterns of compliance? But these gains have been achieved at the cost of a severe narrowing of the intellectual agenda. The chapters in this volume suggest at least four areas where that agenda needs to be expanded—none of which will come as a great surprise to lawyers.

In the first place there is the importance of the systemic and integrated nature of the legal order. In contrast to the institutionalist focus on single-issue areas and overt bargaining, international law has to be understood as an integrated institution and as an interconnected normative system in which historical development and the evolution of specific legal doctrines or concepts over time play a crucial role. The content of a norm and the degree of obligation that attaches to it is therefore related to its place within this broader normative order. This notion of international law as a system recurs in many places in this collection: Gowlland-Debbas, for example, stresses the 'manner in which legal norms are produced, generated, and articulated with each other'. It is also central to Vaughan Lowe's argument about the completeness of the international legal order. (To the non-lawyer, the doubts raised by this claim concern not the internal completeness but rather the question of how one might judge whether this complete system is in fact 'adequate for the needs of the society to which it applies' or is actually able 'to accommodate most international transactions'.)[10]

Second, the role of norms, including legal norms, cannot be understood solely in instrumental terms. They may provide benefits and fulfil functions, but they are also norms that human actors consider to be *binding*. They involve an internally felt obligation and not merely a contractual commitment—what Hart referred to as the 'internal aspect of norms'. This implies that an observer's account of the existence of a norm will always be deficient without an appreciation that some individuals understand the rule as setting a common standard for assessing the behaviour of all involved.

A third, related, area is that legal norms are necessarily evaluative. It is certainly the case that both the strength and the fragility of international law derive from the need to maintain connections with both murky practice and normative aspiration. On the one hand, both the procedural and substantive rules of international law must remain connected to concrete institutions, to power-political structures, and to the often very rough trade of international politics. But to have any normative bite, these rules must be counterfactually valid and involve intersubjectively shared and institutionalized normative reflection on the often illegal practices of States and other

---

[10] See p. 237.

actors. Moreover, in an ever-changing world international law can never remain static and lawyers cannot avoid trying to keep pushing out the normative boat—that is, after all, what having a normative agenda is all about. International law, then, represents a particular form of practice, of reasoning, and of argumentation in which this dialogue between fact and value is carried out.

Finally, as Kratochwil's chapter highlights, legal norms fulfil many different kinds of roles, which cannot be adequately captured by an exclusive focus on regulatory rules designed to constrain the choices of actors. Moreover, norms are not simply instrumentally driven but rather have an internal logic of their own. This is why patterns of judicialized politics are so important to understanding the politics of relatively well-structured institutions such as the EU or the WTO. All of this points to the difficulty of understanding legal norms in terms of dominant positivist social scientific models and one-dimensional understandings of causality.

But if there remains an unavoidable need to hold on to the specificity of law as a social institution, neither is it possible to evade the complexity and specificity of politics. In the first place, international law forms only part of a much broader set of intersubjective understandings and conceptual structures that shape international relations. Often the norms that have real political impact are not legal (or are only indirectly related to the legal order). In some cases these have to do with procedural norms and practices—for example, norms concerning the balance of power, spheres of influence, or practices of crisis-management. All of these were central to the international politics of the Cold War but have not disappeared in the post-Cold War world. Thus shared expectations concerning spheres of influence (both agreed and contested) shape security politics in many parts of the world. And, although we now talk of contact groups and peace implementation councils, patterns of hierarchical management and the acceptance of special status for major States remain a common feature of international politics in the 1990s, as Arthur Watts notes in his chapter.

In other cases, specific legal principles or legal rules form part of a broader cluster of norms whose political importance cannot be understood solely from the perspective of international law. Thus the political impact of national self-determination as both a political ideology and as an international political norm was immense well before it began to be absorbed within the international legal order and well beyond its specifically legal application. Indeed, for very good reasons, international law has treated the norm of self-determination in extremely cautious and highly selective ways. Sustainable development, discussed in the chapter by Vaughan Lowe, provides a further example. Sustainable development is again best viewed as a cluster of related norms and concepts. It emerged on the back of the rise of environmental pressure groups. Its political importance grew within international environmental negotiations (especially during the Rio process) perhaps above all because of its elastic meaning. More recently its substantive content has been overwhelmingly shaped by powerful transnational and transgovernmental networks, both within the non-governmental organization world but, more importantly, in and around the international financial institutions where it has served as a cover for incorporating environmental concerns but without challenging dominant modes of economic analysis. Of course its incorporation into the international legal order is important. But it is only one aspect of its broader political role and by no means the most obviously influential.

A final example concerns humanitarian intervention. This represents a long tradition of moral and political debate (and one which partially contradicts Philip Allott's view of the classical Vattelian order as a 'morality-free zone'). As with self-determination, international law has been very cautious in suggesting that a doctrine of humanitarian intervention either does exist within international law, or should exist. However, it is a normative tradition which illustrates powerfully how inherited conceptual structures and patterns of argumentation shape contemporary political debates. Thus the debate over Western bombing of Serbia needs to be understood at least in part as a clash between conflicting principles in which ideas of humanitarian intervention have played a central role, rather than a simple clash between law on the one hand and crude politics on the other. There is a great deal of politics involved in those cases when law may be seen as 'winning out over politics' (e.g. the *Pinochet case*); but there is also a great deal of law and principled argument in cases that point in the other direction (e.g. the use of force and the bombing campaign in Kosovo).[11]

International order is made up of far more than simply law. There remains in much legal writing the implication that the progressive development of international law would in and of itself lead to a more stable and perhaps equitable world. And yet much of what makes for international order stands outside the domain of law and would not be helped by legal regulation. Some disputes are unsuited either to framing or to resolution in legal terms. It is often legitimacy rather than legality that may be the politically defining factor and legitimacy may in turn be based more on the capacity for effective action than on the possession of a decisive legal case. Order may well depend on the capacity to deploy effective military power, even in circumstances where such resort is not clearly regulated by law or by the United Nations. Equally, and far more commonly, the management of many aspects of international life depends quite directly on hierarchy and unequal power in ways that sit uneasily with the norms and proclaimed standards of the international legal order. Finally, many problems derive not simply from the weakness of international institutions but from the blurring of their political and legal roles—as discussed in the chapters on the legal roles of the Security Council by Gowlland-Debbas and Georg Nolte.

However elusive it may be, the concept of the political remains meaningful. Realists were wrong to believe in the inevitability of conflict, especially violent conflict, and in the impossibility of any form of progress in international relations. But they were right to stress that the degree to which the structure of power and interests, the extent of inequality, the divergences of cultures and value systems, and the rigidities of political language often make the resolution of conflicts difficult if not impossible. Political life is the necessary condition for ordering otherwise irre-

---

[11]   I owe this formulation to Adam Roberts. See also A. Roberts, 'NATO's "Humanitarian War" over Kosovo,' (Autumn 1999) 41(3) Survival 102.

solvable social and intergroup conflicts—precisely those conflicts that cannot be resolved through market exchange, through moral dialogue, or through legal argument. It is also the arena where the practical results of different moral visions are to be negotiated and rationally constructed if they are not to be imposed by coercion and unequal power—although law may certainly form one element in this process of negotiation.

The persistent recalcitrance of international politics derives in large part from the weakness of the political order on the back of which the ever-increasing normative ambitions of international law are to be achieved. One aspect of this weakness follows from what Antonio Cassese calls 'the end of a magnificent illusion'—namely that the UN Charter system could provide an effective answer to the use of aggressive force and an effective instrument for the management of other conflicts. Equally illusory has been the idea that this failure was somehow due to the Cold War and that the end of the Cold War would open up a new age of international co-operation. Although the 1990s has witnessed a remarkable expansion in the role of the United Nations in the management of international security, the old obstacles to a full-blown collective security system remain all too visible. Moreover, as in the past, where collective action has been possible (as in the Gulf, Bosnia, Haiti, or Somalia), it has depended, to an uncomfortable extent, on the political interests of the United States and its allies and on the military capabilities built up in the course of the Cold War. An effective *system* of collective security has therefore remained out of reach, although the collective *element* in security management has expanded (as in the role of regional alliances or coalitions, international peacekeeping forces, and UN authorizations of the use of force).

These weaknesses do not mean that the normative aspirations of international law do not matter. It is impossible to think seriously about international relations today without reference to norms prohibiting the aggressive use of force or proscribing genocide, or upholding self-determination and human rights. Such norms have a powerful political as well as a moral reality. Even on purely pragmatic grounds, States need to justify their actions in terms of these norms and to seek legal endorsement and legitimacy from those international bodies that are the repositories of those norms—which is one of the reasons why even the United States cannot avoid having to deal with the United Nations. But it is to say, first, that the aspirations of this normatively ambitious international society remain deeply contaminated by the interests and values of powerful States and of the private actors that they may represent; and, second, that international law can only ignore the persistence of this structural contamination at the cost of empty formalization. The character of international law will always be influenced by the broader distribution of power both within the international political system and the global economy.

During the Cold War period, the problem lay in the very intensity of bipolar confrontation and the ideological crusading that it engendered on both sides. At times (for example, in the debates on the use of force in the mid-1980s) this placed enormous strains on the international legal system. In the post-Cold War world, the problem lies in the inequality of power distribution and the temptations to unilateralism to which hegemony naturally gives rise—especially when the hegemon is as ideologically driven as is the case with the United States. Inequality is partly a matter of the distribution of State power, both material and ideational. But it also flows from the close links between globalization and inequality: in terms of the distribution of the costs and benefits of economic globalization; in terms of the dominant position of powerful States in setting the ground rules of the global economy and in choosing when, how, and if markets are to be regulated; and in terms of the ever-widening differential capacity of States to adapt to the demands of a global economy.

2. GLOBALIZATION AND THE INTERNATIONAL LEGAL ORDER

The chapters in this volume provide clear evidence of the changing character of the international legal order. As is well known, the international legal order developed within the classical European State system was largely concerned with elaborating limited rules of coexistence. This *pluralist* conception of international law and society was built around the goal of coexistence and reflected an ethic of difference. It was to be constructed around the mutual recognition of sovereignty and aimed at the creation of certain minimalist rules, understandings, and institutions designed to limit the inevitable conflict that was to be expected within such a fragmented political system. These rules and norms provided a structure of coexistence, built on the mutual recognition of States as independent and legally equal members of society, on the unavoidable reliance on self-preservation and self-help, and on freedom to promote their own ends subject to minimal constraints. The dominant values of this society of States were, to quote Vattel, 'the maintenance of order and the preservation of liberty'.

In the course of the century such views have been challenged by more far-reaching, maximalist, or *solidarist* conceptions of the legal order. Four dimensions of change are especially important. The first has to do with the content of norms. In contrast to mere coexistence, the norms of this more solidarist law involve more extensive schemes of co-operation to safeguard peace and security (for example, prohibiting aggression or broadening understandings of what constitutes threats to peace and security); to solve common problems (such as tackling environmental challenges or managing the global economy in the interests of greater stability or equity); and to sustain common values (such as the promotion of self-determination, human rights, or political democracy). This expansion has been driven both by moral change and by material and pragmatic imperatives. As is noted in several of the essays in this volume, globalization has led to increased demands for co-operation in the many areas where governments simply cannot regulate alone.

The second dimension concerns the source of these norms. In a traditional pluralist conception, the dominant norms are created by States and depend directly on the consent of States. In a solidarist conception, the process of norm creation is opened to a wider range of actors, both States and non-State groups; and there is an easing of the degree to which States can only be bound by rules to which they have given their explicit consent—a move from consent to consensus. In many areas it has become increasingly difficult to withhold consent within an ever denser and more complex legal order. The third dimension has to do with the justification and evaluation of norms. Alongside the old idea that actors create and uphold law because it provides them with functional benefits, the post-1945 period has seen the emergence of a range of internationally agreed core principles—respect for fundamental human rights, prohibition of aggression, self-determination—which may underpin some notion of a world common good and some broader basis for evaluating specific rules. This may be viewed in terms of the surreptitious return of natural law ideas or of a philosophically anchorless, but nevertheless reasonably solid, pragmatic consensus. The fourth dimension has to do with moves towards the more effective implementation of these norms and the variety of attempts to move beyond the traditionally very 'soft' compliance mechanisms and to give more effective teeth to the norms of this more ambitious society.

The end of the Cold War and what many view as the increased pace of globalization have witnessed a further expansion of the normative ambitions of international law. Globalization and increasing economic and human interconnections between societies; the increasing seriousness of ecological challenges; democratization and changing notions of political legitimacy; the continued growth of transnational economic actors and the emergence of a dense and increasingly active transnational civil society; the decline in use of large-scale military force between major States together with the parallel expansion of many other forms of social violence; and the extent to which the State is under challenge as a legitimate and effective building-block of international order—all these developments have led inexorably to the belief that international order should be reconceived and reconceptualized. Order is increasingly held to involve the creation of international rules that affect very deeply the domestic structures and organization of States, that invest individuals and groups within States with rights and duties, and which seek to embody some notion of a global common good.

Sovereignty in the sense of freedom to make choices as to economic, political, or social systems or external behaviour has been severely constrained. Sovereignty in the sense of the power of a State over its nationals has been eroded by human rights law and the increased availability of a variety of national courts and international tribunals. Taken together these changes have clouded the notion of international law as a pure State-privileging system. It is precisely the cumulative impact of these changes that has led to the emergence of a third image of international law—the idea of *an emerging law of a transnational society*. This image builds on many of the trends already visible in the contemporary international legal system: the pluralism of the norm-creating processes; the role of private market actors and civil society groups in articulating values which are then assimilated in inter-State institutions; and the increased range of informal, yet norm-governed, governance mechanisms often built around complex networks, both transnational and transgovernmental.

Out of this comes the idea that traditional inter-State law needs to be subsumed within a broader process in which old distinctions between public and private international law and between municipal and international law are being steadily eroded. Thus, on this view, we increasingly find a variety of different kinds of norms made by a wide variety of actors (States, international organizations, multinational enterprises, non-governmental organizations, and private individuals) in a wide variety of public and private, domestic and international, fora, and diffused, internalized, and enforced through a variety of material and symbolic incentives. Again, globalization is seen as intensifying this change and leading to a range of different ways in which norms emerge and converge: partly through traditional inter-State negotiations but involving an increasing range of non-governmental actors; partly through processes of societal convergence that may be the result of increased regulatory competition or pressure from international bodies; and partly by non-State actors acting more or less autonomously (the development of detailed operational norms by market actors in fields as diverse as accounting standards or environmental standards). As a result, the interpretative community involved in law-creation and implementation is broadened very significantly and we can accordingly posit the idea of the law of a transnational civil society—regulating States but not dependent on States for its existence, content, or implementation.

The chapters in this collection have been concerned with debating exactly how these different images of international law may best be conceptualized; how far practice has in fact shifted from one to another; and what the legal, political, and moral implications of such shifts may be. Let me briefly pick out four issues of particular importance.

Globalization and the State

All of the chapters reflect awareness of the challenges that these developments pose for mainstream international law. Vaughan Lowe, for example, notes the manner in which the norms and processes of classical international law are being adopted elsewhere: 'The techniques and principles of public international law are being borrowed most obviously and applied in the dealings and legal relations of private companies and non-governmental organizations and, more generally, in the internal legal orders of States'. Or again: 'The conceptual framework of international law is likely to become diffused throughout the vast web of non-State international dealings.'[12] Arthur Watts expresses the concern that '[T]he consequences of globalization cannot be adequately regulated by reference to a legal order which is based on sovereignty and territory, the very concepts that are being outmoded by that same globalization'.[13]

The dominant line of the essays in this volume is that States are still the primary

---

[12] See p. 253.   [13] See p. 38.

actors although their role may be reduced by globalization. According to Edward Kwakwa, 'predictions of the end of the State fly in the face of reality'.[14] And for Stern: 'As long as there is no world army or police force, States remain the *unique vectors of law creation and enforcement*.'[15] Stern also underscores the false dichotomy of States and markets and the extent to which complex markets depend for their functioning on a dense system of rules and regulations. Thus, whilst global financial markets can impose huge costs on States, the stable (let alone equitable) operation of international financial systems depends on an inter-State system with well-respected rules and in which the principal national economies are under the control of competent and effective States. Stern also points to the degree to which the practices and norms of international commercial relations depend on States for enforcement and for the core structures of rights on which they depend.

Prescriptively, both Stern and Kwakwa are even clearer on the importance of the State and of State-based regulation. For Kwakwa, the orderliness, transparency, and efficiency of the global economy can only be produced by a rules-based regulatory system. For Stern, 'it is increasingly evident that "savage liberalism" cannot bring prosperity and justice to the people of the world'. In terms of what is actually being done, the picture is more complex. Kwakwa's main concern is to underline the asymmetry of control over the global economic system and he stresses the extent to which the rules of the global economy are set by the powerful. Most developing States are 'rule-takers' or 'paradigm receiving States' as he puts it. His chapter also underscores the difficulties faced by developing countries in seeking to influence the institutions in and around which an ever-expanding range of norms, rules, and regulations are negotiated: the complexity of the institutions and the high level of resources needed to participate effectively, the degree to which both formal and informal governance structures work in favour of the strong, and the ability of the strong to choose the fora that most suit their interests.

Stern considers various modes of management for the global economy. She rejects the idea of the expansion of national legal systems and, in particular, the 'imperial imposition of a national legal order' involved in the extraterritorial application of US law. She also sees little real merit in the creation of non-statal regulatory systems, not least because of their ultimate dependence on States and State power. Finally, she argues strongly in favour of the reassertion of international institutional regulation: 'there is no solution apart from the *creation of a truly world-wide international law system of regulation*' (emphasis in original).[15]

The most challenging arguments for statist perspectives on globalization and for mainstream approaches to international law are provided by Anne-Marie Slaughter. In her chapter Slaughter argues, first, that traditional debates on global governance place far too much emphasis on formal inter-State institutions; and second, that they are handicapped by an old-fashioned conception of States and State institutions. 'In fact, the State is not disappearing; it is disaggregating into its component institutions.

[14] See p. 268.   [15] See p. 283.

The primary State actors in the international realm are no longer foreign ministries and heads of states, but the same government institutions that dominate domestic politics: administrative agencies, courts, and legislatures.'[16]

So the thrust of her chapter is to explore what she sees as the expanding role of regulatory transgovernmental networks. 'Courts, administrative agencies, legislators, and heads of State are all networking with their foreign counterparts. Each of these institutions has the capacity not only to represent "the national interest" in interactions with its foreign counterparts, but also to act on a subset of interests arising from its particular domestic function that are likely to be shared by its foreign counterparts.'[16] She looks in detail at both formal transgovernmental regulatory organizations (such as the Basle Committee on Banking Supervision) and agreements between the domestic regulatory agencies of States that cover a very wide range of issue-areas including securities regulation, commodities regulation, anti-trust, environmental regulation, and health policy.

Slaughter suggests that these networks penetrate sovereignty very effectively and draw on a selective range of public/private actors. They are informal, fast, flexible, and secret and can adapt quickly to new problems and new situations. They are established by regulatory agencies rather than political bodies, thereby avoiding 'a great deal of cumbersome and formal international negotiating procedure'.[17] They are effective above all because of the close links between norm development and norm implementation: 'the actors who make the rules or formulate the principles guiding governmental networks are the same actors who have the power to enforce them'.[19] It is certainly the case that this picture captures an important part of the complex processes by which norms are created, diffused, and implemented. It is also clear that this picture is very hard for traditional conceptions of international law to cope with. It cannot, for example, be easily understood in terms of consent or some notion of the delegation of sovereign will.

Slaughter deals at length, and persuasively, with the criticism that networks of this kind will lead to the emergence of an unaccountable transnational technocracy and that networks are displacing international organizations and instituting a minimalist global agenda. Yet two sets of questions persist.

The first concerns the criteria for judging the effectiveness of such networks. In the Asian financial crisis, for example, one might argue that transgovernmental regulatory networks and the private financial interests with which they were closely involved were indeed able to manage the crisis 'effectively'—i.e. without recourse to too much governmental action or to a new round of institution-building. But this 'success' can be seen as reflecting the power of private economic interests anxious to protect their own freedom of action and to resist the restrictions that more formal international regulation would bring with it. This freedom of action is in turn related to their domestic political power within the United States and the importance of the finance and financial services sector to the US economy. To put the point more

[16] See p. 206.   [17] See p. 208.

generally: a liberal theory of transnational law cannot simply stress the importance of societal interests. There has to be some judgement that both the process by which private interests are aggregated and the substantive norms that result from that process are compatible with liberal values.

The second doubt has to do with the charge that such networks represent a 'device whereby the most powerful countries penetrate the defences of national sovereignty to impose their policy templates on everyone else'. Slaughter recognizes that this poses the 'sharpest challenge'. But it is not clear how far she has taken the potential range of difficulties on board. There is very little reason for believing that all States are equally able to operate effectively within these networks. The extent of the relevant expertise and resources possessed by the United States increases the like-lihood that its norms will win out. Equally it is in the nature of hegemony that power brings options: to act unilaterally, imposing a particular set of regulatory standards via the exercise of direct power; to exploit different forms of conditionality (discussed below); or to press for formal regulation through international institutions. Nor does the experience of multilateralism in the 1990s provide much ground for believing that the United States is likely to be entrapped within such networks or to be constrained from imposing its will or at least having the dominant voice.

None of this is to deny the importance of regulatory networks nor to deny that many of the processes of norm diffusion, socialization, and internalization involve liberal notions of learning, emulation, and persuasion. But they also involve power and coercion and structurally unlevel playing fields. Again, to make the point more generally: technocratic approaches to governance, especially in the economic field, tend to ask which organizational forms are best suited to which governance functions. The more important political question, however, involves asking whose interests are being served by which governance mechanisms and whose values protected and promoted.

Pluralism and Process

Interdependence and globalization have opened up transnational civil society as an arena for political action. The infrastructure of increased economic interdependence (new systems of communication and transportation), and the extent to which new technologies (satellites, computer networks, etc.) have increased the costs and diffi-culty of governments controlling flows of information, have facilitated the diffusion of values, knowledge, and ideas, and enhanced the ability of like-minded groups to organize across national boundaries.

Stephen Toope's chapter explores the role of various networks in what he terms governance theory, stressing the degree to which their influence depends on specialist knowledge, on commitment, on clearly defined interests, and on access to decision-makers. Across many of the other chapters of this book we see evidence of the role of networks in an increasingly pluralist process of norm creation and implementation. One category concerns what have come to be called epistemic communities, whose power and influence derive from claims to technocratic knowledge and from the power of the environment or economic ideas. A second category involves legal policy networks, acting in both specific issue-areas and more generally, as what Oscar Schachter famously termed the 'invisible' college of international lawyers. This 'college' is not really invisible but is a historically created and institutionally embedded network based on a shared interpretative discourse and perhaps on a set of normative commitments. In this regard, Stephen Toope calls for more conscious recognition of the role of international lawyers in the advocacy of substantive norms and procedural innovations. The third category, and the one best represented in this collection, concerns human rights networks, whose influence does not derive from narrow economic incentives nor from power-political interests, but rather from ideas and values that are felt directly, if still unevenly, by individual human beings.

Christine Chinkin's chapter highlights the recognition on the part of international lawyers of the increased importance of social movements. She concentrates her analysis on the human rights networks that confront the global subordination of women and their roles in standard setting and in the application and implementation of standards. She traces the ability of non-governmental organizations to gain access to State-controlled arenas, as well as the input by NGOs into the State-based reporting systems and individual complaint mechanisms.

It is clear that the human rights regime has provided both institutional platforms and normative handholds for weaker actors (both States and non-State groups) to press their interests. The programmatic use of soft law, the space provided for experts and working groups, and the broader role of NGOs have helped to open up the process of norm creation and development. State control over this process has been diluted and a degree of political space has been created for the elaboration and promotion of a new range of rights (for example, rights of future generations, rights related to the status of women, rights to cultural identity, rights to development and a clean environment). Chinkin's chapter notes the notable success of the recognition of women's rights within the human rights legal order: 'it has been due to the instrumentality of NGOs and the increasing accommodation of their demands that the concept of civil society has infiltrated the formal structures of the international legal system.'[18]

But her essay also raises doubts and concerns. She notes, for example, the degree to which States have maintained control over the entry of others into the process of law-making; and their unwillingness to undertake high-cost actions in the direction of greater pluralism. There is, she suggests, much symbolic politics, but also a good deal of gatekeeping and closed agendas. As she notes, 'Although NGOs have made significant inroads, States retain a tight grip on the formal law-making processes while apparently ceding ground.'[19] Moreover, as always with the politics of transnationalism, questions of power and autonomy are complex. Not only may NGOs be co-opted by States, but a central dimension of State power lies in the capacity to forge

[18] See p. 163.   [19] See p. 168.

coalitions and alliances with NGOs. In addition, NGOs have tended to be most effective when formal institutions function well.

More generally, it is important to recognize that civil society is an arena of politics in which power plays an important role. Makau wa Mutua points to the power of Western NGOs in promoting certain basic Western liberal values via transnational civil society. 'In reality, however, INGOs [international non-governmental organizations] have been highly partial: their work has concentrated historically on those countries that have not attained the stable and functioning democracies of the West, the standard for liberal democracy.'[20] Chinkin also notes that '[T]here is also the risk that enhancing the role of international civil society might entrench the bias in favour of the agendas of NGOs from the North where civil society is vibrant and directed towards governmental action. In other societies an active civil society may be suppressed, not yet have emerged, or be ambivalent as to the role of the State as the protector of rights.'[21] Despite the rhetoric of authenticity of many NGOs, there appear to be no good grounds for believing that transnational civil society works necessarily to protect diversity and pluralism rather than to challenge and even suppress it.

Universality

An expansion in the density and depth of the norms of international society always raises the question of membership and admission: how are the criteria for full membership to be decided? how are States to be treated that fail to achieve the specified standards? Moreover, differences in historical experience and cultural traditions become more salient as international law comes to involve the creation of rules that affect very deeply the domestic structures and organization of States, that invest individuals and groups within States with rights and duties, and which seek to embody some notion of a common good (human rights, democratization, the environment, the construction of more elaborate and intrusive inter-State security orders).

The problems of universality enter into this collection most directly in the chapter by Makau wa Mutua on human rights. Mutua underscores the European and Western character of the human rights corpus which, he argues, necessarily undercuts the concept of universality. He argues that the traditional legal debate has obscured 'the political character of the norms that it seeks to universalize'. He traces the close connections between human rights instruments and Western liberal political theory; the particular role of Western human rights NGOs; the degree to which the creation of the human rights system depended on the power of Europe and the United States; the degree to which non-Western ideals and notions of rights or duties are not explored in a full or inclusive manner; and finally, the priority given to certain categories of rights and the selectivity of human rights conditionality.

This critique is well taken although it does perhaps downplay the extent to which the international and transnational culture of human rights involves a widely shared

---

[20] See p. 186.   [21] See p. 172.

common language, an inclusive moral vocabulary, and an authoritative and well-developed normative structure from which very few groups are prepared to try and exempt themselves. It is, of course, shaped by its historical origins within a particular culture; but it is open, dynamic, and resistant to permanent capture by a particular interest or power-political grouping. Nevertheless, Mutua's chapter highlights three important areas of concern. In the first place, as liberally driven international law moves towards treating different States differently on the basis of their domestic values, then the whole notion of the legal order as a primary instrument for mediating cultural difference comes under strain. Second, there is the tension within liberalism itself—between the imperialist promotion of one set of universally valid values on the one hand, and the commitment to equality, diversity, and difference on the other.

Third, there is the paradox that the successful promotion of 'universal' or 'global' values, even if they are to some degree genuinely shared, will often depend on the willingness of particularly powerful States to promote them and will work to reinforce the already marked inequality of power and status amongst States and regions. The best alternative is to stress the importance of open and legitimate processes by which difference can be mediated, adopting the position identified by Mutua as that of the cultural agnostics: 'What they hold dear is the opportunity for all major cultural blocs to negotiate the normative content of human rights law and the purposes for which the discourse should legitimately be deployed.'[22]

Power and the Legal Order

Powerful States, even hegemonic States, need a structured legal order. As Arthur Watts points out: 'Power carries responsibility, and even the short-sighted must see that the alternative to the rule of law is anarchy and disorder, even chaos. Except possibly in a short-term revolutionary context, the interests of *no* State can prosper in such circumstances.'[23] As noted earlier, strong States need law and institutions to share burdens and to reduce the costs of promoting their interests by coercion. Even imperfectly legitimated power is likely to be much more effective than crude coercion. Moreover, the increasing complexity of collective action problems, often made necessary by globalization, makes institutions unavoidable. For powerful States, the trade-off in multilateralism is to invest institutions with sufficient autonomy to be both effective and legitimate on the one hand, whilst maintaining as high a degree of control and insulation as possible on the other. Finally, as we have seen, an increasing number of international rules have to do with the way in which societies are organized domestically. To be effective, international institutions must rely on a wider group of actors. As Edward Kwakwa points out, it is important for everyone that developing countries have the *'institutional capacity to enforce internally the rules of the game promulgated internationally'*.[24] Here the trade-off for the powerful is

[22] See p. 196.   [23] See p. 35.   [24] See p. 269.

between the attractions (and real benefits) of managing international problems on the basis of hierarchical modes of governance on the one hand as against this increasingly structural need for deeper involvement and wider participation on the other.

All of these factors give weaker States a degree of political purchase. They help explain how law can often help to erode power hierarchies and to provide a degree of empowerment and protection. Moreover, as several contributors note in this volume, once created, rule-based systems such as the WTO dispute settlement system provide relatively weak States with significant benefits. For Stern, this represents a *'retreat of politics and an advancement of law'*.[25] International law is not therefore simply a direct manifestation of the actual relations of social power. But it is still heavily influenced by patterns of power and the degree of inequality within the international system places strain on the international legal order in at least three ways.

In the first place, there is the asymmetry of commitment. Large and powerful States have options. They have the power to shape the agenda of international law and international institutions and to use direct coercive power in support of their own interests. Very importantly they have the power to influence whether a particular issue is to be regulated on an inter-State basis and to influence the manner of its regulation. As Watts puts it: 'for them, rather than international law being the framework which controls what they do, it is their actions which shape the law.'[26] The concern with hegemonic power emerges more starkly still in Koskenniemi's chapter in which he suggests that the United States is uncomfortable with the idea of law as a system of fixed rules. 'The language of "governance" (in contrast to government), of the management of "regimes", of ensuring "compliance", is the language of a powerful and confident actor with an enviable amount of resources to back up its policies.'[27]

Second, there are the problems of legitimacy and normative coherence that arise as international law edges towards harder mechanisms of compliance or even enforcement. Many moves in this direction are fully compatible with a stable legal order, as with the expansion of International tribunals. But other possibilities are far more problematic. As Stern's chapter argues, there is no consensus at present in favour of the extraterritorial application of US law, or of the idea that a single government should take it upon itself to enact and enforce international law—even in cases where that law may be deficient or where the Security Council is unable to act. As she puts it, 'The deficiencies of international law are no excuse for its violation.'[28]

Further problems arise from the degree to which conditionality has become increasingly implicated in the diffusion and implementation of international legal norms —that is, the institutionalized application of conditions to inter-State flows of economic resources as a means of inducing domestic policy change. Here it is important to note the critical move away from conditionality as forming part of a specific economic bargain or contract (as was at least arguably the case with IMF economic conditionality in the 1980s) and towards using conditionality to promote norms that

[25] See p. 294. [26] See p. 34. [27] See p. 57. [28] See p. 288.

are wholly unrelated to a specific flow of resources—in terms of human rights, democracy and good governance, levels of military spending or policy on nuclear proliferation, and environmental policies. Such forms of explicit political conditionality have now become institutionalized in the policies of major States as well as in those of international financial institutions. A further important category of conditionality arises from the formalized establishment of criteria for admission to a particular economic or political grouping: the notion that membership of an alliance, economic bloc, or international institution depends on the form of government or respect for human rights, or a particular set of economic norms and standards.

Vaughan Lowe recognizes that the device of conditionality is an 'important characteristic of contemporary international law'. But it is a characteristic which surely raises many troublesome problems, resting as it does on the choices and power of a small group of powerful States and being applied in a wholly selective and unreciprocal manner. This kind of coercive enforcement must place strain on the normative coherence of the system and on the consensualism that still lies at the heart of the inherited legal order.

The third and final problem concerns the tension between the reality of unequal power and the striving of the international legal order to identify and promote some shared set of values and purposes. It has become increasingly common to claim that the particular legal rules developed by States should be judged against some shared notion of a world common good or some generally acknowledged set of shared values or moral purposes. Both Gowlland-Debbas and Toope suggest that it is possible to speak of law as embodying an objective community interest or set of shared purposes. For Allott, the prime purpose of international law *ought* to be to identify and promote the international public interest that can be applied universally.

And yet the internal weaknesses of the legal order and, even more, the problematic linkages between international law and international politics render any such search extremely hazardous. There appears to be no alternative but to maintain a pragmatic balance within international law between process and substance— between the value of substantive norms and the legitimacy of the process by which they are arrived at. Much of international law has to do with the creation of a framework of shared understandings, institutions, and practices by which substantive rules can be created and through which clashes of interest and conflicting values can be mediated. Many legal rules are constitutive of actors. Such norms determine who are legitimate actors and structure the processes by which those actors interact and by which other norms are developed. Other sets of process rules determine what law is and how both political facts and moral claims are received into law. In a very important sense the political and ethical claims of international law rest on the contention that it is the *only* set of globally institutionalized processes by which norms can be negotiated on the basis of dialogue and consent, rather than being simply imposed by the most powerful.

Process can never be the whole story for at least three reasons. In the first place, our own ethical commitments demand that we take to the table our own values and seek to promote and uphold them. Second, even on grounds of efficiency, some commitment to equity and fairness may be necessary to secure the effectiveness and legitimacy of co-operative endeavours and shared institutions. And third, the density, scope, and complexity of the agreements, norms, and rules in which States and societies are already enmeshed provide some basis for positing a community interest or a shared set of purposes and values against which new substantive norms may be judged—the idea of an objective community interest or of the common interest of global society.

But—and it is a tremendously important but—the ease with which this putative international or global public interest may be captured or contaminated by the power and special interests of particular States; the utter unobviousness of what substantive norms ought to be once we move down from high-minded sloganizing (the importance of peace and security, of sustainability, of democracy and human rights, of global economic justice); the extent to which understandings of these issues do in fact diverge so substantially not only as a result of cultural heterogeneity but, more importantly, due to hugely different historical experiences and material circumstances—all of these factors underpin the importance of a commitment to legal processes and to taming the unequal political order within which those processes are embedded.

Index

Abi-Saab, Georges 312
Absolutism 72
Abu Dhabi 208
Abus de droit 246, 218, 306
African Charter on Human Rights and Peoples' Rights 169
Agenda 21 118
Ago, Roberto 285, 301
Agreement on Government Procurement 243
Alabama Arbitration 22
Albania 261
Allott, Philip 69–89, 92–3, 101–3, 218, 331, 334, 346
Alston, Philip 142, 194, 196, 198–9, 202
Amnesty International 157–8
Apartheid 171
Arbitration 262
Aristide, Jean-Bertrand 165
Aristotle 49, 67
Arms Trade 248
Aron, Raymond 28
Asian Financial Crisis 340
Asquith, Lord 208
Association of South-East Asian Nations 243
Augsburg, Treaty of 78
Australia 187
Ayala, Balthazar 222

Balance of Power 23, 330, 333
Baldwin, Roger 156
Balkans 11
Bananas 239
Bank for International Settlements 181–4
Basel Committee on Banking Supervision 181–4
Beijing Conference on Women 141, 143
Belarussia 197
Belgium 187, 203
Benenson, Peter 157
Bentham, Jeremy 37
Benvenisti, Eyal 109–29, 329
Berlin, Isaiah 46
Bianchi, Andrea 145
Blackhurst, Richard 229
Bloch, Ernst 32
Bosnia 12, 287–91, 304, 319, 335
Boutros Ghali, Boutros 263, 312
Brazil 233, 239
Bretton Woods 54, 204, 232
Brichambaut, Marc Perrin de 269–76, 317, 324
British School, *see* English School
Brunnée, Jutta 93, 105–6
Bruntland Commission 220

Bull, Hedley 28, 38, 92
Bush, George 171, 198

Cairo Conference on Population and Development 133
Camdessus, Michel 254, 266
Canada 105, 187, 297
Capital Markets 230, 248
Capitalism 86–7, 153
Caradon, Lord 294
Carr, E. H. 28, 37
Carter, Jimmy 170–1
Cassese, Antonio 335
Castlereagh, Lord 315, 326
Causal Mechanism 36
Chayes, Abram & Antonia 177, 194, 203
Chemical Weapons 240–1
Chile 187, 203, 348
China 8, 172, 305
Chinkin, Christine 131–2, 342–3
Civil Society 134–6, 140, 142, 144, 145, 337, 343
Clinton, Bill 171, 178
Cold War 28, 29, 85, 86, 110, 138, 156, 158, 171, 173, 270, 276, 333, 335, 337
Collective Action Theory 111
Coleman, James 329
Common Heritage of Mankind 212
Common Interest 73–4, 81, 101
Common Pool Resources 111–29
Communism 171
Compliance 57, 60–2, 92–3, 107, 133, 189, 240–1, 284, 332, 337, 345
Conditionality 345, 346
Constitutionalism 72–3, 76, 111, 151–2, 162–6
Constitutive Norms 48, 346
Constructivism 30, 37, 53, 58, 93–9, 102, 105, 107, 330
Continental Shelf 212, 223
Cooke, Peter 183
Corporations, Transnational 132, 143, 177–8, 193, 202, 225, 229, 235, 248, 261–2, 338
Corruption 230–1, 240, 242–3
Countermeasures 285, 293, 307, 312
Crawford, James 301
Crimes Against Humanity 258
Critical Legal Studies 30, 43, 44, 45, 48
Cuba 257–8
Cultural Relativism 153, 161–2
Customary International Law 15, 76–83, 93, 139–40, 152, 208, 212, 216–17, 223, 251, 259–60, 273–4, 288, 294, 300, 305–6, 324–6
Czechoslovakia 109, 121–2, 215

Dahl, Robert 247
D'Amato Act 255–6
Danube River 109–12, 120–1, 129, 215
Democracy 87, 132, 150, 154, 159, 165, 169,
    171–4, 180, 196, 267, 321, 325, 336–7,
    343, 346, 347
Descartes, Renates 66
Developing Countries 227–46, 339
Diplomacy 13, 33, 78, 84–5, 88, 223
Diplomatic Bag 214
Diplomatic Immunity 8, 214, 289
Domestic Law 293, 320
Domestic Politics 109–29
Donnelly, John 163
Dray, William 63
Drugs Traffic 248
Dulles, John Foster 275
Dworkin, Ronald 42, 43, 45, 49, 280

Economy 85, 177–205, 227–68, 336, 339–40
Elections 151
Electronic Commerce 230, 236–7
English School 56
Environment 91, 104–29, 197, 201, 208–9,
    212–15, 231, 283, 289, 321, 333
Epistemic Communities 117, 280
Epistemology 62–8
Equity 216, 218, 347
Erga omnes 138, 274, 283
Eritrea 9
Ethiopia 9
Ethnic Cleansing, *see* Genocide
European Bank for Reconstruction and
    Development 254
European Communities 6
European Convention on Human Rights 6,
    303
European Court of Human Rights 14, 303,
    320
European Court of Justice 265
European Union 58, 86, 187, 196–7, 239, 245,
    264–5, 293, 333
Exclusive Economic Zone 212, 214
Expropriation 213, 218

Falk, Richard 131
Financial Markets, *see* Capital Markets
Finland 187
Finnemore, Martha 95
First World War 35, 37, 39, 60
Fitzmaurice, Gerald 28
Force, Use of 10, 11, 82, 99, 260, 283, 287–90,
    312, 319, 323, 335
Foreign Direct Investment 230–1, 235–6,
    241–4, 249
France 28, 155, 187, 203, 249, 250, 262
Franck, Thomas 57, 160, 165

French Revolution 78
Fuller, Lon 100, 102
Functionalism 61

Game Theory 46, 112, 329
Gendreau, Monique Chemillier 267
General Agreement on Tariffs and Trade 232,
    237–9, 265–6
General Agreement on Trade in Services 232
General System of Preferences 241, 253
Genocide 289, 296, 300, 323, 335
Germany 11, 17–34, 49, 320
Ghai, Yash 168
Globalization 10, 121, 131–2, 143, 146–7,
    177–80, 199, 228–31, 240, 243, 246–68,
    327, 336–9, 341, 344
Goldberg, Arthur 294
Governance 93–4, 96–7, 105–6, 132, 172, 178,
    181, 191, 193–4, 200, 204, 329
Government Networks 177–205
Gowlland-Debbas, Vera 277–313, 321–4, 329,
    331–2, 334, 346
Greenpeace 219
Group of Fifteen 243
Grotius, Hugo 91, 222
Grundnorm 41, 278
Guy, Paul 184

Haas, Peter 96, 105
Haiti 165, 335
Hart, H. L. A. 63, 220, 278, 313, 332
Hauriou, Maurice 248
Hegel, G. W. F. 87, 91
Hegemony 30, 34, 54, 95, 101, 201, 230, 331,
    336, 341, 344–5
Helman, Gerard 202
Helms-Burton Act 245, 255–61
Henkin, Louis 57, 160–1, 163–4, 170
Herdegen, Matthias 320
Hinsley, F. H. 28
Hobbes, Thomas 22, 27, 32, 39, 50, 55, 56, 77
Hoffmann, Stanley 26, 27
Holmes, Stephen 202
Holy Alliance 315, 326
Hong Kong 244
Honore, A. M. 63
Human Rights 13, 117, 131–175, 181, 197–8,
    201, 267, 283, 289–90, 292, 300, 303,
    305–6, 320–1, 335–7, 342–3, 346–7
Human Rights Watch 156–7
Humanitarian Intervention, *see* Intervention
Humanitarian Law 289–90, 292, 295, 300, 306,
    321, 323–4
Hume, David 52, 65
Hungary 109–10, 121–2, 215
Huntington, Samuel 154
Hurrell, Andrew 327–47

Idealism 44, 100
Indeterminacy 36, 45, 47, 48, 49, 51
India 233, 287
Indonesia 171–2
Innocent Passage 214
Institutionalism 58, 59, 329
International Association of Insurance Supervisors 185–6
International Bank for Reconstruction and Development, *see* World Bank
International Center for the Settlement of Investment Disputes 225
International Commission of Jurists 157
International Committee of the Red Cross 306
International Court of Justice 13, 82, 109–10, 117, 120–2, 129, 137–9, 215–16, 219, 221, 224, 251, 261, 269–70, 273–4, 284, 294, 299, 306–10, 316–17, 322
International Covenant on Civil and Political Rights 163–4
International Criminal Court 14, 134, 141–5, 295–301, 311, 323
International Criminal Tribunal for the Former Yugoslavia 14, 133–4, 271–5, 295, 300, 307, 316, 322
International Criminal Tribunal for Rwanda 14, 133–4, 271–2, 295, 316, 322
International Joint Commission 105
International Labor Organization 244
International Law Commission 85, 223, 271, 285, 295, 301
International League for Human Rights 156
International Monetary Fund 132, 146, 170, 180, 196, 212, 232–4, 253–4, 265, 345
International Organization of Security Commissioners 184–5
International Relations 27–30, 32–3, 36–9, 52–3, 72, 91–110, 145, 177, 327–333
Internet 230, 249, 261, 263, 267
Interpretation 42, 51–2, 122, 279, 287–8, 293, 300, 305, 308, 318–20, 325, 331, 338, 342
Interstitial Norms 213–26
Intervening Variable 52
Intervention 11–13, 174, 220, 241, 261, 287, 325, 334
Investment, *see* Foreign Direct Investment
Iran 171, 249, 255–61
Iraq 7, 11, 172, 273, 289, 291–3, 297, 299, 304, 319, 322–3, 326, 335
Israel 113–14, 123–4, 287
Italy 11, 187

Jackson, John 239
Japan 86, 187, 234
Jellinek, Otto 19

Jennings, Robert 258, 306–7, 309
Joint Forum on Financial Conglomerates 186–7
Jordan 113–14
Jordan River 113
Jospin, Lionel 256
Judicial Review 307–8, 310, 317–18, 320
Jurisdiction 13, 208, 256–7, 263, 272, 276, 290, 293, 296, 307–8, 316, 318
Jus Cogens 12, 41, 282–3, 305–6

Kahn, Philippe 263
Kaiser, Karl 197
Kant, Immanuel 22, 51, 77, 91, 96, 103
Kelsen, Hans 19, 22, 31, 32, 38, 220, 278–9, 296, 317, 321
Kennan, George 28
Kennedy, David 39, 43
Kennedy, Duncan 44, 48
Kennedy, John F. 58
Kenya 172
Keohane, Robert 31
Koh, Harold 145
Koskenniemi, Martti 17–34, 43–4, 92–3, 101–2, 106–7, 194, 252, 327, 331, 345
Kosovo 12, 289–90, 316, 334
Kratochwil, Friedrich 35–68, 97–103, 327–30, 333
Kuttner, Robert 180
Kutz, Christopher 49
Kuwait 7, 273, 289–93, 299, 322, 326
Kwakwa, Edward 227–46, 339, 344

Laband, Paul 19
Lagarde, Paul 262
Lang, Jack 248
Larosière, Jacques de 254
Lasswell, Harold 91, 100
Lauterpacht, Elihu 297
Lauterpacht, Hersch 302
Law and Economics 44
Lawyers Committee for Human Rights 157
League of Nations 18, 21, 25, 137, 223
Legal Autopoesis 278–81
Legalism 37, 39, 49, 101
Legitimacy 57, 105, 143, 195–7, 221, 242, 253, 265–6, 302, 312, 330–1, 334–7, 344, 346–7
Legitimate Expectations 83
Leibniz, Georg Wilhelm 87
Less Developed Countries, *see* Developed Countries
Lex mercatoria 262–3
Liberal Millenarianism 17, 33
Liberalism 30, 34, 37, 53, 59–61, 149–205, 330–1, 339, 341
Libya 255–61, 271, 290, 294, 310
Locke, John 77, 162

Lowe, Vaughan 207–26, 332–3, 338, 346
Luxembourg 203

McDougal, Myres 41–2, 91, 100, 221
Machiavelli, Niccolo 40, 72–3
Maine, Henry 210
Malawi 172
Malaysia 187, 230
Memoranda of Understanding 179, 185,
      188–92, 203
MERCOSUR 243, 265
Mexico 201, 233
Mohammed, Mahathir 230
Monroe Doctrine 18
Montreal Protocol on the Ozone Layer 106
Morality 8, 22, 24, 27–8, 31–3, 38, 57, 72–3,
      221, 283, 313, 330–1, 334–5, 346
Moravcik, Andrew 59
Morgenthau, Hans 17–34, 37, 92, 327–8
Morocco 172
Muller, Huib 182
Multilateral Agreement on Investment 235–6,
      248–9
Mutua, Makau wa 149–75, 343–4
Mutual Legal Assistance Treaties 189–92

Namibia 270
Natural Law 23, 72, 337
Negotiation 81, 84, 113, 117, 123–4, 141, 188,
      190, 335, 338
Neier, Aryeh 157
Neo-Liberal Institutionalism 59, 93–6, 101, 105
New Haven School 28, 100–1, 330
New International Economic Order 253
Nicolson, Harold 84
Nietzsche, Friedrich Wilhelm 21, 23
Nigeria 325
Nobel Peace Prize 157
Nolte, Georg 315–26, 334
Non-Governmental Organizations 117, 123,
      129, 133–46, 150, 152, 155–60, 168,
      172, 178, 193, 196–7, 202, 204, 225,
      261–2, 306, 333, 338, 342
Non liquet 210–11
Non-Justiciability 210
Non-State Actors 132, 134, 142–3, 145–6, 308,
      337–8, 342
Normativity 99
North American Free Trade Agreement 200–1,
      265
North Atlantic Treaty Organization 153
Nuclear Weapons 272, 284, 287, 293, 346
Nuremberg Tribunal 312

Okere, B. Obinna 167
Opinio juris 76, 139, 212, 216–18, 259–60, 273,
      300, 324, 326

Oppenheim, Lassa 40
Ordre public, see Public Order
Organization for Economic Cooperation and
      Development 200, 233, 235–6, 248–50
Organization for Security and Cooperation in
      Europe 197
Organization for the Prohibition of Chemical
      Weapons 240–1
Oyejide, Ademola 233

Pakistan 259, 287
Palestine 133–4, 287
Peacekeeping 10, 335
Perez, Antonio 194
Permanent Court of Arbitration 211
Permanent Court of International Justice 77, 208
Personality, International Legal 144, 208
Peters, R. S. 67
Picciotto, Sol 194
Pinochet, Augusto 202, 334
Piracy 258
Plato 91
Pluralism 36
Pope, Alexander 87
Popper, Karl 64
Positivism 24, 53, 65, 101, 131, 145, 152, 166,
      317, 328, 333
Postmodernism 30
Public Opinion 24
Public/Private Distinction 48
Public Policy 281–6, 300–2, 311–13
Pufendorf, Samuel 51, 91
Putnam, Robert 112

Raison d'état 72, 78
Rape 301
Rationalism 53–6, 59
Ratner, Steven 202
Rawls, John 60
Realism 27–8, 30, 37–8, 44, 59, 65, 92, 94,
      327–30, 334
Realism, Legal 43
Realpolitik 100
Reasonableness 216, 218
Rebus sic stantibus 120
Reciprocity 13
Recognition 9, 291, 324
Regimes/Regime Theory 36, 52–5, 57, 58, 59,
      60, 82, 95–9, 103–7, 281, 345
Reisman, Michael 198
Reparations 92, 301
Reprisals 285, 303
Reputation 54–5, 241
Rhodesia 289–91, 299
Ricardo, David 250
Rio Conference on the Environment 118, 137
Roberts, Adam 252

Roosevelt, Franklin 27
Rorty, Richard 45
Rousseau, Jean-Jacques 91
Ruggieri, Renato 48
Rule of Law 7, 18
Rule of Recognition 41
Rule Scepticism 36
Ruggie, John Gerard 99
Russia 316
Rwanda 272, 289
Ryle, Gilbert 67

Safe Havens 11
Sanctions 13, 22, 24, 60, 231, 241, 256–8, 275, 284–313
Saudi Arabia 187
Schachter, Oscar 149–50, 267, 309, 342
Schmitt, Carl 17–34
Schumpeter, Joseph 154
Schwebel, Stephen 122
Second World War 37, 39, 54, 91, 100, 149–50
Self-Defense 11, 13, 214, 299
Self-Determination 9, 125, 138, 283, 289, 300, 318, 333–7
Semantics 50–2
Shared Resources, *see* Common Pool Resources
Shared Understandings 40–1, 97–8, 102–3, 317, 319, 331–3, 346
Shklar, Judith 38
Siberian Pipeline Dispute 256
Sierra Leone 325
Simmonds, Nigel 40–1, 50
Singapore 244, 297
Slaughter, Anne-Marie 33, 60, 93, 96, 105, 117–205, 264, 329, 339–41
Slovakia 121
Social Movements 131, 133, 136, 147, 342
Socialism 153, 166
Soft Law 83, 126, 140, 207, 280, 342
Somalia 12, 289, 335
South Africa 171, 187
South Korea 171, 233
Sovereignty 5, 10, 33, 111, 131, 135, 151, 162, 177, 180, 191, 201, 203–4, 208, 240–1, 248–9, 264–5, 284, 336–8, 340
Soviet Union 58, 153, 165, 202
Spain 202–3
Spheres of Influence 333
State of Nature 56
State Responsibility 145–6, 208, 271, 273, 283, 285, 288–90, 293, 302, 305, 322–4
Statehood 208
Steiner, Henry 159–60, 163–5
Stern, Brigitte 245, 247–68, 329, 345
Stresemann, Gustav 20–1
Suarez, Francisco 222
Subsidiarity 128, 200, 260

Subsidies 238
Sub-State Actors 123–8
Sunk Costs 54–5
Sustainable Development 215–17, 219, 333
Suy, Eric 310
Sweden 203
Switzerland 190–2, 203

Terrorism 258, 260, 271, 290, 292
Toope, Stephen 91–108, 329, 341–2, 346
Trade, International 212, 228, 230–3, 237–68, 292–3
Transgovernmental Networks 33, 177–205, 340
Treaties 15, 48, 58, 76–81, 93, 100, 109–10, 115–16, 120, 122–3, 140, 152, 189, 208, 212, 218–19, 251, 274, 281–3, 287–8, 293–4, 297, 305–6
Trégouët, René 263, 267
Truman, Harry S. 223
Teubner, Gunther 280

UNITA 275, 290
United Kingdom 6, 86, 155, 202–3, 261, 298, 316, 323
United Nations 25, 150, 155–6, 161, 196, 200, 232–3, 269–326, 334
United Nations Charter 10, 12, 14, 82, 99, 135, 219, 223, 260, 269–326, 335
United Nations Compensation Commission 292, 322
United Nations Conference on Trade and Development 231, 234
United Nations Economic and Social Council 135, 141, 146
United Nations General Assembly 223, 273, 299–300, 306, 324–5
United Nations High Commissioner for Human Rights 169
United Nations Human Rights Commission 135
United Nations Human Rights Committee 218
United Nations Security Council 10–12, 146, 218–19, 253, 260, 269–326, 334
United States 24, 26–7, 30, 58, 84, 86, 105, 142, 155–6, 170–1, 183, 187, 190–2, 194, 196, 199–200, 204–5, 223, 230, 232, 234, 239, 245, 255–60, 298, 304–5, 323, 328, 335–6, 340–1, 343, 345
Uniting for Peace 304
Universal Declaration of Human Rights 154–5, 157, 161, 163–4, 173
Unjust Enrichment 218
Uruguay Round 237

Vattel, Émeric de 77, 334, 336
Venezuela 239
Versailles, Treaty of 18, 20, 22, 39, 84
Victoria, Francisco 222

Vienna Conference on Human Rights 133
Vienna, Congress of 81
Vienna Convention on the Law of Treaties 77
Vietnam 26, 170

Walsh, David 186
Waltz, Kenneth 28
Watercourse Law 104–8
Watts, Arthur 5–16, 54, 328, 333, 338, 344–5
Weapons of Mass Destruction 321
Weber, Max 29, 66, 282
Weeramantry, Christopher 215–16
Weil, Prosper 284
Weimar Republic 17–34
Wendt, Alexander 58, 99
Wight, Martin 28
Willets, Peter 136
Wilson, Woodrow 12, 27, 39, 84
Wittgenstein, Ludwig 47, 52, 66–7
Women's Rights 133–47, 342

World Bank 132, 141, 146, 153, 170, 172, 180,
   187, 196, 202, 212, 232, 234, 240, 248,
   253, 265
World Court Project 138
World Health Organization 138, 306
World Intellectual Property Organization 200,
   234, 244
World Trade Organization 14, 132, 146, 196,
   200, 231, 233–4, 236–9, 243–5, 248,
   250, 264–6, 333, 345

Year 2000 Network 186–8
Yee, Albert 66
Young, Iris 103
Young, Oran 96, 105
Yugoslavia 11–12, 272, 289–91, 309, 334

Zaire 153, 167, 169–70
Zaring, David 181, 188–9